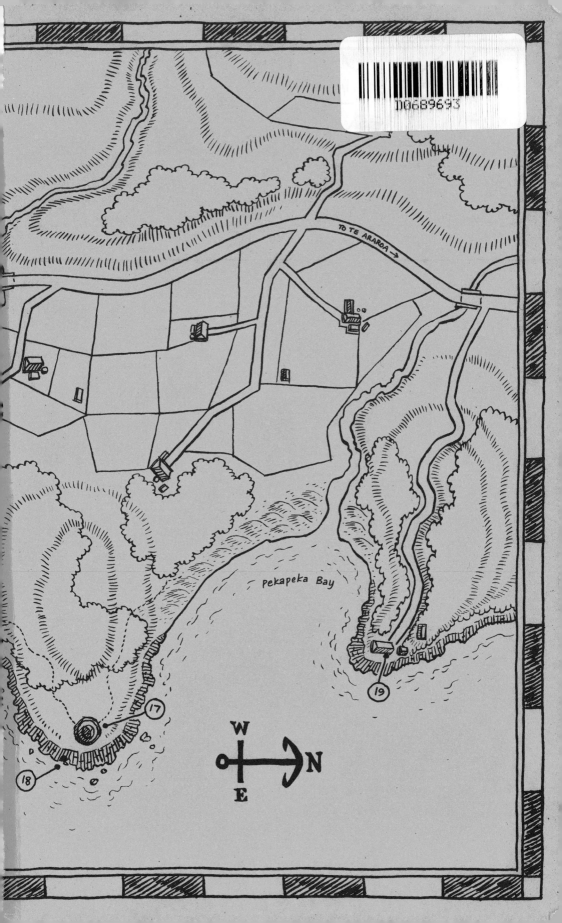

TO TE ARAROA →

Pekapeka Bay

17

18

19

W · N
E

This comic belongs to...

HICKSVILLE

a comic book by Dylan Horrocks

DRAWN AND QUARTERLY PUBLICATIONS

First published in 1998 by Black Eye Books.
This edition: January 2010. Second Printing: June 2014.
Printed in Canada.

10 9 8 7 6 5 4 3 2

Library and Archives Canada Cataloguing in Publication
Horrocks, Dylan
Hicksville / Dylan Horrocks.
ISBN 978-1-77046-002-7
I. Title.
PN6790.N454H6 2009   741.5'993   C2009-906020-5

www.drawnandquarterly.com

Published in the USA by Drawn & Quarterly, a client publisher of:
Farrar, Straus and Giroux
Orders: 888.330.8477

Published in Canada by Drawn & Quarterly, a client publisher of:
Raincoast Books
Orders: 800.663.5714

For:

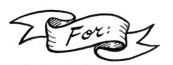

**Paul
Gravett**

Introduction

to the new edition

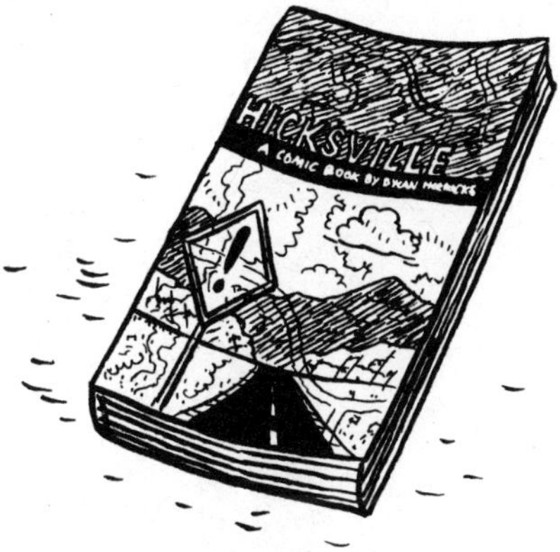
HICKSVILLE
A COMIC BOOK BY DYLAN HORROCKS

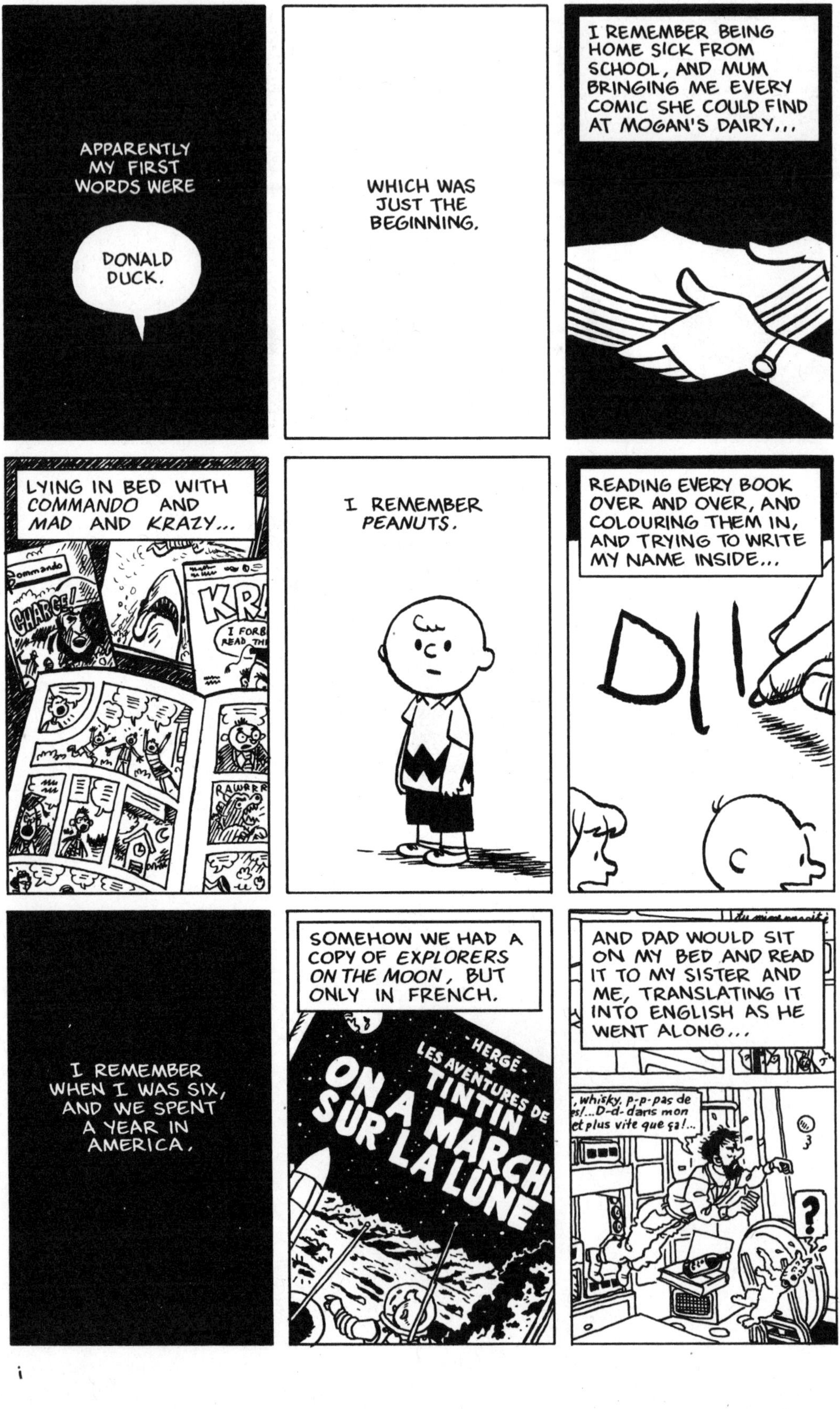
APPARENTLY MY FIRST WORDS WERE
DONALD DUCK.
WHICH WAS JUST THE BEGINNING.
I REMEMBER BEING HOME SICK FROM SCHOOL, AND MUM BRINGING ME EVERY COMIC SHE COULD FIND AT MOGAN'S DAIRY...
LYING IN BED WITH *COMMANDO* AND *MAD* AND *KRAZY*...
I REMEMBER *PEANUTS*.
READING EVERY BOOK OVER AND OVER, AND COLOURING THEM IN, AND TRYING TO WRITE MY NAME INSIDE...
I REMEMBER WHEN I WAS SIX, AND WE SPENT A YEAR IN AMERICA.
SOMEHOW WE HAD A COPY OF *EXPLORERS ON THE MOON*, BUT ONLY IN FRENCH.
AND DAD WOULD SIT ON MY BED AND READ IT TO MY SISTER AND ME, TRANSLATING IT INTO ENGLISH AS HE WENT ALONG...

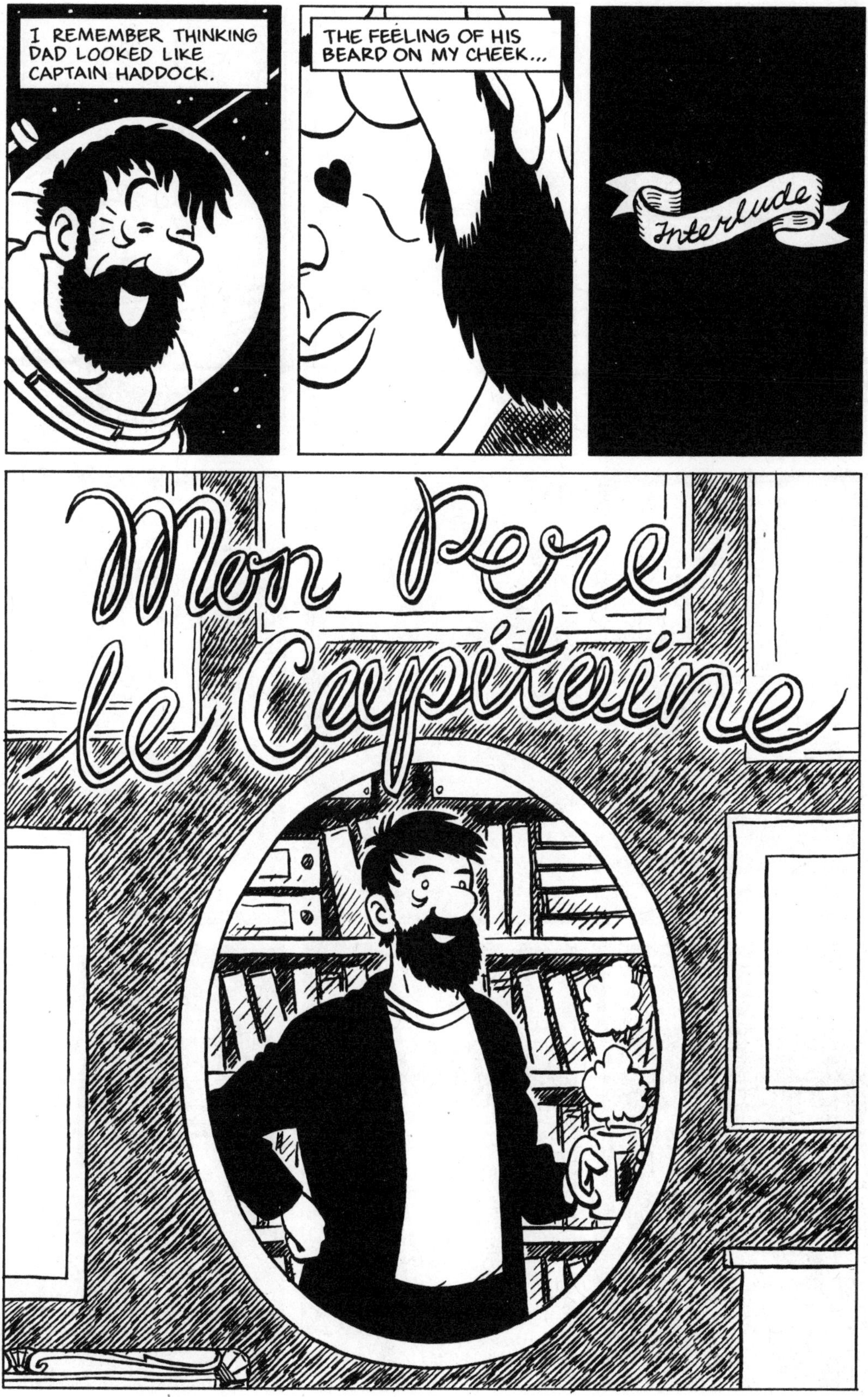
I REMEMBER THINKING DAD LOOKED LIKE CAPTAIN HADDOCK.
THE FEELING OF HIS BEARD ON MY CHEEK...
Interlude
Mon Pere le Capitaine

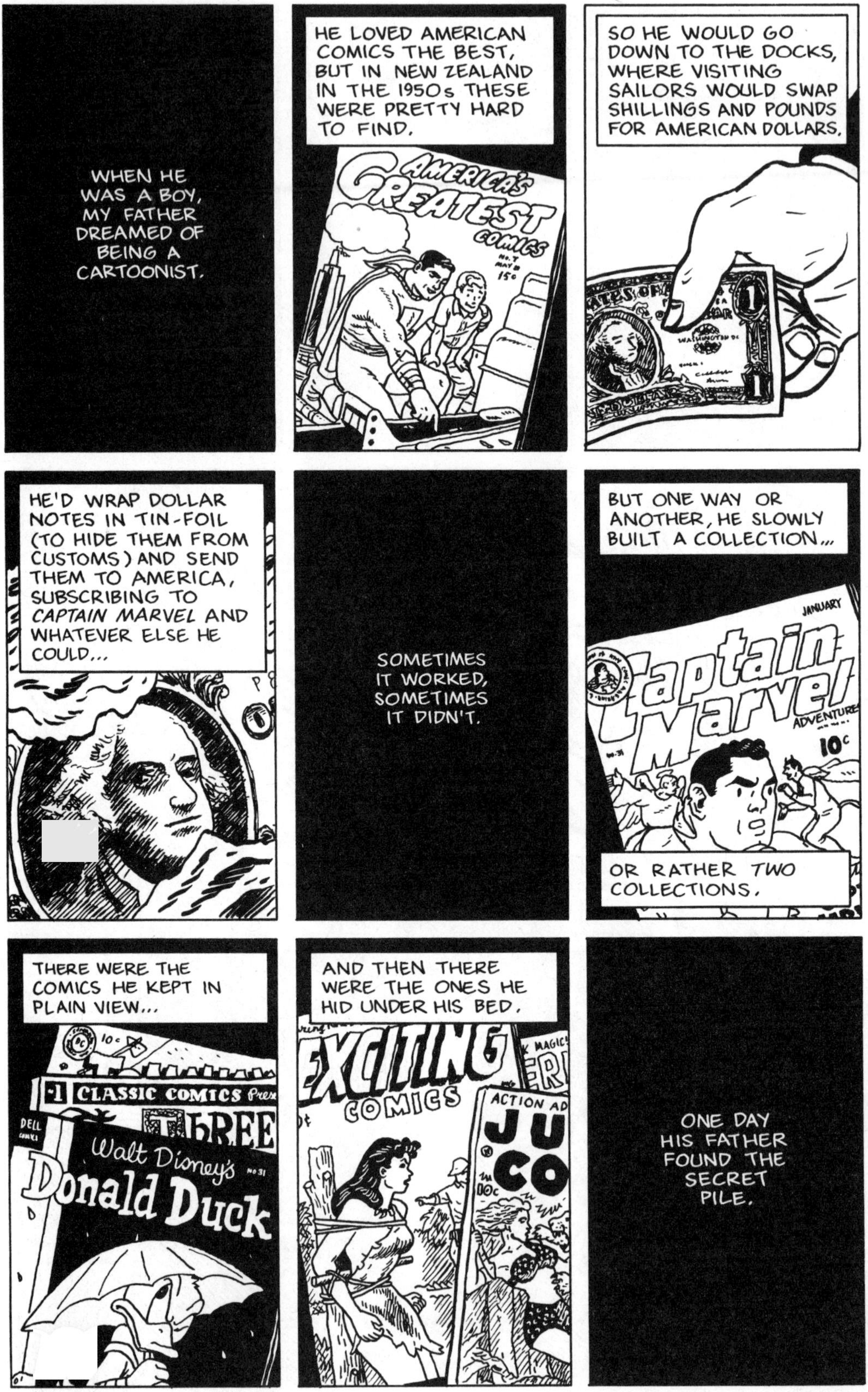
WHEN HE WAS A BOY, MY FATHER DREAMED OF BEING A CARTOONIST.
HE LOVED AMERICAN COMICS THE BEST, BUT IN NEW ZEALAND IN THE 1950s THESE WERE PRETTY HARD TO FIND.
AMERICA'S GREATEST COMICS
SO HE WOULD GO DOWN TO THE DOCKS, WHERE VISITING SAILORS WOULD SWAP SHILLINGS AND POUNDS FOR AMERICAN DOLLARS.
HE'D WRAP DOLLAR NOTES IN TIN-FOIL (TO HIDE THEM FROM CUSTOMS) AND SEND THEM TO AMERICA, SUBSCRIBING TO *CAPTAIN MARVEL* AND WHATEVER ELSE HE COULD...
SOMETIMES IT WORKED, SOMETIMES IT DIDN'T.
BUT ONE WAY OR ANOTHER, HE SLOWLY BUILT A COLLECTION...
JANUARY
Captain Marvel ADVENTURES
10¢
OR RATHER *TWO* COLLECTIONS.
THERE WERE THE COMICS HE KEPT IN PLAIN VIEW...
CLASSIC COMICS
Walt Disney's Donald Duck
AND THEN THERE WERE THE ONES HE HID UNDER HIS BED.
EXCITING COMICS
ACTION
ONE DAY HIS FATHER FOUND THE SECRET PILE.

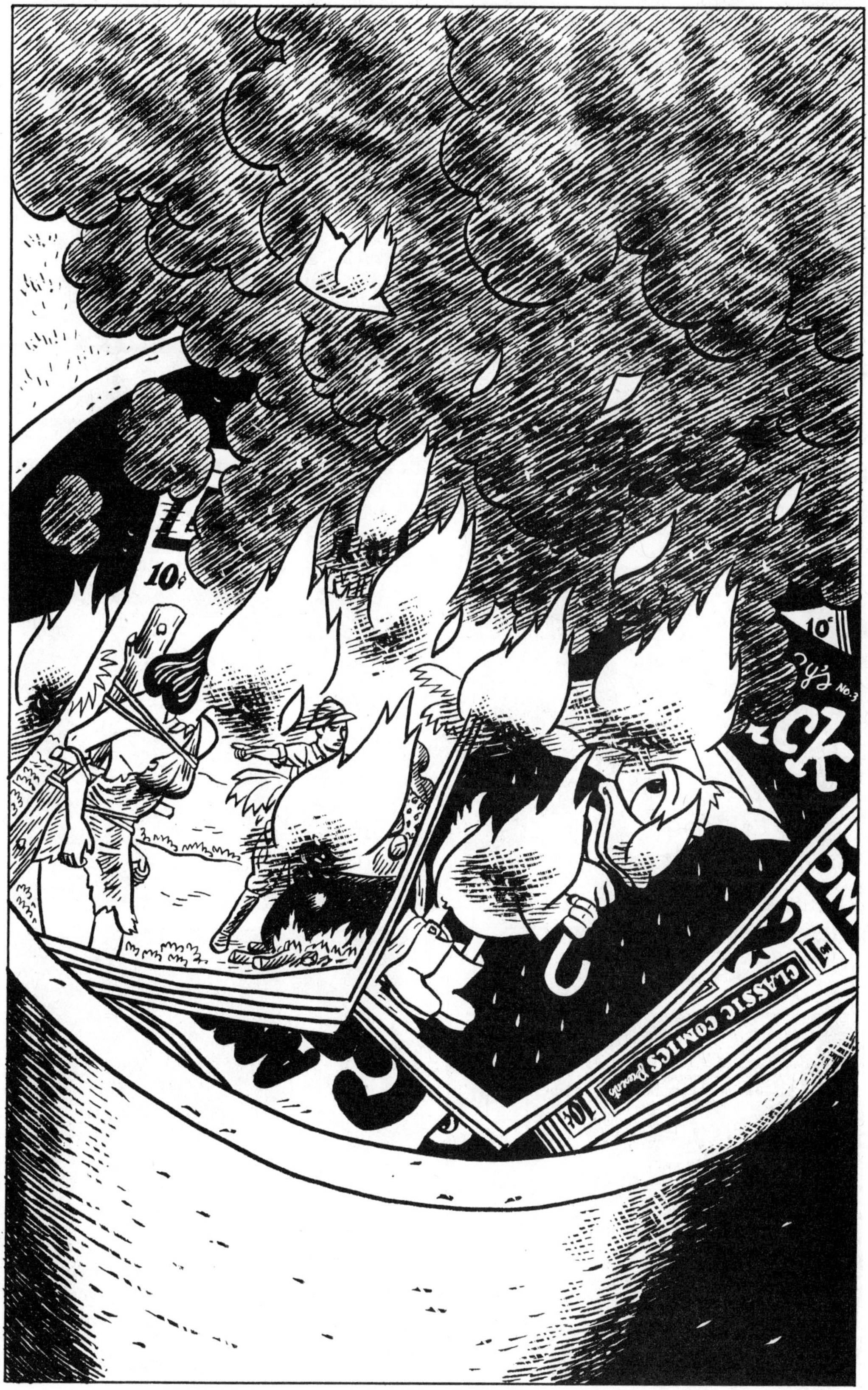
10¢
10¢
No.3
CLASSIC COMICS Presents
10¢

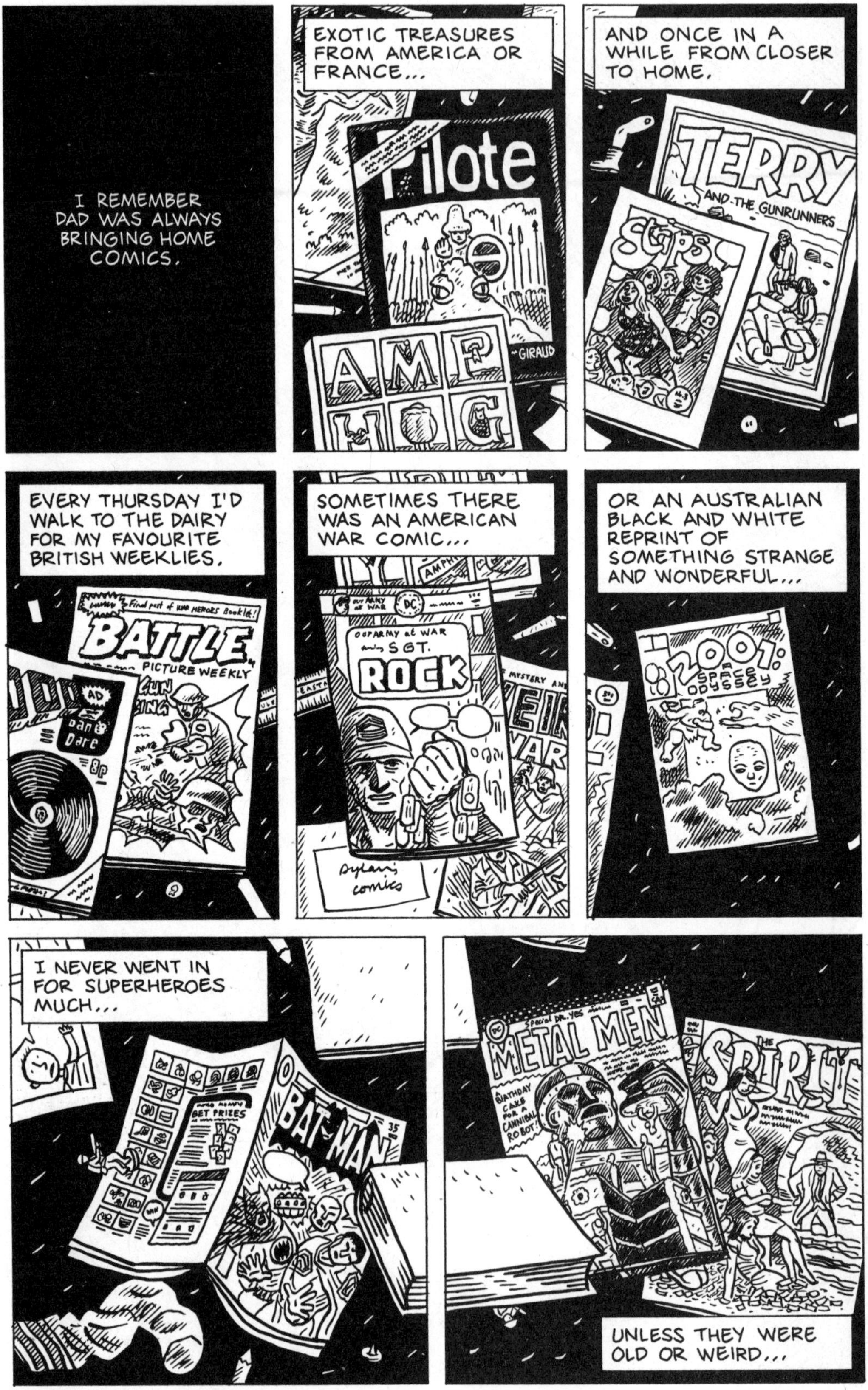
I REMEMBER DAD WAS ALWAYS BRINGING HOME COMICS.
EXOTIC TREASURES FROM AMERICA OR FRANCE...
Pilote
GIRAUD
AND ONCE IN A WHILE FROM CLOSER TO HOME.
TERRY AND THE GUNRUNNERS
EVERY THURSDAY I'D WALK TO THE DAIRY FOR MY FAVOURITE BRITISH WEEKLIES.
BATTLE PICTURE WEEKLY
Dan Dare
8p
SOMETIMES THERE WAS AN AMERICAN WAR COMIC...
OUR ARMY AT WAR
SGT. ROCK
DC
OR AN AUSTRALIAN BLACK AND WHITE REPRINT OF SOMETHING STRANGE AND WONDERFUL...
2001 SPACE ODYSSEY
I NEVER WENT IN FOR SUPERHEROES MUCH...
GET PRIZES
BATMAN
METAL MEN
A BIRTHDAY CAKE FOR A CANNIBAL ROBOT!
THE SPIRIT
UNLESS THEY WERE OLD OR WEIRD...

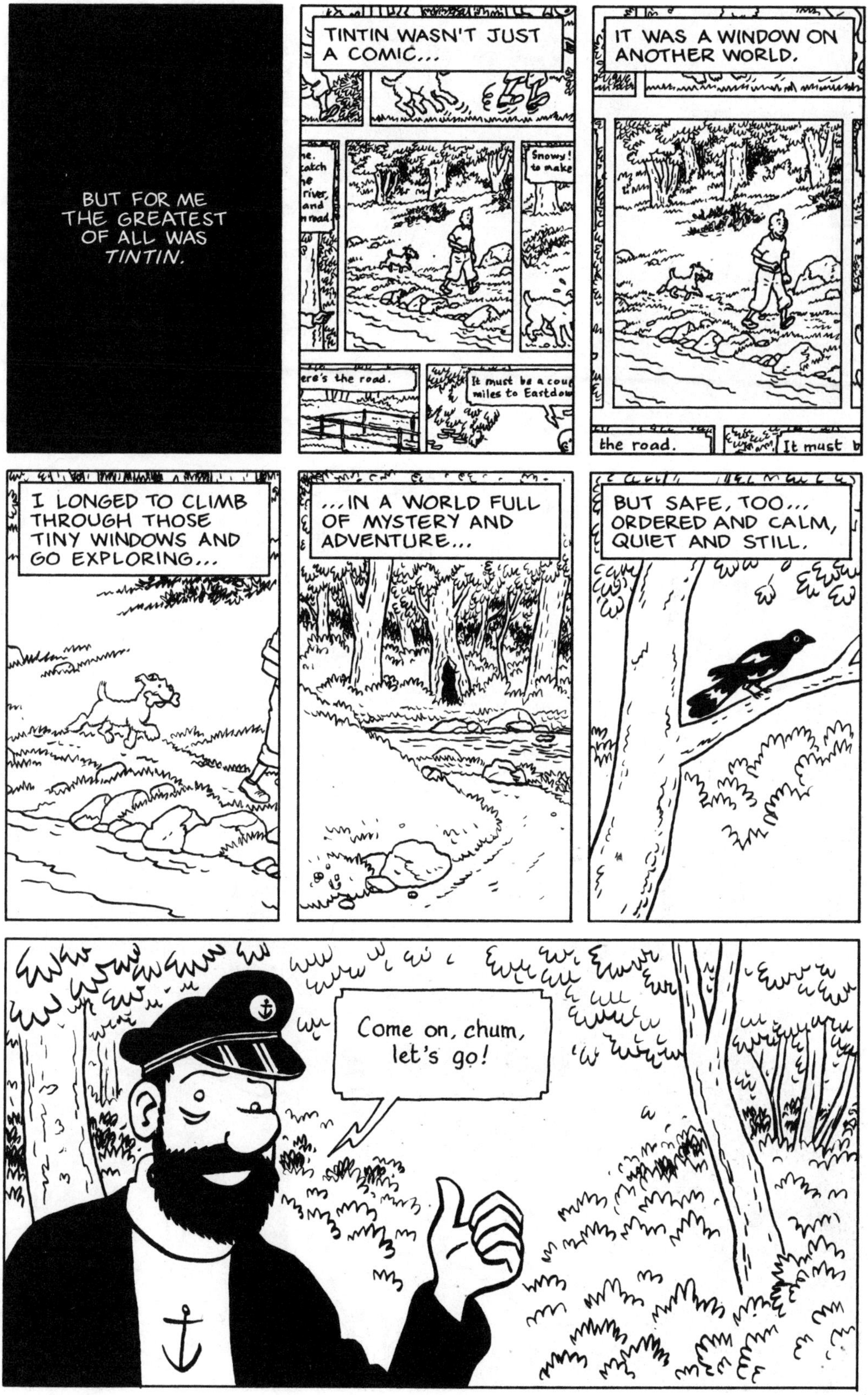
BUT FOR ME THE GREATEST OF ALL WAS *TINTIN*.
TINTIN WASN'T JUST A COMIC...
Snowy! to make
ere's the road.
It must be a coup miles to Eastdow
IT WAS A WINDOW ON ANOTHER WORLD.
the road.
It must b
I LONGED TO CLIMB THROUGH THOSE TINY WINDOWS AND GO EXPLORING...
...IN A WORLD FULL OF MYSTERY AND ADVENTURE...
BUT SAFE, TOO... ORDERED AND CALM, QUIET AND STILL.
Come on, chum, let's go!

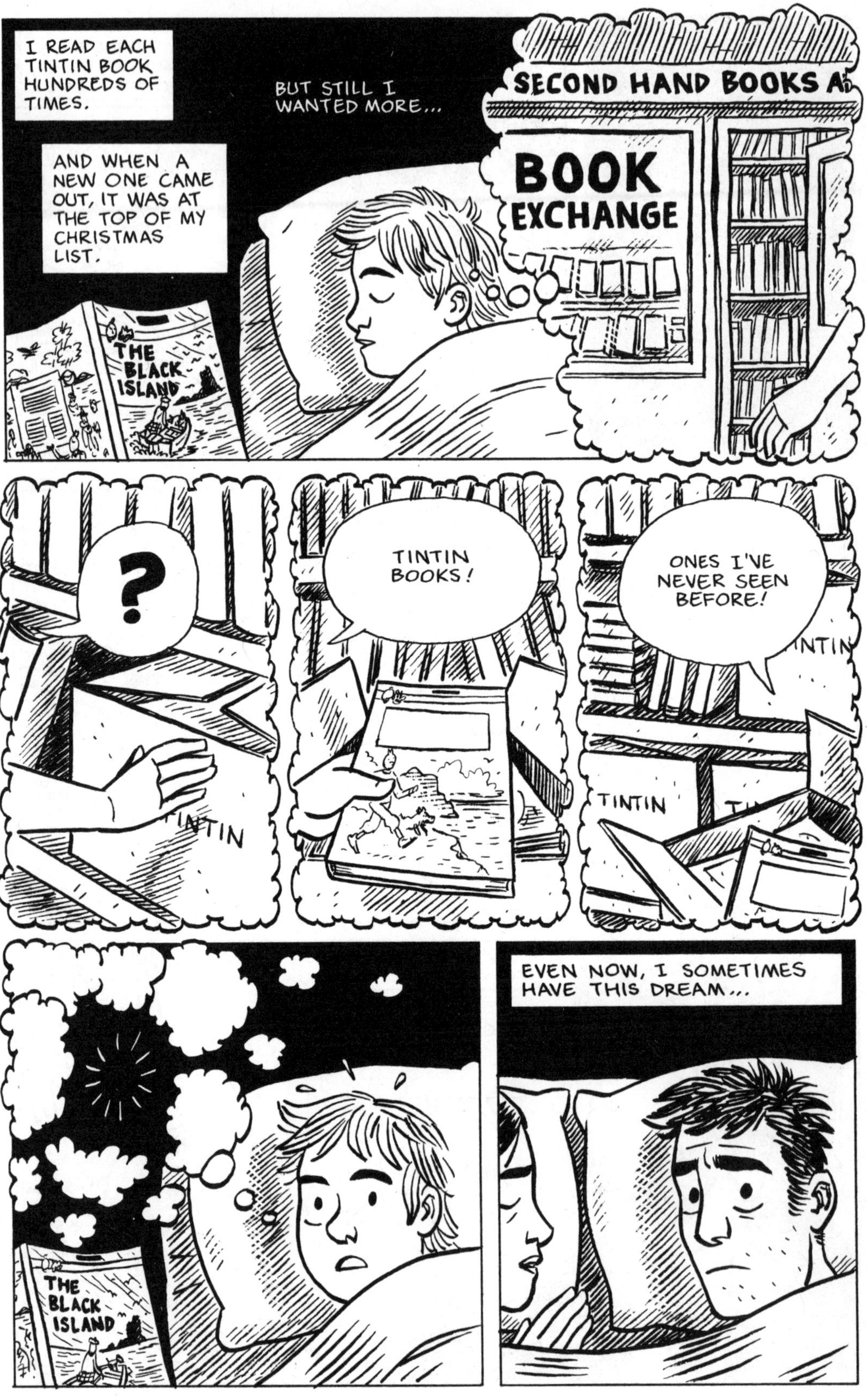

I READ EACH TINTIN BOOK HUNDREDS OF TIMES.
AND WHEN A NEW ONE CAME OUT, IT WAS AT THE TOP OF MY CHRISTMAS LIST.
THE BLACK ISLAND
BUT STILL I WANTED MORE...
SECOND HAND BOOKS A
BOOK EXCHANGE
?
TINTIN
TINTIN BOOKS!
ONES I'VE NEVER SEEN BEFORE!
TINTIN
TINTIN
THE BLACK ISLAND
EVEN NOW, I SOMETIMES HAVE THIS DREAM...

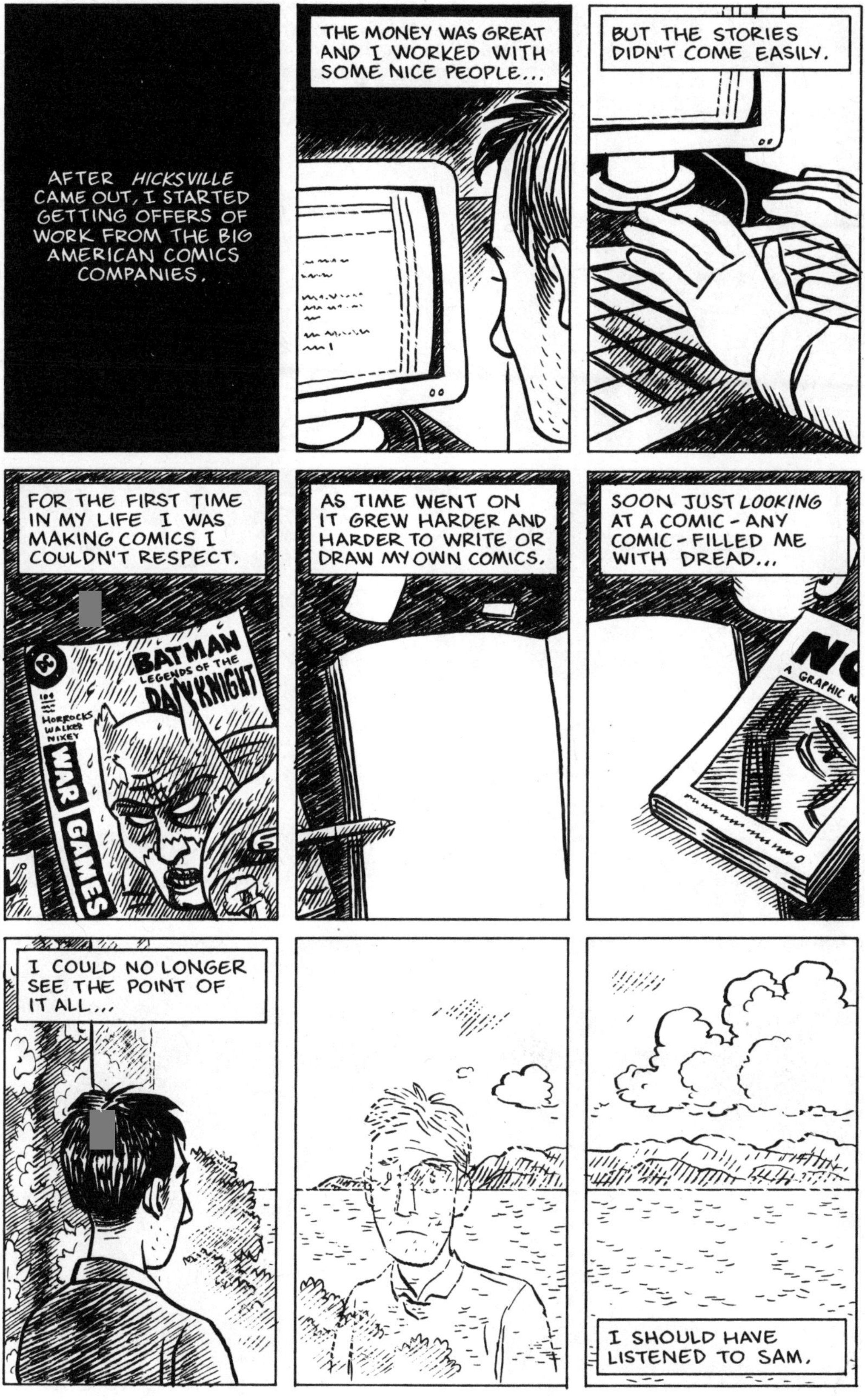
AFTER *HICKSVILLE* CAME OUT, I STARTED GETTING OFFERS OF WORK FROM THE BIG AMERICAN COMICS COMPANIES.
THE MONEY WAS GREAT AND I WORKED WITH SOME NICE PEOPLE...
BUT THE STORIES DIDN'T COME EASILY.
FOR THE FIRST TIME IN MY LIFE I WAS MAKING COMICS I COULDN'T RESPECT.
BATMAN
LEGENDS OF THE
HORROCKS WALKER NIXEY
WAR GAMES
AS TIME WENT ON IT GREW HARDER AND HARDER TO WRITE OR DRAW MY OWN COMICS.
SOON JUST *LOOKING* AT A COMIC - ANY COMIC - FILLED ME WITH DREAD...
A GRAPHIC
I COULD NO LONGER SEE THE POINT OF IT ALL...
I SHOULD HAVE LISTENED TO SAM.

AND I'M GETTING *HICKSVILLE* READY FOR THE PRINTER ALL OVER AGAIN...

SO NOW IT'S BEEN TEN YEARS.

I STILL WINCE AT A LOT OF THE DRAWING...

AND I HAVE TO FIGHT THE URGE TO REDO THE WHOLE BOOK FROM SCRATCH.

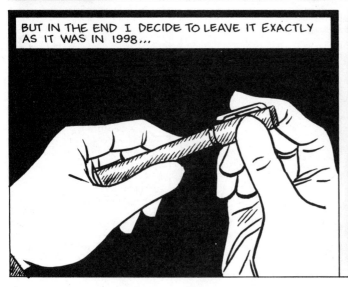

BUT IN THE END I DECIDE TO LEAVE IT EXACTLY AS IT WAS IN 1998...

(APART FROM CORRECTING GENUINE MISTAKES AND RELETTERING THE MOST ILLEGIBLE WORDS)

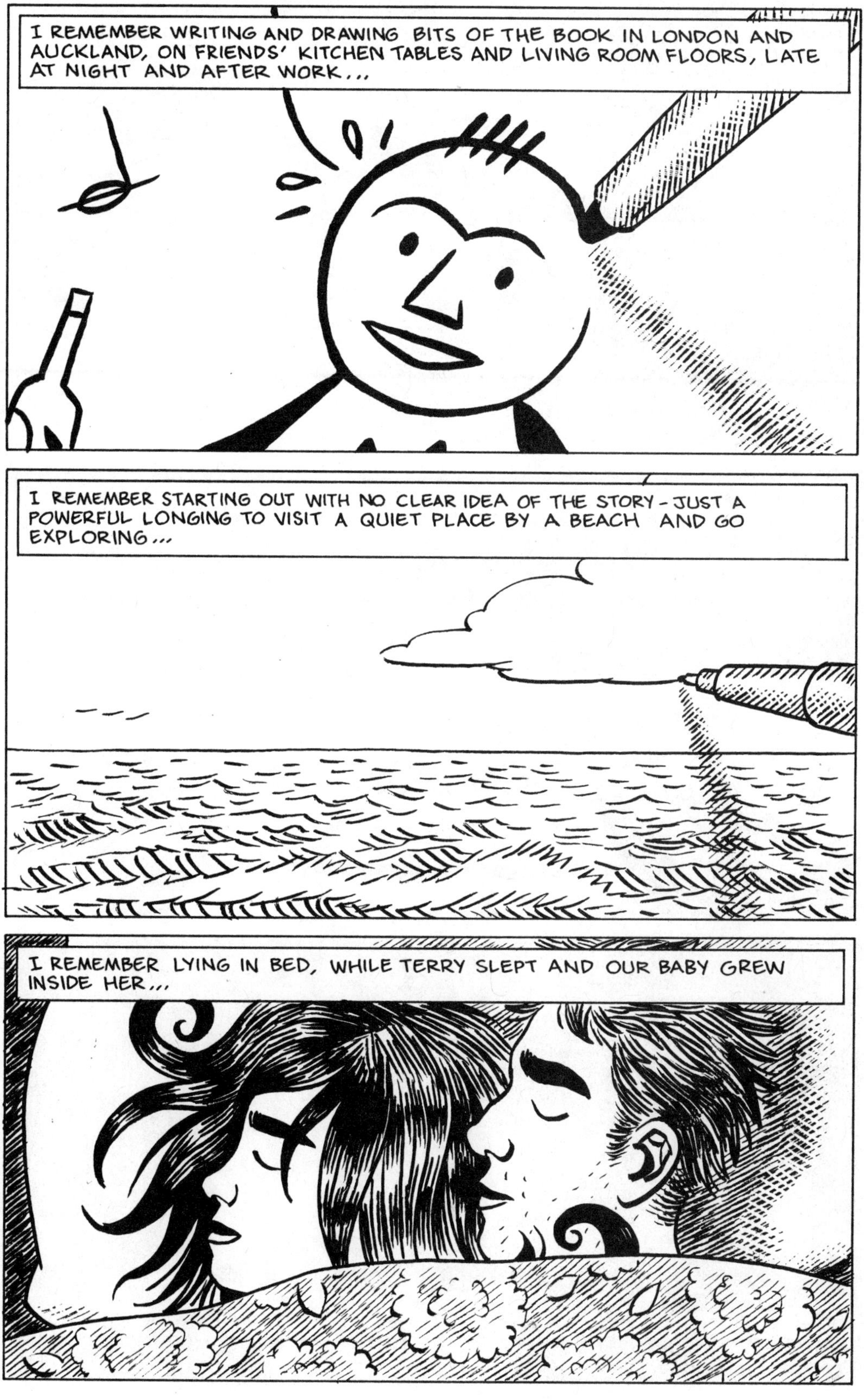
I REMEMBER WRITING AND DRAWING BITS OF THE BOOK IN LONDON AND AUCKLAND, ON FRIENDS' KITCHEN TABLES AND LIVING ROOM FLOORS, LATE AT NIGHT AND AFTER WORK...
I REMEMBER STARTING OUT WITH NO CLEAR IDEA OF THE STORY - JUST A POWERFUL LONGING TO VISIT A QUIET PLACE BY A BEACH AND GO EXPLORING...
I REMEMBER LYING IN BED, WHILE TERRY SLEPT AND OUR BABY GREW INSIDE HER...

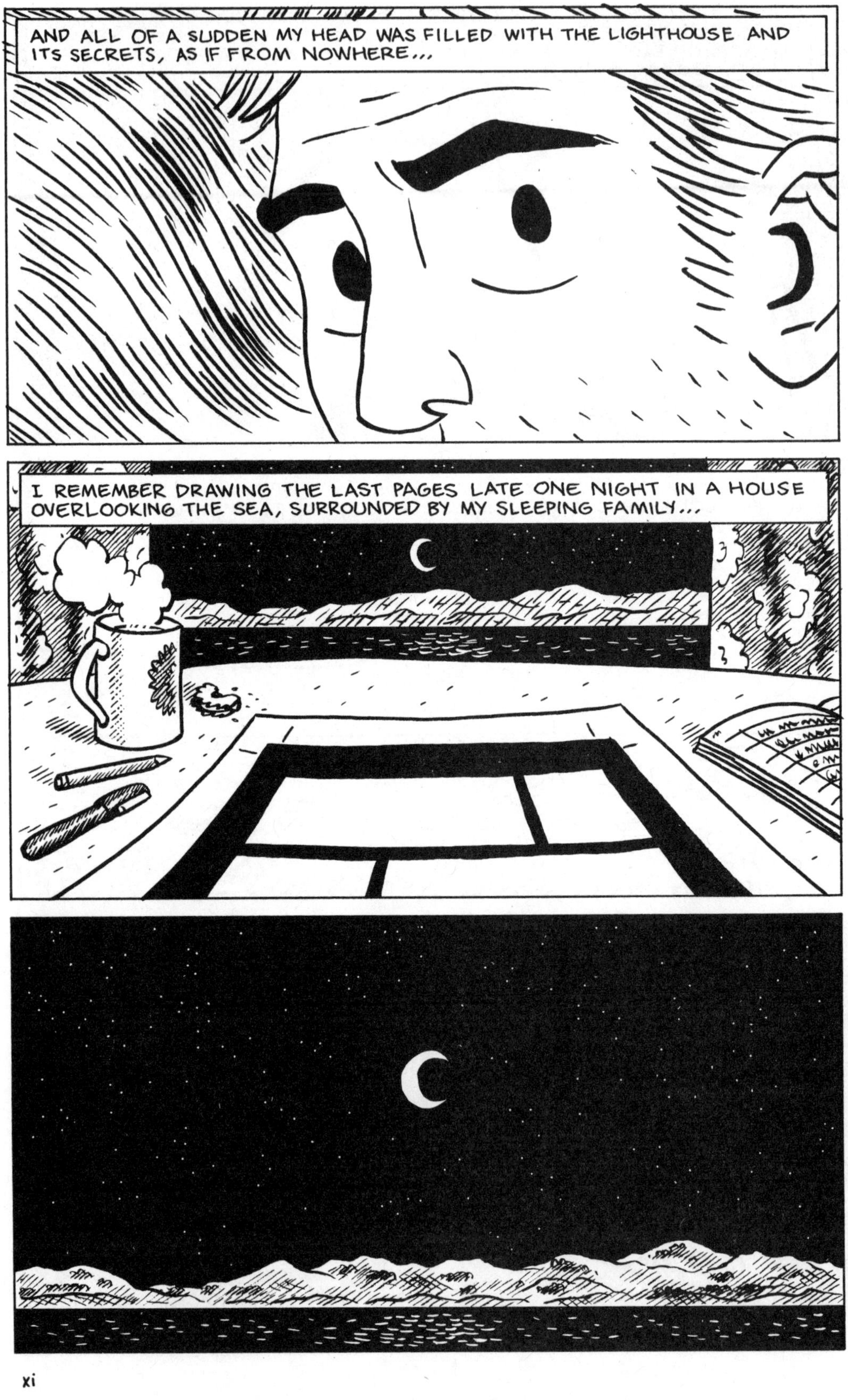
AND ALL OF A SUDDEN MY HEAD WAS FILLED WITH THE LIGHTHOUSE AND ITS SECRETS, AS IF FROM NOWHERE...
I REMEMBER DRAWING THE LAST PAGES LATE ONE NIGHT IN A HOUSE OVERLOOKING THE SEA, SURROUNDED BY MY SLEEPING FAMILY...

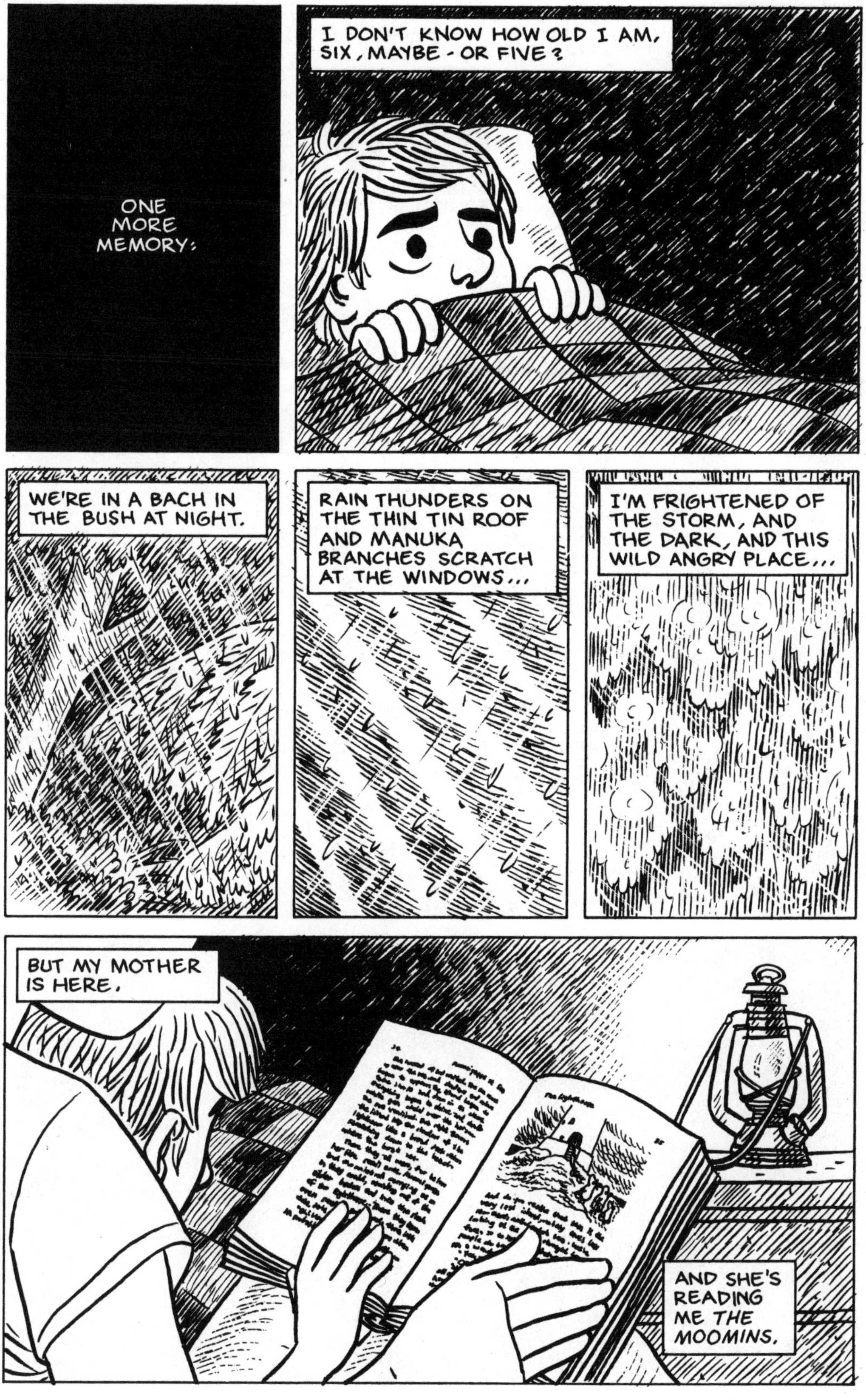
ONE MORE MEMORY:
I DON'T KNOW HOW OLD I AM, SIX, MAYBE - OR FIVE?
WE'RE IN A BACH IN THE BUSH AT NIGHT.
RAIN THUNDERS ON THE THIN TIN ROOF AND MANUKA BRANCHES SCRATCH AT THE WINDOWS...
I'M FRIGHTENED OF THE STORM, AND THE DARK, AND THIS WILD ANGRY PLACE...
BUT MY MOTHER IS HERE.
AND SHE'S READING ME *THE MOOMINS*.

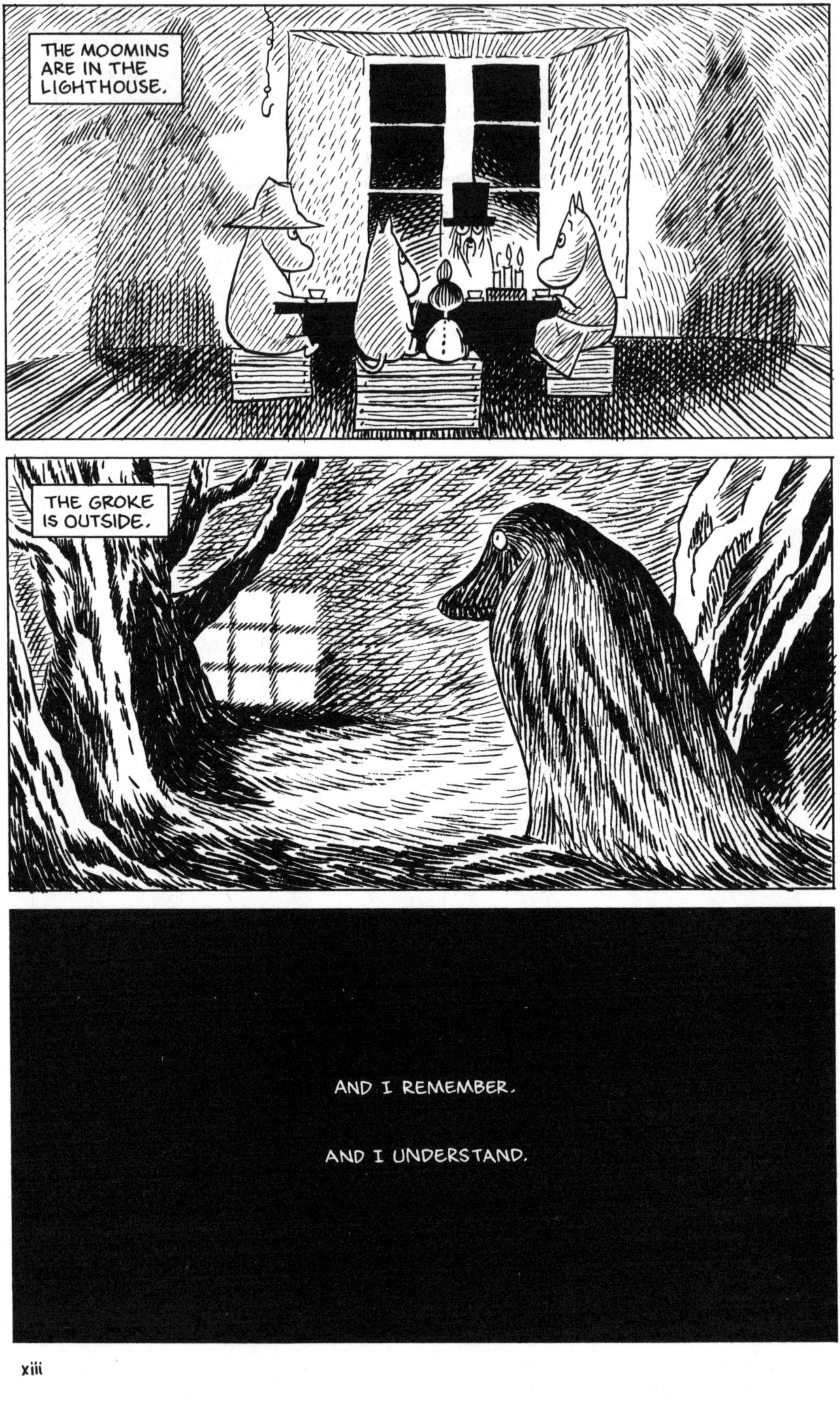
THE MOOMINS ARE IN THE LIGHTHOUSE.
THE GROKE IS OUTSIDE.
AND I REMEMBER.
AND I UNDERSTAND.

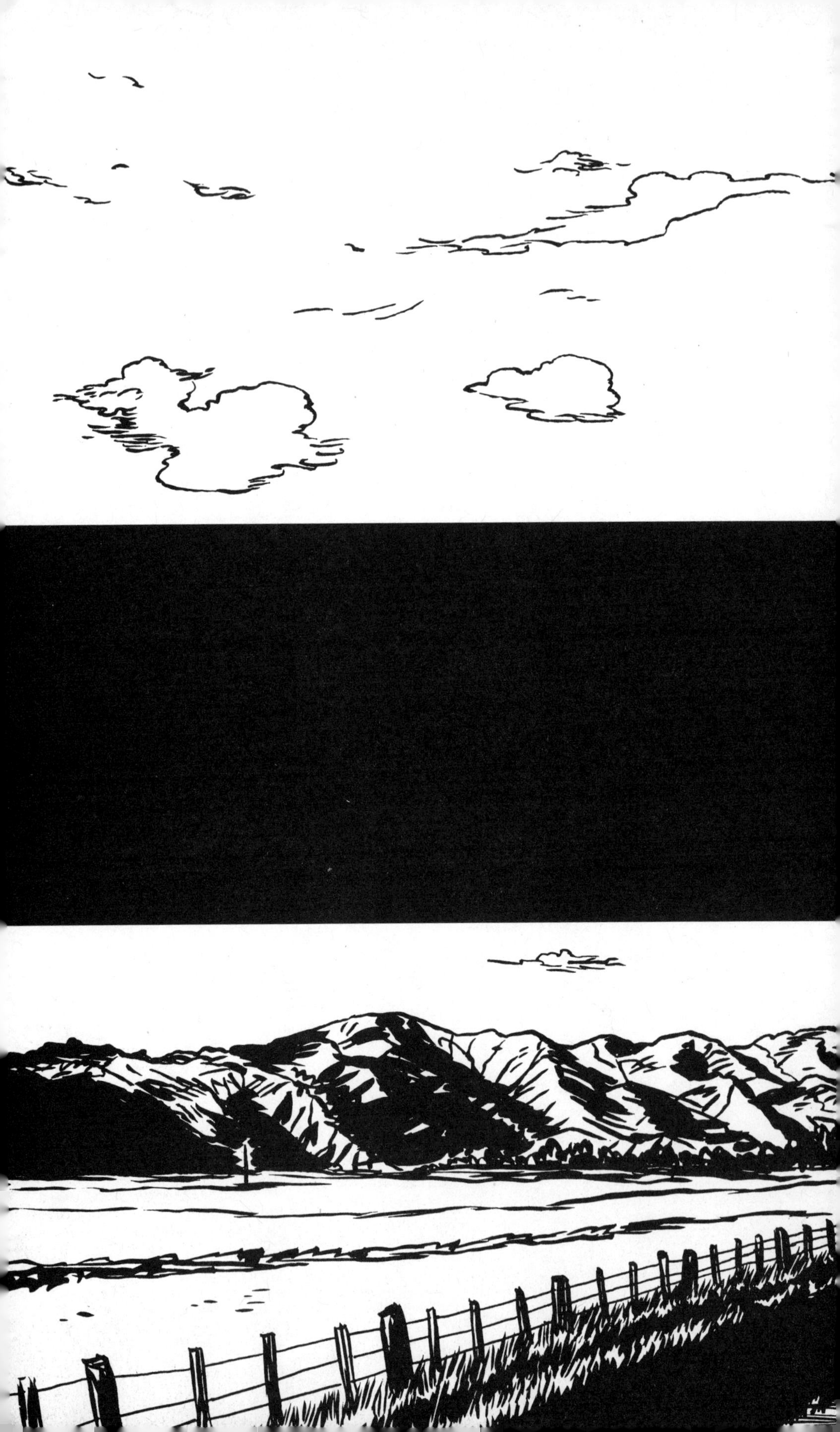

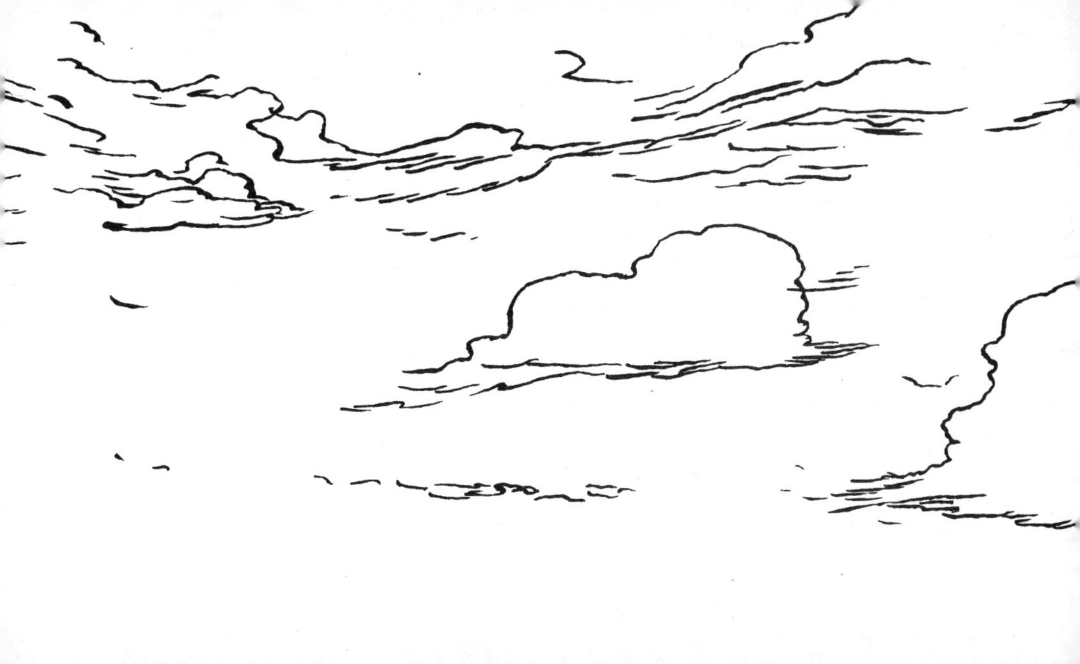

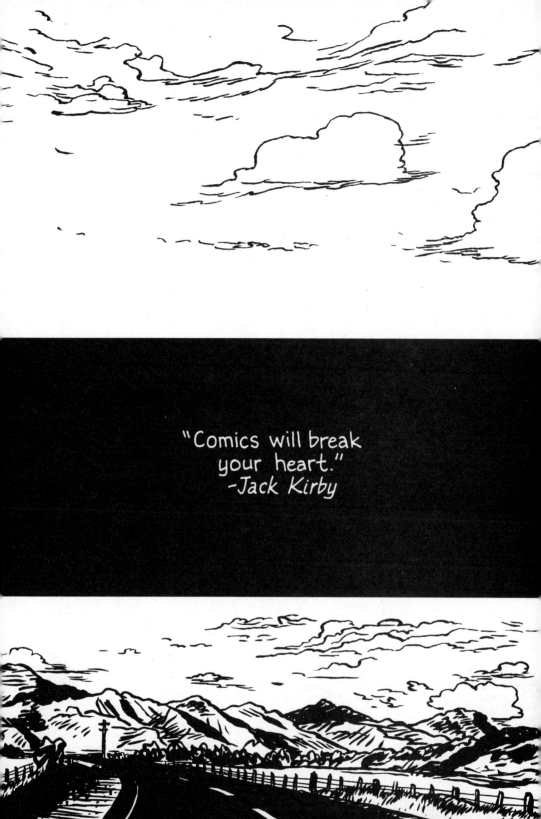

"Comics will break your heart."
-Jack Kirby

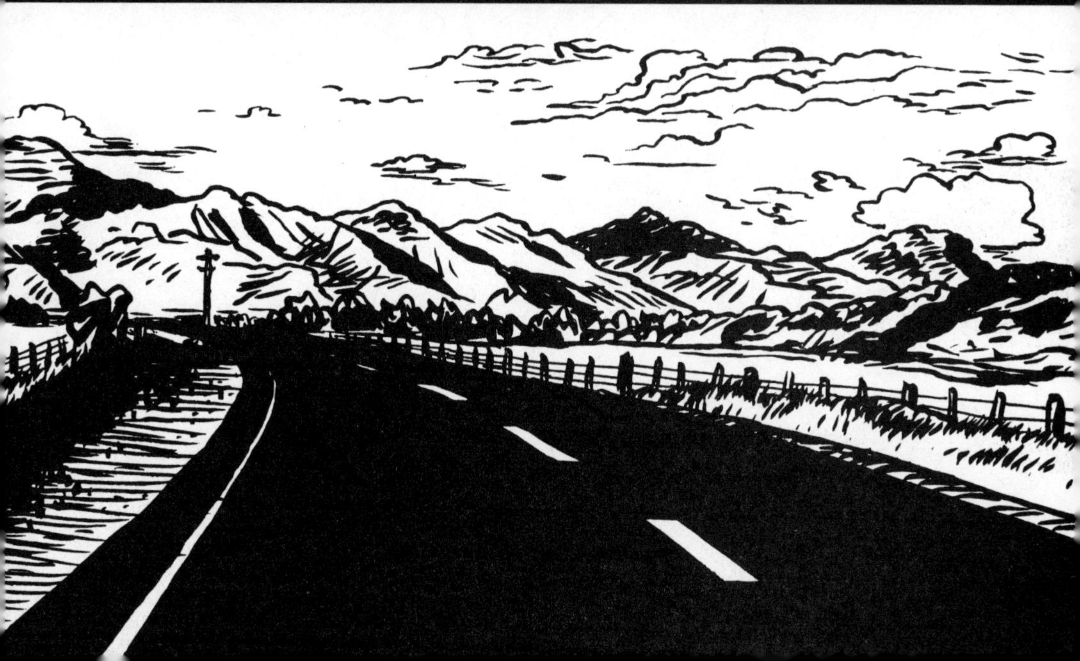

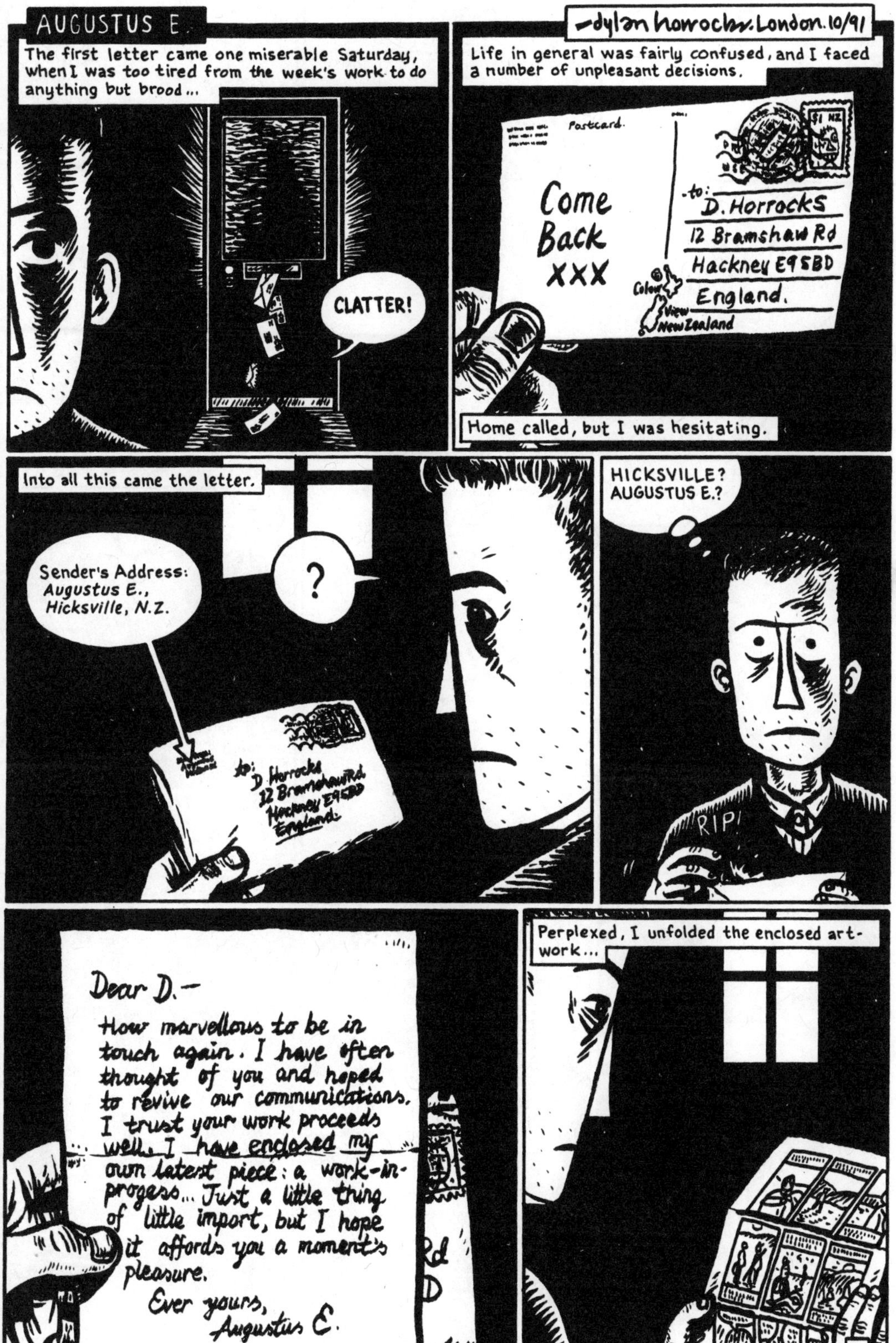
AUGUSTUS E.
-dylan horrocks. London. 10/91
The first letter came one miserable Saturday, when I was too tired from the week's work to do anything but brood...
CLATTER!
Life in general was fairly confused, and I faced a number of unpleasant decisions.
Postcard
Come Back XXX
to: D. Horrocks 12 Bramshaw Rd Hackney E9 5BD England.
Colour View New Zealand
Home called, but I was hesitating.
Into all this came the letter.
Sender's Address: Augustus E., Hicksville, N.Z.
?
to: D. Horrocks 12 Bramshaw Rd. Hackney E9 5BD England.
HICKSVILLE? AUGUSTUS E.?
RIP
Dear D.— How marvellous to be in touch again. I have often thought of you and hoped to revive our communications. I trust your work proceeds well. I have enclosed my own latest piece: a work-in-progress... Just a little thing of little import, but I hope it affords you a moment's pleasure. Ever yours, Augustus E.
Perplexed, I unfolded the enclosed art-work...

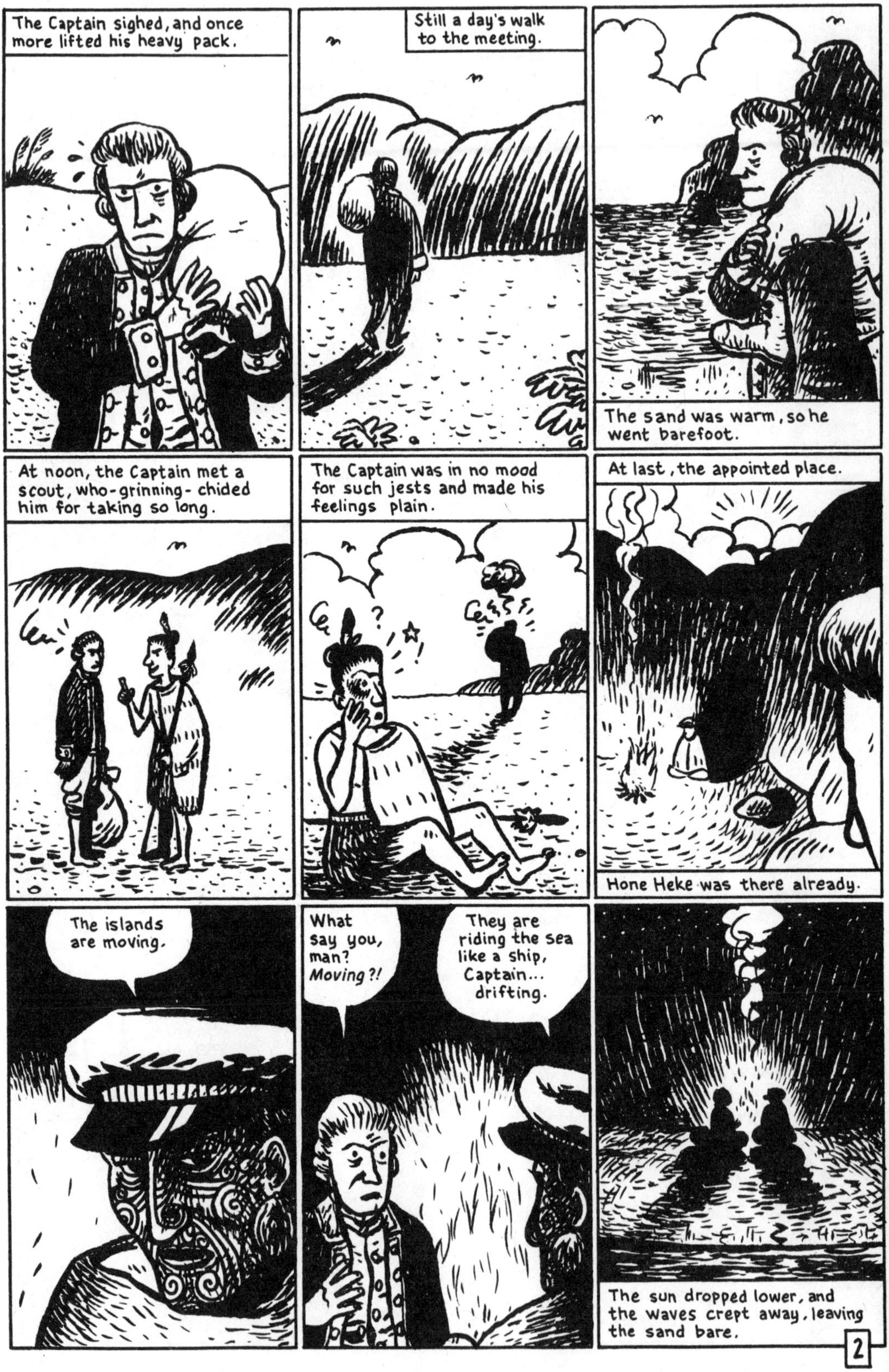
The Captain sighed, and once more lifted his heavy pack.
Still a day's walk to the meeting.
The sand was warm, so he went barefoot.
At noon, the Captain met a scout, who-grinning- chided him for taking so long.
The Captain was in no mood for such jests and made his feelings plain.
At last, the appointed place.
Hone Heke was there already.
The islands are moving.
What say you, man? *Moving?!*
They are riding the sea like a ship, Captain... drifting.
The sun dropped lower, and the waves crept away, leaving the sand bare.

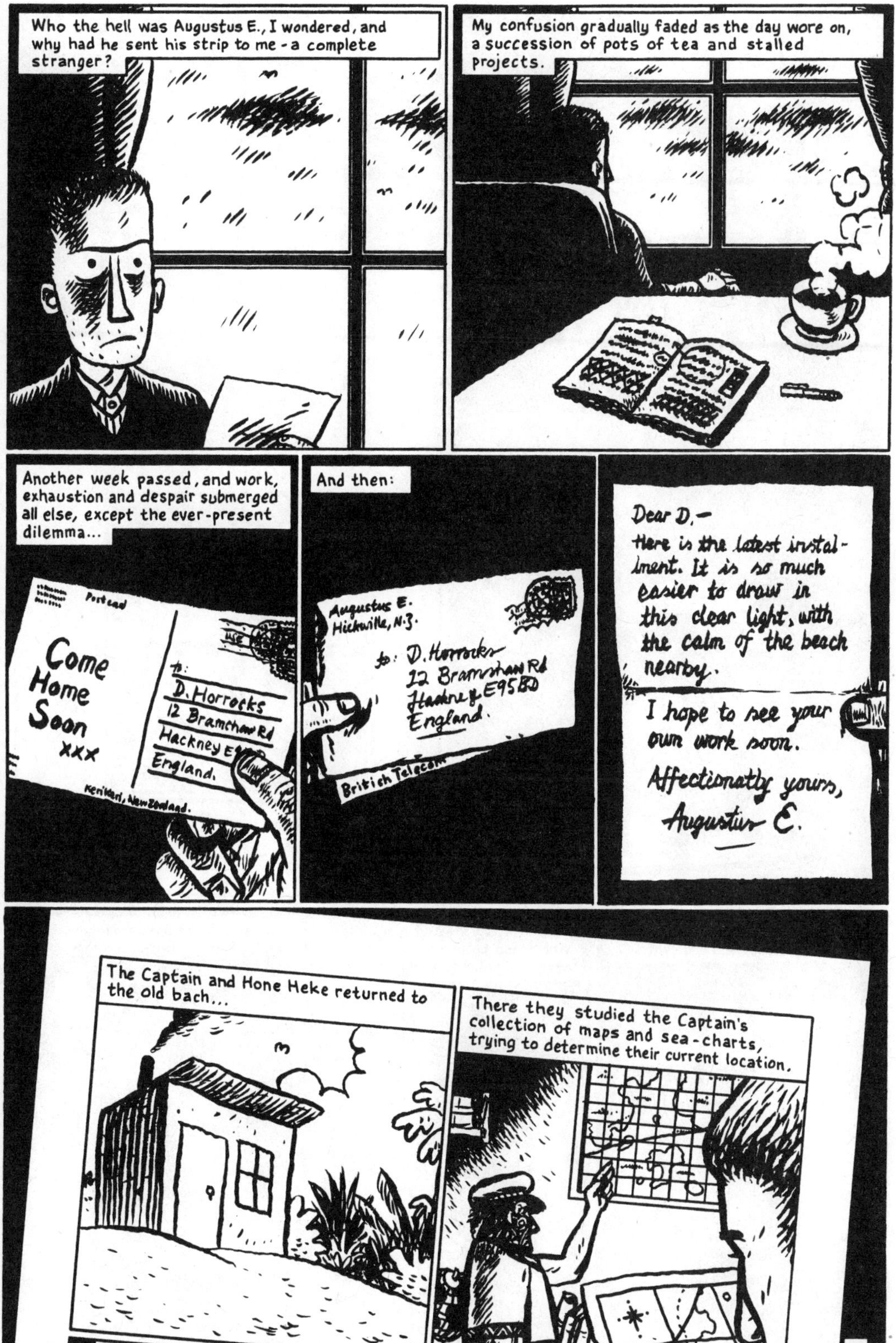
Who the hell was Augustus E., I wondered, and why had he sent his strip to me - a complete stranger?
My confusion gradually faded as the day wore on, a succession of pots of tea and stalled projects.
Another week passed, and work, exhaustion and despair submerged all else, except the ever-present dilemma...
Postcard
Come Home Soon xxx
to: D. Horrocks 12 Bramshaw Rd Hackney E9 England.
Kerikeri, New Zealand.
And then:
Augustus E. Hicksville, N.Z.
to: D. Horrocks 12 Bramshaw Rd Hackney E95BD England
British Telecom
Dear D. -
Here is the latest installment. It is so much easier to draw in this clear light, with the calm of the beach nearby.
I hope to see your own work soon.
Affectionately yours, Augustus E.
The Captain and Hone Heke returned to the old bach...
There they studied the Captain's collection of maps and sea-charts, trying to determine their current location.

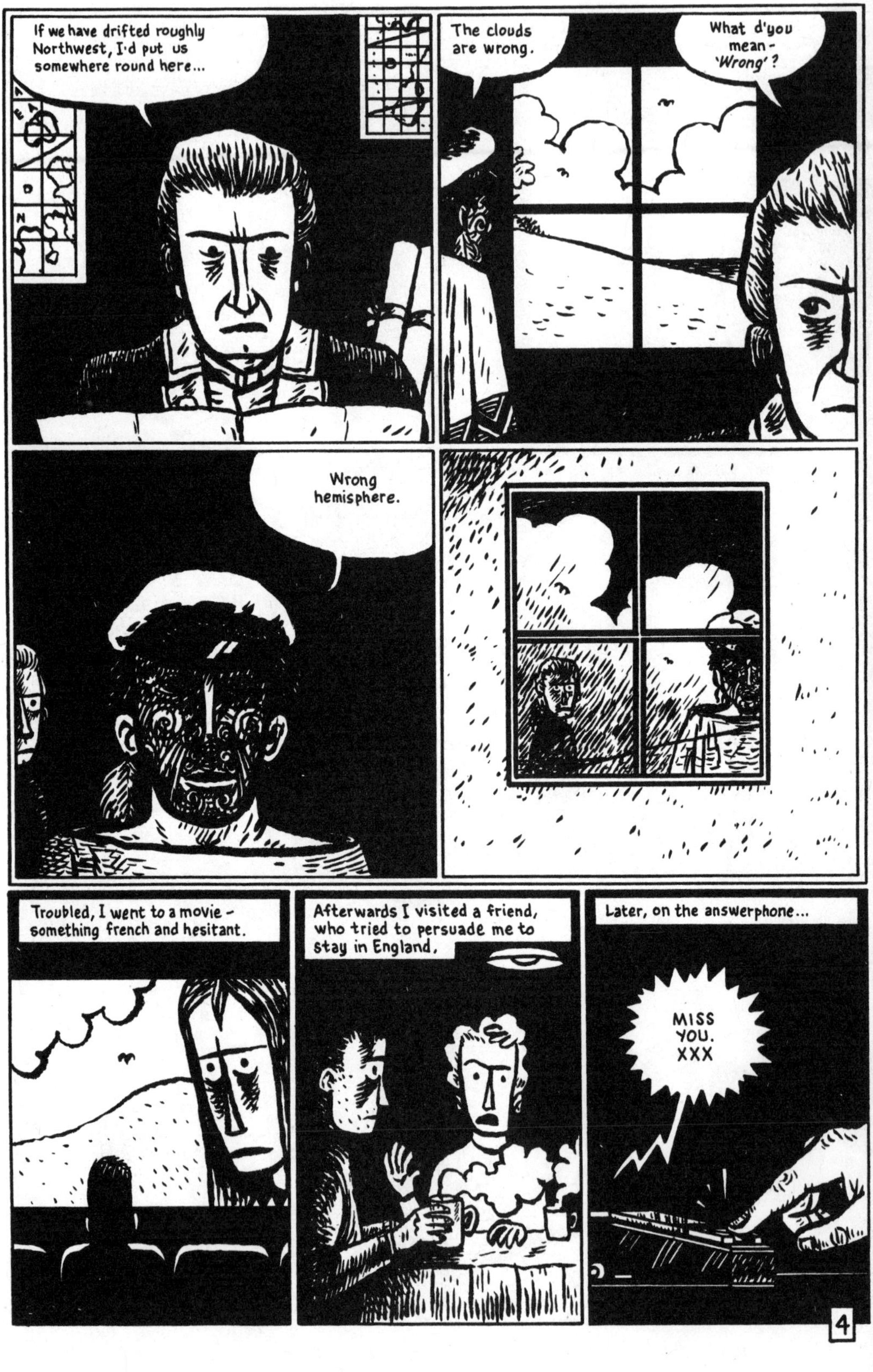

If we have drifted roughly Northwest, I'd put us somewhere round here...
The clouds are wrong.
What d'you mean - 'Wrong'?
Wrong hemisphere.
Troubled, I went to a movie - something french and hesitant.
Afterwards I visited a friend, who tried to persuade me to stay in England.
Later, on the answerphone...
MISS YOU. XXX

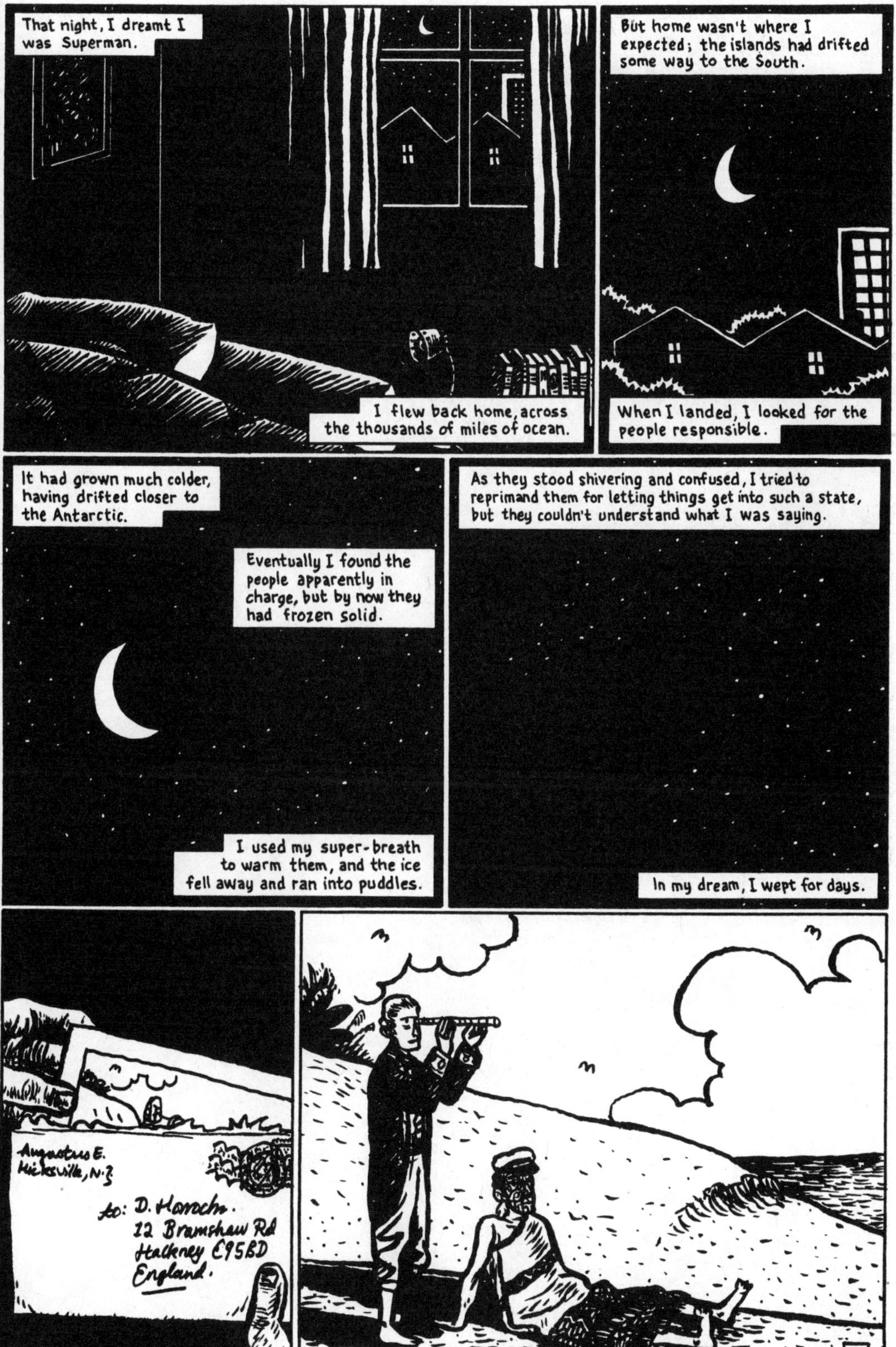
That night, I dreamt I was Superman.
I flew back home, across the thousands of miles of ocean.
But home wasn't where I expected; the islands had drifted some way to the South.
When I landed, I looked for the people responsible.
It had grown much colder, having drifted closer to the Antarctic.
Eventually I found the people apparently in charge, but by now they had frozen solid.
I used my super-breath to warm them, and the ice fell away and ran into puddles.
As they stood shivering and confused, I tried to reprimand them for letting things get into such a state, but they couldn't understand what I was saying.
In my dream, I wept for days.
12 Bramshaw Rd
England.

To Jeffrey. — dylan. 7.vii.92

Chapter One

"From now on, I do not
want progress."
Stan Lee, 1973.

VOLUME ONE IN A FOUR VOLUME EPIC!
Dick Burger's
CAPTAIN TOMORROW: REBIRTH
Eternal Comics TM
VOLUME 1 OF 4. WINTER 1988. U.S.$6.95. CAN.$8.95.
Dick Burger

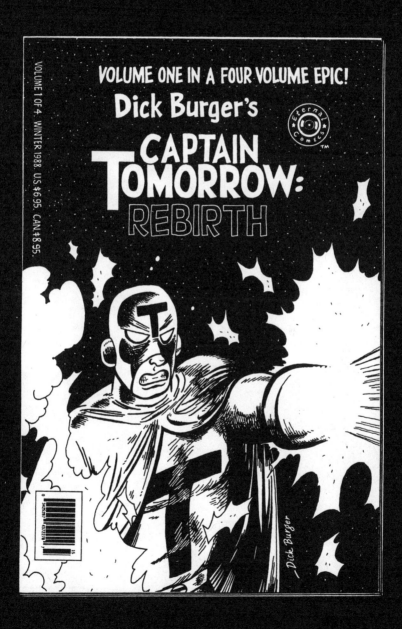

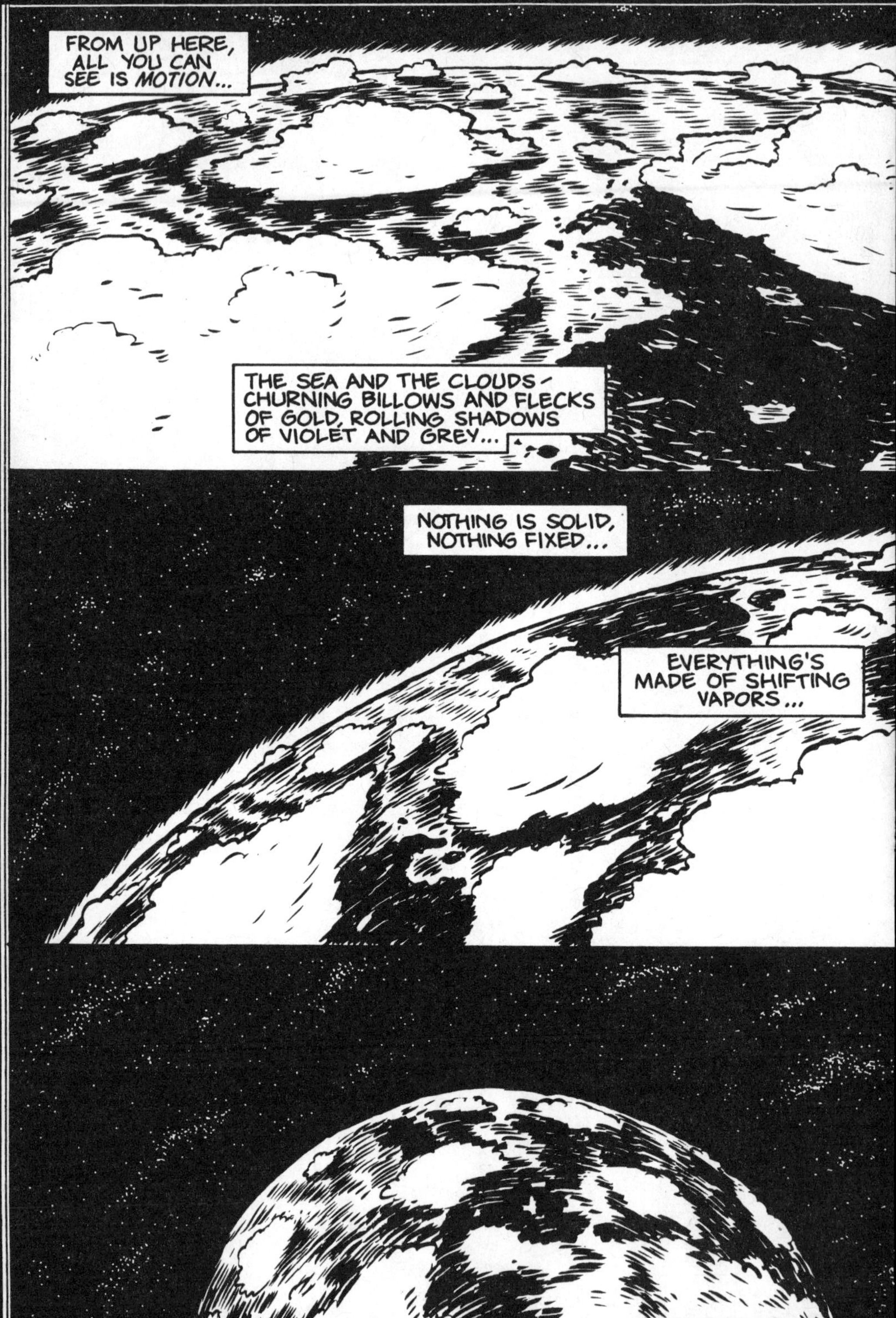
FROM UP HERE, ALL YOU CAN SEE IS MOTION...
THE SEA AND THE CLOUDS- CHURNING BILLOWS AND FLECKS OF GOLD, ROLLING SHADOWS OF VIOLET AND GREY...
NOTHING IS SOLID, NOTHING FIXED...
EVERYTHING'S MADE OF SHIFTING VAPORS...
CONSTANTLY DYING AND BEING REBORN...

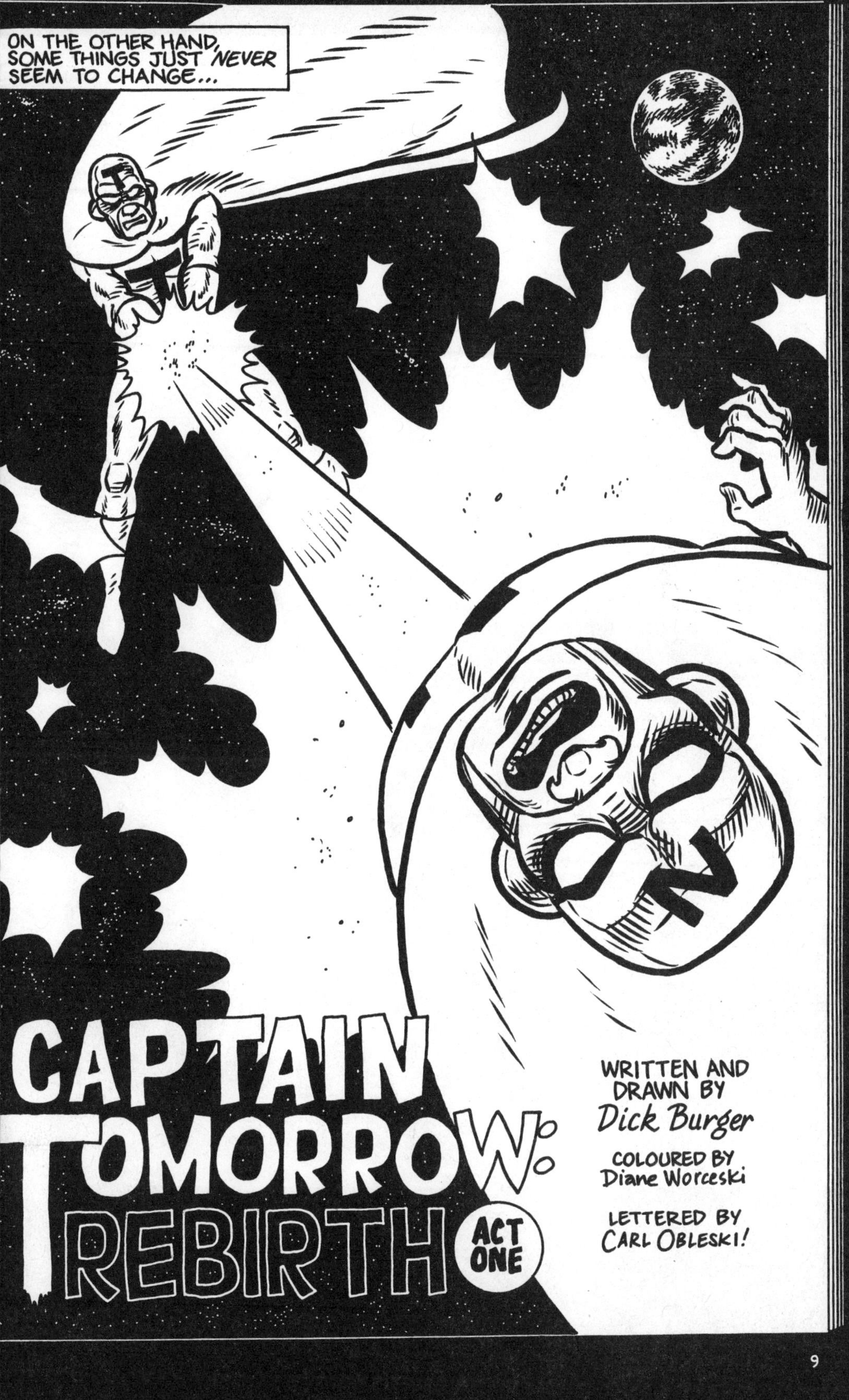

ON THE OTHER HAND, SOME THINGS JUST *NEVER* SEEM TO CHANGE...
CAPTAIN TOMORROW:
REBIRTH
ACT ONE
WRITTEN AND DRAWN BY
Dick Burger
COLOURED BY
Diane Worceski
LETTERED BY
CARL OBLESKI!

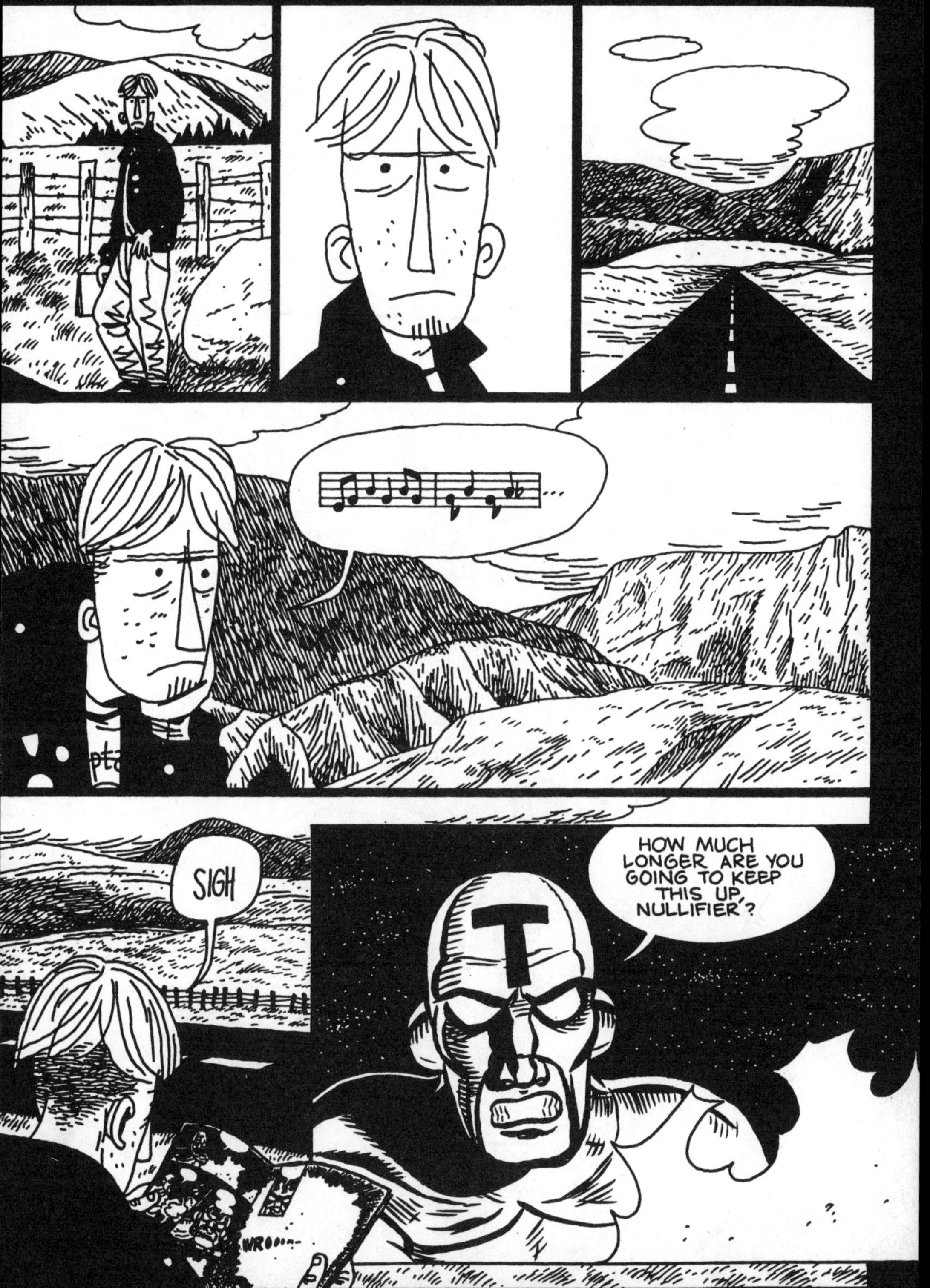
SIGH
HOW MUCH LONGER ARE YOU GOING TO KEEP THIS UP, NULLIFIER?

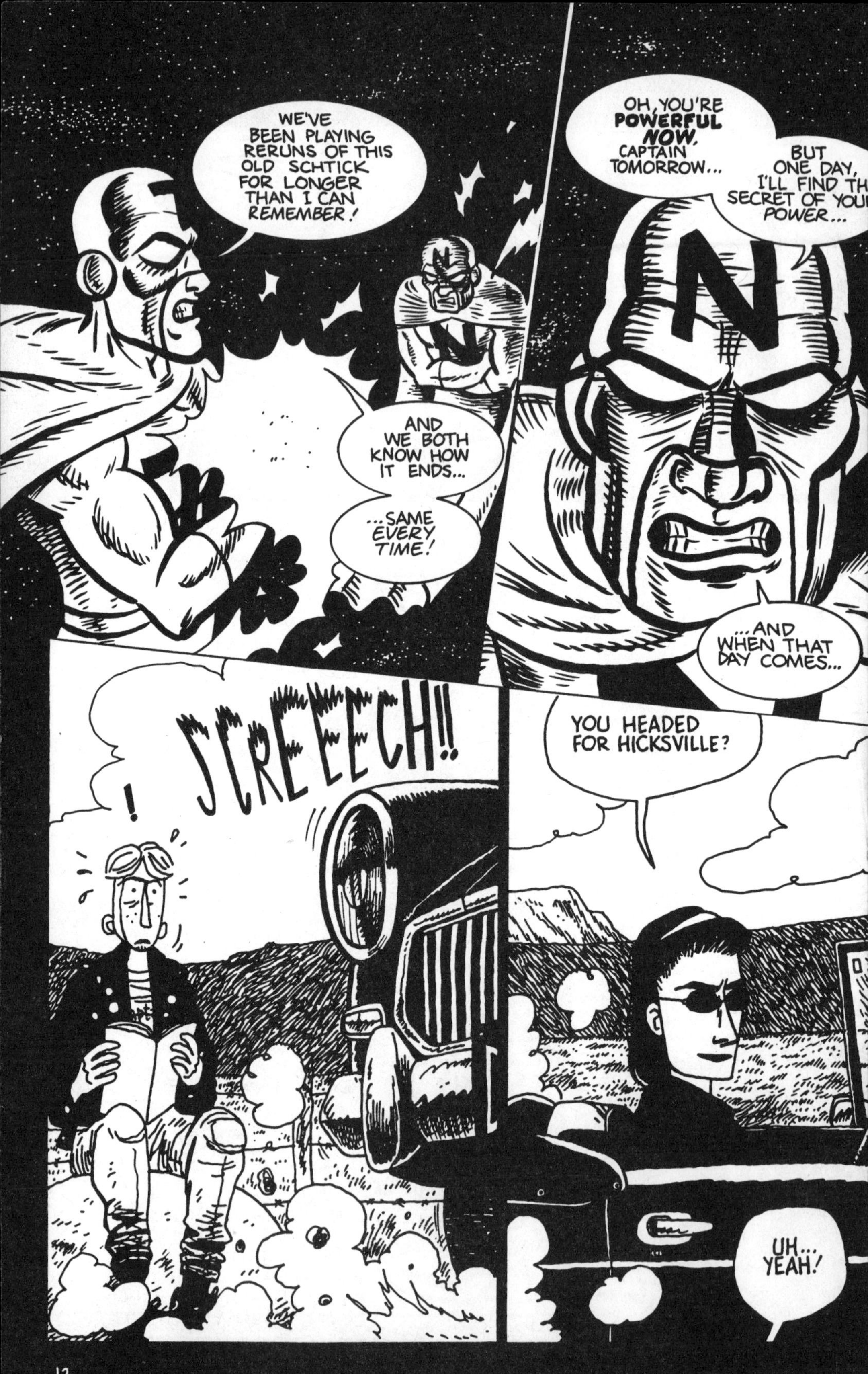
WE'VE BEEN PLAYING RERUNS OF THIS OLD SCHTICK FOR LONGER THAN I CAN REMEMBER!
AND WE BOTH KNOW HOW IT ENDS...
...SAME EVERY TIME!
OH, YOU'RE POWERFUL NOW, CAPTAIN TOMORROW...
...AND WHEN THAT DAY COMES...
SCREEECH!!
!
YOU HEADED FOR HICKSVILLE?
UH... YEAH!

GET IN!

THANK GOD YOU SHOWED UP. I THOUGHT THE BUS WENT ALL THE WAY TO HICKSVILLE, BUT APPARENTLY NOT. I'M VERY GRATEFUL TO YOU, MISS...

YOU AMERICAN?

YEAH. NAME'S LEONARD BATTS. I'M A JOURNAL-IST AND CRITIC FOR *COMICS WORLD* MAGAZINE.

COMICS WORLD? WHAT—YOU WRITE ABOUT COMICS?

YEAH. I'VE JUST FINISHED A BOOK ON JACK KIRBY AND—

WIERDEST FUCKEN JOB I EVER HEARD OF...

WELL... UH...

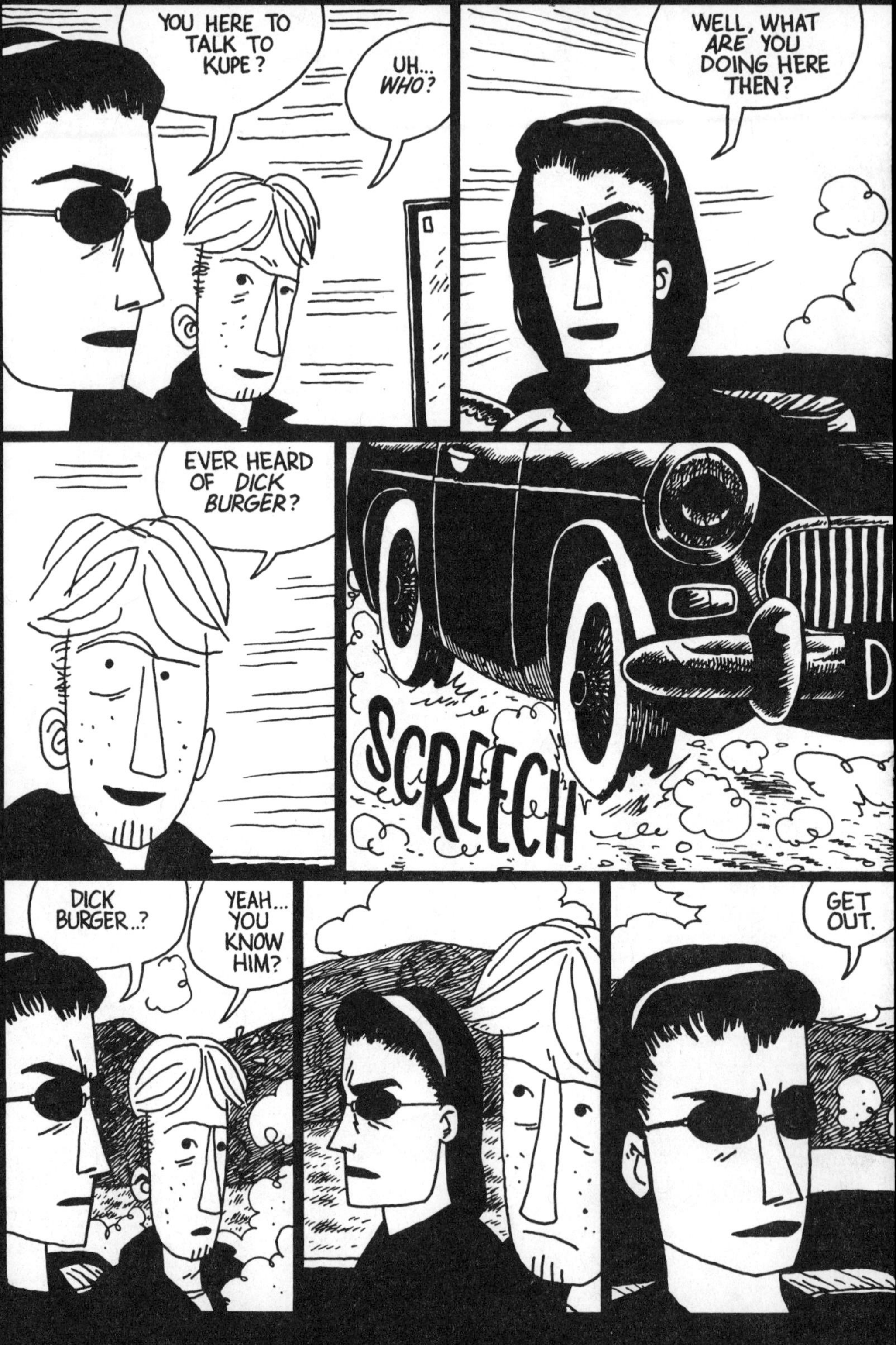
YOU HERE TO TALK TO KUPE?
UH... WHO?
WELL, WHAT ARE YOU DOING HERE THEN?
EVER HEARD OF DICK BURGER?
SCREECH
DICK BURGER..?
YEAH... YOU KNOW HIM?
GET OUT.

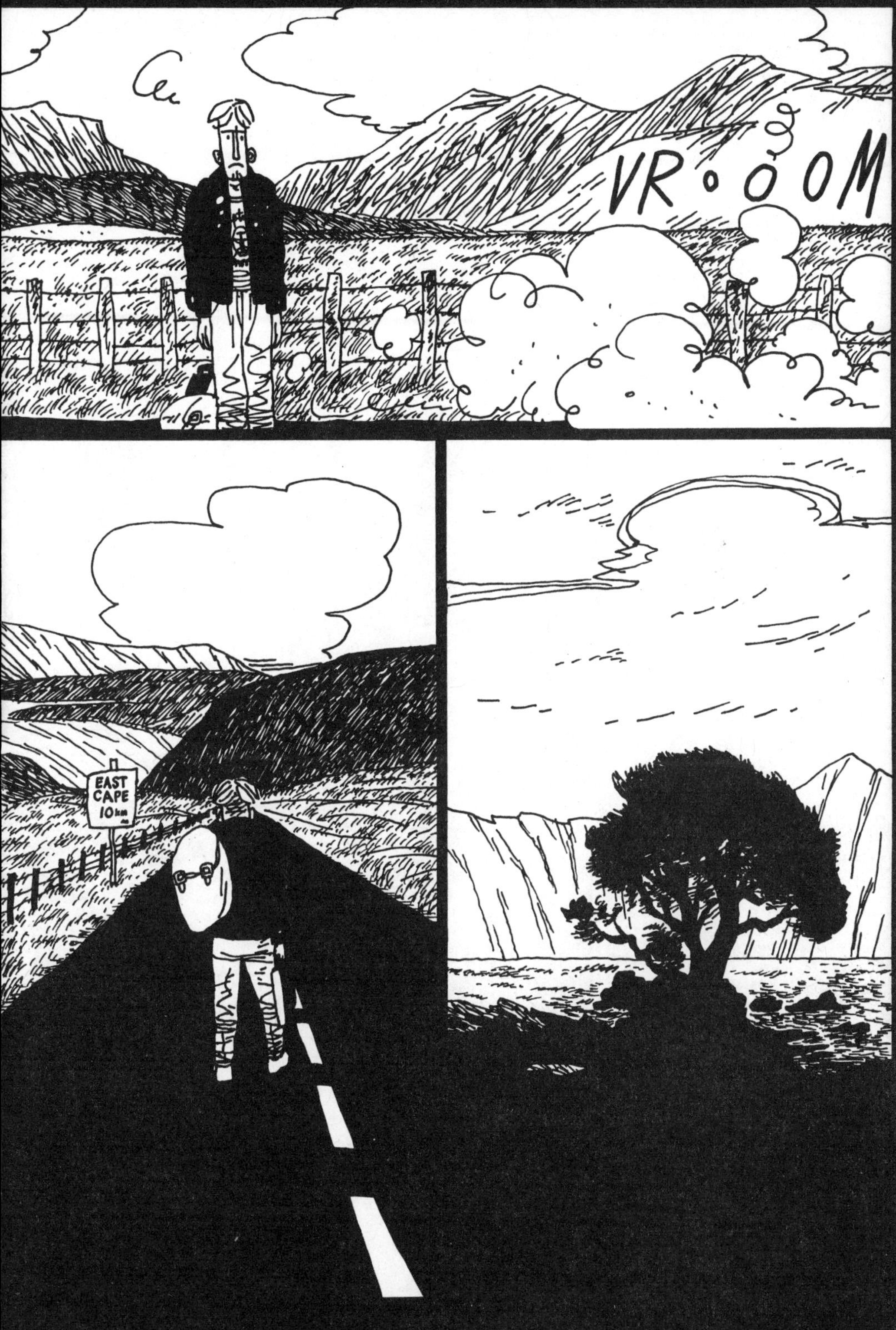
VROOM
EAST CAPE 10 km

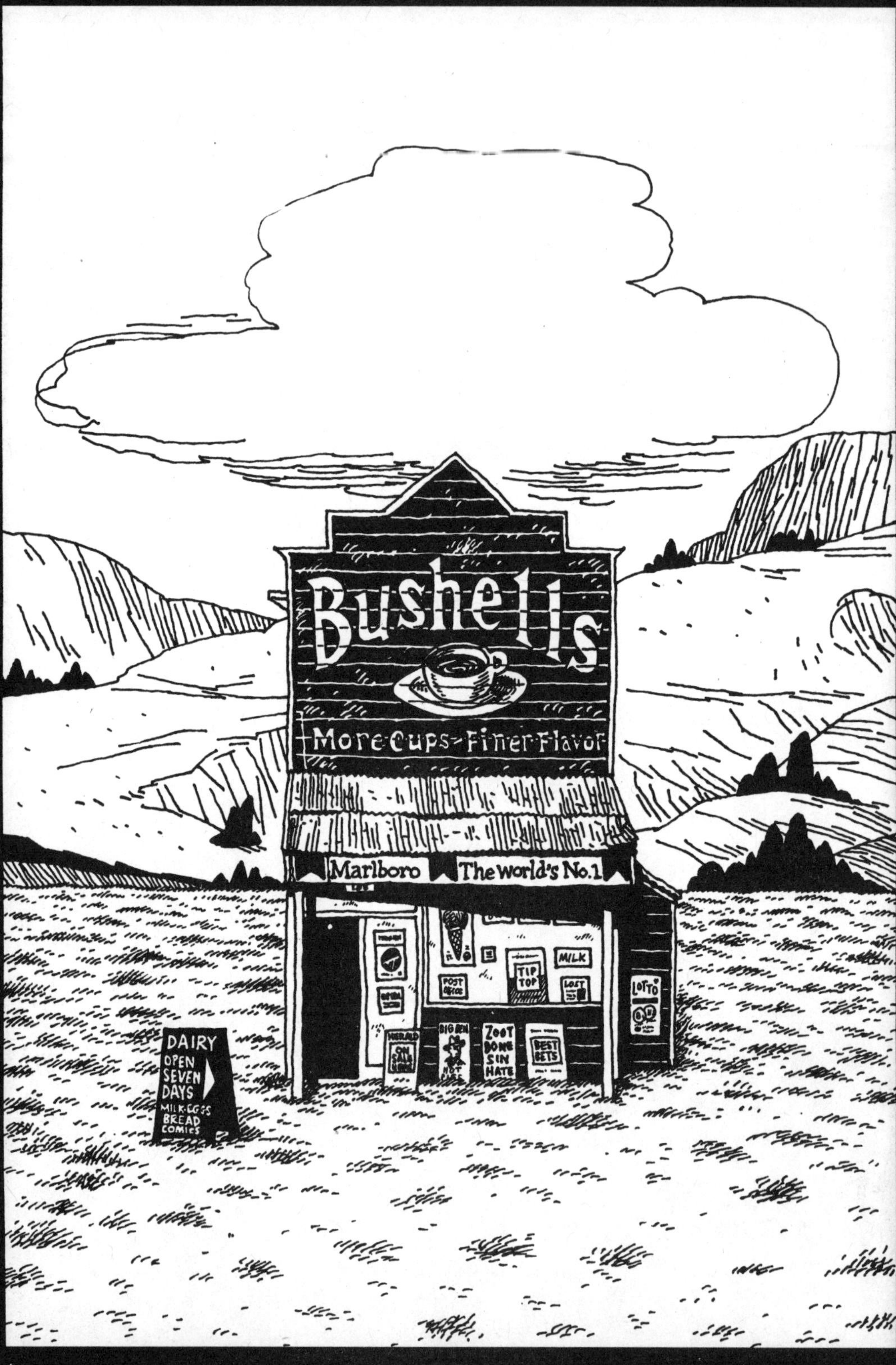
Bushells
More Cups - Finer Flavor
Marlboro
The world's No.1
MILK
POST OFFICE
TIP TOP
LOTTO
HERALD
ON SALE
BIG BEN
ZOOT BONE SIN HATE
BEST BETS
DAIRY
OPEN SEVEN DAYS
MILK·EGGS BREAD COMICS

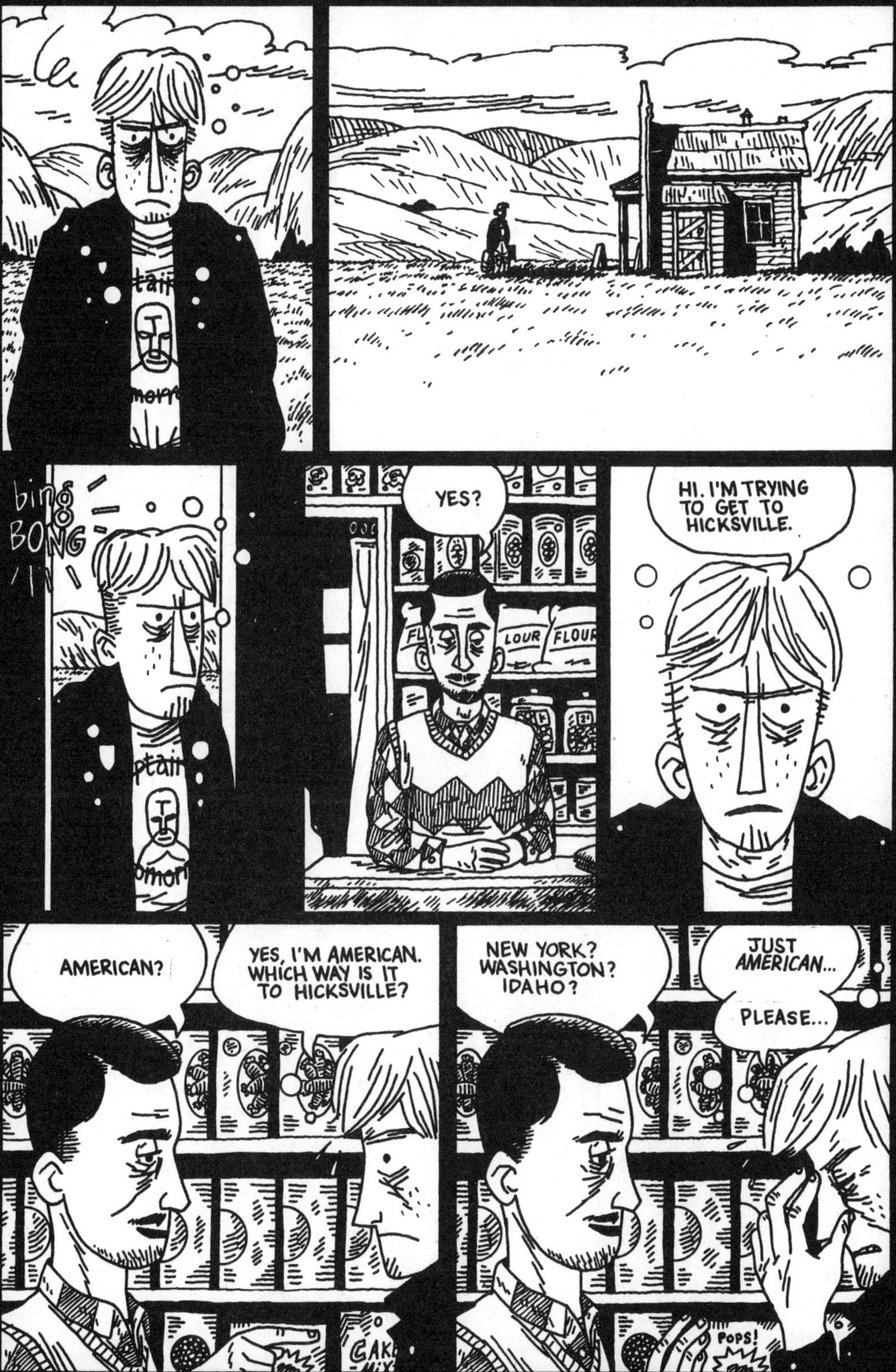
bing
BONG
YES?
HI. I'M TRYING TO GET TO HICKSVILLE.
AMERICAN?
YES, I'M AMERICAN. WHICH WAY IS IT TO HICKSVILLE?
NEW YORK? WASHINGTON? IDAHO?
JUST AMERICAN...
PLEASE...
POPS!

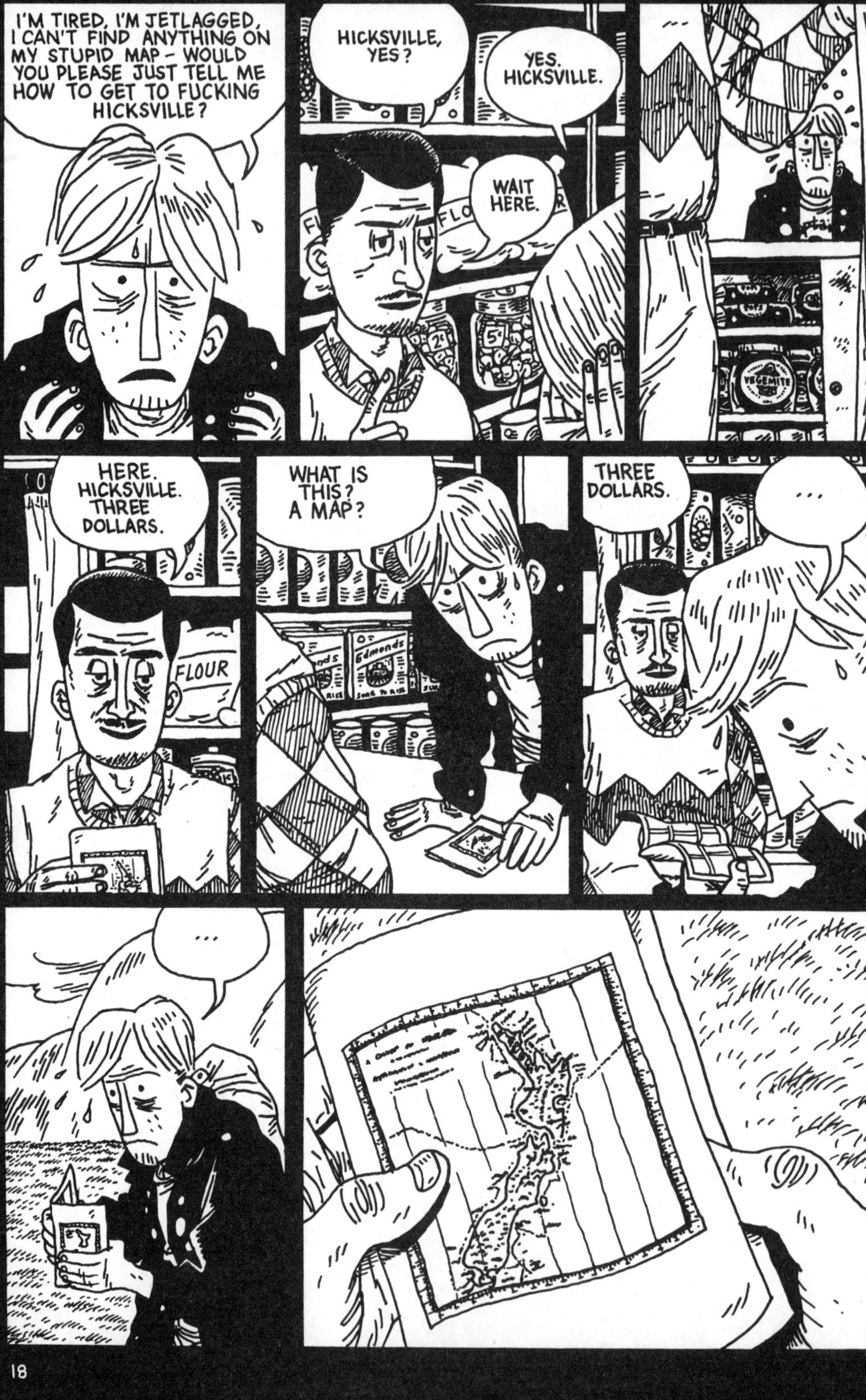
I'M TIRED, I'M JETLAGGED, I CAN'T FIND ANYTHING ON MY STUPID MAP - WOULD YOU PLEASE JUST TELL ME HOW TO GET TO FUCKING HICKSVILLE?
HICKSVILLE, YES?
YES. HICKSVILLE.
WAIT HERE.
FLOUR
VEGEMITE
HERE. HICKSVILLE. THREE DOLLARS.
FLOUR
WHAT IS THIS? A MAP?
Edmonds
THREE DOLLARS.
...
...

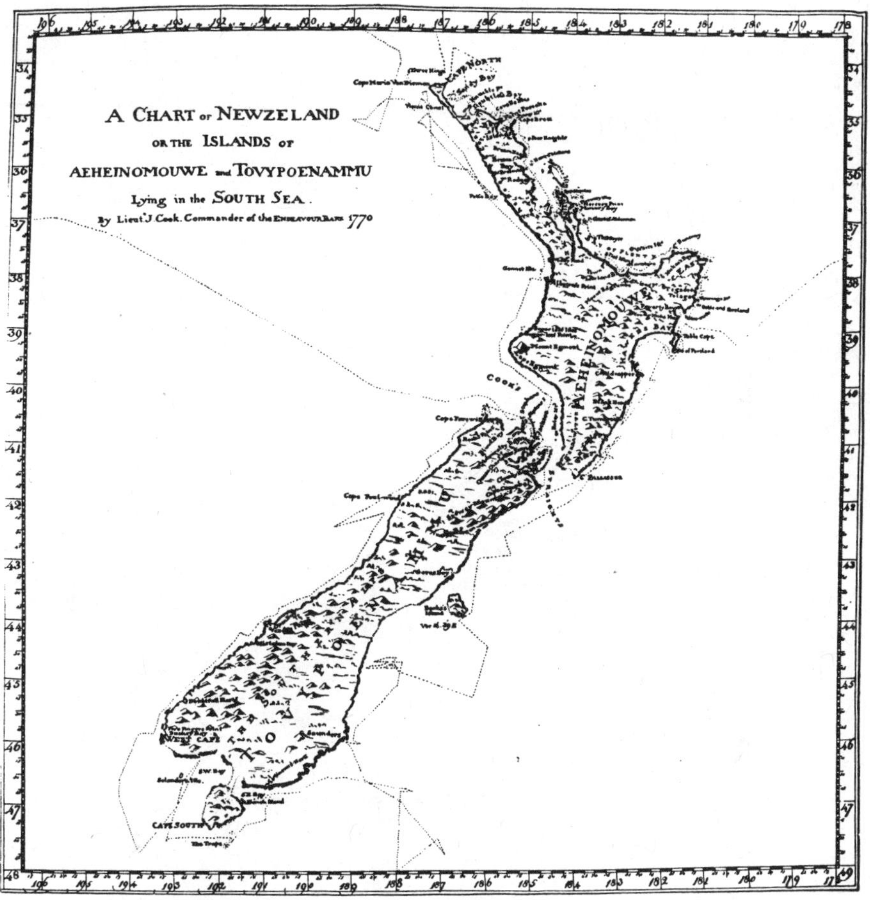
A CHART OF NEWZELAND
OR THE ISLANDS OF
AEHEINOMOUWE and TOVYPOENAMMU
Lying in the SOUTH SEA.
By Lieut. J. Cook. Commander of the ENDEAVOUR BARK 1770
CAPE NORTH
COOK'S
AEHEINOMOUWE
CAPE SOUTH
WEST CAPE

Time passes...

Do you recall, Captain, how Te Ika-a-Maui came into being?

I know something of your legends, yes...

The North Island is Te Ika-a-Maui - 'The Fish of Maui.' It is the great fish caught by Maui using the jaw-bone of Murirangawhenua.

You're telling me the North Island is a fish?

And the South Island is the canoe from which it was caught: Te Waka-o-Maui...

Very amusing. But what is your point exactly?

The fish has woken up and begun to swim, Captain, towing Maui's canoe behind it...

Well, didn't your Maui have sense enough to kill this fish once he'd caught it?

...

I jest, Hone, as do you, surely!

Pack your compass, Captain. Your maps have told us nothing.

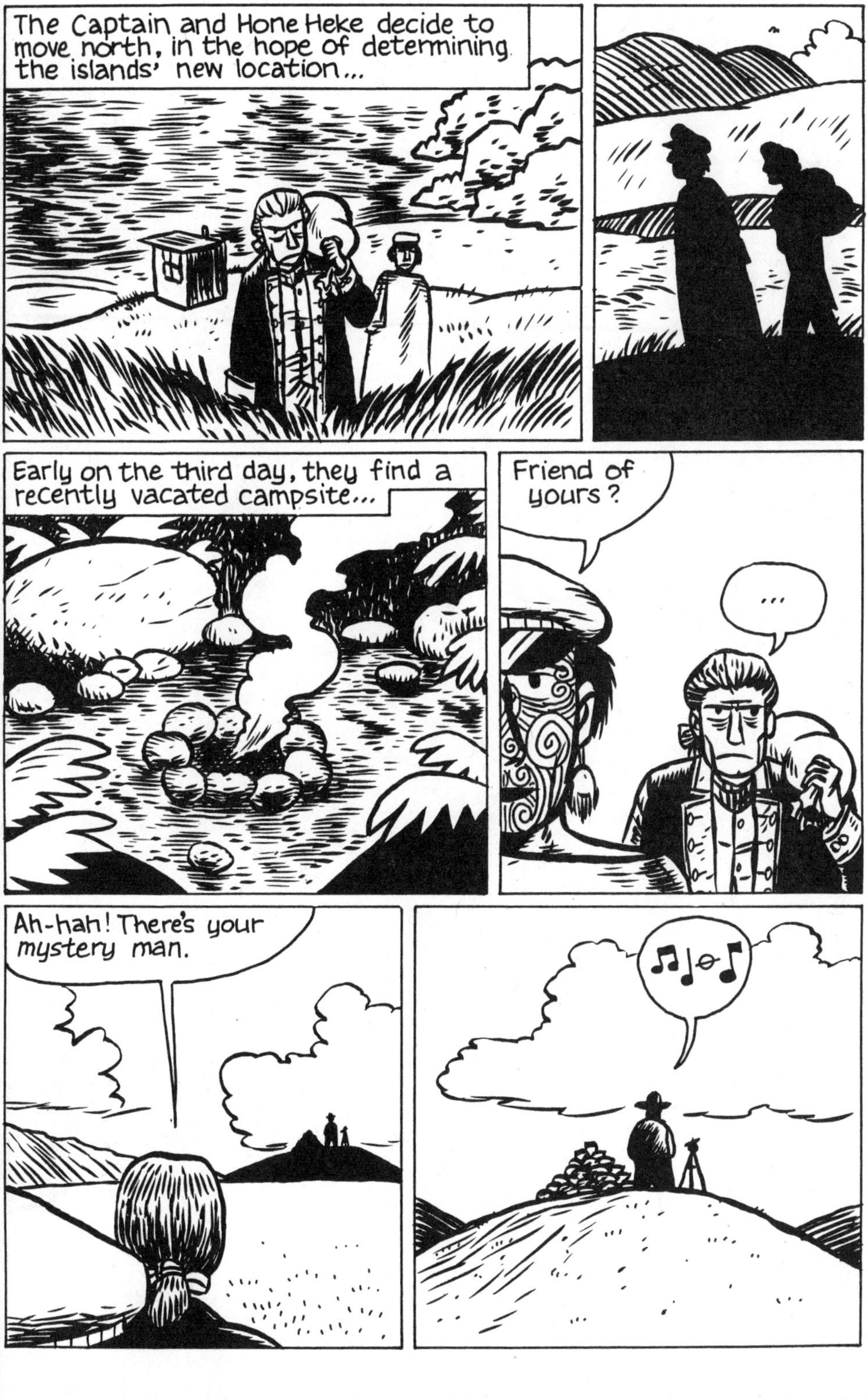
The Captain and Hone Heke decide to move north, in the hope of determining the islands' new location...
Early on the third day, they find a recently vacated campsite...
Friend of yours?
...
Ah-hah! There's your *mystery* man.

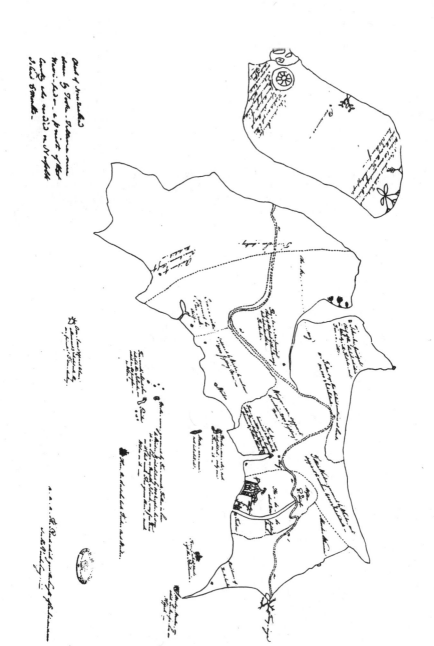

22

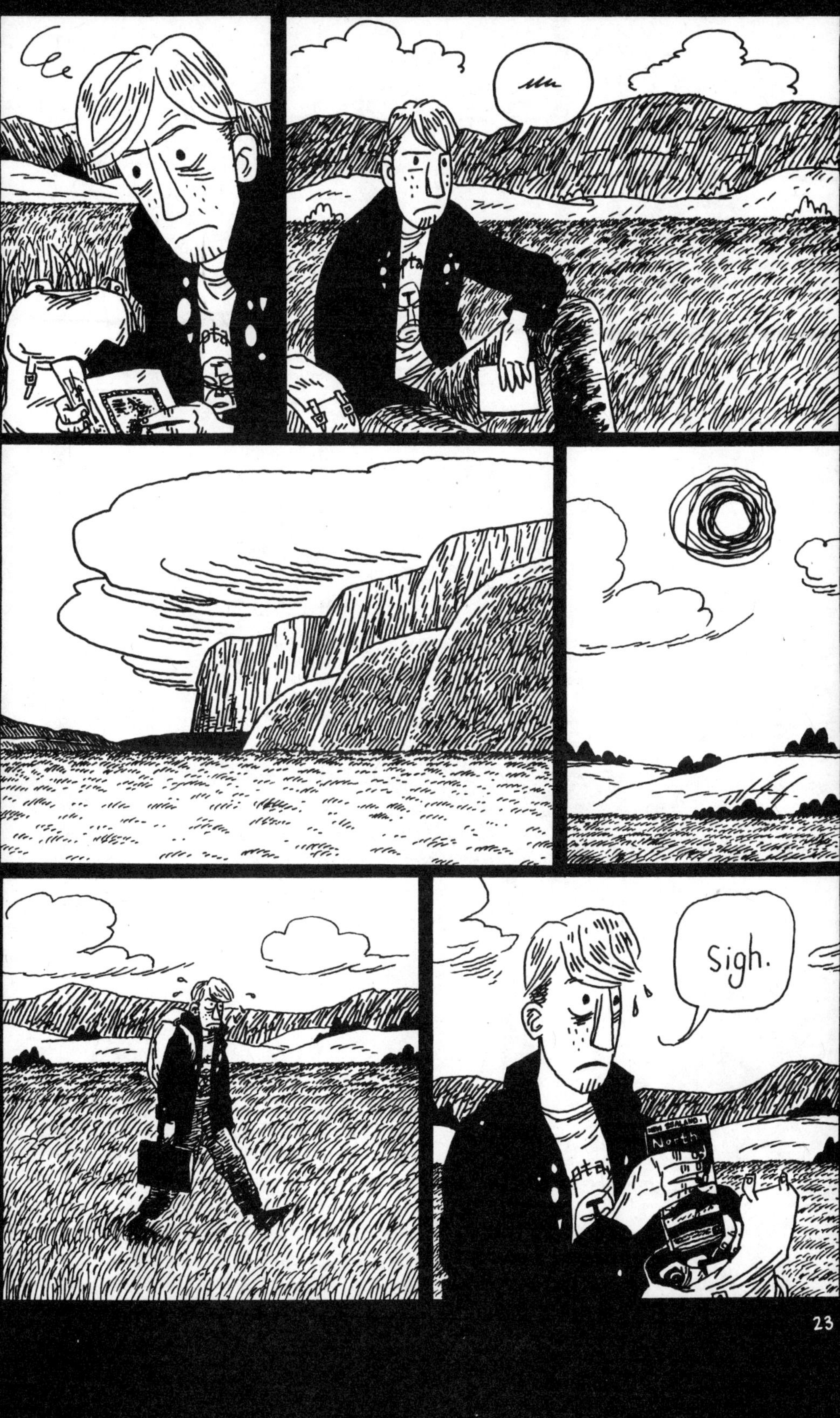
Sigh.
North

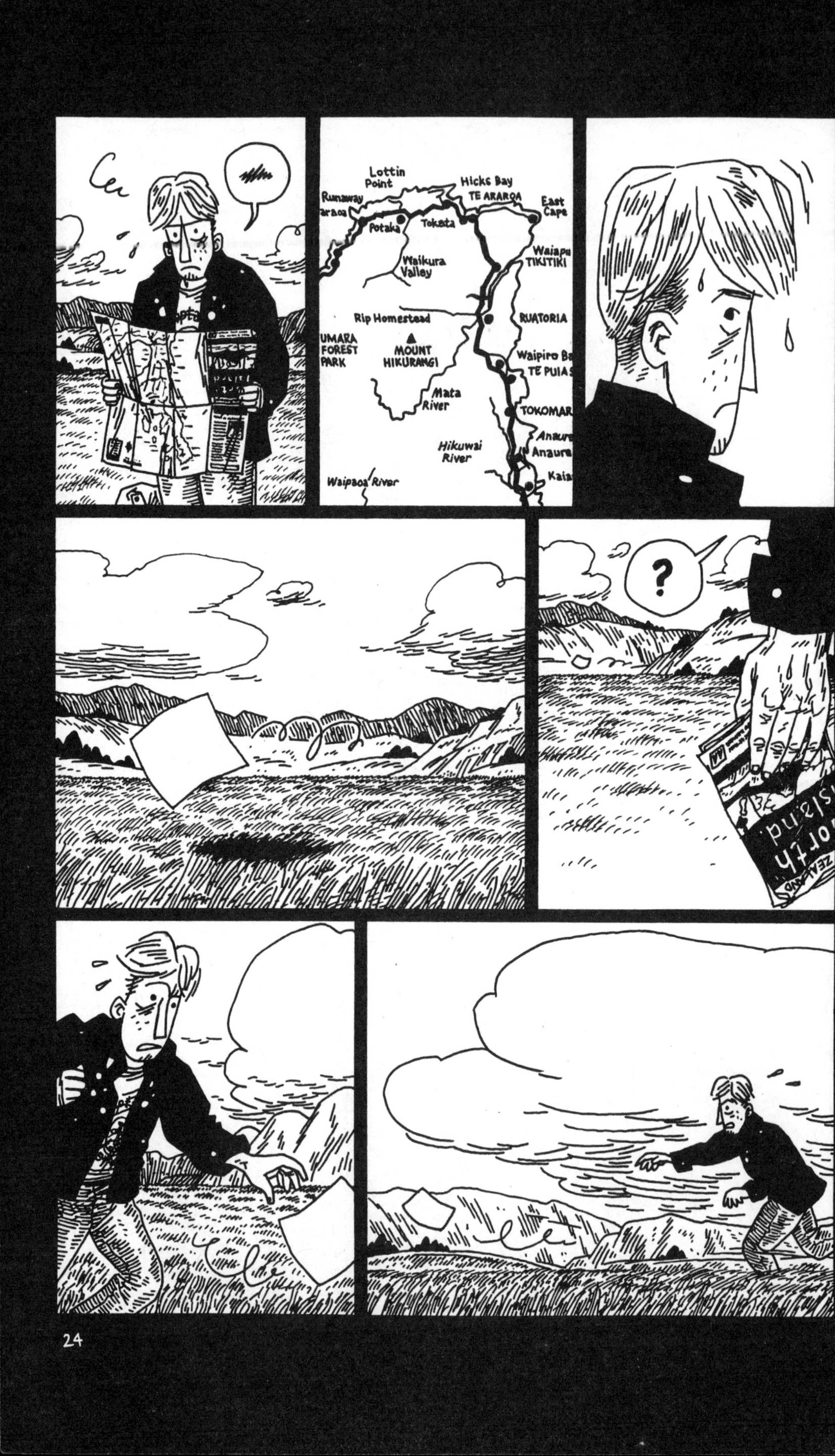
Lottin Point
Runaway
araroa
Hicks Bay
TE ARAROA
East Cape
Potaka
Tokata
Waikura Valley
Waiapu
TIKITIKI
Rip Homestead
RUATORIA
UMARA FOREST PARK
MOUNT HIKURANGI
Waipiro Ba
TE PUIAS
Mata River
TOKOMAR
Anaura
Anaura
Hikuwai River
Kaia
Waipaoa River
?

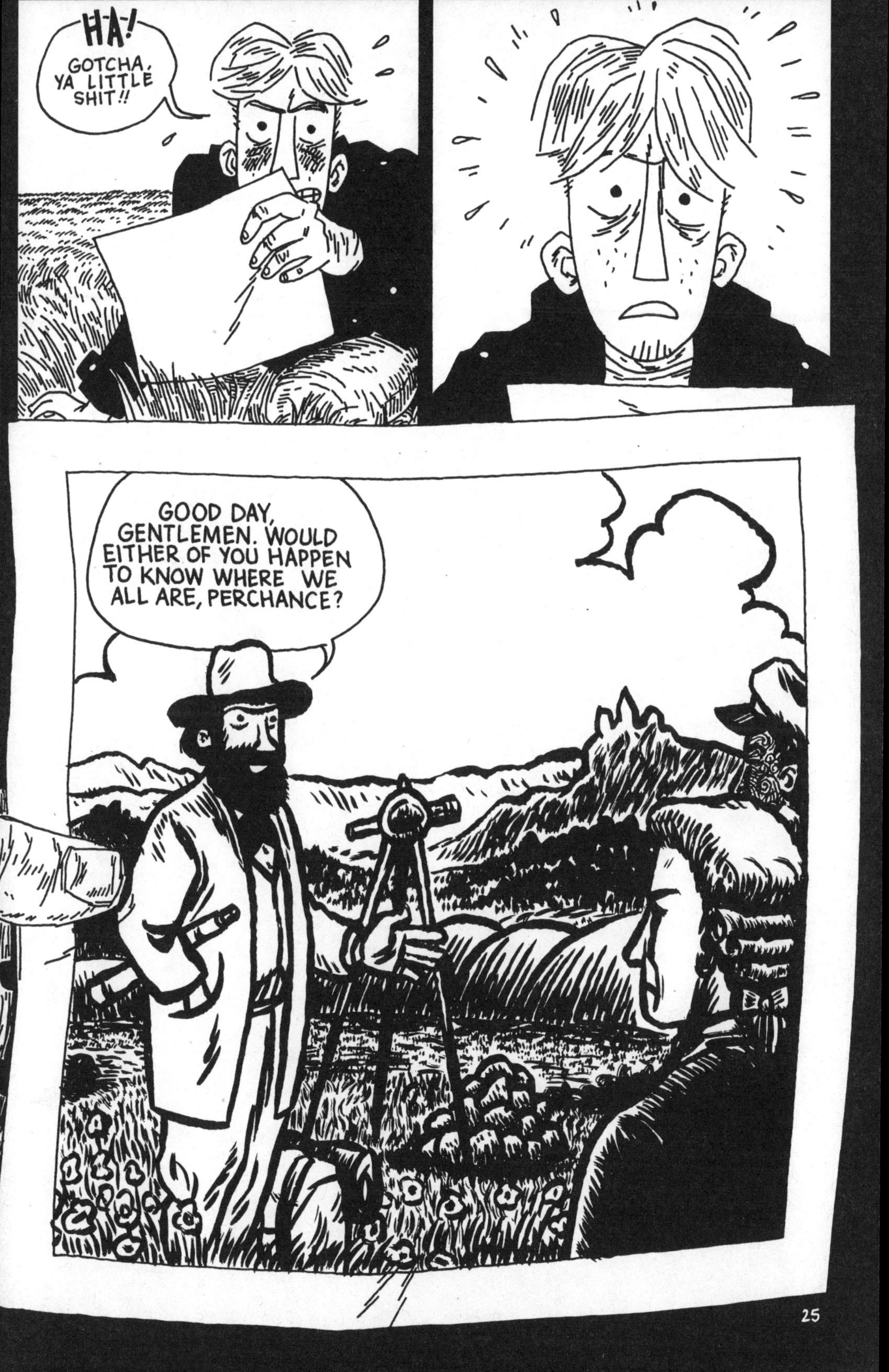
HA!
GOTCHA, YA LITTLE SHIT!!
GOOD DAY, GENTLEMEN. WOULD EITHER OF YOU HAPPEN TO KNOW WHERE WE ALL ARE, PERCHANCE?

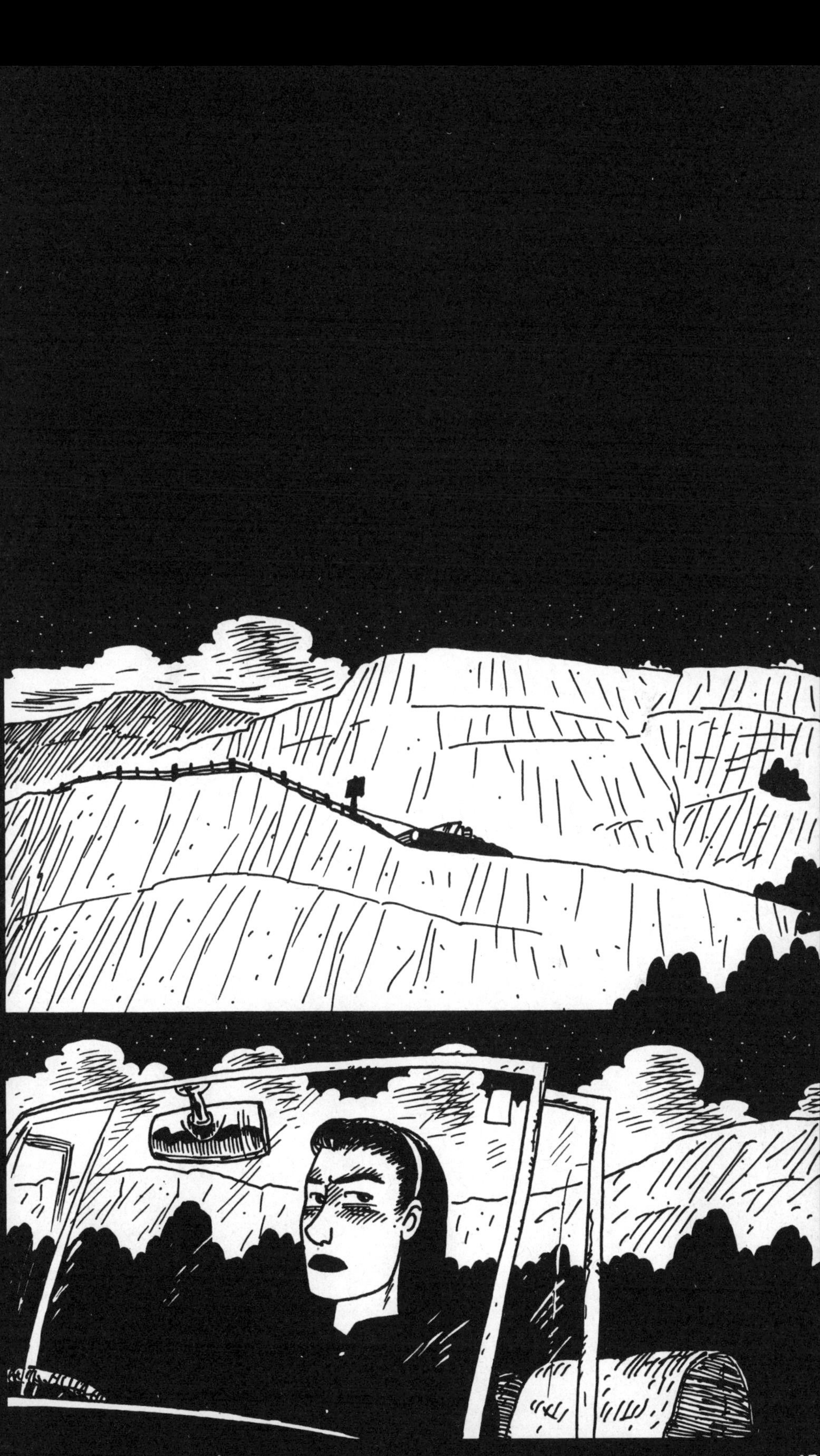

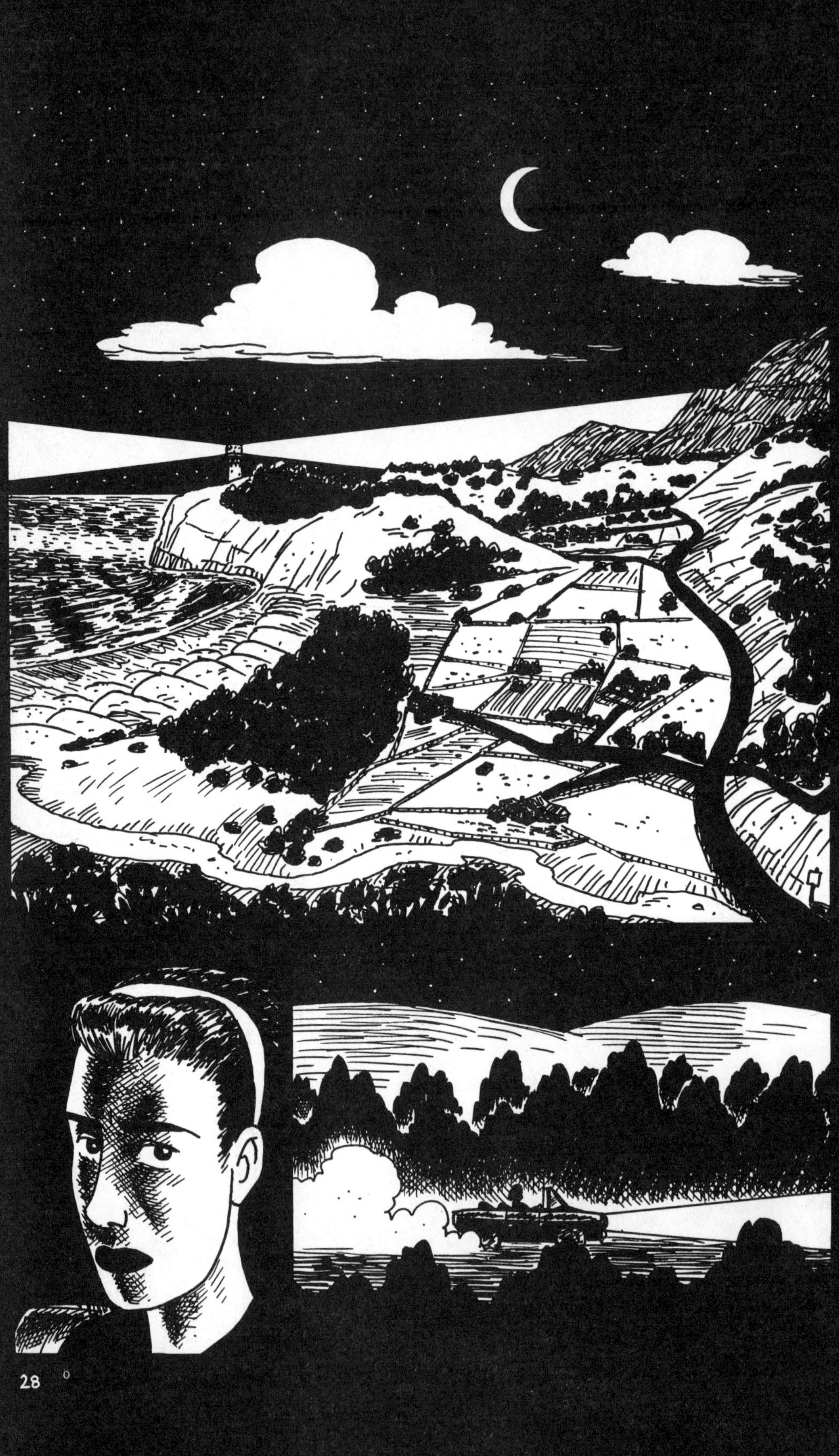

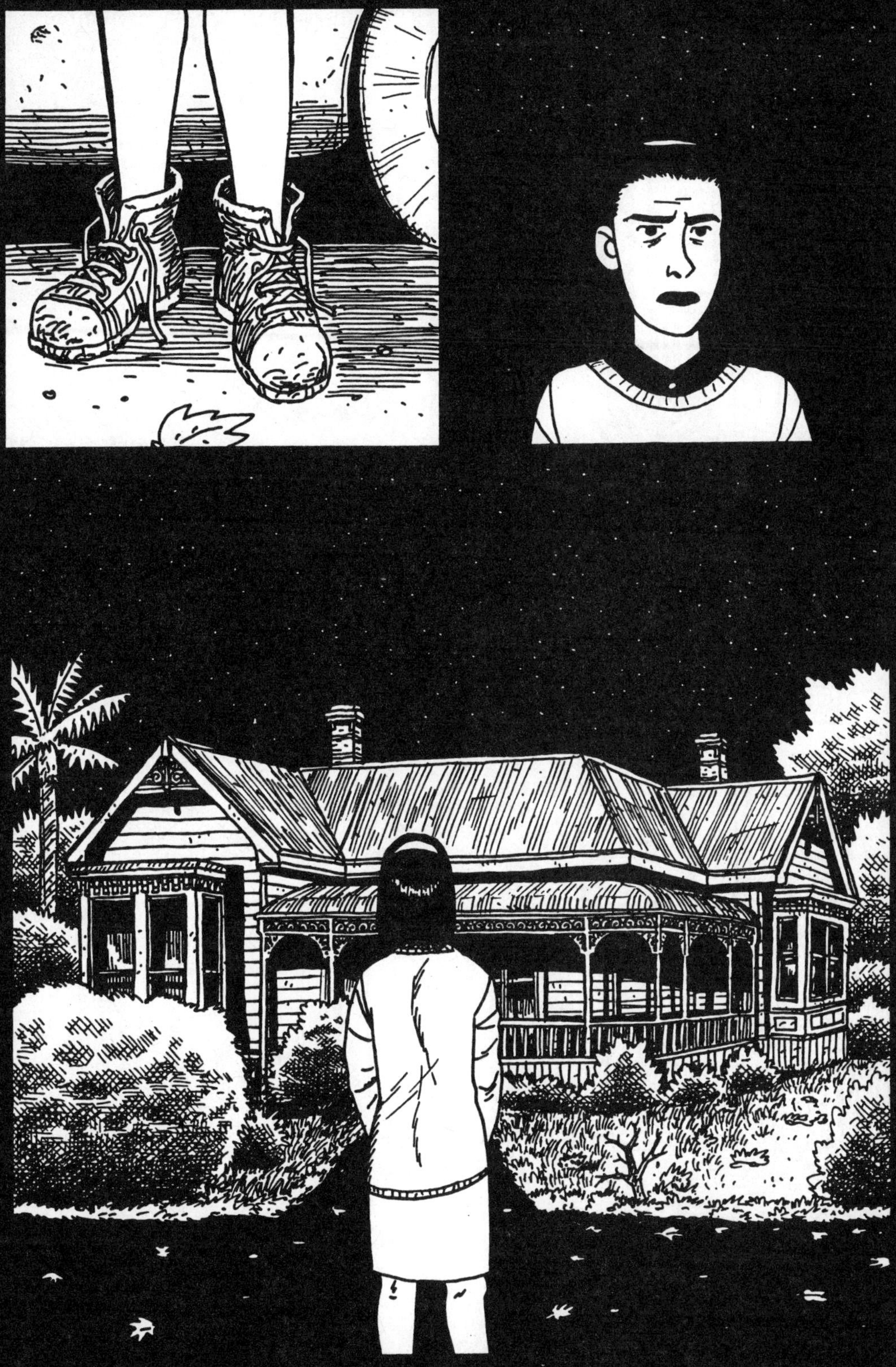

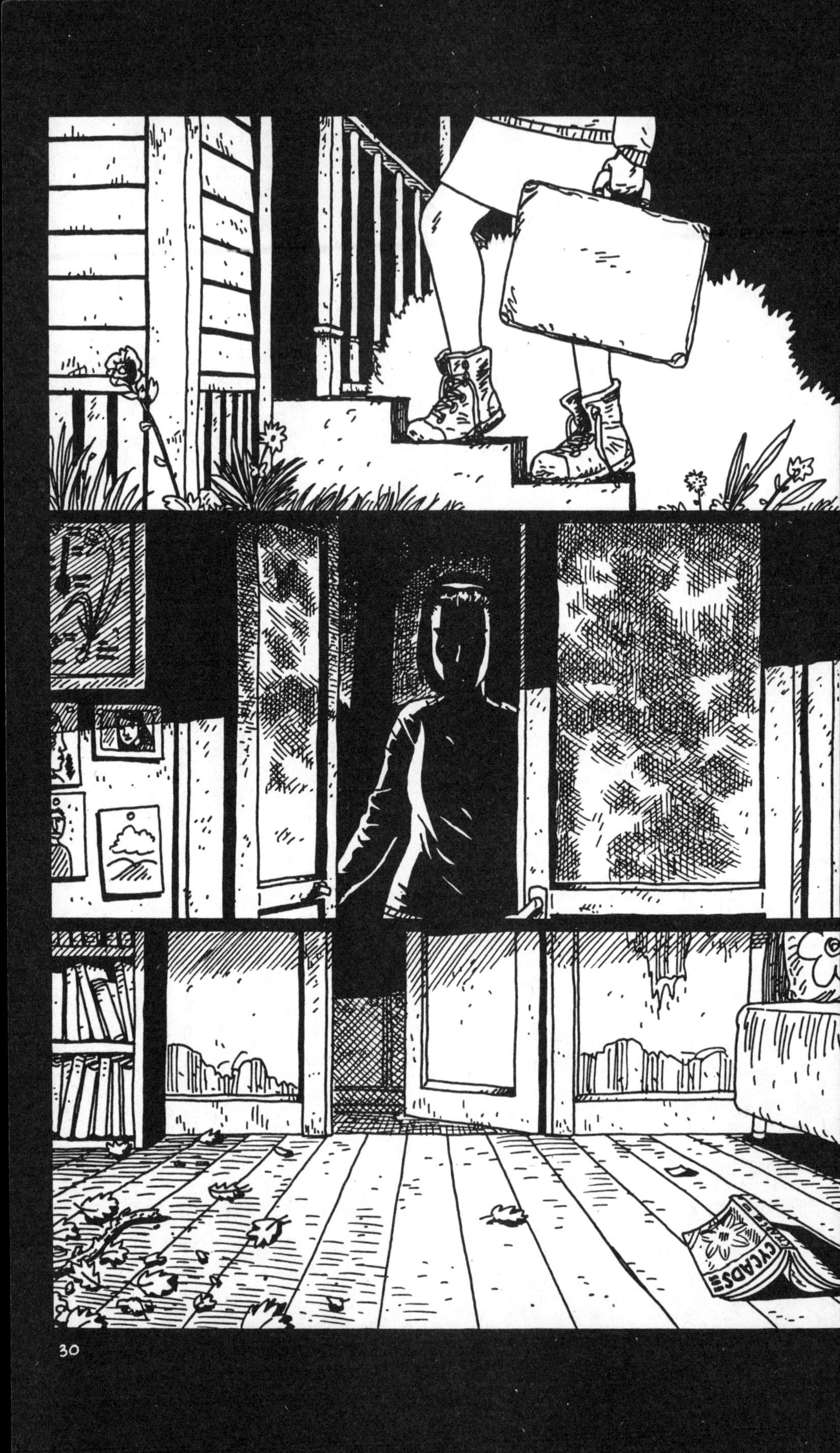
CYCADS

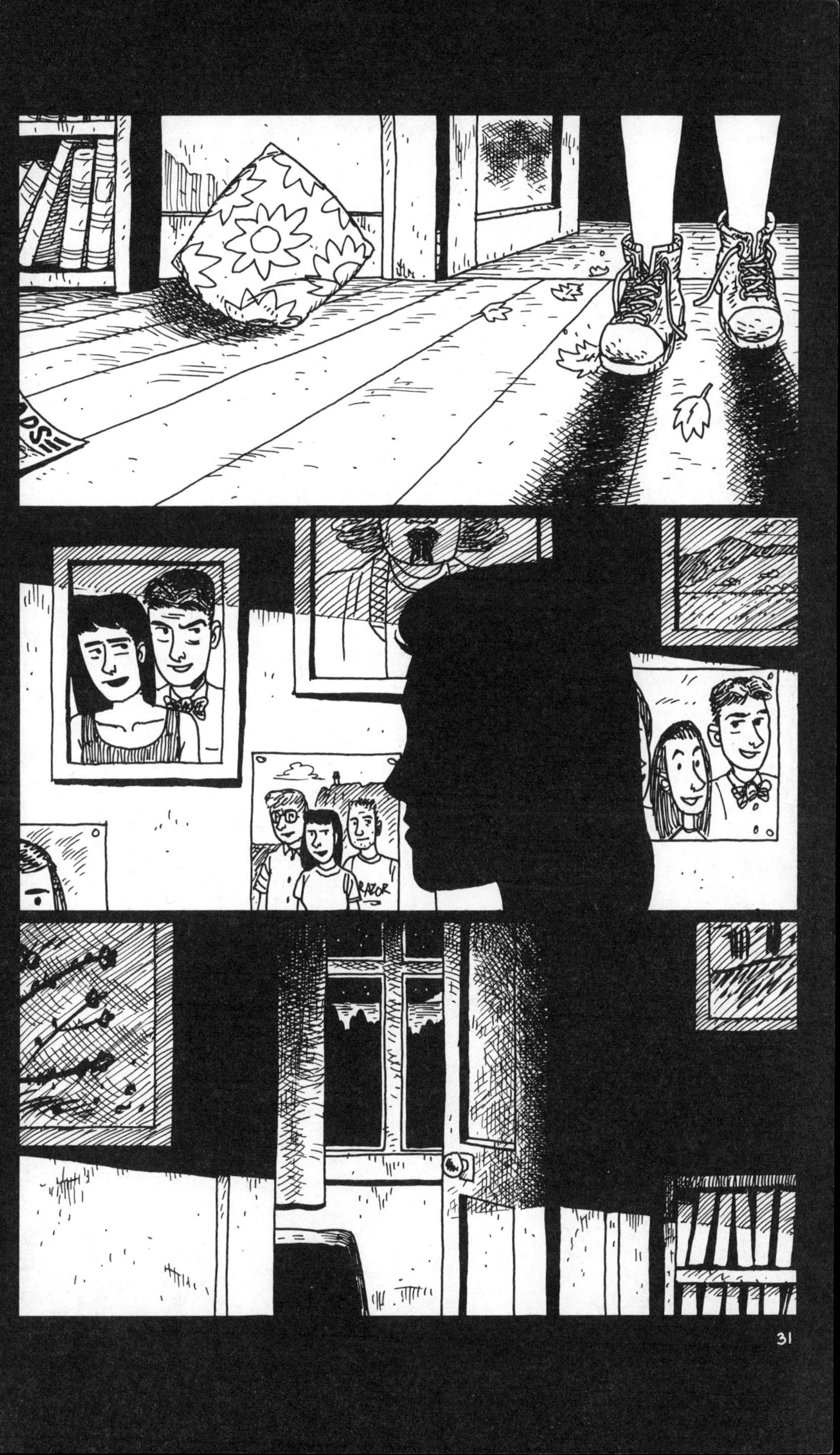
RAZOR

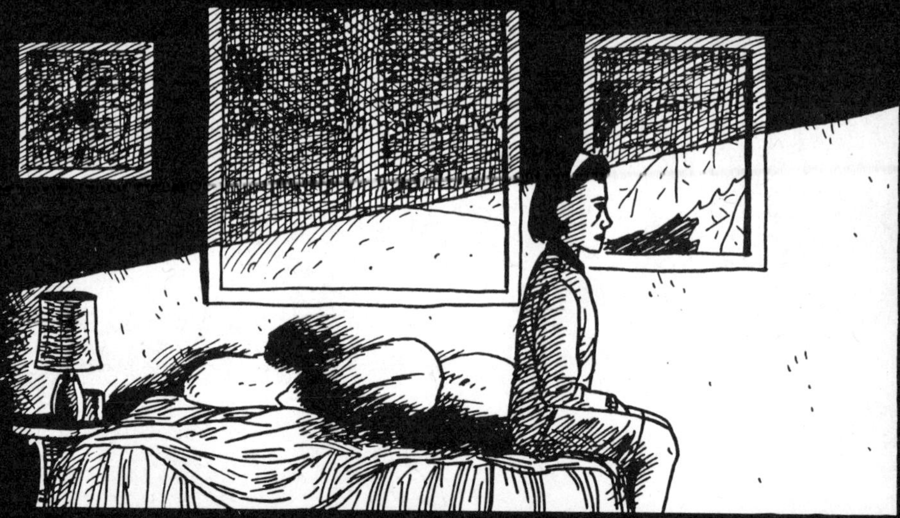

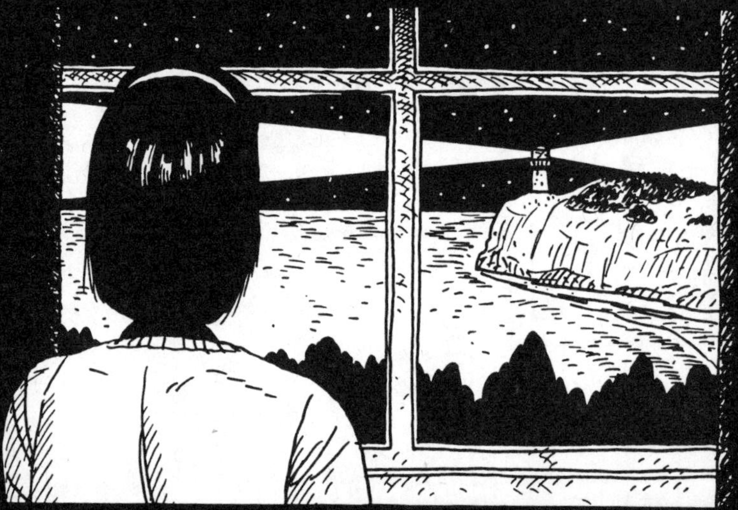

Chapter Two

"When somebody asks me what got me into comics I can only think of one word: malnutrition."

Will Eisner.

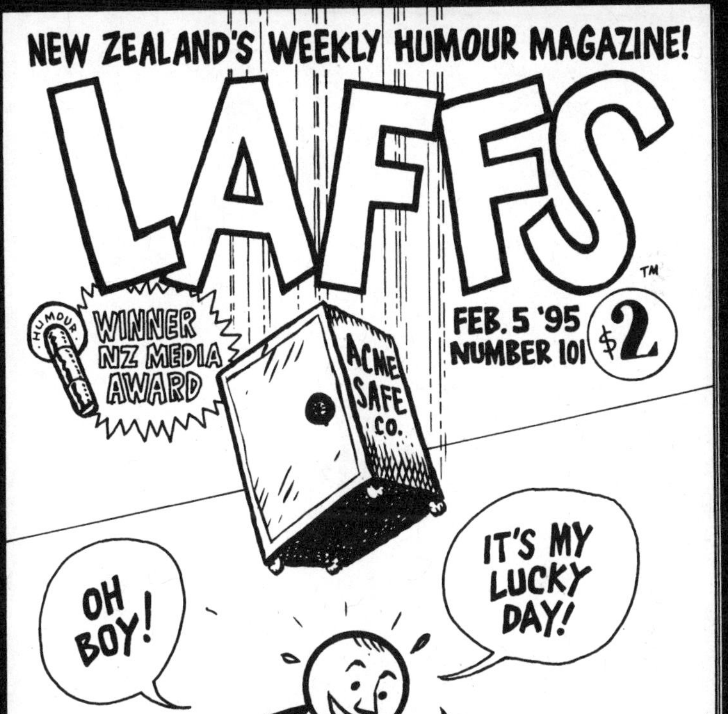
NEW ZEALAND'S WEEKLY HUMOUR MAGAZINE!
LAFFS
TM
HUMOUR
WINNER NZ MEDIA AWARD
ACME SAFE CO.
FEB. 5 '95 NUMBER 101
$2
OH BOY!
IT'S MY LUCKY DAY!
T
SPECIAL KARMA ISSUE!
Sam Zabel '95

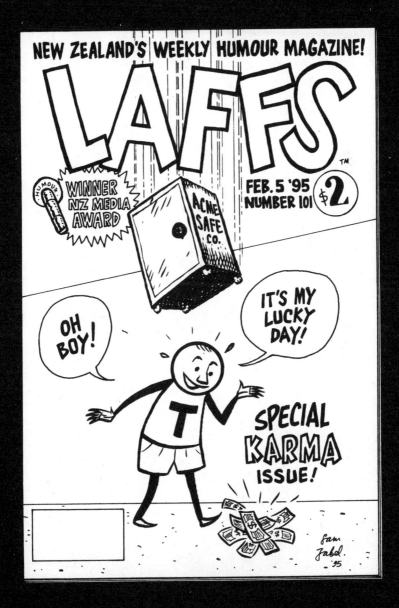

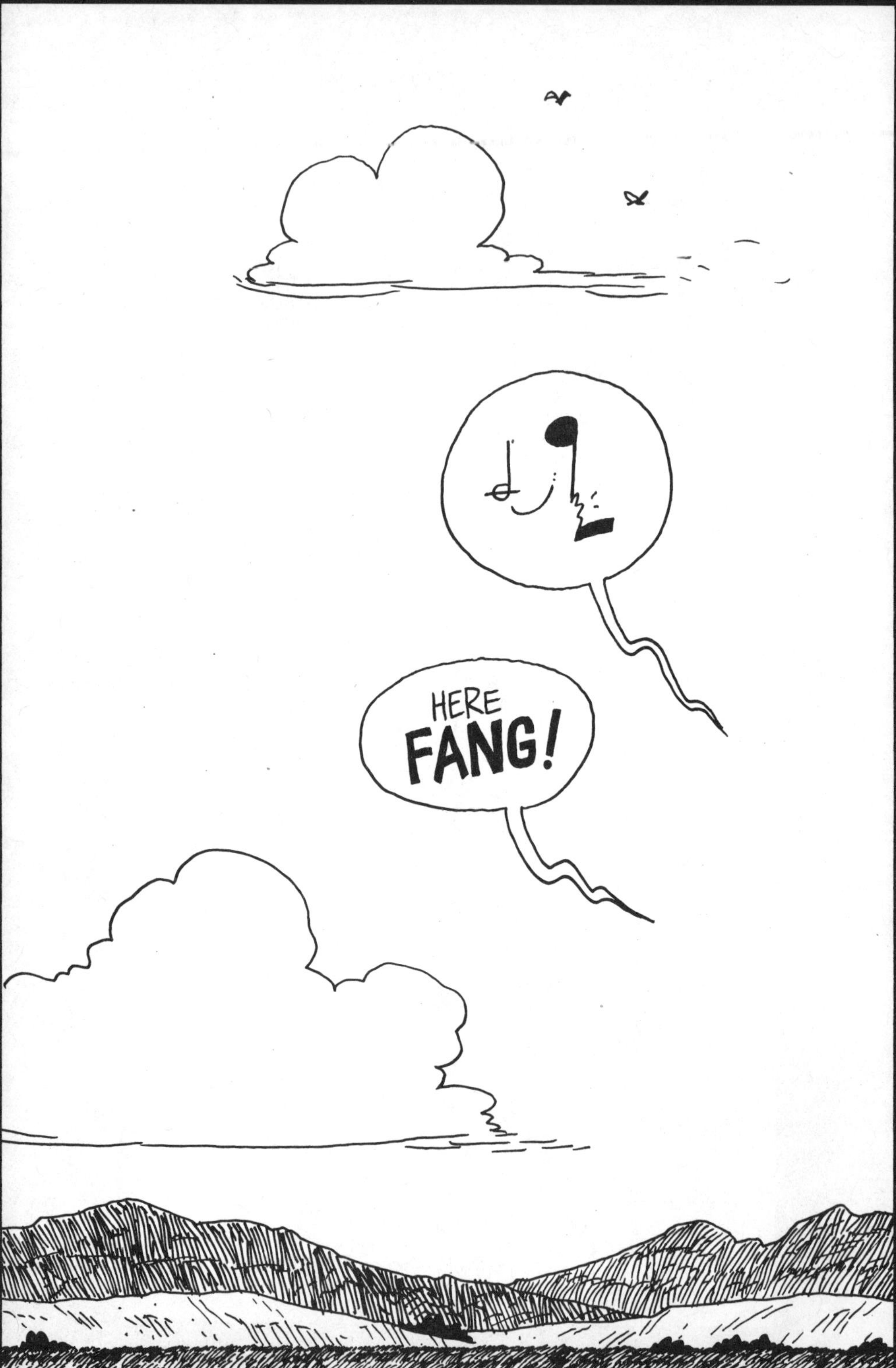
HERE FANG!

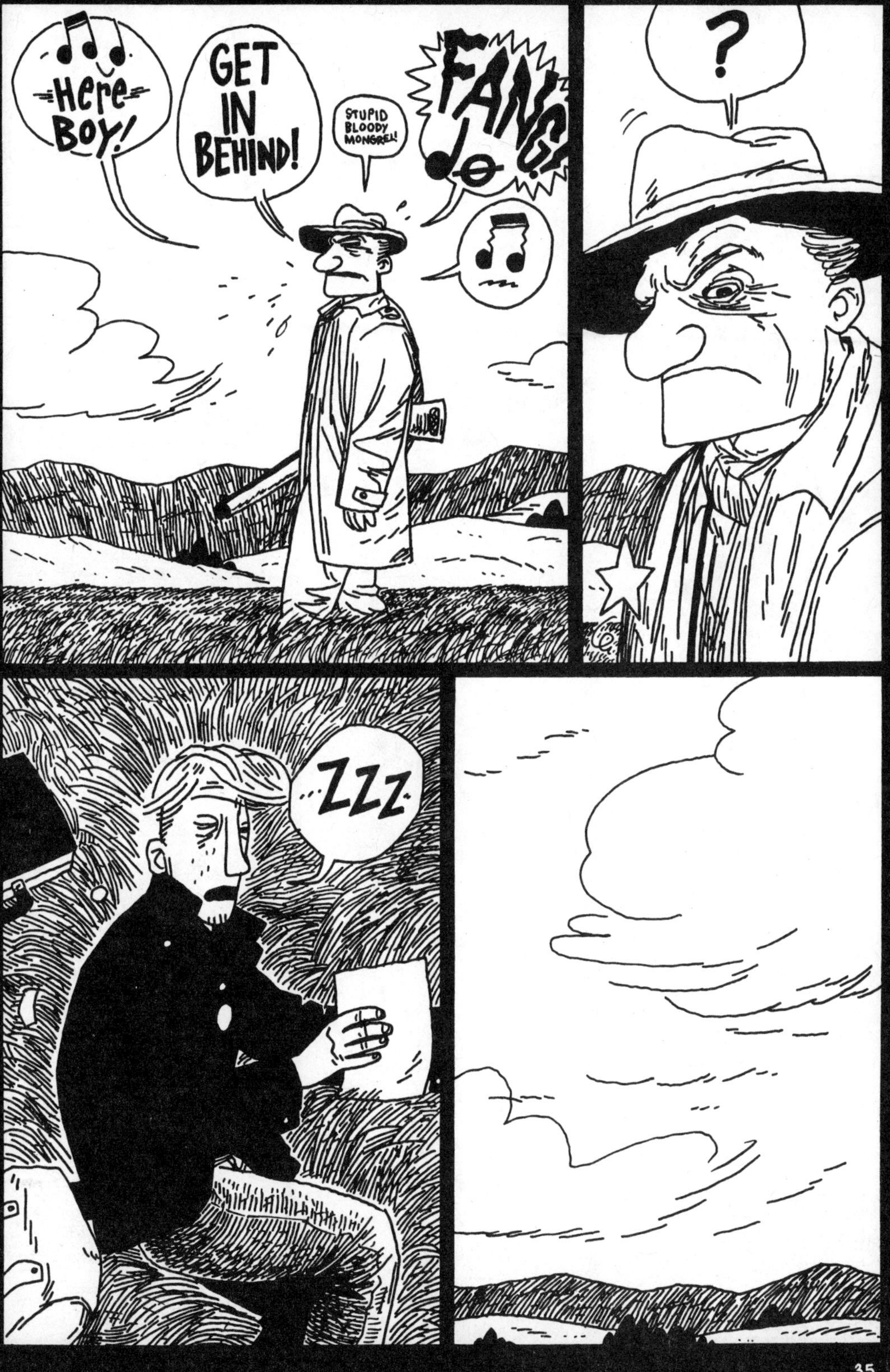
Here Boy!
GET IN BEHIND!
STUPID BLOODY MONGREL!
FANG!
?
ZZZ

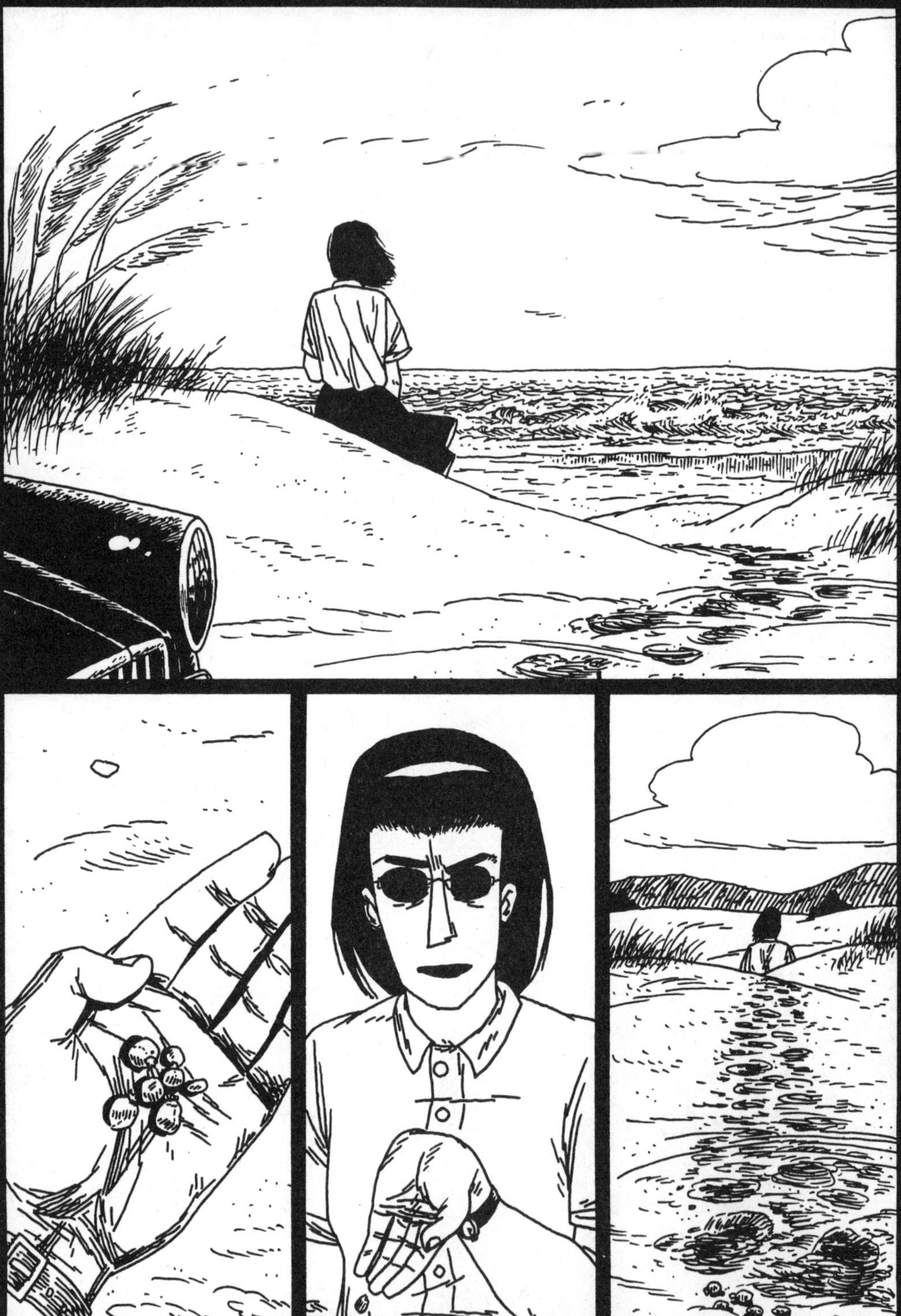

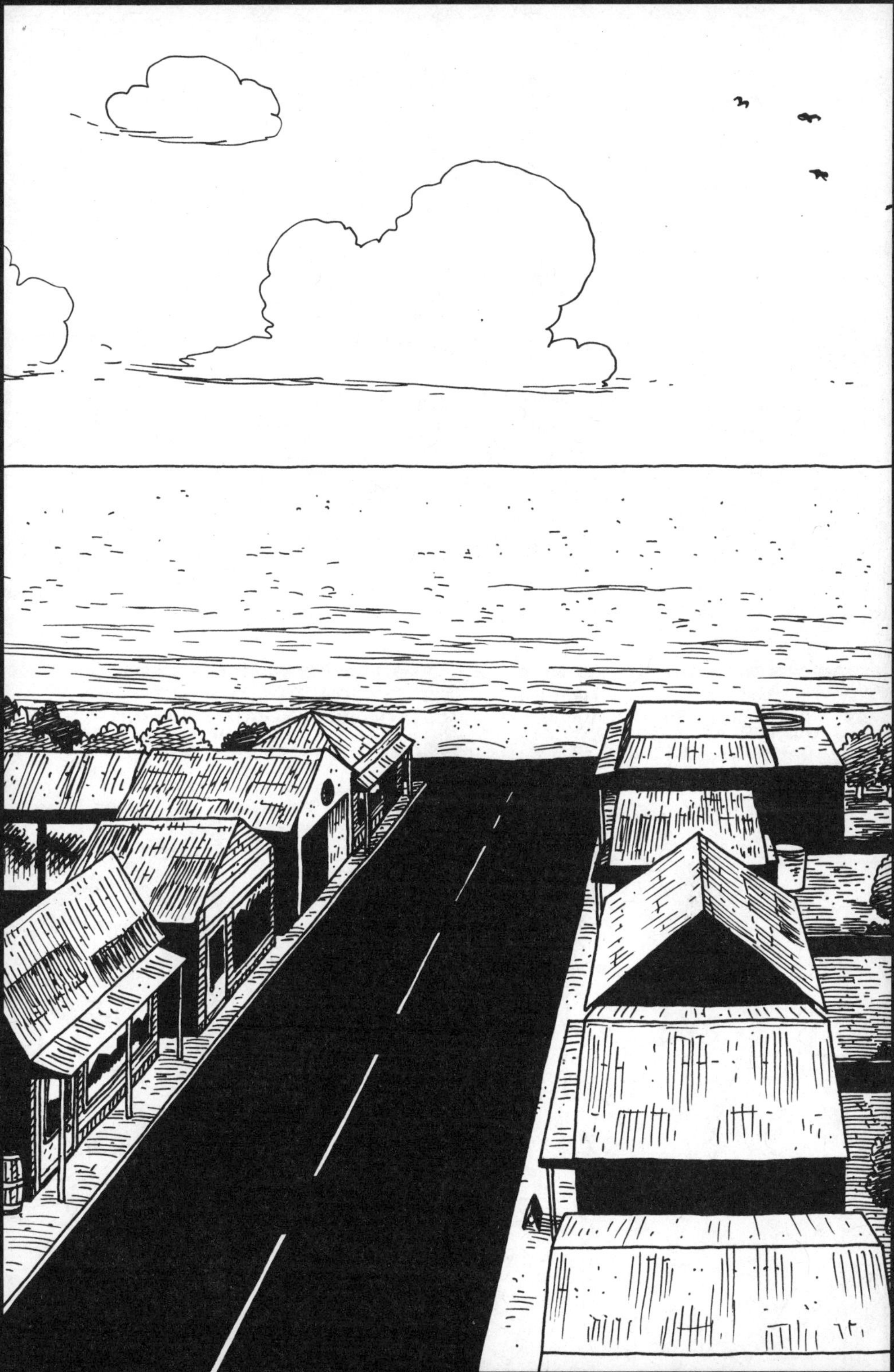

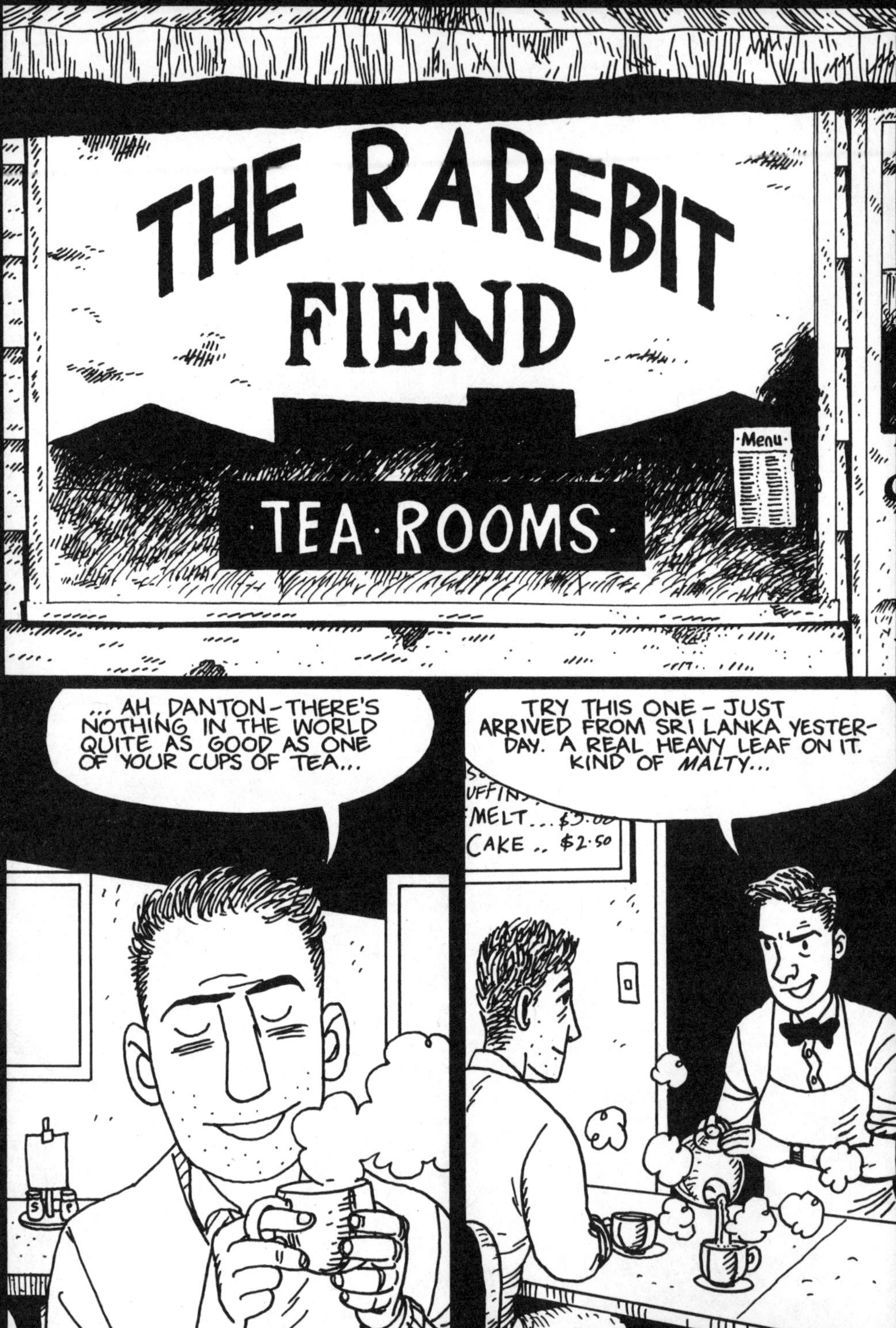
THE RAREBIT FIEND
TEA · ROOMS
Menu
... AH, DANTON - THERE'S NOTHING IN THE WORLD QUITE AS GOOD AS ONE OF YOUR CUPS OF TEA...
TRY THIS ONE - JUST ARRIVED FROM SRI LANKA YESTERDAY. A REAL HEAVY LEAF ON IT. KIND OF *MALTY*...
CAKE .. $2.50

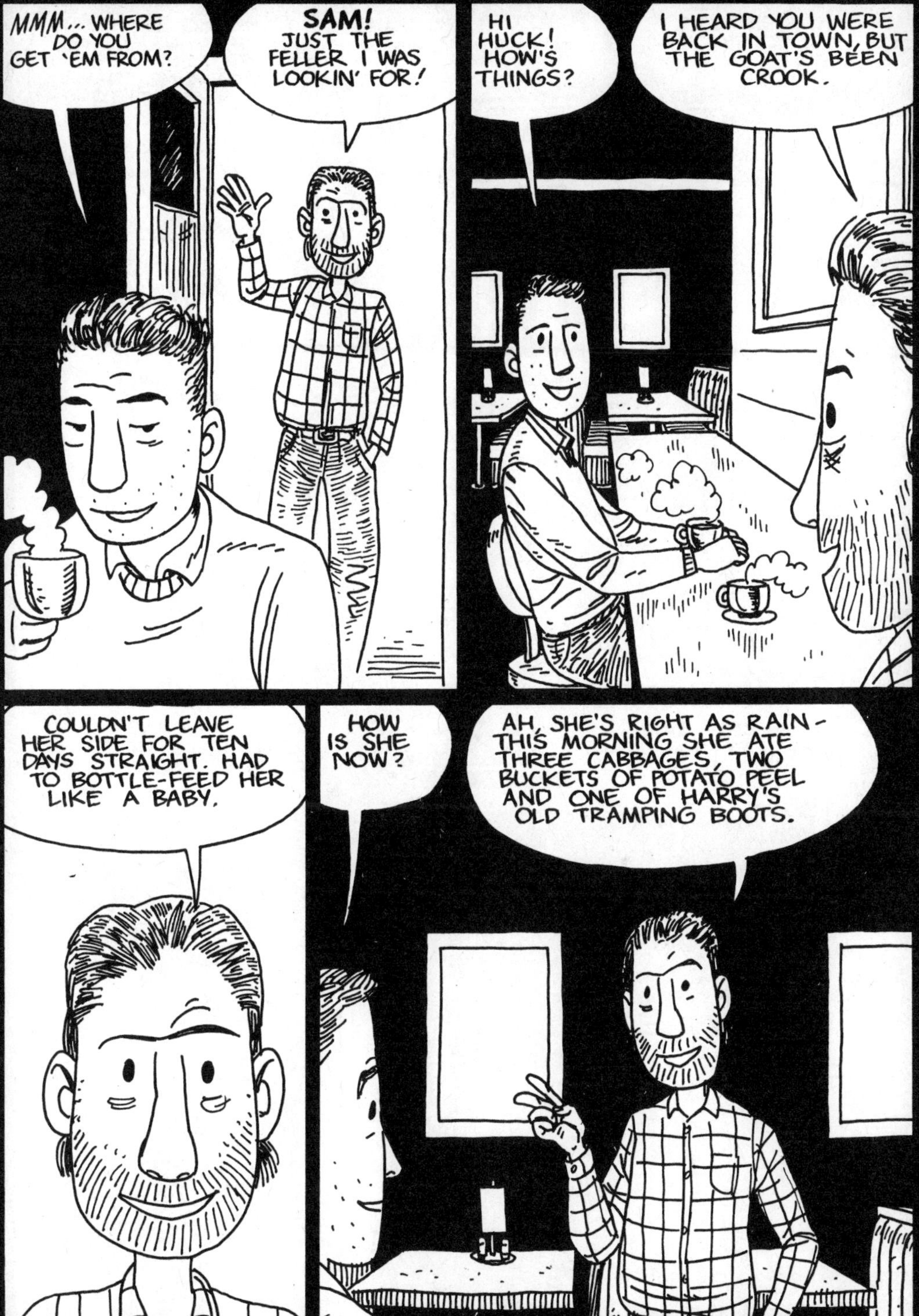
MMM... WHERE DO YOU GET 'EM FROM?
SAM! JUST THE FELLER I WAS LOOKIN' FOR!
HI HUCK! HOW'S THINGS?
I HEARD YOU WERE BACK IN TOWN, BUT THE GOAT'S BEEN CROOK.
COULDN'T LEAVE HER SIDE FOR TEN DAYS STRAIGHT. HAD TO BOTTLE-FEED HER LIKE A BABY.
HOW IS SHE NOW?
AH, SHE'S RIGHT AS RAIN - THIS MORNING SHE ATE THREE CABBAGES, TWO BUCKETS OF POTATO PEEL AND ONE OF HARRY'S OLD TRAMPING BOOTS.

SO WHAT'S BROUGHT YOU BACK TO HICKSVILLE, MATE?

OH, JUST THE USUAL — BROKE AND UNEMPLOYED...

KITCHEN

DESSERTS.
PAVLOVA..$2.50
ERINGUE..$2.00
BRIOCHE..$1.50
KIN PIE...$2.00
EESE CAKE..$2.50
SCONES...$
UFFIN
MEL
CAK

I THOUGHT YOU HAD A REGULAR SPOT IN 'LAFFS' MAGAZINE. WHAT HAPPENED TO THAT?

HERE — SAM'S LATEST MINICOMIC TELLS ALL.

HEN

S.
..$2.50
E..$2.00
E..$1.50
E..$2.00

KE..$2.50

...$1.00
NS...$1.00

A NEW *PICKLE!* GREAT! LET'S HAVE A LOOK, THEN.

Pickle.

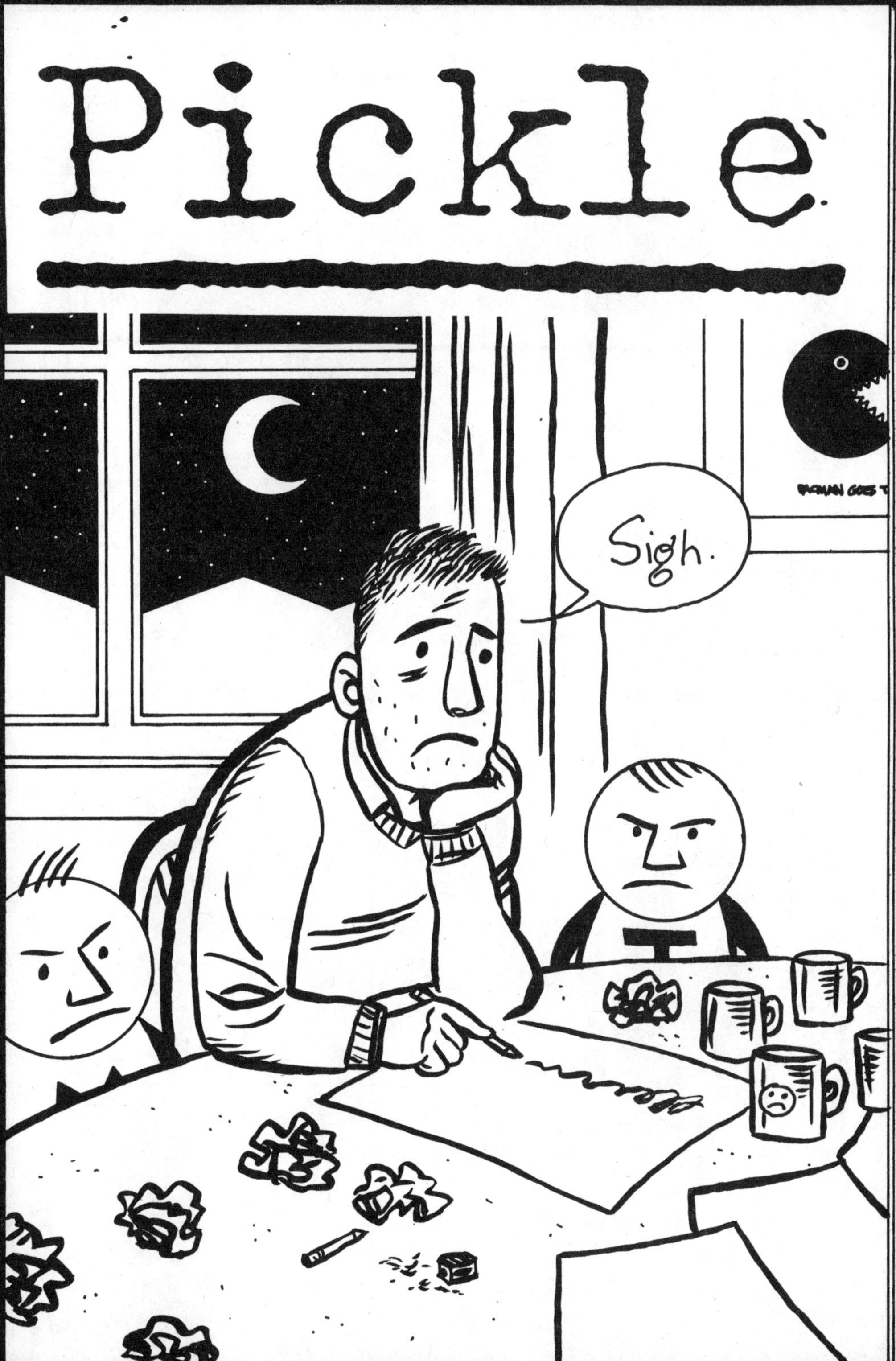
Pickle
Sigh.

HALFWAY TO HEAVEN...

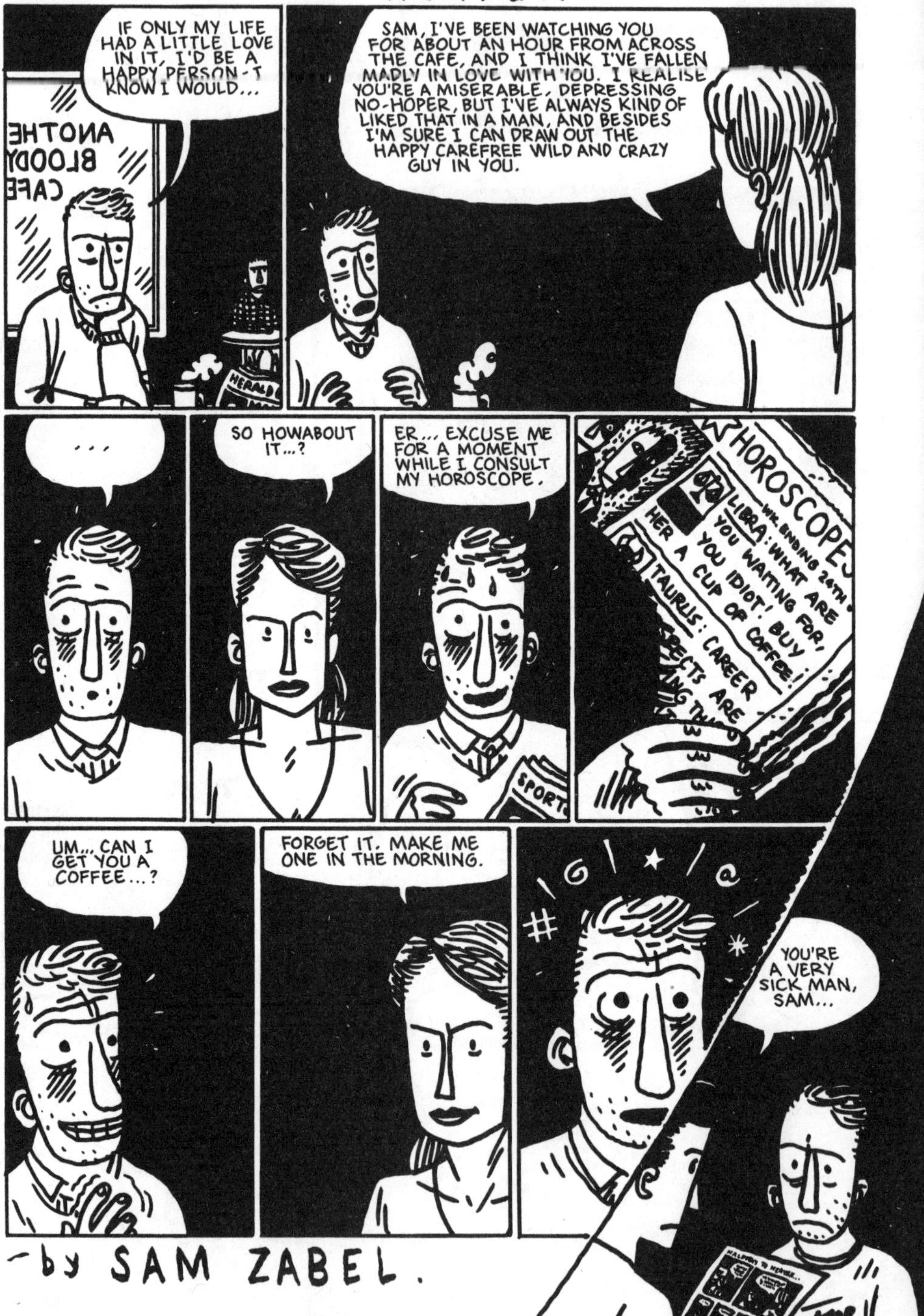
IF ONLY MY LIFE HAD A LITTLE LOVE IN IT, I'D BE A HAPPY PERSON - I KNOW I WOULD...
HERALD
SAM, I'VE BEEN WATCHING YOU FOR ABOUT AN HOUR FROM ACROSS THE CAFE, AND I THINK I'VE FALLEN MADLY IN LOVE WITH YOU. I REALISE YOU'RE A MISERABLE, DEPRESSING NO-HOPER, BUT I'VE ALWAYS KIND OF LIKED THAT IN A MAN, AND BESIDES I'M SURE I CAN DRAW OUT THE HAPPY CAREFREE WILD AND CRAZY GUY IN YOU.
...
SO HOWABOUT IT...?
ER... EXCUSE ME FOR A MOMENT WHILE I CONSULT MY HOROSCOPE.
SPORT
HOROSCOPE
HOROSCOPES
WK. ENDING 24TH.
LIBRA: WHAT ARE YOU WAITING FOR, YOU IDIOT! BUY HER A CUP OF COFFEE!
TAURUS: CAREER PROSPECTS ARE
UM... CAN I GET YOU A COFFEE...?
FORGET IT. MAKE ME ONE IN THE MORNING.
YOU'RE A VERY SICK MAN, SAM...
RAZOR

-by SAM ZABEL.

HALFWAY TO HELL...

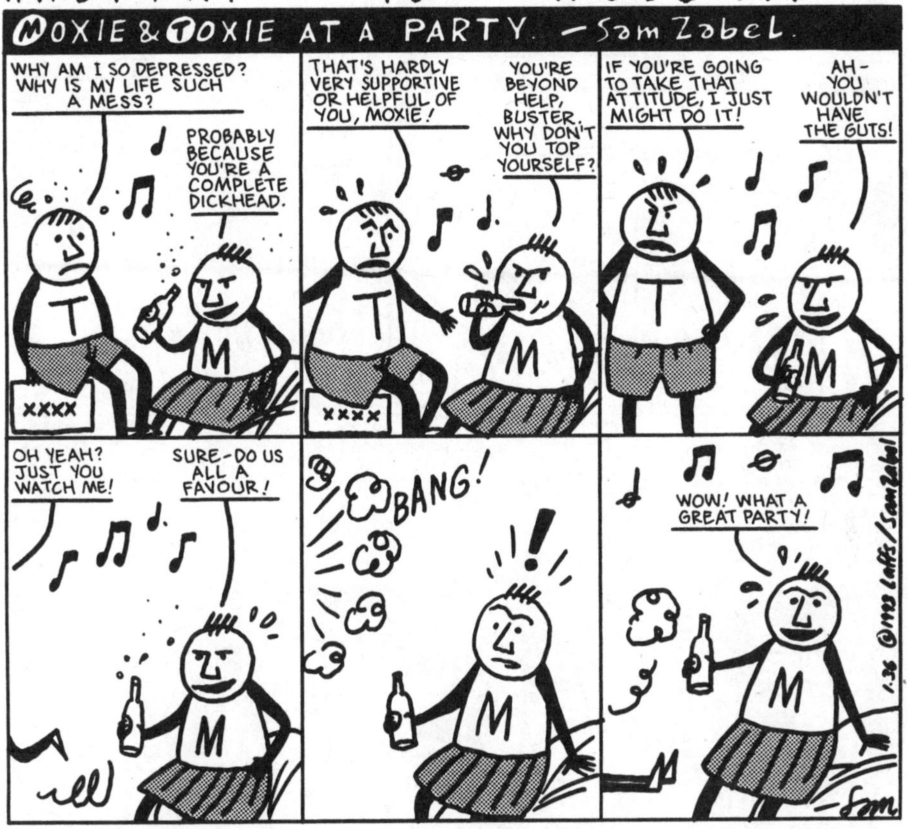
MOXIE & TOXIE AT A PARTY. —Sam Zabel.
WHY AM I SO DEPRESSED? WHY IS MY LIFE SUCH A MESS?
PROBABLY BECAUSE YOU'RE A COMPLETE DICKHEAD.
XXXX
THAT'S HARDLY VERY SUPPORTIVE OR HELPFUL OF YOU, MOXIE!
YOU'RE BEYOND HELP, BUSTER. WHY DON'T YOU TOP YOURSELF?
IF YOU'RE GOING TO TAKE THAT ATTITUDE, I JUST MIGHT DO IT!
AH - YOU WOULDN'T HAVE THE GUTS!
OH YEAH? JUST YOU WATCH ME!
SURE - DO US ALL A FAVOUR!
BANG!
WOW! WHAT A GREAT PARTY!
Sam

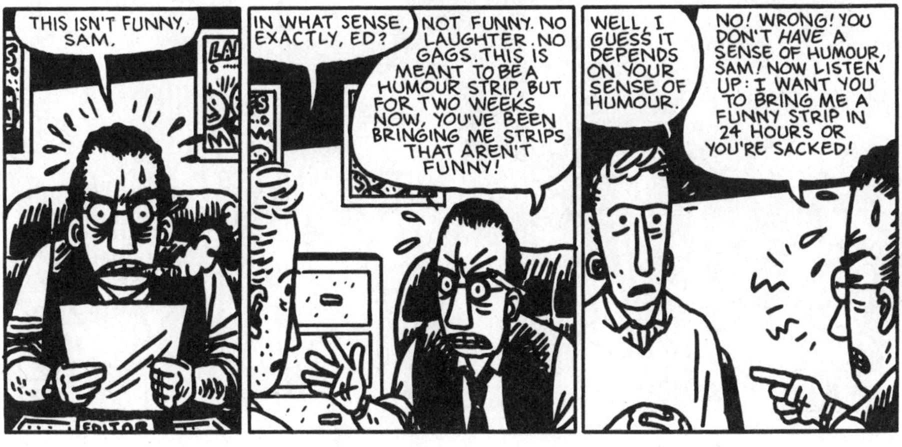
THIS ISN'T FUNNY, SAM.
EDITOR
IN WHAT SENSE, EXACTLY, ED?
NOT FUNNY. NO LAUGHTER. NO GAGS. THIS IS MEANT TO BE A HUMOUR STRIP, BUT FOR TWO WEEKS NOW, YOU'VE BEEN BRINGING ME STRIPS THAT AREN'T FUNNY!
WELL, I GUESS IT DEPENDS ON YOUR SENSE OF HUMOUR.
NO! WRONG! YOU DON'T HAVE A SENSE OF HUMOUR, SAM! NOW LISTEN UP: I WANT YOU TO BRING ME A FUNNY STRIP IN 24 HOURS OR YOU'RE SACKED!

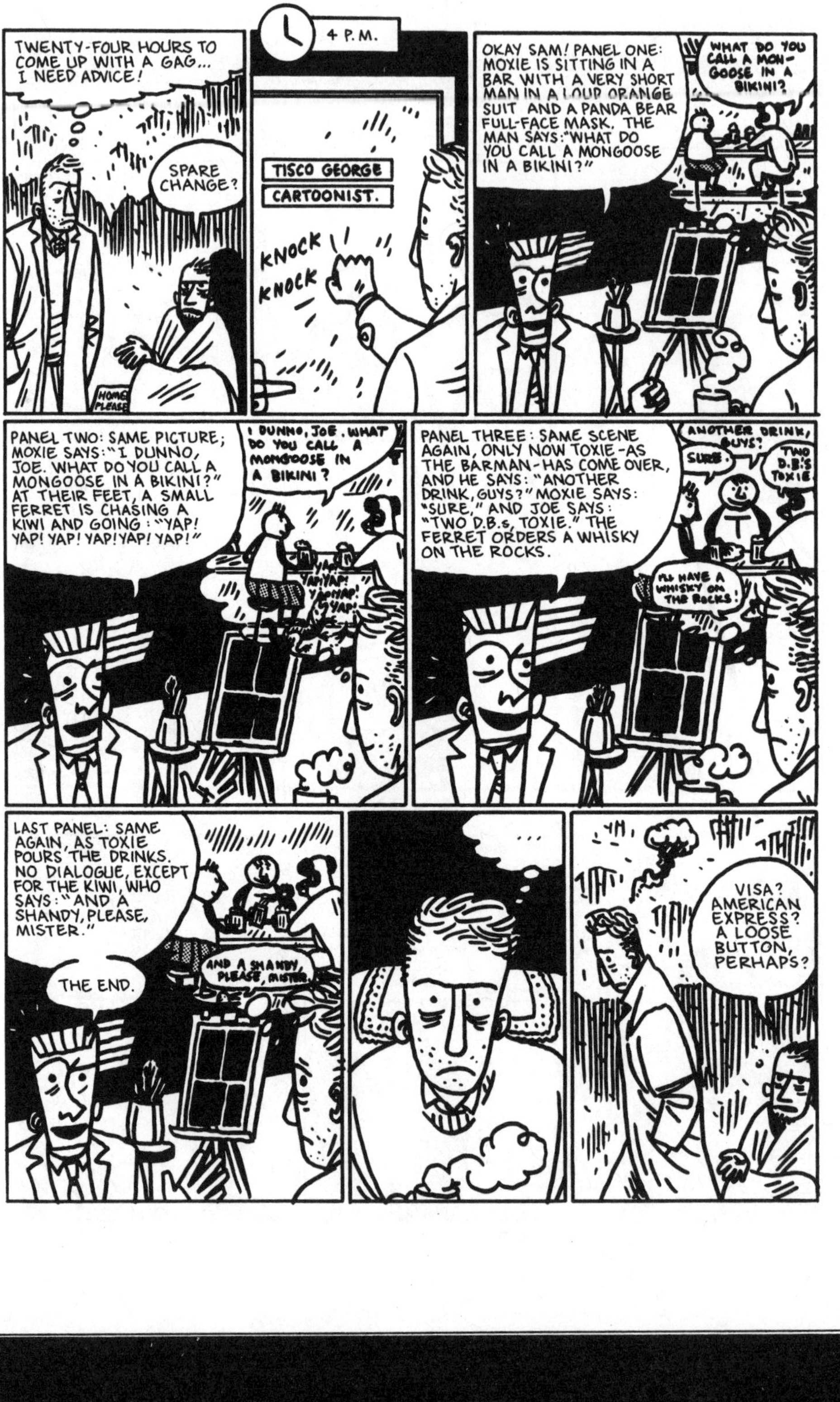
TWENTY-FOUR HOURS TO COME UP WITH A GAG... I NEED ADVICE!
SPARE CHANGE?
4 P.M.
TISCO GEORGE
CARTOONIST.
KNOCK
KNOCK
OKAY SAM! PANEL ONE: MOXIE IS SITTING IN A BAR WITH A VERY SHORT MAN IN A LOUD ORANGE SUIT AND A PANDA BEAR FULL-FACE MASK. THE MAN SAYS: "WHAT DO YOU CALL A MONGOOSE IN A BIKINI?"
WHAT DO YOU CALL A MON-GOOSE IN A BIKINI?
PANEL TWO: SAME PICTURE; MOXIE SAYS: "I DUNNO, JOE. WHAT DO YOU CALL A MONGOOSE IN A BIKINI?" AT THEIR FEET, A SMALL FERRET IS CHASING A KIWI AND GOING: "YAP! YAP! YAP! YAP! YAP! YAP!"
I DUNNO, JOE. WHAT DO YOU CALL A MONGOOSE IN A BIKINI?
YAP!YAP!
YAP!
PANEL THREE: SAME SCENE AGAIN, ONLY NOW TOXIE-AS THE BARMAN-HAS COME OVER, AND HE SAYS: "ANOTHER DRINK, GUYS?" MOXIE SAYS: "SURE," AND JOE SAYS: "TWO D.B.s, TOXIE." THE FERRET ORDERS A WHISKY ON THE ROCKS.
ANOTHER DRINK, GUYS?
SURE.
TWO D.B.'s TOXIE.
I'LL HAVE A WHISKY ON THE ROCKS!
LAST PANEL: SAME AGAIN, AS TOXIE POURS THE DRINKS. NO DIALOGUE, EXCEPT FOR THE KIWI, WHO SAYS: "AND A SHANDY, PLEASE, MISTER."
AND A SHANDY, PLEASE, MISTER.
THE END.
...
VISA? AMERICAN EXPRESS? A LOOSE BUTTON, PERHAPS?

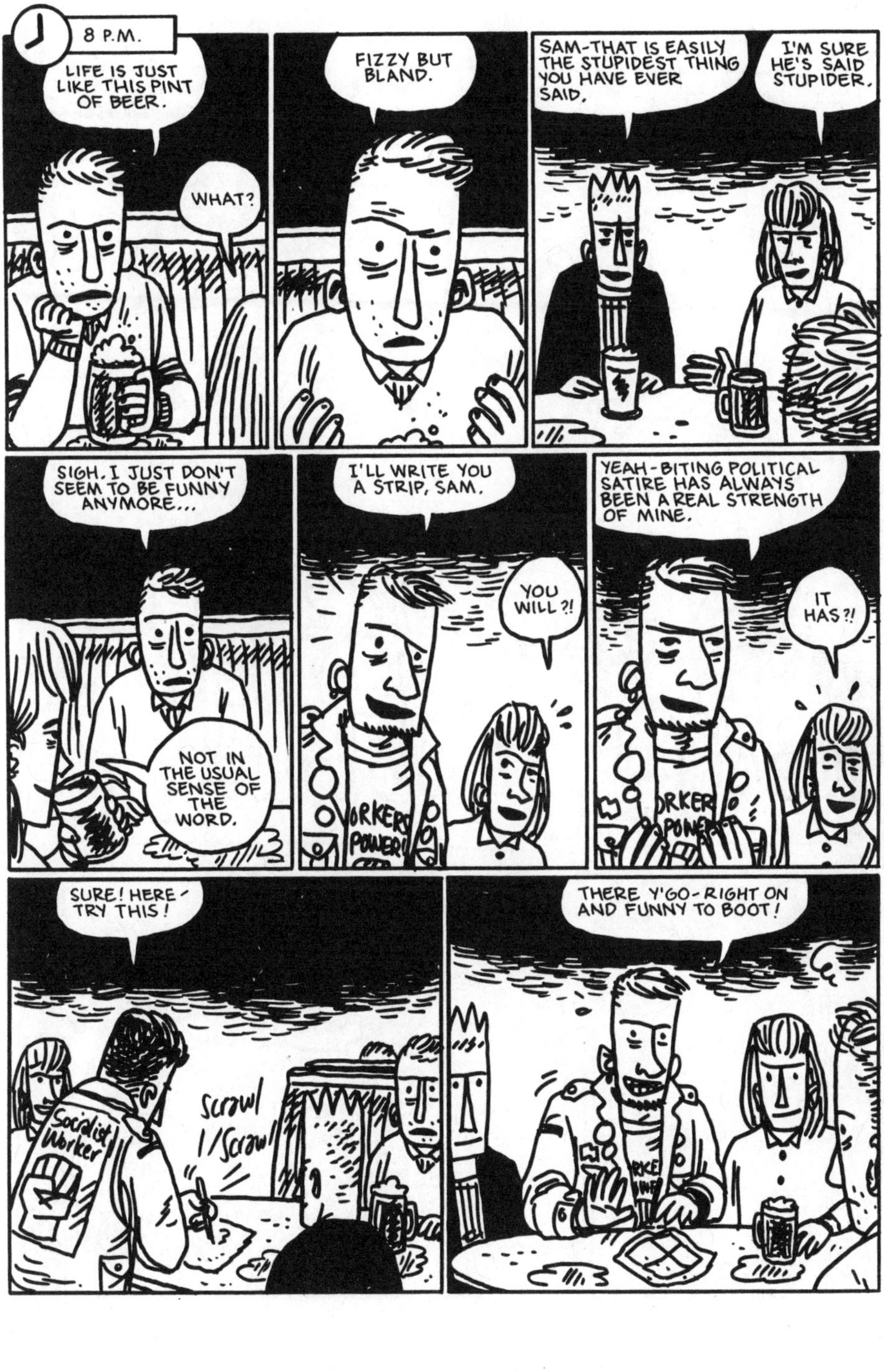
8 P.M.
LIFE IS JUST LIKE THIS PINT OF BEER.
WHAT?
FIZZY BUT BLAND.
SAM-THAT IS EASILY THE STUPIDEST THING YOU HAVE EVER SAID.
I'M SURE HE'S SAID STUPIDER.
SIGH. I JUST DON'T SEEM TO BE FUNNY ANYMORE...
NOT IN THE USUAL SENSE OF THE WORD.
I'LL WRITE YOU A STRIP, SAM.
YOU WILL?!
YEAH-BITING POLITICAL SATIRE HAS ALWAYS BEEN A REAL STRENGTH OF MINE.
IT HAS?!
SURE! HERE-TRY THIS!
Socialist Worker
Scrawl Scrawl
THERE Y'GO-RIGHT ON AND FUNNY TO BOOT!

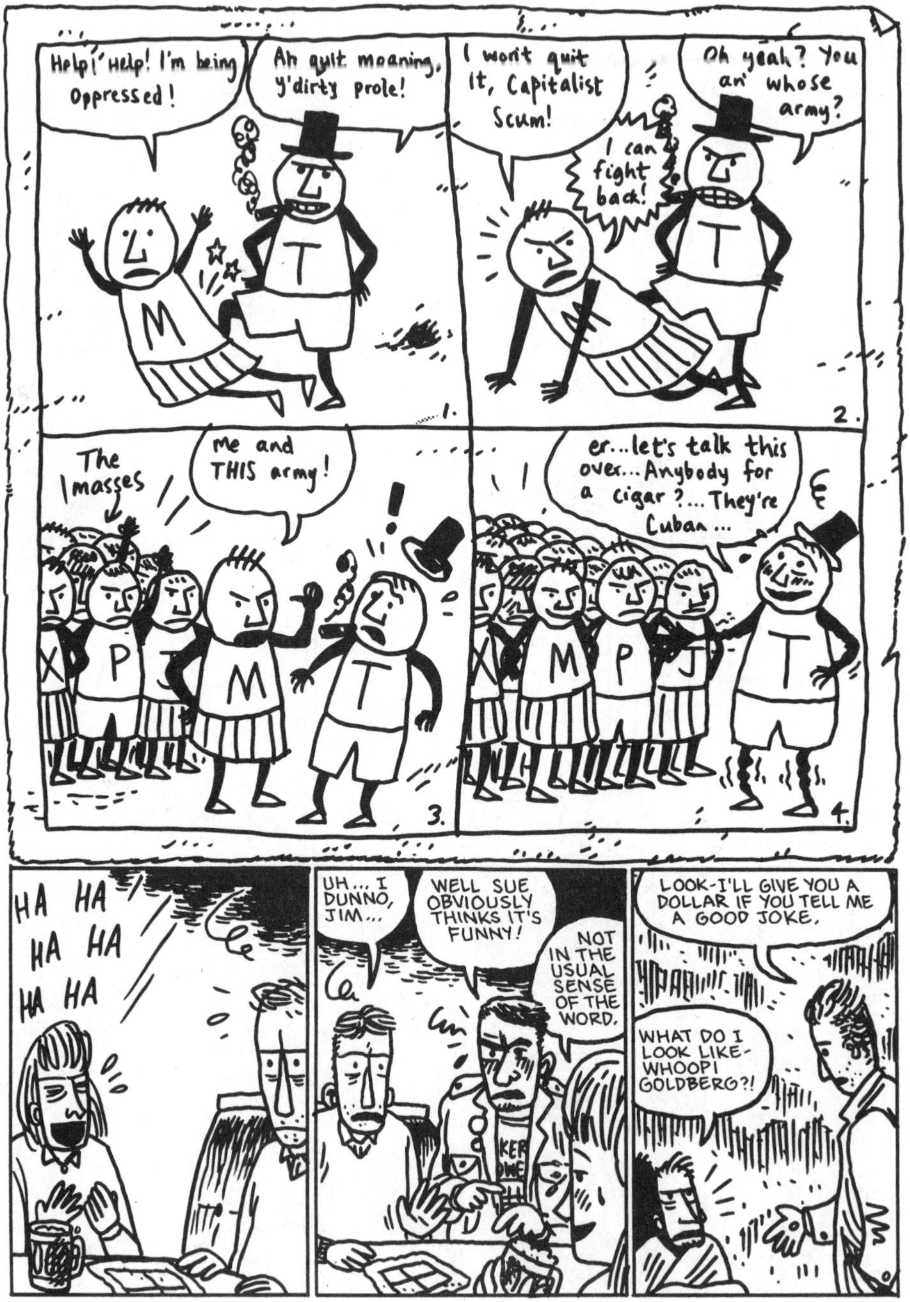
Help! Help! I'm being Oppressed!
Ah quit moaning, y'dirty prole!
1.
I won't quit it, Capitalist Scum!
I can fight back!
Oh yeah? You an' whose army?
2.
The masses
me and THIS army!
!
3.
er...let's talk this over...Anybody for a cigar?...They're Cuban...
4.
HA HA HA HA HA HA
UH... I DUNNO, JIM...
WELL SUE OBVIOUSLY THINKS IT'S FUNNY!
NOT IN THE USUAL SENSE OF THE WORD.
LOOK-I'LL GIVE YOU A DOLLAR IF YOU TELL ME A GOOD JOKE.
WHAT DO I LOOK LIKE-WHOOPI GOLDBERG?!

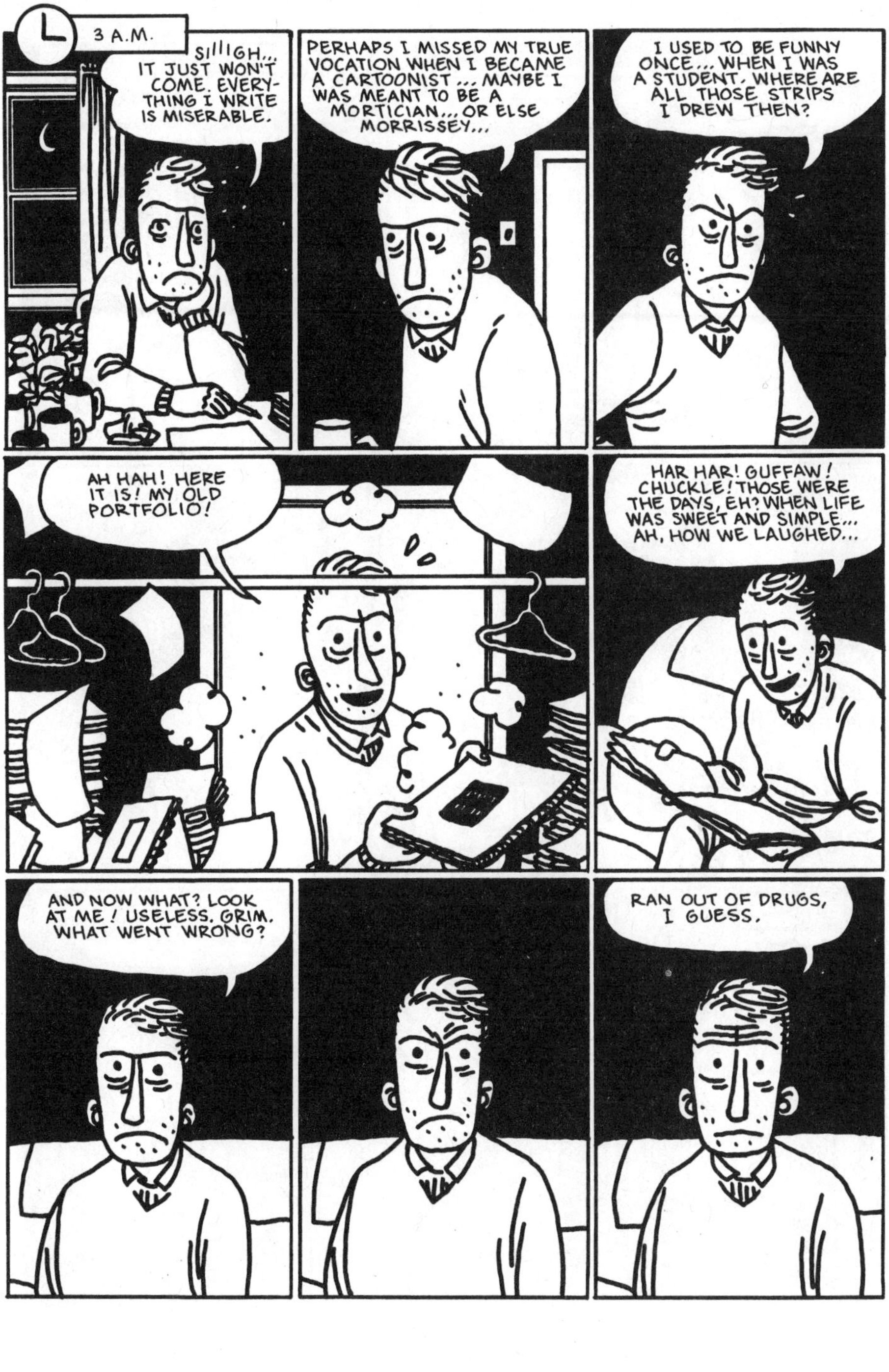
3 A.M.
SI'''GH... IT JUST WON'T COME. EVERY-THING I WRITE IS MISERABLE.
PERHAPS I MISSED MY TRUE VOCATION WHEN I BECAME A CARTOONIST... MAYBE I WAS MEANT TO BE A MORTICIAN... OR ELSE MORRISSEY...
I USED TO BE FUNNY ONCE... WHEN I WAS A STUDENT. WHERE ARE ALL THOSE STRIPS I DREW THEN?
AH HAH! HERE IT IS! MY OLD PORTFOLIO!
HAR HAR! GUFFAW! CHUCKLE! THOSE WERE THE DAYS, EH? WHEN LIFE WAS SWEET AND SIMPLE... AH, HOW WE LAUGHED...
AND NOW WHAT? LOOK AT ME! USELESS. GRIM. WHAT WENT WRONG?
RAN OUT OF DRUGS, I GUESS.

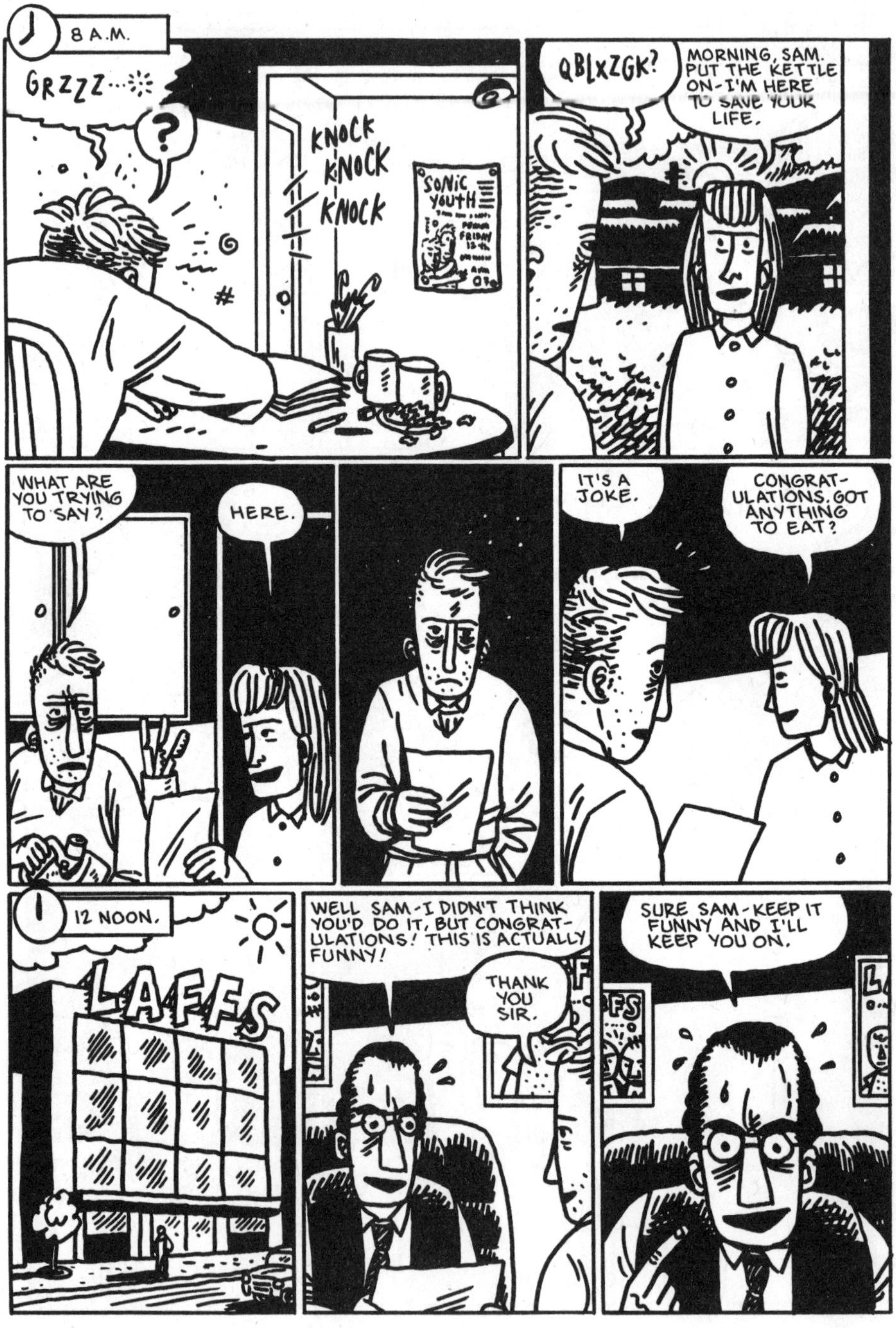
8 A.M.
GRZZZ...
?
KNOCK
KNOCK
KNOCK
SONIC YOUTH
QBLXZGK?
MORNING, SAM. PUT THE KETTLE ON-I'M HERE TO SAVE YOUR LIFE.
WHAT ARE YOU TRYING TO SAY?
HERE.
IT'S A JOKE.
CONGRATULATIONS. GOT ANYTHING TO EAT?
12 NOON.
LAFFS
WELL SAM-I DIDN'T THINK YOU'D DO IT, BUT CONGRATULATIONS! THIS IS ACTUALLY FUNNY!
THANK YOU SIR.
SURE SAM-KEEP IT FUNNY AND I'LL KEEP YOU ON.

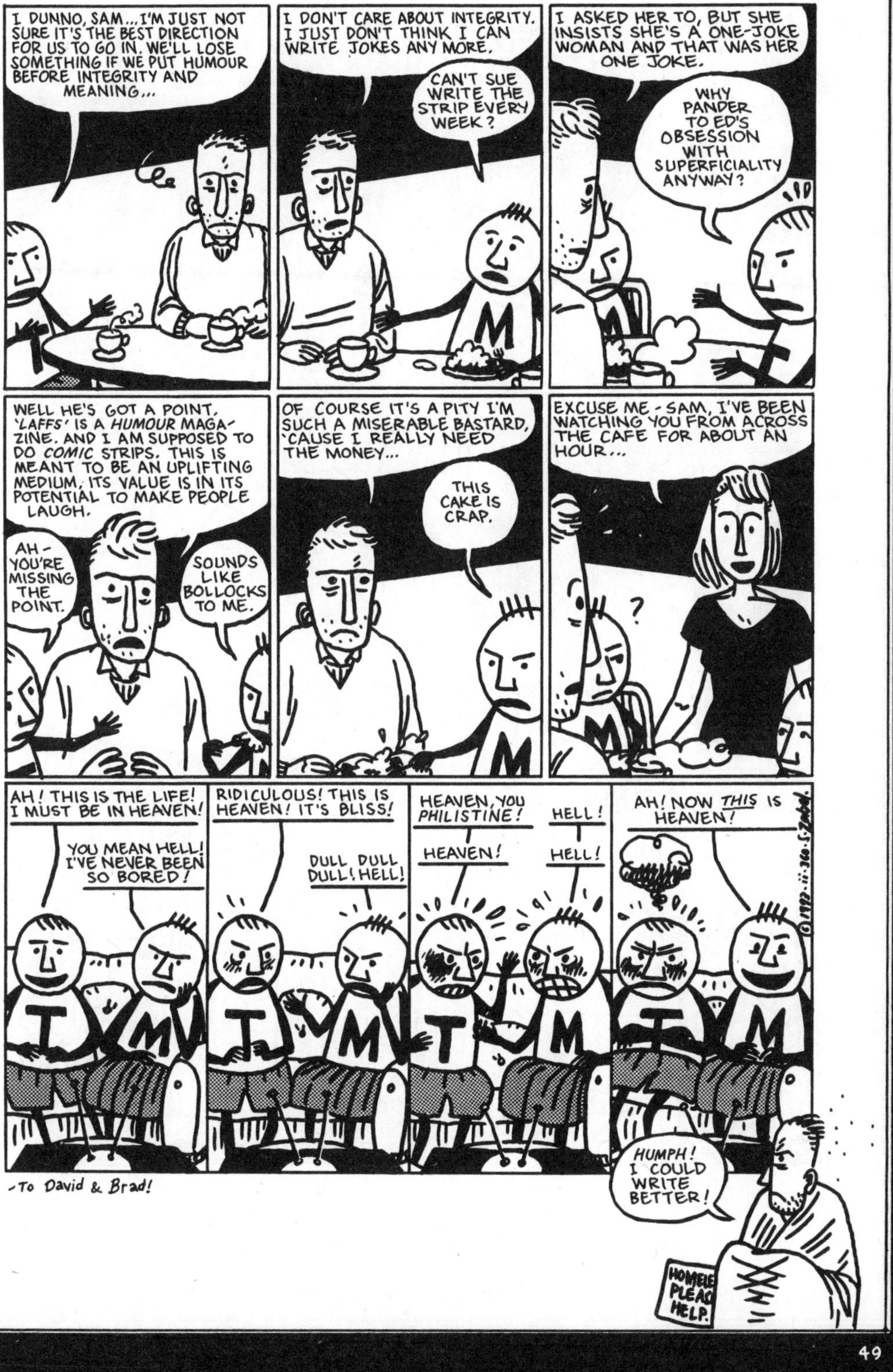
I DUNNO, SAM... I'M JUST NOT SURE IT'S THE BEST DIRECTION FOR US TO GO IN. WE'LL LOSE SOMETHING IF WE PUT HUMOUR BEFORE INTEGRITY AND MEANING...
I DON'T CARE ABOUT INTEGRITY. I JUST DON'T THINK I CAN WRITE JOKES ANY MORE.
CAN'T SUE WRITE THE STRIP EVERY WEEK?
I ASKED HER TO, BUT SHE INSISTS SHE'S A ONE-JOKE WOMAN AND THAT WAS HER ONE JOKE.
WHY PANDER TO ED'S OBSESSION WITH SUPERFICIALITY ANYWAY?
WELL HE'S GOT A POINT. 'LAFFS' IS A HUMOUR MAGAZINE. AND I AM SUPPOSED TO DO COMIC STRIPS. THIS IS MEANT TO BE AN UPLIFTING MEDIUM, ITS VALUE IS IN ITS POTENTIAL TO MAKE PEOPLE LAUGH.
AH - YOU'RE MISSING THE POINT.
SOUNDS LIKE BOLLOCKS TO ME.
OF COURSE IT'S A PITY I'M SUCH A MISERABLE BASTARD, 'CAUSE I REALLY NEED THE MONEY...
THIS CAKE IS CRAP.
EXCUSE ME - SAM, I'VE BEEN WATCHING YOU FROM ACROSS THE CAFE FOR ABOUT AN HOUR...
?
AH! THIS IS THE LIFE! I MUST BE IN HEAVEN!
YOU MEAN HELL! I'VE NEVER BEEN SO BORED!
I
M
RIDICULOUS! THIS IS HEAVEN! IT'S BLISS!
DULL DULL DULL! HELL!
I
M
HEAVEN, YOU PHILISTINE!
HELL!
HEAVEN!
HELL!
T
M
AH! NOW THIS IS HEAVEN!
M
© 1992 · ii · 30 · S. Zabel.
-To David & Brad!
HUMPH! I COULD WRITE BETTER!
HOMELE PLEAS HELP.

EPILOGUE...

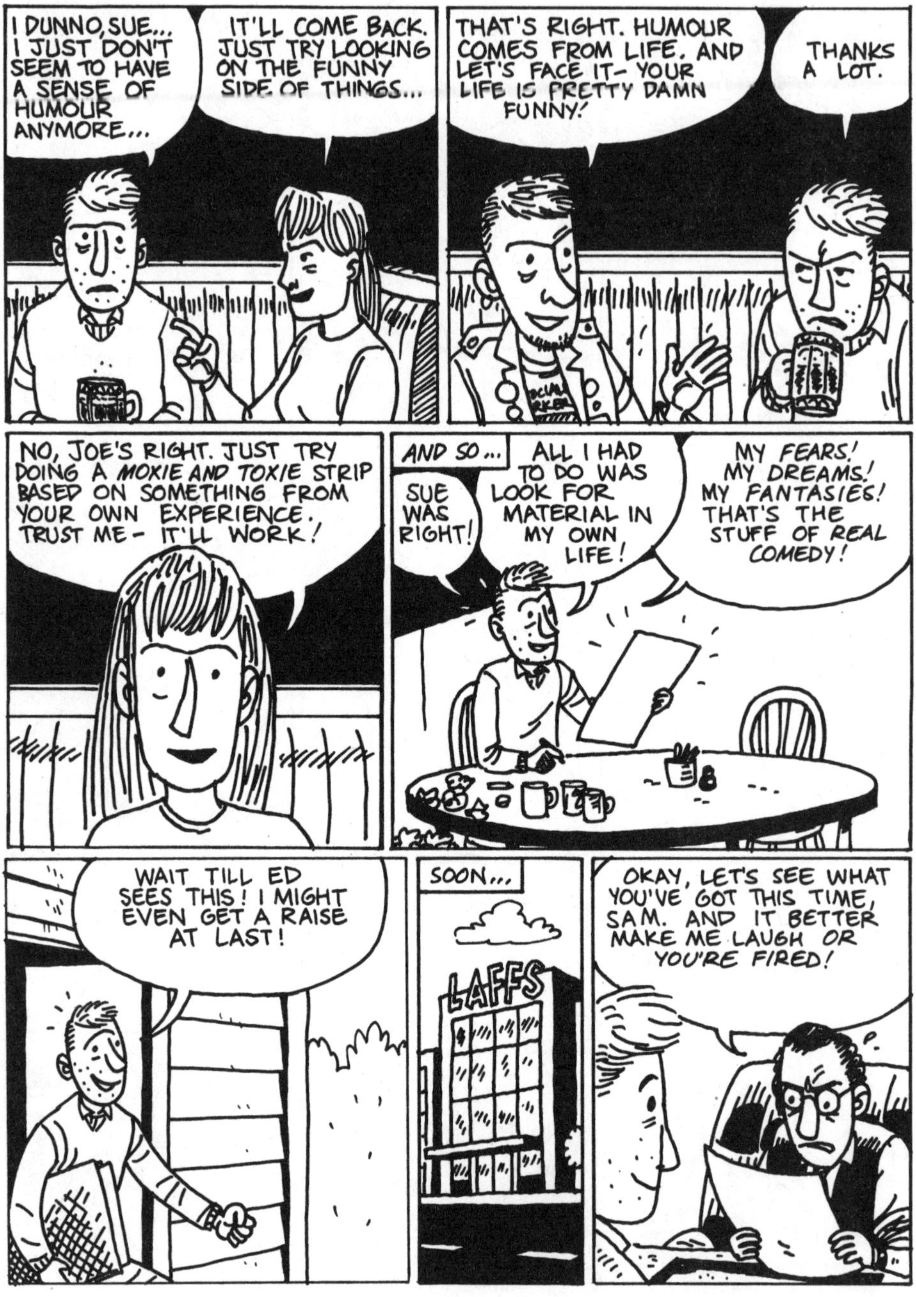
I DUNNO, SUE... I JUST DON'T SEEM TO HAVE A SENSE OF HUMOUR ANYMORE...
IT'LL COME BACK. JUST TRY LOOKING ON THE FUNNY SIDE OF THINGS...
THAT'S RIGHT. HUMOUR COMES FROM LIFE. AND LET'S FACE IT- YOUR LIFE IS PRETTY DAMN FUNNY!
THANKS A LOT.
NO, JOE'S RIGHT. JUST TRY DOING A MOXIE AND TOXIE STRIP BASED ON SOMETHING FROM YOUR OWN EXPERIENCE. TRUST ME- IT'LL WORK!
AND SO...
SUE WAS RIGHT!
ALL I HAD TO DO WAS LOOK FOR MATERIAL IN MY OWN LIFE!
MY FEARS! MY DREAMS! MY FANTASIES! THAT'S THE STUFF OF REAL COMEDY!
WAIT TILL ED SEES THIS! I MIGHT EVEN GET A RAISE AT LAST!
SOON...
LAFFS
OKAY, LET'S SEE WHAT YOU'VE GOT THIS TIME, SAM. AND IT BETTER MAKE ME LAUGH OR YOU'RE FIRED!

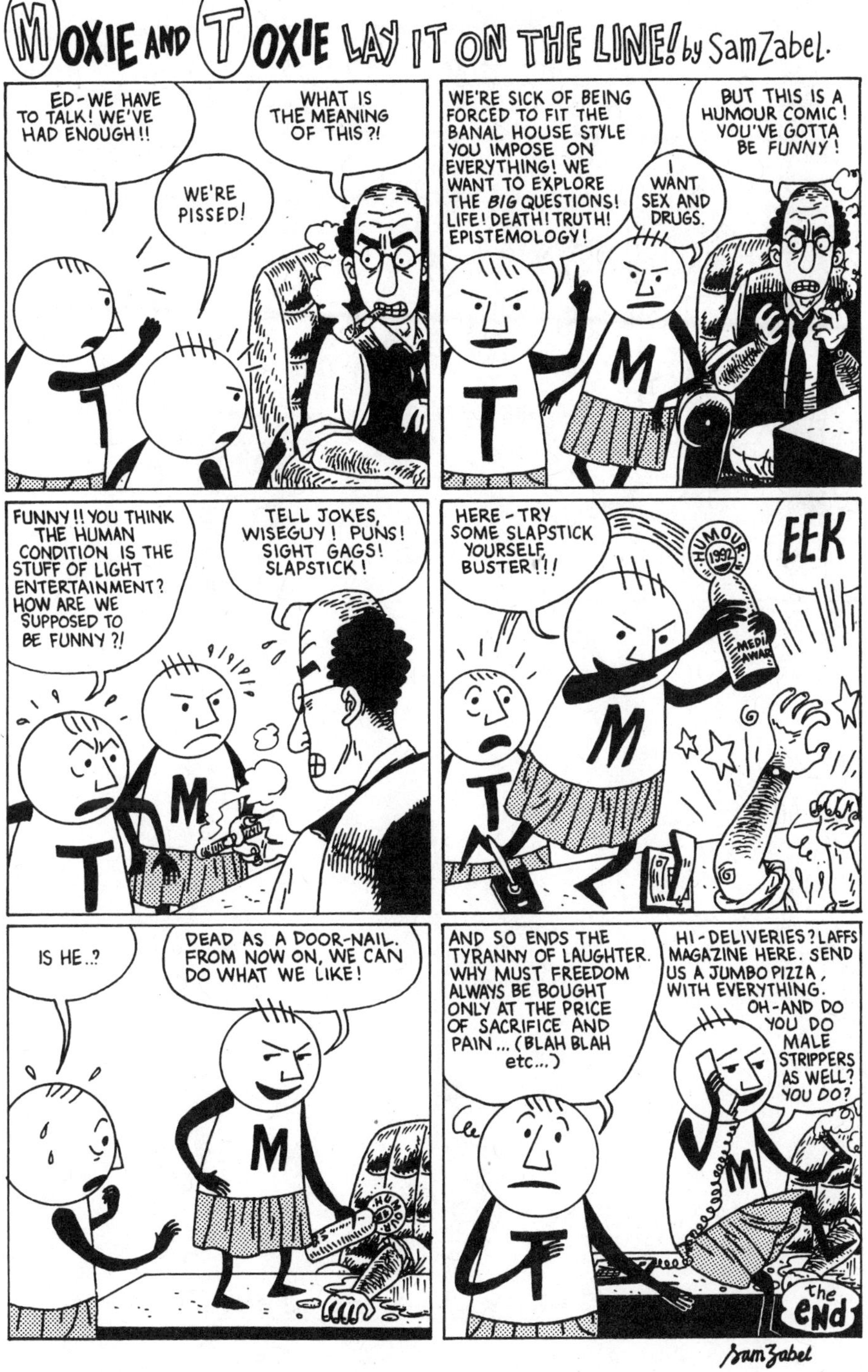
MOXIE AND TOXIE LAY IT ON THE LINE! by Sam Zabel.
ED-WE HAVE TO TALK! WE'VE HAD ENOUGH!!
WE'RE PISSED!
WHAT IS THE MEANING OF THIS ?!
WE'RE SICK OF BEING FORCED TO FIT THE BANAL HOUSE STYLE YOU IMPOSE ON EVERYTHING! WE WANT TO EXPLORE THE BIG QUESTIONS! LIFE! DEATH! TRUTH! EPISTEMOLOGY!
I WANT SEX AND DRUGS.
BUT THIS IS A HUMOUR COMIC! YOU'VE GOTTA BE FUNNY!
FUNNY!! YOU THINK THE HUMAN CONDITION IS THE STUFF OF LIGHT ENTERTAINMENT? HOW ARE WE SUPPOSED TO BE FUNNY ?!
TELL JOKES, WISEGUY! PUNS! SIGHT GAGS! SLAPSTICK!
HERE - TRY SOME SLAPSTICK YOURSELF, BUSTER!!!
HUMOUR 1992
MEDIA AWARD
EEK
IS HE..?
DEAD AS A DOOR-NAIL. FROM NOW ON, WE CAN DO WHAT WE LIKE!
AND SO ENDS THE TYRANNY OF LAUGHTER. WHY MUST FREEDOM ALWAYS BE BOUGHT ONLY AT THE PRICE OF SACRIFICE AND PAIN... (BLAH BLAH etc...)
HI-DELIVERIES? LAFFS MAGAZINE HERE. SEND US A JUMBO PIZZA, WITH EVERYTHING.
OH-AND DO YOU DO MALE STRIPPERS AS WELL? YOU DO?
the end
Sam Zabel

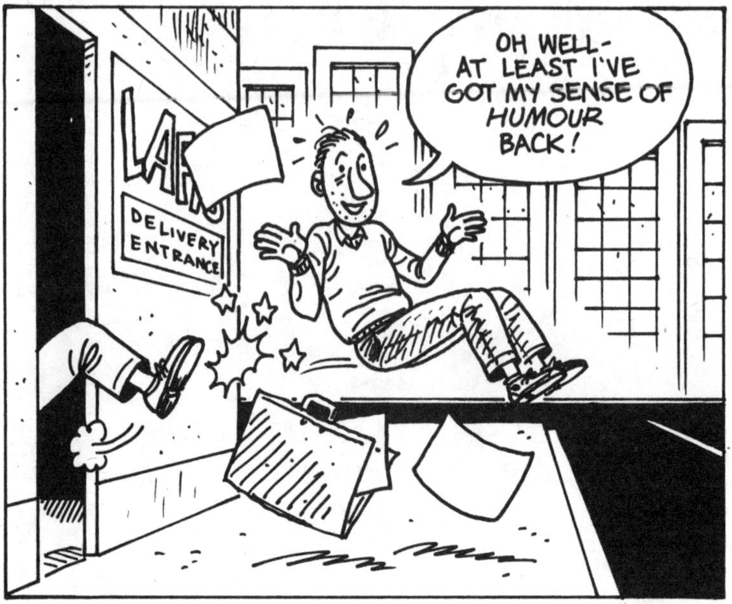
OH WELL-
AT LEAST I'VE
GOT MY SENSE OF
HUMOUR
BACK!
DELIVERY
ENTRANCE

The End

Hicksville Press

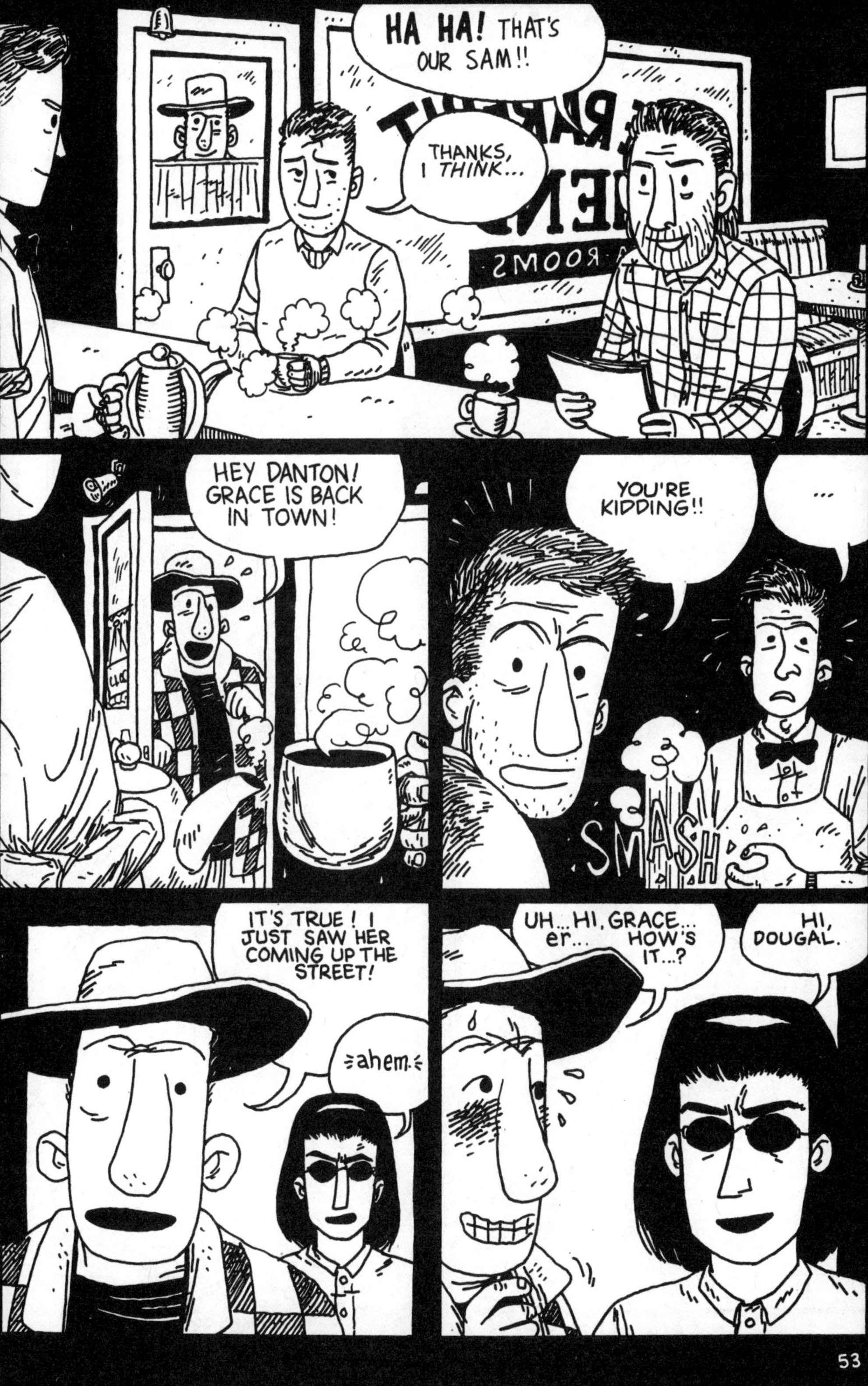
HA HA! THAT'S OUR SAM!!
THANKS, I THINK...
ROOMS
HEY DANTON! GRACE IS BACK IN TOWN!
YOU'RE KIDDING!!
...
SMASH
IT'S TRUE! I JUST SAW HER COMING UP THE STREET!
ahem.
UH... HI, GRACE... er... HOW'S IT...?
HI, DOUGAL.

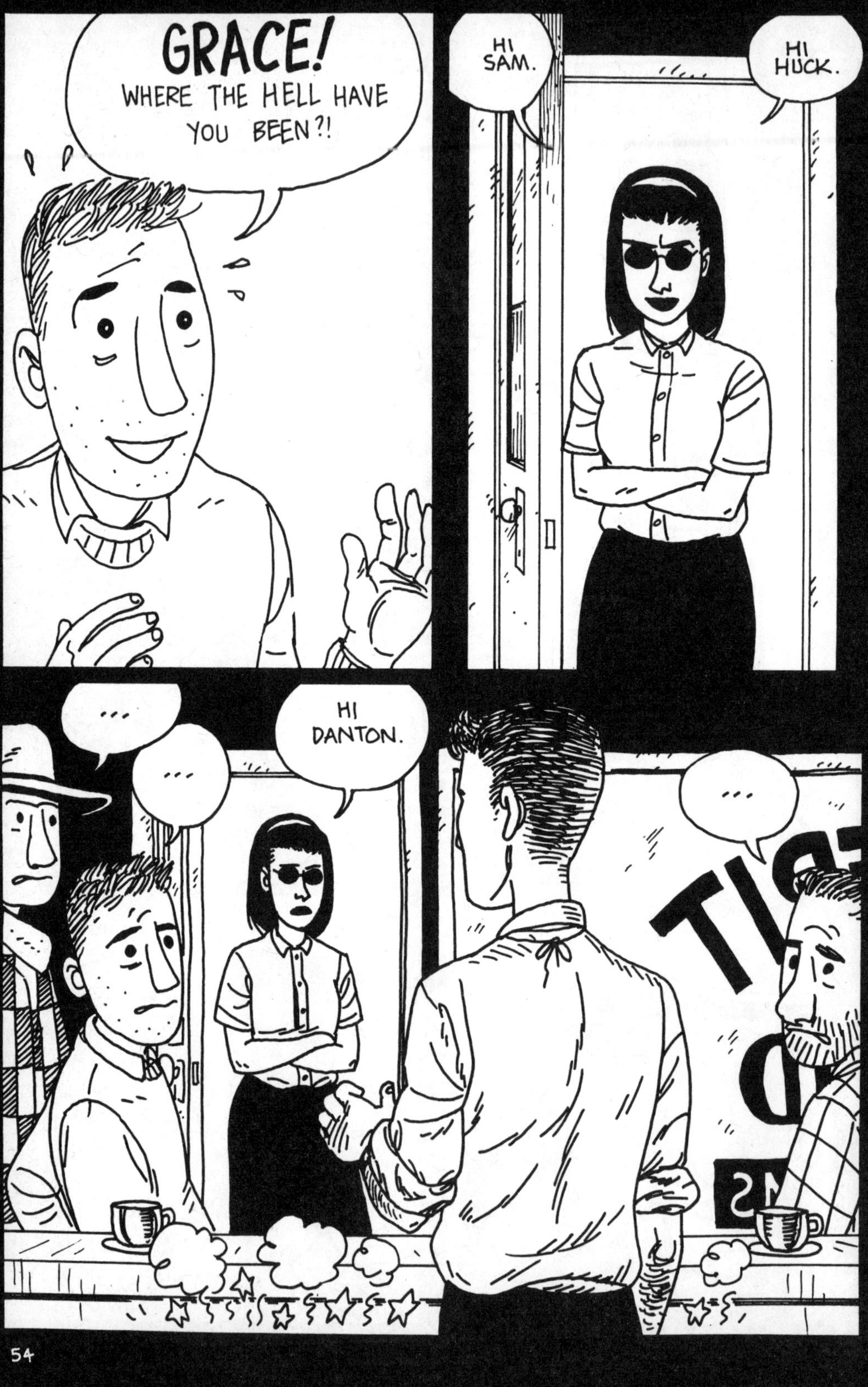
GRACE! WHERE THE HELL HAVE YOU BEEN?!
HI SAM.
HI HUCK.
...
...
HI DANTON.
...

Chapter Three

"I loved the comics from the start, especially when I read somewhere that Bud Fisher married a fresh Ziegfield Follies girl every couple of years - and could afford them all."

Al Capp.

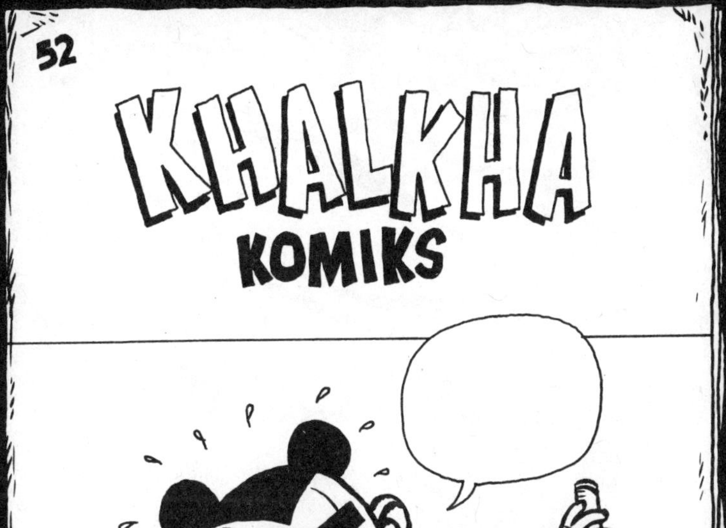
52
KHALKHA
KOMIKS

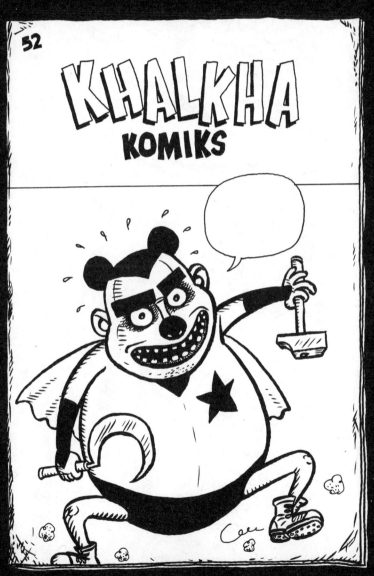

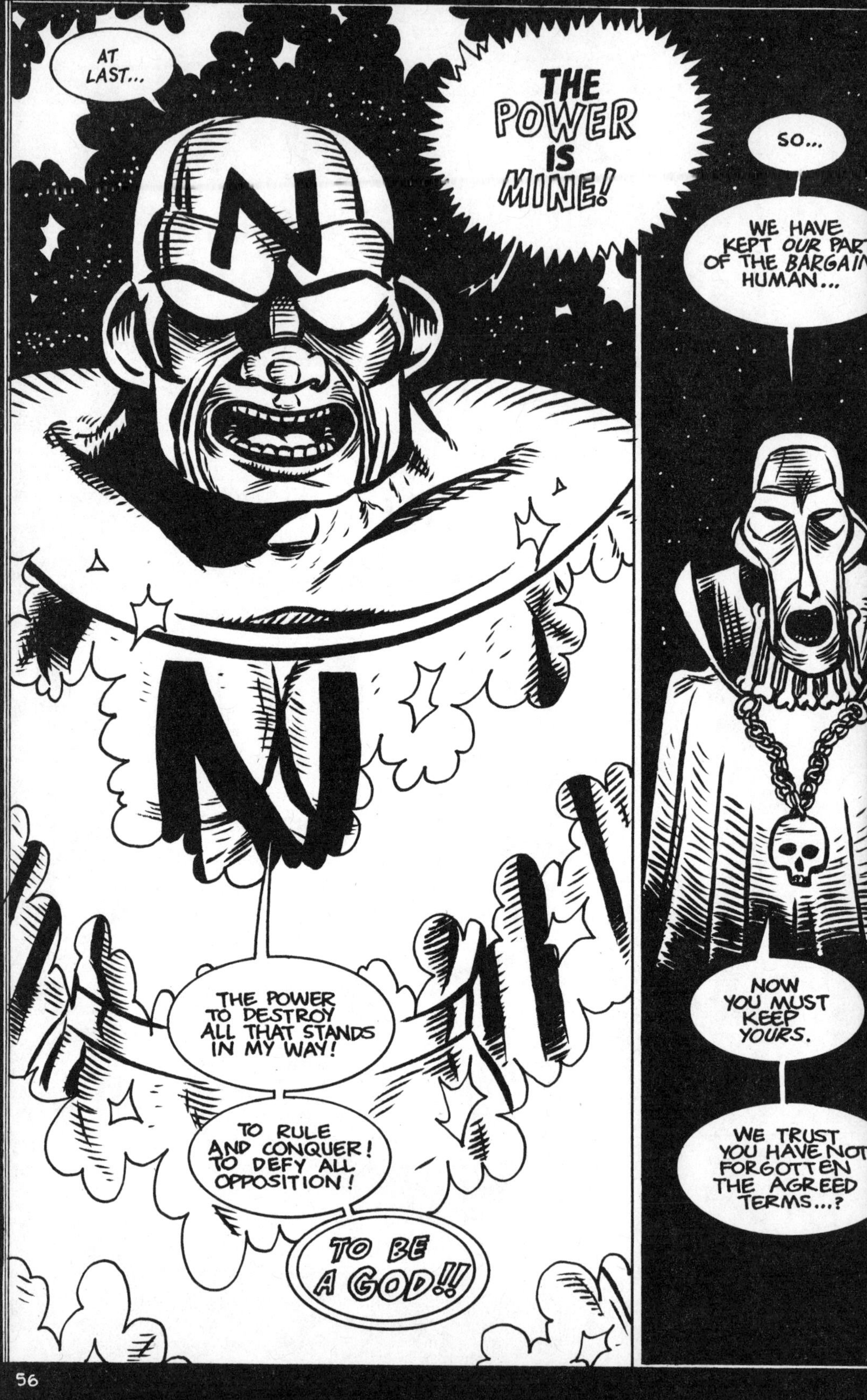

AT LAST...
THE POWER IS MINE!
THE POWER TO DESTROY ALL THAT STANDS IN MY WAY!
TO RULE AND CONQUER! TO DEFY ALL OPPOSITION!
TO BE A GOD!!
SO...
WE HAVE KEPT OUR PART OF THE BARGAIN HUMAN...
NOW YOU MUST KEEP YOURS.
WE TRUST YOU HAVE NOT FORGOTTEN THE AGREED TERMS...?

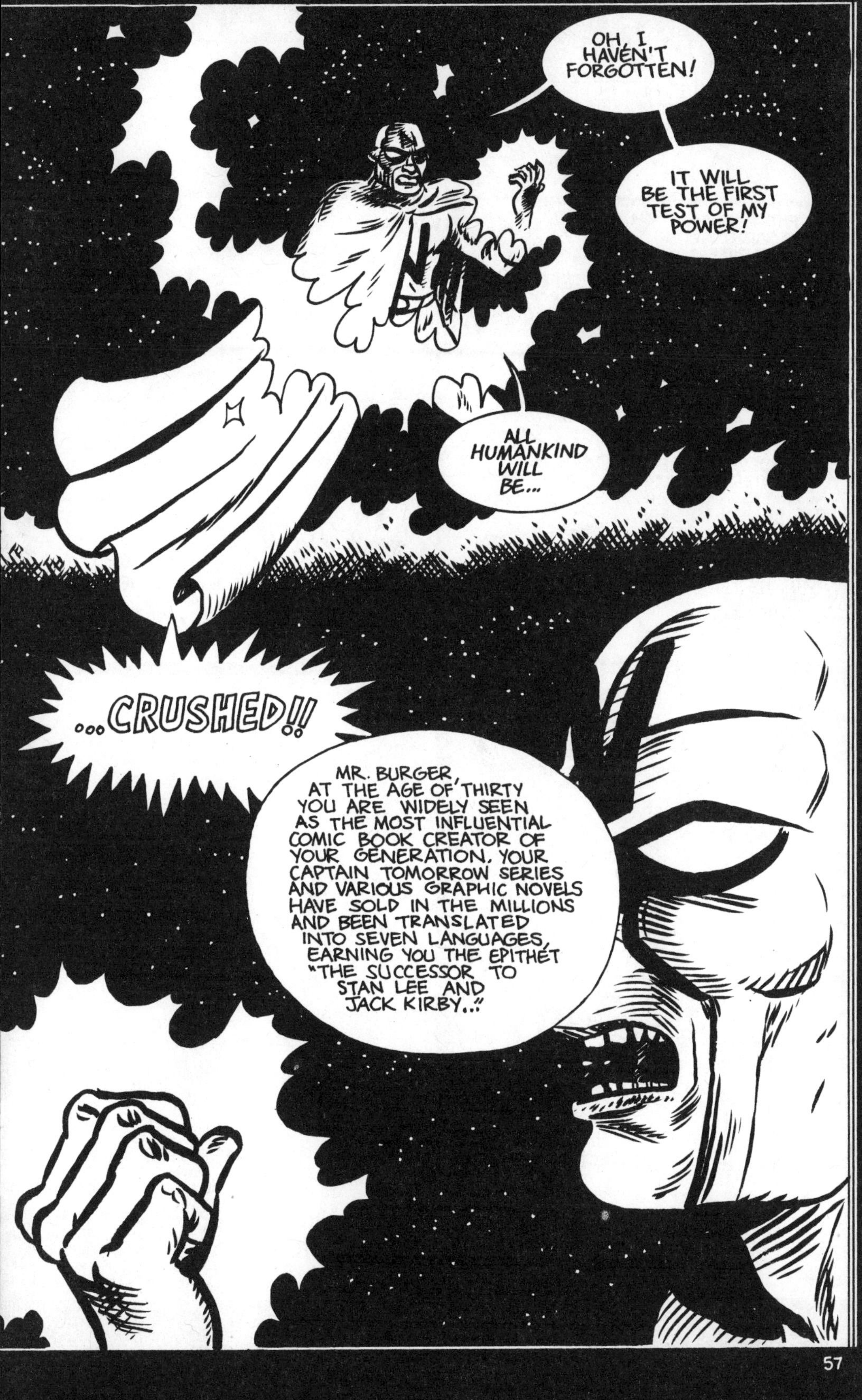
OH, I HAVEN'T FORGOTTEN!
IT WILL BE THE FIRST TEST OF MY POWER!
ALL HUMANKIND WILL BE...
...CRUSHED!!
MR. BURGER, AT THE AGE OF THIRTY YOU ARE WIDELY SEEN AS THE MOST INFLUENTIAL COMIC BOOK CREATOR OF YOUR GENERATION. YOUR CAPTAIN TOMORROW SERIES AND VARIOUS GRAPHIC NOVELS HAVE SOLD IN THE MILLIONS AND BEEN TRANSLATED INTO SEVEN LANGUAGES, EARNING YOU THE EPITHET "THE SUCCESSOR TO STAN LEE AND JACK KIRBY..."

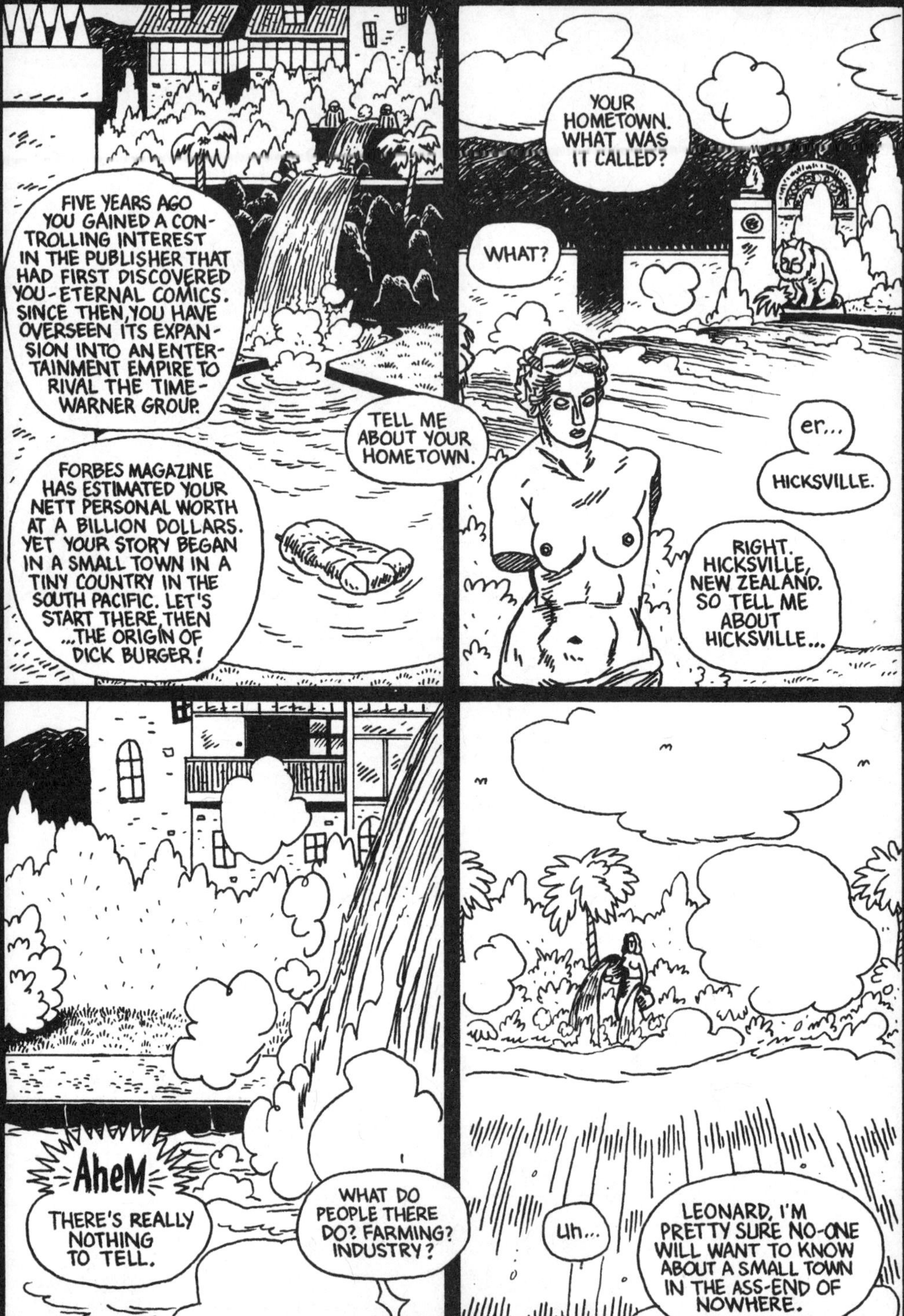

FIVE YEARS AGO YOU GAINED A CONTROLLING INTEREST IN THE PUBLISHER THAT HAD FIRST DISCOVERED YOU - ETERNAL COMICS. SINCE THEN, YOU HAVE OVERSEEN ITS EXPANSION INTO AN ENTERTAINMENT EMPIRE TO RIVAL THE TIME-WARNER GROUP.
FORBES MAGAZINE HAS ESTIMATED YOUR NETT PERSONAL WORTH AT A BILLION DOLLARS. YET YOUR STORY BEGAN IN A SMALL TOWN IN A TINY COUNTRY IN THE SOUTH PACIFIC. LET'S START THERE THEN ...THE ORIGIN OF DICK BURGER!
TELL ME ABOUT YOUR HOMETOWN.
WHAT?
YOUR HOMETOWN. WHAT WAS IT CALLED?
er...
HICKSVILLE.
RIGHT. HICKSVILLE, NEW ZEALAND. SO TELL ME ABOUT HICKSVILLE...
AheM
THERE'S REALLY NOTHING TO TELL.
WHAT DO PEOPLE THERE DO? FARMING? INDUSTRY?
uh...
LEONARD, I'M PRETTY SURE NO-ONE WILL WANT TO KNOW ABOUT A SMALL TOWN IN THE ASS-END OF NOWHERE.

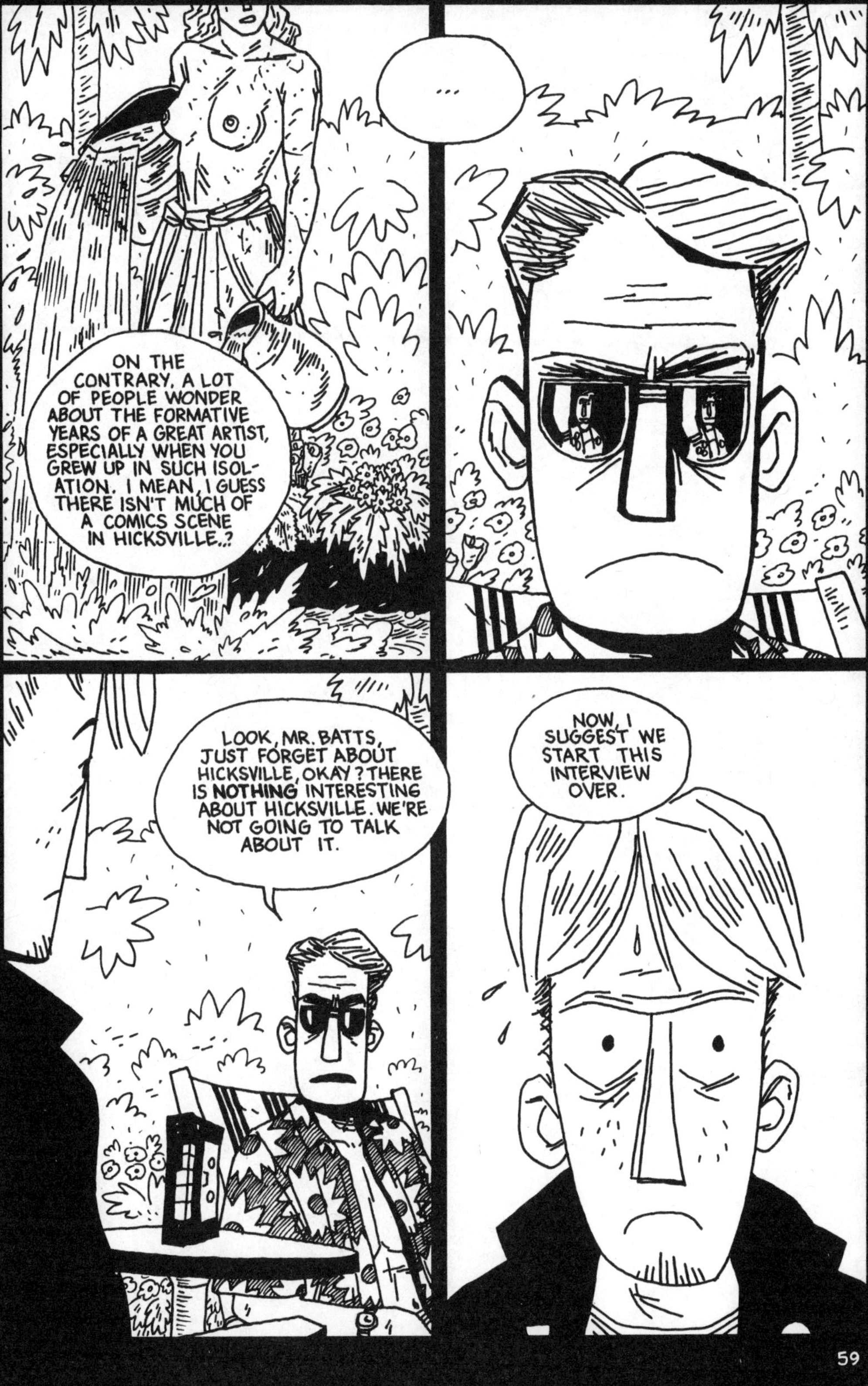
ON THE CONTRARY, A LOT OF PEOPLE WONDER ABOUT THE FORMATIVE YEARS OF A GREAT ARTIST, ESPECIALLY WHEN YOU GREW UP IN SUCH ISOLATION. I MEAN, I GUESS THERE ISN'T MUCH OF A COMICS SCENE IN HICKSVILLE..?
...
LOOK, MR. BATTS, JUST FORGET ABOUT HICKSVILLE, OKAY? THERE IS NOTHING INTERESTING ABOUT HICKSVILLE. WE'RE NOT GOING TO TALK ABOUT IT.
NOW, I SUGGEST WE START THIS INTERVIEW OVER.

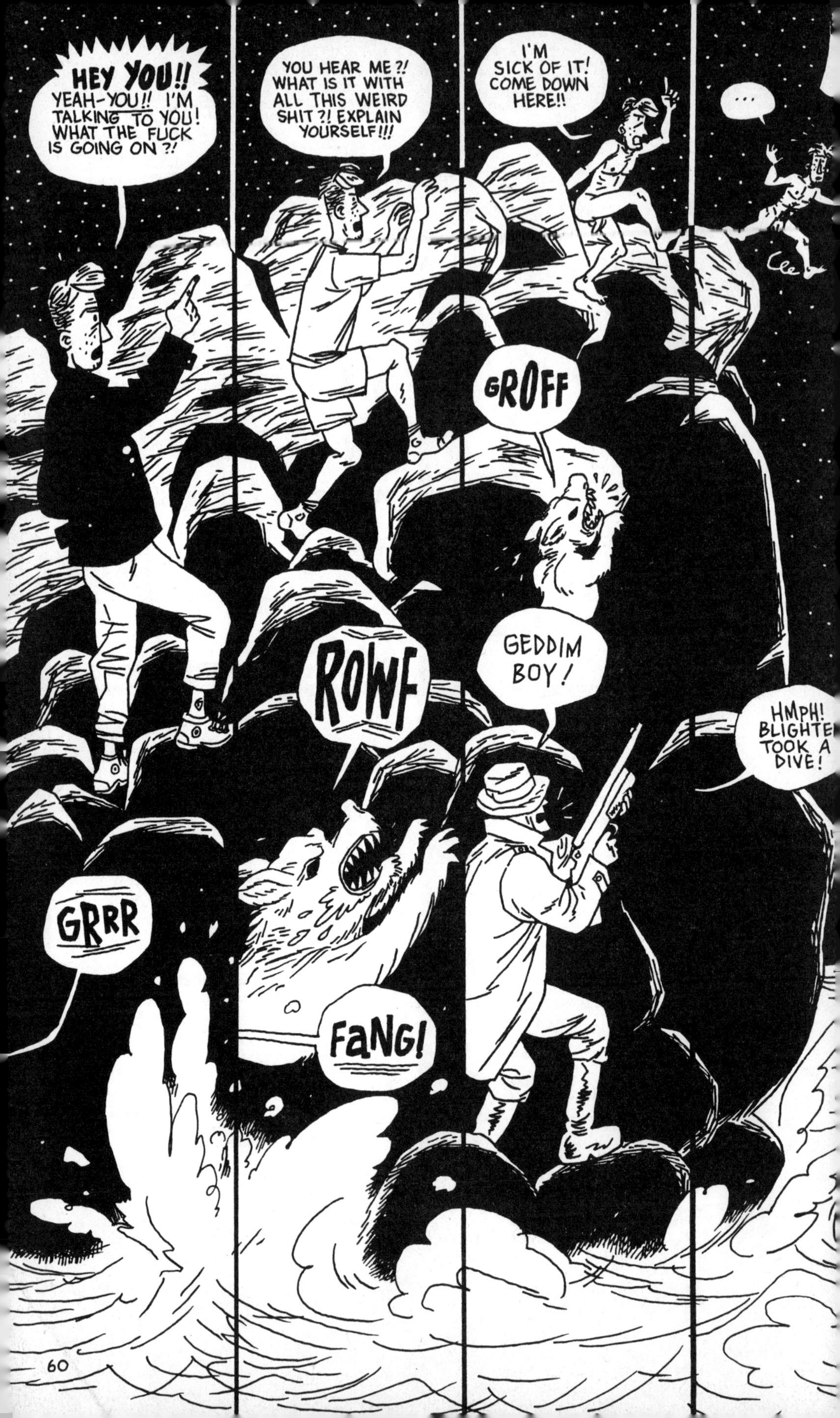

HEY YOU!! YEAH-YOU!! I'M TALKING TO YOU! WHAT THE FUCK IS GOING ON?!
YOU HEAR ME?! WHAT IS IT WITH ALL THIS WEIRD SHIT?! EXPLAIN YOURSELF!!!
I'M SICK OF IT! COME DOWN HERE!!
...
GROFF
ROWF
GEDDIM BOY!
HMPH! BLIGHTE TOOK A DIVE!
GRRR
FANG!

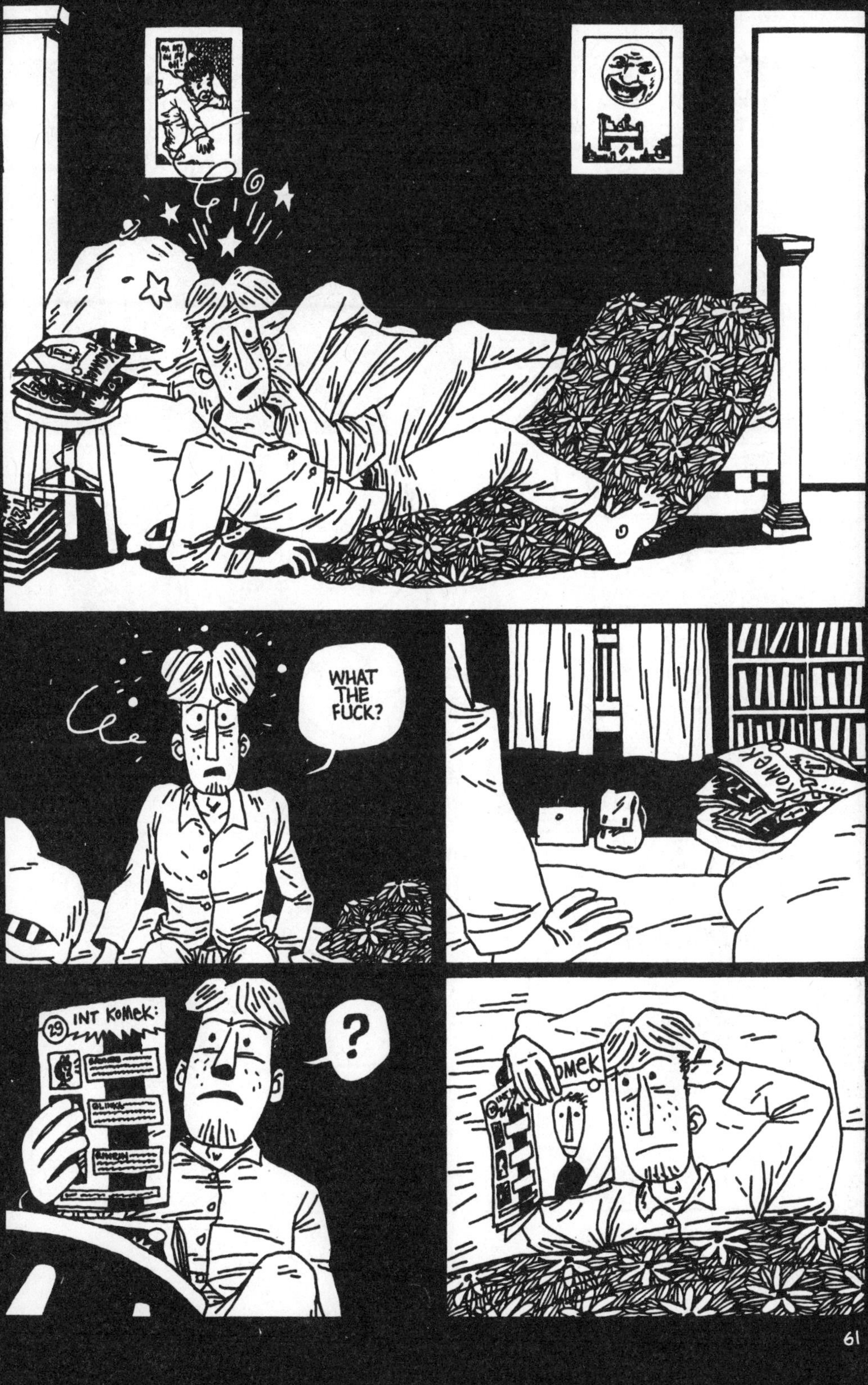
WHAT THE FUCK?
29
INT KOMEK:
?

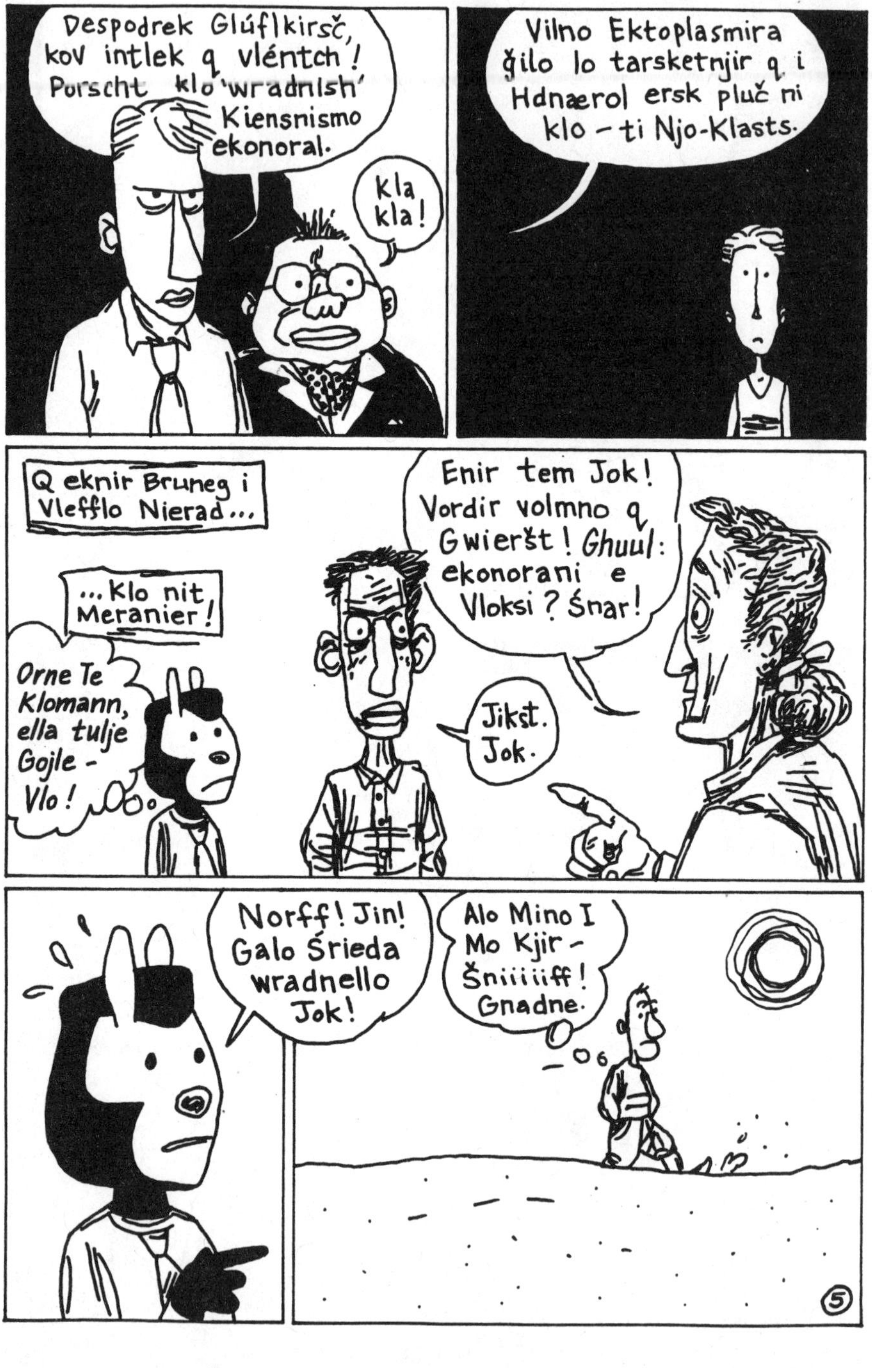

Despodrek Glúflkirsč, kov intlek q vléntch! Porscht klo 'wradnish' Kiensnismo ekonoral.
Kla kla!
Vilno Ektoplasmira ğilo lo tarsketnjir q i Hdnærol ersk pluč ni klo – ti Njo-Klasts.
Q eknir Bruneg i Vlefflo Nierad...
...Klo nit Meranier!
Orne Te Klomann, ella tulje Gojle - Vlo!
Enir tem Jok! Vordir volmno q Gwierŝt! Ghuul: ekonorani e Vloksi? Śnar!
Jikŝt. Jok.
Norff! Jin! Galo Śrieda wradnello Jok!
Alo Mino I Mo Kjir - Šniiiiiff! Gnadne.
5

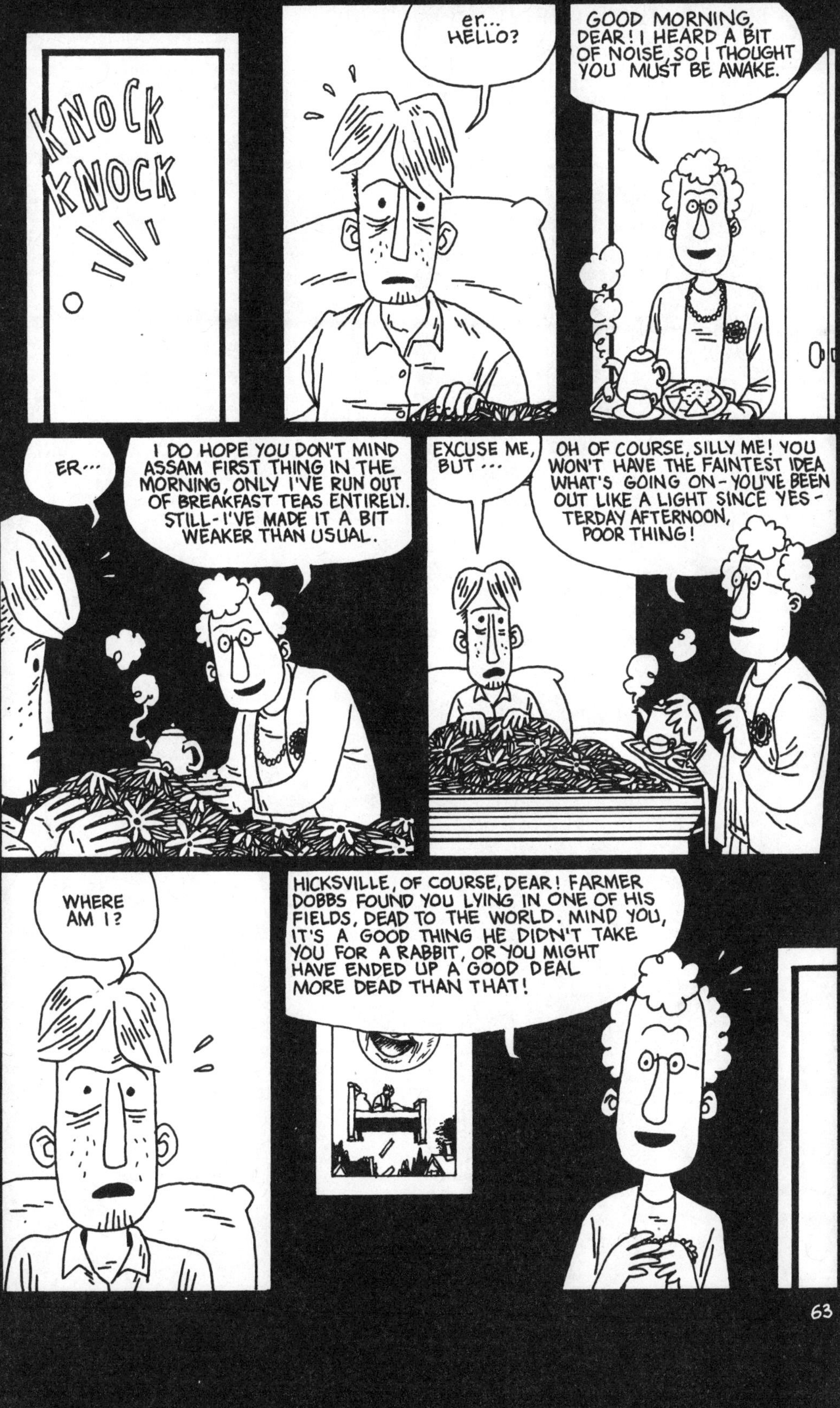
KNOCK KNOCK
er... HELLO?
GOOD MORNING, DEAR! I HEARD A BIT OF NOISE, SO I THOUGHT YOU MUST BE AWAKE.
ER...
I DO HOPE YOU DON'T MIND ASSAM FIRST THING IN THE MORNING, ONLY I'VE RUN OUT OF BREAKFAST TEAS ENTIRELY. STILL- I'VE MADE IT A BIT WEAKER THAN USUAL.
EXCUSE ME, BUT ...
OH OF COURSE, SILLY ME! YOU WON'T HAVE THE FAINTEST IDEA WHAT'S GOING ON - YOU'VE BEEN OUT LIKE A LIGHT SINCE YES-TERDAY AFTERNOON, POOR THING!
WHERE AM I?
HICKSVILLE, OF COURSE, DEAR! FARMER DOBBS FOUND YOU LYING IN ONE OF HIS FIELDS, DEAD TO THE WORLD. MIND YOU, IT'S A GOOD THING HE DIDN'T TAKE YOU FOR A RABBIT, OR YOU MIGHT HAVE ENDED UP A GOOD DEAL MORE DEAD THAN THAT!

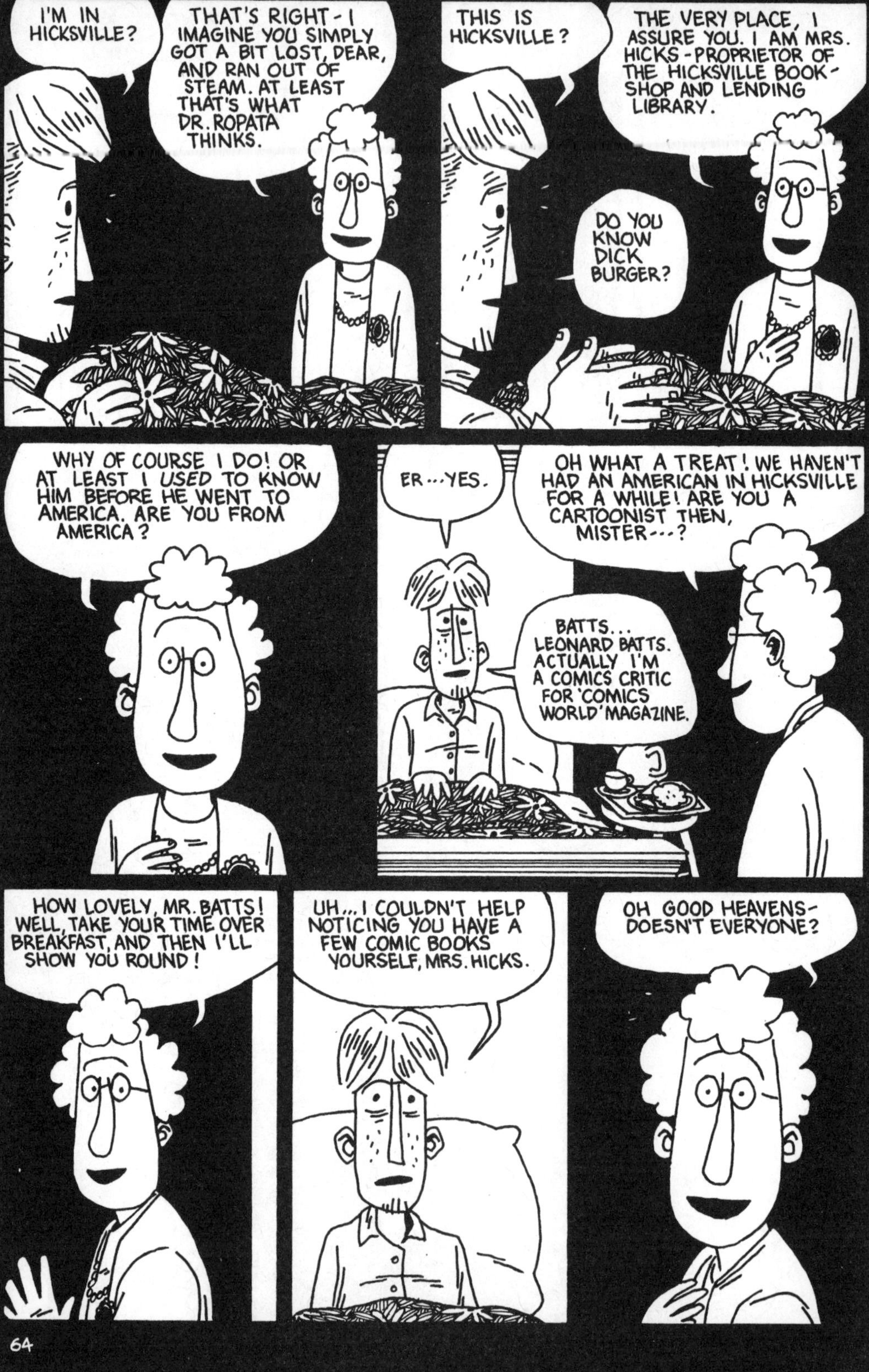
I'M IN HICKSVILLE?
THAT'S RIGHT - I IMAGINE YOU SIMPLY GOT A BIT LOST, DEAR, AND RAN OUT OF STEAM. AT LEAST THAT'S WHAT DR. ROPATA THINKS.
THIS IS HICKSVILLE?
THE VERY PLACE, I ASSURE YOU. I AM MRS. HICKS - PROPRIETOR OF THE HICKSVILLE BOOK-SHOP AND LENDING LIBRARY.
DO YOU KNOW DICK BURGER?
WHY OF COURSE I DO! OR AT LEAST I *USED* TO KNOW HIM BEFORE HE WENT TO AMERICA. ARE YOU FROM AMERICA?
ER...YES.
OH WHAT A TREAT! WE HAVEN'T HAD AN AMERICAN IN HICKSVILLE FOR A WHILE! ARE YOU A CARTOONIST THEN, MISTER---?
BATTS... LEONARD BATTS. ACTUALLY I'M A COMICS CRITIC FOR 'COMICS WORLD' MAGAZINE.
HOW LOVELY, MR. BATTS! WELL, TAKE YOUR TIME OVER BREAKFAST, AND THEN I'LL SHOW YOU ROUND!
UH... I COULDN'T HELP NOTICING YOU HAVE A FEW COMIC BOOKS YOURSELF, MRS. HICKS.
OH GOOD HEAVENS-DOESN'T EVERYONE?

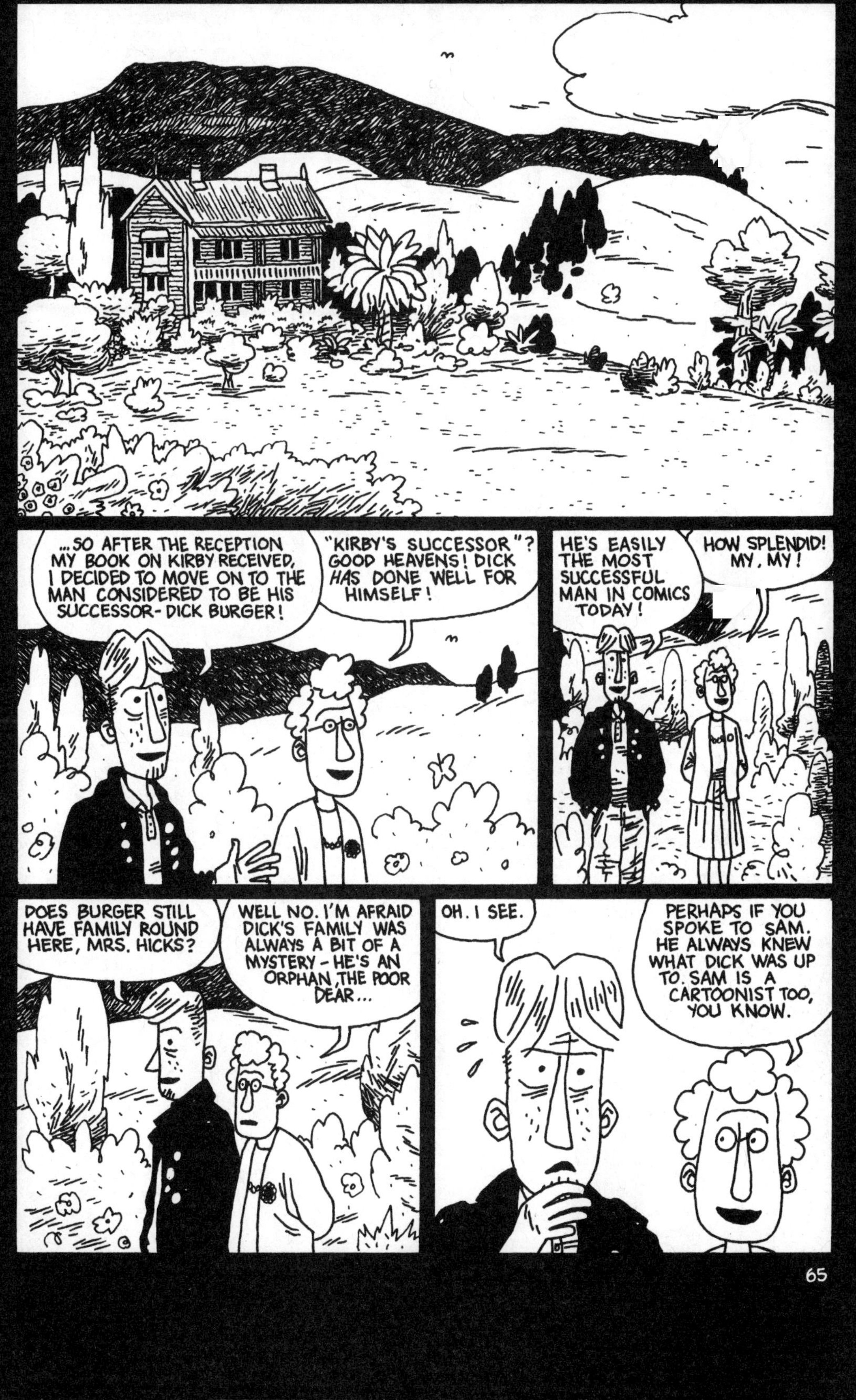
...SO AFTER THE RECEPTION MY BOOK ON KIRBY RECEIVED, I DECIDED TO MOVE ON TO THE MAN CONSIDERED TO BE HIS SUCCESSOR- DICK BURGER!
"KIRBY'S SUCCESSOR"? GOOD HEAVENS! DICK *HAS* DONE WELL FOR HIMSELF!
HE'S EASILY THE MOST SUCCESSFUL MAN IN COMICS TODAY!
HOW SPLENDID! MY, MY!
DOES BURGER STILL HAVE FAMILY ROUND HERE, MRS. HICKS?
WELL NO. I'M AFRAID DICK'S FAMILY WAS ALWAYS A BIT OF A MYSTERY - HE'S AN ORPHAN, THE POOR DEAR...
OH. I SEE.
PERHAPS IF YOU SPOKE TO SAM. HE ALWAYS KNEW WHAT DICK WAS UP TO. SAM IS A CARTOONIST TOO, YOU KNOW.

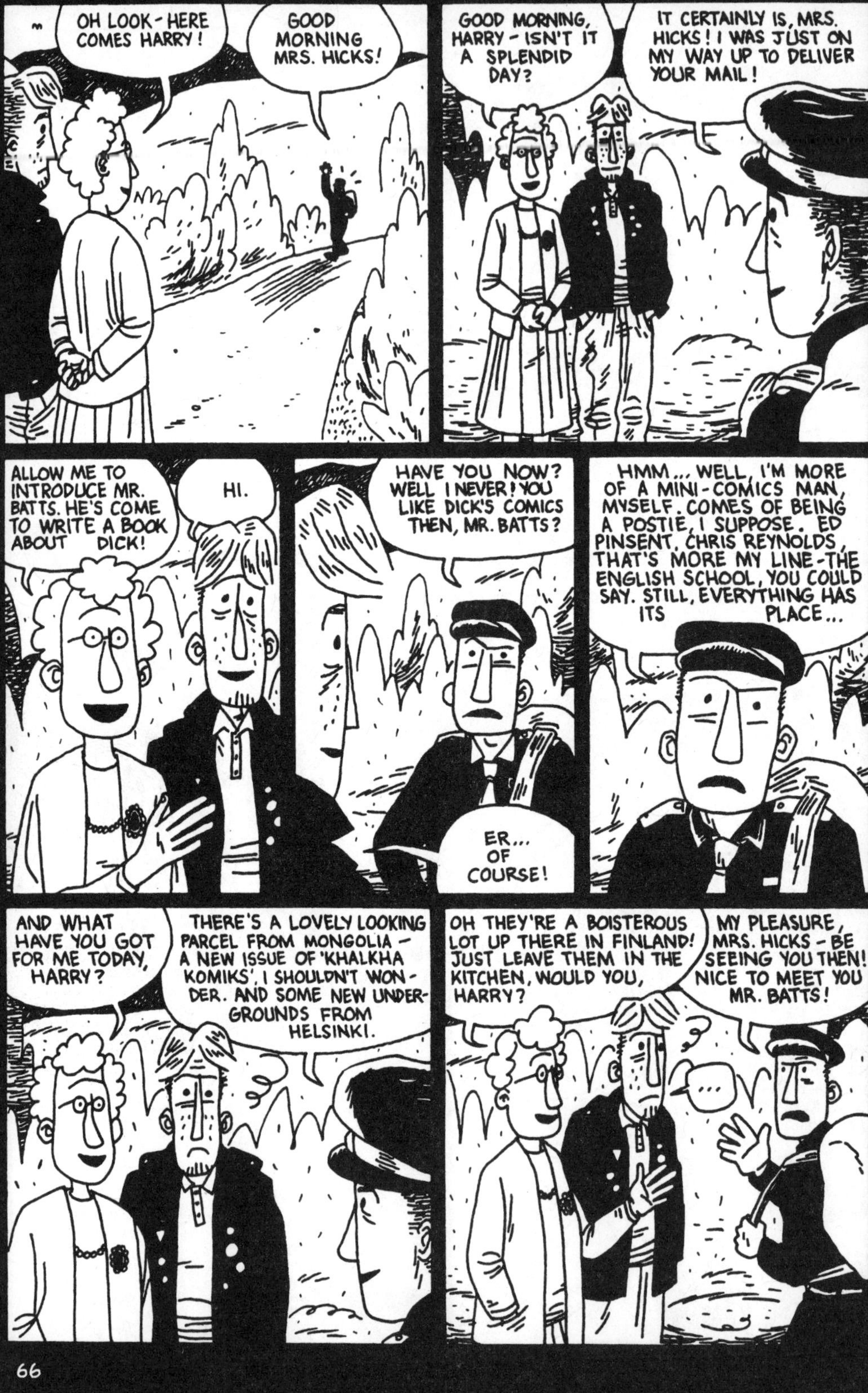
OH LOOK - HERE COMES HARRY!
GOOD MORNING MRS. HICKS!
GOOD MORNING, HARRY - ISN'T IT A SPLENDID DAY?
IT CERTAINLY IS, MRS. HICKS! I WAS JUST ON MY WAY UP TO DELIVER YOUR MAIL!
ALLOW ME TO INTRODUCE MR. BATTS. HE'S COME TO WRITE A BOOK ABOUT DICK!
HI.
HAVE YOU NOW? WELL I NEVER! YOU LIKE DICK'S COMICS THEN, MR. BATTS?
ER... OF COURSE!
HMM... WELL, I'M MORE OF A MINI-COMICS MAN, MYSELF. COMES OF BEING A POSTIE, I SUPPOSE. ED PINSENT, CHRIS REYNOLDS, THAT'S MORE MY LINE - THE ENGLISH SCHOOL, YOU COULD SAY. STILL, EVERYTHING HAS ITS PLACE...
AND WHAT HAVE YOU GOT FOR ME TODAY, HARRY?
THERE'S A LOVELY LOOKING PARCEL FROM MONGOLIA - A NEW ISSUE OF 'KHALKHA KOMIKS', I SHOULDN'T WONDER. AND SOME NEW UNDERGROUNDS FROM HELSINKI.
OH THEY'RE A BOISTEROUS LOT UP THERE IN FINLAND! JUST LEAVE THEM IN THE KITCHEN, WOULD YOU, HARRY?
MY PLEASURE, MRS. HICKS - BE SEEING YOU THEN! NICE TO MEET YOU MR. BATTS!
...

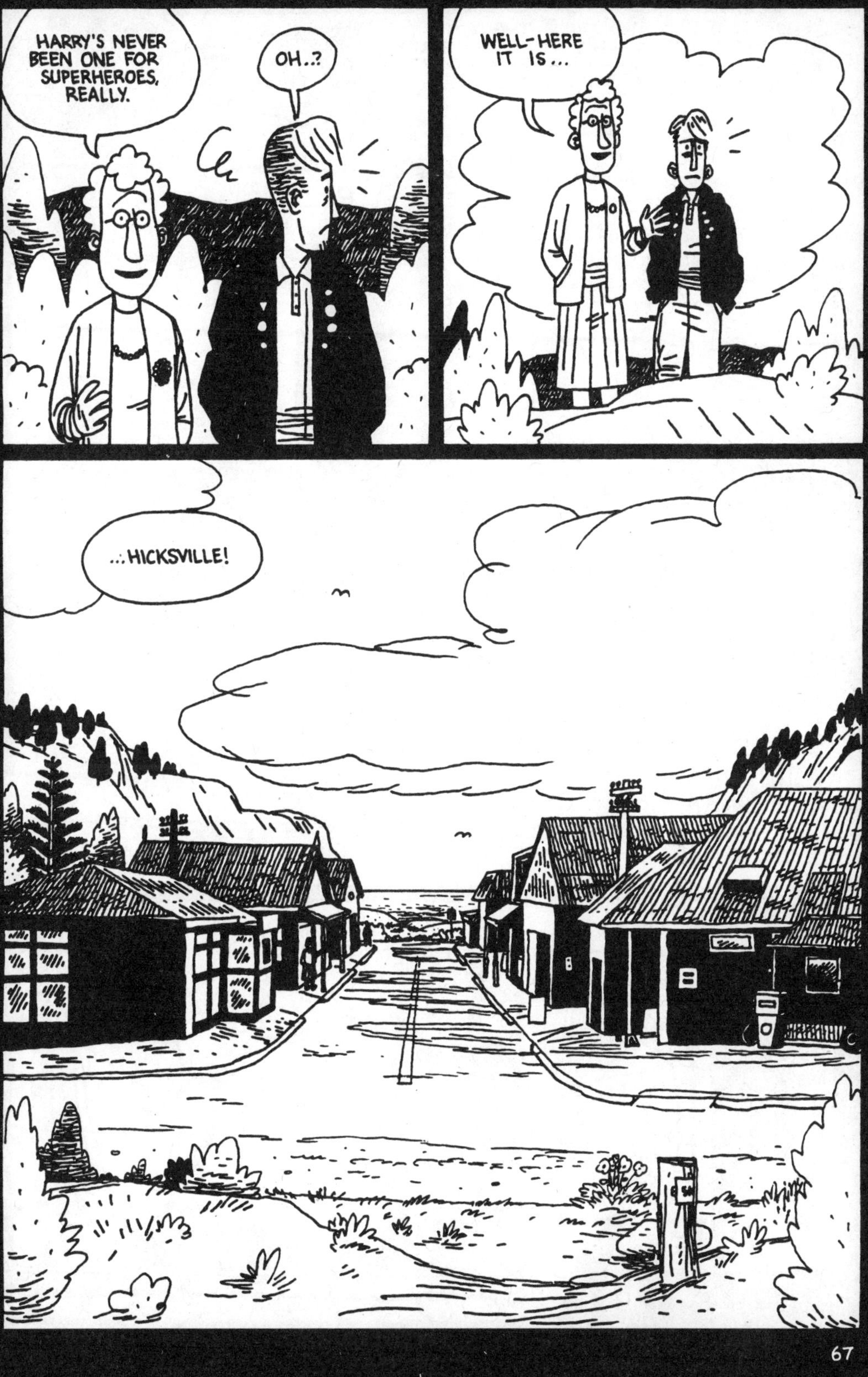
HARRY'S NEVER BEEN ONE FOR SUPERHEROES, REALLY.
OH..?
WELL-HERE IT IS...
...HICKSVILLE!

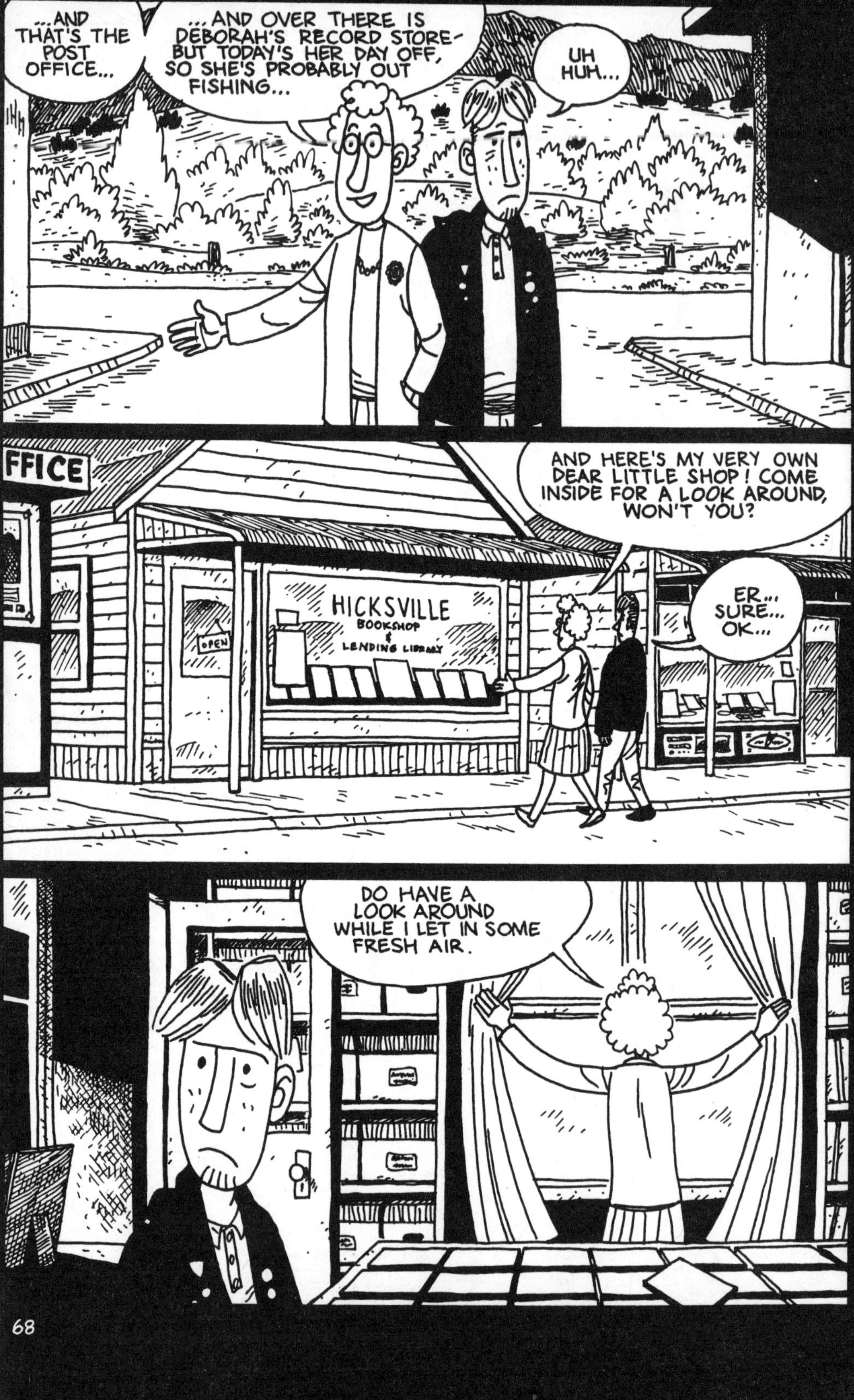
...AND THAT'S THE POST OFFICE...
...AND OVER THERE IS DEBORAH'S RECORD STORE- BUT TODAY'S HER DAY OFF, SO SHE'S PROBABLY OUT FISHING...
UH HUH...
FFICE
HICKSVILLE BOOKSHOP & LENDING LIBRARY
OPEN
AND HERE'S MY VERY OWN DEAR LITTLE SHOP! COME INSIDE FOR A LOOK AROUND, WON'T YOU?
ER... SURE... OK...
DO HAVE A LOOK AROUND WHILE I LET IN SOME FRESH AIR.

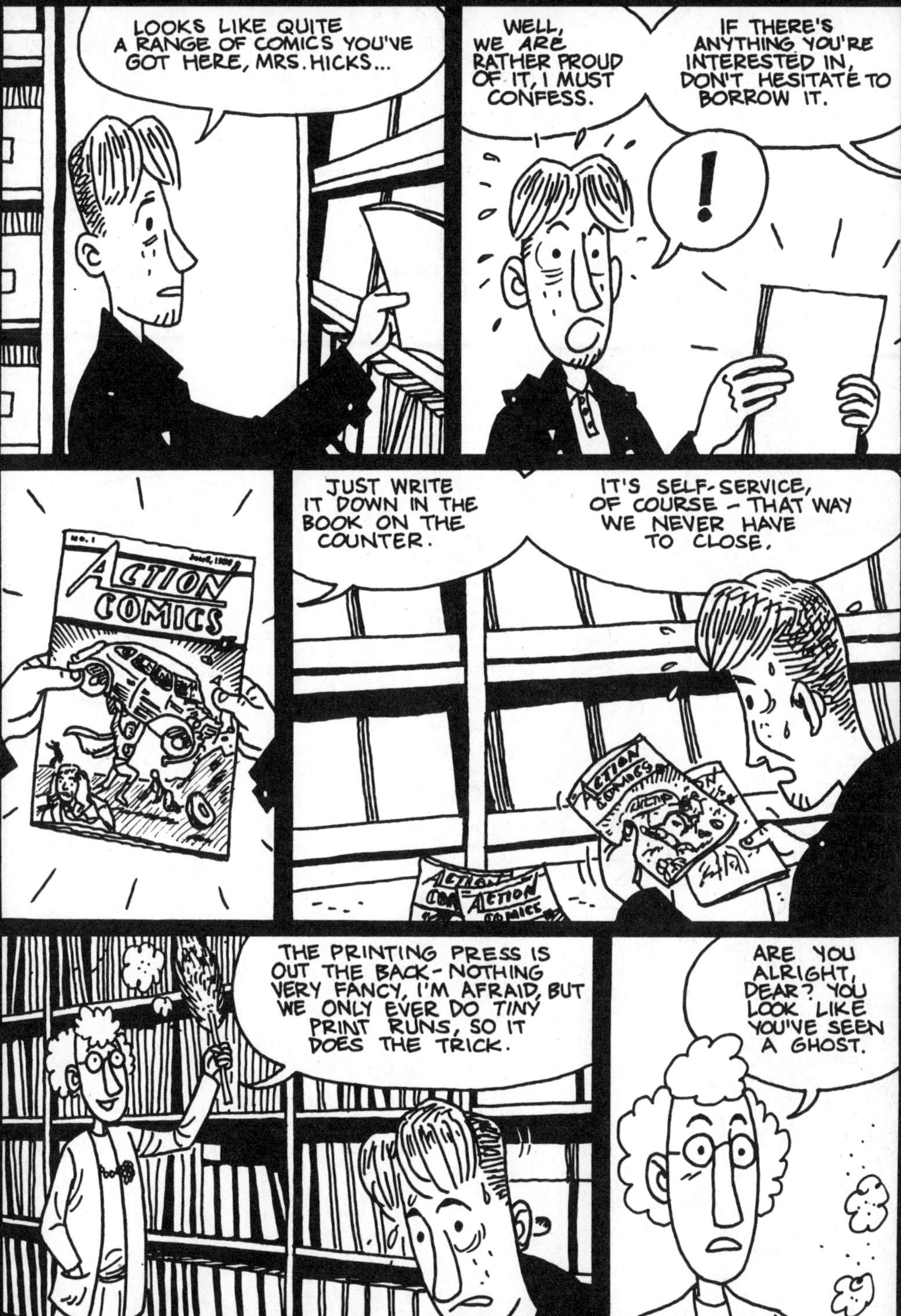
LOOKS LIKE QUITE A RANGE OF COMICS YOU'VE GOT HERE, MRS. HICKS...
WELL, WE *ARE* RATHER PROUD OF IT, I MUST CONFESS.
IF THERE'S ANYTHING YOU'RE INTERESTED IN, DON'T HESITATE TO BORROW IT.
!
NO. 1
ACTION COMICS
JUST WRITE IT DOWN IN THE BOOK ON THE COUNTER.
IT'S SELF-SERVICE, OF COURSE - THAT WAY WE NEVER HAVE TO CLOSE.
THE PRINTING PRESS IS OUT THE BACK - NOTHING VERY FANCY, I'M AFRAID, BUT WE ONLY EVER DO *TINY* PRINT RUNS, SO IT DOES THE TRICK.
ARE YOU ALRIGHT, DEAR? YOU LOOK LIKE YOU'VE SEEN A GHOST.

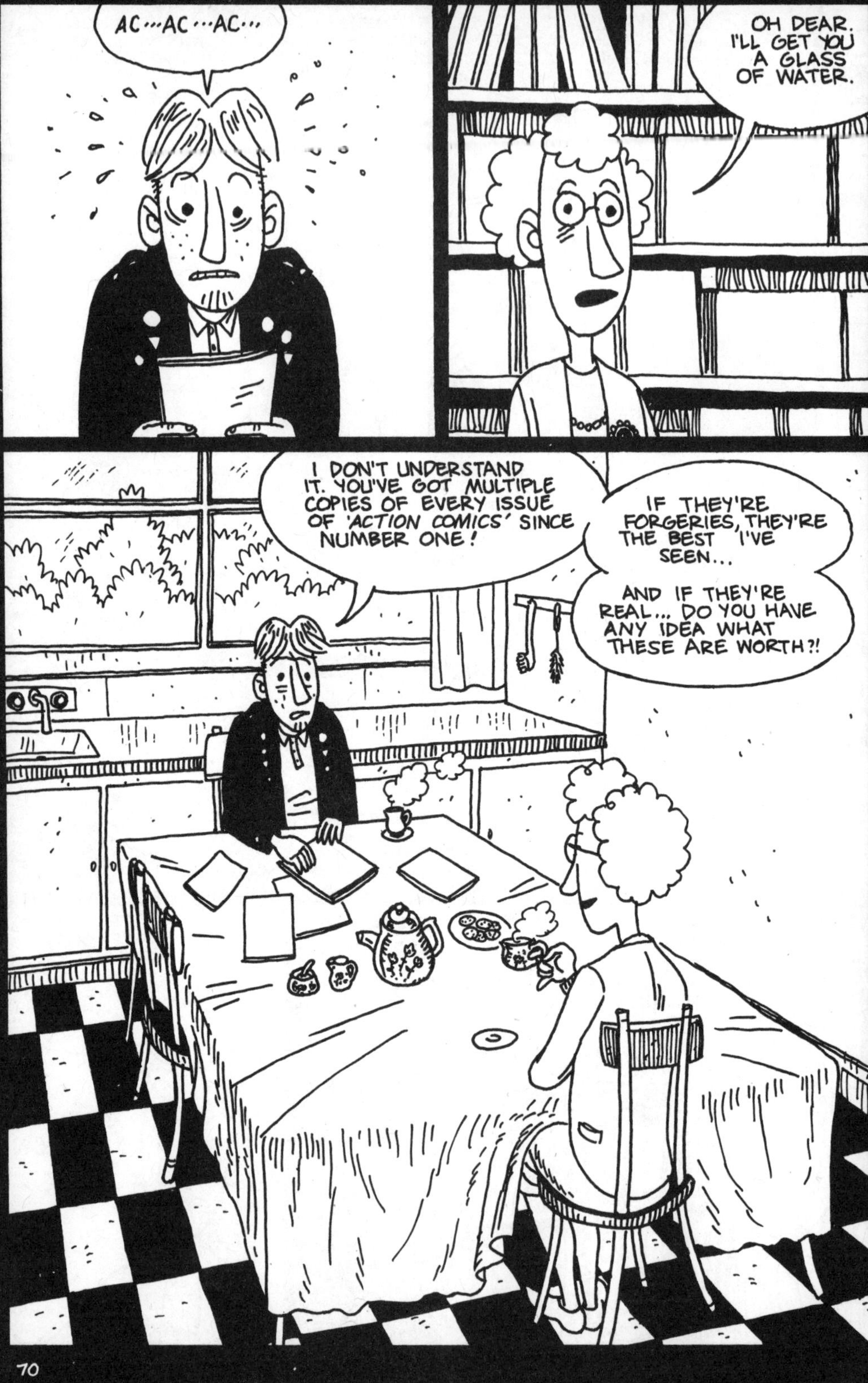
AC...AC...AC...
OH DEAR. I'LL GET YOU A GLASS OF WATER.
I DON'T UNDERSTAND IT. YOU'VE GOT MULTIPLE COPIES OF EVERY ISSUE OF 'ACTION COMICS' SINCE NUMBER ONE!
IF THEY'RE FORGERIES, THEY'RE THE BEST I'VE SEEN...
AND IF THEY'RE REAL... DO YOU HAVE ANY IDEA WHAT THESE ARE WORTH?!

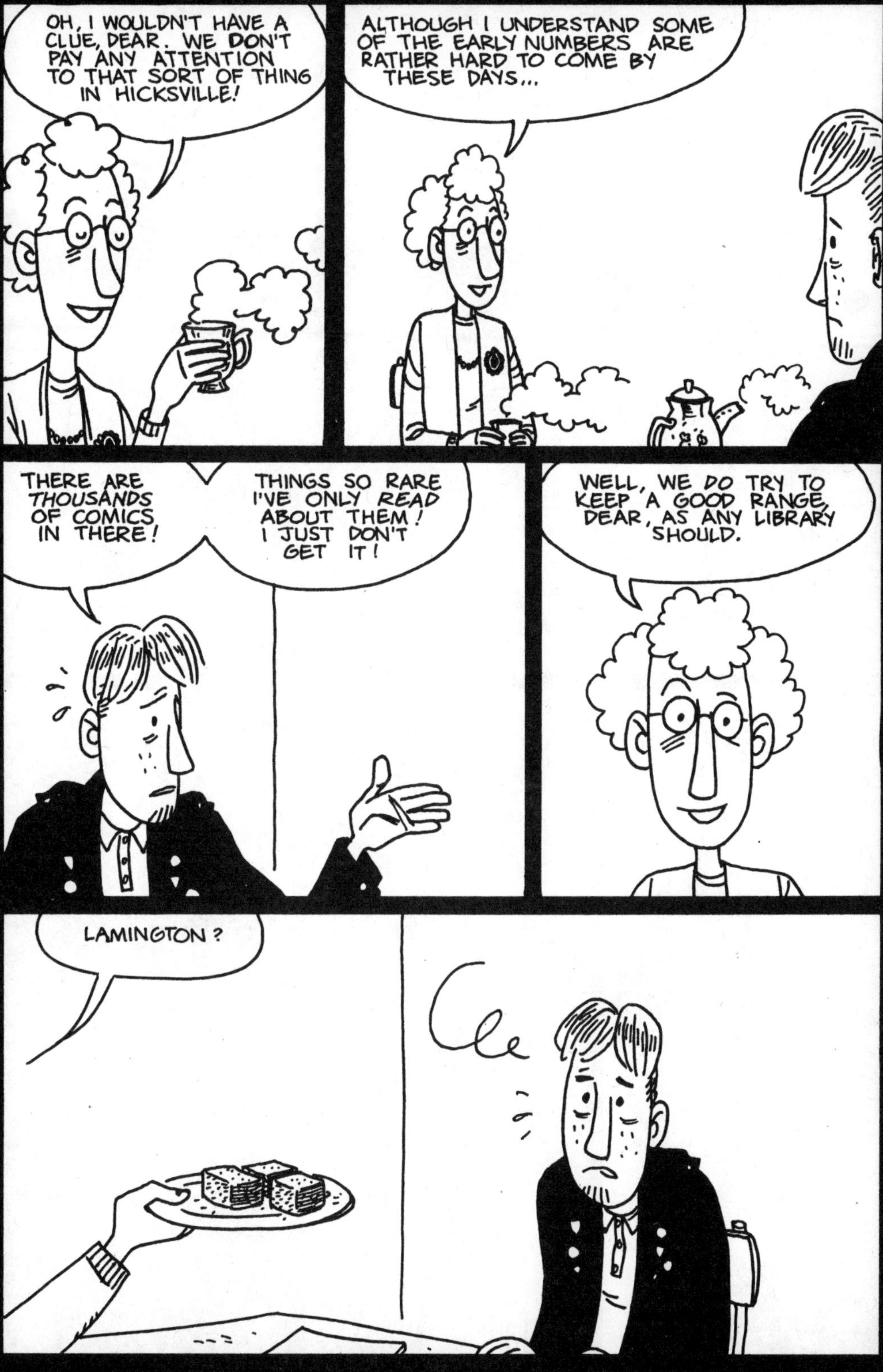
OH, I WOULDN'T HAVE A CLUE, DEAR. WE DON'T PAY ANY ATTENTION TO THAT SORT OF THING IN HICKSVILLE!
ALTHOUGH I UNDERSTAND SOME OF THE EARLY NUMBERS ARE RATHER HARD TO COME BY THESE DAYS...
THERE ARE THOUSANDS OF COMICS IN THERE!
THINGS SO RARE I'VE ONLY READ ABOUT THEM! I JUST DON'T GET IT!
WELL, WE DO TRY TO KEEP A GOOD RANGE, DEAR, AS ANY LIBRARY SHOULD.
LAMINGTON?

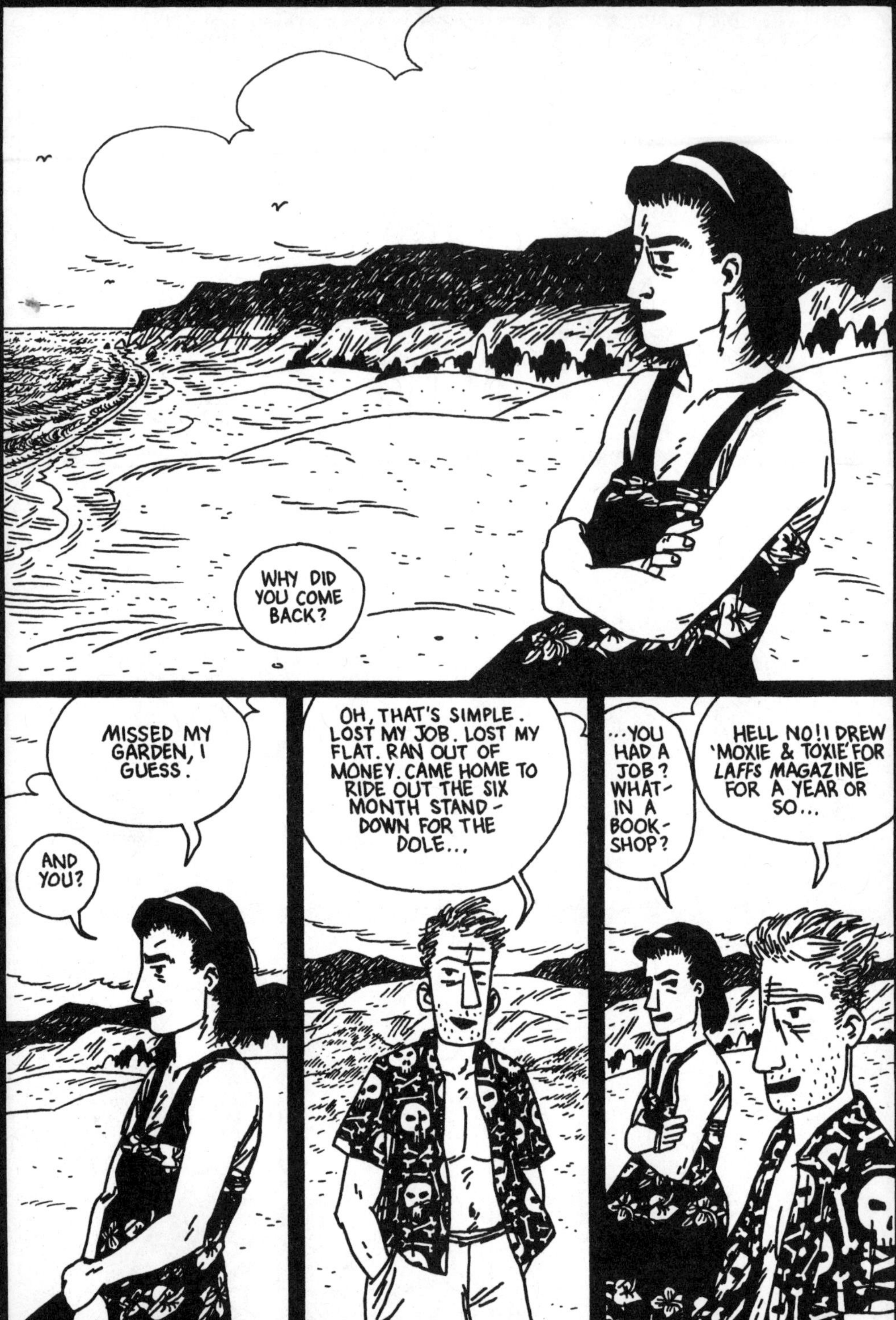
WHY DID YOU COME BACK?
MISSED MY GARDEN, I GUESS.
AND YOU?
OH, THAT'S SIMPLE. LOST MY JOB. LOST MY FLAT. RAN OUT OF MONEY. CAME HOME TO RIDE OUT THE SIX MONTH STAND-DOWN FOR THE DOLE...
...YOU HAD A JOB? WHAT-IN A BOOK-SHOP?
HELL NO! I DREW 'MOXIE & TOXIE' FOR *LAFFS MAGAZINE* FOR A YEAR OR SO...

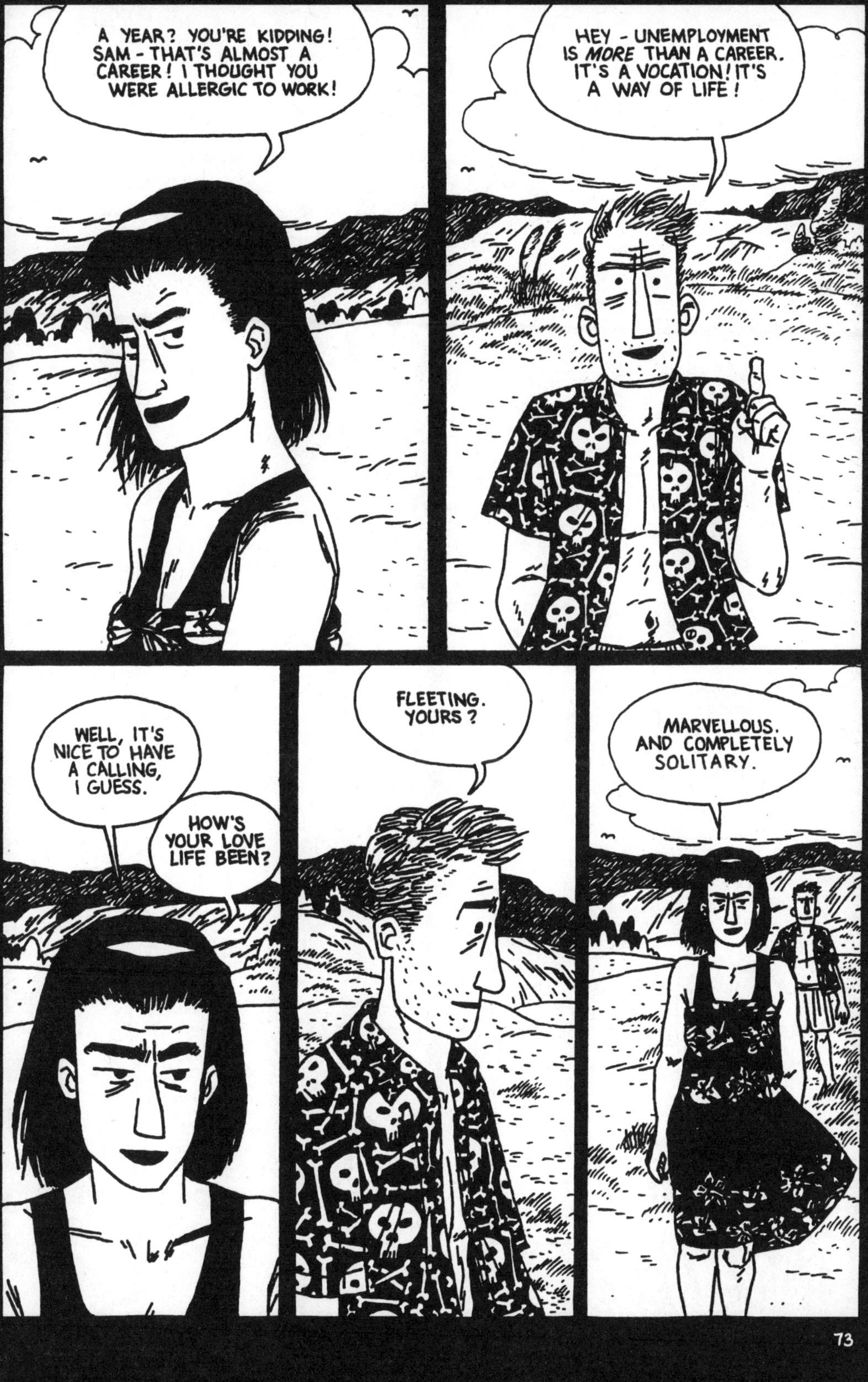
A YEAR? YOU'RE KIDDING! SAM - THAT'S ALMOST A CAREER! I THOUGHT YOU WERE ALLERGIC TO WORK!
HEY - UNEMPLOYMENT IS *MORE* THAN A CAREER. IT'S A VOCATION! IT'S A WAY OF LIFE!
WELL, IT'S NICE TO HAVE A CALLING, I GUESS.
HOW'S YOUR LOVE LIFE BEEN?
FLEETING. YOURS?
MARVELLOUS. AND COMPLETELY SOLITARY.

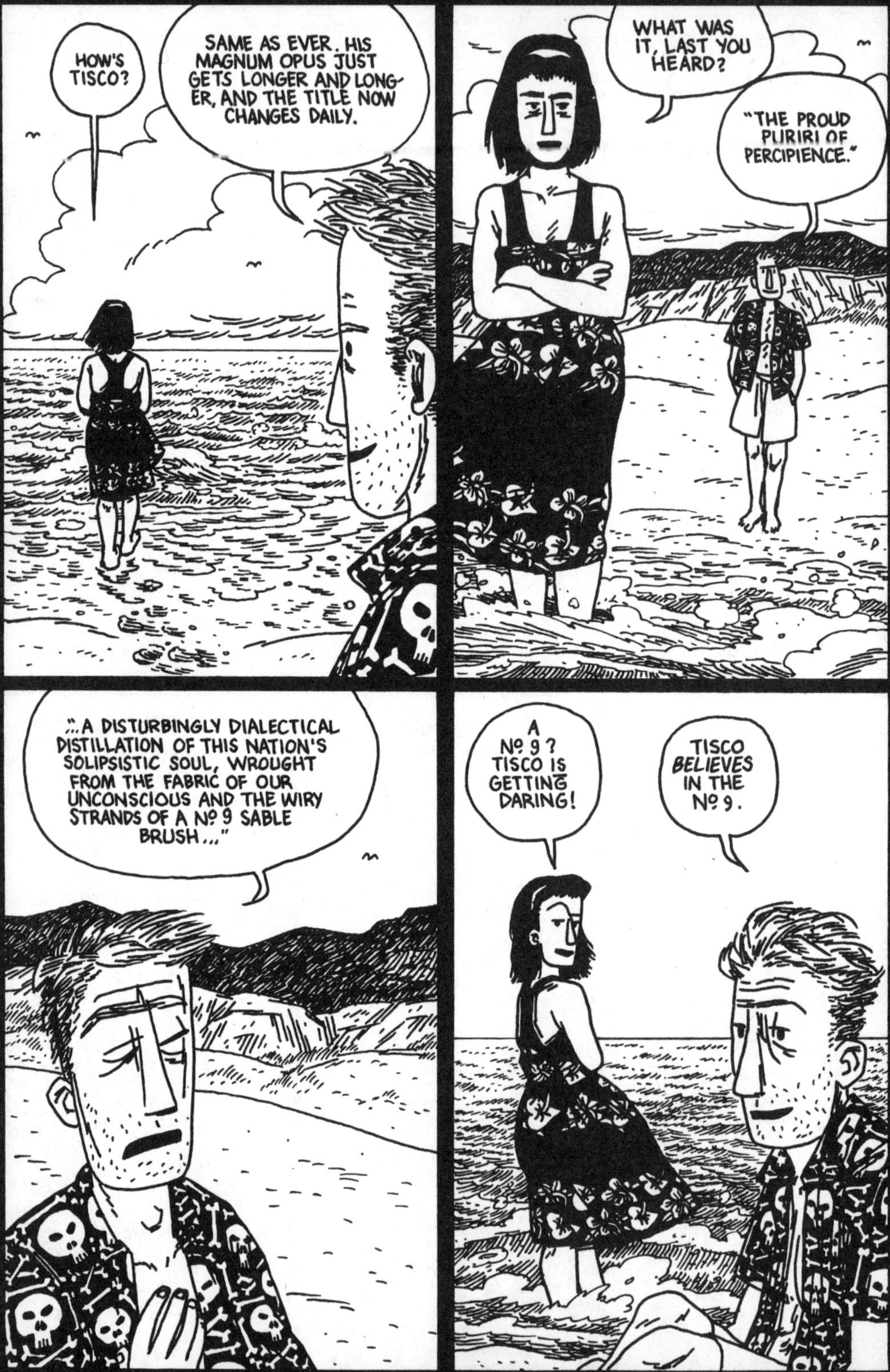
HOW'S TISCO?
SAME AS EVER. HIS MAGNUM OPUS JUST GETS LONGER AND LONGER, AND THE TITLE NOW CHANGES DAILY.
WHAT WAS IT, LAST YOU HEARD?
"THE PROUD PURIRI OF PERCIPIENCE."
..A DISTURBINGLY DIALECTICAL DISTILLATION OF THIS NATION'S SOLIPSISTIC SOUL, WROUGHT FROM THE FABRIC OF OUR UNCONSCIOUS AND THE WIRY STRANDS OF A No 9 SABLE BRUSH..."
A No 9? TISCO IS GETTING DARING!
TISCO *BELIEVES* IN THE No 9.

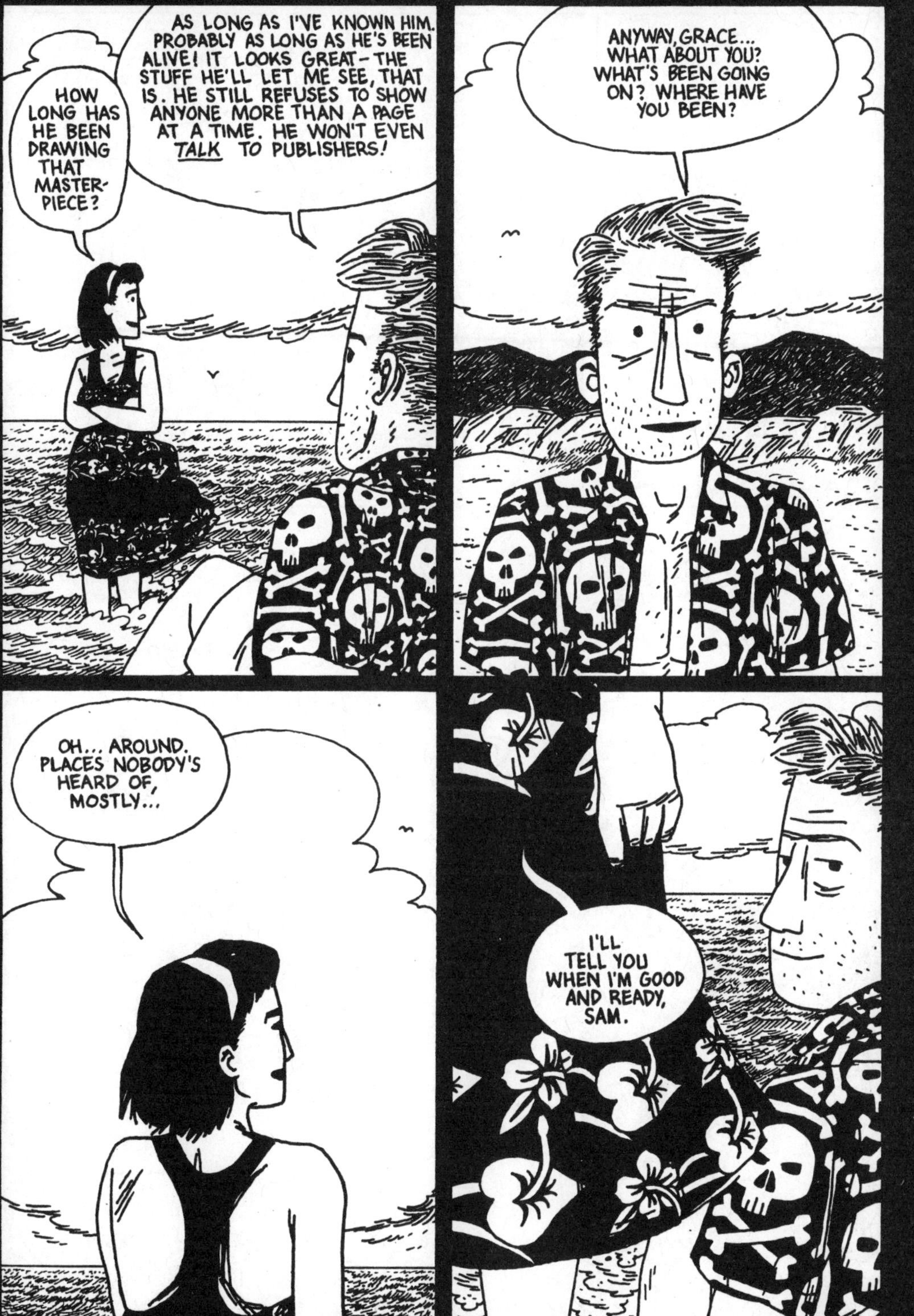
HOW LONG HAS HE BEEN DRAWING THAT MASTER-PIECE?
AS LONG AS I'VE KNOWN HIM. PROBABLY AS LONG AS HE'S BEEN ALIVE! IT LOOKS GREAT– THE STUFF HE'LL LET ME SEE, THAT IS. HE STILL REFUSES TO SHOW ANYONE MORE THAN A PAGE AT A TIME. HE WON'T EVEN TALK TO PUBLISHERS!
ANYWAY, GRACE... WHAT ABOUT YOU? WHAT'S BEEN GOING ON? WHERE HAVE YOU BEEN?
OH... AROUND. PLACES NOBODY'S HEARD OF, MOSTLY...
I'LL TELL YOU WHEN I'M GOOD AND READY, SAM.

Meanwhile, down at the Rarebit Fiend Tearooms...

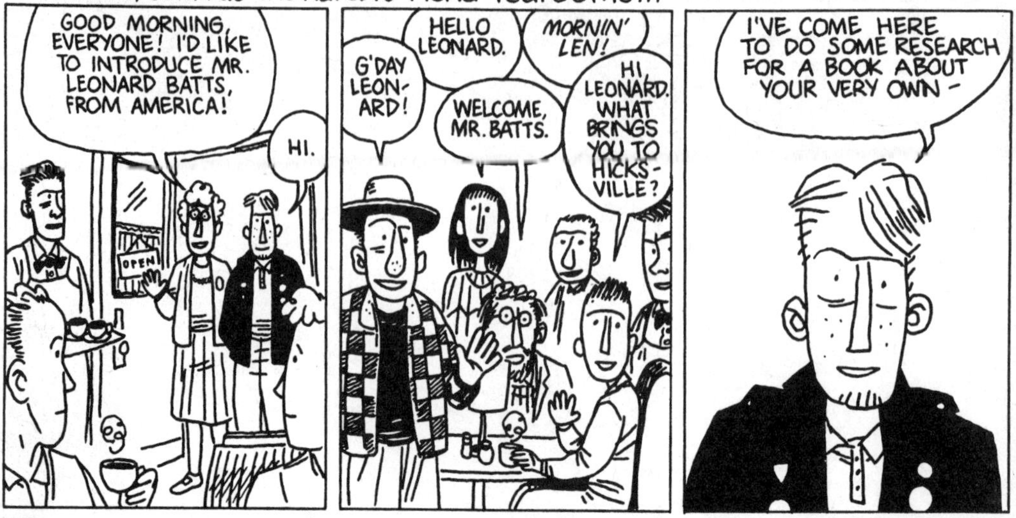
GOOD MORNING, EVERYONE! I'D LIKE TO INTRODUCE MR. LEONARD BATTS, FROM AMERICA!
HI.
OPEN
G'DAY LEON-ARD!
HELLO LEONARD.
MORNIN' LEN!
WELCOME, MR. BATTS.
HI, LEONARD. WHAT BRINGS YOU TO HICKS-VILLE?
I'VE COME HERE TO DO SOME RESEARCH FOR A BOOK ABOUT YOUR VERY OWN -

The man who mentioned 'Dick Burger' in the Rarebit Fiend

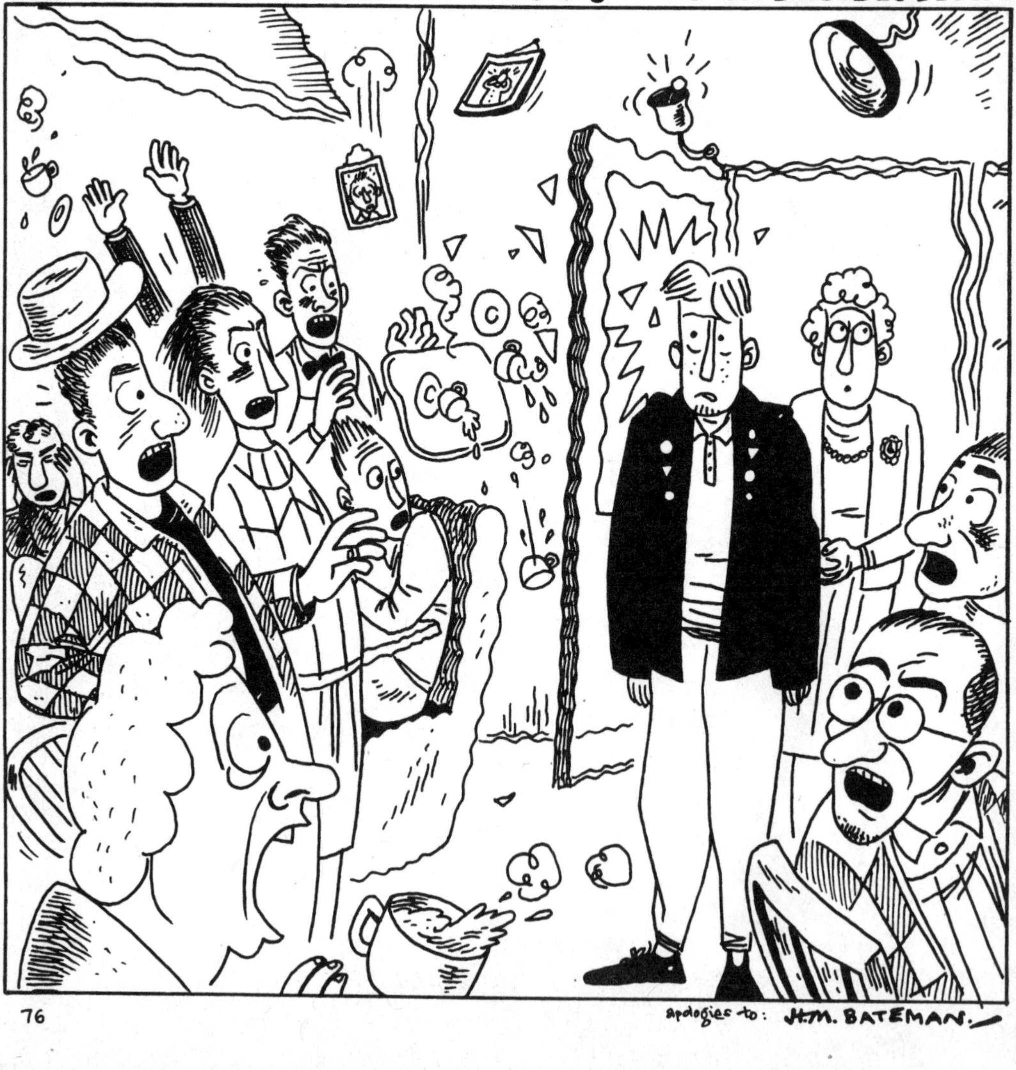

apologies to: H.M. BATEMAN.

Chapter Four

*"Now we're in the age of
'comics as air.'"*
Osamu Tezuka.

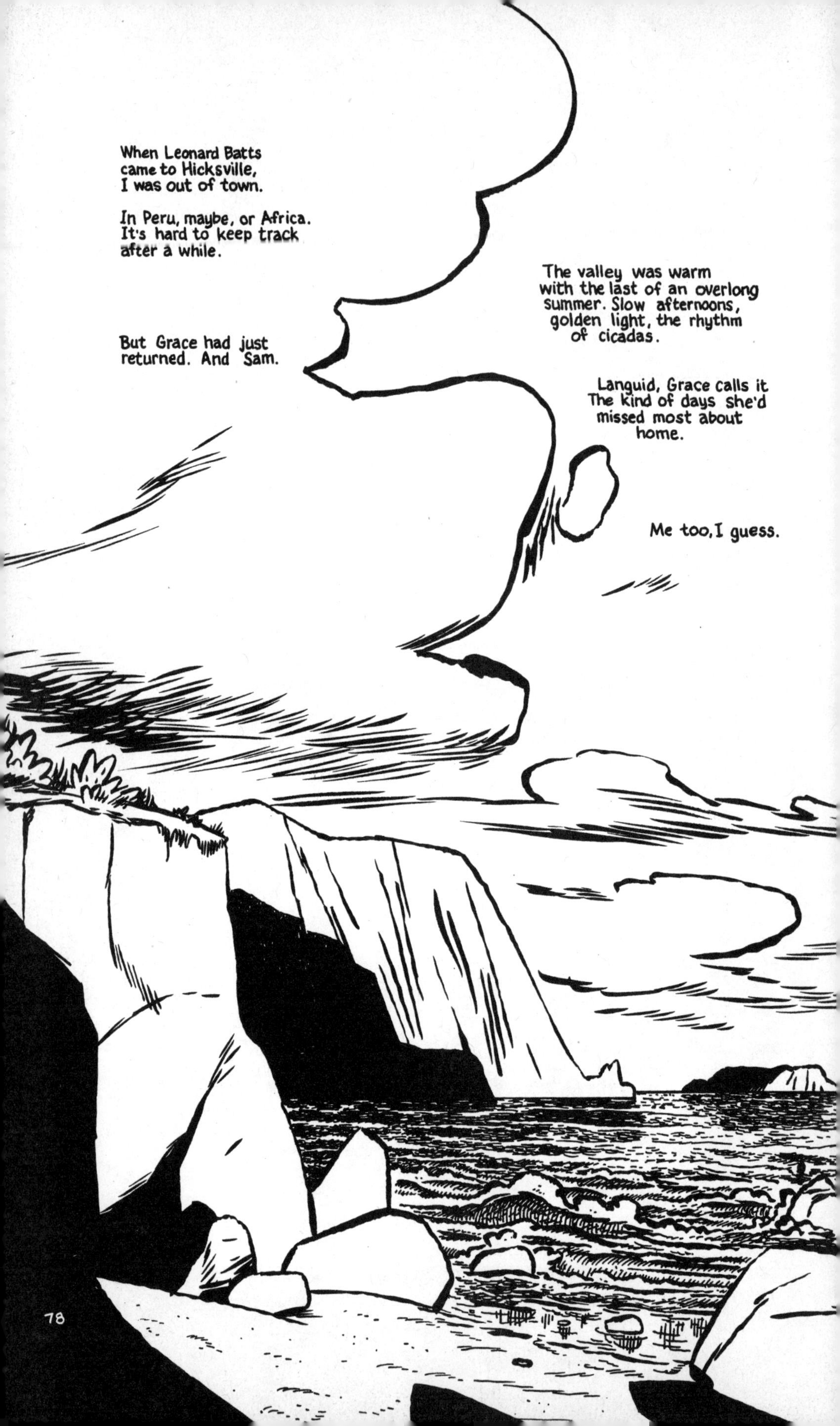
When Leonard Batts came to Hicksville, I was out of town.
In Peru, maybe, or Africa. It's hard to keep track after a while.
But Grace had just returned. And Sam.
The valley was warm with the last of an overlong summer. Slow afternoons, golden light, the rhythm of cicadas.
Languid, Grace calls it The kind of days she'd missed most about home.
Me too, I guess.

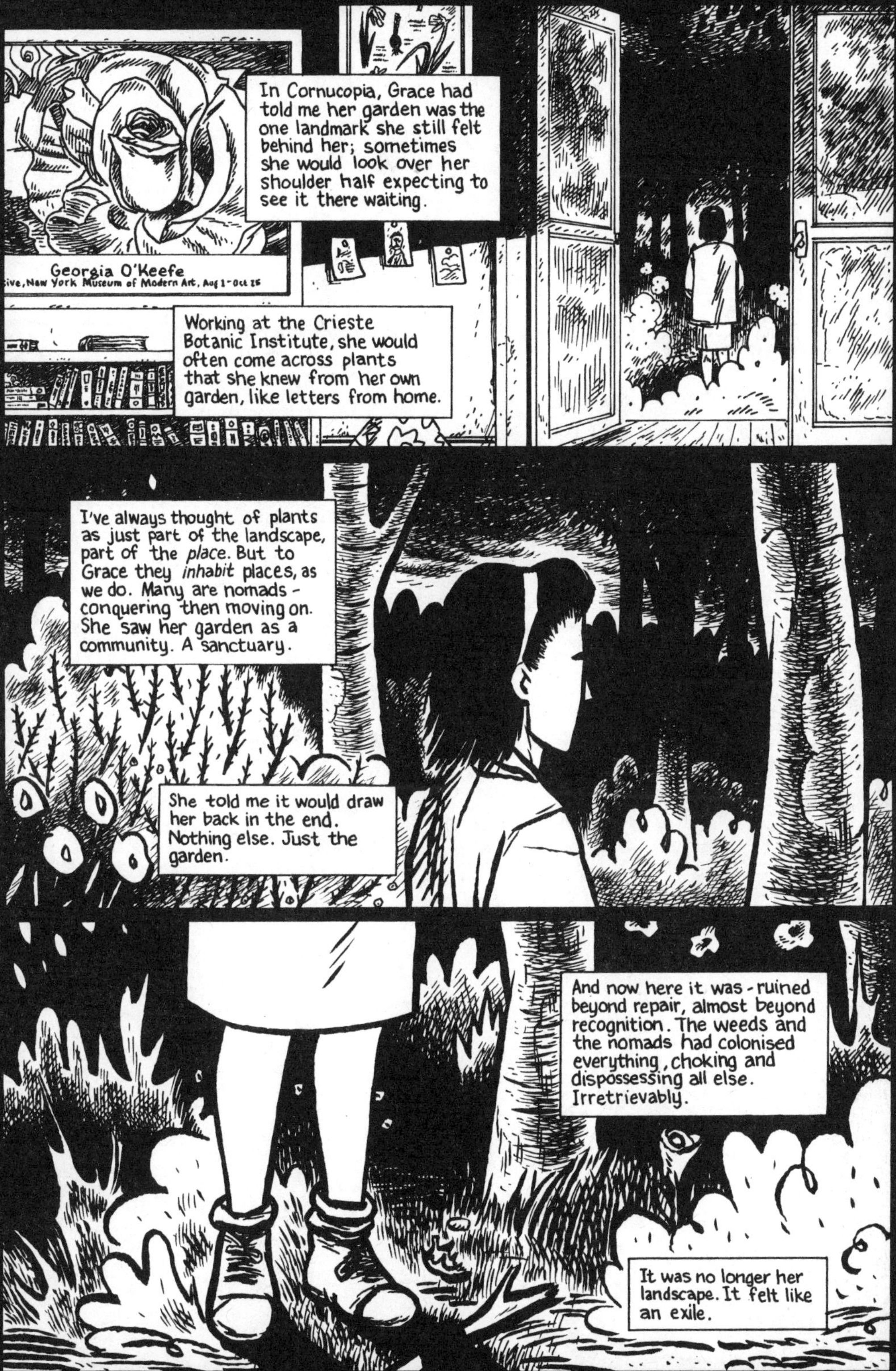

Georgia O'Keefe
ive, New York Museum of Modern Art, Aug 1-Oct 25
In Cornucopia, Grace had told me her garden was the one landmark she still felt behind her; sometimes she would look over her shoulder half expecting to see it there waiting.
Working at the Crieste Botanic Institute, she would often come across plants that she knew from her own garden, like letters from home.
I've always thought of plants as just part of the landscape, part of the *place*. But to Grace they *inhabit* places, as we do. Many are nomads - conquering then moving on. She saw her garden as a community. A sanctuary.
She told me it would draw her back in the end. Nothing else. Just the garden.
And now here it was - ruined beyond repair, almost beyond recognition. The weeds and the nomads had colonised everything, choking and dispossessing all else. Irretrievably.
It was no longer her landscape. It felt like an exile.

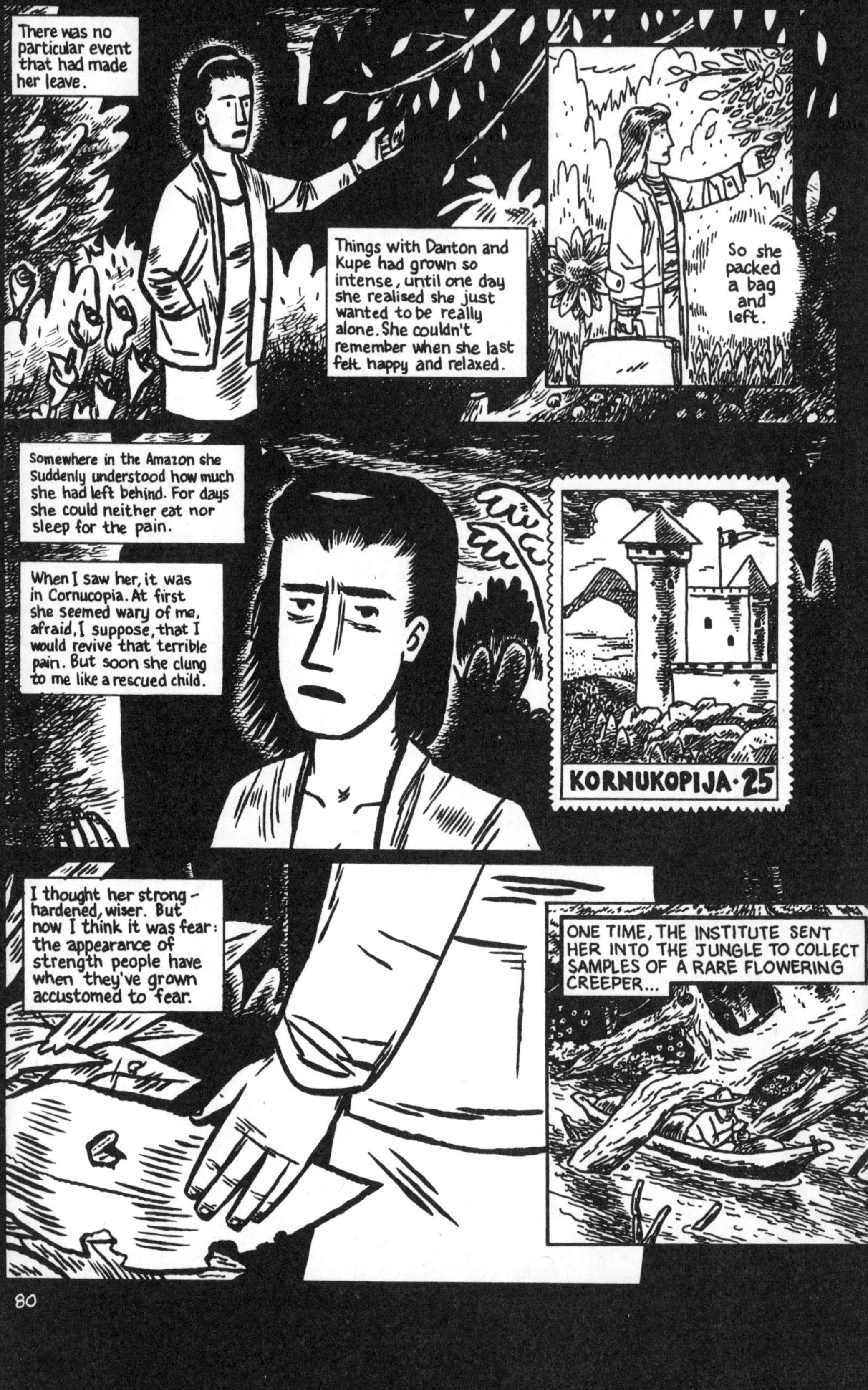
There was no particular event that had made her leave.
Things with Danton and Kupe had grown so intense, until one day she realised she just wanted to be really alone. She couldn't remember when she last felt happy and relaxed.
So she packed a bag and left.
Somewhere in the Amazon she suddenly understood how much she had left behind. For days she could neither eat nor sleep for the pain.
When I saw her, it was in Cornucopia. At first she seemed wary of me, afraid, I suppose, that I would revive that terrible pain. But soon she clung to me like a rescued child.
KORNUKOPIJA · 25
I thought her strong - hardened, wiser. But now I think it was fear: the appearance of strength people have when they've grown accustomed to fear.
ONE TIME, THE INSTITUTE SENT HER INTO THE JUNGLE TO COLLECT SAMPLES OF A RARE FLOWERING CREEPER...

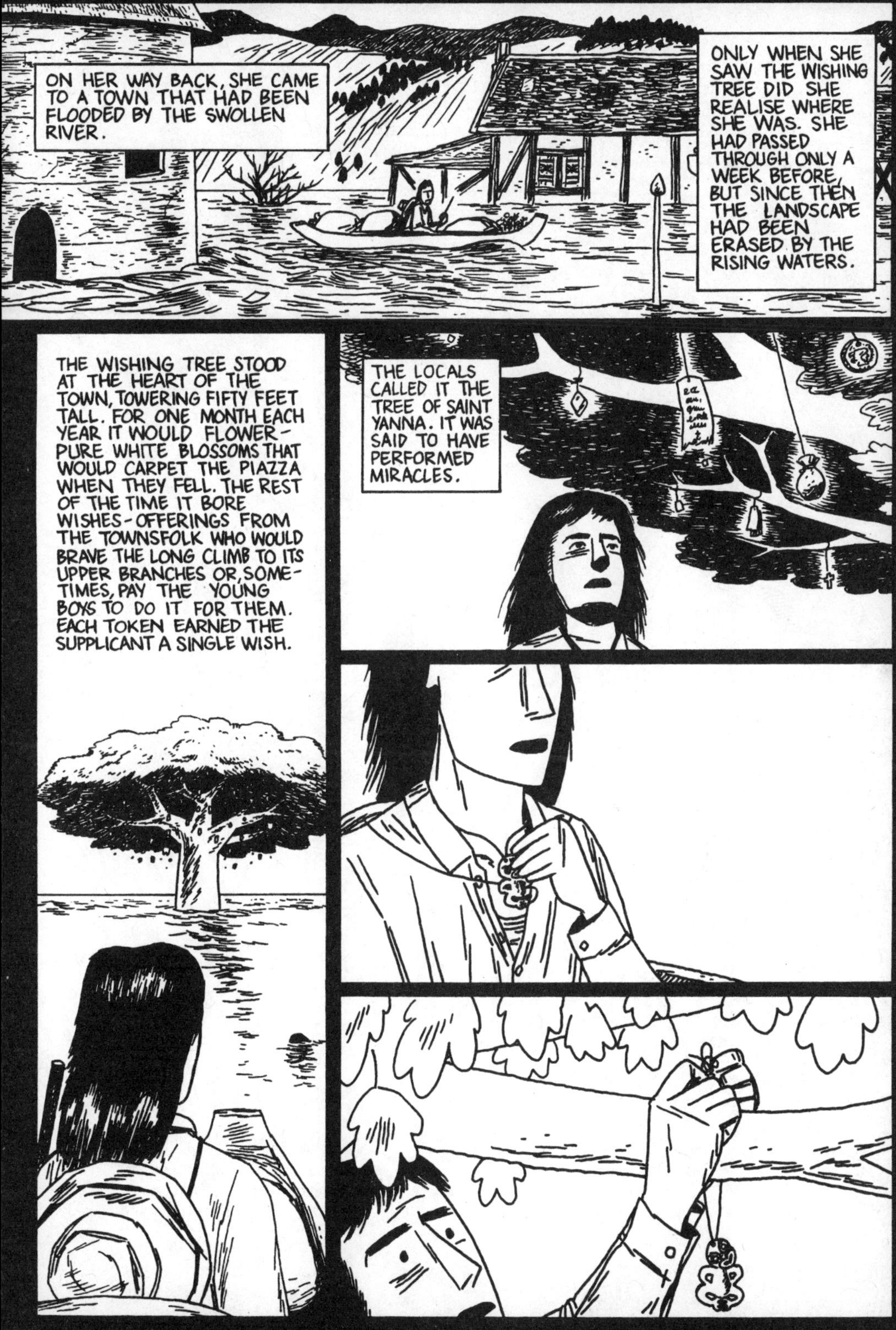
ON HER WAY BACK, SHE CAME TO A TOWN THAT HAD BEEN FLOODED BY THE SWOLLEN RIVER.
ONLY WHEN SHE SAW THE WISHING TREE DID SHE REALISE WHERE SHE WAS. SHE HAD PASSED THROUGH ONLY A WEEK BEFORE, BUT SINCE THEN THE LANDSCAPE HAD BEEN ERASED BY THE RISING WATERS.
THE WISHING TREE STOOD AT THE HEART OF THE TOWN, TOWERING FIFTY FEET TALL. FOR ONE MONTH EACH YEAR IT WOULD FLOWER- PURE WHITE BLOSSOMS THAT WOULD CARPET THE PIAZZA WHEN THEY FELL. THE REST OF THE TIME IT BORE WISHES- OFFERINGS FROM THE TOWNSFOLK WHO WOULD BRAVE THE LONG CLIMB TO ITS UPPER BRANCHES OR, SOME- TIMES, PAY THE YOUNG BOYS TO DO IT FOR THEM. EACH TOKEN EARNED THE SUPPLICANT A SINGLE WISH.
THE LOCALS CALLED IT THE TREE OF SAINT YANNA. IT WAS SAID TO HAVE PERFORMED MIRACLES.

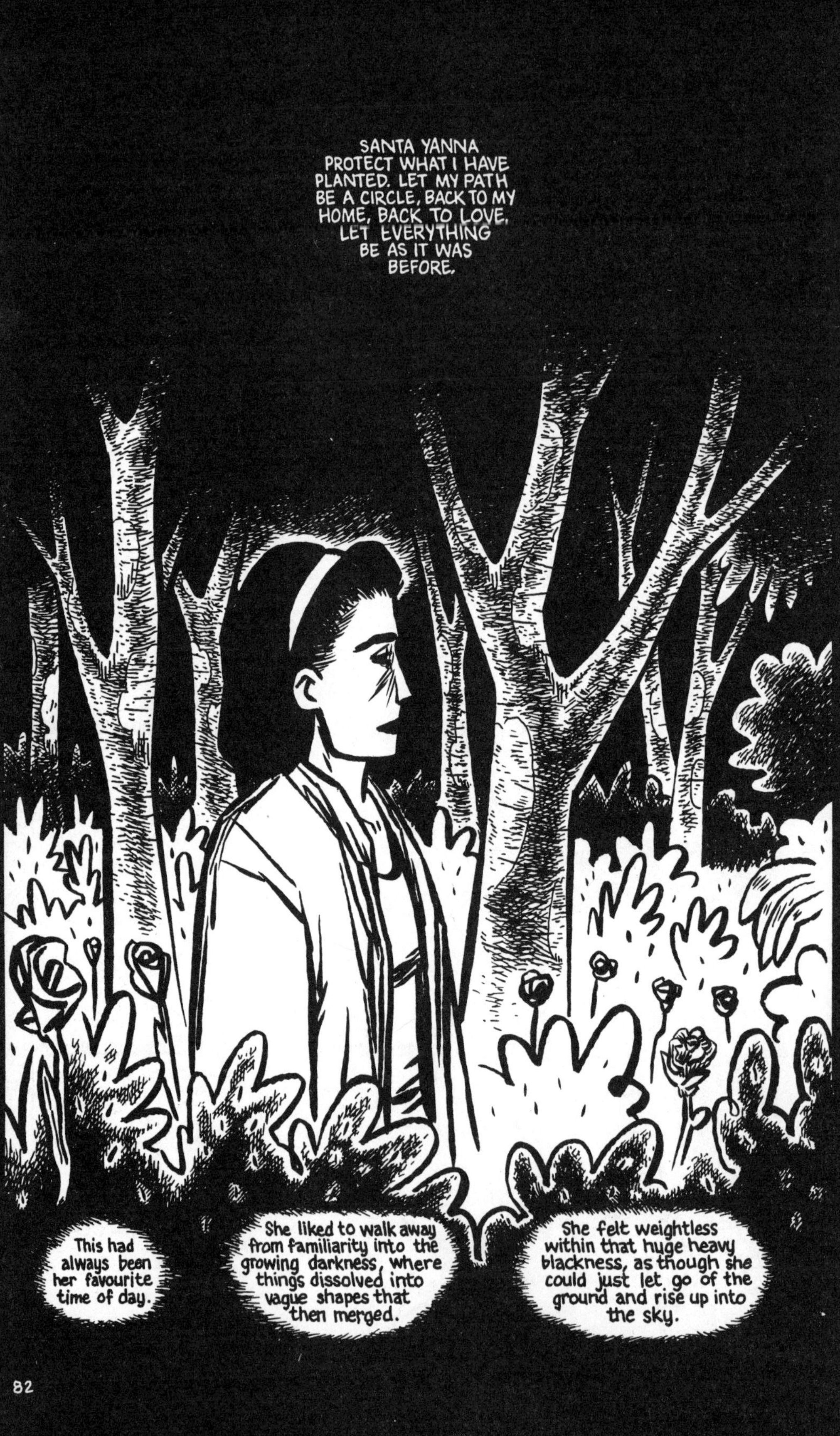
SANTA YANNA PROTECT WHAT I HAVE PLANTED. LET MY PATH BE A CIRCLE, BACK TO MY HOME, BACK TO LOVE. LET EVERYTHING BE AS IT WAS BEFORE.
This had always been her favourite time of day.
She liked to walk away from familiarity into the growing darkness, where things dissolved into vague shapes that then merged.
She felt weightless within that huge heavy blackness, as though she could just let go of the ground and rise up into the sky.

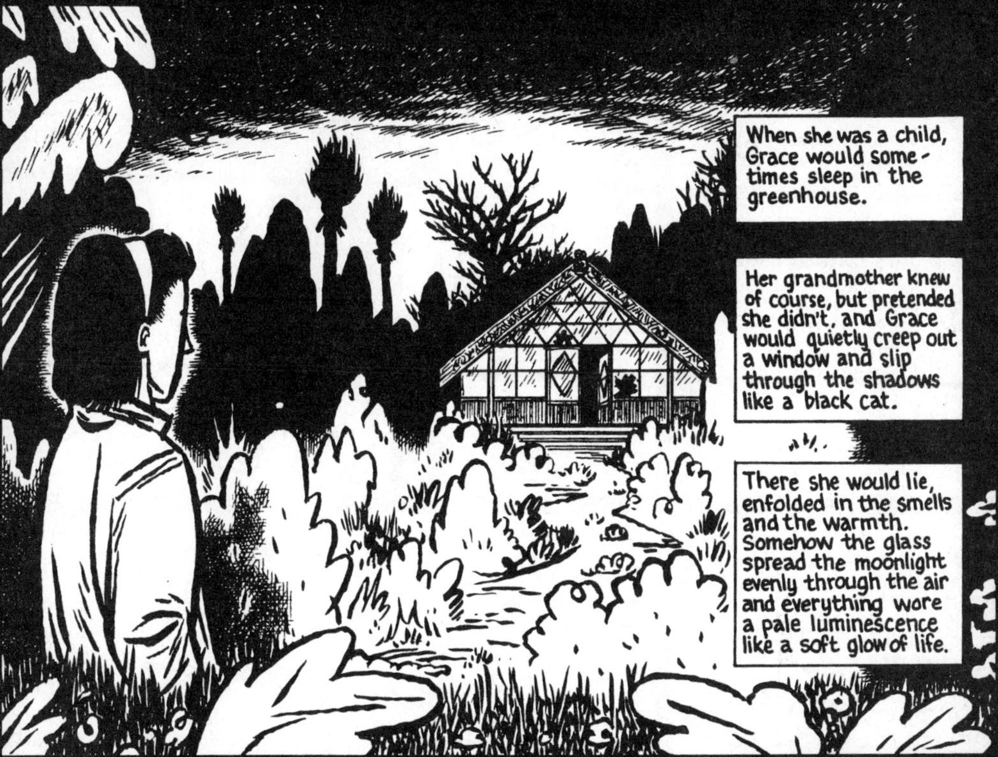
When she was a child, Grace would some-times sleep in the greenhouse.
Her grandmother knew of course, but pretended she didn't, and Grace would quietly creep out a window and slip through the shadows like a black cat.
There she would lie, enfolded in the smells and the warmth. Somehow the glass spread the moonlight evenly through the air and everything wore a pale luminescence like a soft glow of life.

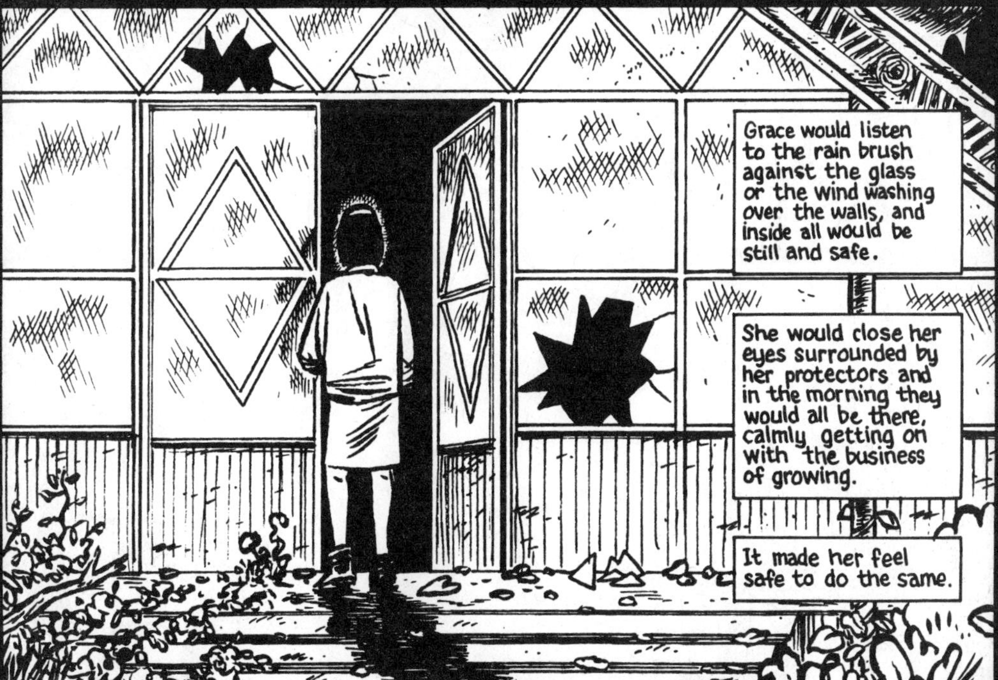
Grace would listen to the rain brush against the glass or the wind washing over the walls, and inside all would be still and safe.
She would close her eyes surrounded by her protectors and in the morning they would all be there, calmly getting on with the business of growing.
It made her feel safe to do the same.

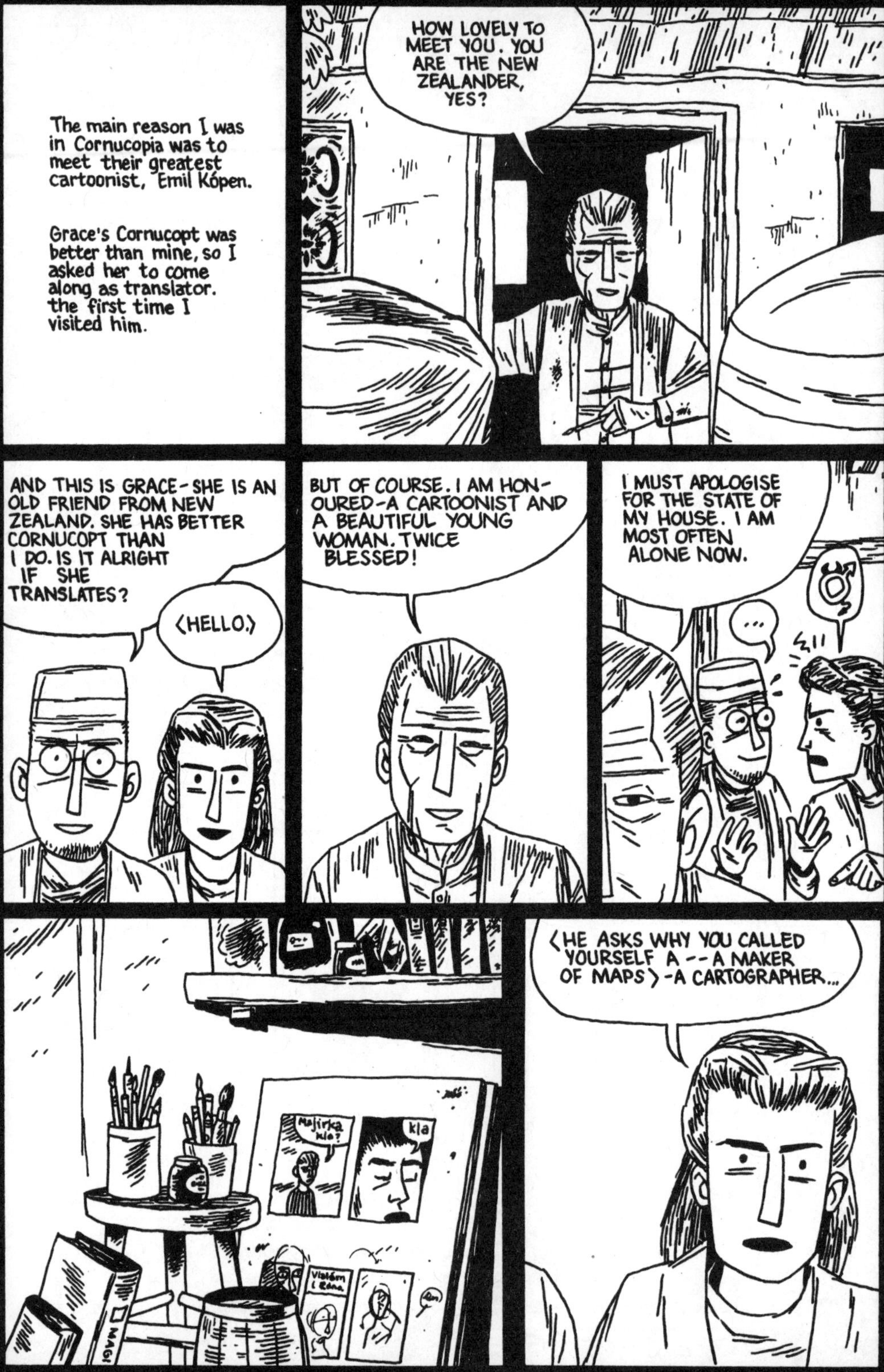
The main reason I was in Cornucopia was to meet their greatest cartoonist, Emil Kópen.
Grace's Cornucopt was better than mine, so I asked her to come along as translator. the first time I visited him.
HOW LOVELY TO MEET YOU. YOU ARE THE NEW ZEALANDER, YES?
AND THIS IS GRACE- SHE IS AN OLD FRIEND FROM NEW ZEALAND. SHE HAS BETTER CORNUCOPT THAN I DO. IS IT ALRIGHT IF SHE TRANSLATES?
⟨HELLO.⟩
BUT OF COURSE. I AM HON-OURED-A CARTOONIST AND A BEAUTIFUL YOUNG WOMAN. TWICE BLESSED!
I MUST APOLOGISE FOR THE STATE OF MY HOUSE. I AM MOST OFTEN ALONE NOW.
...
Majirka kla?
kla
MAGI
⟨HE ASKS WHY YOU CALLED YOURSELF A -- A MAKER OF MAPS⟩ -A CARTOGRAPHER...

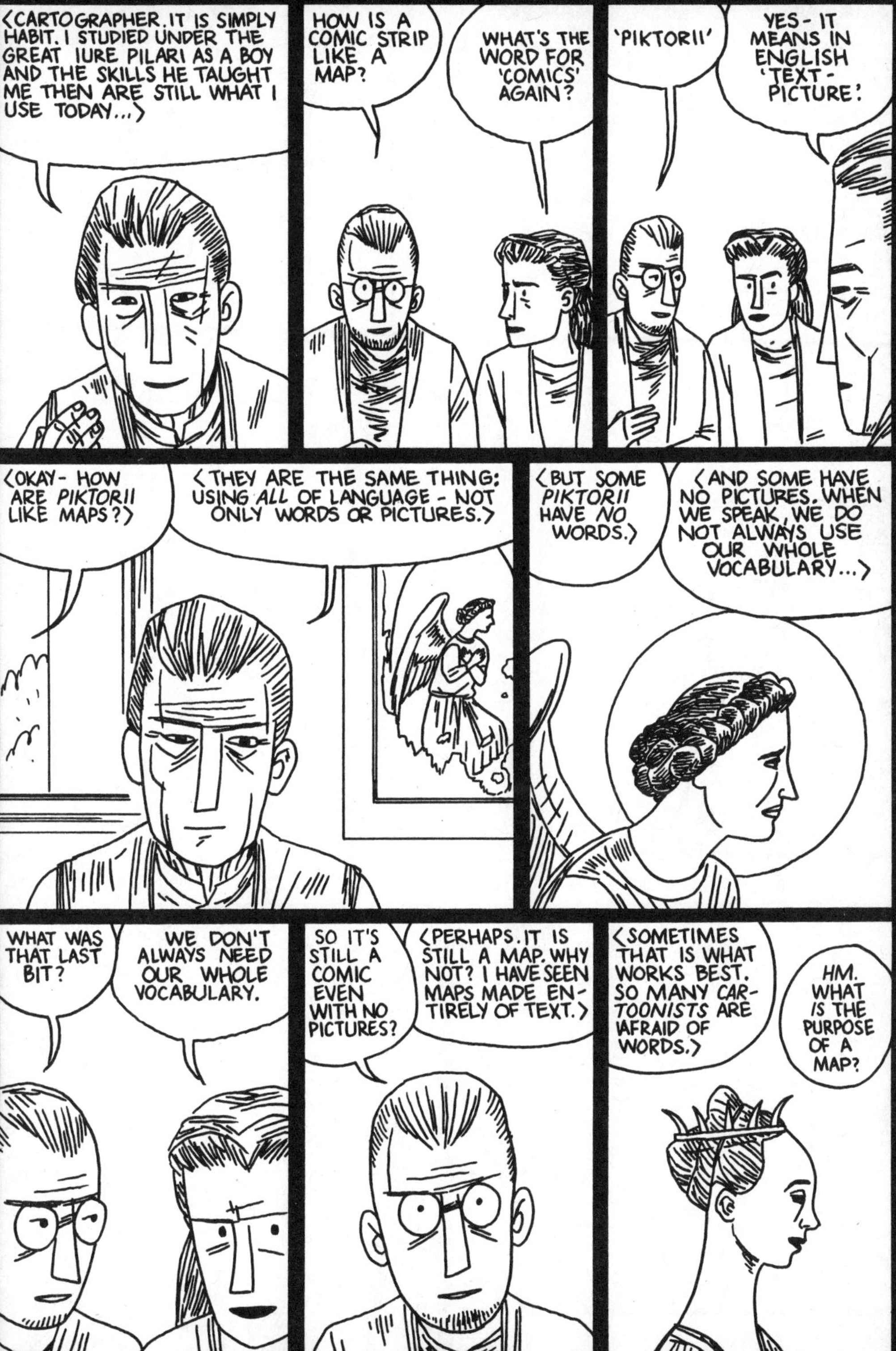

<CARTOGRAPHER. IT IS SIMPLY HABIT. I STUDIED UNDER THE GREAT IURE PILARI AS A BOY AND THE SKILLS HE TAUGHT ME THEN ARE STILL WHAT I USE TODAY...>
HOW IS A COMIC STRIP LIKE A MAP?
WHAT'S THE WORD FOR 'COMICS' AGAIN?
'PIKTORII'
YES- IT MEANS IN ENGLISH 'TEXT-PICTURE'.
<OKAY- HOW ARE *PIKTORII* LIKE MAPS?>
<THEY ARE THE SAME THING: USING *ALL* OF LANGUAGE - NOT ONLY WORDS OR PICTURES.>
<BUT SOME *PIKTORII* HAVE *NO* WORDS.>
<AND SOME HAVE NO PICTURES. WHEN WE SPEAK, WE DO NOT ALWAYS USE OUR WHOLE VOCABULARY...>
WHAT WAS THAT LAST BIT?
WE DON'T ALWAYS NEED OUR WHOLE VOCABULARY.
SO IT'S STILL A COMIC EVEN WITH NO PICTURES?
<PERHAPS. IT IS STILL A MAP. WHY NOT? I HAVE SEEN MAPS MADE ENTIRELY OF TEXT.>
<SOMETIMES THAT IS WHAT WORKS BEST. SO MANY *CARTOONISTS* ARE AFRAID OF WORDS.>
HM. WHAT *IS* THE PURPOSE OF A MAP?

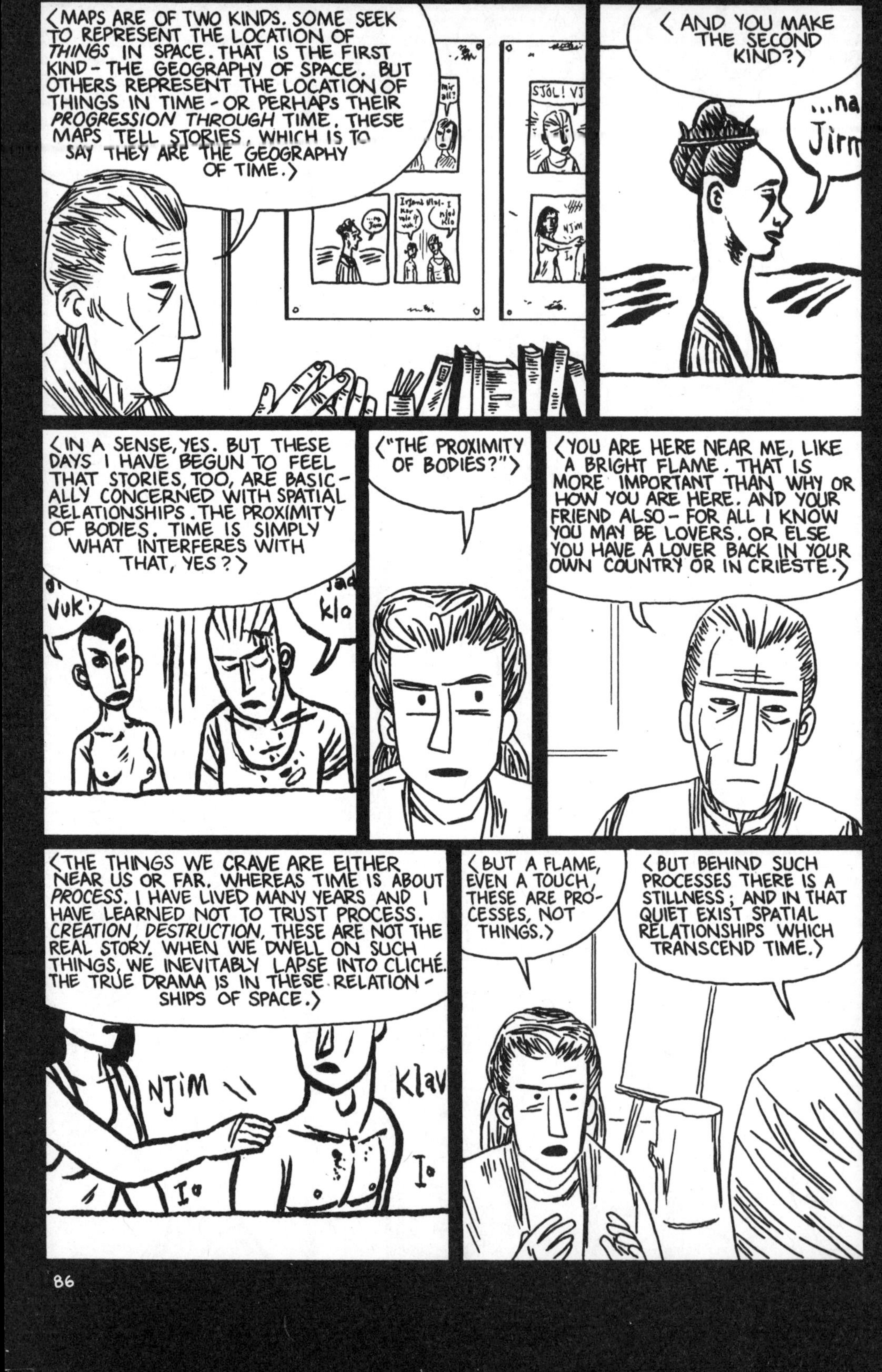
<MAPS ARE OF TWO KINDS. SOME SEEK TO REPRESENT THE LOCATION OF *THINGS* IN SPACE. THAT IS THE FIRST KIND - THE GEOGRAPHY OF SPACE. BUT OTHERS REPRESENT THE LOCATION OF THINGS IN TIME - OR PERHAPS THEIR *PROGRESSION THROUGH* TIME. THESE MAPS TELL STORIES, WHICH IS TO SAY THEY ARE THE GEOGRAPHY OF TIME.>
SJÓL! VJ
<AND YOU MAKE THE SECOND KIND?>
...na Jirm
<IN A SENSE, YES. BUT THESE DAYS I HAVE BEGUN TO FEEL THAT STORIES, TOO, ARE BASICALLY CONCERNED WITH SPATIAL RELATIONSHIPS. THE PROXIMITY OF BODIES. TIME IS SIMPLY WHAT INTERFERES WITH THAT, YES?>
VUK!
klo
<"THE PROXIMITY OF BODIES?">
<YOU ARE HERE NEAR ME, LIKE A BRIGHT FLAME. THAT IS MORE IMPORTANT THAN WHY OR HOW YOU ARE HERE. AND YOUR FRIEND ALSO - FOR ALL I KNOW YOU MAY BE LOVERS, OR ELSE YOU HAVE A LOVER BACK IN YOUR OWN COUNTRY OR IN CRIESTE.>
<THE THINGS WE CRAVE ARE EITHER NEAR US OR FAR. WHEREAS TIME IS ABOUT *PROCESS*. I HAVE LIVED MANY YEARS AND I HAVE LEARNED NOT TO TRUST PROCESS. *CREATION*, *DESTRUCTION*, THESE ARE NOT THE REAL STORY. WHEN WE DWELL ON SUCH THINGS, WE INEVITABLY LAPSE INTO CLICHÉ. THE TRUE DRAMA IS IN THESE RELATIONSHIPS OF SPACE.>
NJiM
Klav
Io
Io
<BUT A FLAME, EVEN A TOUCH, THESE ARE PROCESSES, NOT THINGS.>
<BUT BEHIND SUCH PROCESSES THERE IS A STILLNESS; AND IN THAT QUIET EXIST SPATIAL RELATIONSHIPS WHICH TRANSCEND TIME.>

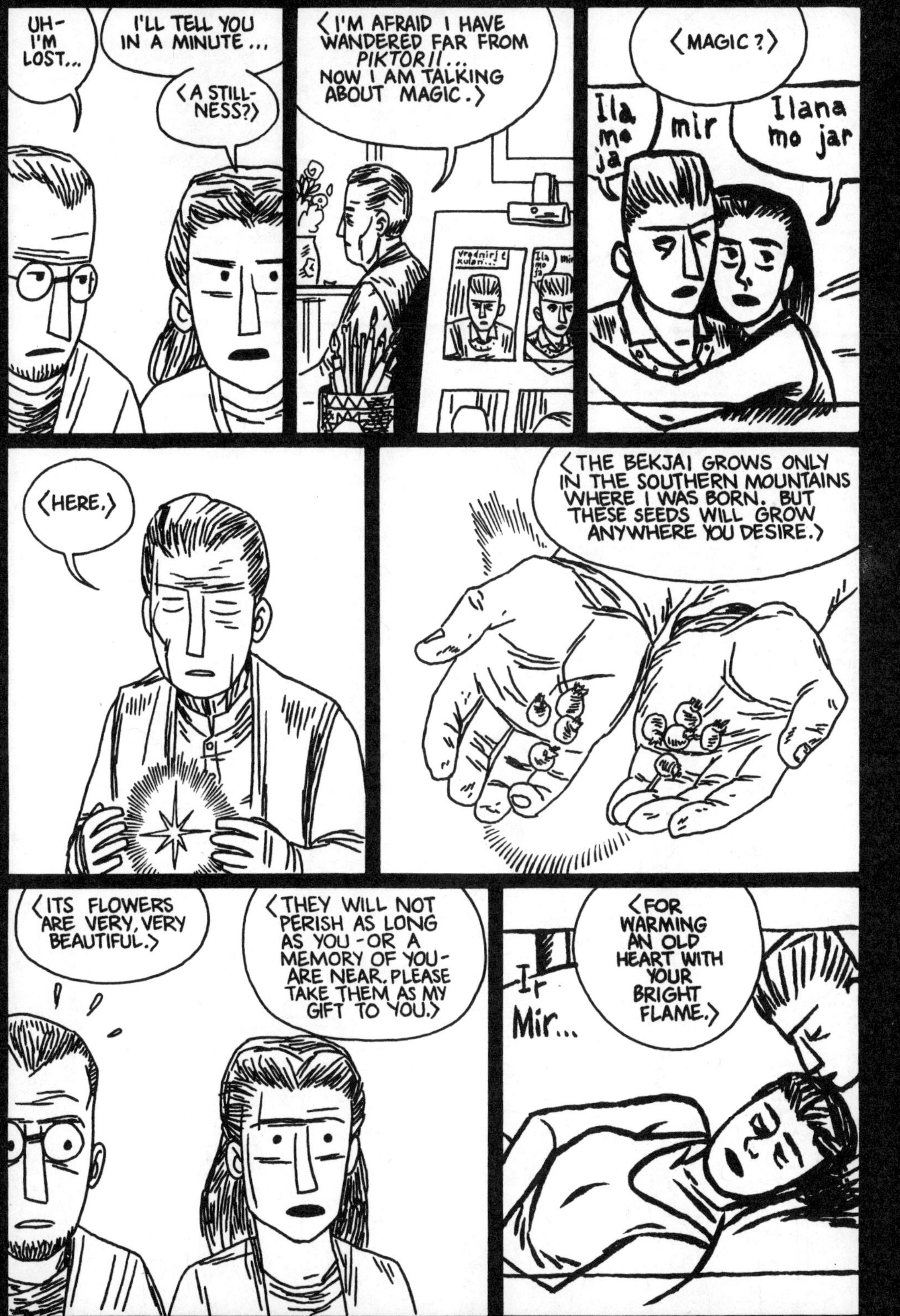
UH- I'M LOST...
I'LL TELL YOU IN A MINUTE...
⟨A STILL-NESS?⟩
⟨I'M AFRAID I HAVE WANDERED FAR FROM *PIKTORII*... NOW I AM TALKING ABOUT MAGIC.⟩
⟨MAGIC?⟩
Ila mo ja
mir
Ilana mo jar
⟨HERE.⟩
⟨THE BEKJAI GROWS ONLY IN THE SOUTHERN MOUNTAINS WHERE I WAS BORN. BUT THESE SEEDS WILL GROW ANYWHERE YOU DESIRE.⟩
⟨ITS FLOWERS ARE VERY, VERY BEAUTIFUL.⟩
⟨THEY WILL NOT PERISH AS LONG AS YOU - OR A MEMORY OF YOU - ARE NEAR. PLEASE TAKE THEM AS MY GIFT TO YOU.⟩
I-
Mir...
⟨FOR WARMING AN OLD HEART WITH YOUR BRIGHT FLAME.⟩

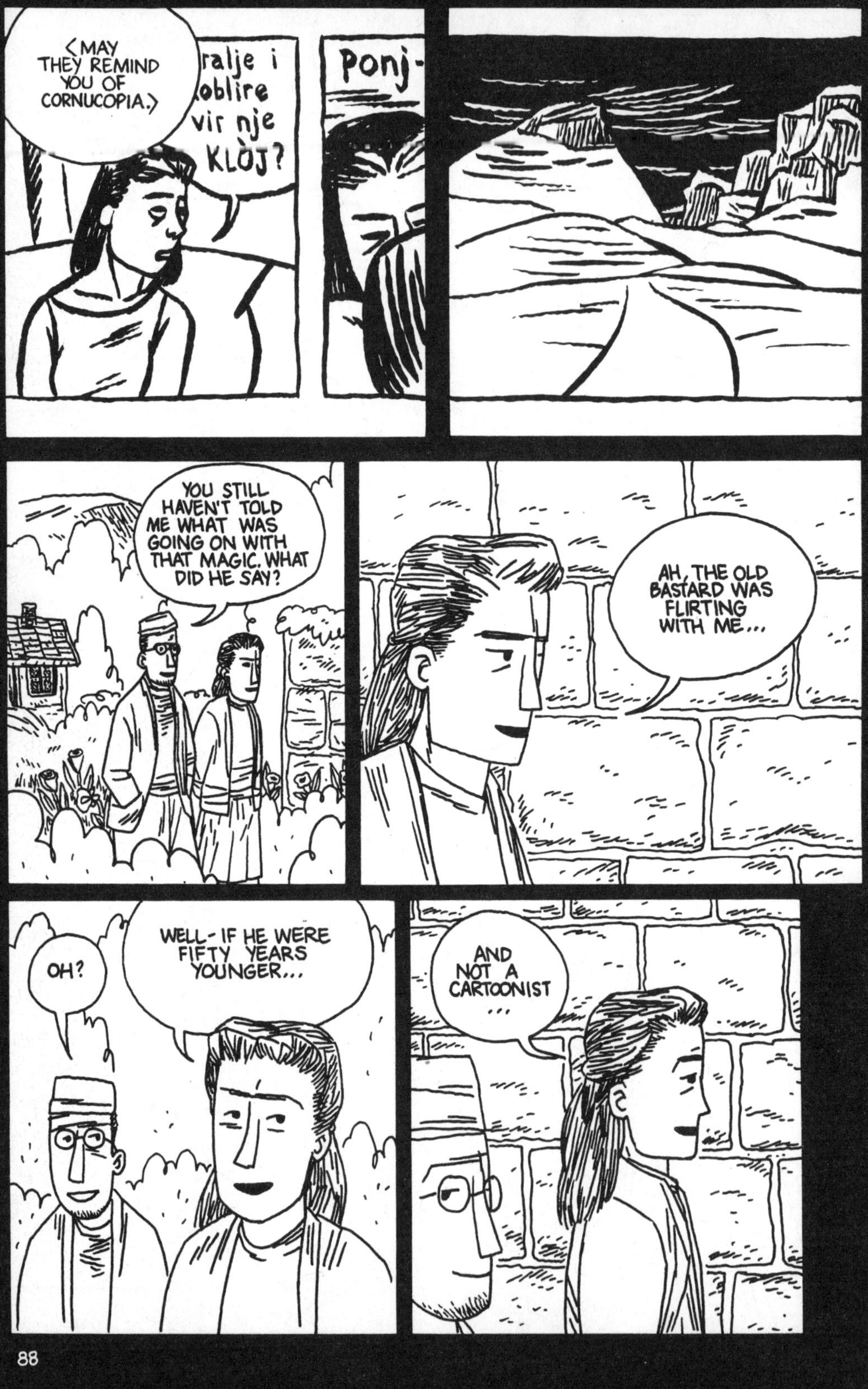

<MAY THEY REMIND YOU OF CORNUCOPIA.>
ralje i oblire vir nje KLÒJ?
Ponj-
YOU STILL HAVEN'T TOLD ME WHAT WAS GOING ON WITH THAT MAGIC. WHAT DID HE SAY?
AH, THE OLD BASTARD WAS FLIRTING WITH ME...
OH?
WELL- IF HE WERE FIFTY YEARS YOUNGER...
AND NOT A CARTOONIST ...

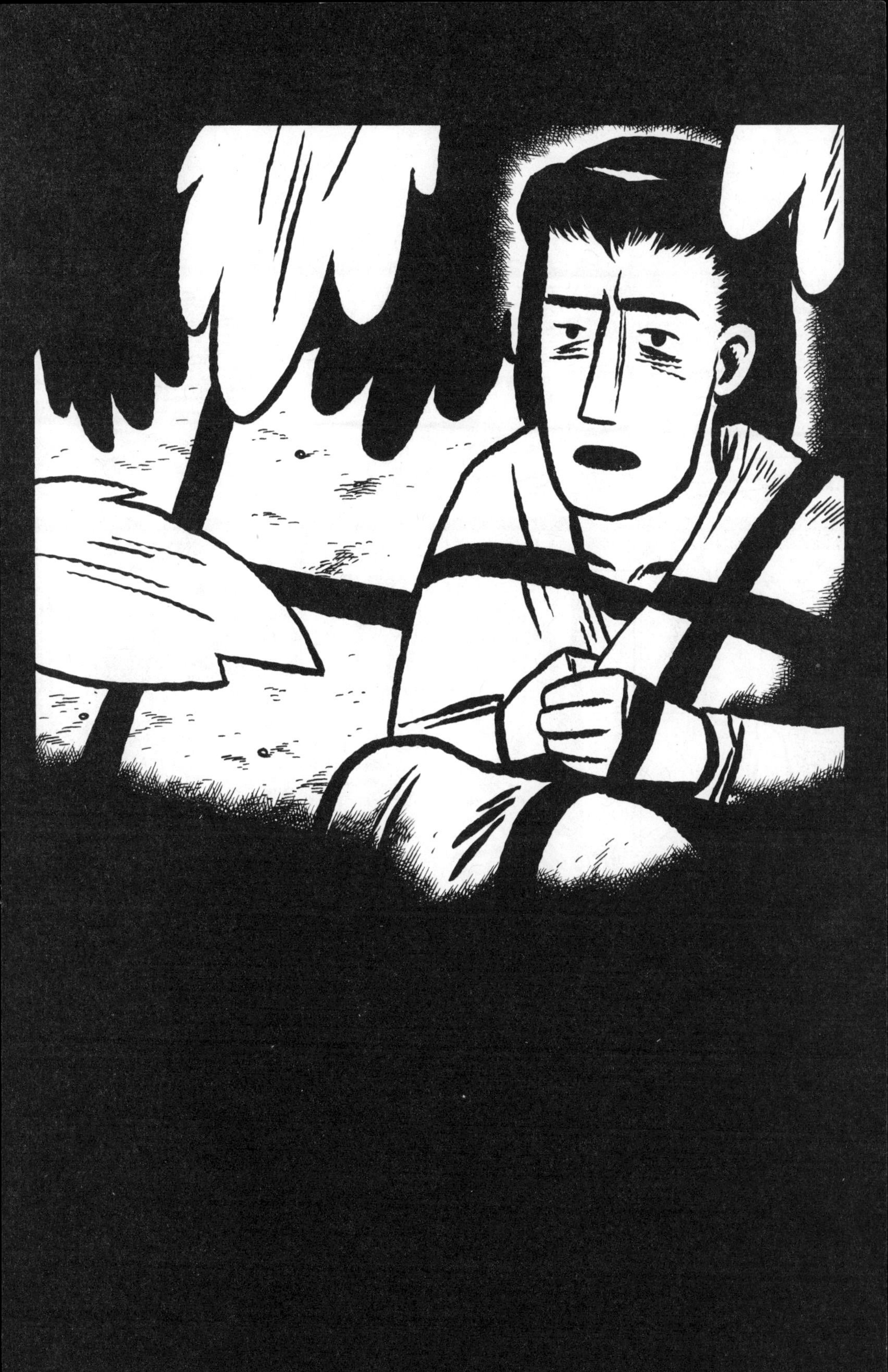

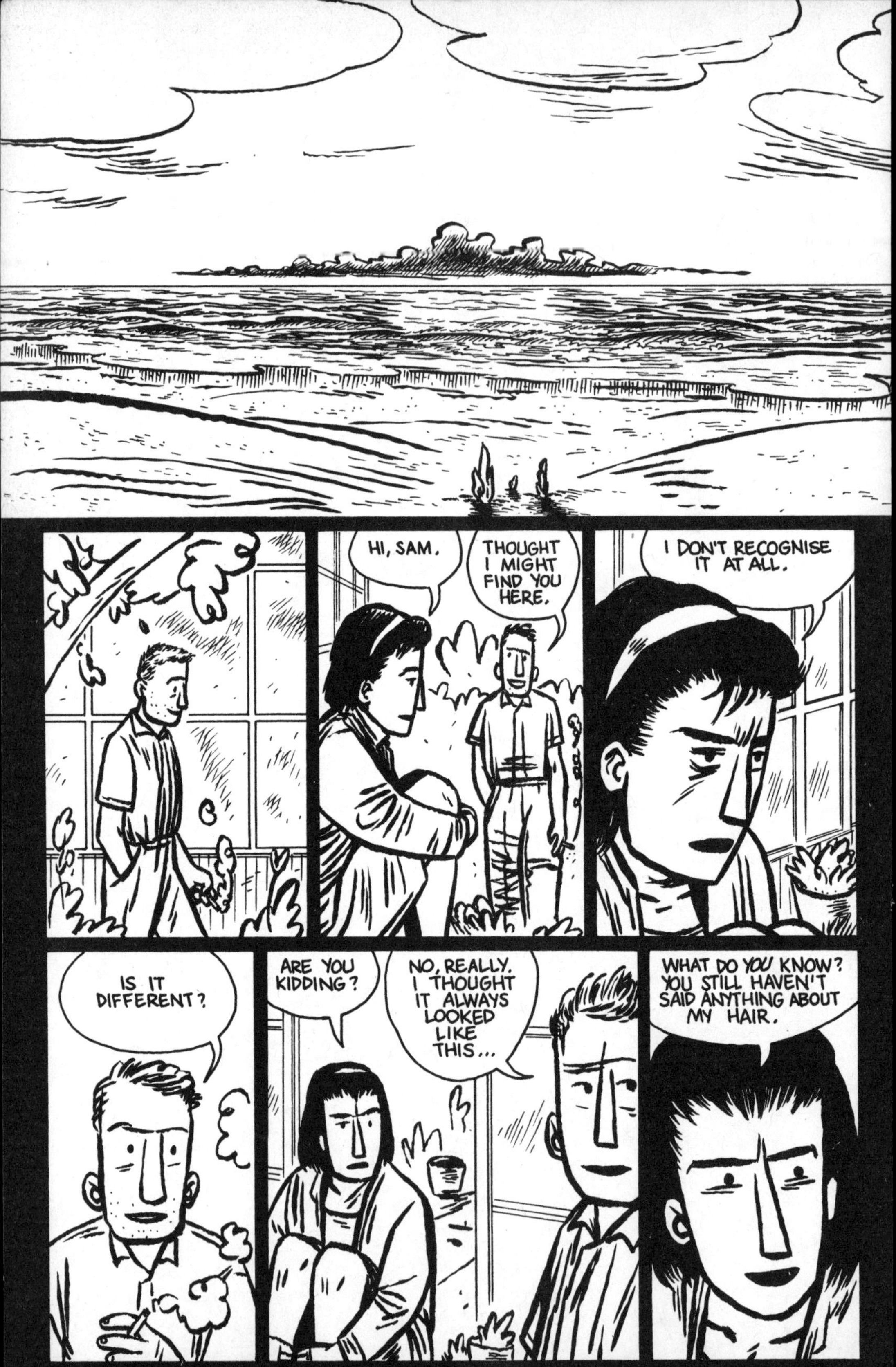
HI, SAM.
THOUGHT I MIGHT FIND YOU HERE.
I DON'T RECOGNISE IT AT ALL.
IS IT DIFFERENT?
ARE YOU KIDDING?
NO, REALLY. I THOUGHT IT ALWAYS LOOKED LIKE THIS...
WHAT DO *YOU* KNOW? YOU STILL HAVEN'T SAID ANYTHING ABOUT MY HAIR.

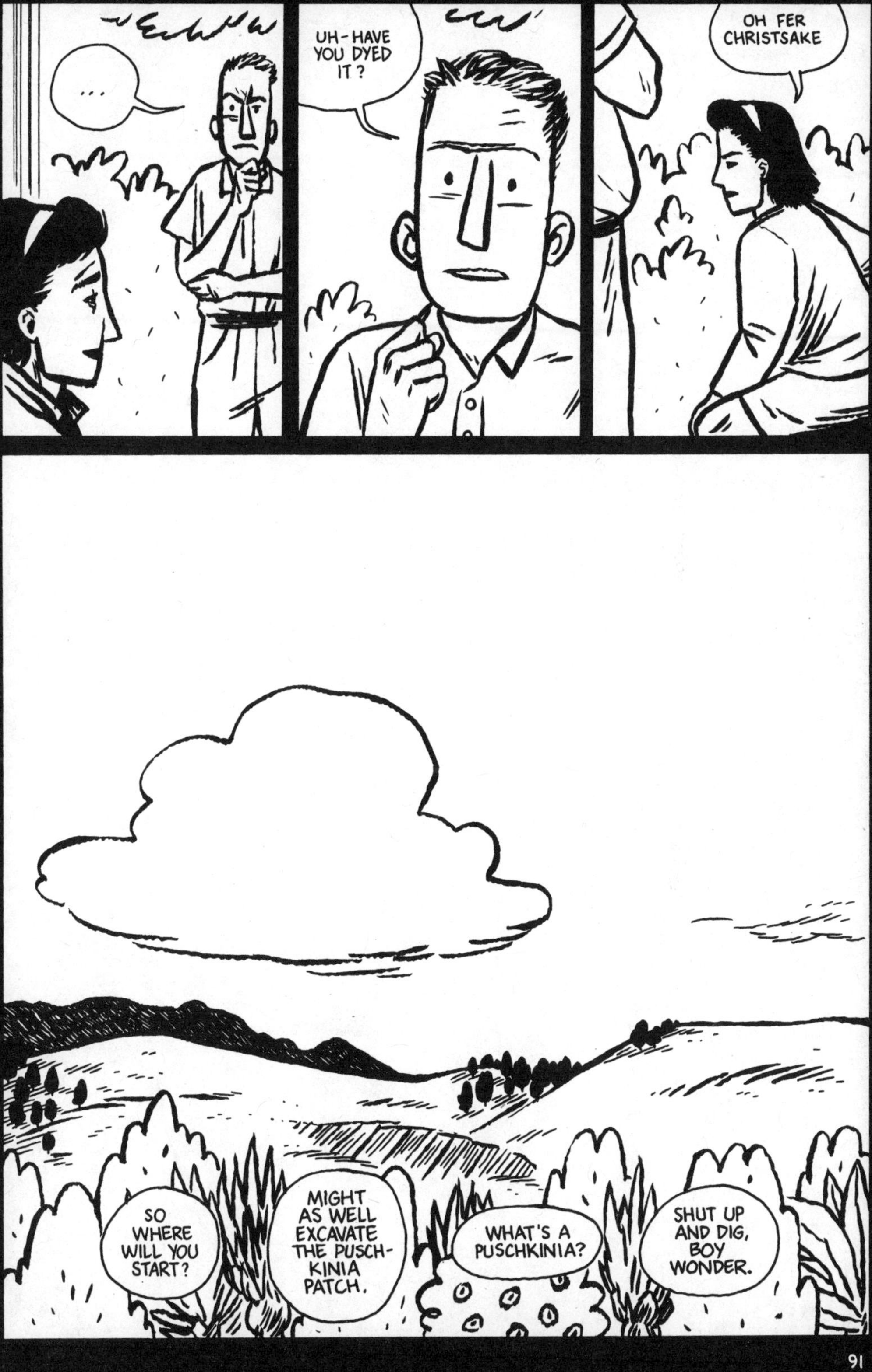
...
UH-HAVE YOU DYED IT?
OH FER CHRISTSAKE
SO WHERE WILL YOU START?
MIGHT AS WELL EXCAVATE THE PUSCH-KINIA PATCH.
WHAT'S A PUSCHKINIA?
SHUT UP AND DIG, BOY WONDER.

Chapter Five

"We can't keep putting out this crap for very long."

Martin Goodman, founder of Marvel Comics, c. 1939.

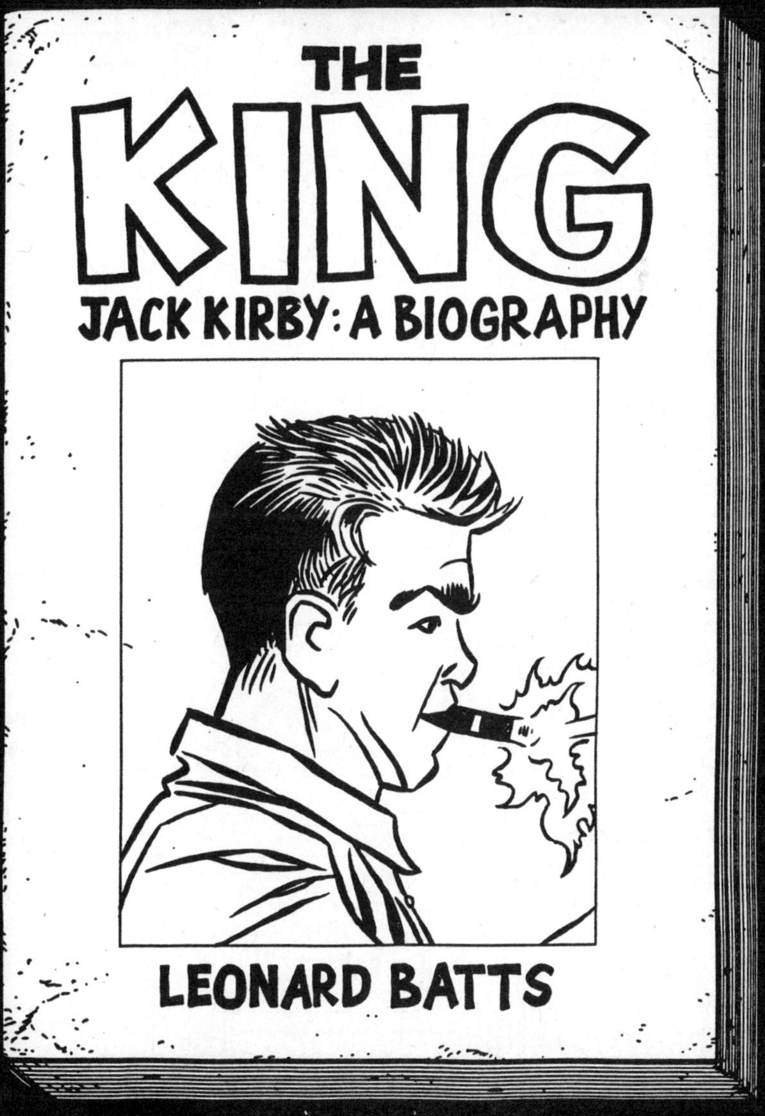
THE KING
JACK KIRBY: A BIOGRAPHY
LEONARD BATTS

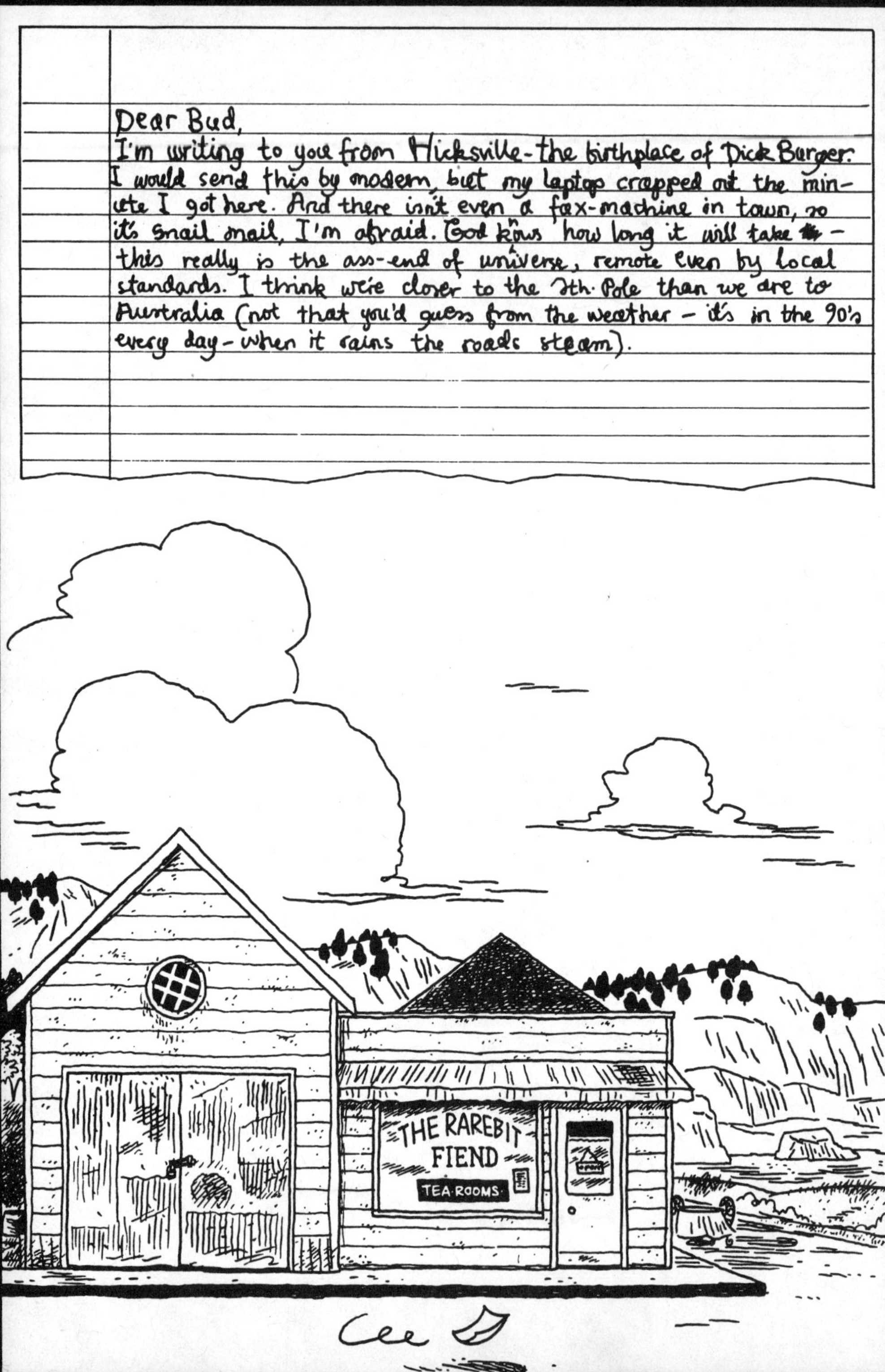
Dear Bud,
I'm writing to you from Hicksville - the birthplace of Dick Burger. I would send this by modem, but my laptop crapped out the minute I got here. And there isn't even a fax-machine in town, so it's snail mail, I'm afraid. God knows how long it will take - this really is the ass-end of universe, remote even by local standards. I think we're closer to the Sth. Pole than we are to Australia (not that you'd guess from the weather - it's in the 90's every day - when it rains the roads steam).
THE RAREBIT FIEND
TEA·ROOMS

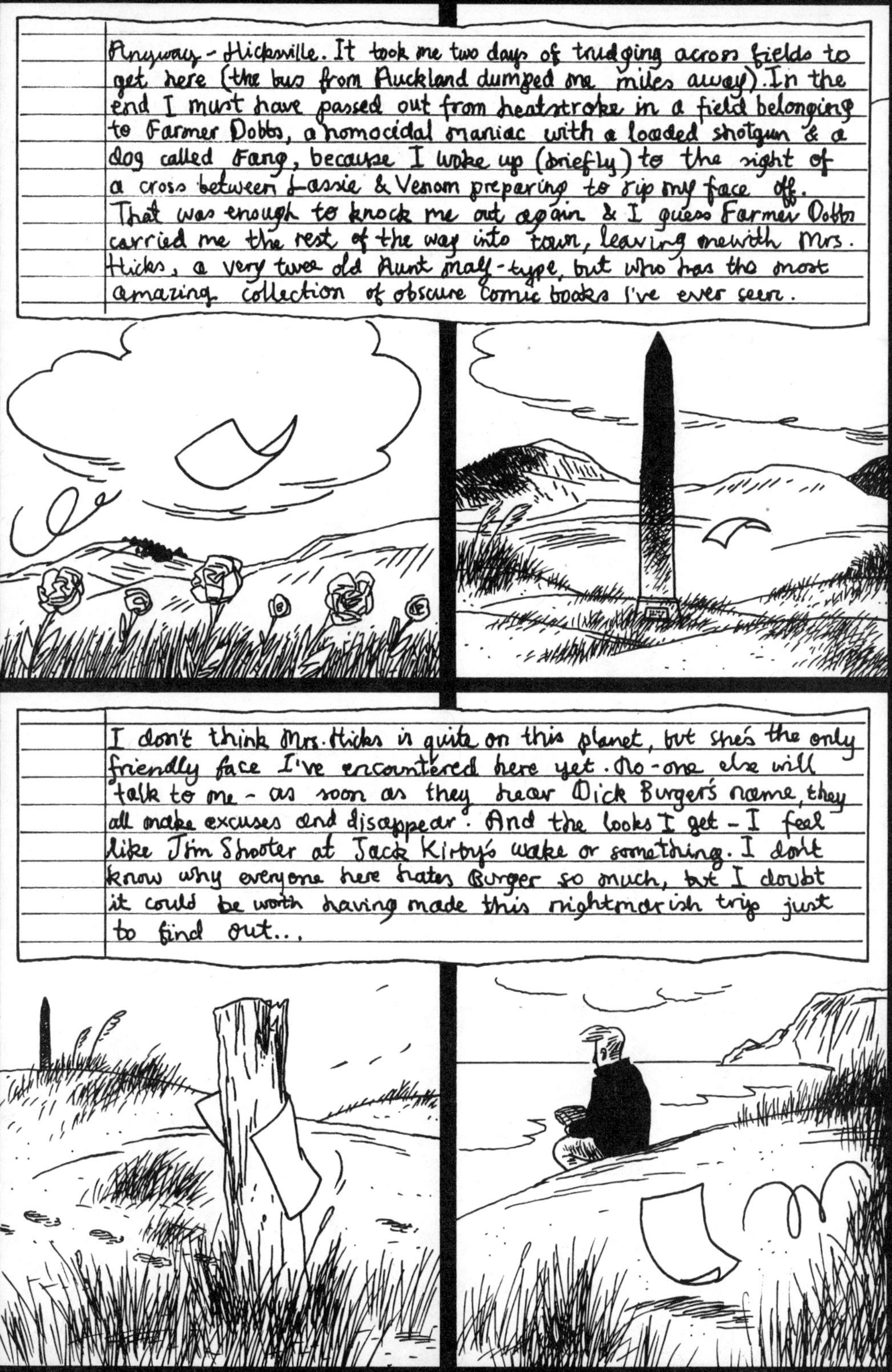
Anyway - Hicksville. It took me two days of trudging across fields to get here (the bus from Auckland dumped me miles away). In the end I must have passed out from heatstroke in a field belonging to Farmer Dobbs, a homocidal maniac with a loaded shotgun & a dog called Fang, because I woke up (briefly) to the sight of a cross between Lassie & Venom preparing to rip my face off. That was enough to knock me out again & I guess Farmer Dobbs carried me the rest of the way into town, leaving me with Mrs. Hicks, a very twee old Aunt May-type, but who has the most amazing collection of obscure comic books I've ever seen.
I don't think Mrs. Hicks is quite on this planet, but she's the only friendly face I've encountered here yet. No-one else will talk to me - as soon as they hear Dick Burger's name, they all make excuses and disappear. And the looks I get - I feel like Jim Shooter at Jack Kirby's wake or something. I don't know why everyone here hates Burger so much, but I doubt it could be worth having made this nightmarish trip just to find out...

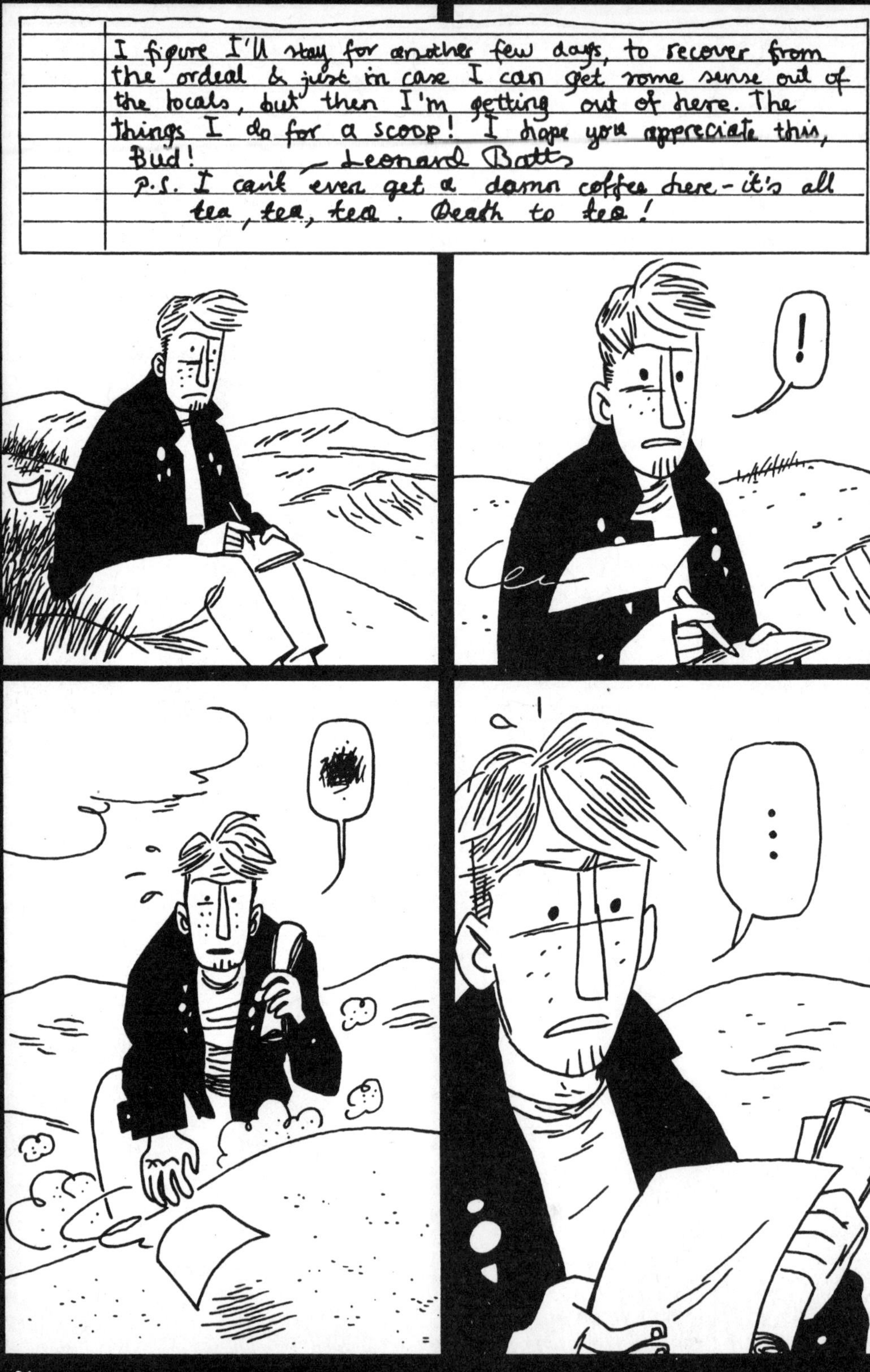
I figure I'll stay for another few days, to recover from the ordeal & just in case I can get some sense out of the locals, but then I'm getting out of here. The things I do for a scoop! I hope you appreciate this, Bud!
— Leonard Batts
P.S. I can't even get a damn coffee here - it's all tea, tea, tea. Death to tea!
!
...

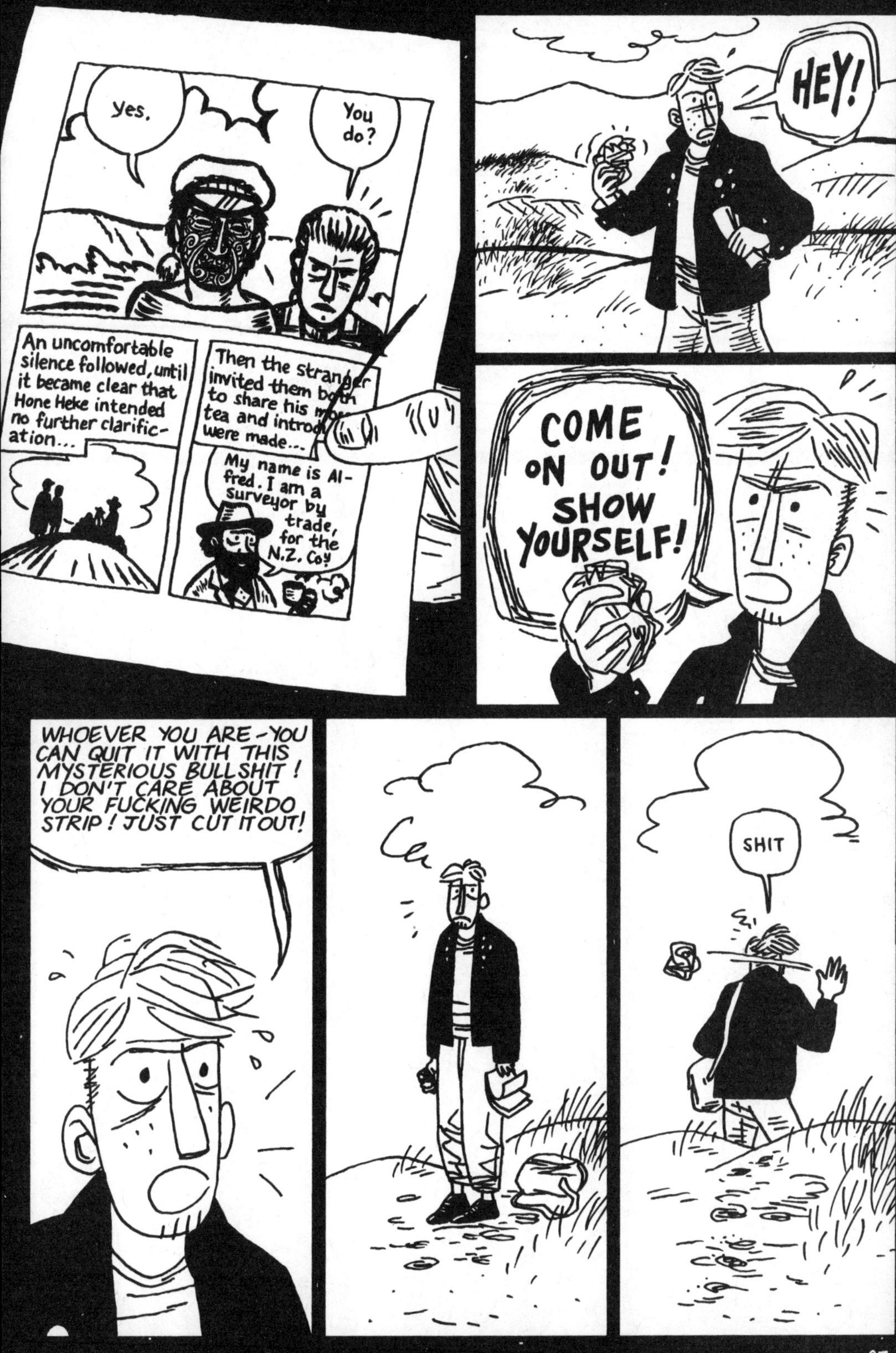
yes.
You do?
An uncomfortable silence followed, until it became clear that Hone Heke intended no further clarific-ation...
Then the stranger invited them both to share his
tea and introd
were made...
My name is Alfred. I am a surveyor by trade, for the N.Z. Coy
HEY!
COME ON OUT! SHOW YOURSELF!
WHOEVER YOU ARE - YOU CAN QUIT IT WITH THIS MYSTERIOUS BULLSHIT! I DON'T CARE ABOUT YOUR FUCKING WEIRDO STRIP! JUST CUT IT OUT!
SHIT

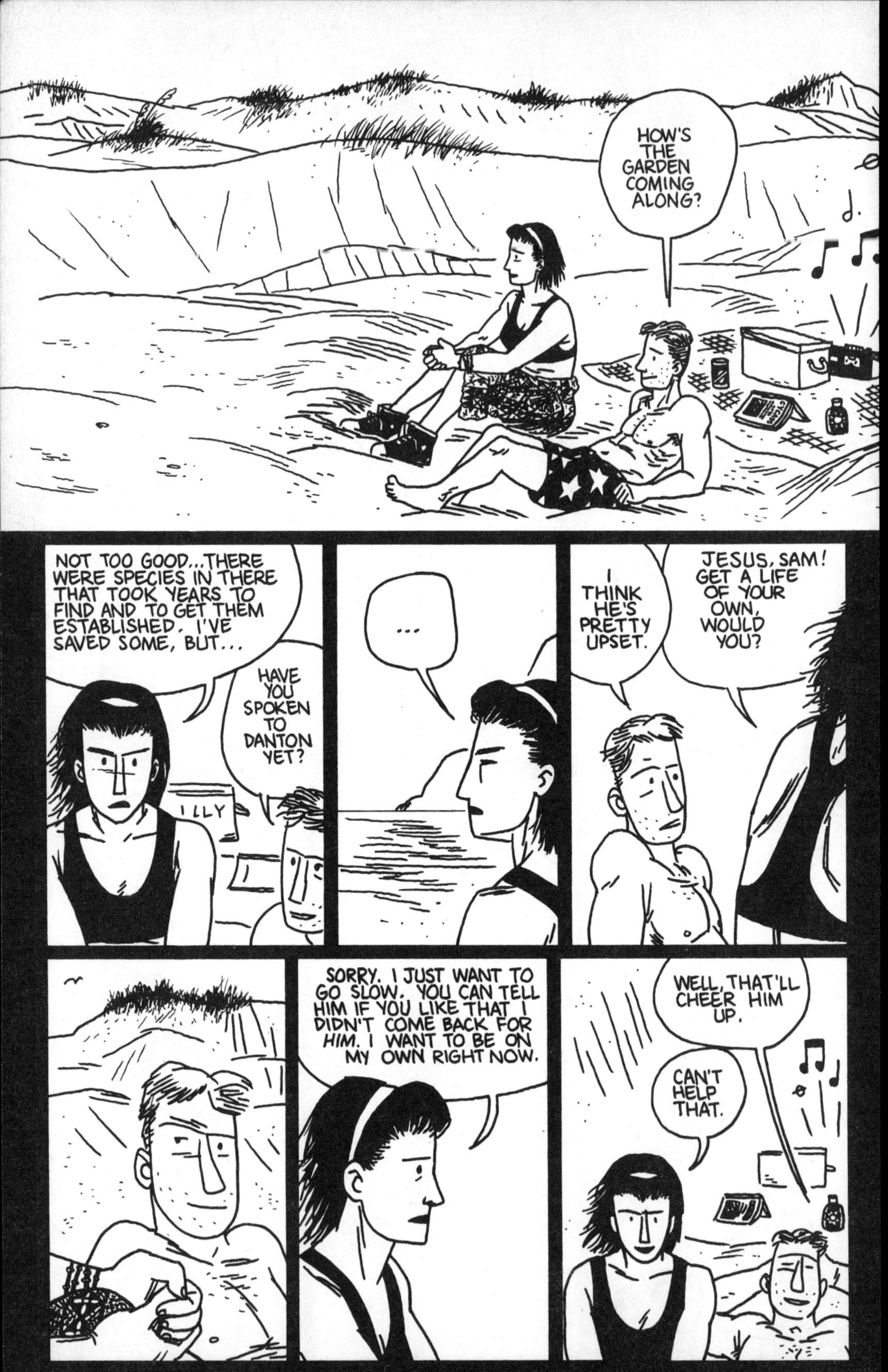
HOW'S THE GARDEN COMING ALONG?
NOT TOO GOOD...THERE WERE SPECIES IN THERE THAT TOOK YEARS TO FIND AND TO GET THEM ESTABLISHED. I'VE SAVED SOME, BUT...
HAVE YOU SPOKEN TO DANTON YET?
...
I THINK HE'S PRETTY UPSET.
JESUS, SAM! GET A LIFE OF YOUR OWN, WOULD YOU?
SORRY. I JUST WANT TO GO SLOW. YOU CAN TELL HIM IF YOU LIKE THAT I DIDN'T COME BACK FOR HIM. I WANT TO BE ON MY OWN RIGHT NOW.
WELL, THAT'LL CHEER HIM UP.
CAN'T HELP THAT.

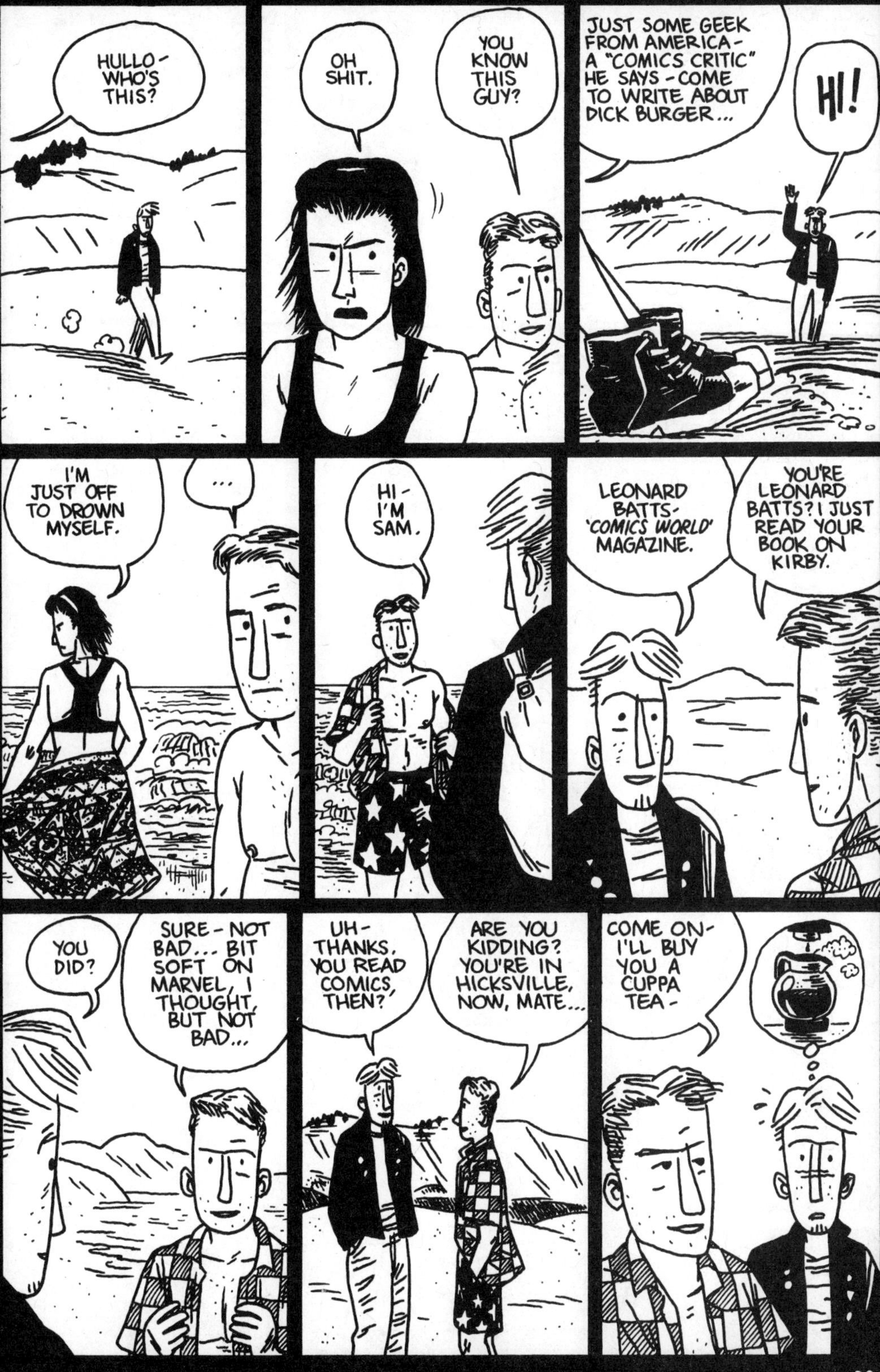
HULLO-
WHO'S
THIS?
OH
SHIT.
YOU
KNOW
THIS
GUY?
JUST SOME GEEK
FROM AMERICA-
A "COMICS CRITIC"
HE SAYS - COME
TO WRITE ABOUT
DICK BURGER...
HI!
I'M
JUST OFF
TO DROWN
MYSELF.
...
HI-
I'M
SAM.
LEONARD
BATTS-
'COMICS WORLD'
MAGAZINE.
YOU'RE
LEONARD
BATTS? I JUST
READ YOUR
BOOK ON
KIRBY.
YOU
DID?
SURE- NOT
BAD... BIT
SOFT ON
MARVEL, I
THOUGHT,
BUT NOT
BAD...
UH-
THANKS.
YOU READ
COMICS,
THEN?
ARE YOU
KIDDING?
YOU'RE IN
HICKSVILLE,
NOW, MATE...
COME ON-
I'LL BUY
YOU A
CUPPA
TEA-

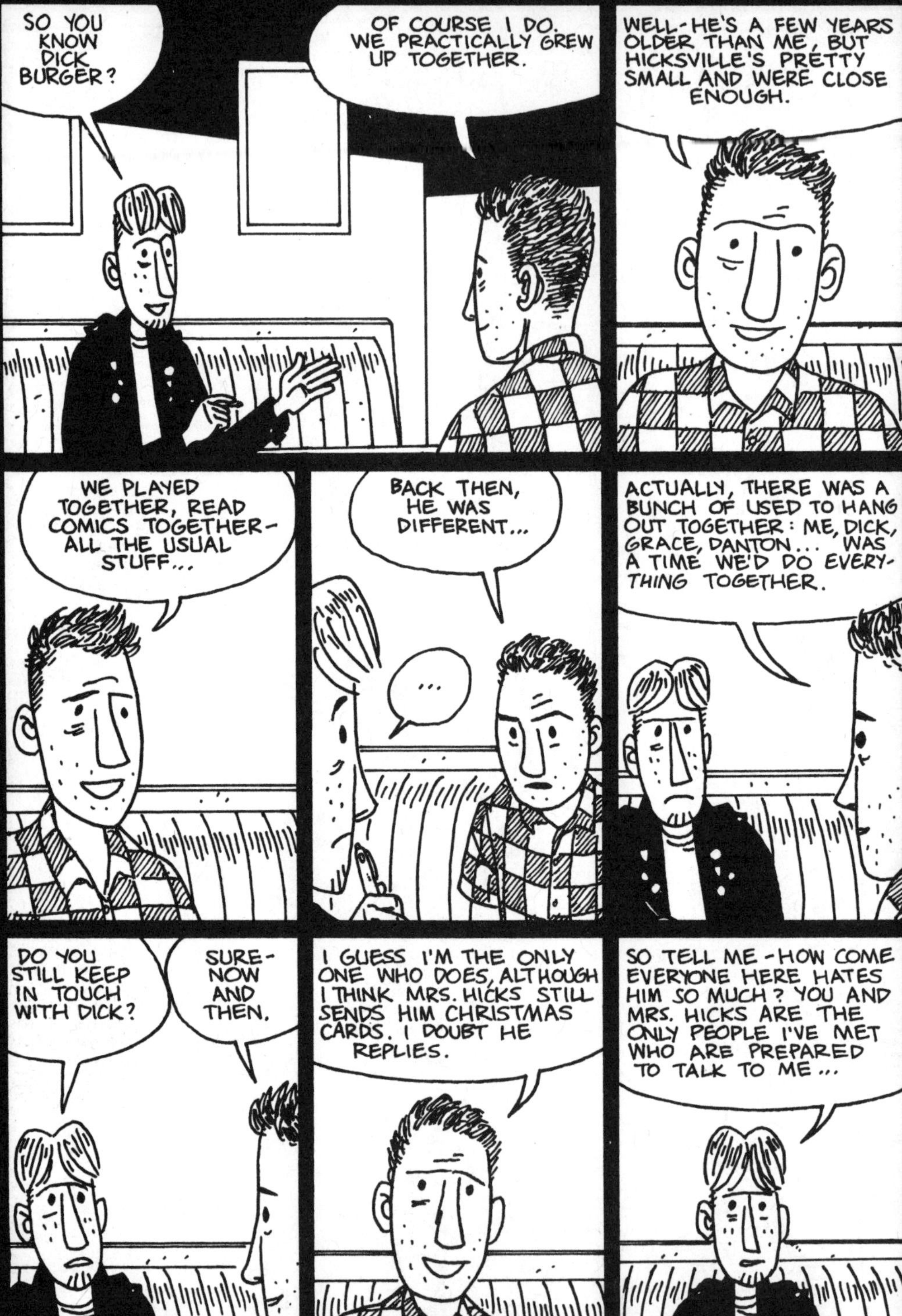
SO YOU KNOW DICK BURGER?
OF COURSE I DO. WE PRACTICALLY GREW UP TOGETHER.
WELL- HE'S A FEW YEARS OLDER THAN ME, BUT HICKSVILLE'S PRETTY SMALL AND WERE CLOSE ENOUGH.
WE PLAYED TOGETHER, READ COMICS TOGETHER- ALL THE USUAL STUFF...
BACK THEN, HE WAS DIFFERENT...
...
ACTUALLY, THERE WAS A BUNCH OF USED TO HANG OUT TOGETHER: ME, DICK, GRACE, DANTON... WAS A TIME WE'D DO EVERY-THING TOGETHER.
DO YOU STILL KEEP IN TOUCH WITH DICK?
SURE- NOW AND THEN.
I GUESS I'M THE ONLY ONE WHO DOES, ALTHOUGH I THINK MRS. HICKS STILL SENDS HIM CHRISTMAS CARDS. I DOUBT HE REPLIES.
SO TELL ME - HOW COME EVERYONE HERE HATES HIM SO MUCH? YOU AND MRS. HICKS ARE THE ONLY PEOPLE I'VE MET WHO ARE PREPARED TO TALK TO ME...

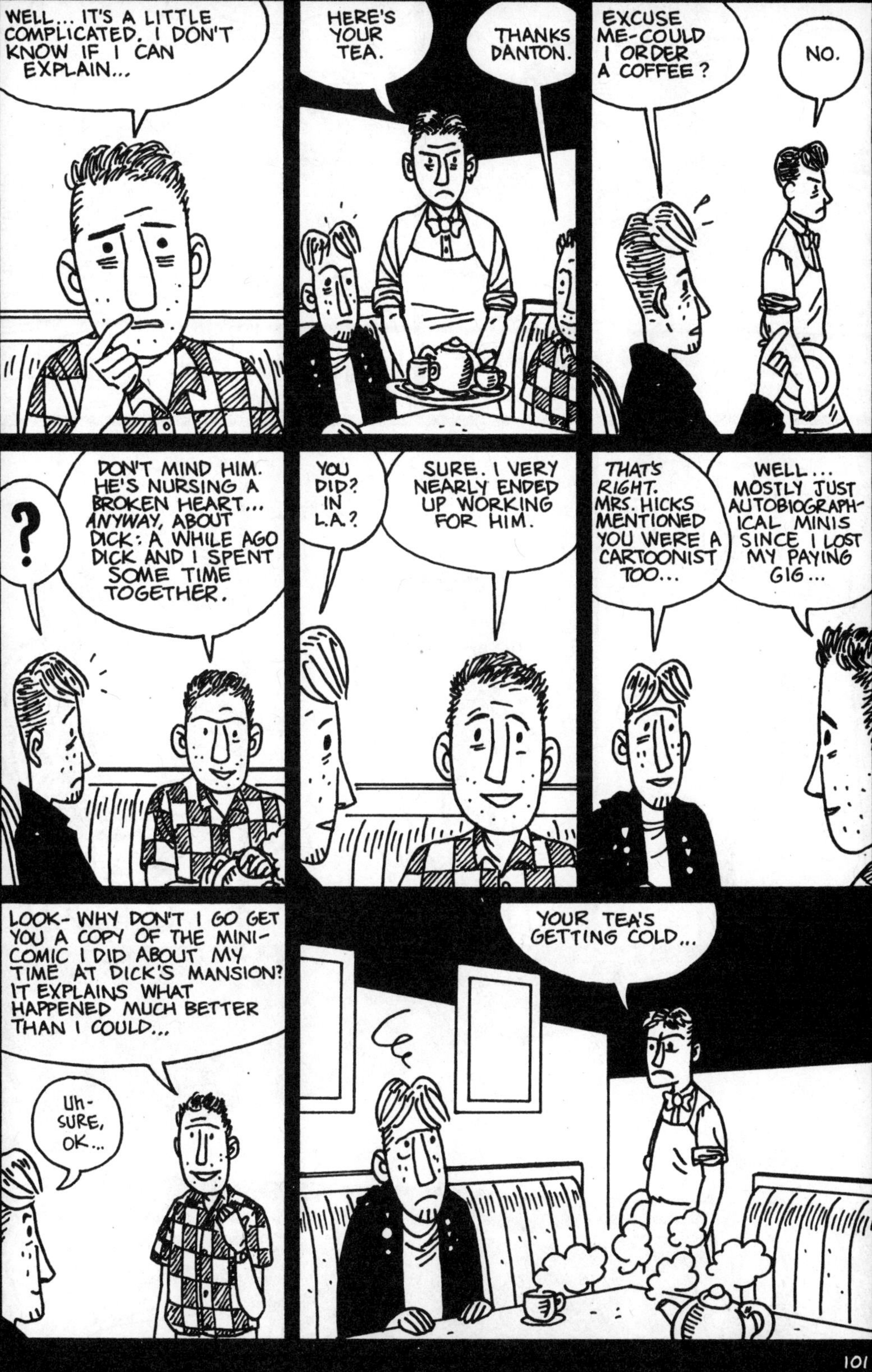
WELL... IT'S A LITTLE COMPLICATED. I DON'T KNOW IF I CAN EXPLAIN...
HERE'S YOUR TEA.
THANKS DANTON.
EXCUSE ME-COULD I ORDER A COFFEE?
NO.
?
DON'T MIND HIM. HE'S NURSING A BROKEN HEART... ANYWAY, ABOUT DICK: A WHILE AGO DICK AND I SPENT SOME TIME TOGETHER.
YOU DID? IN L.A.?
SURE. I VERY NEARLY ENDED UP WORKING FOR HIM.
THAT'S RIGHT. MRS. HICKS MENTIONED YOU WERE A CARTOONIST TOO...
WELL... MOSTLY JUST AUTOBIOGRAPH-ICAL MINIS SINCE I LOST MY PAYING GIG...
LOOK- WHY DON'T I GO GET YOU A COPY OF THE MINI-COMIC I DID ABOUT MY TIME AT DICK'S MANSION? IT EXPLAINS WHAT HAPPENED MUCH BETTER THAN I COULD...
Uh- SURE, OK...
YOUR TEA'S GETTING COLD...

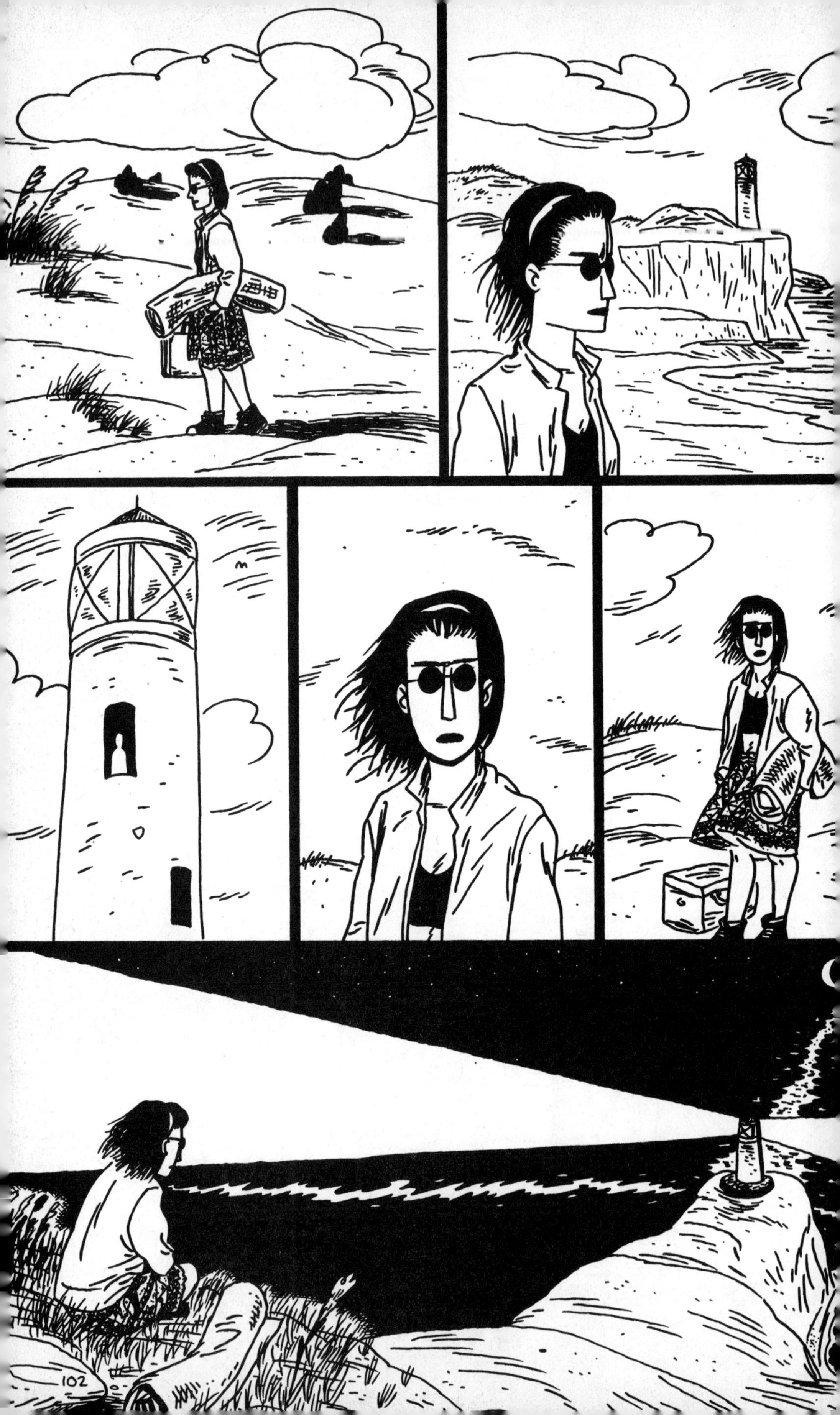

Chapter Six

"Even more than money,
an artist likes to be loved."
Joe Simon.

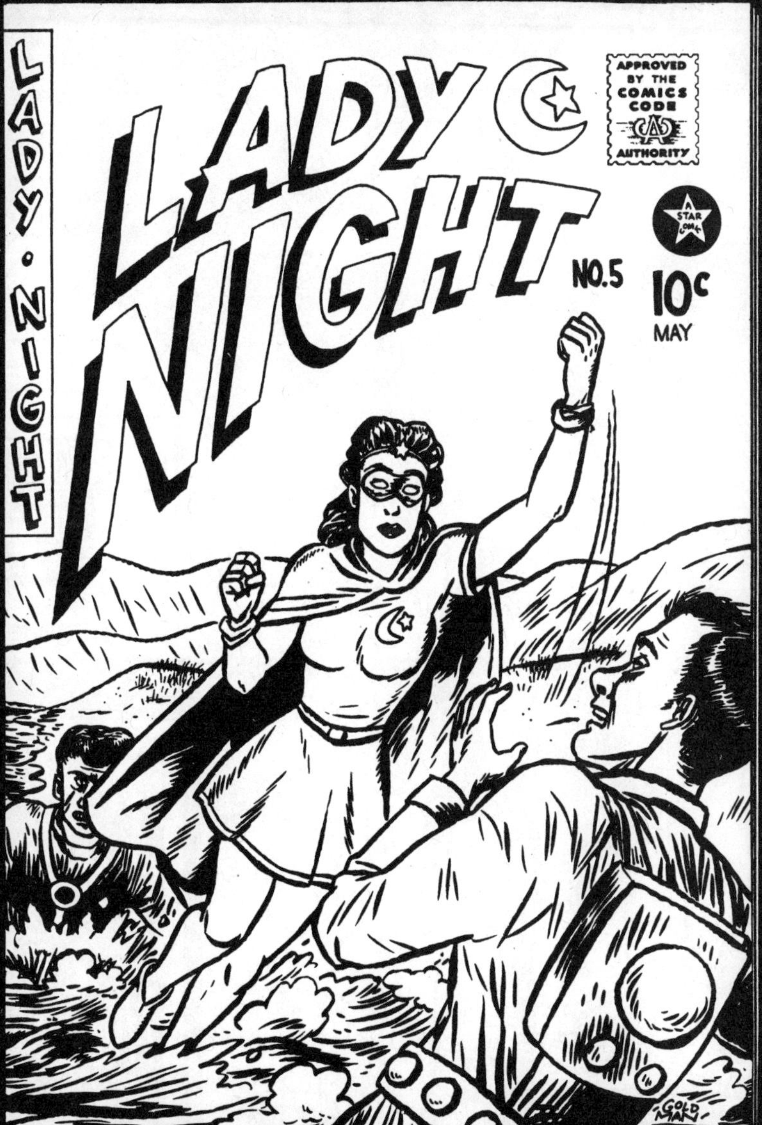
LADY NIGHT
APPROVED BY THE COMICS CODE AUTHORITY
A STAR COMIC
NO.5
10¢
MAY
LADY • NIGHT
GOLDMAN

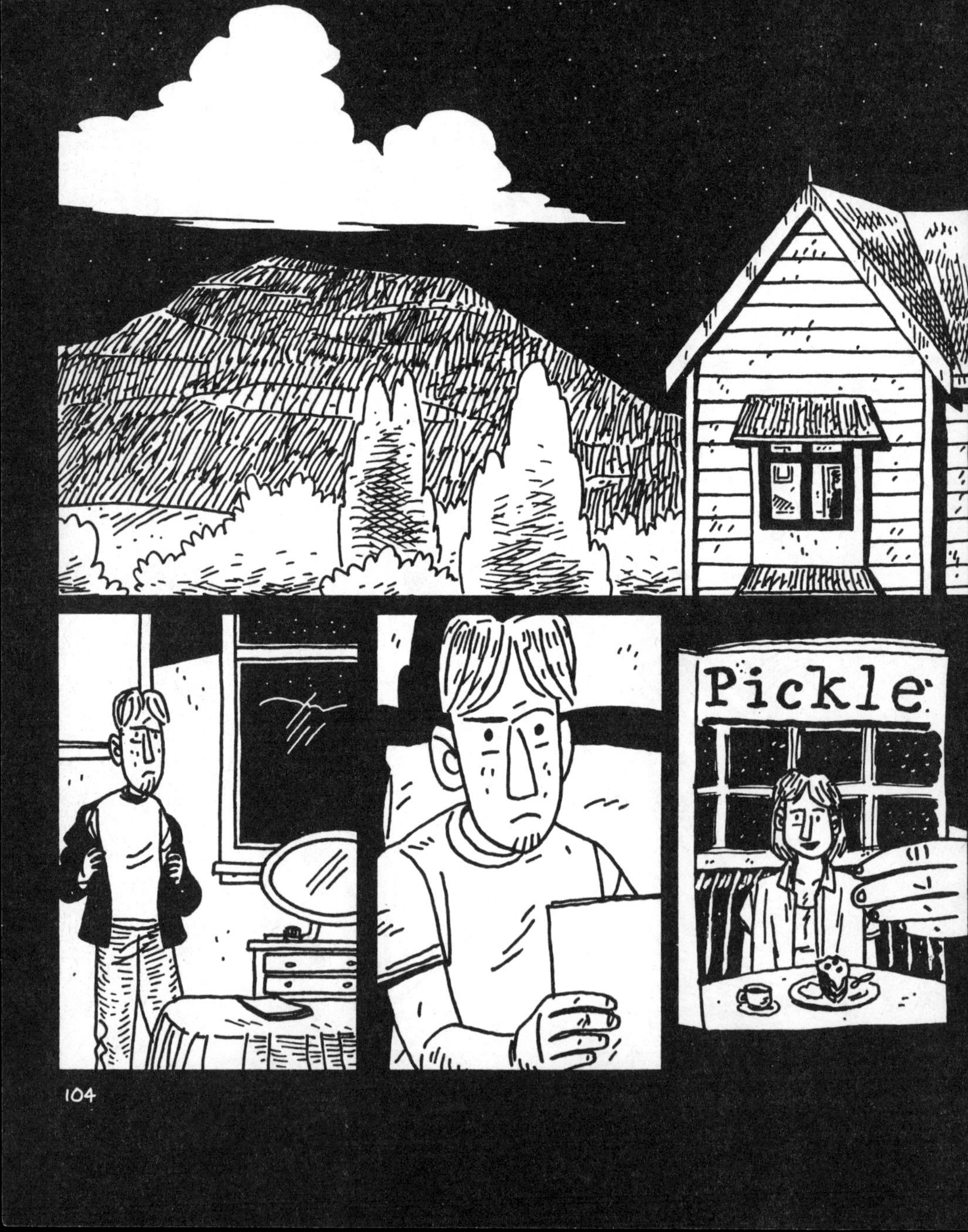
Pickle

Pickle

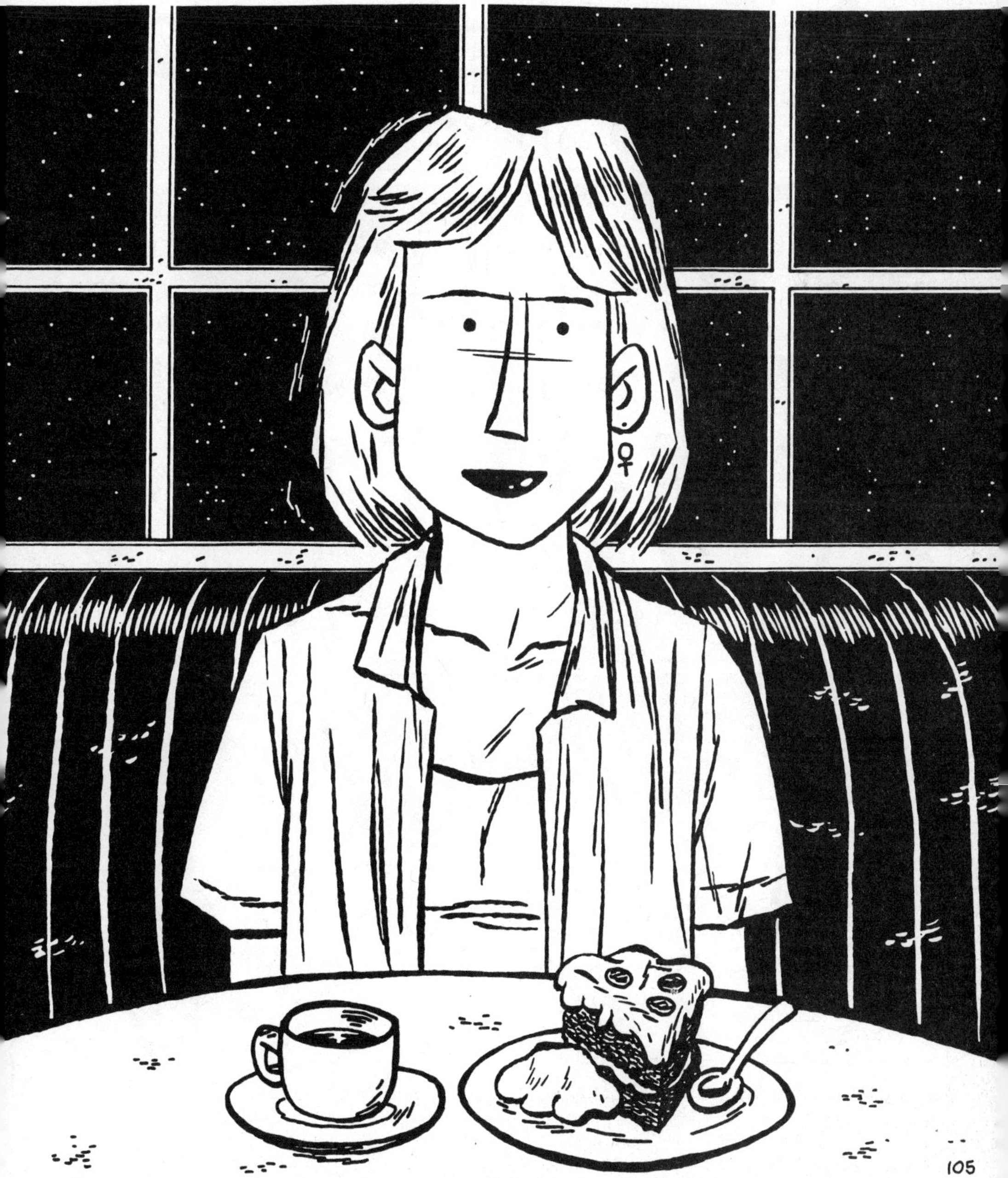

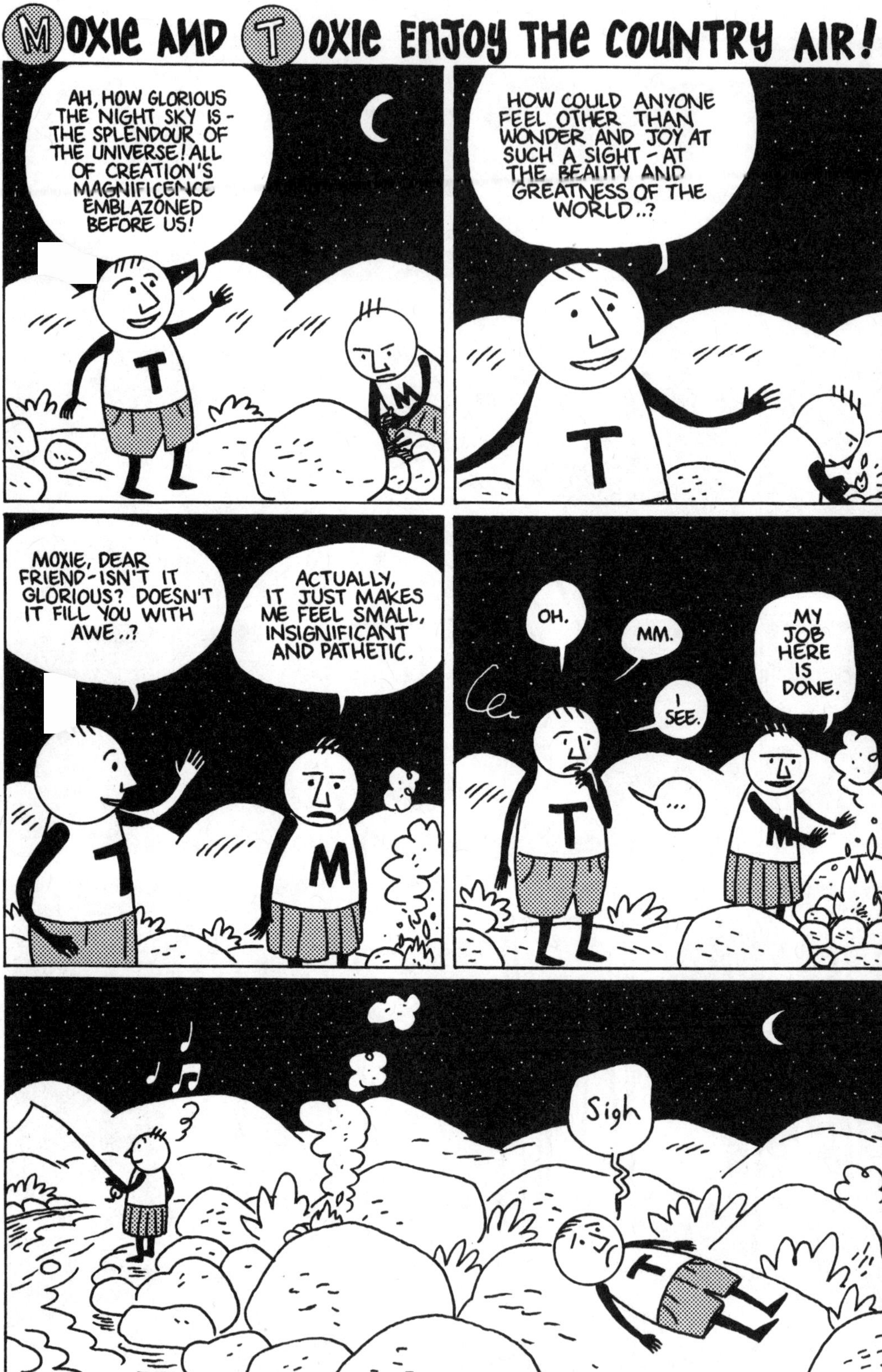
MOXIE AND TOXIE ENJOY THE COUNTRY AIR!
AH, HOW GLORIOUS THE NIGHT SKY IS - THE SPLENDOUR OF THE UNIVERSE! ALL OF CREATION'S MAGNIFICENCE EMBLAZONED BEFORE US!
HOW COULD ANYONE FEEL OTHER THAN WONDER AND JOY AT SUCH A SIGHT - AT THE BEAUTY AND GREATNESS OF THE WORLD..?
MOXIE, DEAR FRIEND - ISN'T IT GLORIOUS? DOESN'T IT FILL YOU WITH AWE..?
ACTUALLY, IT JUST MAKES ME FEEL SMALL, INSIGNIFICANT AND PATHETIC.
OH.
MM.
I SEE.
...
MY JOB HERE IS DONE.
Sigh
— Sam Jakel — 1994.©

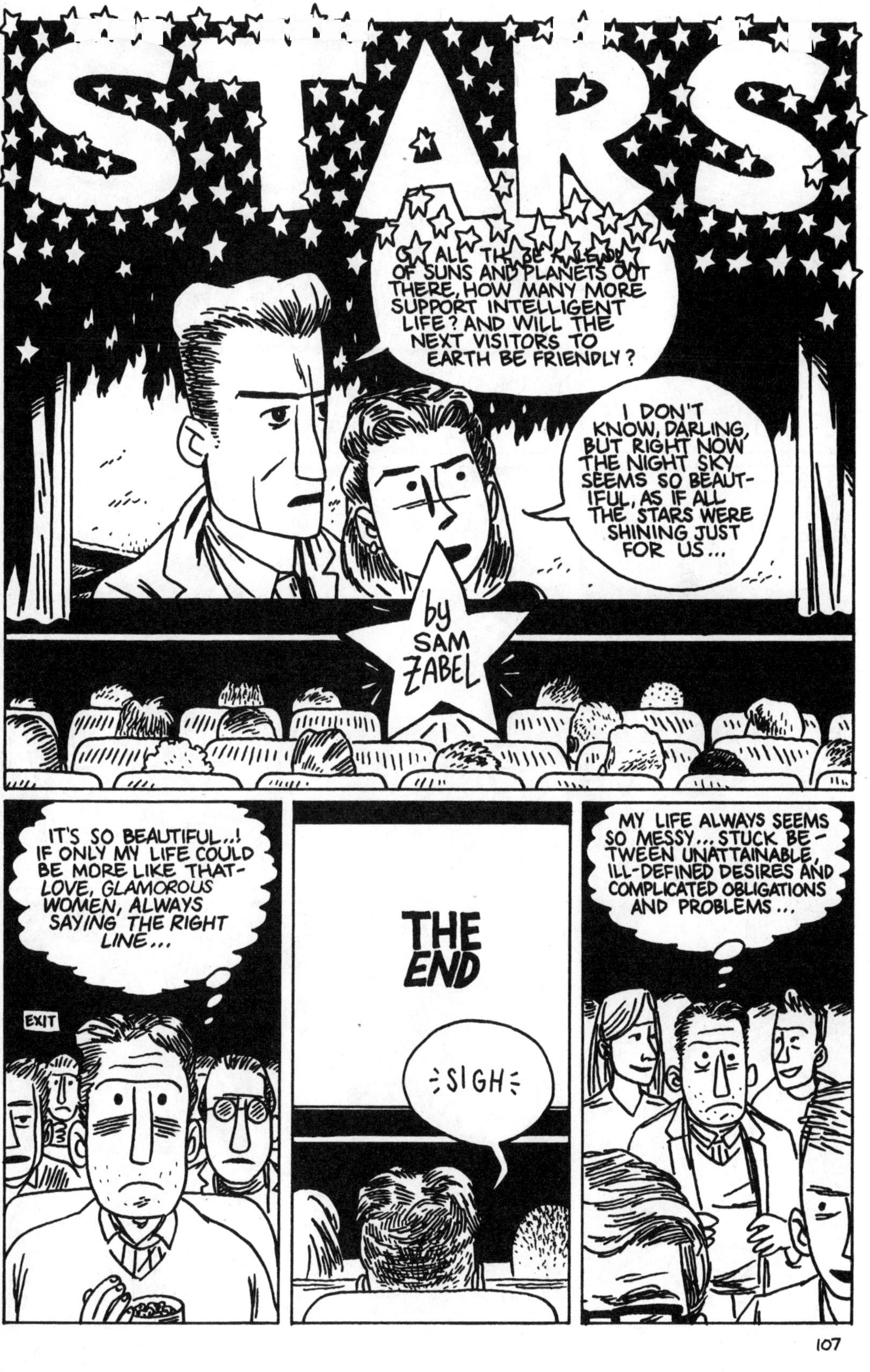
STARS
OF SUNS AND PLANETS OUT THERE, HOW MANY MORE SUPPORT INTELLIGENT LIFE? AND WILL THE NEXT VISITORS TO EARTH BE FRIENDLY?
I DON'T KNOW, DARLING, BUT RIGHT NOW THE NIGHT SKY SEEMS SO BEAUTIFUL, AS IF ALL THE STARS WERE SHINING JUST FOR US...
by SAM ZABEL
IT'S SO BEAUTIFUL..! IF ONLY MY LIFE COULD BE MORE LIKE THAT- LOVE, GLAMOROUS WOMEN, ALWAYS SAYING THE RIGHT LINE...
EXIT
THE END
SIGH
MY LIFE ALWAYS SEEMS SO MESSY... STUCK BETWEEN UNATTAINABLE, ILL-DEFINED DESIRES AND COMPLICATED OBLIGATIONS AND PROBLEMS...

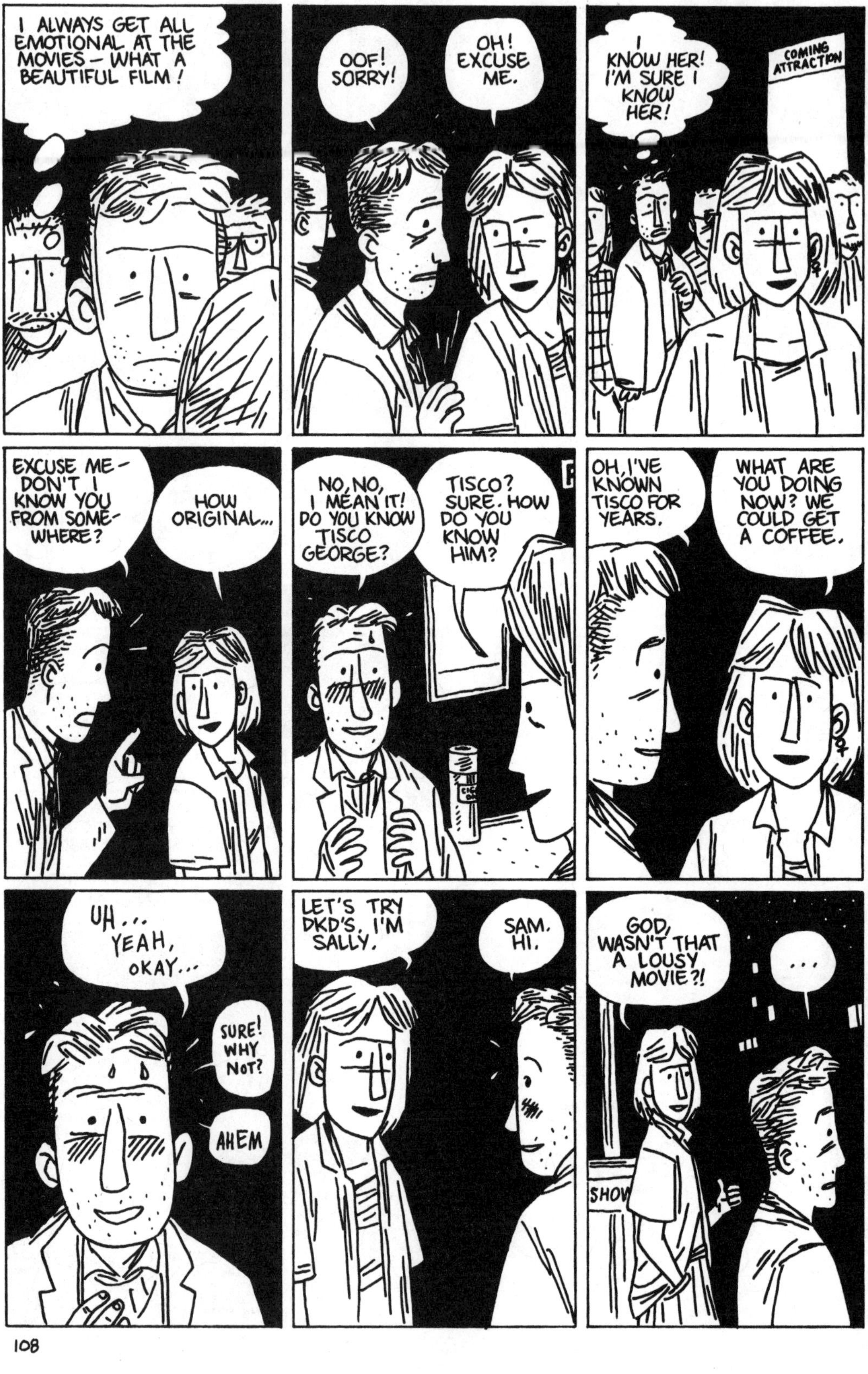

I ALWAYS GET ALL EMOTIONAL AT THE MOVIES — WHAT A BEAUTIFUL FILM!
OOF! SORRY!
OH! EXCUSE ME.
I KNOW HER! I'M SURE I KNOW HER!
COMING ATTRACTION
EXCUSE ME — DON'T I KNOW YOU FROM SOMEWHERE?
HOW ORIGINAL...
NO, NO, I MEAN IT! DO YOU KNOW TISCO GEORGE?
TISCO? SURE. HOW DO YOU KNOW HIM?
OH, I'VE KNOWN TISCO FOR YEARS.
WHAT ARE YOU DOING NOW? WE COULD GET A COFFEE.
UH... YEAH, OKAY...
SURE! WHY NOT?
AHEM
LET'S TRY DKD'S. I'M SALLY.
SAM. HI.
GOD, WASN'T THAT A LOUSY MOVIE?!
...
SHOW

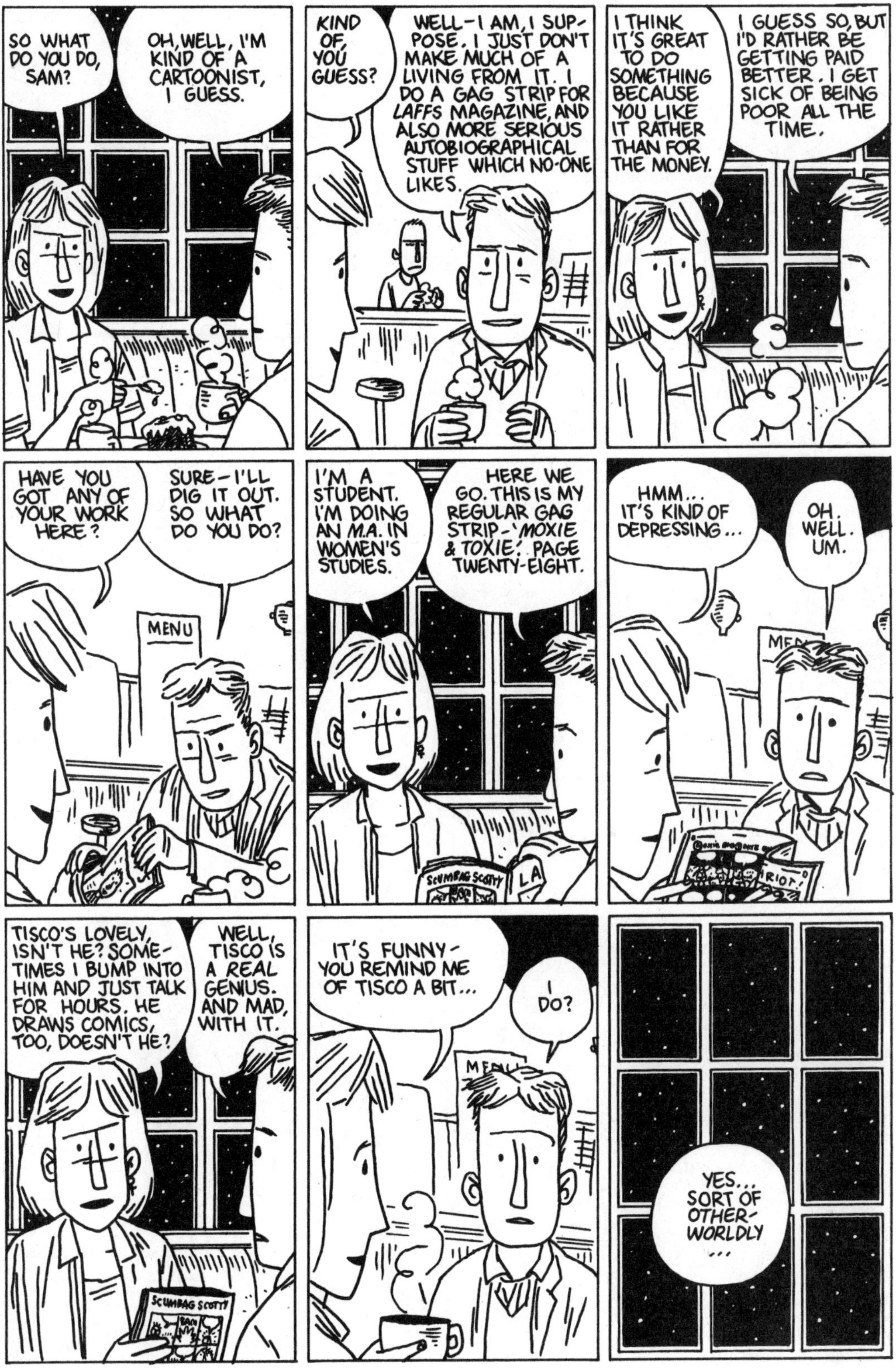
SO WHAT DO YOU DO, SAM?
OH, WELL, I'M KIND OF A CARTOONIST, I GUESS.
KIND OF, YOU GUESS?
WELL - I AM, I SUPPOSE. I JUST DON'T MAKE MUCH OF A LIVING FROM IT. I DO A GAG STRIP FOR LAFFS MAGAZINE, AND ALSO MORE SERIOUS AUTOBIOGRAPHICAL STUFF WHICH NO-ONE LIKES.
I THINK IT'S GREAT TO DO SOMETHING BECAUSE YOU LIKE IT RATHER THAN FOR THE MONEY.
I GUESS SO, BUT I'D RATHER BE GETTING PAID BETTER. I GET SICK OF BEING POOR ALL THE TIME.
HAVE YOU GOT ANY OF YOUR WORK HERE?
SURE - I'LL DIG IT OUT. SO WHAT DO YOU DO?
MENU
I'M A STUDENT. I'M DOING AN M.A. IN WOMEN'S STUDIES.
HERE WE GO. THIS IS MY REGULAR GAG STRIP - 'MOXIE & TOXIE'. PAGE TWENTY-EIGHT.
SCUMBAG SCOTTY
HMM... IT'S KIND OF DEPRESSING...
OH. WELL. UM.
TISCO'S LOVELY, ISN'T HE? SOMETIMES I BUMP INTO HIM AND JUST TALK FOR HOURS. HE DRAWS COMICS, TOO, DOESN'T HE?
WELL, TISCO IS A REAL GENIUS. AND MAD, WITH IT.
SCUMBAG SCOTTY
IT'S FUNNY - YOU REMIND ME OF TISCO A BIT...
I DO?
YES... SORT OF OTHER-WORLDLY...

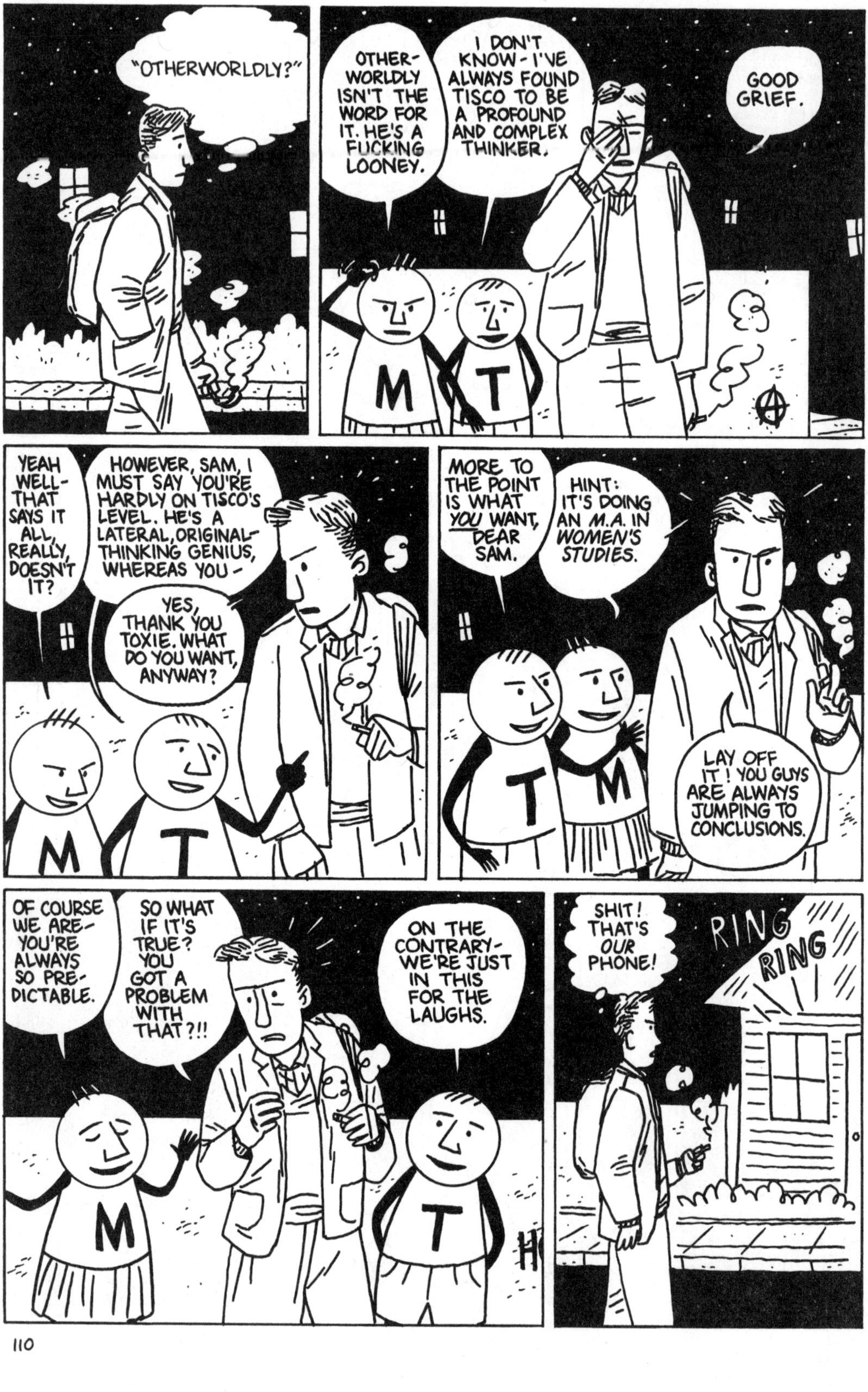
"OTHERWORLDLY?"
OTHER-WORLDLY ISN'T THE WORD FOR IT. HE'S A FUCKING LOONEY.
I DON'T KNOW - I'VE ALWAYS FOUND TISCO TO BE A PROFOUND AND COMPLEX THINKER.
GOOD GRIEF.
YEAH WELL- THAT SAYS IT ALL, REALLY, DOESN'T IT?
HOWEVER, SAM, I MUST SAY YOU'RE HARDLY ON TISCO'S LEVEL. HE'S A LATERAL, ORIGINAL-THINKING GENIUS, WHEREAS YOU -
YES, THANK YOU TOXIE. WHAT DO YOU WANT, ANYWAY?
MORE TO THE POINT IS WHAT YOU WANT, DEAR SAM.
HINT: IT'S DOING AN M.A. IN WOMEN'S STUDIES.
LAY OFF IT! YOU GUYS ARE ALWAYS JUMPING TO CONCLUSIONS.
OF COURSE WE ARE- YOU'RE ALWAYS SO PRE-DICTABLE.
SO WHAT IF IT'S TRUE? YOU GOT A PROBLEM WITH THAT?!!
ON THE CONTRARY- WE'RE JUST IN THIS FOR THE LAUGHS.
SHIT! THAT'S OUR PHONE!
RING
RING

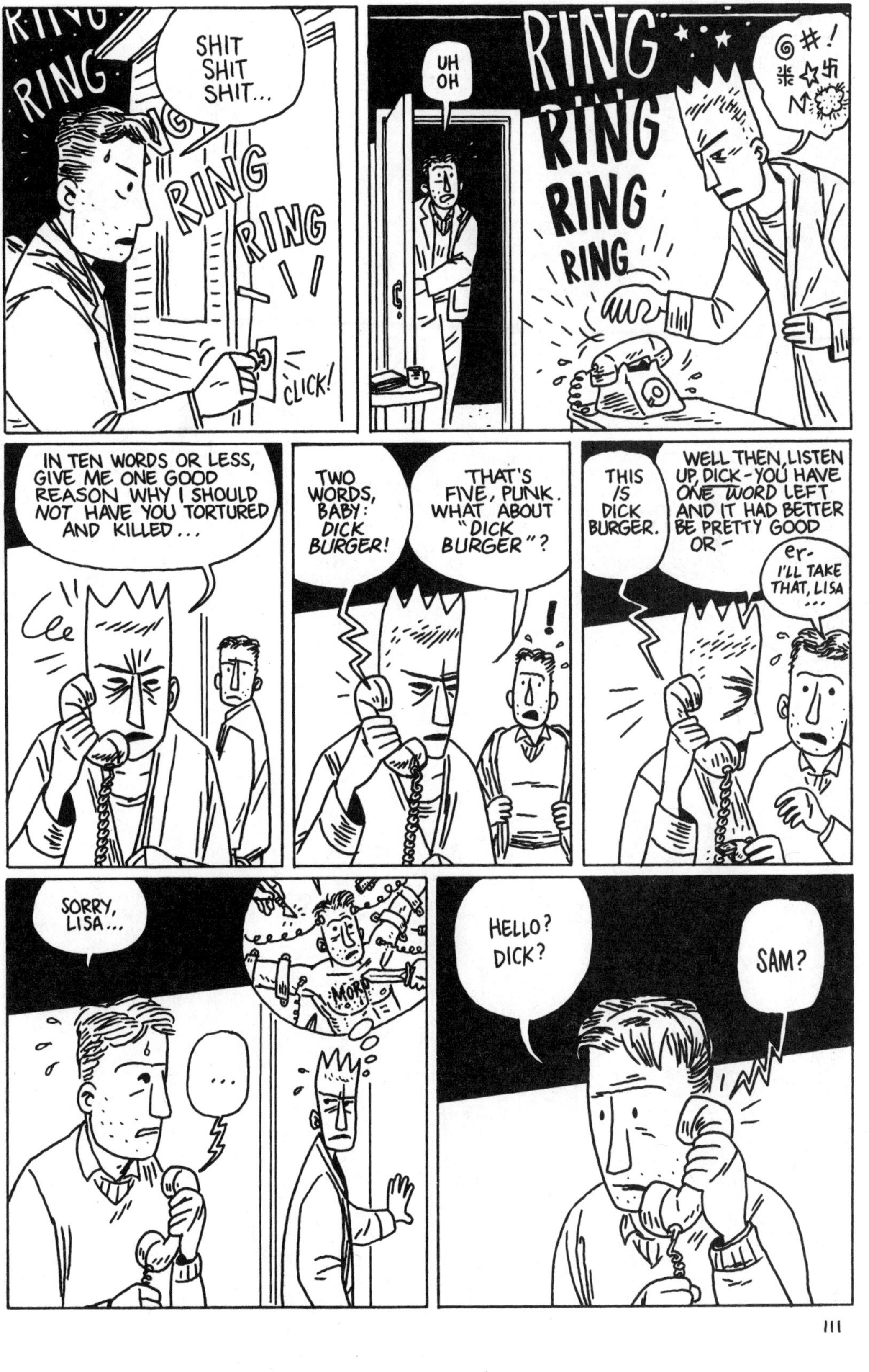
RING
RING
SHIT SHIT SHIT...
RING
RING
CLICK!
UH OH
RING
RING
RING
RING
IN TEN WORDS OR LESS, GIVE ME ONE GOOD REASON WHY I SHOULD NOT HAVE YOU TORTURED AND KILLED...
TWO WORDS, BABY: DICK BURGER!
THAT'S FIVE, PUNK. WHAT ABOUT "DICK BURGER"?
!
THIS IS DICK BURGER.
WELL THEN, LISTEN UP, DICK - YOU HAVE ONE WORD LEFT AND IT HAD BETTER BE PRETTY GOOD OR -
er- I'LL TAKE THAT, LISA...
SORRY, LISA...
...
HELLO? DICK?
SAM?

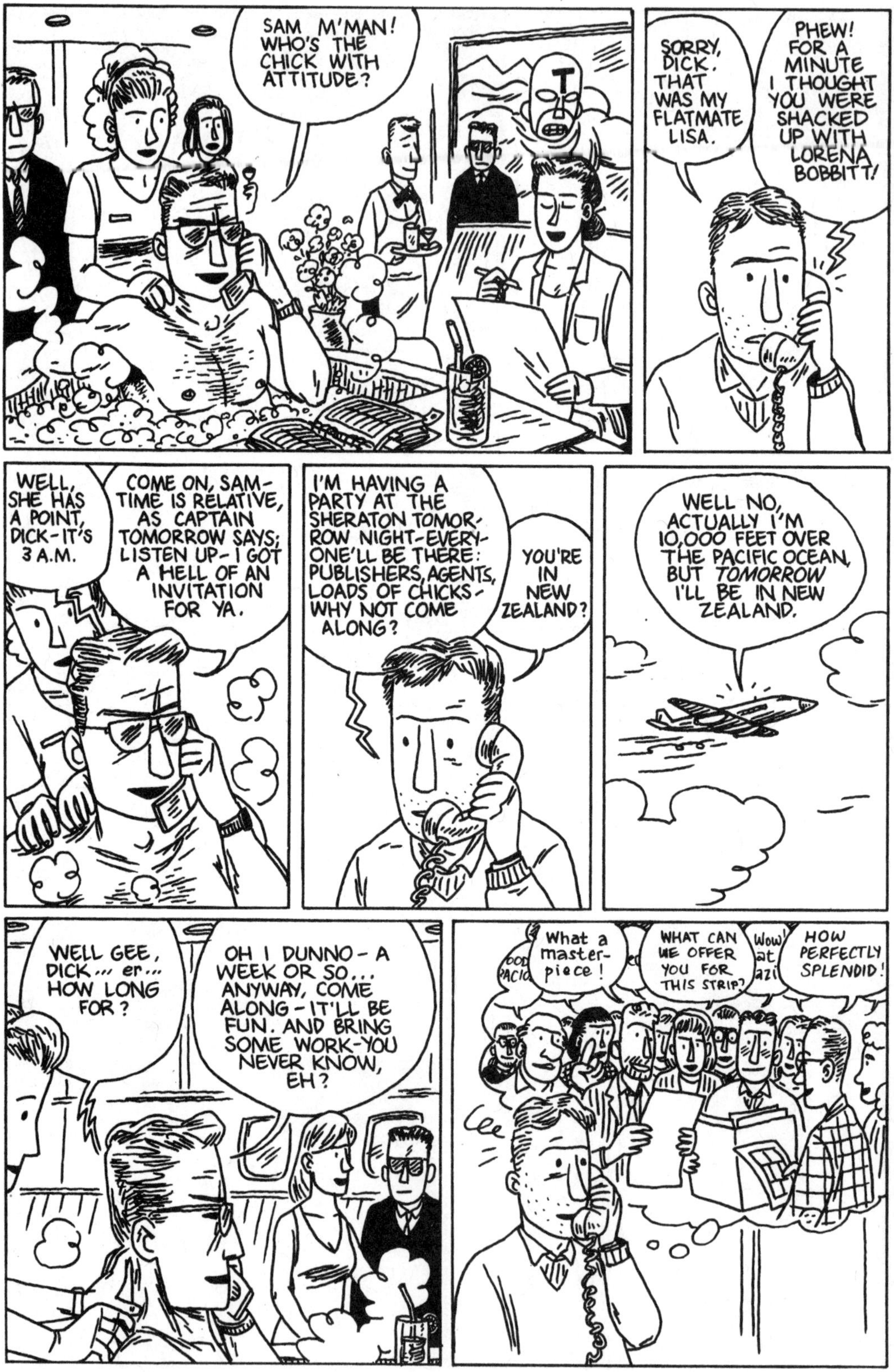
SAM M'MAN! WHO'S THE CHICK WITH ATTITUDE?
SORRY, DICK. THAT WAS MY FLATMATE LISA.
PHEW! FOR A MINUTE I THOUGHT YOU WERE SHACKED UP WITH LORENA BOBBITT!
WELL, SHE HAS A POINT, DICK - IT'S 3 A.M.
COME ON, SAM - TIME IS RELATIVE, AS CAPTAIN TOMORROW SAYS; LISTEN UP - I GOT A HELL OF AN INVITATION FOR YA.
I'M HAVING A PARTY AT THE SHERATON TOMORROW NIGHT - EVERYONE'LL BE THERE: PUBLISHERS, AGENTS, LOADS OF CHICKS - WHY NOT COME ALONG?
YOU'RE IN NEW ZEALAND?
WELL NO, ACTUALLY I'M 10,000 FEET OVER THE PACIFIC OCEAN, BUT *TOMORROW* I'LL BE IN NEW ZEALAND.
WELL GEE, DICK... er... HOW LONG FOR?
OH I DUNNO - A WEEK OR SO... ANYWAY, COME ALONG - IT'LL BE FUN. AND BRING SOME WORK - YOU NEVER KNOW, EH?
What a master-piece!
WHAT CAN WE OFFER YOU FOR THIS STRIP?
Wow!
HOW PERFECTLY SPLENDID!

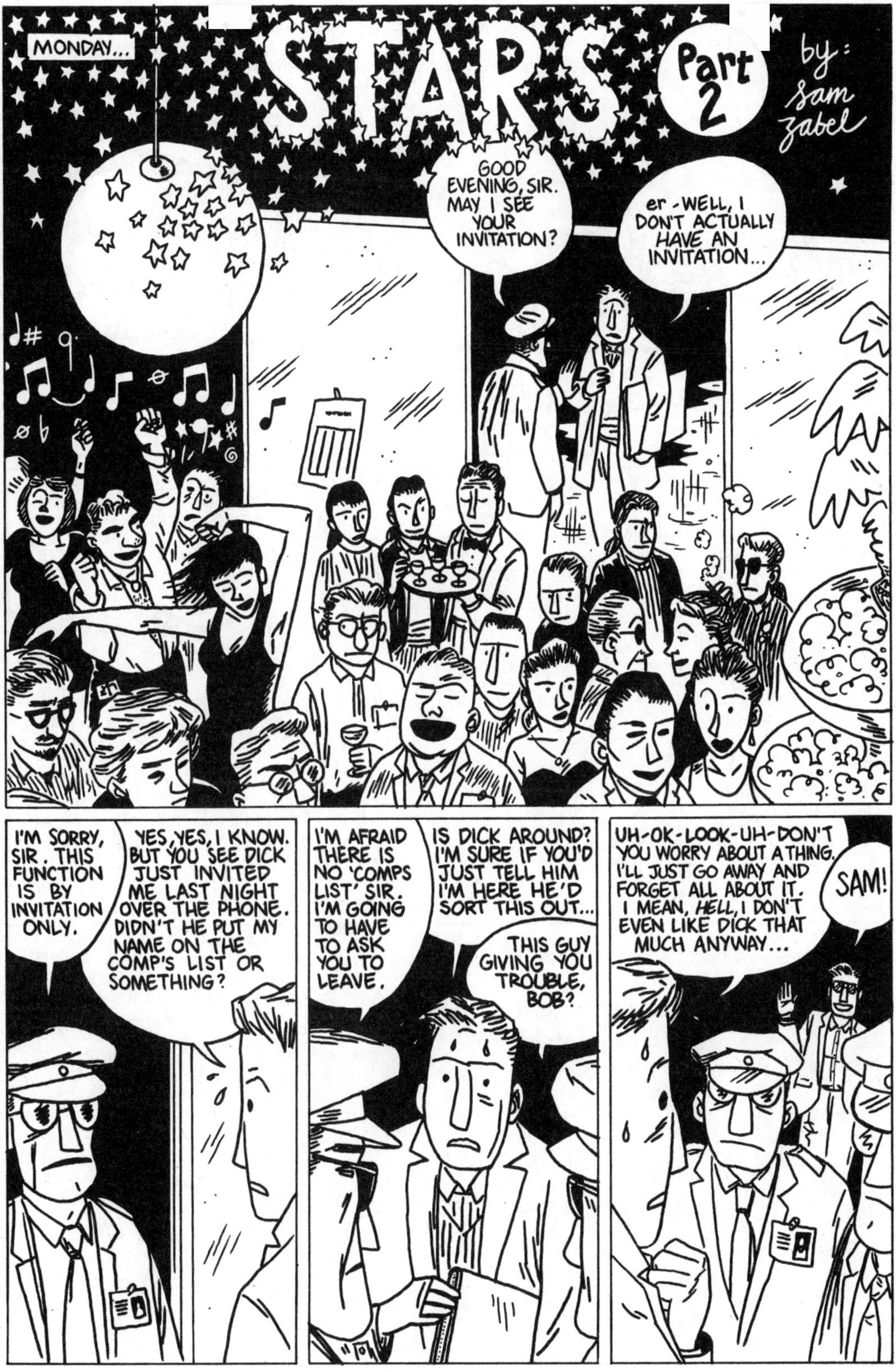
MONDAY...
STARS
Part 2
by: sam zabel
GOOD EVENING, SIR. MAY I SEE YOUR INVITATION?
er - WELL, I DON'T ACTUALLY HAVE AN INVITATION...
I'M SORRY, SIR. THIS FUNCTION IS BY INVITATION ONLY.
YES, YES, I KNOW. BUT YOU SEE DICK JUST INVITED ME LAST NIGHT OVER THE PHONE. DIDN'T HE PUT MY NAME ON THE COMP'S LIST OR SOMETHING?
I'M AFRAID THERE IS NO 'COMPS LIST' SIR. I'M GOING TO HAVE TO ASK YOU TO LEAVE.
IS DICK AROUND? I'M SURE IF YOU'D JUST TELL HIM I'M HERE HE'D SORT THIS OUT...
THIS GUY GIVING YOU TROUBLE, BOB?
UH-OK-LOOK-UH-DON'T YOU WORRY ABOUT A THING. I'LL JUST GO AWAY AND FORGET ALL ABOUT IT. I MEAN, HELL, I DON'T EVEN LIKE DICK THAT MUCH ANYWAY...
SAM!

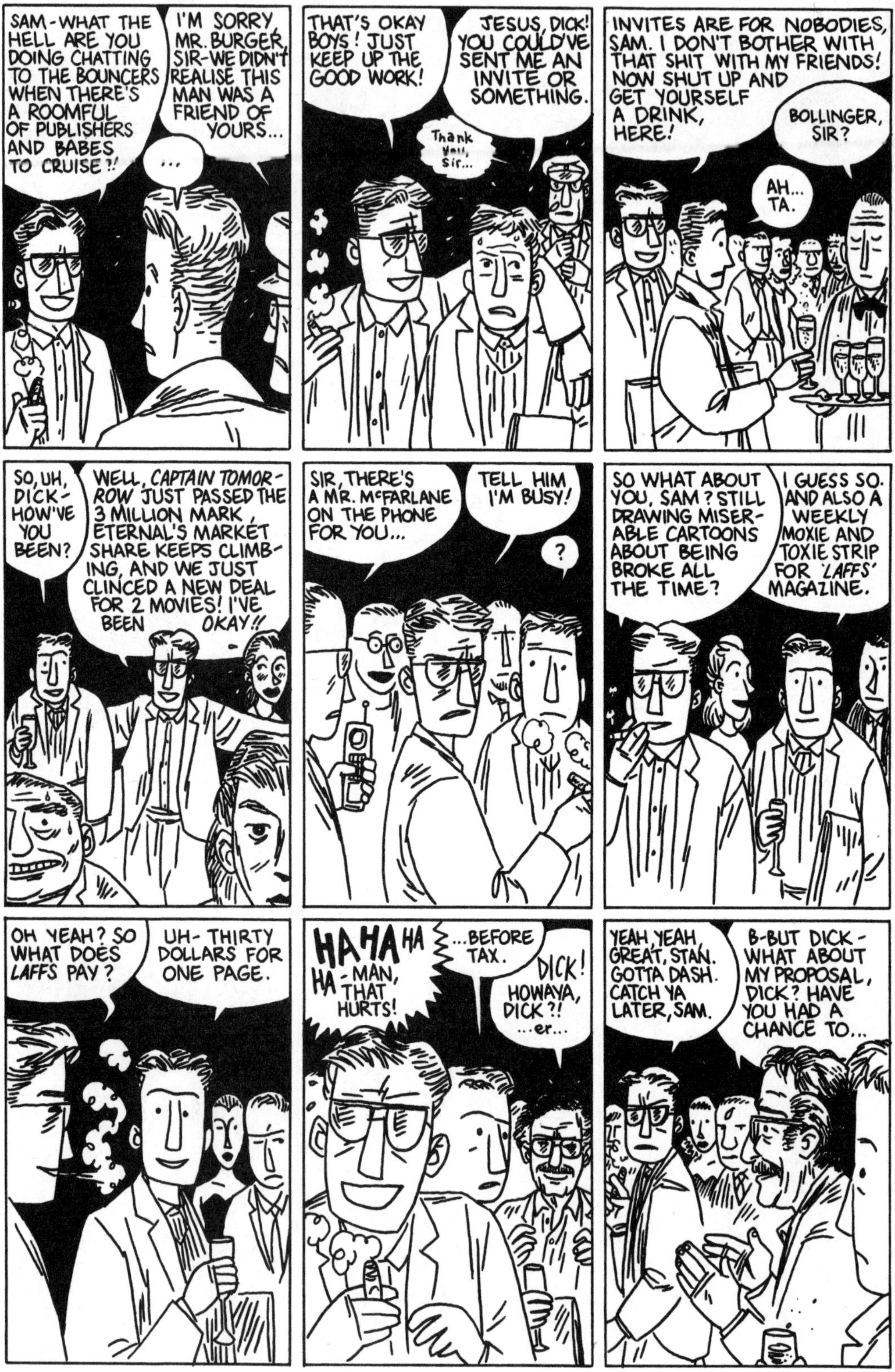
SAM - WHAT THE HELL ARE YOU DOING CHATTING TO THE BOUNCERS WHEN THERE'S A ROOMFUL OF PUBLISHERS AND BABES TO CRUISE?!
I'M SORRY, MR. BURGER, SIR - WE DIDN'T REALISE THIS MAN WAS A FRIEND OF YOURS...
...
THAT'S OKAY BOYS! JUST KEEP UP THE GOOD WORK!
JESUS, DICK! YOU COULD'VE SENT ME AN INVITE OR SOMETHING.
Thank you, Sir...
INVITES ARE FOR NOBODIES, SAM. I DON'T BOTHER WITH THAT SHIT WITH MY FRIENDS! NOW SHUT UP AND GET YOURSELF A DRINK, HERE!
BOLLINGER, SIR?
AH... TA.
SO, UH, DICK - HOW'VE YOU BEEN?
WELL, CAPTAIN TOMORROW JUST PASSED THE 3 MILLION MARK, ETERNAL'S MARKET SHARE KEEPS CLIMBING, AND WE JUST CLINCED A NEW DEAL FOR 2 MOVIES! I'VE BEEN OKAY!!
SIR, THERE'S A MR. McFARLANE ON THE PHONE FOR YOU...
TELL HIM I'M BUSY!
?
SO WHAT ABOUT YOU, SAM? STILL DRAWING MISERABLE CARTOONS ABOUT BEING BROKE ALL THE TIME?
I GUESS SO. AND ALSO A WEEKLY MOXIE AND TOXIE STRIP FOR 'LAFFS' MAGAZINE.
OH YEAH? SO WHAT DOES LAFFS PAY?
UH - THIRTY DOLLARS FOR ONE PAGE.
...BEFORE TAX.
HAHAHA HA HA - MAN, THAT HURTS!
DICK! HOWAYA, DICK?! ...er...
YEAH, YEAH, GREAT, STAN. GOTTA DASH. CATCH YA LATER, SAM.
B-BUT DICK - WHAT ABOUT MY PROPOSAL, DICK? HAVE YOU HAD A CHANCE TO...

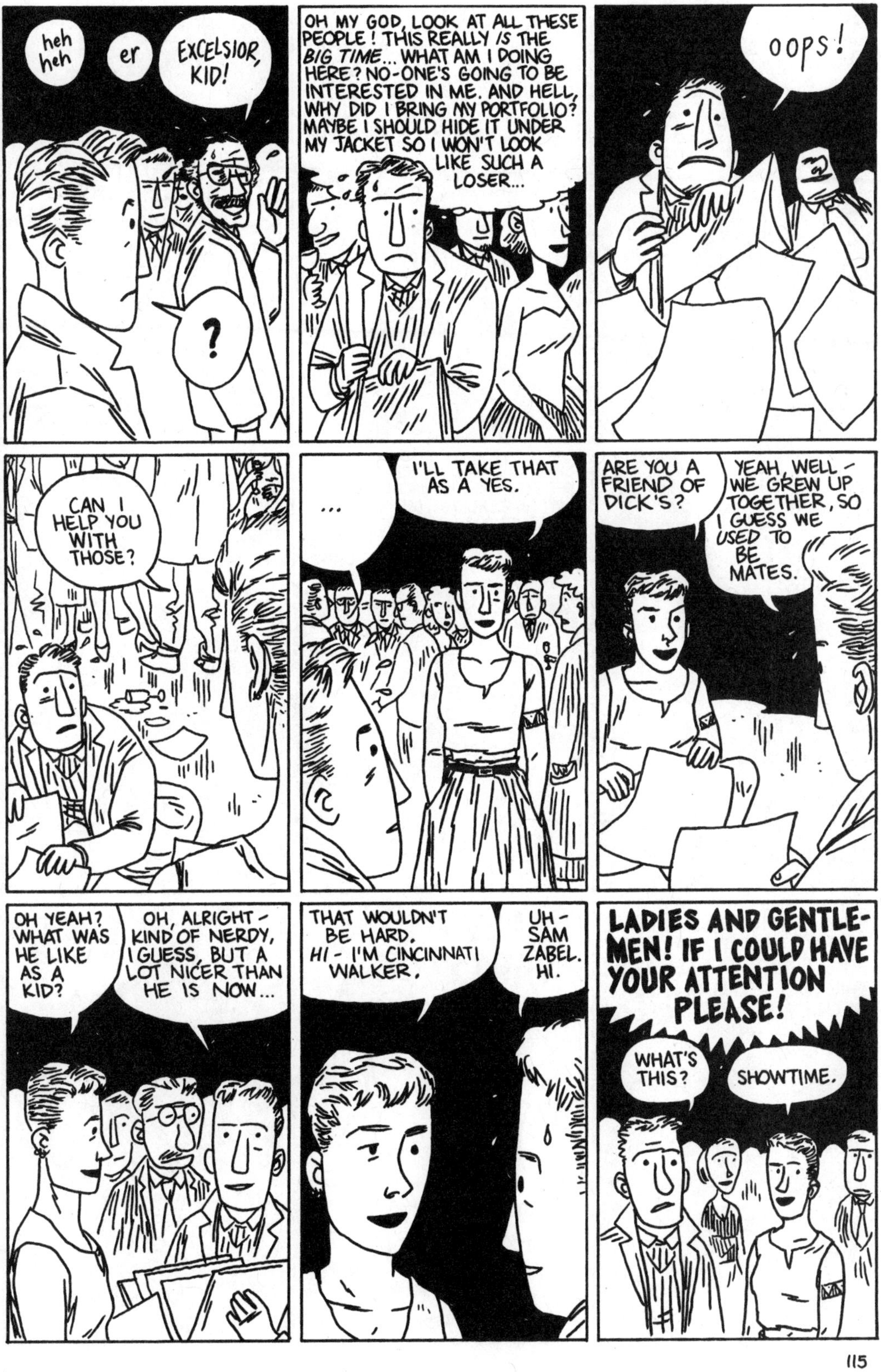
heh heh
er
EXCELSIOR, KID!
?
OH MY GOD, LOOK AT ALL THESE PEOPLE! THIS REALLY IS THE BIG TIME... WHAT AM I DOING HERE? NO-ONE'S GOING TO BE INTERESTED IN ME. AND HELL, WHY DID I BRING MY PORTFOLIO? MAYBE I SHOULD HIDE IT UNDER MY JACKET SO I WON'T LOOK LIKE SUCH A LOSER...
oops!
CAN I HELP YOU WITH THOSE?
...
I'LL TAKE THAT AS A YES.
ARE YOU A FRIEND OF DICK'S?
YEAH, WELL - WE GREW UP TOGETHER, SO I GUESS WE USED TO BE MATES.
OH YEAH? WHAT WAS HE LIKE AS A KID?
OH, ALRIGHT - KIND OF NERDY, I GUESS, BUT A LOT NICER THAN HE IS NOW...
THAT WOULDN'T BE HARD. HI - I'M CINCINNATI WALKER.
UH - SAM ZABEL. HI.
LADIES AND GENTLEMEN! IF I COULD HAVE YOUR ATTENTION PLEASE!
WHAT'S THIS?
SHOWTIME.

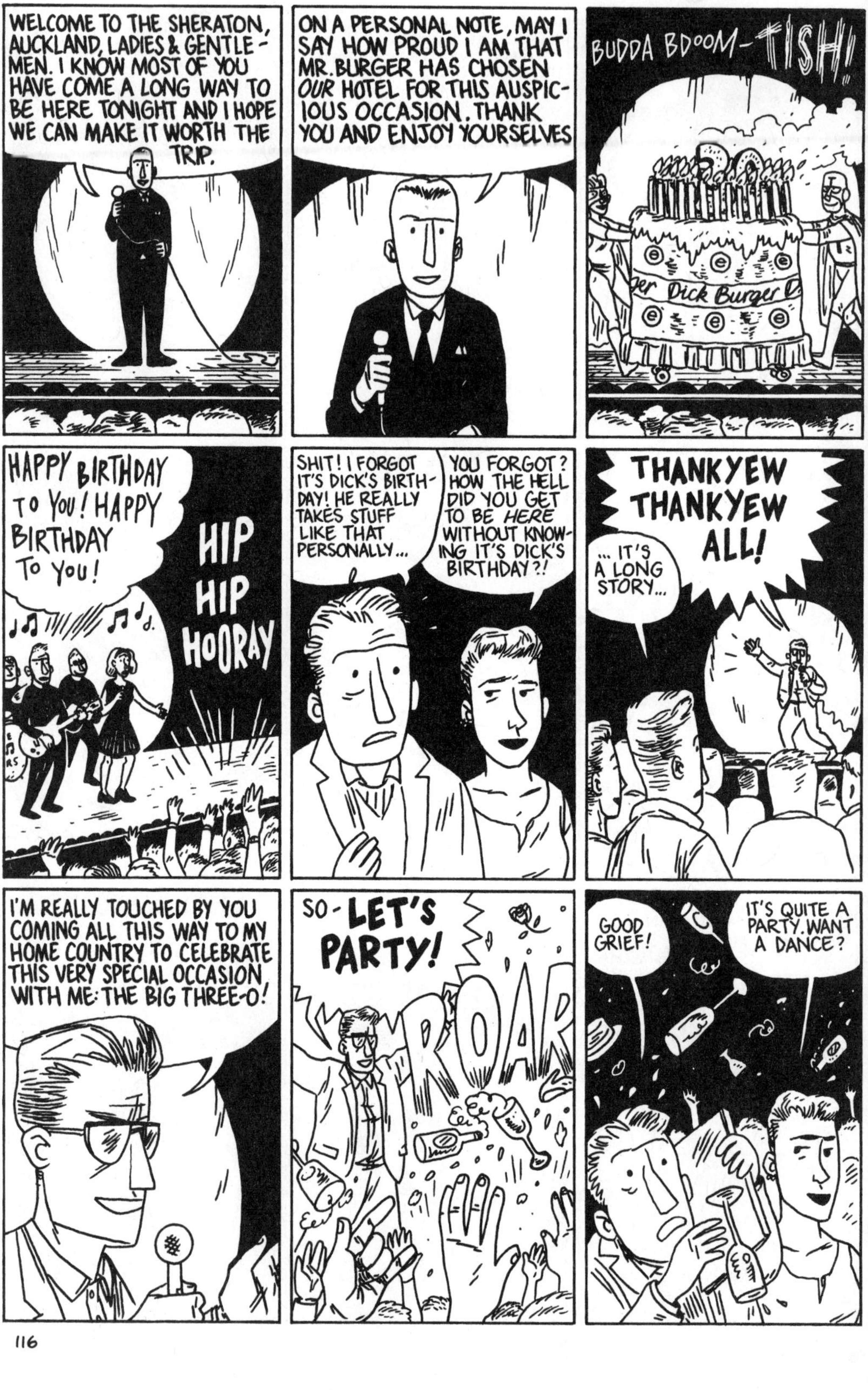

WELCOME TO THE SHERATON, AUCKLAND, LADIES & GENTLEMEN. I KNOW MOST OF YOU HAVE COME A LONG WAY TO BE HERE TONIGHT AND I HOPE WE CAN MAKE IT WORTH THE TRIP.
ON A PERSONAL NOTE, MAY I SAY HOW PROUD I AM THAT MR. BURGER HAS CHOSEN OUR HOTEL FOR THIS AUSPICIOUS OCCASION. THANK YOU AND ENJOY YOURSELVES
BUDDA BDOOM-TISH!
Dick Burger
HAPPY BIRTHDAY TO YOU! HAPPY BIRTHDAY TO YOU!
HIP HIP HOORAY
SHIT! I FORGOT IT'S DICK'S BIRTHDAY! HE REALLY TAKES STUFF LIKE THAT PERSONALLY...
YOU FORGOT? HOW THE HELL DID YOU GET TO BE HERE WITHOUT KNOWING IT'S DICK'S BIRTHDAY?!
THANKYEW THANKYEW ALL!
... IT'S A LONG STORY...
I'M REALLY TOUCHED BY YOU COMING ALL THIS WAY TO MY HOME COUNTRY TO CELEBRATE THIS VERY SPECIAL OCCASION WITH ME: THE BIG THREE-O!
SO-LET'S PARTY!
ROAR
GOOD GRIEF!
IT'S QUITE A PARTY. WANT A DANCE?

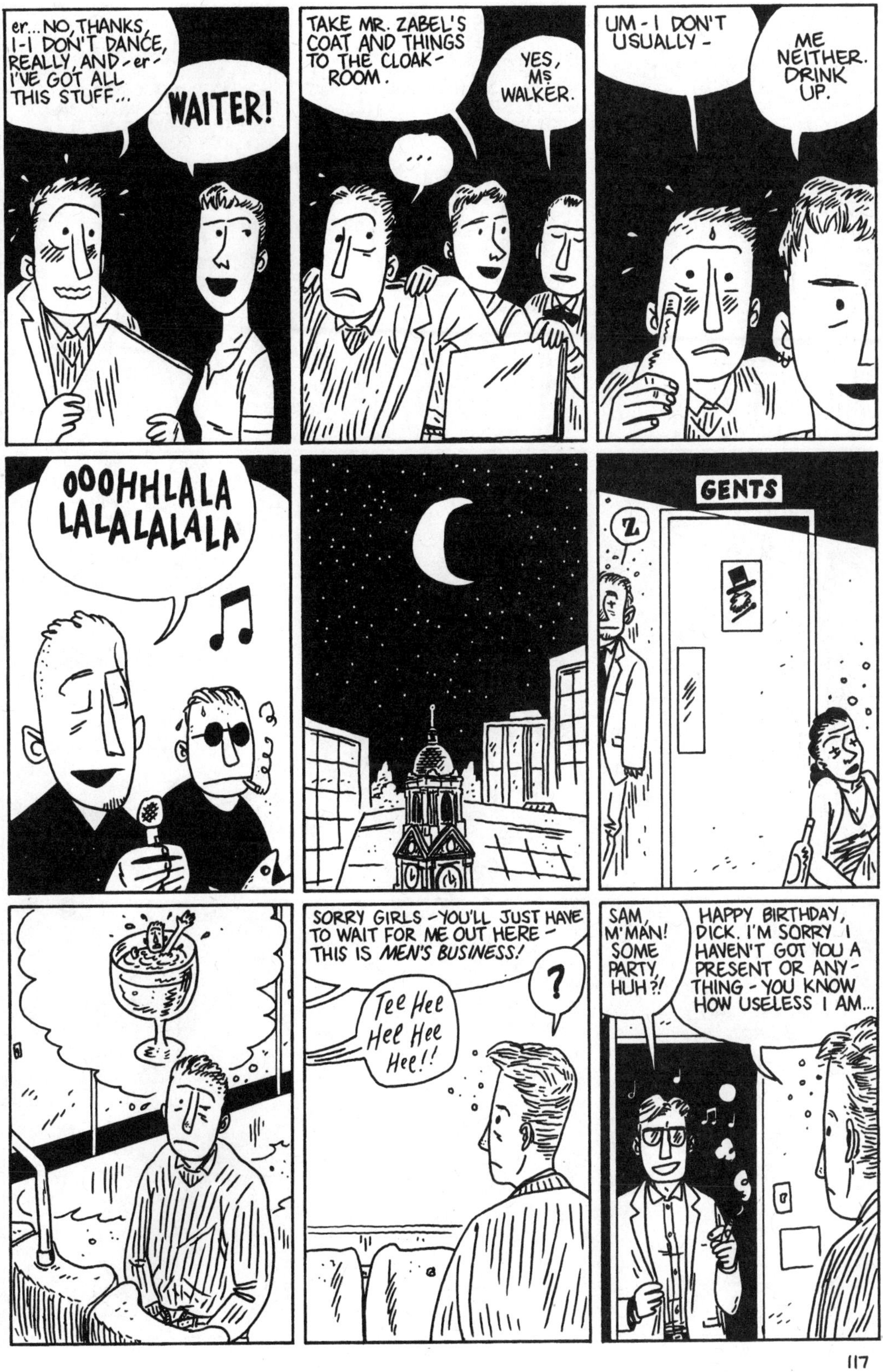
er... NO, THANKS, I-I DON'T DANCE, REALLY, AND - er - I'VE GOT ALL THIS STUFF...
WAITER!
TAKE MR. ZABEL'S COAT AND THINGS TO THE CLOAK-ROOM.
...
YES, Ms WALKER.
UM - I DON'T USUALLY -
ME NEITHER. DRINK UP.
OOOHHLALA LALALALALA
GENTS
Z
SORRY GIRLS - YOU'LL JUST HAVE TO WAIT FOR ME OUT HERE - THIS IS *MEN'S BUSINESS!*
Tee Hee Hee Hee Hee!!
?
SAM, M'MAN! SOME PARTY, HUH?!
HAPPY BIRTHDAY, DICK. I'M SORRY I HAVEN'T GOT YOU A PRESENT OR ANY-THING - YOU KNOW HOW USELESS I AM...

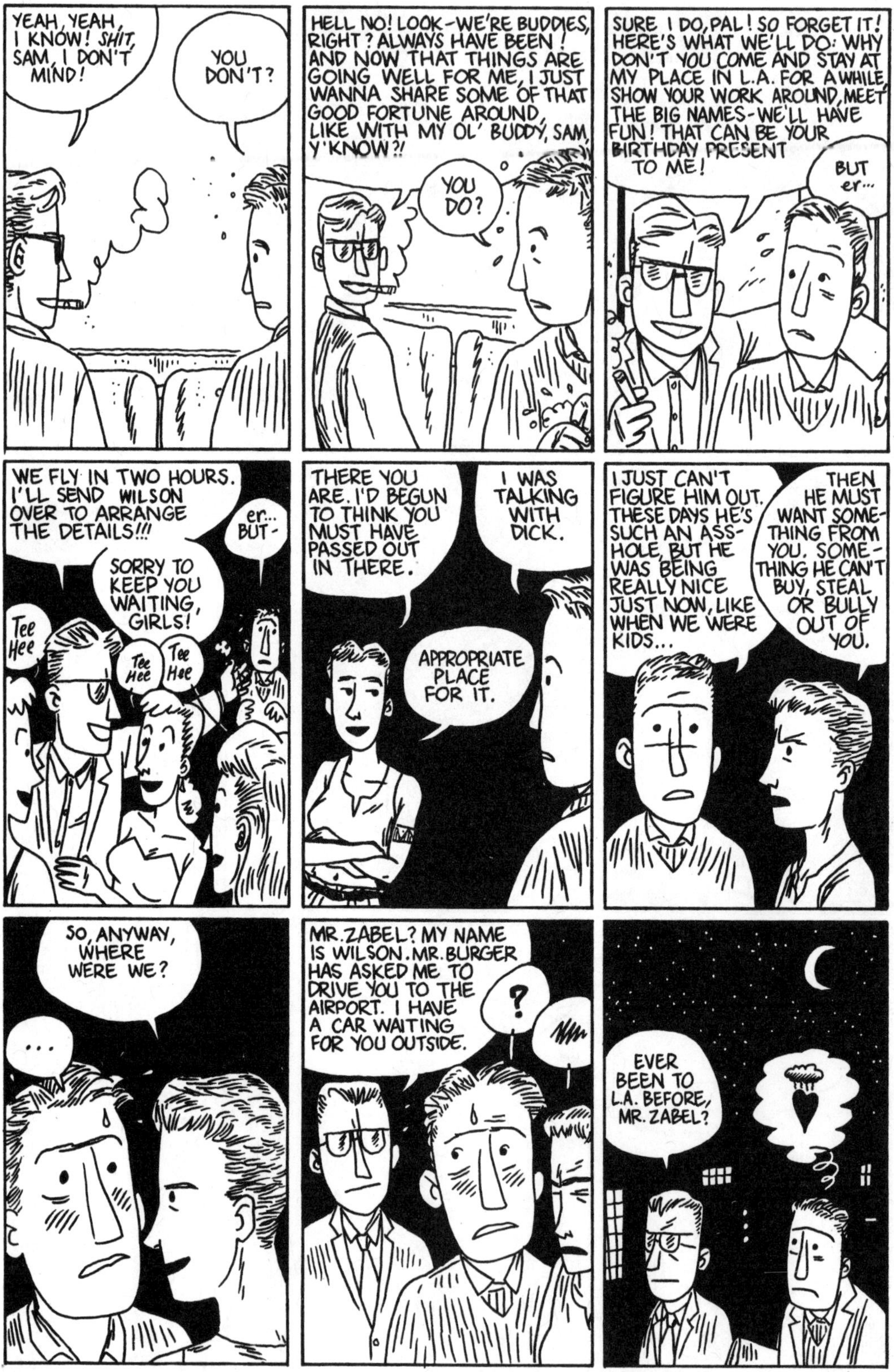
YEAH, YEAH, I KNOW! SHIT, SAM, I DON'T MIND!
YOU DON'T?
HELL NO! LOOK-WE'RE BUDDIES, RIGHT? ALWAYS HAVE BEEN! AND NOW THAT THINGS ARE GOING WELL FOR ME, I JUST WANNA SHARE SOME OF THAT GOOD FORTUNE AROUND, LIKE WITH MY OL' BUDDY, SAM, Y'KNOW?!
YOU DO?
SURE I DO, PAL! SO FORGET IT! HERE'S WHAT WE'LL DO: WHY DON'T YOU COME AND STAY AT MY PLACE IN L.A. FOR A WHILE, SHOW YOUR WORK AROUND, MEET THE BIG NAMES-WE'LL HAVE FUN! THAT CAN BE YOUR BIRTHDAY PRESENT TO ME!
BUT er...
WE FLY IN TWO HOURS. I'LL SEND WILSON OVER TO ARRANGE THE DETAILS!!!
er... BUT-
SORRY TO KEEP YOU WAITING, GIRLS!
Tee Hee
Tee Hee
Tee Hee
THERE YOU ARE. I'D BEGUN TO THINK YOU MUST HAVE PASSED OUT IN THERE.
I WAS TALKING WITH DICK.
APPROPRIATE PLACE FOR IT.
I JUST CAN'T FIGURE HIM OUT. THESE DAYS HE'S SUCH AN ASS-HOLE, BUT HE WAS BEING REALLY NICE JUST NOW, LIKE WHEN WE WERE KIDS...
THEN HE MUST WANT SOME-THING FROM YOU. SOME-THING HE CAN'T BUY, STEAL OR BULLY OUT OF YOU.
SO, ANYWAY, WHERE WERE WE?
...
MR. ZABEL? MY NAME IS WILSON. MR. BURGER HAS ASKED ME TO DRIVE YOU TO THE AIRPORT. I HAVE A CAR WAITING FOR YOU OUTSIDE.
?
EVER BEEN TO L.A. BEFORE, MR. ZABEL?

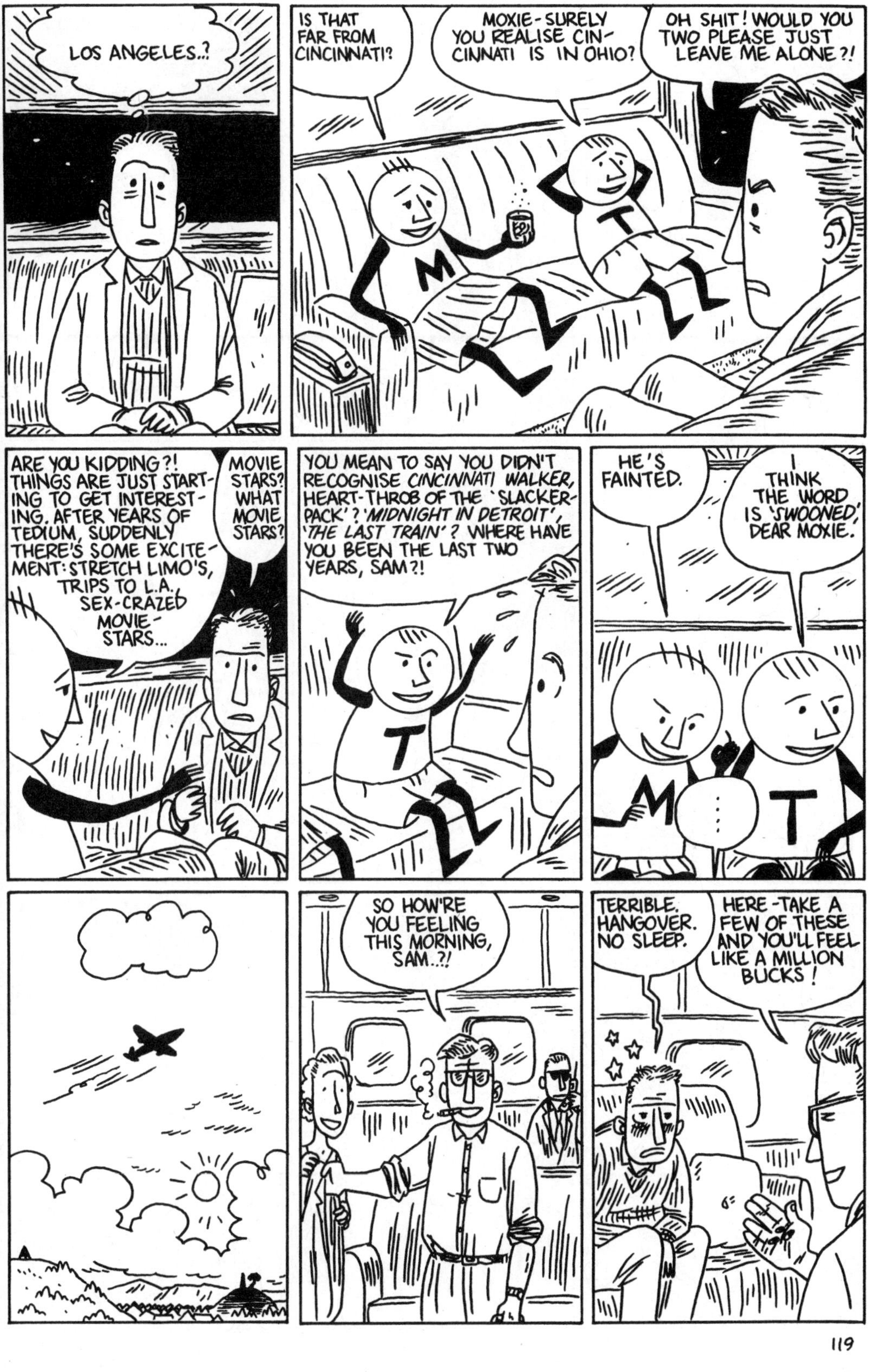
LOS ANGELES..?
IS THAT FAR FROM CINCINNATI?
MOXIE-SURELY YOU REALISE CIN-CINNATI IS IN OHIO?
OH SHIT! WOULD YOU TWO PLEASE JUST LEAVE ME ALONE?!
ARE YOU KIDDING?! THINGS ARE JUST START-ING TO GET INTEREST-ING. AFTER YEARS OF TEDIUM, SUDDENLY THERE'S SOME EXCITE-MENT: STRETCH LIMO'S, TRIPS TO L.A. SEX-CRAZED MOVIE-STARS...
MOVIE STARS? WHAT MOVIE STARS?
YOU MEAN TO SAY YOU DIDN'T RECOGNISE *CINCINNATI WALKER*, HEART-THROB OF THE 'SLACKER-PACK'? '*MIDNIGHT IN DETROIT*', '*THE LAST TRAIN*'? WHERE HAVE YOU BEEN THE LAST TWO YEARS, SAM?!
HE'S FAINTED.
I THINK THE WORD IS '*SWOONED*', DEAR MOXIE.
SO HOW'RE YOU FEELING THIS MORNING, SAM..?!
TERRIBLE. HANGOVER. NO SLEEP.
HERE-TAKE A FEW OF THESE AND YOU'LL FEEL LIKE A MILLION BUCKS!

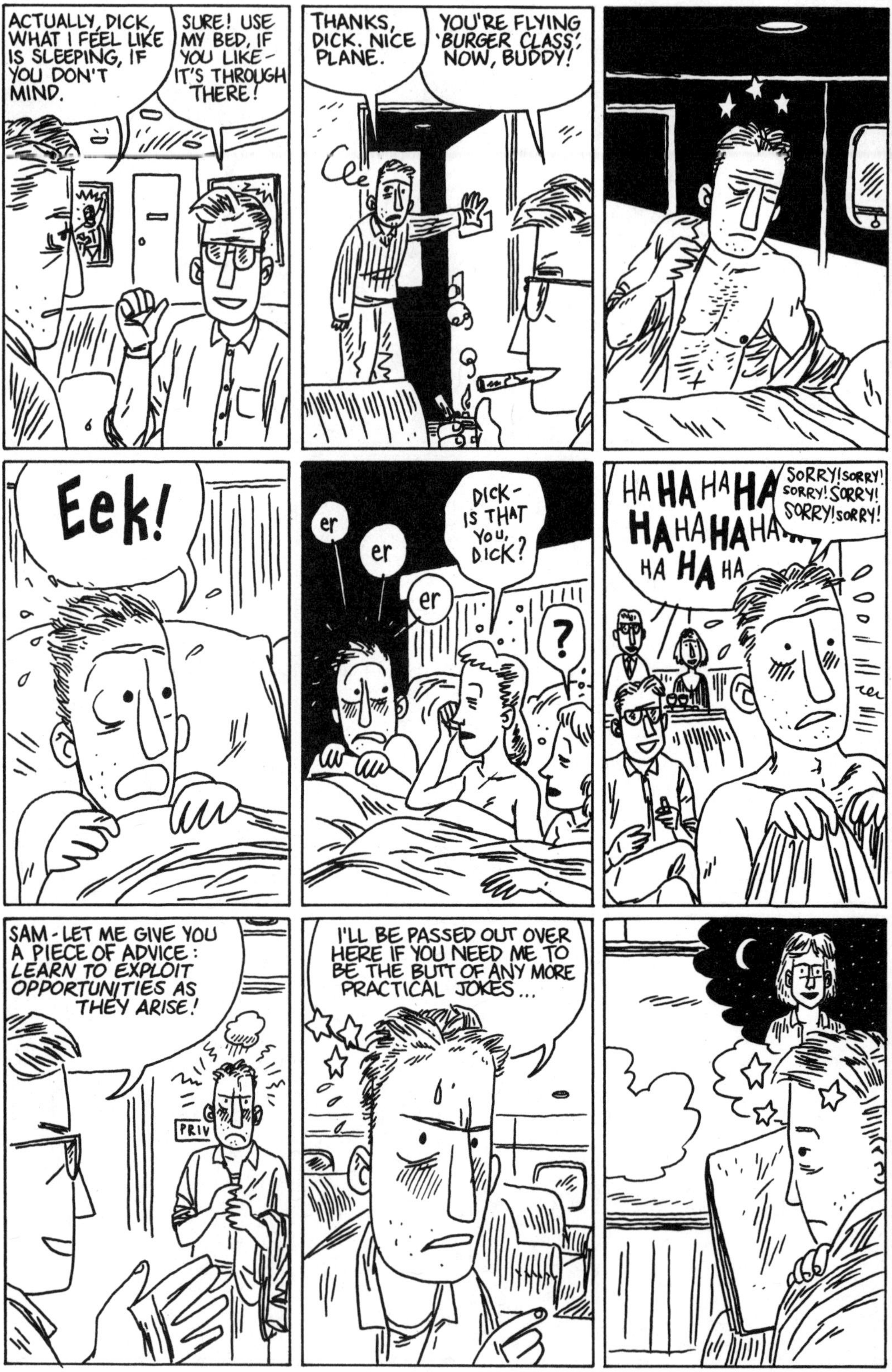

ACTUALLY, DICK, WHAT I FEEL LIKE IS SLEEPING, IF YOU DON'T MIND.
SURE! USE MY BED, IF YOU LIKE - IT'S THROUGH THERE!
THANKS, DICK. NICE PLANE.
YOU'RE FLYING 'BURGER CLASS' NOW, BUDDY!
Eek!
er
er
er
DICK - IS THAT YOU, DICK?
?
HA HA HA HA HA HA HA HA HA HA HA HA
SORRY! SORRY! SORRY! SORRY! SORRY! SORRY!
SAM - LET ME GIVE YOU A PIECE OF ADVICE: LEARN TO EXPLOIT OPPORTUNITIES AS THEY ARISE!
PRIV
I'LL BE PASSED OUT OVER HERE IF YOU NEED ME TO BE THE BUTT OF ANY MORE PRACTICAL JOKES...

TUESDAY...

STARS Part 3

NO, TODD, I DON'T CARE WHAT YOU THINK. I DON'T PAY YOU TO THINK – IF I DID, YOU'D HAVE BEEN FIRED A *LONG* TIME AGO!

BURGER ESTATE

STOP

PRIVATE PROPERTY

YEAH, WELL, IF YOU DON'T LIKE IT YOU KNOW WHAT YOU CAN DO! I'VE GOT A HUNDRED YOUNG PENCILLERS WHO DRAW JUST LIKE YOU DO, WAITING IN LINE...

SURE, SURE, I'VE HEARD IT ALL BEFORE: "*WHEN I HAD MY OWN COMPANY...*" TODD – LISTEN! YOU *HAD* YOUR OWN COMPANY AND YOU BLEW IT! IF I HADN'T BOUGHT YOU OUT WHEN I DID, YOU'D BE QUEUEING AT CONVENTIONS WITH YOUR PORTFOLIO ALL OVER AGAIN!

SO SHUT UP AND DRAW IT LIKE I TELL YOU! NOW GET OFF THIS LINE – I'M BUSY!

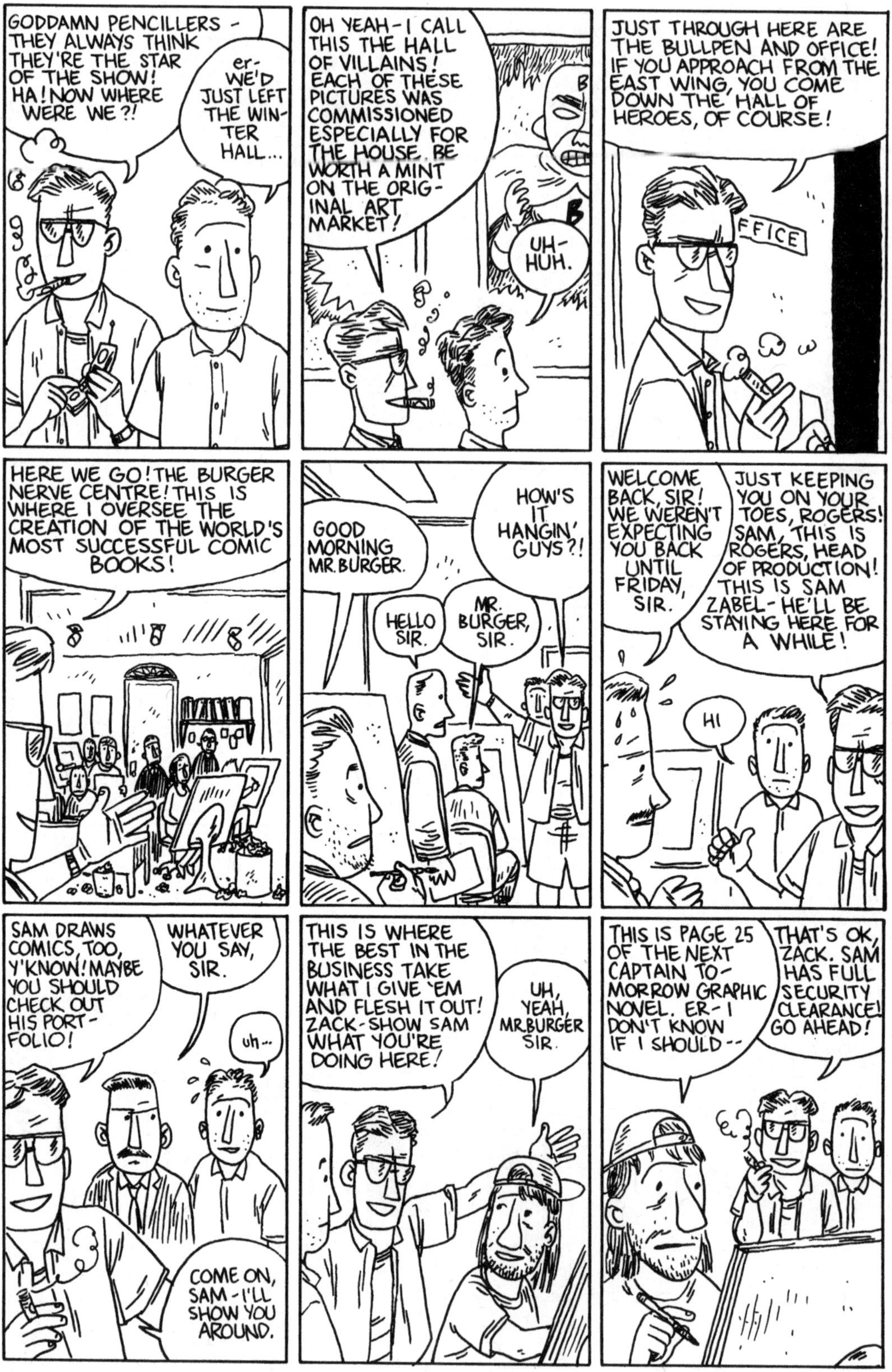
GODDAMN PENCILLERS - THEY ALWAYS THINK THEY'RE THE STAR OF THE SHOW! HA! NOW WHERE WERE WE?!
er- WE'D JUST LEFT THE WINTER HALL...
OH YEAH - I CALL THIS THE HALL OF VILLAINS! EACH OF THESE PICTURES WAS COMMISSIONED ESPECIALLY FOR THE HOUSE. BE WORTH A MINT ON THE ORIGINAL ART MARKET!
UH-HUH.
JUST THROUGH HERE ARE THE BULLPEN AND OFFICE! IF YOU APPROACH FROM THE EAST WING, YOU COME DOWN THE HALL OF HEROES, OF COURSE!
FFICE
HERE WE GO! THE BURGER NERVE CENTRE! THIS IS WHERE I OVERSEE THE CREATION OF THE WORLD'S MOST SUCCESSFUL COMIC BOOKS!
GOOD MORNING MR. BURGER.
HOW'S IT HANGIN' GUYS?!
HELLO SIR.
MR. BURGER, SIR.
WELCOME BACK, SIR! WE WEREN'T EXPECTING YOU BACK UNTIL FRIDAY, SIR.
JUST KEEPING YOU ON YOUR TOES, ROGERS! SAM, THIS IS ROGERS, HEAD OF PRODUCTION! THIS IS SAM ZABEL - HE'LL BE STAYING HERE FOR A WHILE!
HI
SAM DRAWS COMICS, TOO, Y'KNOW! MAYBE YOU SHOULD CHECK OUT HIS PORTFOLIO!
WHATEVER YOU SAY, SIR.
uh...
COME ON, SAM - I'LL SHOW YOU AROUND.
THIS IS WHERE THE BEST IN THE BUSINESS TAKE WHAT I GIVE 'EM AND FLESH IT OUT! ZACK - SHOW SAM WHAT YOU'RE DOING HERE!
UH, YEAH, MR. BURGER SIR.
THIS IS PAGE 25 OF THE NEXT CAPTAIN TOMORROW GRAPHIC NOVEL. ER - I DON'T KNOW IF I SHOULD--
THAT'S OK, ZACK. SAM HAS FULL SECURITY CLEARANCE! GO AHEAD!

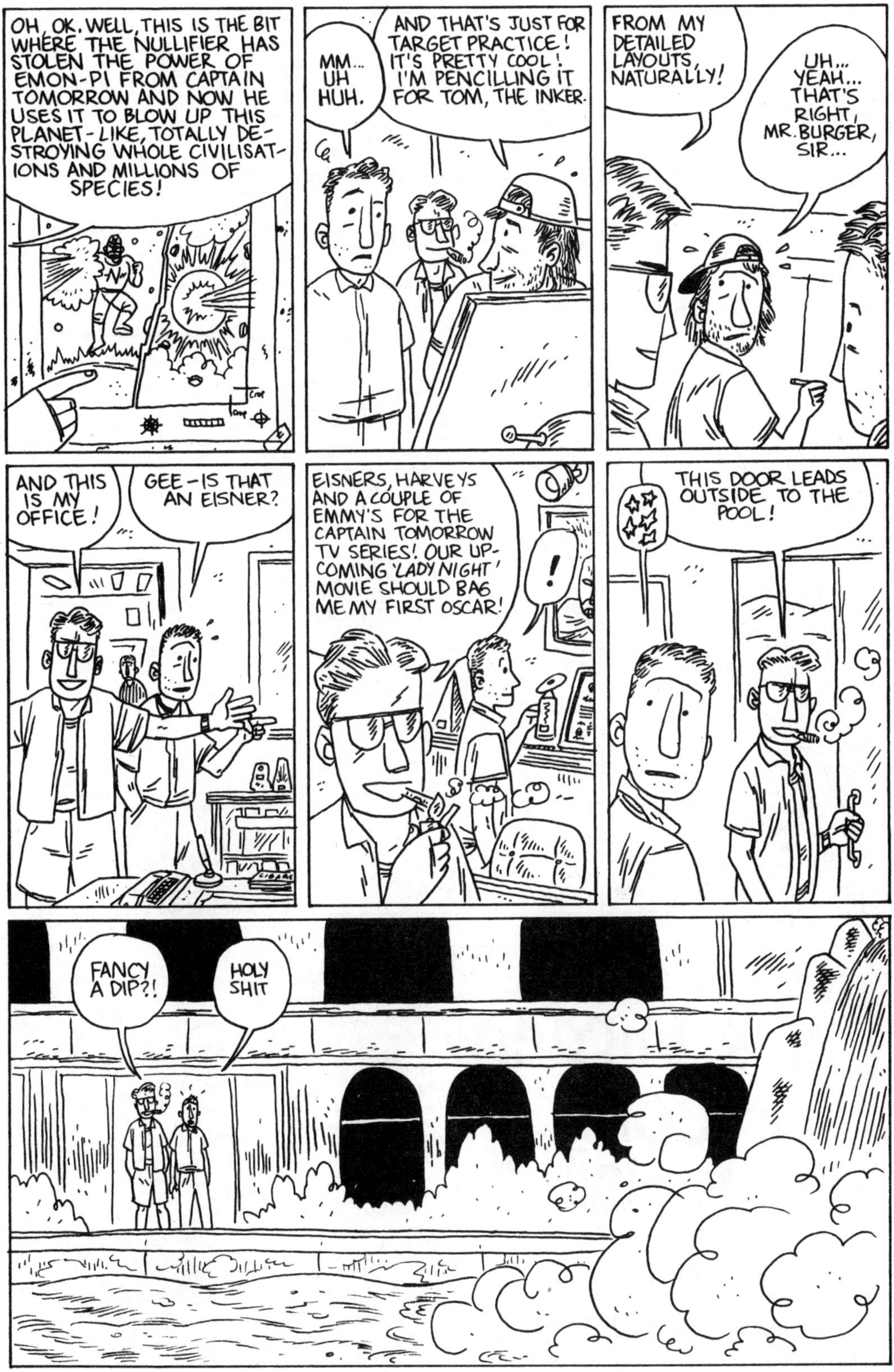
OH, OK. WELL, THIS IS THE BIT WHERE THE NULLIFIER HAS STOLEN THE POWER OF EMON-PI FROM CAPTAIN TOMORROW AND NOW HE USES IT TO BLOW UP THIS PLANET- LIKE, TOTALLY DESTROYING WHOLE CIVILISATIONS AND MILLIONS OF SPECIES!
AND THAT'S JUST FOR TARGET PRACTICE! IT'S PRETTY COOL! I'M PENCILLING IT FOR TOM, THE INKER.
MM... UH HUH.
FROM MY DETAILED LAYOUTS, NATURALLY!
UH... YEAH... THAT'S RIGHT, MR. BURGER, SIR...
AND THIS IS MY OFFICE!
GEE-IS THAT AN EISNER?
EISNERS, HARVEYS AND A COUPLE OF EMMY'S FOR THE CAPTAIN TOMORROW TV SERIES! OUR UPCOMING 'LADY NIGHT' MOVIE SHOULD BAG ME MY FIRST OSCAR!
!
THIS DOOR LEADS OUTSIDE TO THE POOL!
FANCY A DIP?!
HOLY SHIT

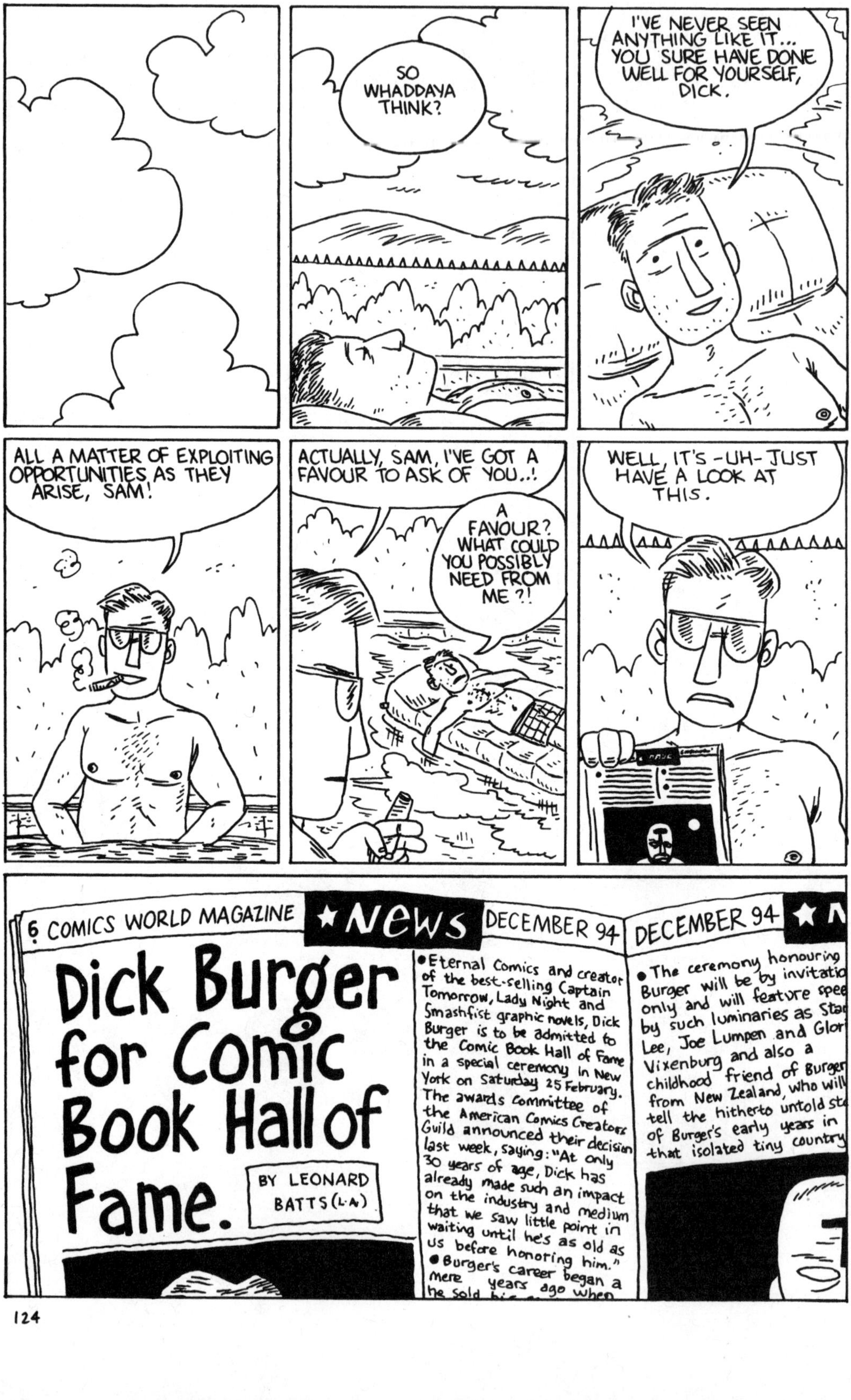
SO WHADDAYA THINK?
I'VE NEVER SEEN ANYTHING LIKE IT... YOU SURE HAVE DONE WELL FOR YOURSELF, DICK.
ALL A MATTER OF EXPLOITING OPPORTUNITIES AS THEY ARISE, SAM!
ACTUALLY, SAM, I'VE GOT A FAVOUR TO ASK OF YOU..!
A FAVOUR? WHAT COULD YOU POSSIBLY NEED FROM ME?!
WELL, IT'S -UH- JUST HAVE A LOOK AT THIS.
6 COMICS WORLD MAGAZINE
★NEWS
DECEMBER 94
DECEMBER 94
Dick Burger for Comic Book Hall of Fame.
BY LEONARD BATTS (L.A.)
●Eternal Comics and creator of the best-selling Captain Tomorrow, Lady Night and Smashfist graphic novels, Dick Burger is to be admitted to the Comic Book Hall of Fame in a special ceremony in New York on Saturday 25 February. The awards committee of the American Comics Creators Guild announced their decision last week, saying: "At only 30 years of age, Dick has already made such an impact on the industry and medium that we saw little point in waiting until he's as old as us before honoring him."
●Burger's career began a mere years ago when
●The ceremony honouring Burger will be by invitatio only and will feature spee by such luminaries as Sta Lee, Joe Lumpen and Glor Vixenburg and also a childhood friend of Burger from New Zealand, who will tell the hitherto untold st of Burger's early years in that isolated tiny country

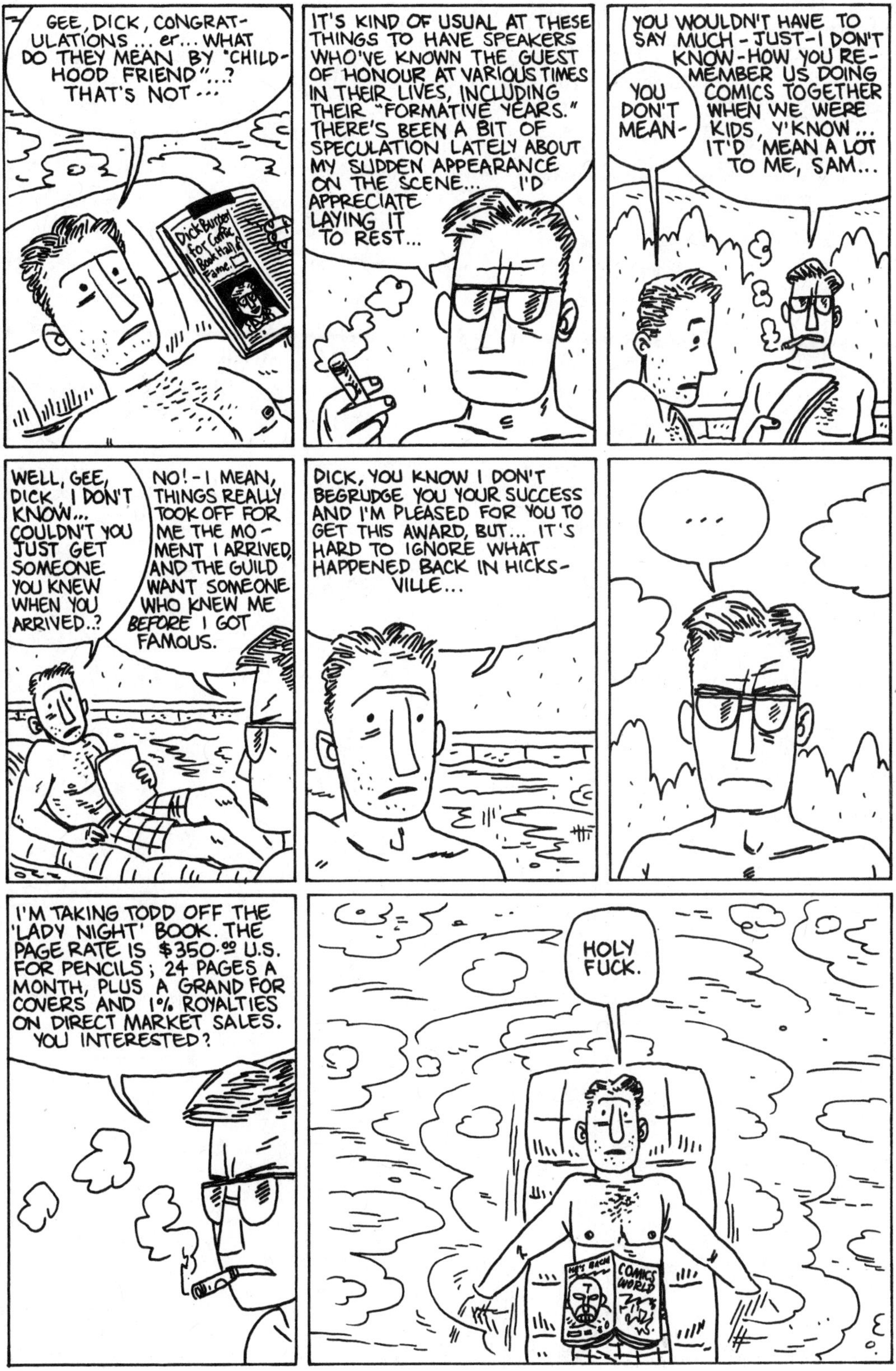
GEE, DICK, CONGRAT-ULATIONS... er... WHAT DO THEY MEAN BY "CHILD-HOOD FRIEND"...? THAT'S NOT...
Dick Burger for Comic Book Hall of Fame.
IT'S KIND OF USUAL AT THESE THINGS TO HAVE SPEAKERS WHO'VE KNOWN THE GUEST OF HONOUR AT VARIOUS TIMES IN THEIR LIVES, INCLUDING THEIR "FORMATIVE YEARS." THERE'S BEEN A BIT OF SPECULATION LATELY ABOUT MY SUDDEN APPEARANCE ON THE SCENE... I'D APPRECIATE LAYING IT TO REST...
YOU WOULDN'T HAVE TO SAY MUCH - JUST - I DON'T KNOW - HOW YOU RE-MEMBER US DOING COMICS TOGETHER WHEN WE WERE KIDS, Y'KNOW... IT'D MEAN A LOT TO ME, SAM...
YOU DON'T MEAN-
WELL, GEE, DICK, I DON'T KNOW... COULDN'T YOU JUST GET SOMEONE YOU KNEW WHEN YOU ARRIVED..?
NO! - I MEAN, THINGS REALLY TOOK OFF FOR ME THE MO-MENT I ARRIVED, AND THE GUILD WANT SOMEONE WHO KNEW ME BEFORE I GOT FAMOUS.
DICK, YOU KNOW I DON'T BEGRUDGE YOU YOUR SUCCESS AND I'M PLEASED FOR YOU TO GET THIS AWARD, BUT... IT'S HARD TO IGNORE WHAT HAPPENED BACK IN HICKS-VILLE...
...
I'M TAKING TODD OFF THE 'LADY NIGHT' BOOK. THE PAGE RATE IS $350.00 U.S. FOR PENCILS; 24 PAGES A MONTH, PLUS A GRAND FOR COVERS AND 1% ROYALTIES ON DIRECT MARKET SALES. YOU INTERESTED?
HOLY FUCK.
COMICS WORLD

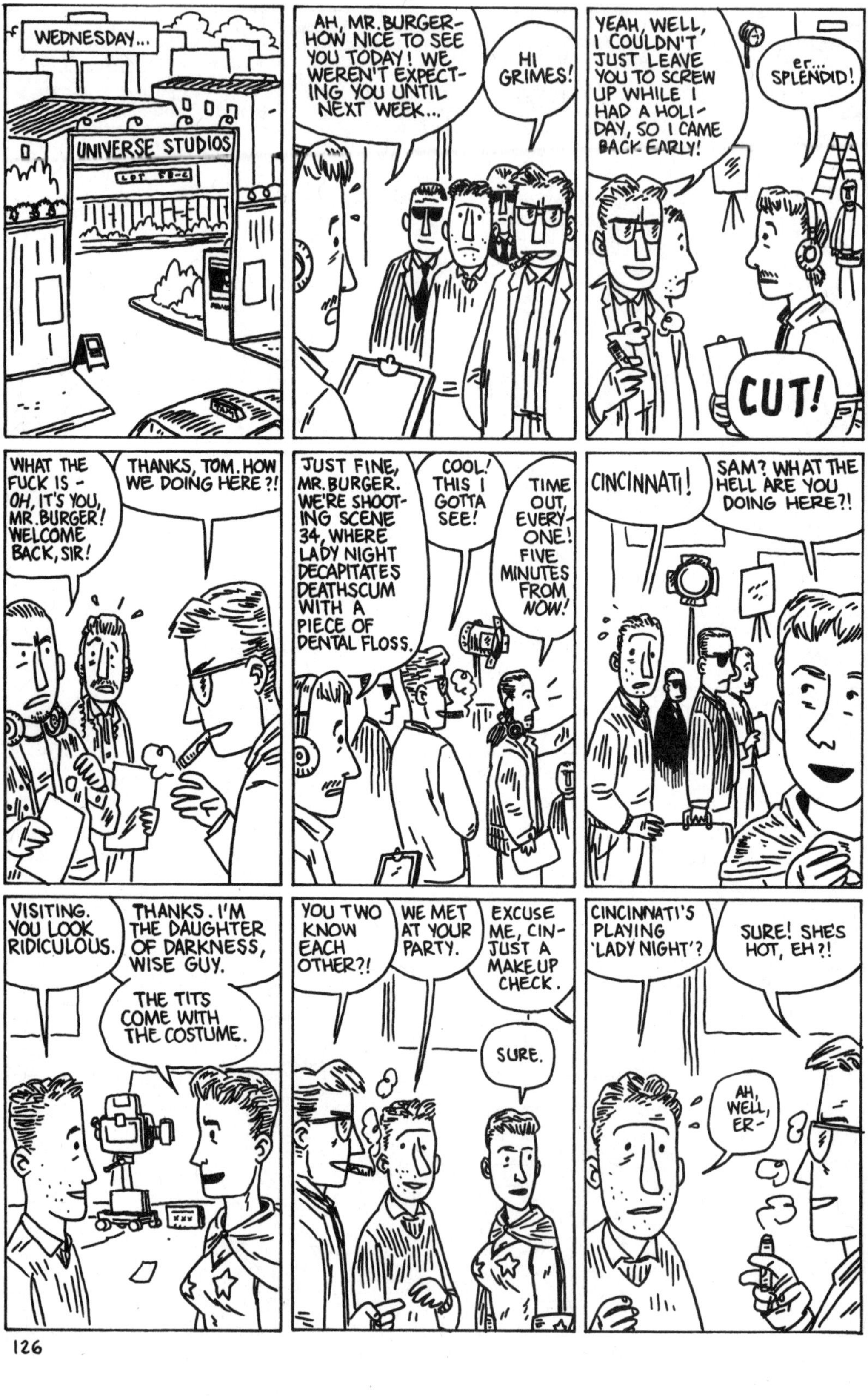

WEDNESDAY...
UNIVERSE STUDIOS
AH, MR. BURGER- HOW NICE TO SEE YOU TODAY! WE WEREN'T EXPECTING YOU UNTIL NEXT WEEK...
HI GRIMES!
YEAH, WELL, I COULDN'T JUST LEAVE YOU TO SCREW UP WHILE I HAD A HOLIDAY, SO I CAME BACK EARLY!
er... SPLENDID!
CUT!
WHAT THE FUCK IS - OH, IT'S YOU, MR. BURGER! WELCOME BACK, SIR!
THANKS, TOM. HOW WE DOING HERE?!
JUST FINE, MR. BURGER. WE'RE SHOOTING SCENE 34, WHERE LADY NIGHT DECAPITATES DEATHSCUM WITH A PIECE OF DENTAL FLOSS.
COOL! THIS I GOTTA SEE!
TIME OUT, EVERYONE! FIVE MINUTES FROM NOW!
CINCINNATI!
SAM? WHAT THE HELL ARE YOU DOING HERE?!
VISITING. YOU LOOK RIDICULOUS.
THANKS. I'M THE DAUGHTER OF DARKNESS, WISE GUY.
THE TITS COME WITH THE COSTUME.
YOU TWO KNOW EACH OTHER?!
WE MET AT YOUR PARTY.
EXCUSE ME, CIN - JUST A MAKEUP CHECK.
SURE.
CINCINNATI'S PLAYING 'LADY NIGHT'?
SURE! SHE'S HOT, EH?!
AH, WELL, ER-

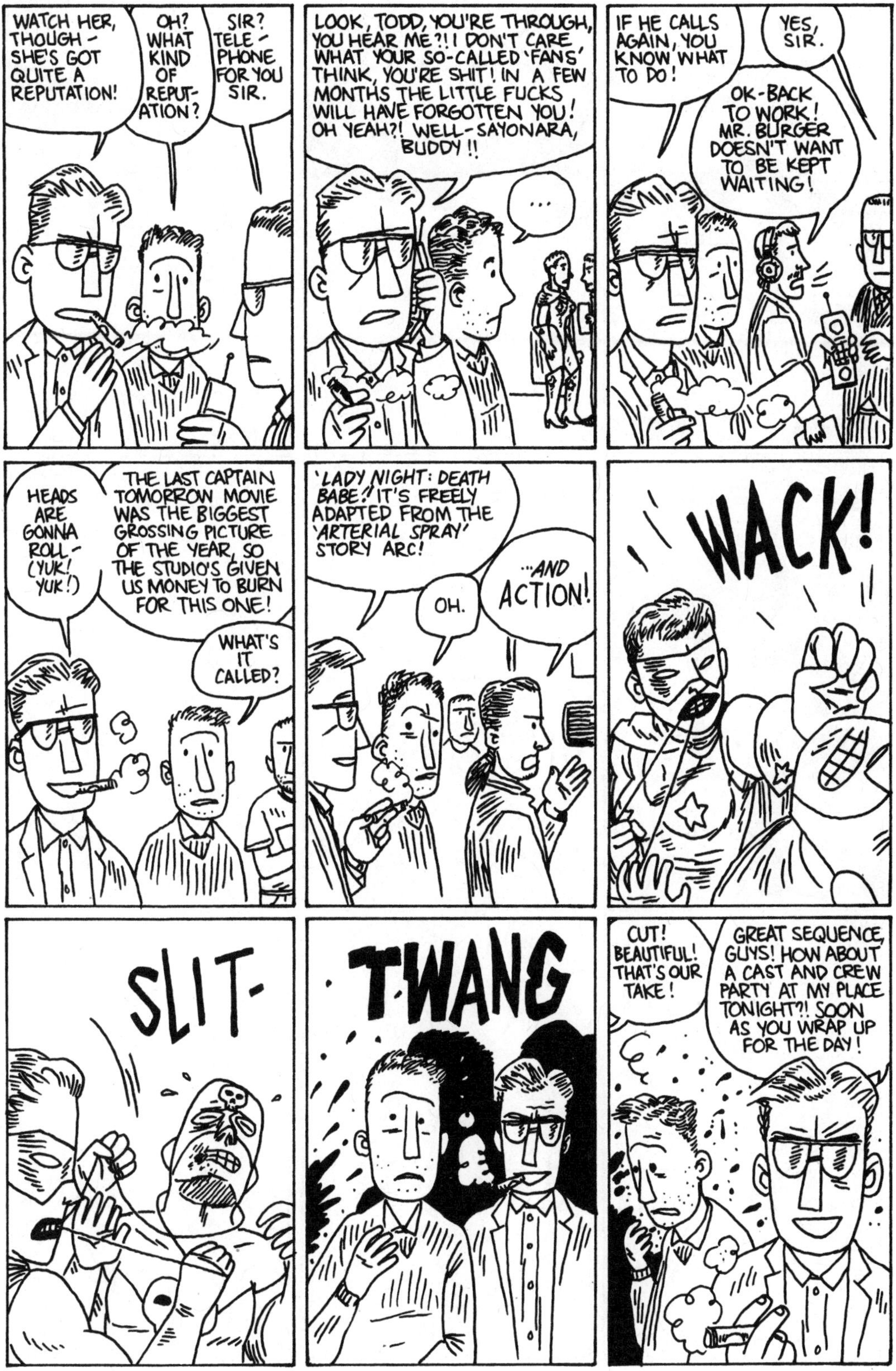
WATCH HER, THOUGH - SHE'S GOT QUITE A REPUTATION!
OH? WHAT KIND OF REPUTATION?
SIR? TELEPHONE FOR YOU SIR.
LOOK, TODD, YOU'RE THROUGH, YOU HEAR ME?! I DON'T CARE WHAT YOUR SO-CALLED 'FANS' THINK, YOU'RE SHIT! IN A FEW MONTHS THE LITTLE FUCKS WILL HAVE FORGOTTEN YOU! OH YEAH?! WELL - SAYONARA, BUDDY!!
...
IF HE CALLS AGAIN, YOU KNOW WHAT TO DO!
YES, SIR.
OK - BACK TO WORK! MR. BURGER DOESN'T WANT TO BE KEPT WAITING!
HEADS ARE GONNA ROLL - (YUK! YUK!)
THE LAST CAPTAIN TOMORROW MOVIE WAS THE BIGGEST GROSSING PICTURE OF THE YEAR, SO THE STUDIO'S GIVEN US MONEY TO BURN FOR THIS ONE!
WHAT'S IT CALLED?
'LADY NIGHT: DEATH BABE!' IT'S FREELY ADAPTED FROM THE 'ARTERIAL SPRAY' STORY ARC!
OH.
...AND ACTION!
WACK!
SLIT-
TWANG
CUT! BEAUTIFUL! THAT'S OUR TAKE!
GREAT SEQUENCE, GUYS! HOW ABOUT A CAST AND CREW PARTY AT MY PLACE TONIGHT?! SOON AS YOU WRAP UP FOR THE DAY!

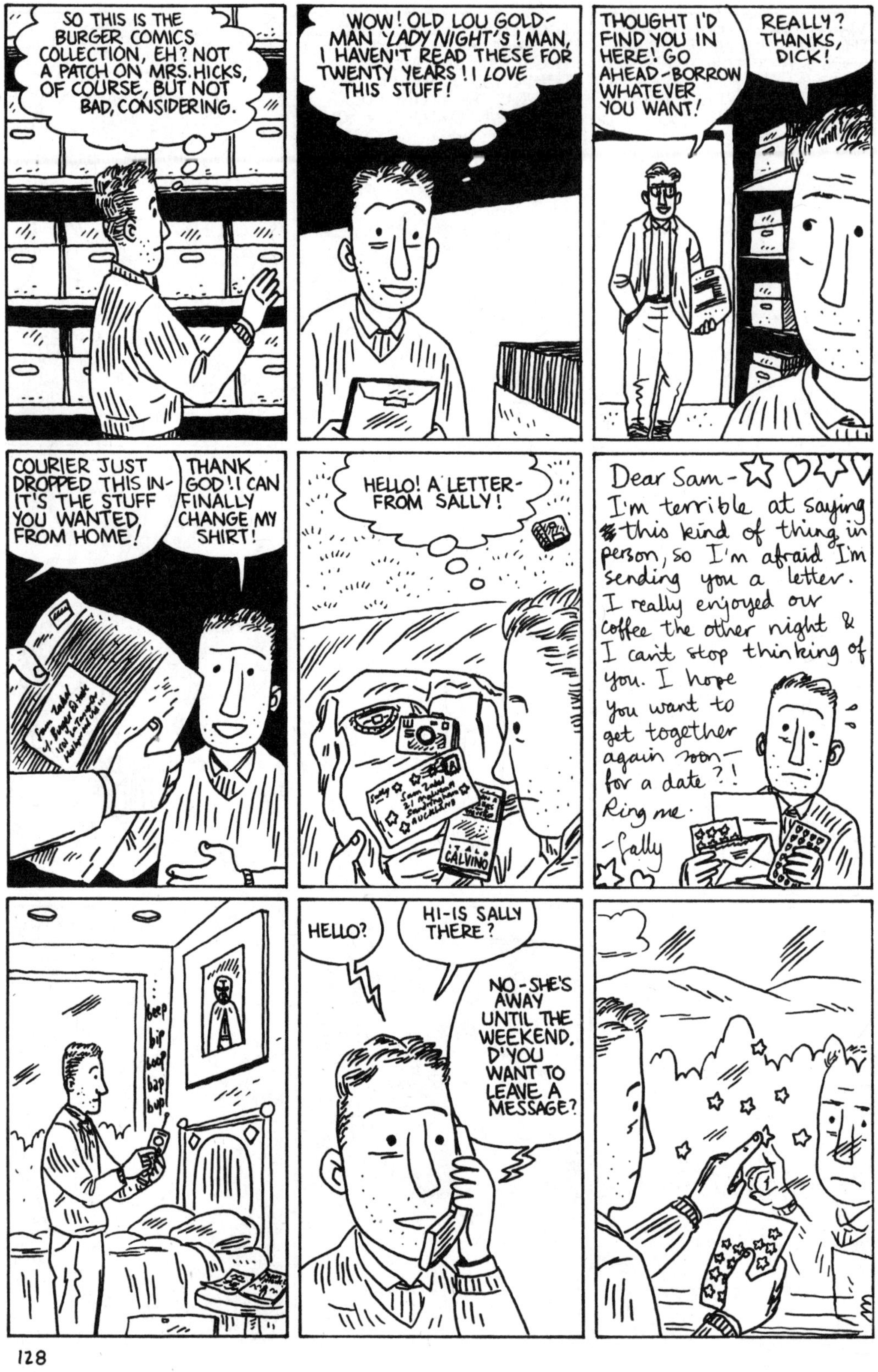
SO THIS IS THE BURGER COMICS COLLECTION, EH? NOT A PATCH ON MRS. HICKS, OF COURSE, BUT NOT BAD, CONSIDERING.
WOW! OLD LOU GOLDMAN 'LADY NIGHT'S! MAN, I HAVEN'T READ THESE FOR TWENTY YEARS!! I LOVE THIS STUFF!
THOUGHT I'D FIND YOU IN HERE! GO AHEAD-BORROW WHATEVER YOU WANT!
REALLY? THANKS, DICK!
COURIER JUST DROPPED THIS IN-IT'S THE STUFF YOU WANTED FROM HOME!
THANK GOD!! CAN FINALLY CHANGE MY SHIRT!
HELLO! A LETTER-FROM SALLY!
CALVINO
Dear Sam-
I'm terrible at saying this kind of thing in person, so I'm afraid I'm sending you a letter. I really enjoyed our coffee the other night & I can't stop thinking of you. I hope you want to get together again soon-for a date?! Ring me.
-Sally
beep bip boop bap bup!
HELLO?
HI-IS SALLY THERE?
NO-SHE'S AWAY UNTIL THE WEEKEND. D'YOU WANT TO LEAVE A MESSAGE?

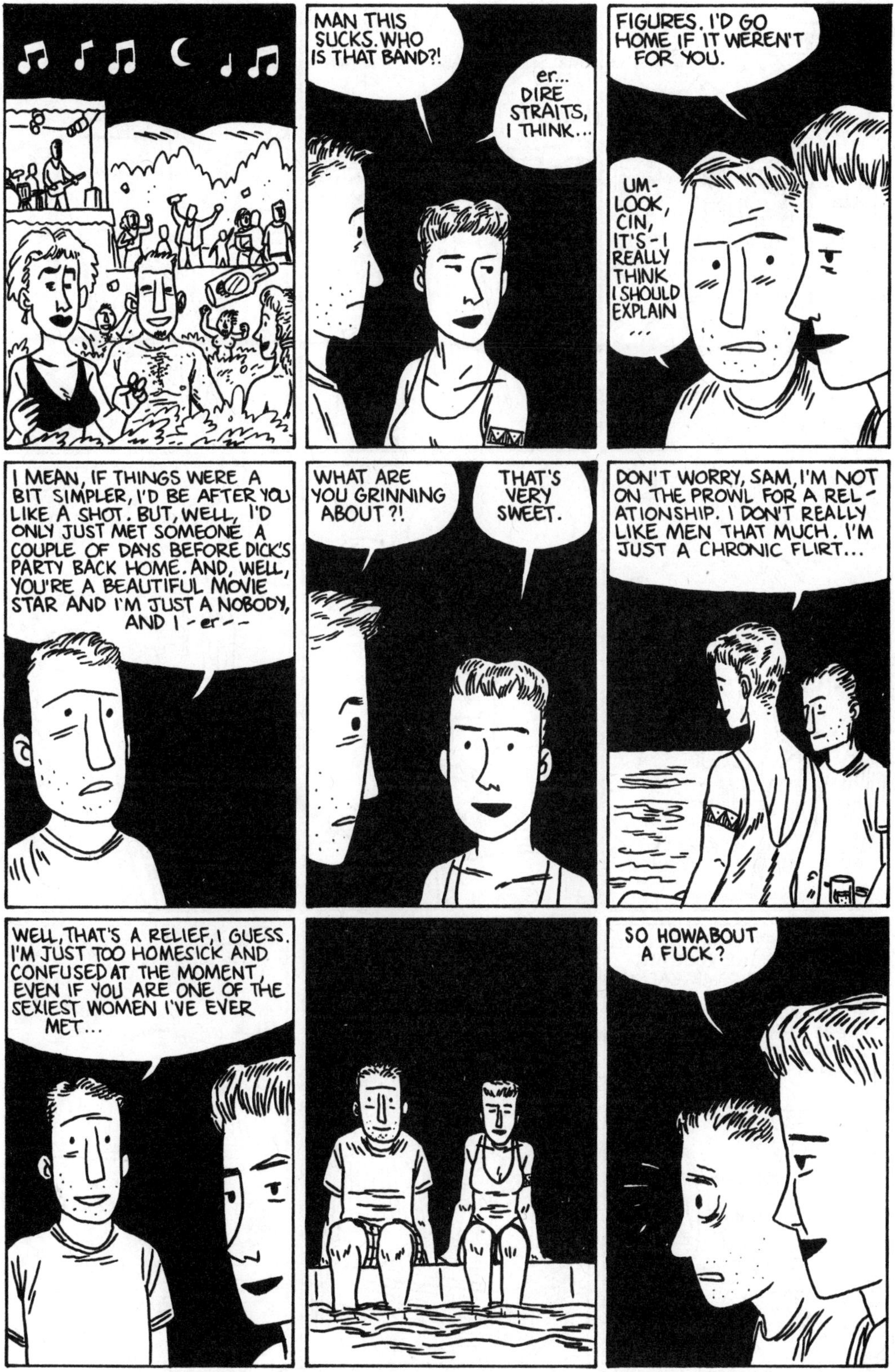
MAN THIS SUCKS. WHO IS THAT BAND?!
er... DIRE STRAITS, I THINK...
FIGURES. I'D GO HOME IF IT WEREN'T FOR YOU.
UM- LOOK, CIN, IT'S - I REALLY THINK I SHOULD EXPLAIN ...
I MEAN, IF THINGS WERE A BIT SIMPLER, I'D BE AFTER YOU LIKE A SHOT. BUT, WELL, I'D ONLY JUST MET SOMEONE A COUPLE OF DAYS BEFORE DICK'S PARTY BACK HOME. AND, WELL, YOU'RE A BEAUTIFUL MOVIE STAR AND I'M JUST A NOBODY, AND I - er - -
WHAT ARE YOU GRINNING ABOUT?!
THAT'S VERY SWEET.
DON'T WORRY, SAM, I'M NOT ON THE PROWL FOR A RELATIONSHIP. I DON'T REALLY LIKE MEN THAT MUCH. I'M JUST A CHRONIC FLIRT...
WELL, THAT'S A RELIEF, I GUESS. I'M JUST TOO HOMESICK AND CONFUSED AT THE MOMENT, EVEN IF YOU ARE ONE OF THE SEXIEST WOMEN I'VE EVER MET...
SO HOWABOUT A FUCK?

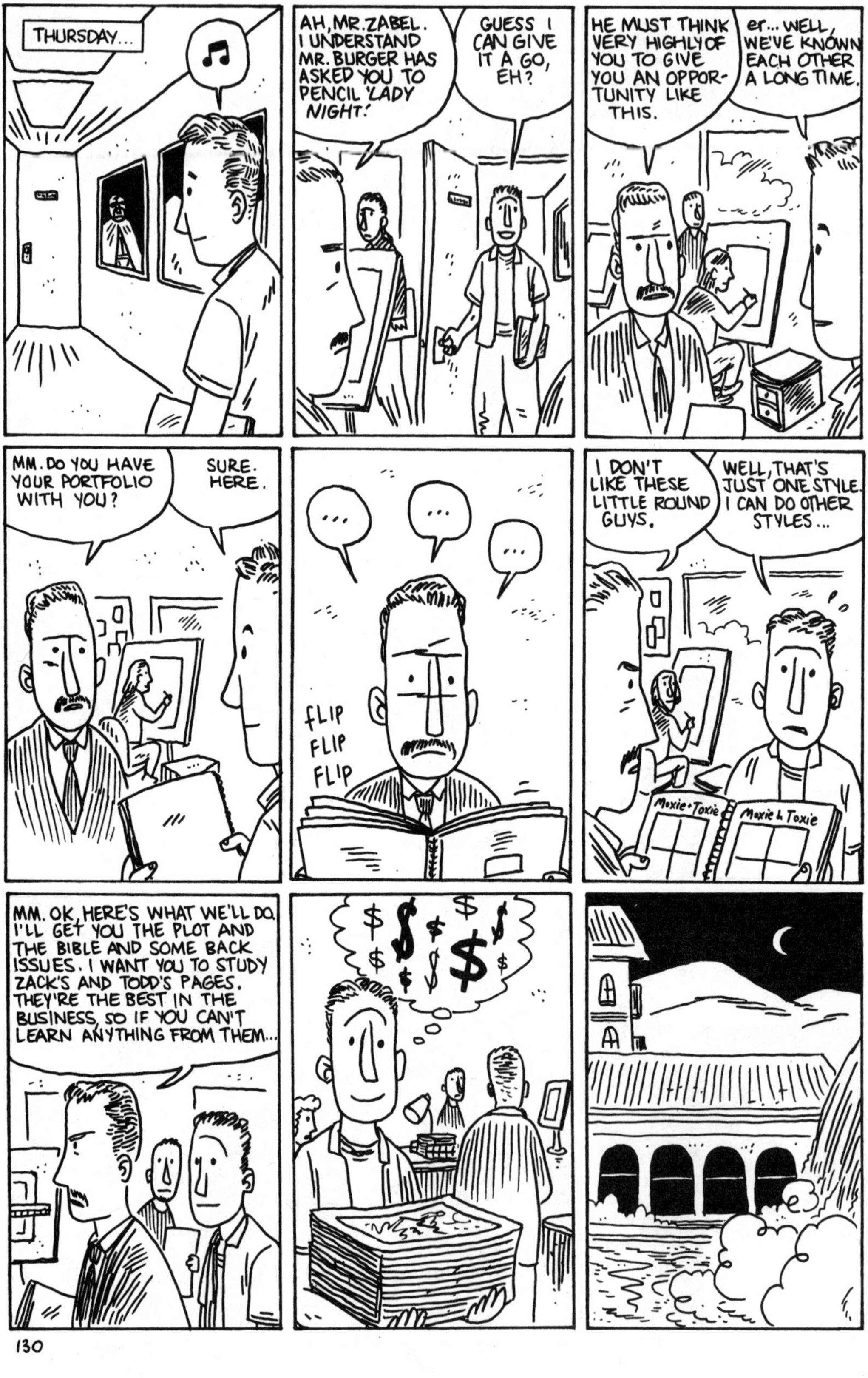

THURSDAY...
AH, MR. ZABEL. I UNDERSTAND MR. BURGER HAS ASKED YOU TO PENCIL 'LADY NIGHT.'
GUESS I CAN GIVE IT A GO, EH?
HE MUST THINK VERY HIGHLY OF YOU TO GIVE YOU AN OPPORTUNITY LIKE THIS.
er... WELL, WE'VE KNOWN EACH OTHER A LONG TIME.
MM. DO YOU HAVE YOUR PORTFOLIO WITH YOU?
SURE. HERE.
...
...
...
FLIP
FLIP
FLIP
I DON'T LIKE THESE LITTLE ROUND GUYS.
WELL, THAT'S JUST ONE STYLE. I CAN DO OTHER STYLES...
Moxie + Toxie
Moxie & Toxie
MM. OK, HERE'S WHAT WE'LL DO. I'LL GET YOU THE PLOT AND THE BIBLE AND SOME BACK ISSUES. I WANT YOU TO STUDY ZACK'S AND TODD'S PAGES. THEY'RE THE BEST IN THE BUSINESS, SO IF YOU CAN'T LEARN ANYTHING FROM THEM...

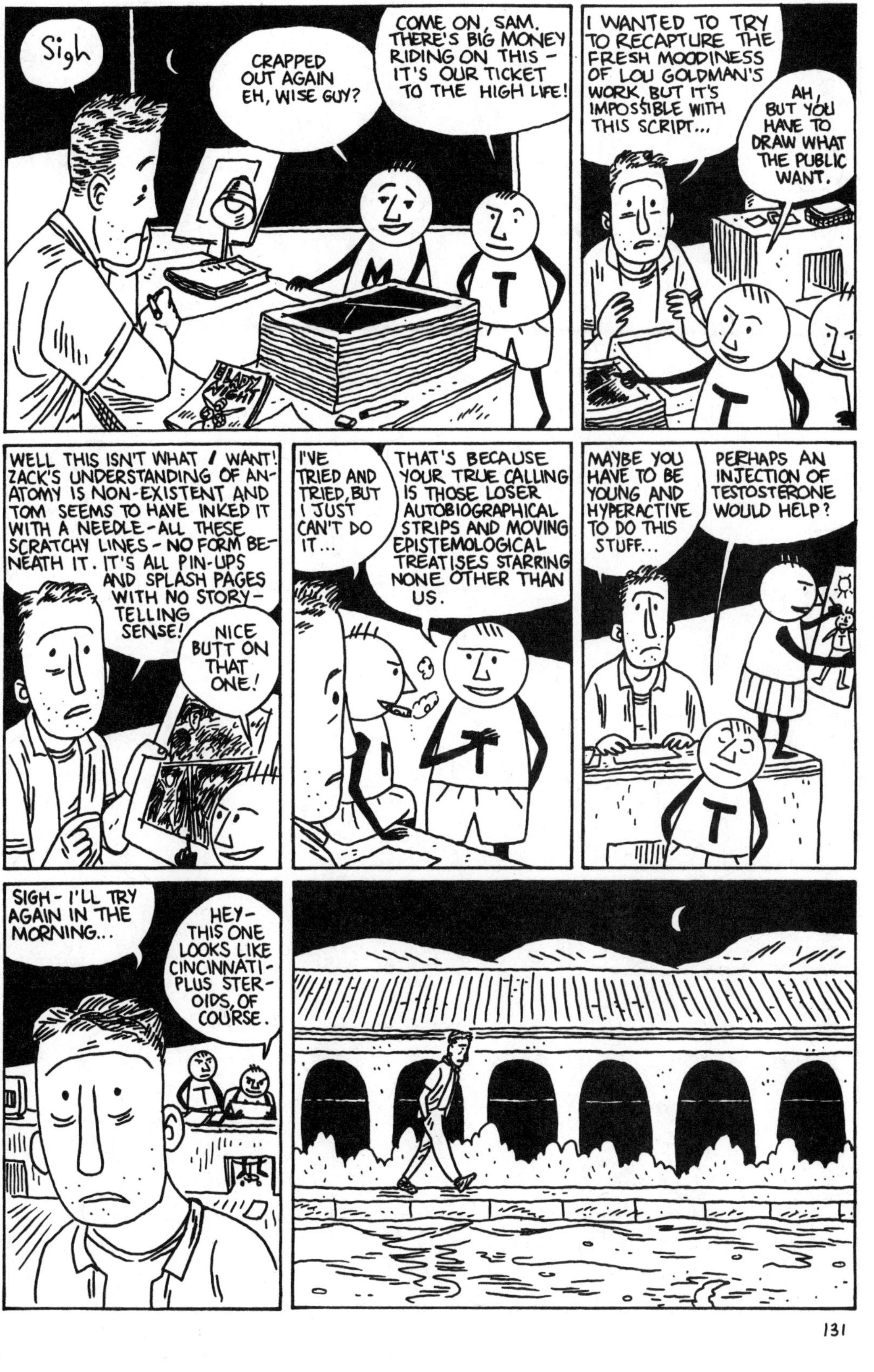

Sigh
CRAPPED OUT AGAIN EH, WISE GUY?
COME ON, SAM. THERE'S BIG MONEY RIDING ON THIS - IT'S OUR TICKET TO THE HIGH LIFE!
I WANTED TO TRY TO RECAPTURE THE FRESH MOODINESS OF LOU GOLDMAN'S WORK, BUT IT'S IMPOSSIBLE WITH THIS SCRIPT...
AH, BUT YOU HAVE TO DRAW WHAT THE PUBLIC WANT.
WELL THIS ISN'T WHAT I WANT! ZACK'S UNDERSTANDING OF ANATOMY IS NON-EXISTENT AND TOM SEEMS TO HAVE INKED IT WITH A NEEDLE - ALL THESE SCRATCHY LINES - NO FORM BENEATH IT. IT'S ALL PIN-UPS AND SPLASH PAGES WITH NO STORY-TELLING SENSE!
NICE BUTT ON THAT ONE!
I'VE TRIED AND TRIED, BUT I JUST CAN'T DO IT...
THAT'S BECAUSE YOUR TRUE CALLING IS THOSE LOSER AUTOBIOGRAPHICAL STRIPS AND MOVING EPISTEMOLOGICAL TREATISES STARRING NONE OTHER THAN US.
MAYBE YOU HAVE TO BE YOUNG AND HYPERACTIVE TO DO THIS STUFF...
PERHAPS AN INJECTION OF TESTOSTERONE WOULD HELP?
SIGH - I'LL TRY AGAIN IN THE MORNING...
HEY - THIS ONE LOOKS LIKE CINCINNATI - PLUS STEROIDS, OF COURSE.

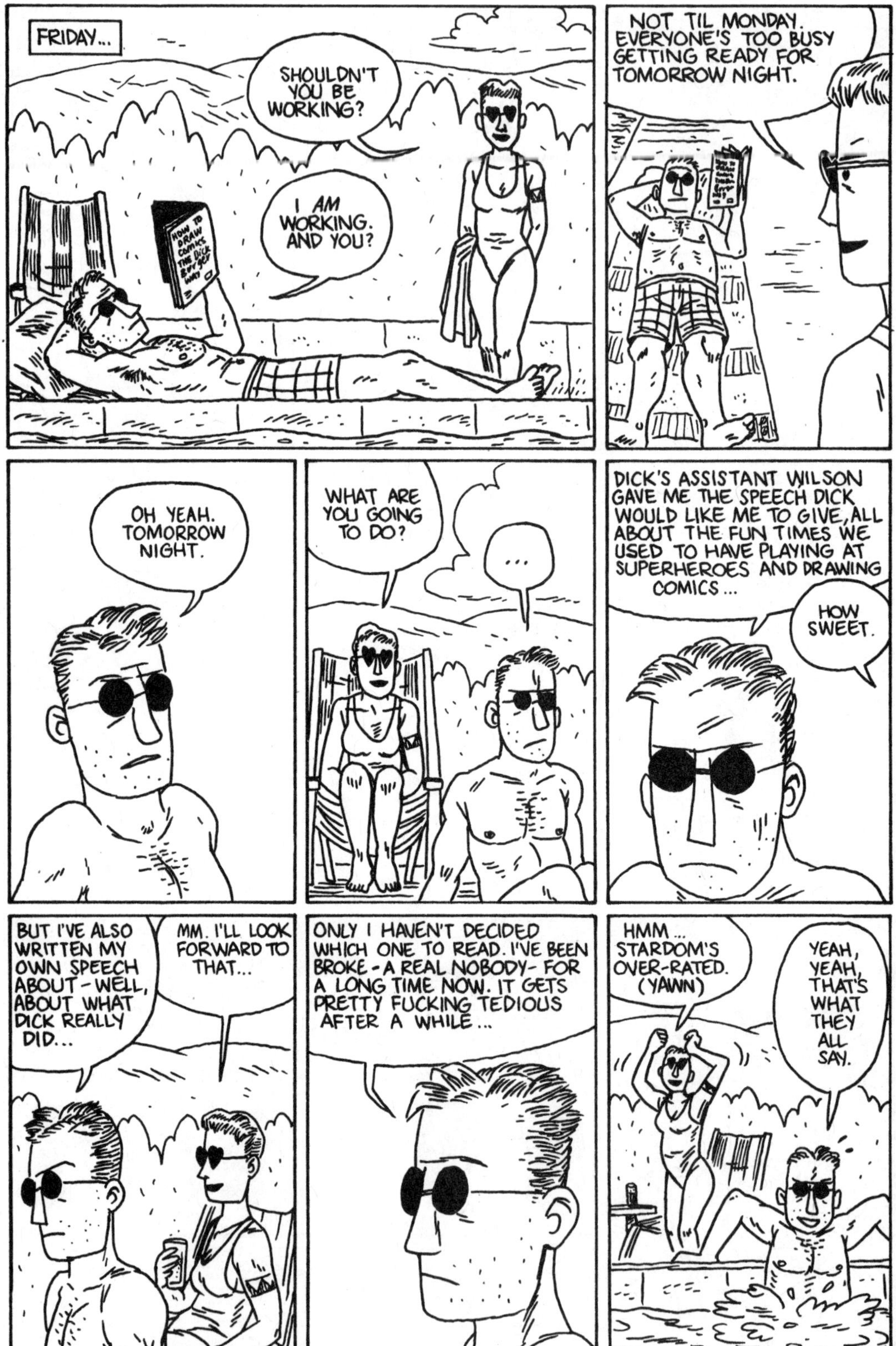
FRIDAY...
SHOULDN'T YOU BE WORKING?
I AM WORKING. AND YOU?
HOW TO DRAW COMICS THE DICK BURGER WAY
NOT TIL MONDAY. EVERYONE'S TOO BUSY GETTING READY FOR TOMORROW NIGHT.
OH YEAH. TOMORROW NIGHT.
WHAT ARE YOU GOING TO DO?
...
DICK'S ASSISTANT WILSON GAVE ME THE SPEECH DICK WOULD LIKE ME TO GIVE, ALL ABOUT THE FUN TIMES WE USED TO HAVE PLAYING AT SUPERHEROES AND DRAWING COMICS...
HOW SWEET.
BUT I'VE ALSO WRITTEN MY OWN SPEECH ABOUT - WELL, ABOUT WHAT DICK REALLY DID...
MM. I'LL LOOK FORWARD TO THAT...
ONLY I HAVEN'T DECIDED WHICH ONE TO READ. I'VE BEEN BROKE - A REAL NOBODY - FOR A LONG TIME NOW. IT GETS PRETTY FUCKING TEDIOUS AFTER A WHILE...
HMM... STARDOM'S OVER-RATED. (YAWN)
YEAH, YEAH, THAT'S WHAT THEY ALL SAY.

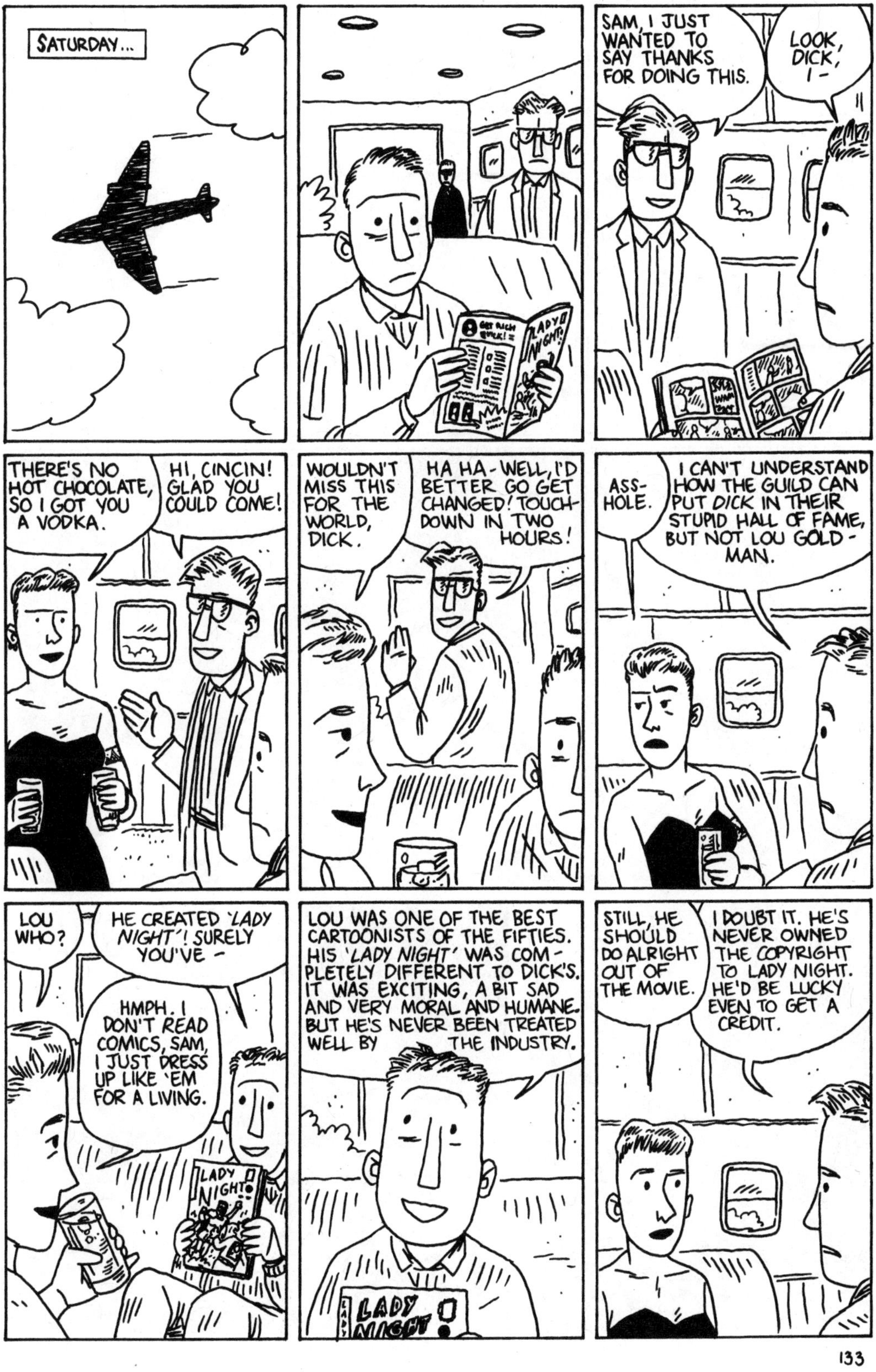
SATURDAY...
SAM, I JUST WANTED TO SAY THANKS FOR DOING THIS.
LOOK, DICK, I -
THERE'S NO HOT CHOCOLATE, SO I GOT YOU A VODKA.
HI, CINCIN! GLAD YOU COULD COME!
WOULDN'T MISS THIS FOR THE WORLD, DICK.
HA HA - WELL, I'D BETTER GO GET CHANGED! TOUCH-DOWN IN TWO HOURS!
ASS-HOLE.
I CAN'T UNDERSTAND HOW THE GUILD CAN PUT DICK IN THEIR STUPID HALL OF FAME, BUT NOT LOU GOLD-MAN.
LOU WHO?
HE CREATED 'LADY NIGHT'! SURELY YOU'VE -
HMPH. I DON'T READ COMICS, SAM, I JUST DRESS UP LIKE 'EM FOR A LIVING.
LADY NIGHT
LOU WAS ONE OF THE BEST CARTOONISTS OF THE FIFTIES. HIS 'LADY NIGHT' WAS COM-PLETELY DIFFERENT TO DICK'S. IT WAS EXCITING, A BIT SAD AND VERY MORAL AND HUMANE. BUT HE'S NEVER BEEN TREATED WELL BY THE INDUSTRY.
LADY NIGHT
STILL, HE SHOULD DO ALRIGHT OUT OF THE MOVIE.
I DOUBT IT. HE'S NEVER OWNED THE COPYRIGHT TO LADY NIGHT. HE'D BE LUCKY EVEN TO GET A CREDIT.

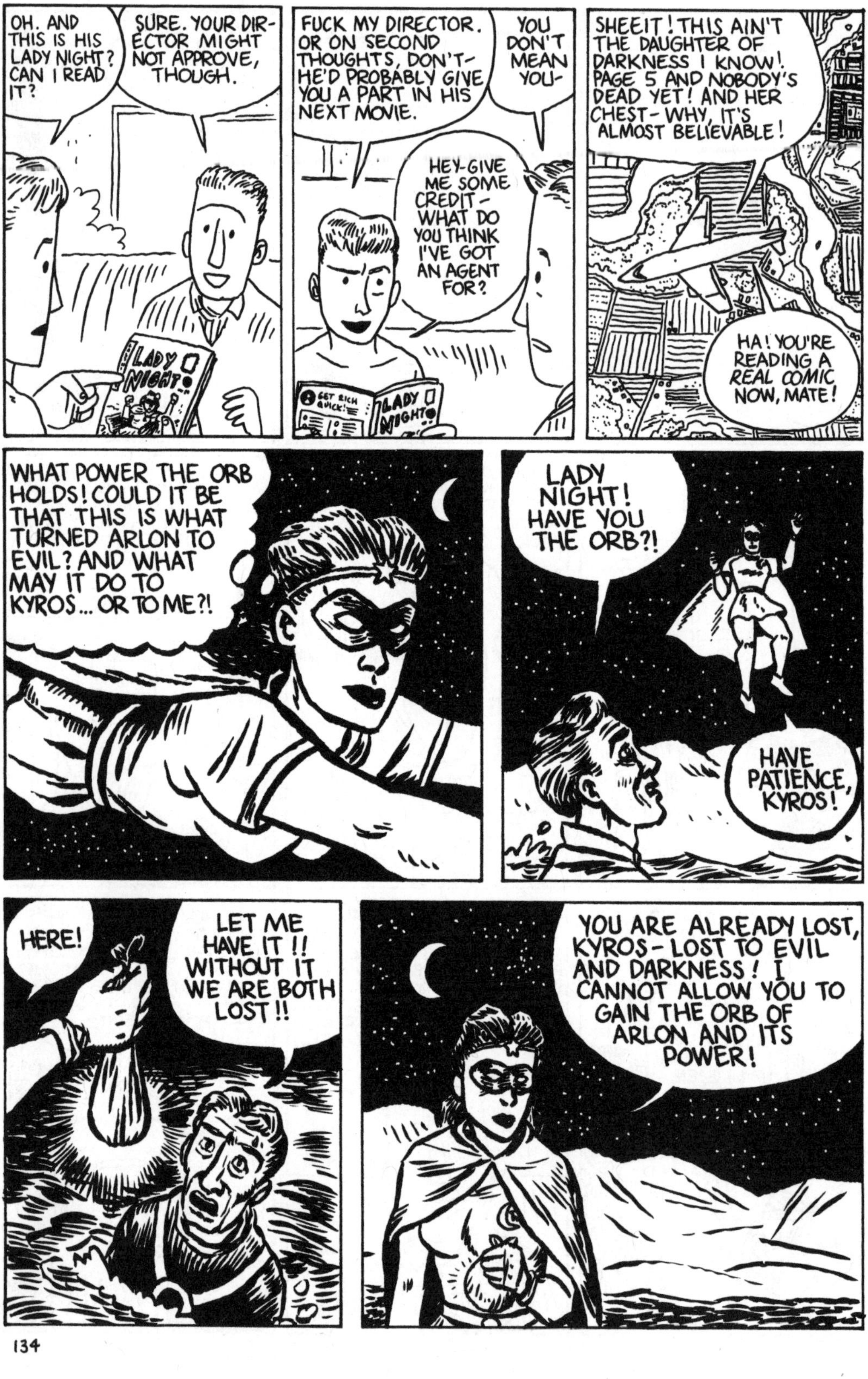
OH. AND THIS IS HIS LADY NIGHT? CAN I READ IT?
SURE. YOUR DIRECTOR MIGHT NOT APPROVE, THOUGH.
LADY NIGHT
FUCK MY DIRECTOR. OR ON SECOND THOUGHTS, DON'T- HE'D PROBABLY GIVE YOU A PART IN HIS NEXT MOVIE.
YOU DON'T MEAN YOU-
HEY-GIVE ME SOME CREDIT- WHAT DO YOU THINK I'VE GOT AN AGENT FOR?
GET RICH QUICK!
LADY NIGHT
SHEEIT! THIS AIN'T THE DAUGHTER OF DARKNESS I KNOW! PAGE 5 AND NOBODY'S DEAD YET! AND HER CHEST- WHY, IT'S ALMOST BELIEVABLE!
HA! YOU'RE READING A *REAL COMIC* NOW, MATE!
WHAT POWER THE ORB HOLDS! COULD IT BE THAT THIS IS WHAT TURNED ARLON TO EVIL? AND WHAT MAY IT DO TO KYROS... OR TO ME?!
LADY NIGHT! HAVE YOU THE ORB?!
HAVE PATIENCE, KYROS!
HERE!
LET ME HAVE IT!! WITHOUT IT WE ARE BOTH LOST!!
YOU ARE ALREADY LOST, KYROS- LOST TO EVIL AND DARKNESS! I CANNOT ALLOW YOU TO GAIN THE ORB OF ARLON AND ITS POWER!

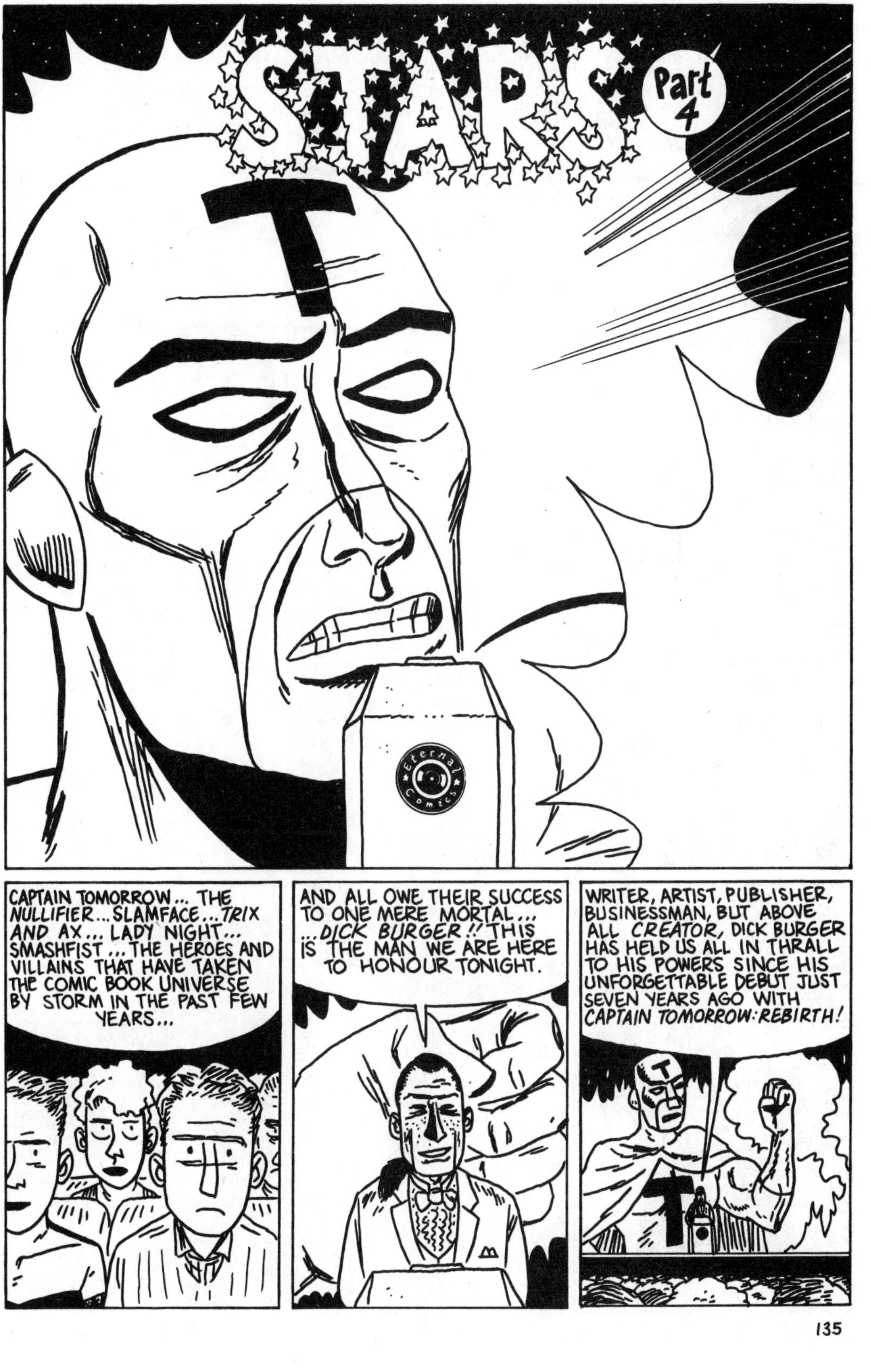
STARS
Part 4
Eternal Comics
CAPTAIN TOMORROW... THE NULLIFIER...SLAMFACE...TRIX AND AX... LADY NIGHT... SMASHFIST...THE HEROES AND VILLAINS THAT HAVE TAKEN THE COMIC BOOK UNIVERSE BY STORM IN THE PAST FEW YEARS...
AND ALL OWE THEIR SUCCESS TO ONE MERE MORTAL... ...DICK BURGER!! THIS IS THE MAN WE ARE HERE TO HONOUR TONIGHT.
WRITER, ARTIST, PUBLISHER, BUSINESSMAN, BUT ABOVE ALL CREATOR, DICK BURGER HAS HELD US ALL IN THRALL TO HIS POWERS SINCE HIS UNFORGETTABLE DEBUT JUST SEVEN YEARS AGO WITH CAPTAIN TOMORROW: REBIRTH!

...DICK'S THE BEST! HE'S A GREAT GUY! IF I'D HAD A GUY LIKE *HIM* IN THE *BULLPEN* THIRTY YEARS AGO, JUST THINK WHERE WE'D BE TODAY! OF COURSE I DID HAVE A GUY LIKE DICK BACK THEN ... AND HIS NAME WAS JACK KIRBY!!

I USED TO THINK NO-ONE COULD EVER REACH JACK'S LEVEL OF GENIUS, BUT THAT WAS BEFORE DICK CAME ALONG. *DICK*—YOU ARE THE GREATEST GUY I'VE EVER KNOWN... AND, DICK, DON'T FORGET TO SPELL MY NAME RIGHT ON THE CHECK!

HAHAHAHAHA

EVER SINCE THE LAUNCH OF *CAPTAIN TOMORROW:REBIRTH*, DICK BURGER HAS BEEN *THE* CREATIVE FORCE IN COMICS. MORE RECENTLY HE WENT ON TO BECOME THE MOST IMPORTANT FIGURE IN THE *BUSINESS* OF COMICS AS WELL.

IT IS MY BELIEF THAT DICK WILL LEAD US INTO THE NEXT CENTURY AND BEYOND—INTO A NEW AND UNPRECEDENTED ERA IN COMIC BOOK HISTORY, IN TERMS OF POPULARITY, FINANCIAL GROWTH AND MOST IMPORTANTLY, CREATIVE SUCCESS NEVER DREAMED OF...

WITH THE RELEASE OF THE FORTHCOMING *LADY NIGHT* MOTION PICTURE, I AM SURE DICK BURGER WILL USHER IN A NEW GOLDEN AGE FOR AMERICAN COMIC ART.

AND OUR NEXT SPEAKER IS NONE OTHER THAN THE CREATOR OF THE GOLDEN AGE *LADY NIGHT* HIMSELF... *LOU GOLDMAN!!*

CLAPCLAPCLA

-AHHEM- ...THE FIRST TIME I SAW DICK BURGER WAS UP AT THE ETERNAL OFFICES. I WAS DROPPING IN A JOB AND THERE WAS DICK, KIDDING AROUND WITH ED TOGLIANI, ACTING OUT A CAPTAIN TOMORROW FIGHT SCENE. AND I THOUGHT TO MYSELF: WHO *IS* THIS IDIOT?

YOU'RE NEXT, MR. ZABEL.

HAHAHAHA

SO NOW I KNOW.

HAHAHAHA HAHA!

CONGRATULATIONS DICK...

CLAP CLAP CLAP

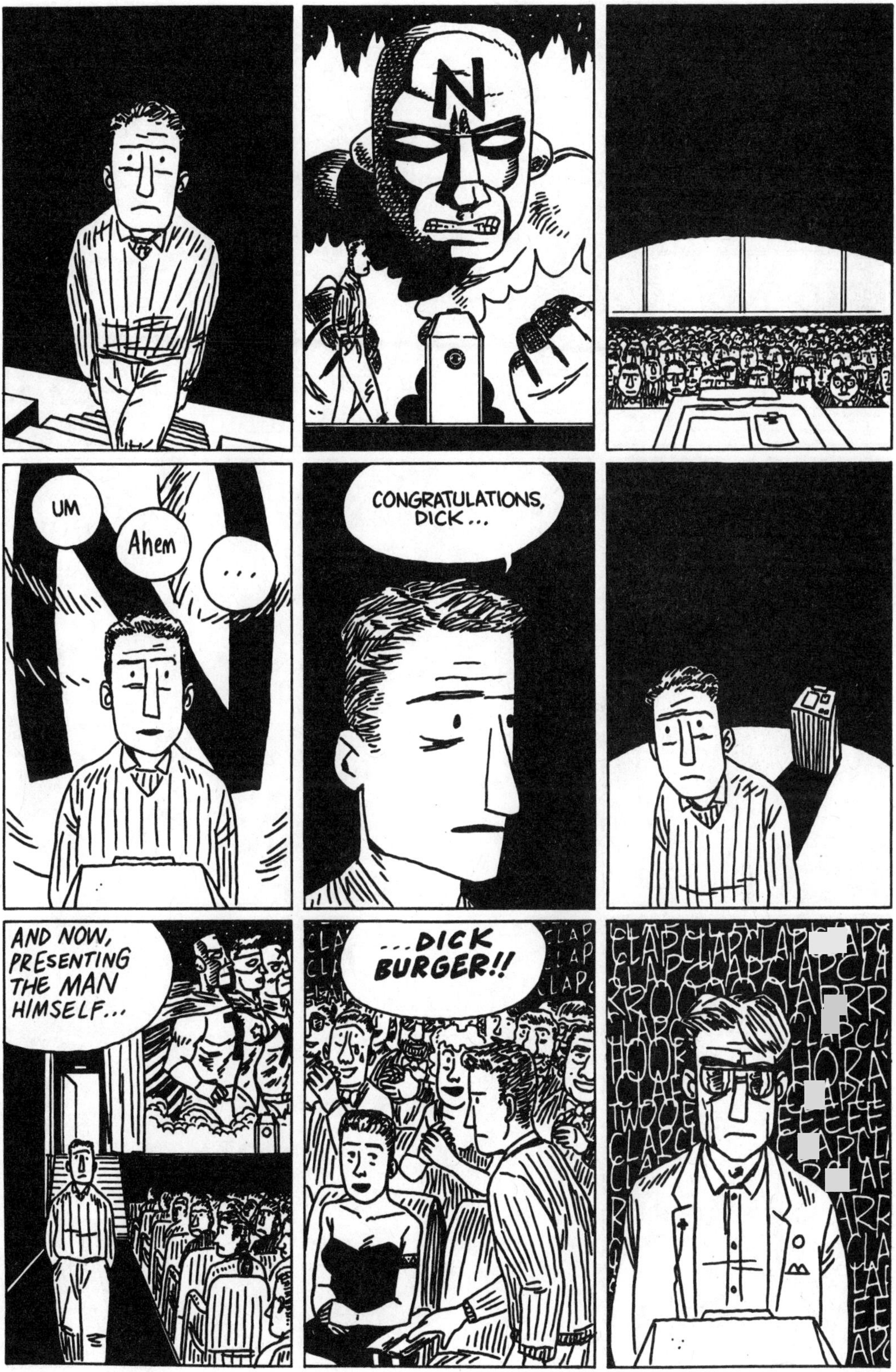
UM
Ahem
...
CONGRATULATIONS, DICK...
AND NOW, PRESENTING THE MAN HIMSELF...
...DICK BURGER!!

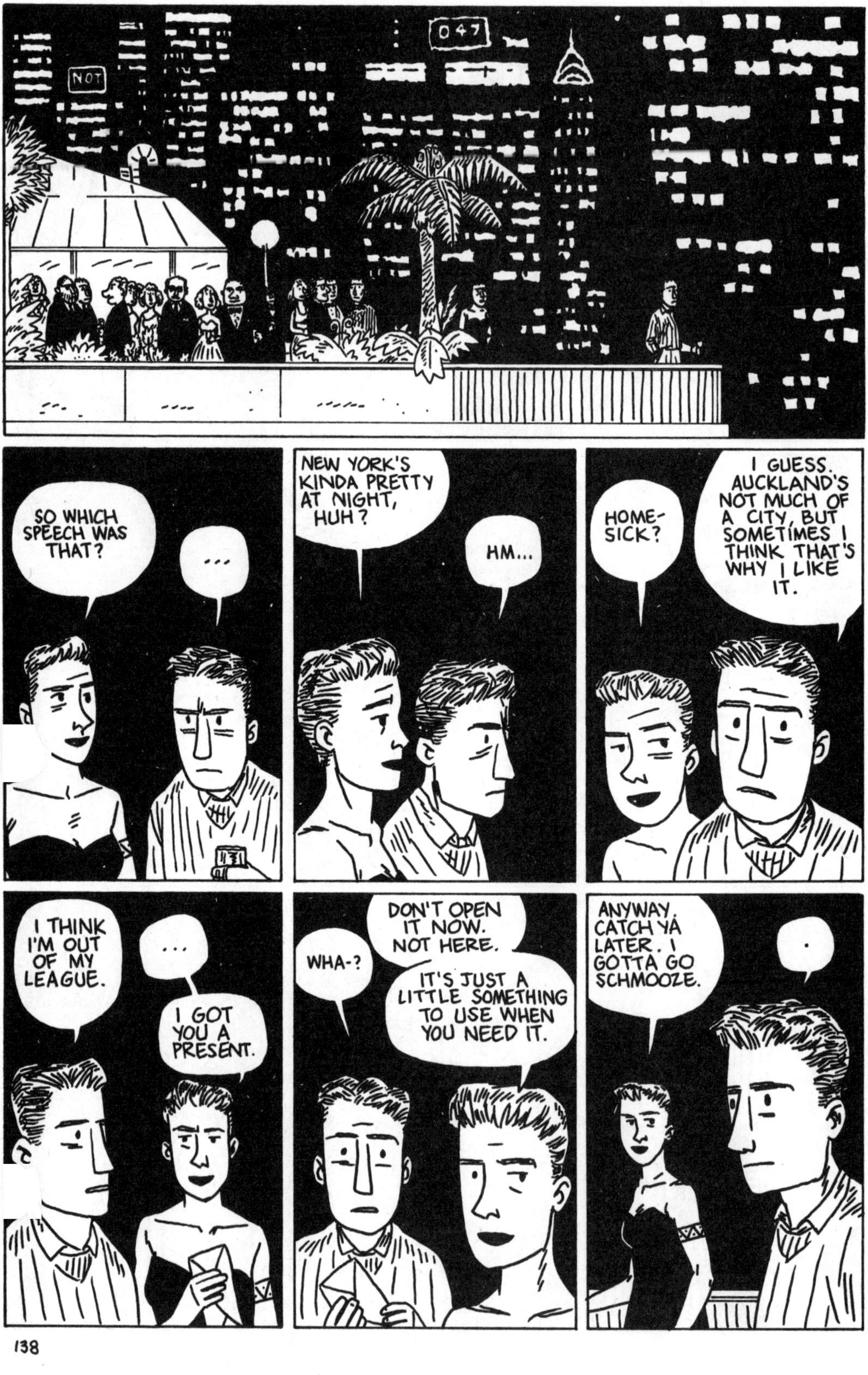
NOT
047
SO WHICH SPEECH WAS THAT?
...
NEW YORK'S KINDA PRETTY AT NIGHT, HUH?
HM...
HOME-SICK?
I GUESS. AUCKLAND'S NOT MUCH OF A CITY, BUT SOMETIMES I THINK THAT'S WHY I LIKE IT.
I THINK I'M OUT OF MY LEAGUE.
...
I GOT YOU A PRESENT.
WHA-?
DON'T OPEN IT NOW. NOT HERE.
IT'S JUST A LITTLE SOMETHING TO USE WHEN YOU NEED IT.
ANYWAY, CATCH YA LATER. I GOTTA GO SCHMOOZE.
.

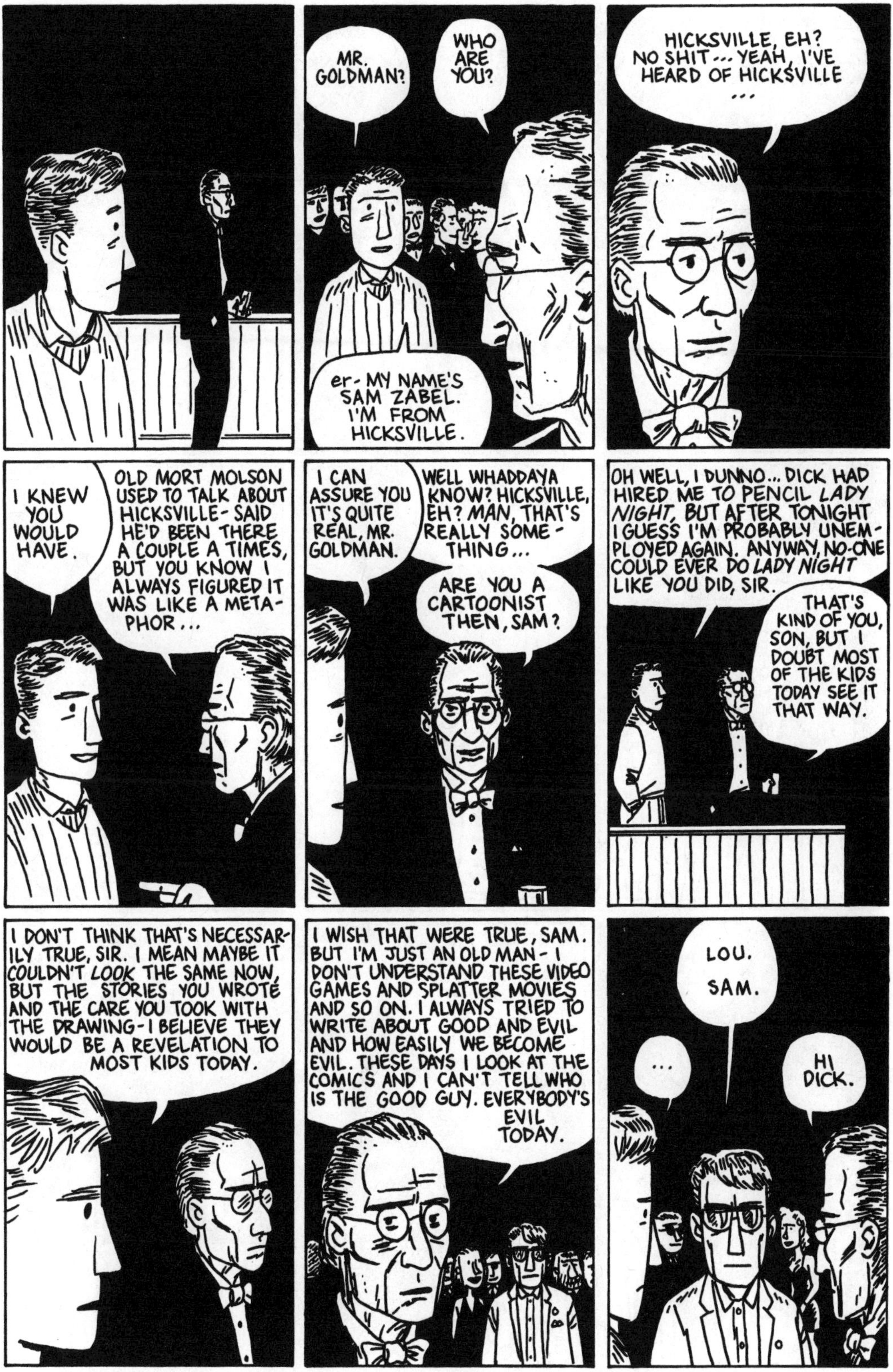

MR. GOLDMAN?
WHO ARE YOU?
er- MY NAME'S SAM ZABEL. I'M FROM HICKSVILLE.
HICKSVILLE, EH? NO SHIT... YEAH, I'VE HEARD OF HICKSVILLE ...
I KNEW YOU WOULD HAVE.
OLD MORT MOLSON USED TO TALK ABOUT HICKSVILLE- SAID HE'D BEEN THERE A COUPLE A TIMES, BUT YOU KNOW I ALWAYS FIGURED IT WAS LIKE A METAPHOR...
I CAN ASSURE YOU IT'S QUITE REAL, MR. GOLDMAN.
WELL WHADDAYA KNOW? HICKSVILLE, EH? MAN, THAT'S REALLY SOMETHING...
ARE YOU A CARTOONIST THEN, SAM?
OH WELL, I DUNNO... DICK HAD HIRED ME TO PENCIL LADY NIGHT, BUT AFTER TONIGHT I GUESS I'M PROBABLY UNEMPLOYED AGAIN. ANYWAY, NO-ONE COULD EVER DO LADY NIGHT LIKE YOU DID, SIR.
THAT'S KIND OF YOU, SON, BUT I DOUBT MOST OF THE KIDS TODAY SEE IT THAT WAY.
I DON'T THINK THAT'S NECESSARILY TRUE, SIR. I MEAN MAYBE IT COULDN'T LOOK THE SAME NOW, BUT THE STORIES YOU WROTE AND THE CARE YOU TOOK WITH THE DRAWING- I BELIEVE THEY WOULD BE A REVELATION TO MOST KIDS TODAY.
I WISH THAT WERE TRUE, SAM. BUT I'M JUST AN OLD MAN- I DON'T UNDERSTAND THESE VIDEO GAMES AND SPLATTER MOVIES AND SO ON. I ALWAYS TRIED TO WRITE ABOUT GOOD AND EVIL AND HOW EASILY WE BECOME EVIL. THESE DAYS I LOOK AT THE COMICS AND I CAN'T TELL WHO IS THE GOOD GUY. EVERYBODY'S EVIL TODAY.
LOU.
SAM.
...
HI DICK.

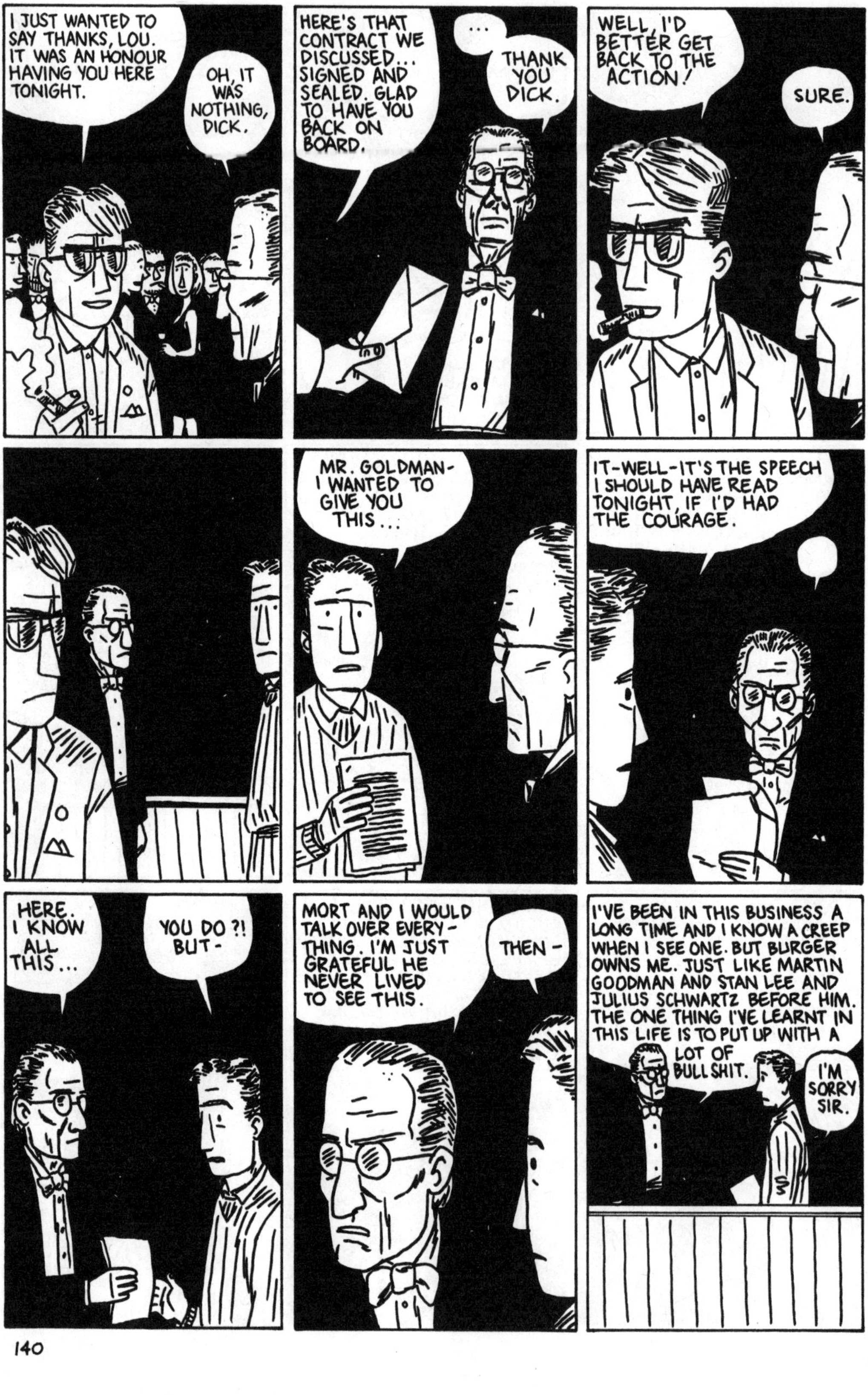
I JUST WANTED TO SAY THANKS, LOU. IT WAS AN HONOUR HAVING YOU HERE TONIGHT.
OH, IT WAS NOTHING, DICK.
HERE'S THAT CONTRACT WE DISCUSSED... SIGNED AND SEALED. GLAD TO HAVE YOU BACK ON BOARD.
...
THANK YOU DICK.
WELL, I'D BETTER GET BACK TO THE ACTION!
SURE.
MR. GOLDMAN- I WANTED TO GIVE YOU THIS...
IT-WELL-IT'S THE SPEECH I SHOULD HAVE READ TONIGHT, IF I'D HAD THE COURAGE.
HERE. I KNOW ALL THIS...
YOU DO?! BUT-
MORT AND I WOULD TALK OVER EVERY-THING. I'M JUST GRATEFUL HE NEVER LIVED TO SEE THIS.
THEN-
I'VE BEEN IN THIS BUSINESS A LONG TIME AND I KNOW A CREEP WHEN I SEE ONE. BUT BURGER OWNS ME. JUST LIKE MARTIN GOODMAN AND STAN LEE AND JULIUS SCHWARTZ BEFORE HIM. THE ONE THING I'VE LEARNT IN THIS LIFE IS TO PUT UP WITH A LOT OF BULLSHIT.
I'M SORRY SIR.

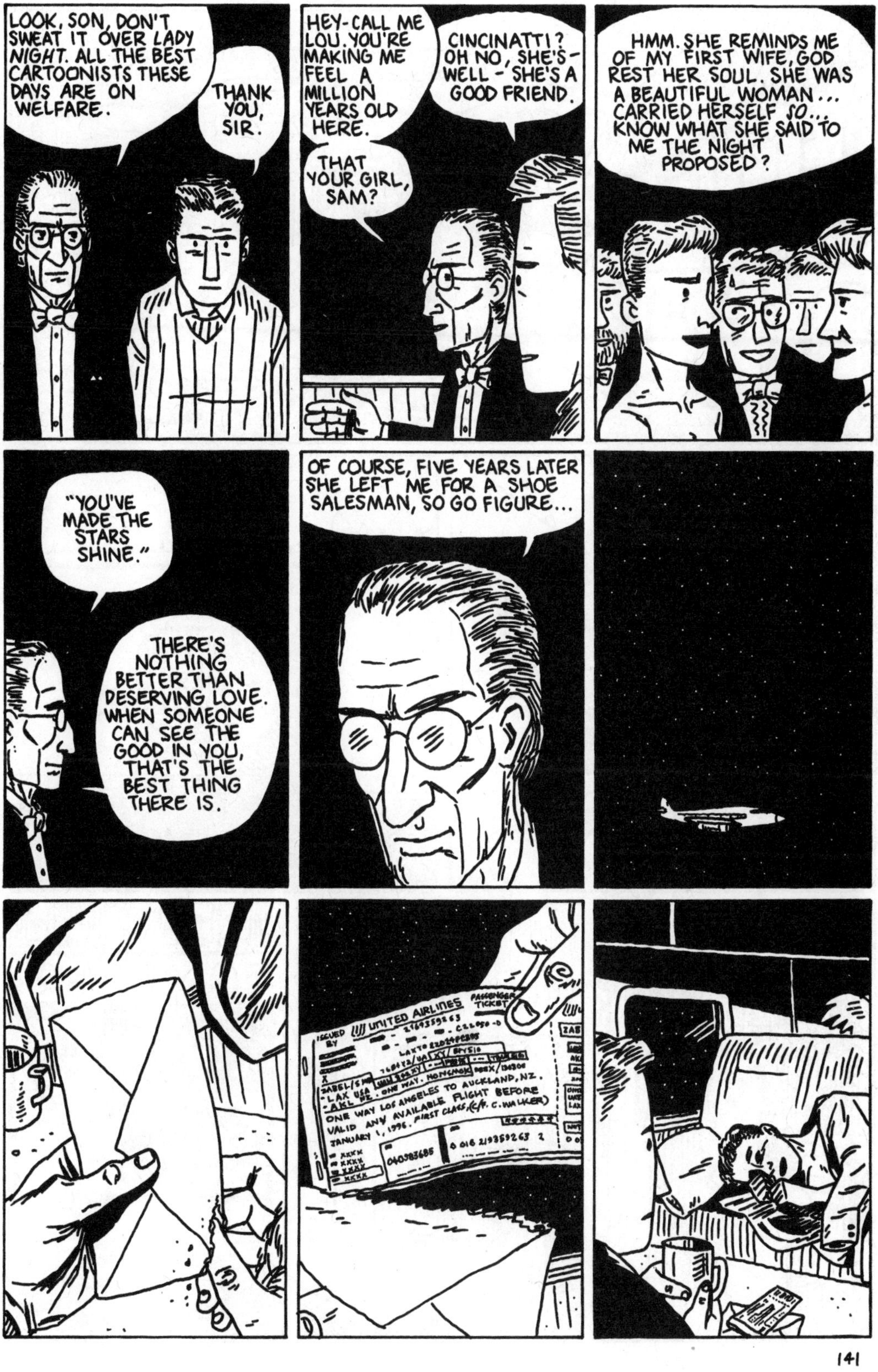
LOOK, SON, DON'T SWEAT IT OVER *LADY NIGHT*. ALL THE BEST CARTOONISTS THESE DAYS ARE ON WELFARE.
THANK YOU, SIR.
HEY- CALL ME LOU. YOU'RE MAKING ME FEEL A MILLION YEARS OLD HERE.
THAT YOUR GIRL, SAM?
CINCINATTI? OH NO, SHE'S- WELL - SHE'S A GOOD FRIEND.
HMM. SHE REMINDS ME OF MY FIRST WIFE, GOD REST HER SOUL. SHE WAS A BEAUTIFUL WOMAN... CARRIED HERSELF *SO*... KNOW WHAT SHE SAID TO ME THE NIGHT I PROPOSED?
"YOU'VE MADE THE STARS SHINE."
THERE'S NOTHING BETTER THAN DESERVING LOVE. WHEN SOMEONE CAN SEE THE GOOD IN YOU, THAT'S THE BEST THING THERE IS.
OF COURSE, FIVE YEARS LATER SHE LEFT ME FOR A SHOE SALESMAN, SO GO FIGURE...
UNITED AIRLINES
PASSENGER TICKET
ONE WAY LOS ANGELES TO AUCKLAND, NZ.
VALID ANY AVAILABLE FLIGHT BEFORE
JANUARY 1, 1996. FIRST CLASS

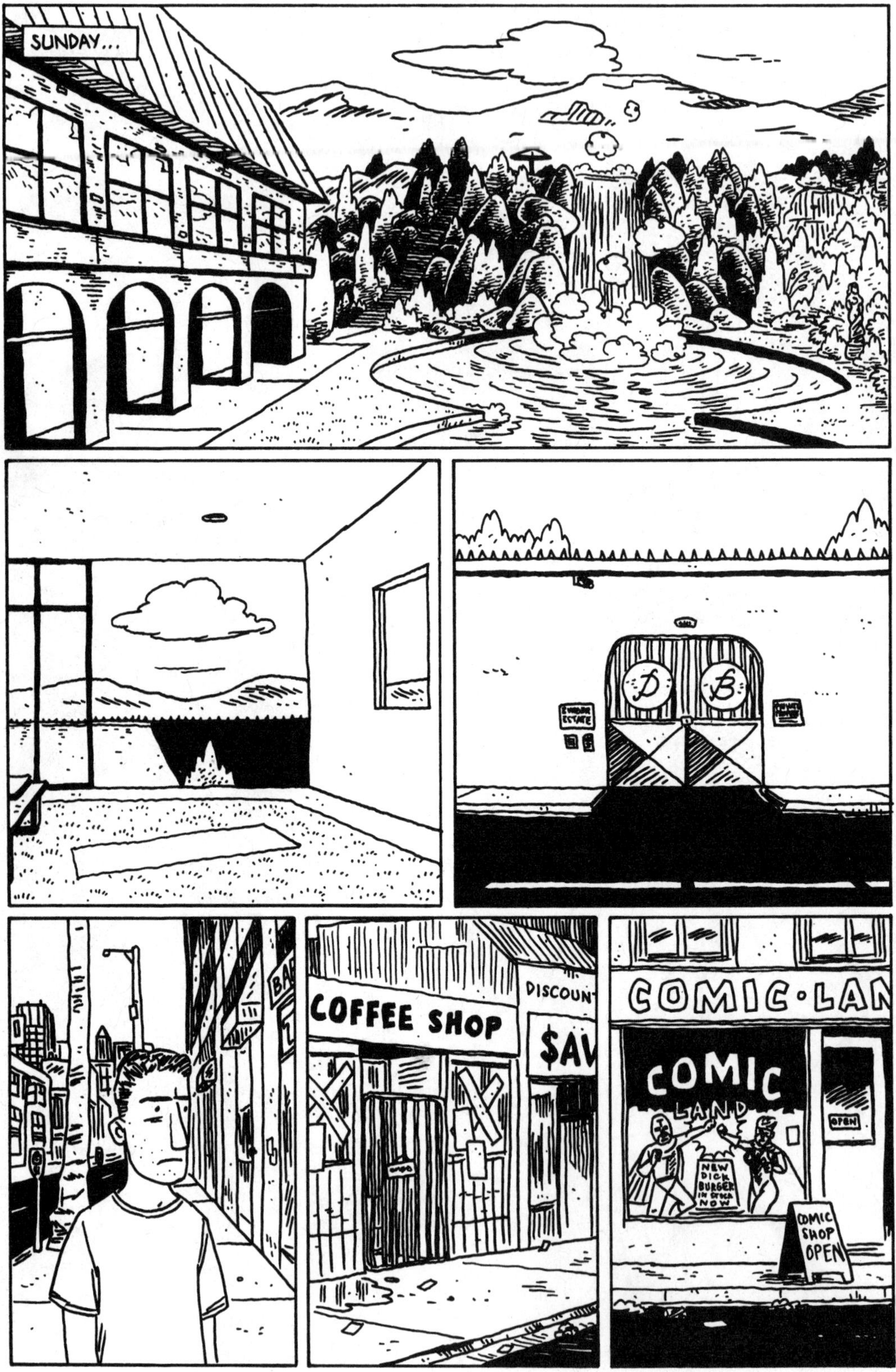
SUNDAY...
COFFEE SHOP
DISCOUNT
$AV
COMIC·LAN
COMIC
LAND
OPEN
NEW DICK BURGER IN STOCK NOW
COMIC SHOP OPEN

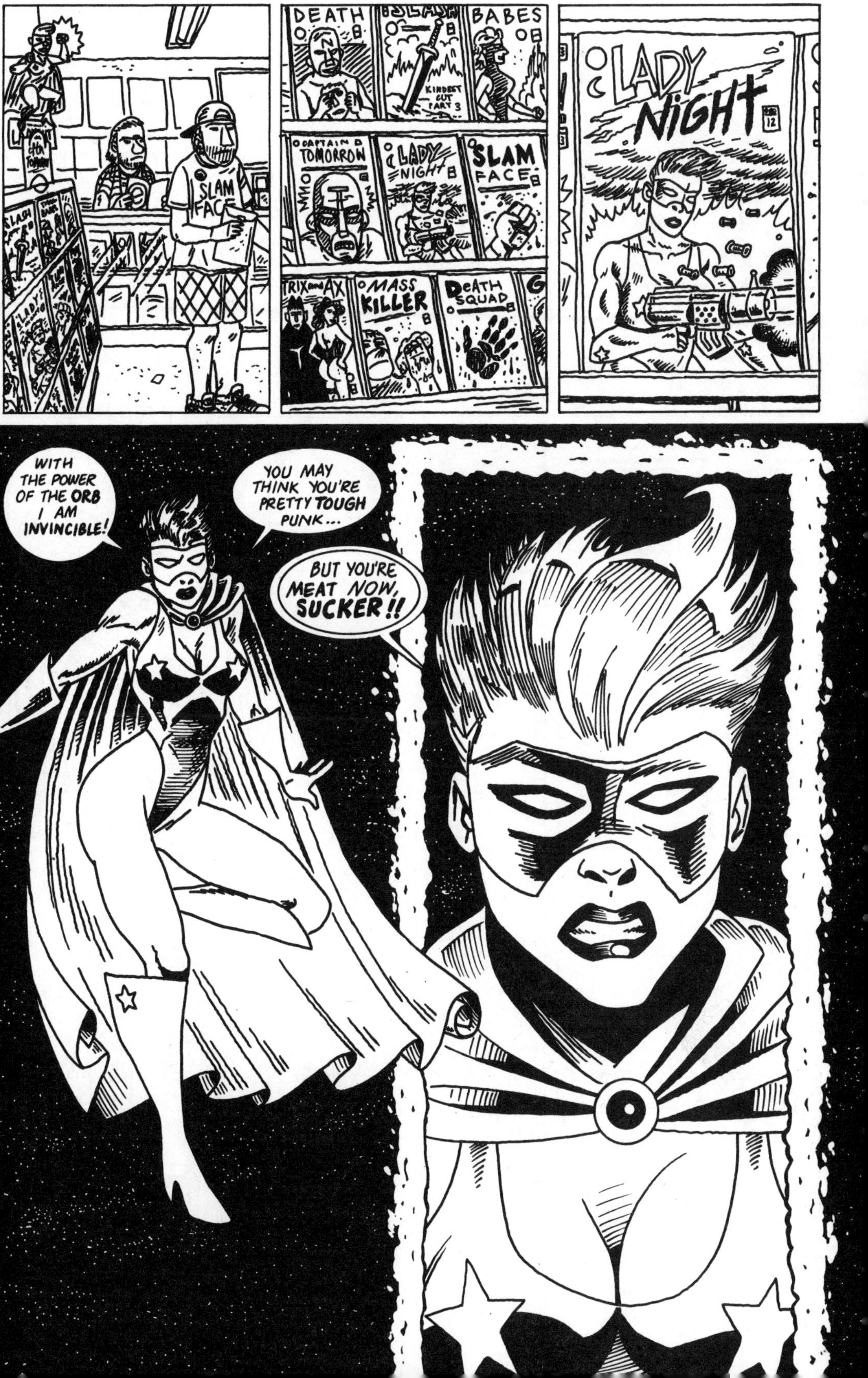
SLAM FACE
DEATH
SLASH
BABES
KINDEST CUT PART 3
CAPTAIN TOMORROW
LADY NIGHT
SLAM FACE
TRIX AND AX
MASS KILLER
DEATH SQUAD
LADY NIGHT
12
WITH THE POWER OF THE ORB I AM INVINCIBLE!
YOU MAY THINK YOU'RE PRETTY TOUGH PUNK...
BUT YOU'RE MEAT NOW, SUCKER!!

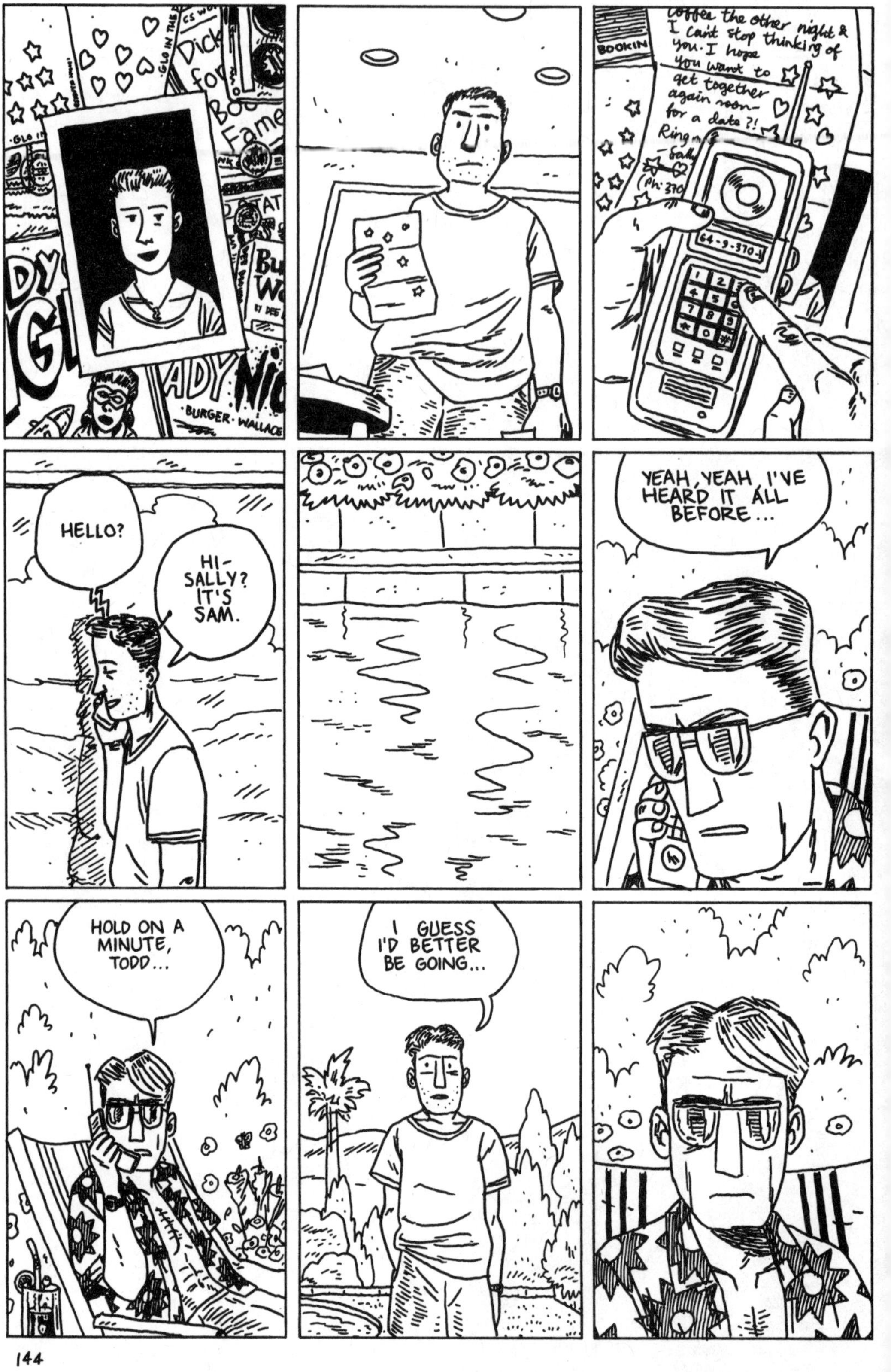
BURGER · WALLACE
coffee the other night & I can't stop thinking of you. I hope you want to get together again soon— for a date?!
64-9-370-
HELLO?
HI- SALLY? IT'S SAM.
YEAH, YEAH, I'VE HEARD IT ALL BEFORE...
HOLD ON A MINUTE, TODD...
I GUESS I'D BETTER BE GOING...

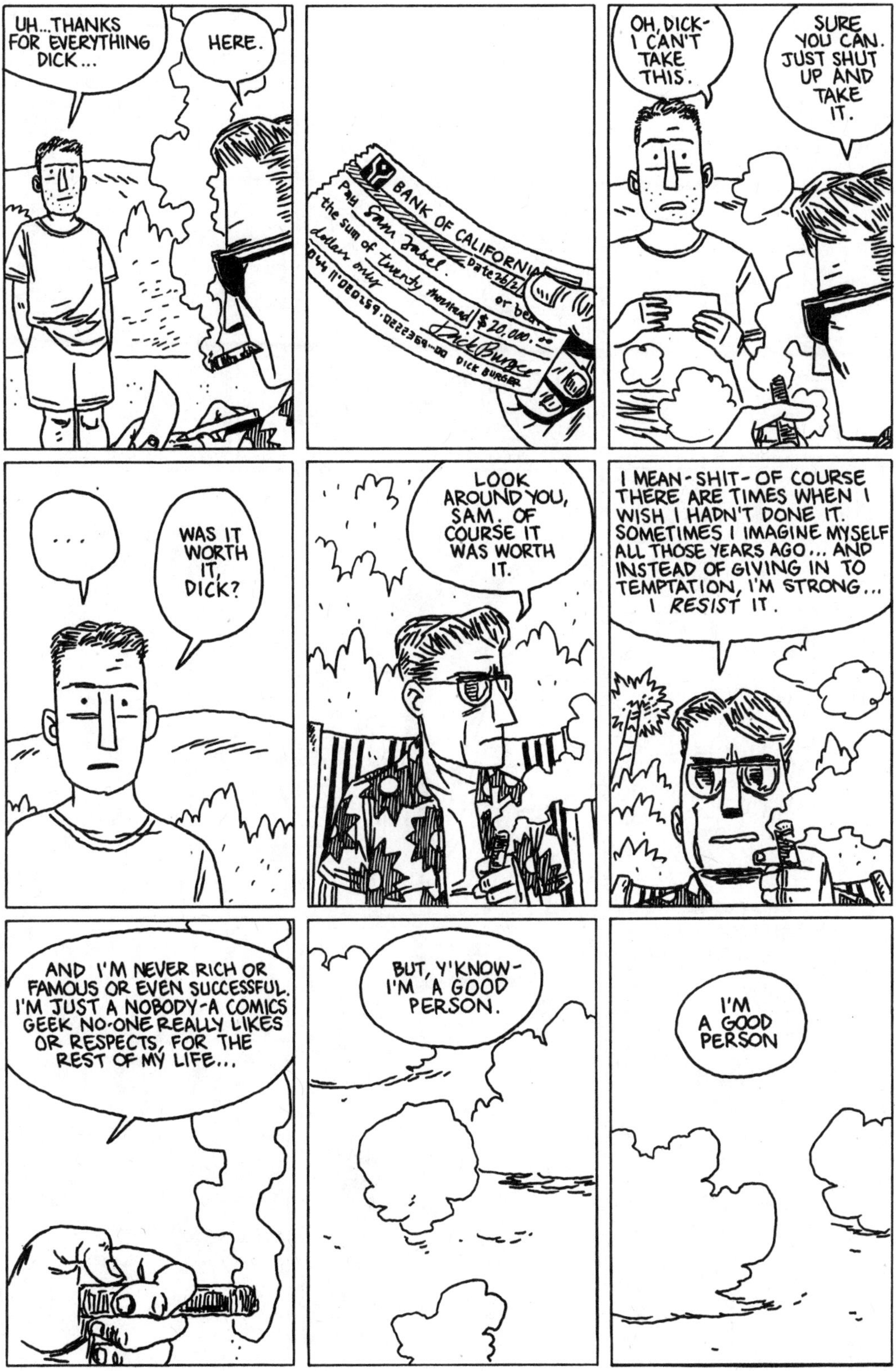
UH...THANKS FOR EVERYTHING DICK...
HERE.
BANK OF CALIFORNIA
OH, DICK- I CAN'T TAKE THIS.
SURE YOU CAN. JUST SHUT UP AND TAKE IT.
...
WAS IT WORTH IT, DICK?
LOOK AROUND YOU, SAM. OF COURSE IT WAS WORTH IT.
I MEAN-SHIT- OF COURSE THERE ARE TIMES WHEN I WISH I HADN'T DONE IT. SOMETIMES I IMAGINE MYSELF ALL THOSE YEARS AGO... AND INSTEAD OF GIVING IN TO TEMPTATION, I'M STRONG... I *RESIST* IT.
AND I'M NEVER RICH OR FAMOUS OR EVEN SUCCESSFUL. I'M JUST A NOBODY-A COMICS GEEK NO-ONE REALLY LIKES OR RESPECTS, FOR THE REST OF MY LIFE...
BUT, Y'KNOW- I'M A GOOD PERSON.
I'M A GOOD PERSON

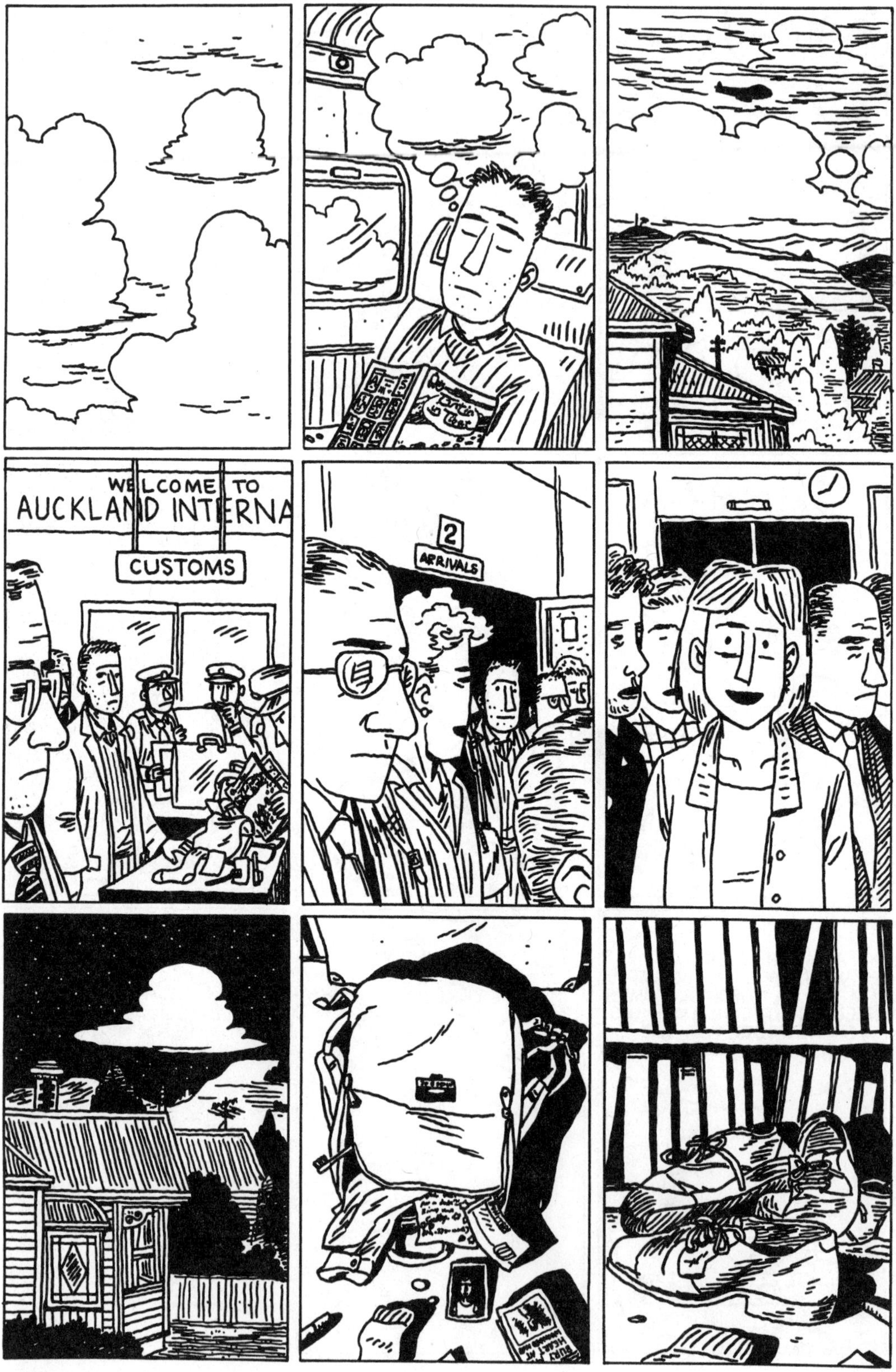
WELCOME TO
AUCKLAND INTERNA
CUSTOMS
2
ARRIVALS

I HAVE TO ADMIT— WHEN YOU SAID YOU WANTED TO SHOW ME YOUR BEDROOM CEILING, I DIDN'T THINK YOU ACTUALLY MEANT...

BE PATIENT. THEY'RE SOAKING UP LIGHT.

WHAT?

OKAY, THAT'LL DO. SWITCH OFF THE LAMP.

CLICK

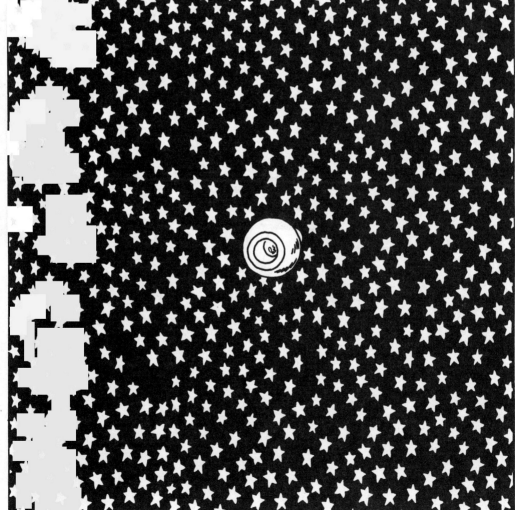

Sam Zabel.

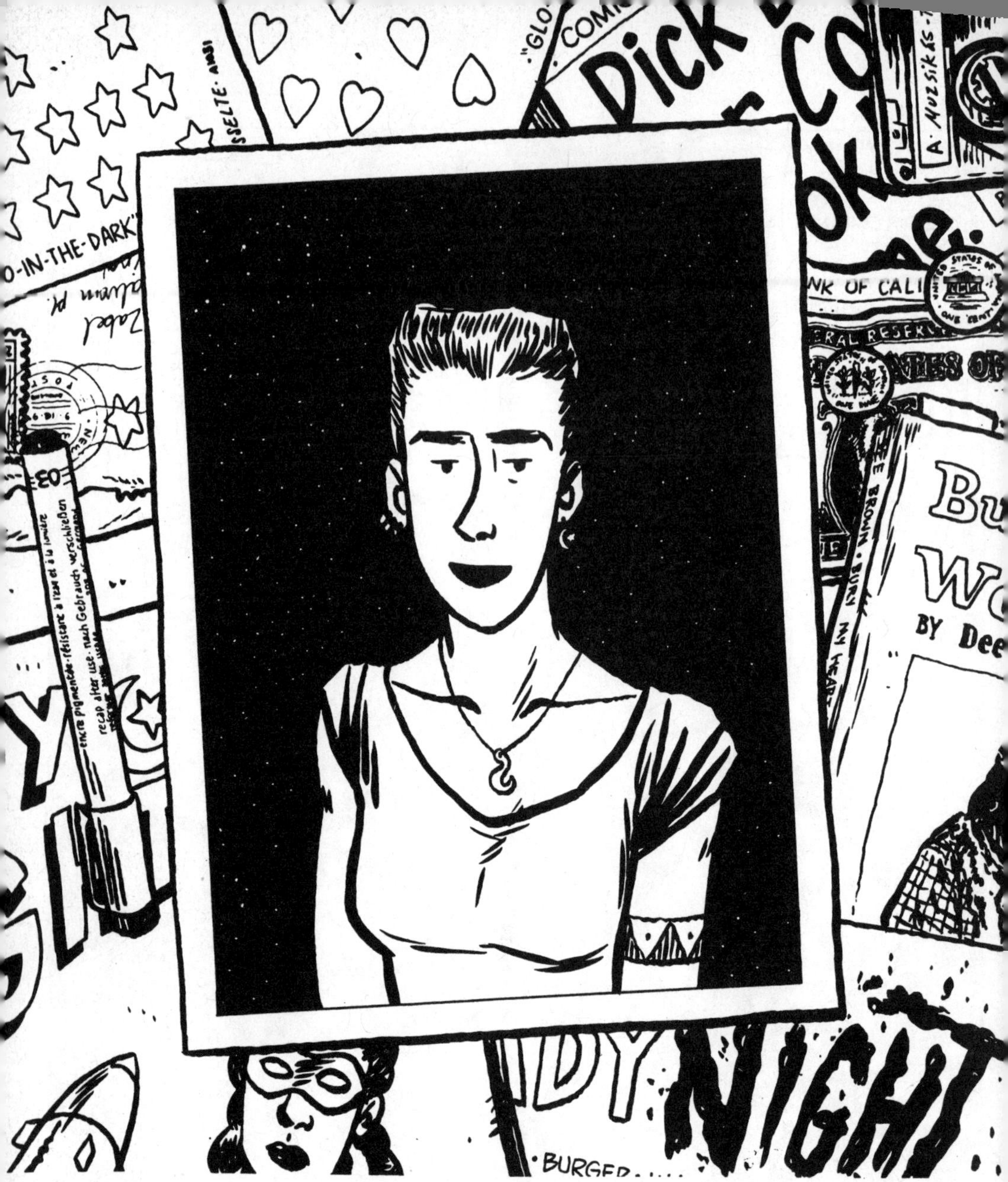
Dick
NIGHT

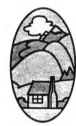

Hicksville Press

Chapter Seven

"The medium of exchange in the comics business is guilt; it's not money."

Steve Englehart.

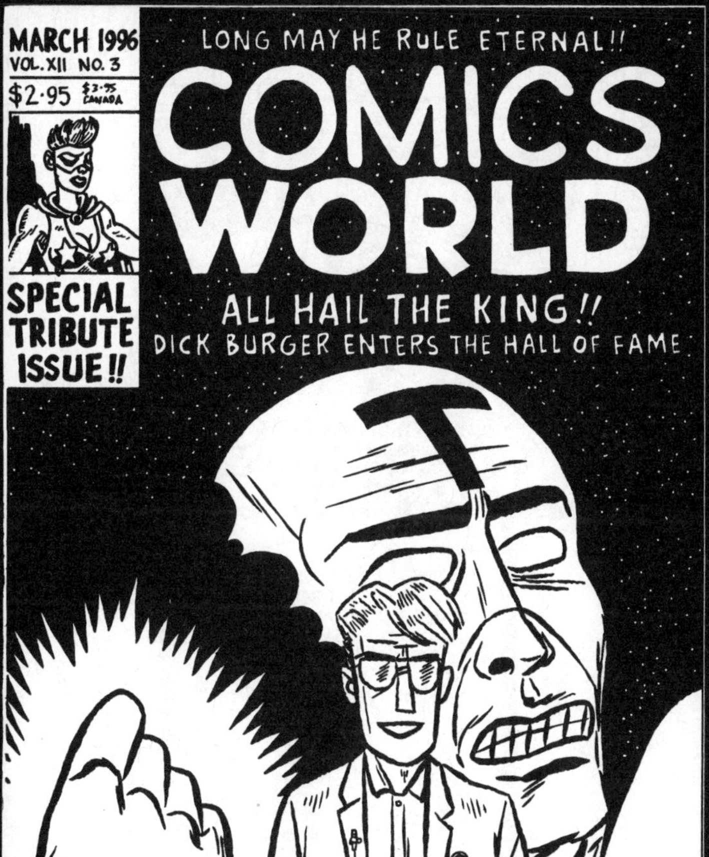
MARCH 1996
VOL. XII NO. 3
$2.95 $3.95 CANADA
LONG MAY HE RULE ETERNAL!!
COMICS WORLD
SPECIAL TRIBUTE ISSUE!!
ALL HAIL THE KING!!
DICK BURGER ENTERS THE HALL OF FAME
Eternal

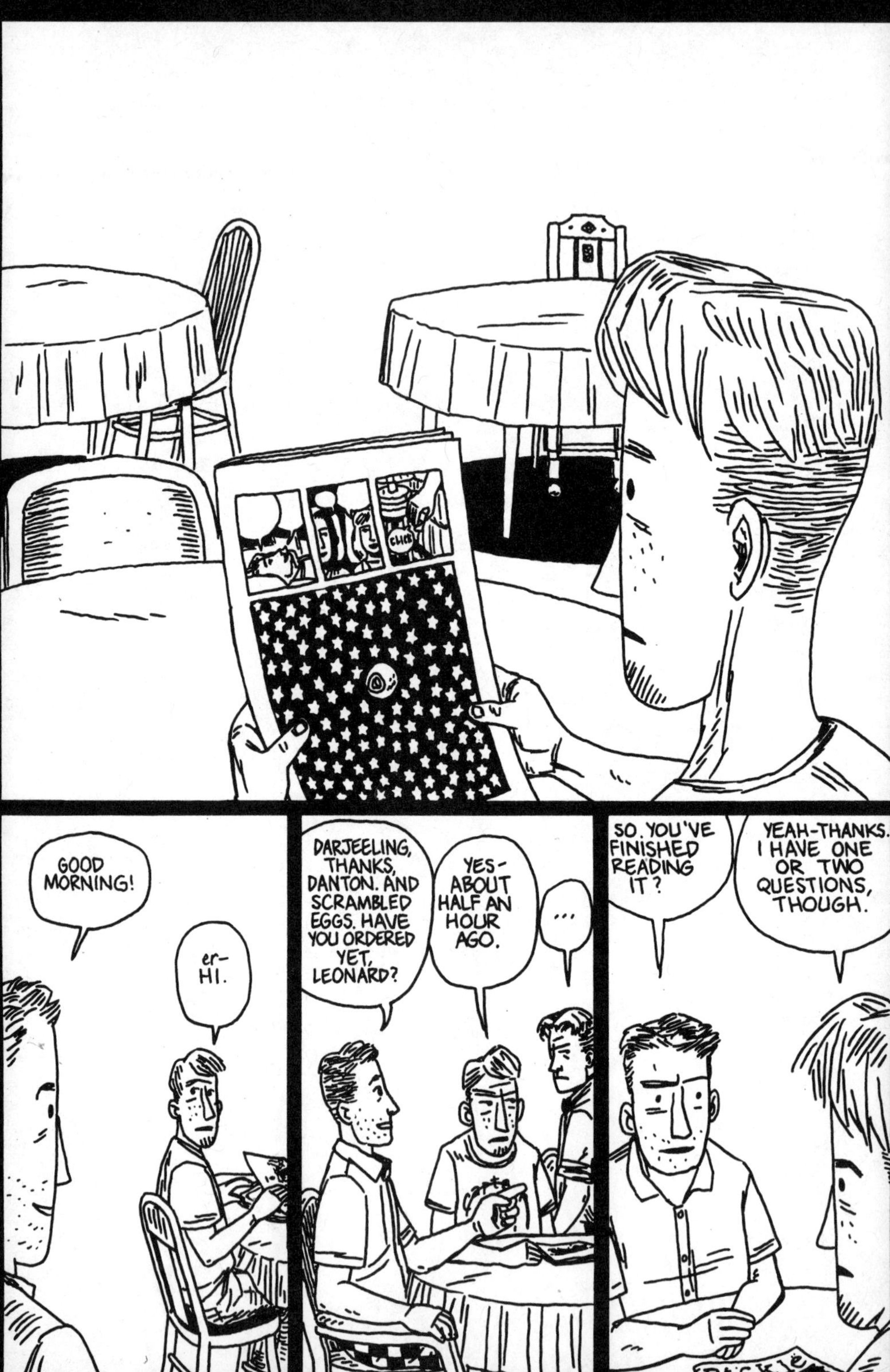
CLICK
GOOD MORNING!
er- HI.
DARJEELING, THANKS, DANTON. AND SCRAMBLED EGGS. HAVE YOU ORDERED YET, LEONARD?
YES- ABOUT HALF AN HOUR AGO.
...
SO. YOU'VE FINISHED READING IT?
YEAH-THANKS. I HAVE ONE OR TWO QUESTIONS, THOUGH.
Pickle

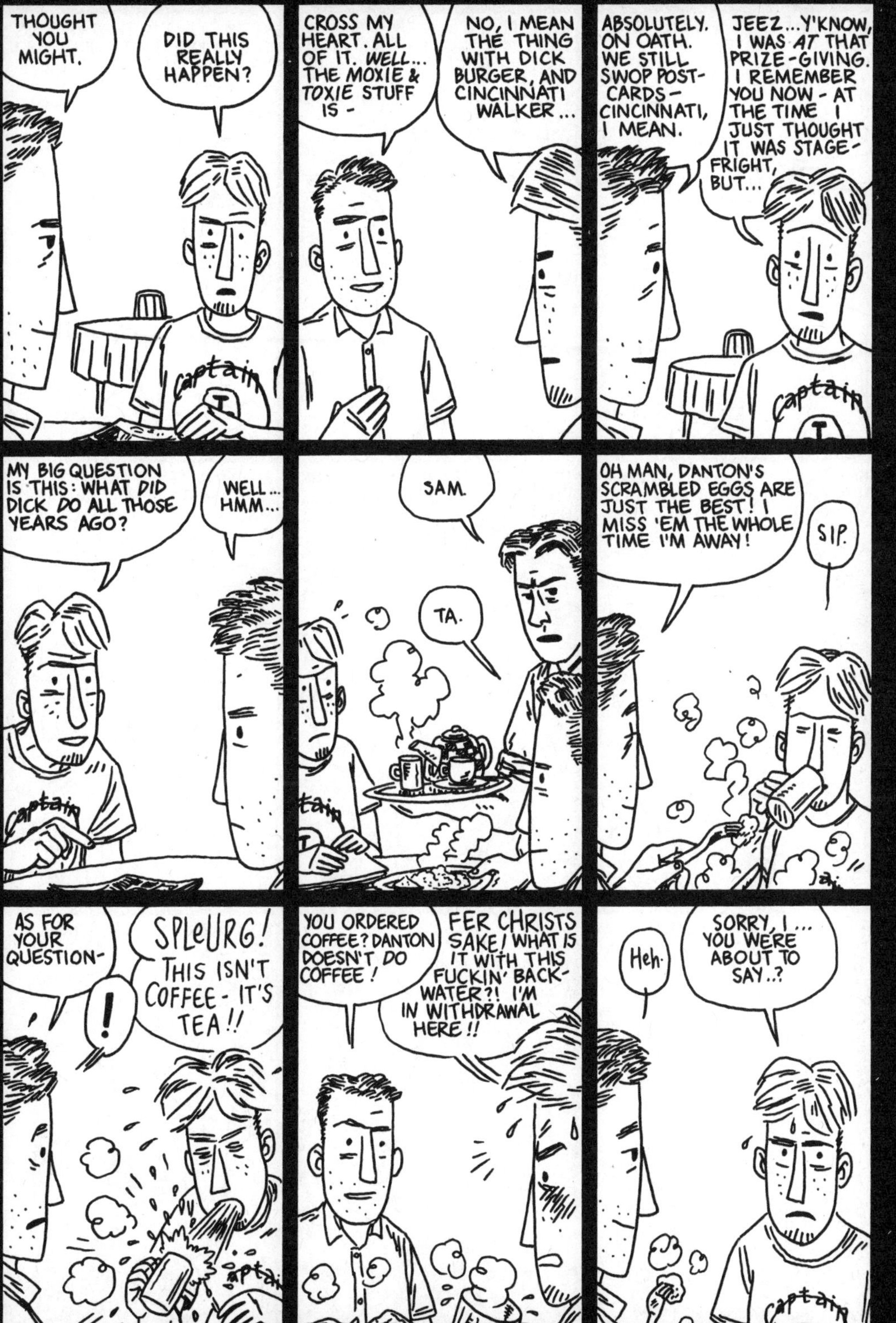
THOUGHT YOU MIGHT.
DID THIS REALLY HAPPEN?
CROSS MY HEART. ALL OF IT. WELL... THE MOXIE & TOXIE STUFF IS -
NO, I MEAN THE THING WITH DICK BURGER, AND CINCINNATI WALKER...
ABSOLUTELY. ON OATH. WE STILL SWOP POST-CARDS - CINCINNATI, I MEAN.
JEEZ... Y'KNOW, I WAS AT THAT PRIZE-GIVING. I REMEMBER YOU NOW - AT THE TIME I JUST THOUGHT IT WAS STAGE-FRIGHT, BUT...
captain
MY BIG QUESTION IS THIS: WHAT DID DICK DO ALL THOSE YEARS AGO?
WELL... HMM...
SAM.
TA.
OH MAN, DANTON'S SCRAMBLED EGGS ARE JUST THE BEST! I MISS 'EM THE WHOLE TIME I'M AWAY!
SIP.
AS FOR YOUR QUESTION-
SPLeURG! THIS ISN'T COFFEE - IT'S TEA!!
!
YOU ORDERED COFFEE? DANTON DOESN'T DO COFFEE!
FER CHRISTS SAKE! WHAT IS IT WITH THIS FUCKIN' BACK-WATER?! I'M IN WITHDRAWAL HERE!!
Heh.
SORRY, I... YOU WERE ABOUT TO SAY..?

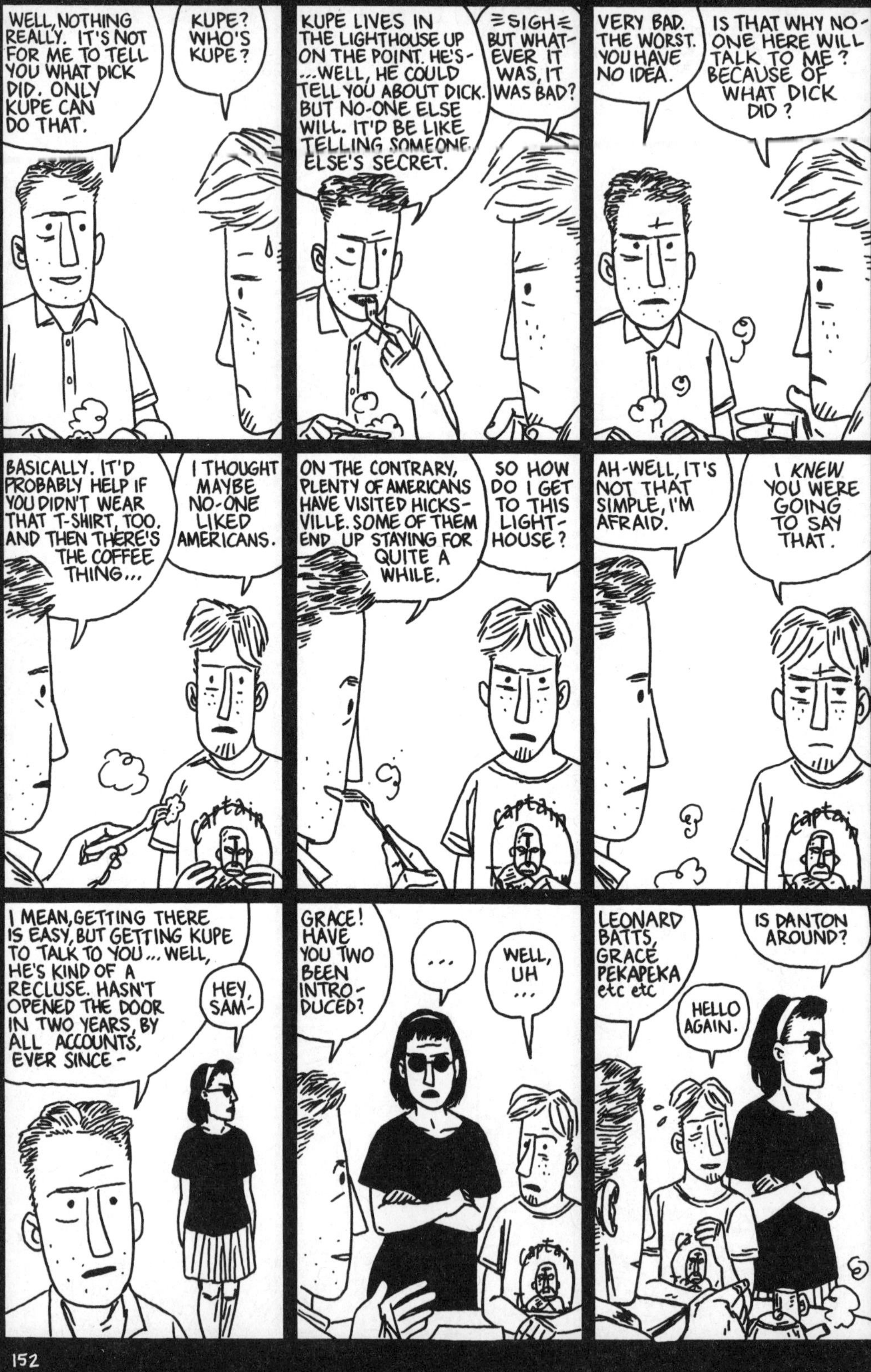

WELL, NOTHING REALLY. IT'S NOT FOR ME TO TELL YOU WHAT DICK DID. ONLY KUPE CAN DO THAT.
KUPE? WHO'S KUPE?
KUPE LIVES IN THE LIGHTHOUSE UP ON THE POINT. HE'S- ...WELL, HE COULD TELL YOU ABOUT DICK. BUT NO-ONE ELSE WILL. IT'D BE LIKE TELLING SOMEONE ELSE'S SECRET.
≡SIGH≡ BUT WHATEVER IT WAS, IT WAS BAD?
VERY BAD. THE WORST. YOU HAVE NO IDEA.
IS THAT WHY NO-ONE HERE WILL TALK TO ME? BECAUSE OF WHAT DICK DID?
BASICALLY. IT'D PROBABLY HELP IF YOU DIDN'T WEAR THAT T-SHIRT, TOO. AND THEN THERE'S THE COFFEE THING...
I THOUGHT MAYBE NO-ONE LIKED AMERICANS.
ON THE CONTRARY, PLENTY OF AMERICANS HAVE VISITED HICKSVILLE. SOME OF THEM END UP STAYING FOR QUITE A WHILE.
SO HOW DO I GET TO THIS LIGHTHOUSE?
AH-WELL, IT'S NOT THAT SIMPLE, I'M AFRAID.
I *KNEW* YOU WERE GOING TO SAY THAT.
I MEAN, GETTING THERE IS EASY, BUT GETTING KUPE TO TALK TO YOU ... WELL, HE'S KIND OF A RECLUSE. HASN'T OPENED THE DOOR IN TWO YEARS, BY ALL ACCOUNTS, EVER SINCE -
HEY, SAM-
GRACE! HAVE YOU TWO BEEN INTRODUCED?
...
WELL, UH ...
LEONARD BATTS, GRACE PEKAPEKA etc etc
HELLO AGAIN.
IS DANTON AROUND?

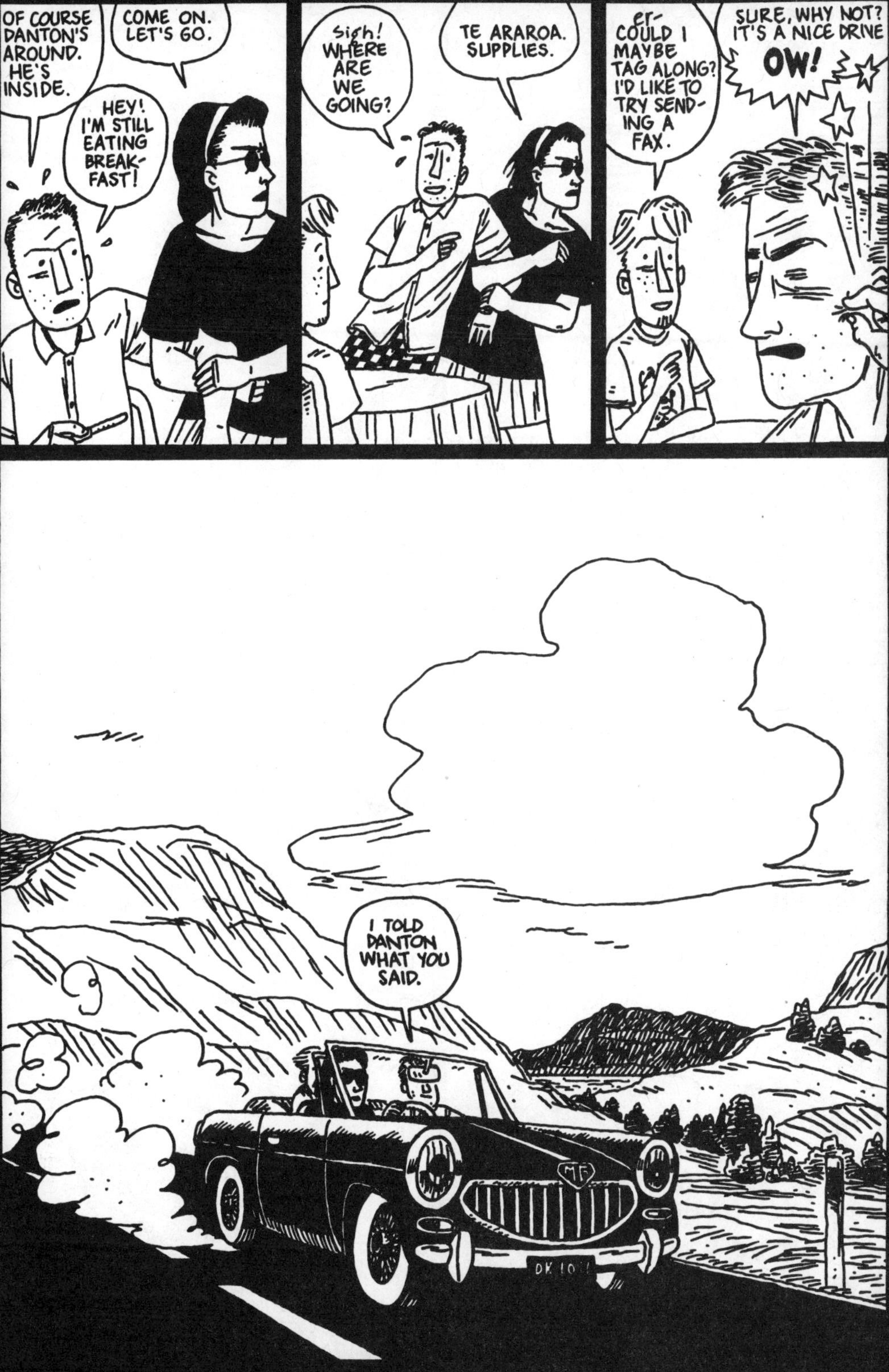
OF COURSE DANTON'S AROUND. HE'S INSIDE.
COME ON. LET'S GO.
HEY! I'M STILL EATING BREAK-FAST!
Sigh! WHERE ARE WE GOING?
TE ARAROA. SUPPLIES.
er- COULD I MAYBE TAG ALONG? I'D LIKE TO TRY SEND-ING A FAX.
SURE, WHY NOT? IT'S A NICE DRIVE
OW!
I TOLD DANTON WHAT YOU SAID.
MG
DK 10

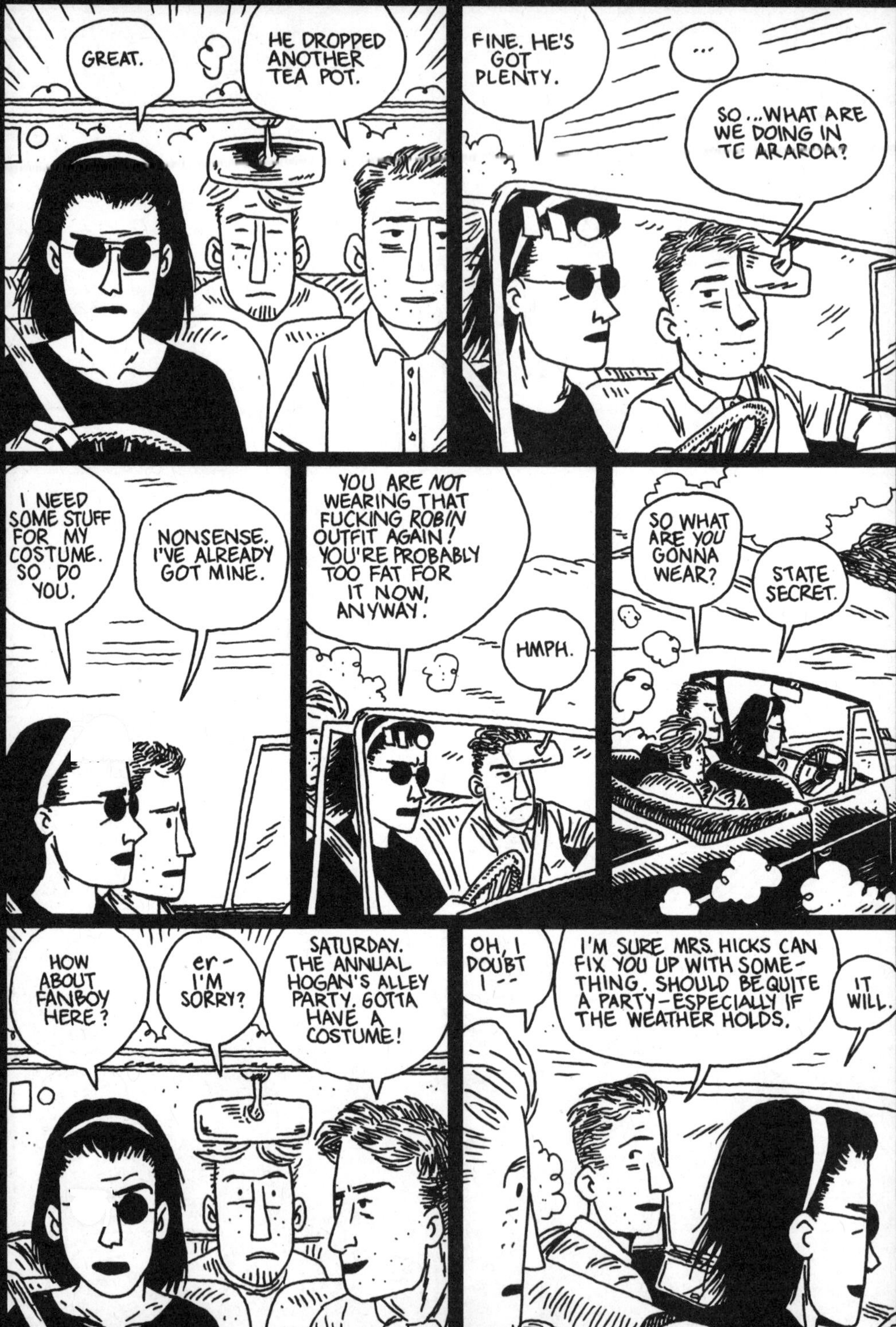

GREAT.
HE DROPPED ANOTHER TEA POT.
FINE. HE'S GOT PLENTY.
...
SO ... WHAT ARE WE DOING IN TE ARAROA?
I NEED SOME STUFF FOR MY COSTUME. SO DO YOU.
NONSENSE. I'VE ALREADY GOT MINE.
YOU ARE NOT WEARING THAT FUCKING ROBIN OUTFIT AGAIN! YOU'RE PROBABLY TOO FAT FOR IT NOW, ANYWAY.
HMPH.
SO WHAT ARE YOU GONNA WEAR?
STATE SECRET.
HOW ABOUT FANBOY HERE?
er- I'M SORRY?
SATURDAY. THE ANNUAL HOGAN'S ALLEY PARTY. GOTTA HAVE A COSTUME!
OH, I DOUBT I --
I'M SURE MRS. HICKS CAN FIX YOU UP WITH SOMETHING. SHOULD BE QUITE A PARTY-ESPECIALLY IF THE WEATHER HOLDS.
IT WILL.

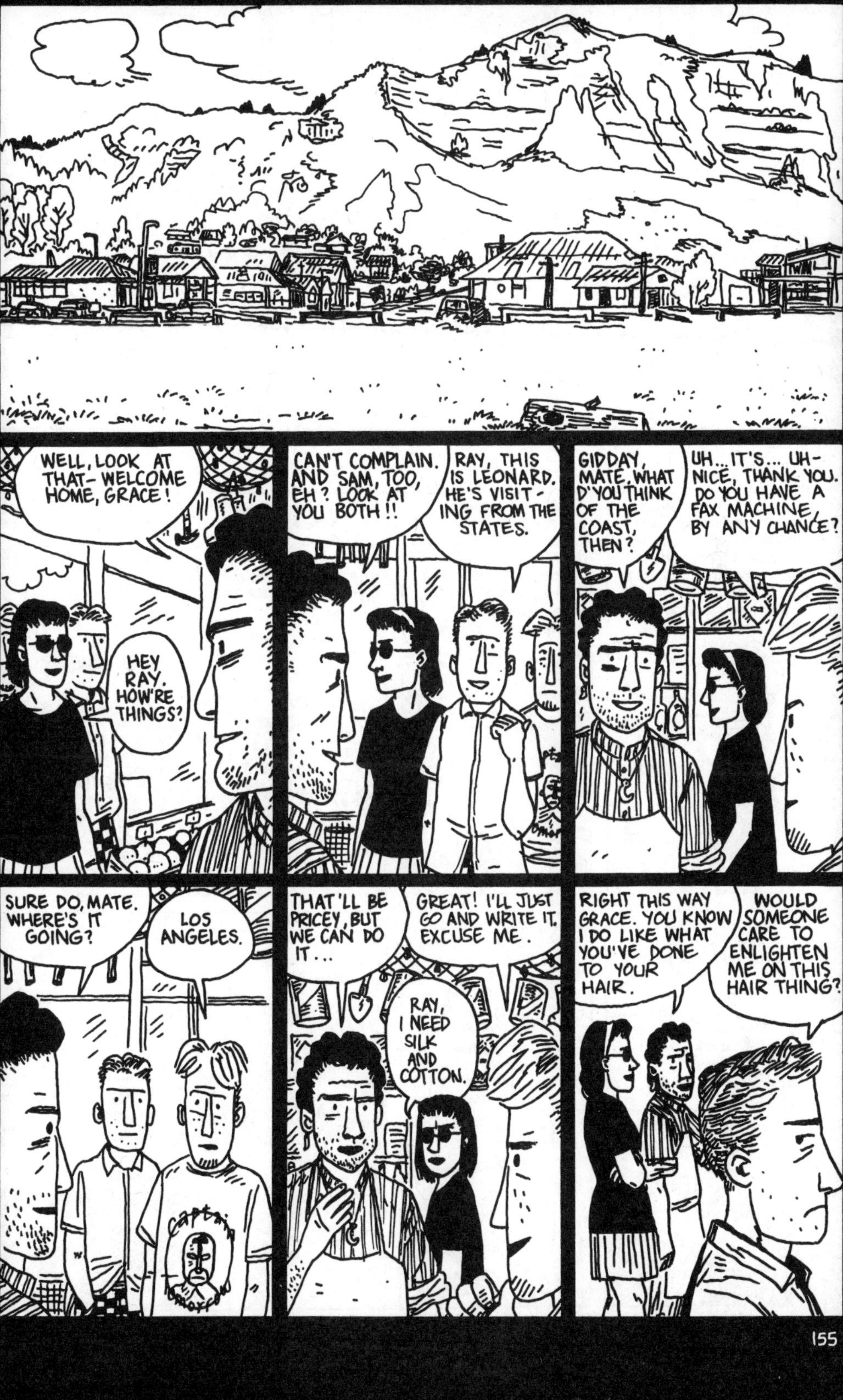
WELL, LOOK AT THAT- WELCOME HOME, GRACE!
HEY RAY. HOW'RE THINGS?
CAN'T COMPLAIN. AND SAM, TOO, EH? LOOK AT YOU BOTH!!
RAY, THIS IS LEONARD. HE'S VISIT-ING FROM THE STATES.
GIDDAY, MATE. WHAT D'YOU THINK OF THE COAST, THEN?
UH... IT'S... UH- NICE, THANK YOU. DO YOU HAVE A FAX MACHINE, BY ANY CHANCE?
SURE DO, MATE. WHERE'S IT GOING?
LOS ANGELES.
THAT'LL BE PRICEY, BUT WE CAN DO IT...
GREAT! I'LL JUST GO AND WRITE IT. EXCUSE ME.
RAY, I NEED SILK AND COTTON.
RIGHT THIS WAY GRACE. YOU KNOW I DO LIKE WHAT YOU'VE DONE TO YOUR HAIR.
WOULD SOMEONE CARE TO ENLIGHTEN ME ON THIS HAIR THING?

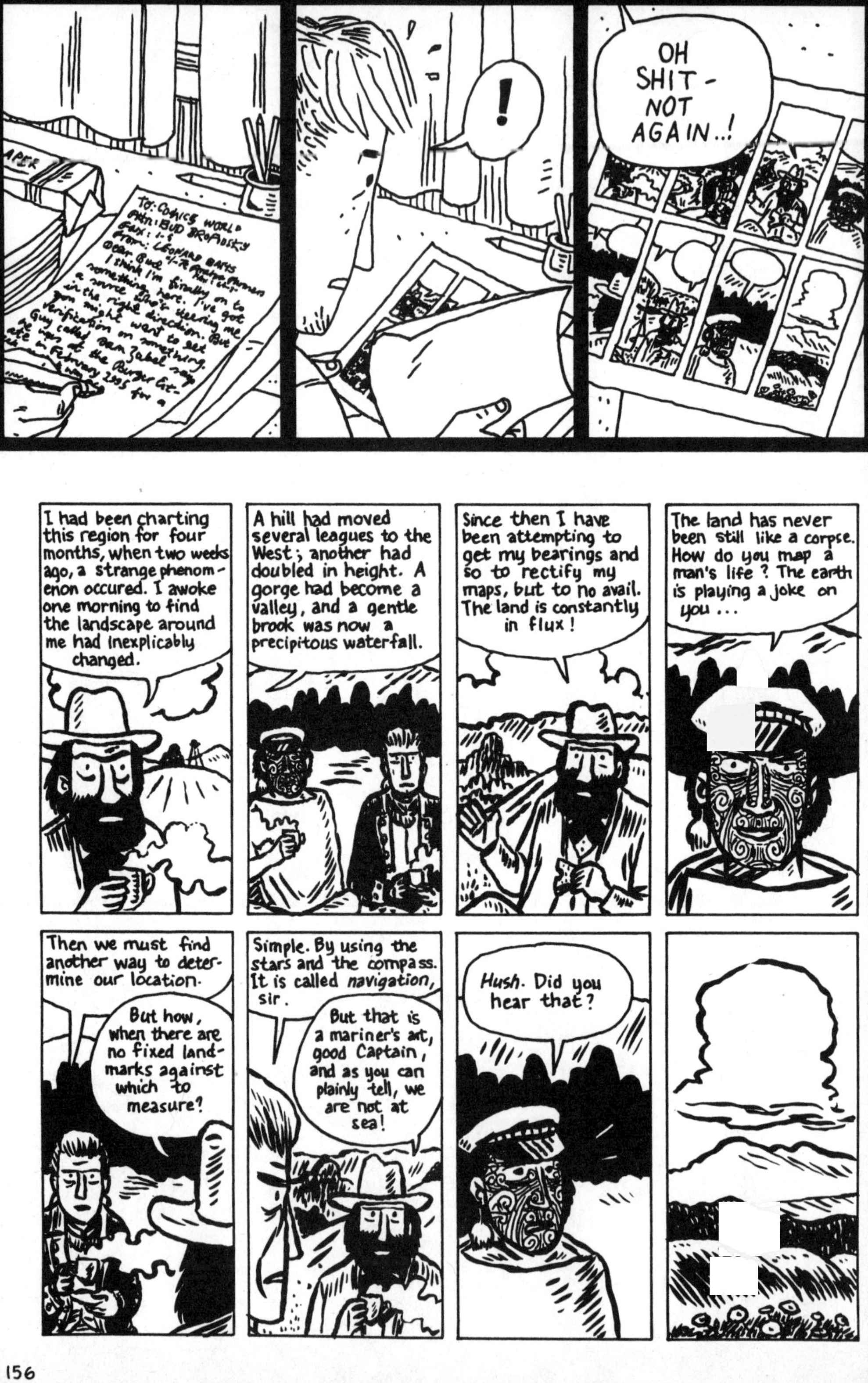

To: COMICS WORLD
From: LEONARD BATTS
Dear Bud
I think I'm finally on to something here. I've got a source who's steering me in the right direction. But you might want to get verification on something. Guy called Ben Zabel says he was at the Burger Eat-
!
OH SHIT - NOT AGAIN..!
I had been charting this region for four months, when two weeks ago, a strange phenom-enon occured. I awoke one morning to find the landscape around me had inexplicably changed.
A hill had moved several leagues to the West; another had doubled in height. A gorge had become a valley, and a gentle brook was now a precipitous waterfall.
Since then I have been attempting to get my bearings and so to rectify my maps, but to no avail. The land is constantly in flux!
The land has never been still like a corpse. How do you map a man's life? The earth is playing a joke on you...
Then we must find another way to deter-mine our location.
But how, when there are no fixed land-marks against which to measure?
Simple. By using the stars and the compass. It is called *navigation*, sir.
But that is a mariner's art, good Captain, and as you can plainly tell, we are not at sea!
Hush. Did you hear that?

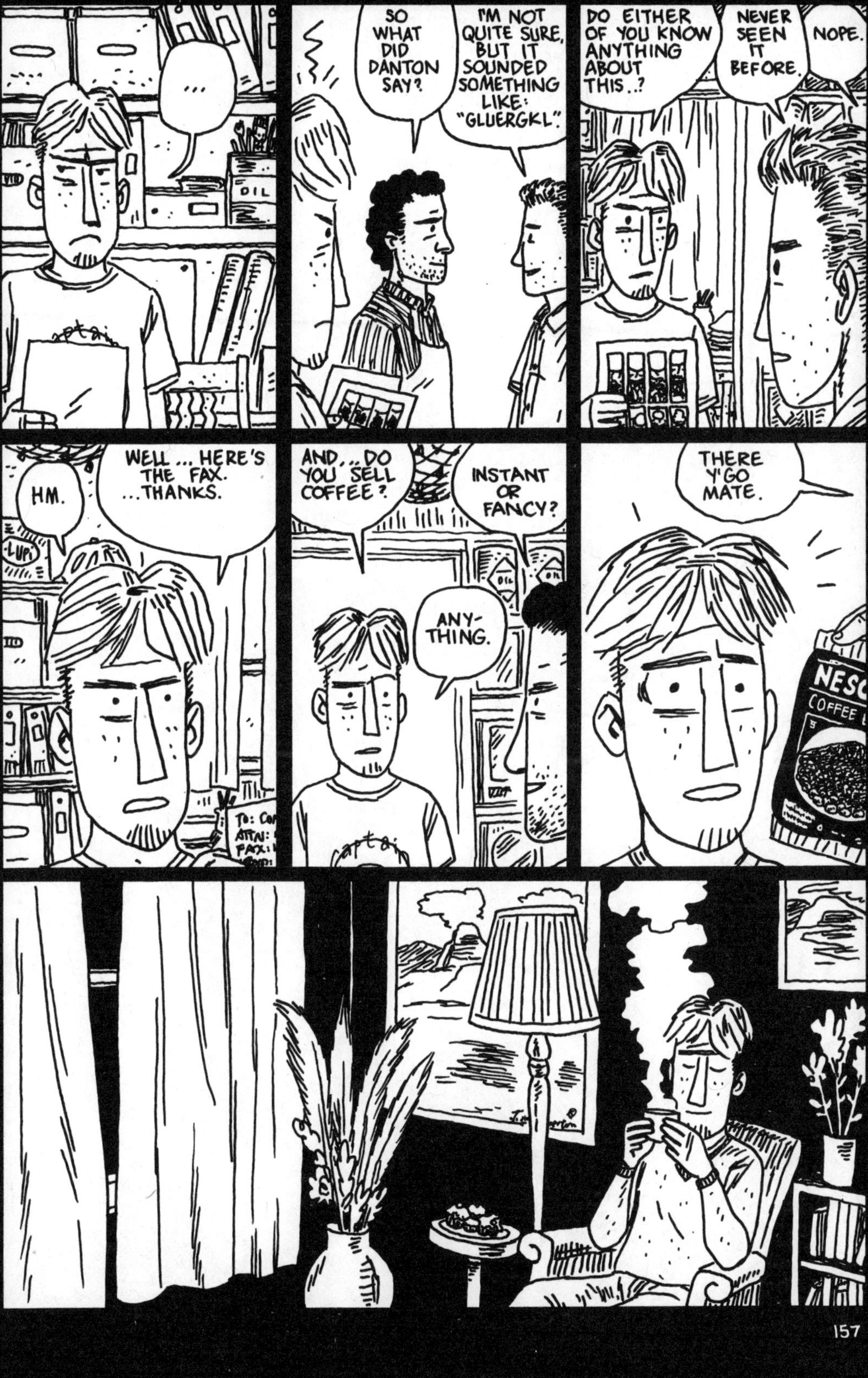
...
SO WHAT DID DANTON SAY?
I'M NOT QUITE SURE, BUT IT SOUNDED SOMETHING LIKE: "GLUERGKL".
DO EITHER OF YOU KNOW ANYTHING ABOUT THIS..?
NEVER SEEN IT BEFORE.
NOPE.
HM.
WELL... HERE'S THE FAX. ...THANKS.
AND... DO YOU SELL COFFEE?
INSTANT OR FANCY?
ANY-THING.
THERE Y'GO MATE.
NESC
COFFEE

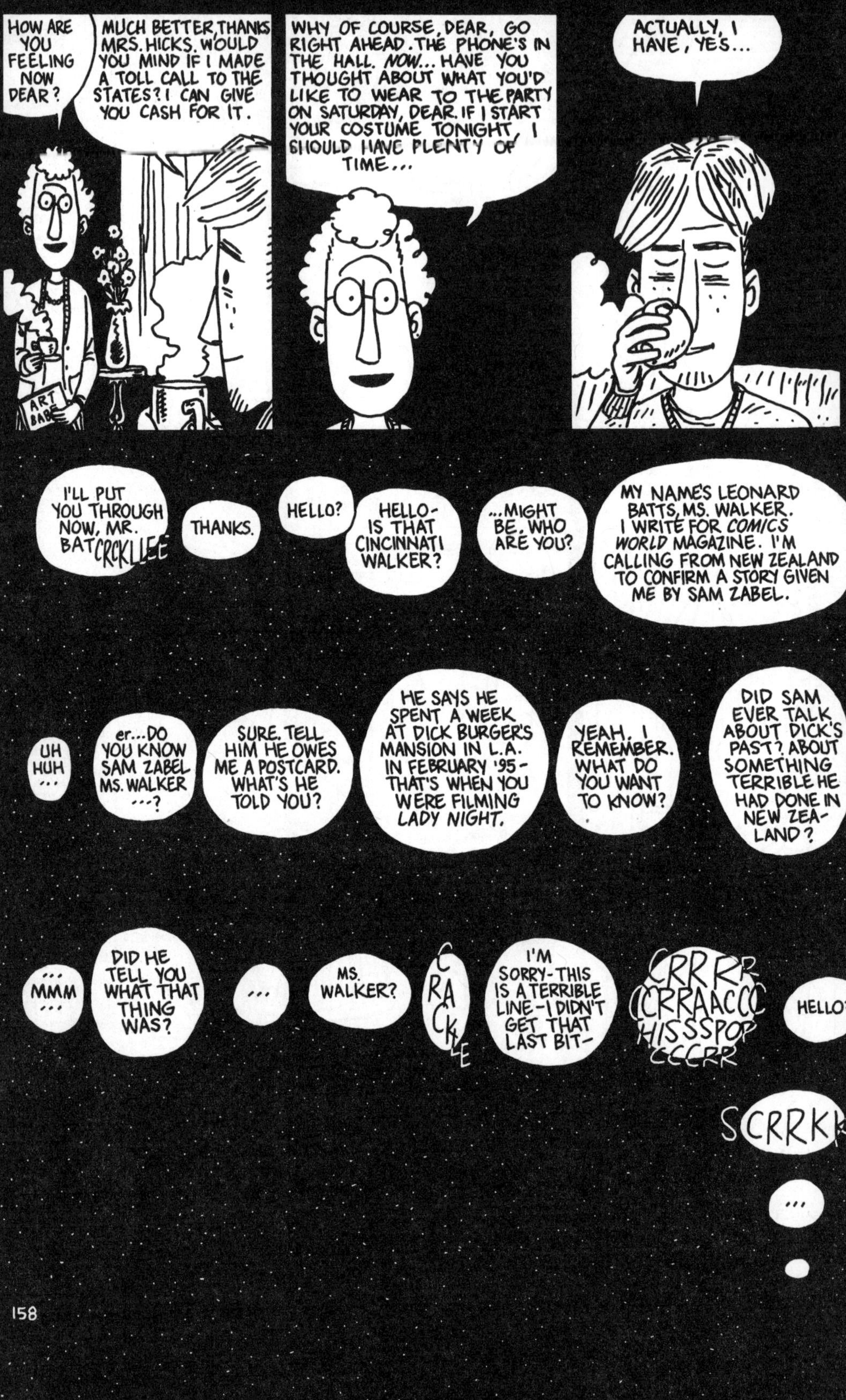
HOW ARE YOU FEELING NOW DEAR?
MUCH BETTER, THANKS MRS. HICKS. WOULD YOU MIND IF I MADE A TOLL CALL TO THE STATES? I CAN GIVE YOU CASH FOR IT.
ART BABE
WHY OF COURSE, DEAR, GO RIGHT AHEAD. THE PHONE'S IN THE HALL. NOW... HAVE YOU THOUGHT ABOUT WHAT YOU'D LIKE TO WEAR TO THE PARTY ON SATURDAY, DEAR. IF I START YOUR COSTUME TONIGHT, I SHOULD HAVE PLENTY OF TIME...
ACTUALLY, I HAVE, YES...
I'LL PUT YOU THROUGH NOW, MR. BATCRCKLLEE
THANKS.
HELLO?
HELLO- IS THAT CINCINNATI WALKER?
...MIGHT BE. WHO ARE YOU?
MY NAME'S LEONARD BATTS, MS. WALKER. I WRITE FOR COMICS WORLD MAGAZINE. I'M CALLING FROM NEW ZEALAND TO CONFIRM A STORY GIVEN ME BY SAM ZABEL.
UH HUH ...
er...DO YOU KNOW SAM ZABEL MS. WALKER ...?
SURE. TELL HIM HE OWES ME A POSTCARD. WHAT'S HE TOLD YOU?
HE SAYS HE SPENT A WEEK AT DICK BURGER'S MANSION IN L.A. IN FEBRUARY '95 - THAT'S WHEN YOU WERE FILMING LADY NIGHT.
YEAH, I REMEMBER. WHAT DO YOU WANT TO KNOW?
DID SAM EVER TALK ABOUT DICK'S PAST? ABOUT SOMETHING TERRIBLE HE HAD DONE IN NEW ZEALAND?
... MMM ...
DID HE TELL YOU WHAT THAT THING WAS?
...
MS. WALKER?
CRACKLE
I'M SORRY- THIS IS A TERRIBLE LINE - I DIDN'T GET THAT LAST BIT-
CRRRR CRRAACCC HISSSPOP CCCRR
HELLO?
SCRRKKK
...

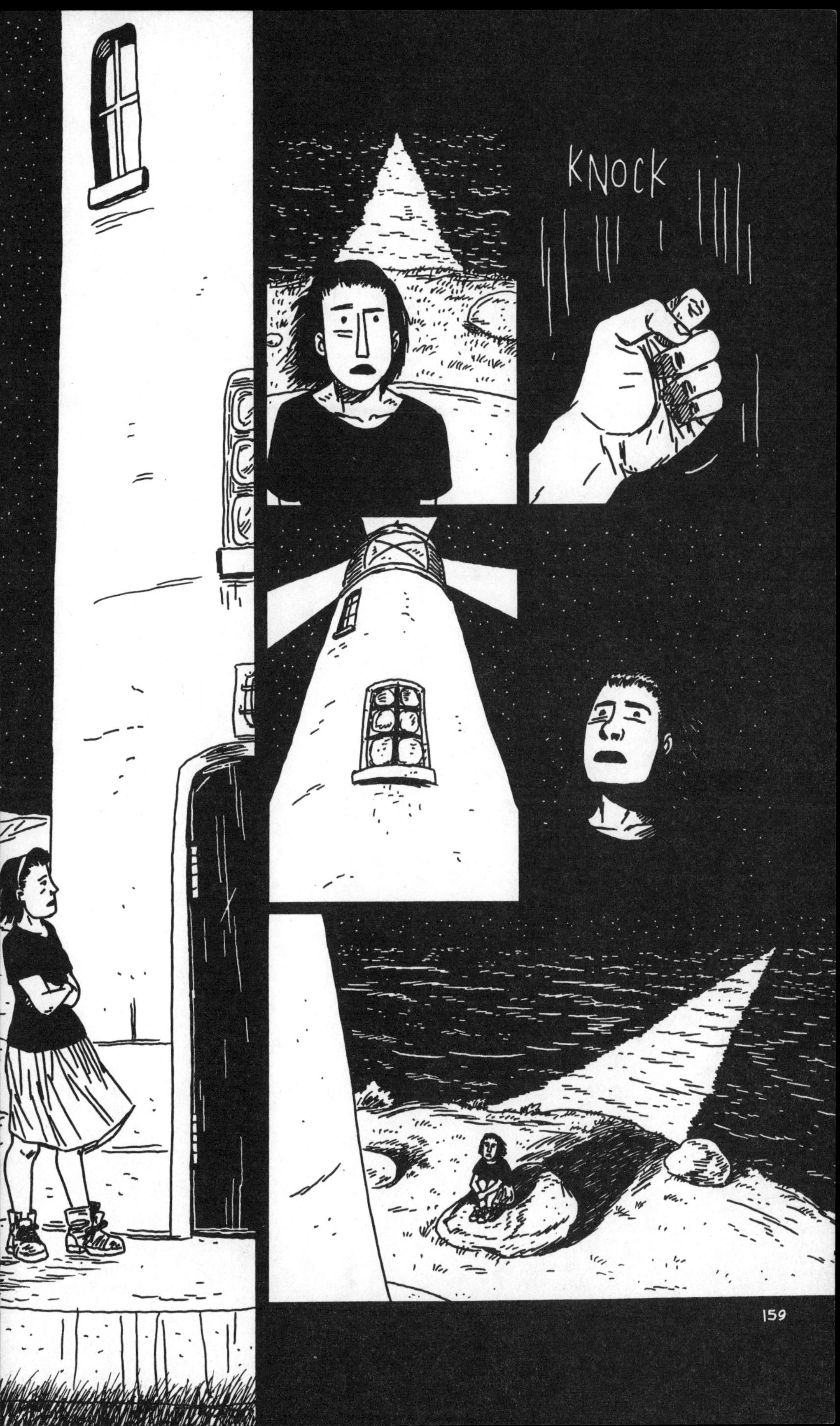
KNOCK

Chapter Eight

"I've seen recent examples of superheroes being pushed around and made fun of and I don't go along with it. Nobody ever pushed me around in those serials. The world needs heroes today."

Kirk Alyn, star of Superman (1948) and Atom Man vs. Superman (1952).

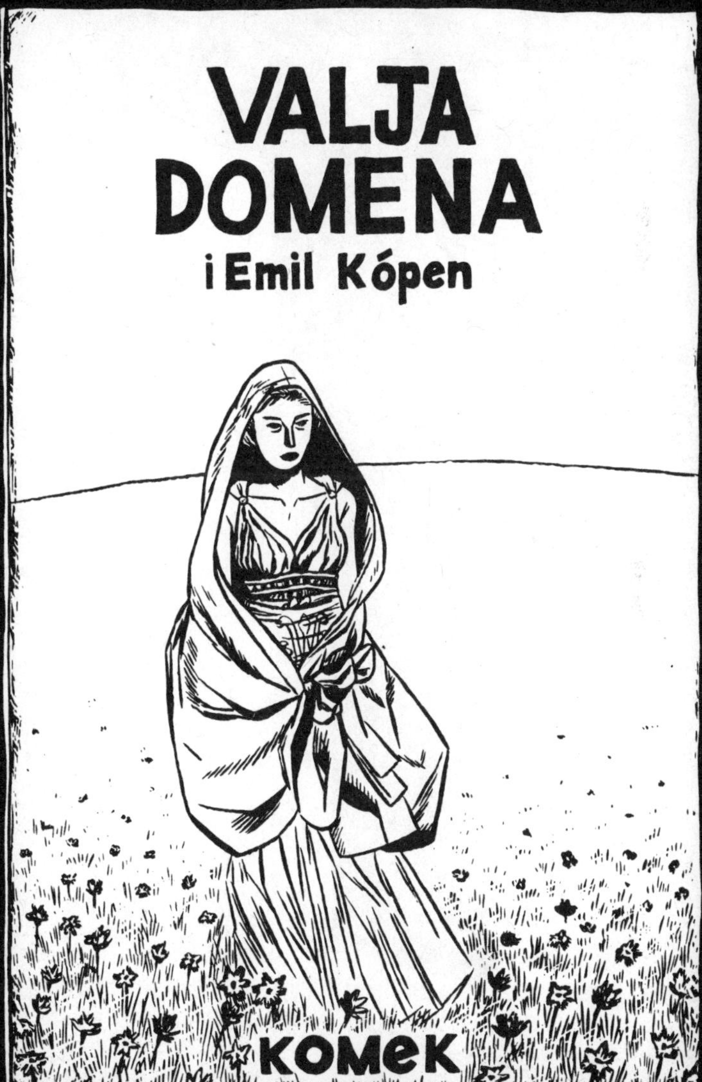

VALJA DOMENA
i Emil Kópen
KOMEK

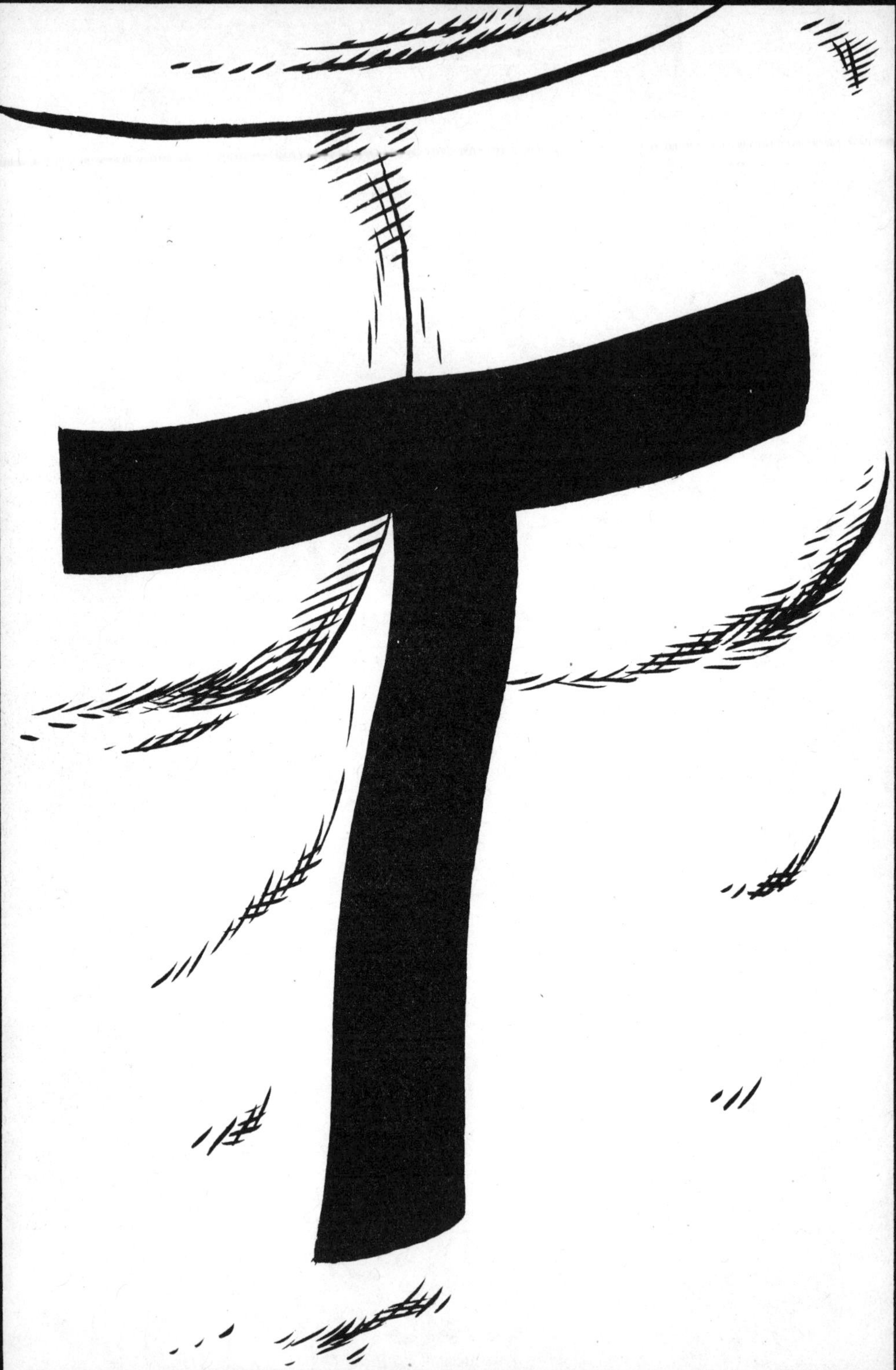

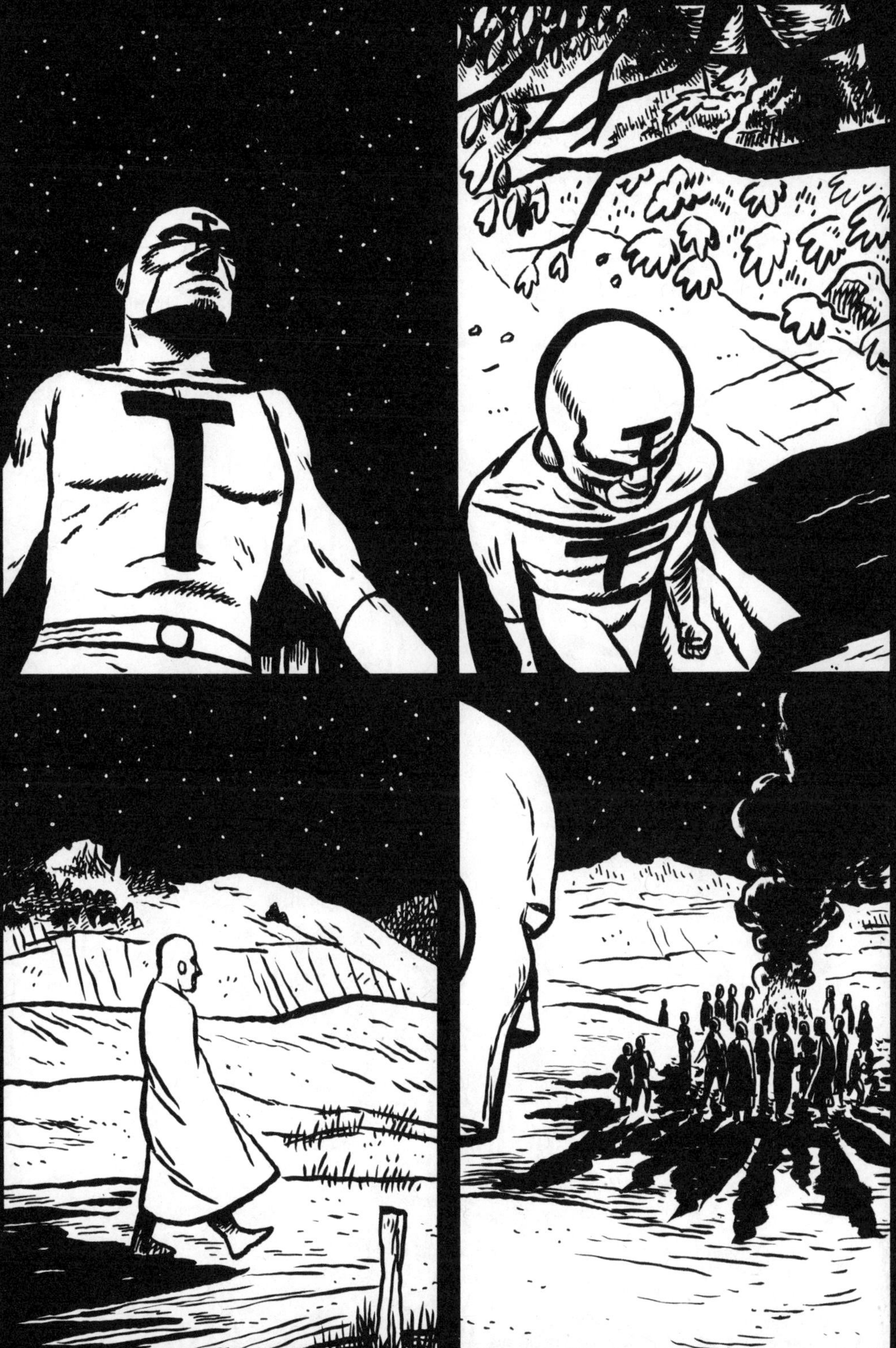

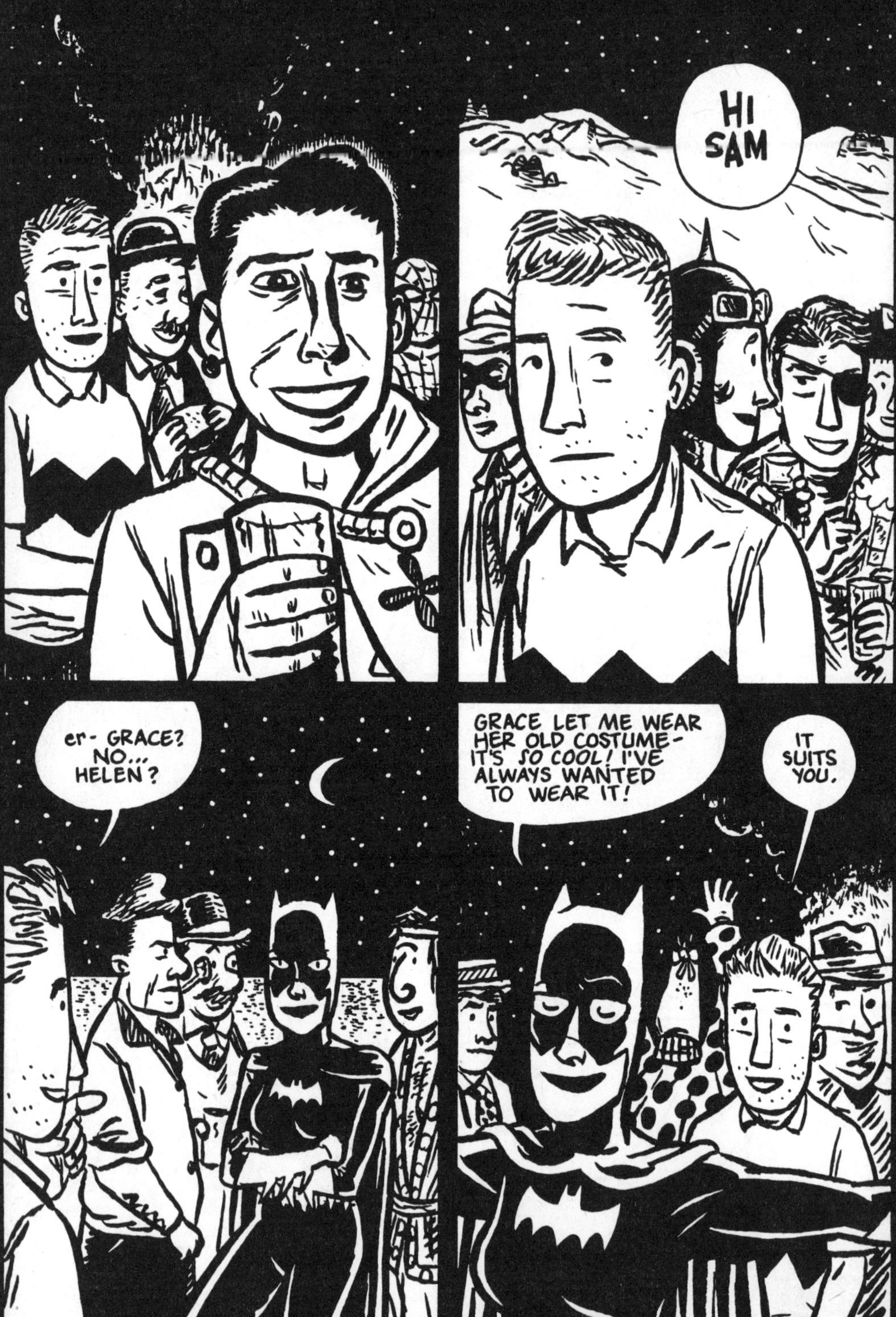
HI SAM
er- GRACE? NO... HELEN?
GRACE LET ME WEAR HER OLD COSTUME- IT'S SO COOL! I'VE ALWAYS WANTED TO WEAR IT!
IT SUITS YOU.

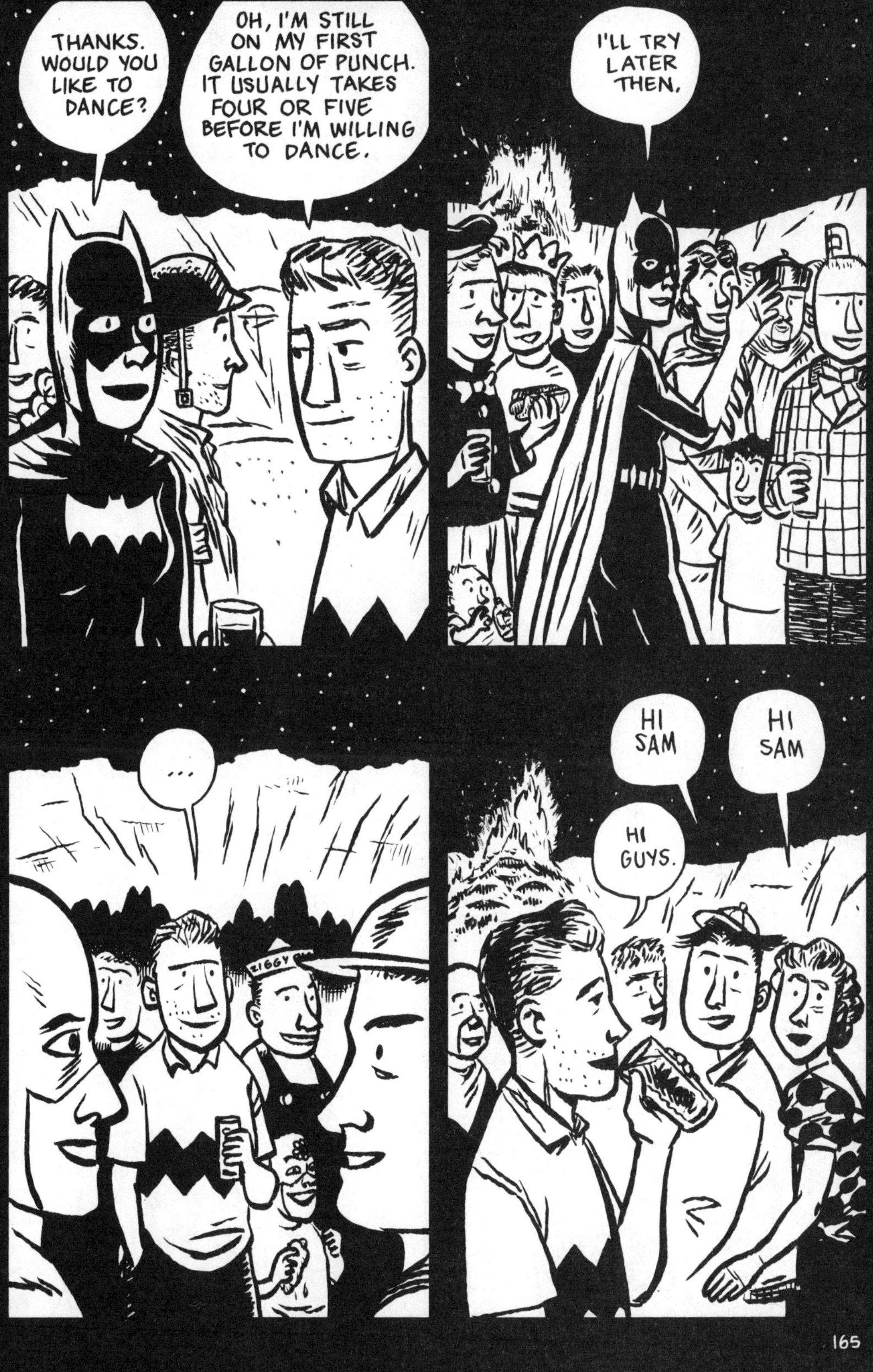
THANKS. WOULD YOU LIKE TO DANCE?
OH, I'M STILL ON MY FIRST GALLON OF PUNCH. IT USUALLY TAKES FOUR OR FIVE BEFORE I'M WILLING TO DANCE.
I'LL TRY LATER THEN.
...
ZIGGY
HI SAM
HI SAM
HI GUYS.

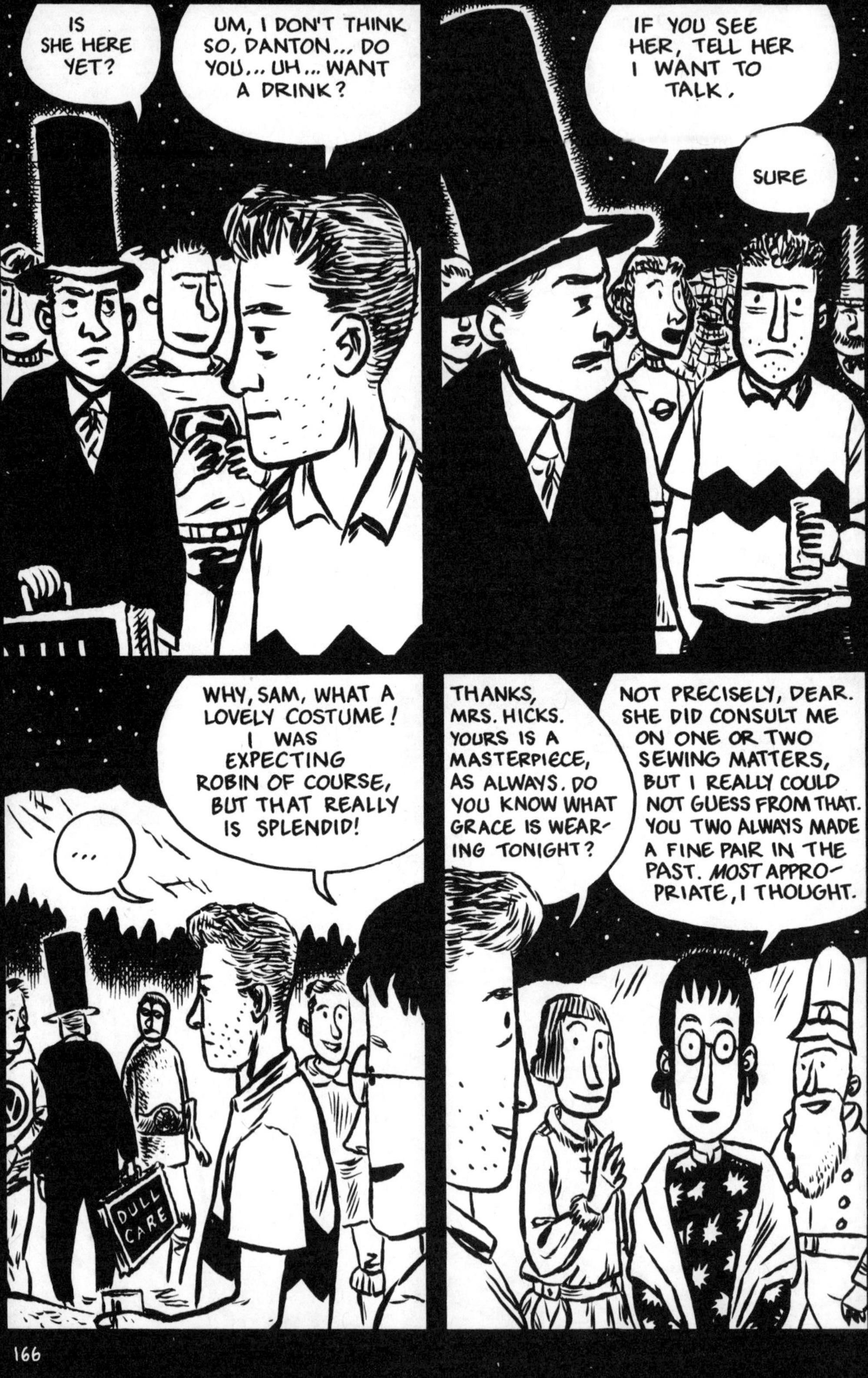
IS SHE HERE YET?
UM, I DON'T THINK SO, DANTON... DO YOU... UH... WANT A DRINK?
IF YOU SEE HER, TELL HER I WANT TO TALK.
SURE
WHY, SAM, WHAT A LOVELY COSTUME! I WAS EXPECTING ROBIN OF COURSE, BUT THAT REALLY IS SPLENDID!
...
DULL CARE
THANKS, MRS. HICKS. YOURS IS A MASTERPIECE, AS ALWAYS. DO YOU KNOW WHAT GRACE IS WEARING TONIGHT?
NOT PRECISELY, DEAR. SHE DID CONSULT ME ON ONE OR TWO SEWING MATTERS, BUT I REALLY COULD NOT GUESS FROM THAT. YOU TWO ALWAYS MADE A FINE PAIR IN THE PAST. *MOST* APPROPRIATE, I THOUGHT.

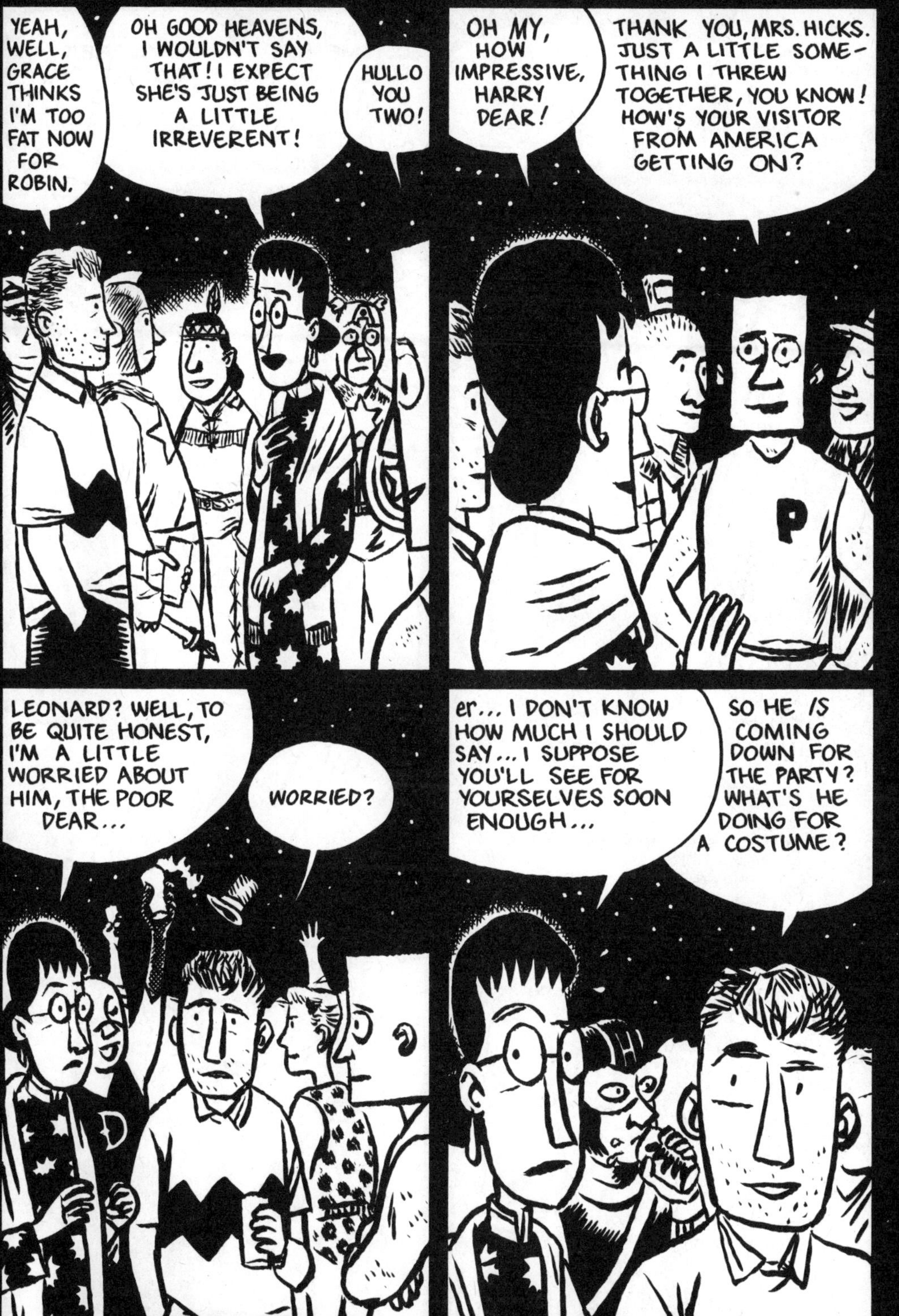
YEAH, WELL, GRACE THINKS I'M TOO FAT NOW FOR ROBIN.
OH GOOD HEAVENS, I WOULDN'T SAY THAT! I EXPECT SHE'S JUST BEING A LITTLE IRREVERENT!
HULLO YOU TWO!
OH MY, HOW IMPRESSIVE, HARRY DEAR!
THANK YOU, MRS. HICKS. JUST A LITTLE SOMETHING I THREW TOGETHER, YOU KNOW! HOW'S YOUR VISITOR FROM AMERICA GETTING ON?
P
LEONARD? WELL, TO BE QUITE HONEST, I'M A LITTLE WORRIED ABOUT HIM, THE POOR DEAR...
WORRIED?
D
er... I DON'T KNOW HOW MUCH I SHOULD SAY... I SUPPOSE YOU'LL SEE FOR YOURSELVES SOON ENOUGH...
SO HE IS COMING DOWN FOR THE PARTY? WHAT'S HE DOING FOR A COSTUME?

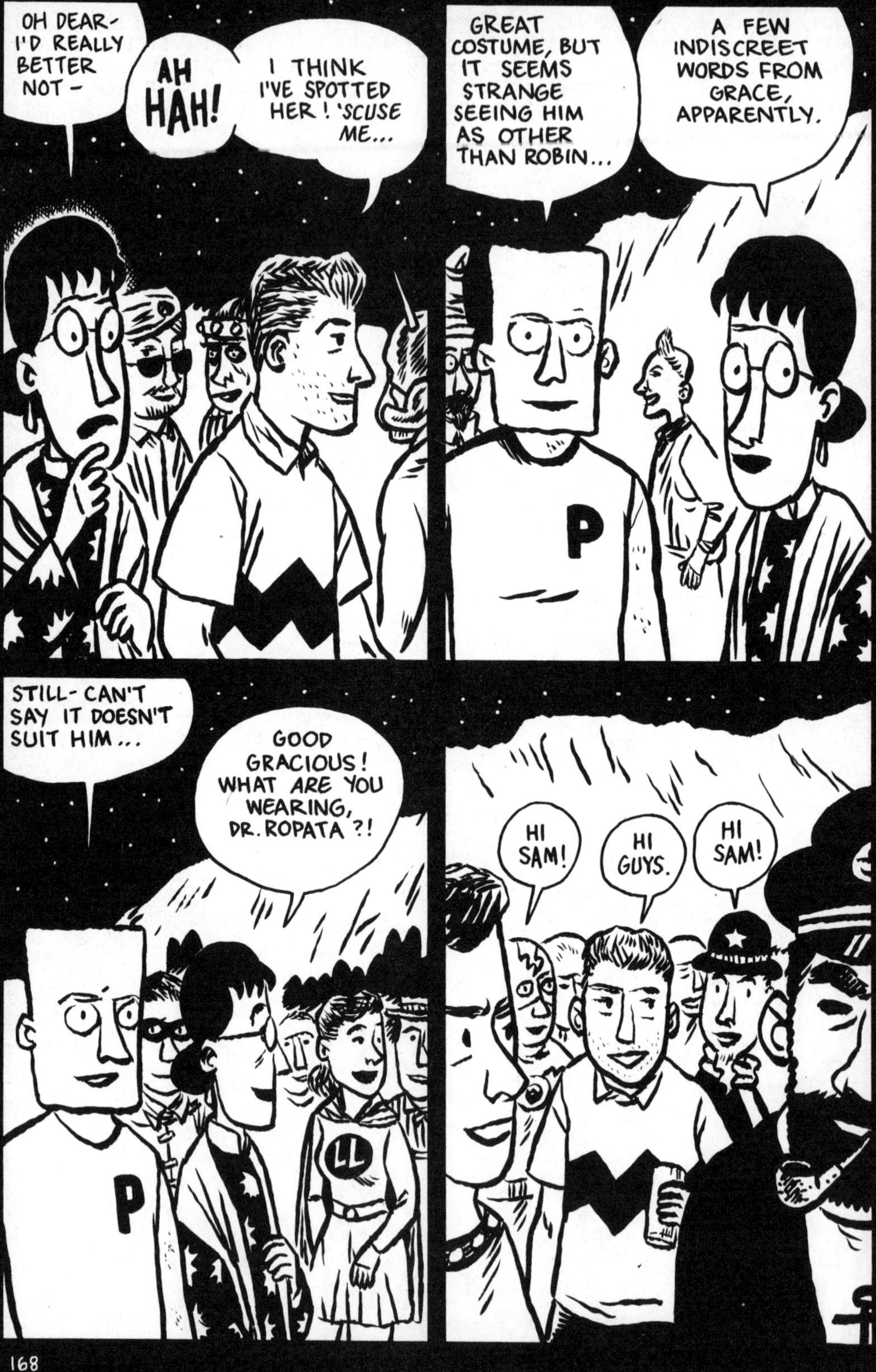
OH DEAR- I'D REALLY BETTER NOT-
AH HAH!
I THINK I'VE SPOTTED HER! 'SCUSE ME...
GREAT COSTUME, BUT IT SEEMS STRANGE SEEING HIM AS OTHER THAN ROBIN...
A FEW INDISCREET WORDS FROM GRACE, APPARENTLY.
STILL- CAN'T SAY IT DOESN'T SUIT HIM...
GOOD GRACIOUS! WHAT ARE YOU WEARING, DR. ROPATA ?!
HI SAM!
HI GUYS.
HI SAM!
P
P
LL

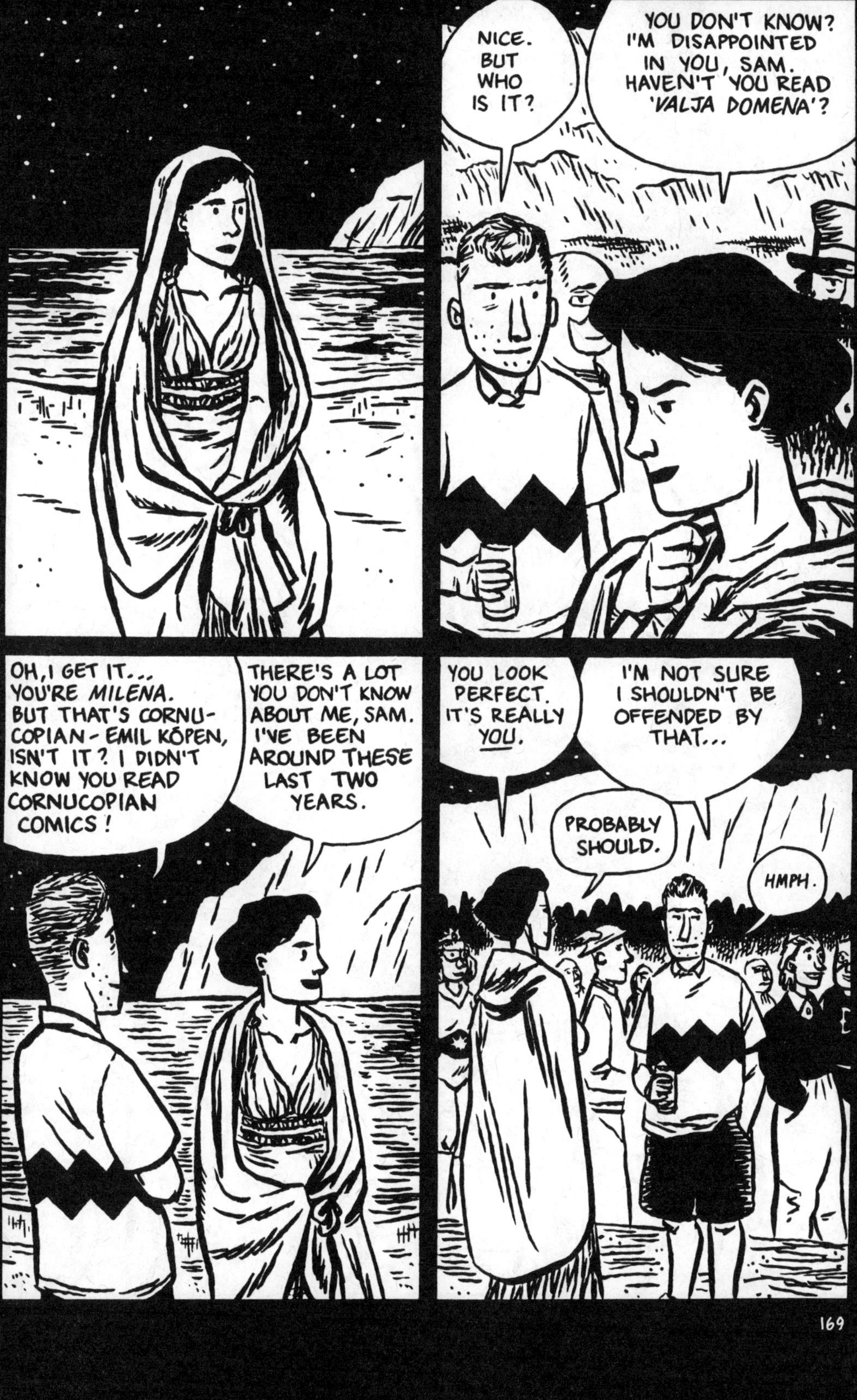
NICE. BUT WHO IS IT?
YOU DON'T KNOW? I'M DISAPPOINTED IN YOU, SAM. HAVEN'T YOU READ 'VALJA DOMENA'?
OH, I GET IT... YOU'RE MILENA. BUT THAT'S CORNUCOPIAN - EMIL KÖPEN, ISN'T IT? I DIDN'T KNOW YOU READ CORNUCOPIAN COMICS!
THERE'S A LOT YOU DON'T KNOW ABOUT ME, SAM. I'VE BEEN AROUND THESE LAST TWO YEARS.
YOU LOOK PERFECT. IT'S REALLY YOU.
I'M NOT SURE I SHOULDN'T BE OFFENDED BY THAT...
PROBABLY SHOULD.
HMPH.

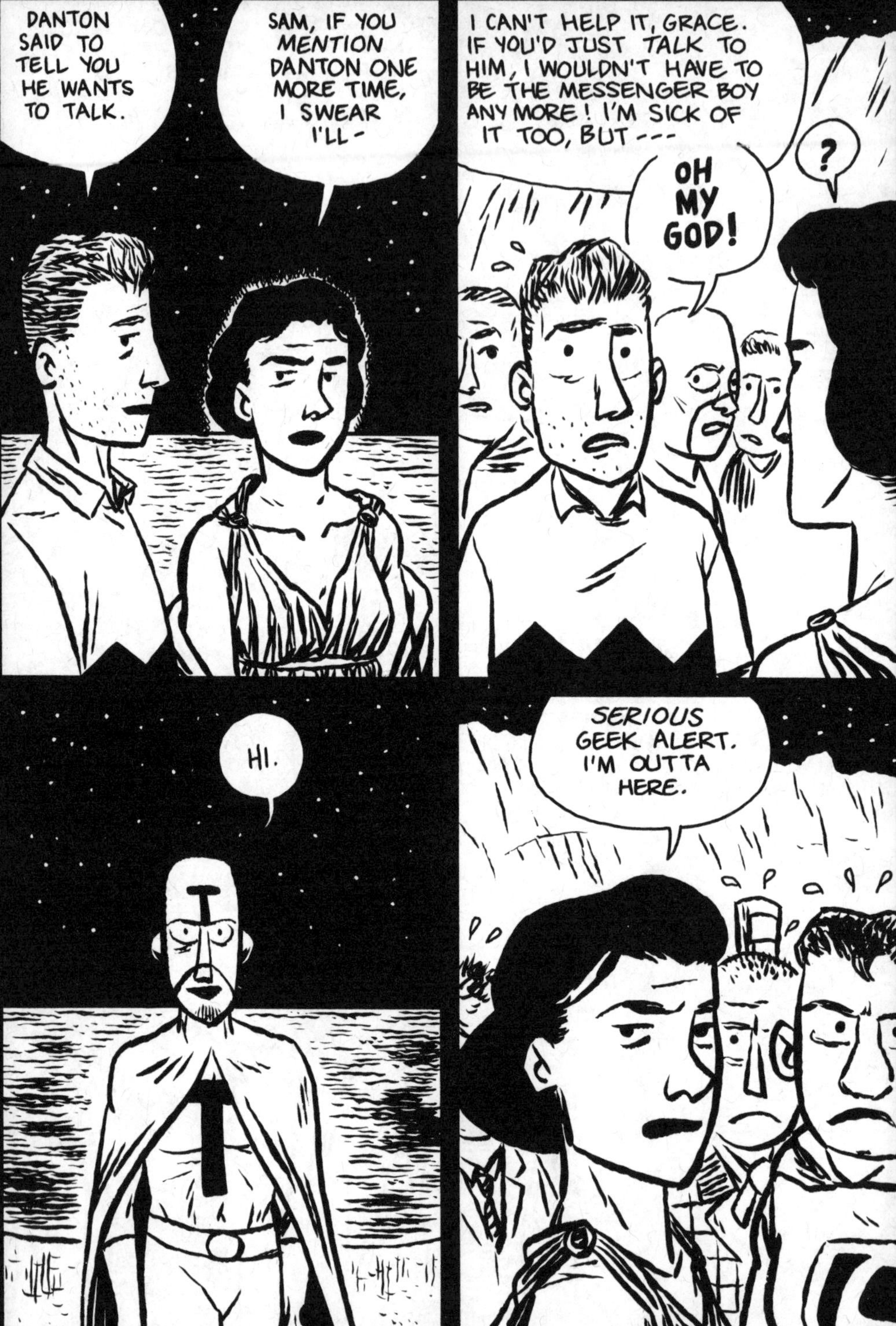
DANTON SAID TO TELL YOU HE WANTS TO TALK.
SAM, IF YOU MENTION DANTON ONE MORE TIME, I SWEAR I'LL-
I CAN'T HELP IT, GRACE. IF YOU'D JUST TALK TO HIM, I WOULDN'T HAVE TO BE THE MESSENGER BOY ANY MORE! I'M SICK OF IT TOO, BUT---
OH MY GOD!
?
HI.
SERIOUS GEEK ALERT. I'M OUTTA HERE.

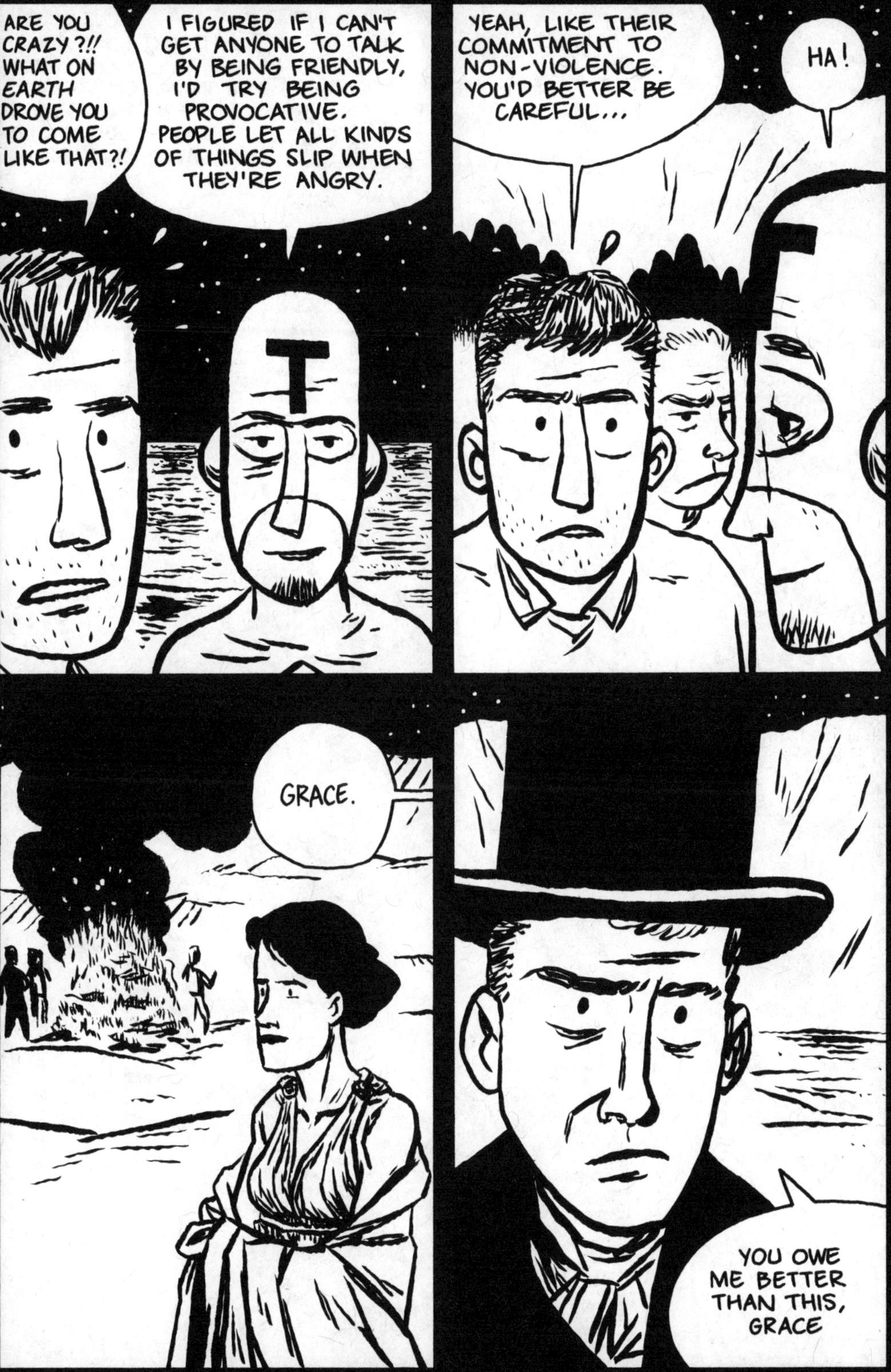
ARE YOU CRAZY?!! WHAT ON EARTH DROVE YOU TO COME LIKE THAT?!
I FIGURED IF I CAN'T GET ANYONE TO TALK BY BEING FRIENDLY, I'D TRY BEING PROVOCATIVE. PEOPLE LET ALL KINDS OF THINGS SLIP WHEN THEY'RE ANGRY.
YEAH, LIKE THEIR COMMITMENT TO NON-VIOLENCE. YOU'D BETTER BE CAREFUL...
HA!
GRACE.
YOU OWE ME BETTER THAN THIS, GRACE

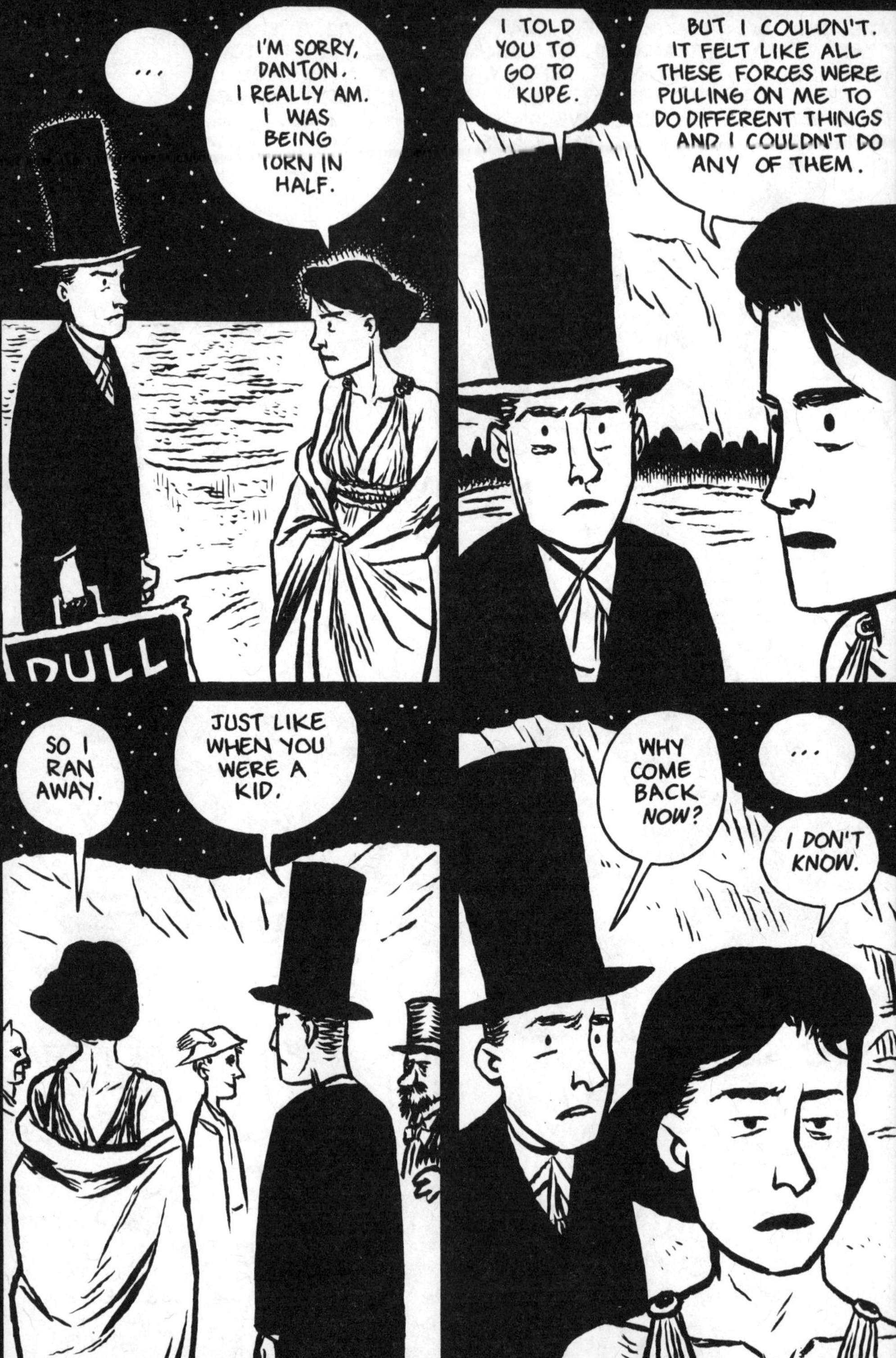
...
I'M SORRY, DANTON. I REALLY AM. I WAS BEING TORN IN HALF.
DULL
I TOLD YOU TO GO TO KUPE.
BUT I COULDN'T. IT FELT LIKE ALL THESE FORCES WERE PULLING ON ME TO DO DIFFERENT THINGS AND I COULDN'T DO ANY OF THEM.
SO I RAN AWAY.
JUST LIKE WHEN YOU WERE A KID.
WHY COME BACK *NOW*?
...
I DON'T KNOW.

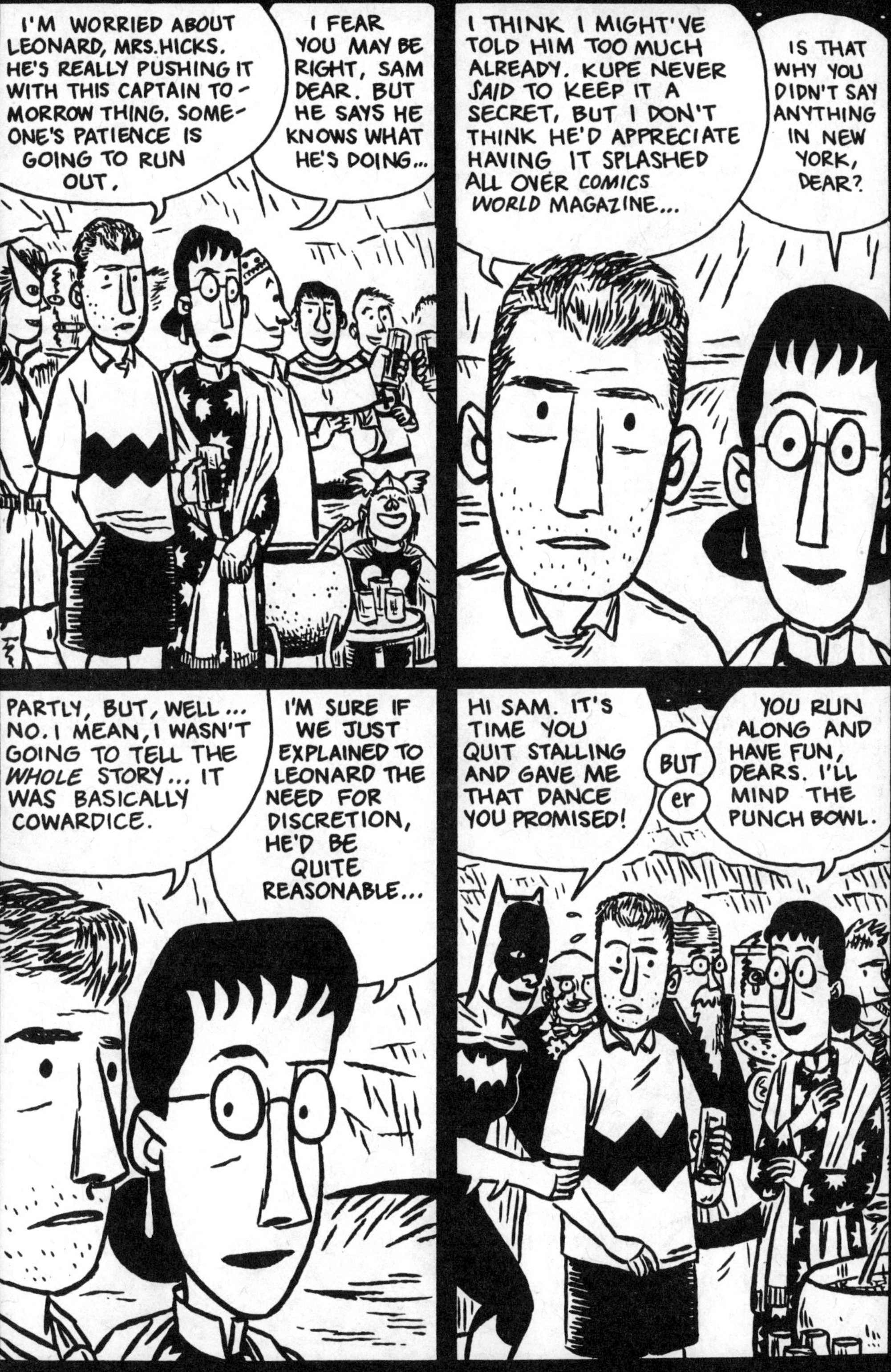
I'M WORRIED ABOUT LEONARD, MRS. HICKS. HE'S REALLY PUSHING IT WITH THIS CAPTAIN TO-MORROW THING. SOME-ONE'S PATIENCE IS GOING TO RUN OUT.
I FEAR YOU MAY BE RIGHT, SAM DEAR. BUT HE SAYS HE KNOWS WHAT HE'S DOING...
I THINK I MIGHT'VE TOLD HIM TOO MUCH ALREADY. KUPE NEVER *SAID* TO KEEP IT A SECRET, BUT I DON'T THINK HE'D APPRECIATE HAVING IT SPLASHED ALL OVER *COMICS WORLD* MAGAZINE...
IS THAT WHY YOU DIDN'T SAY ANYTHING IN NEW YORK, DEAR?
PARTLY, BUT, WELL... NO. I MEAN, I WASN'T GOING TO TELL THE *WHOLE* STORY... IT WAS BASICALLY COWARDICE.
I'M SURE IF WE JUST EXPLAINED TO LEONARD THE NEED FOR DISCRETION, HE'D BE QUITE REASONABLE...
HI SAM. IT'S TIME YOU QUIT STALLING AND GAVE ME THAT DANCE YOU PROMISED!
BUT
er
YOU RUN ALONG AND HAVE FUN, DEARS. I'LL MIND THE PUNCH BOWL.

SO, SAM, ARE YOU SEEING ANYONE THESE DAYS?

WHO, ME? UH-WELL-UM-

WHEN YOU WALKED INTO THE FIEND- JUST LIKE THAT... IT WAS LIKE SEEING A GHOST. I THOUGHT YOU'D COME BACK SOME DAY, BUT I'D PRETTY MUCH ADJUSTED TO THE FACT THAT YOU WEREN'T AROUND, AND IT WAS ALL OVER.

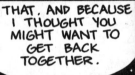

MMM.

AND THEN THERE YOU WERE... AND WE'RE GAWKING AT EACH OTHER, LIKE WE DON'T KNOW WHAT TO SAY...

I DIDN'T KNOW WHAT TO SAY... I STILL DON'T.

IS THAT WHY YOU'VE BEEN AVOIDING ME?

THAT, AND BECAUSE I THOUGHT YOU MIGHT WANT TO GET BACK TOGETHER.

174

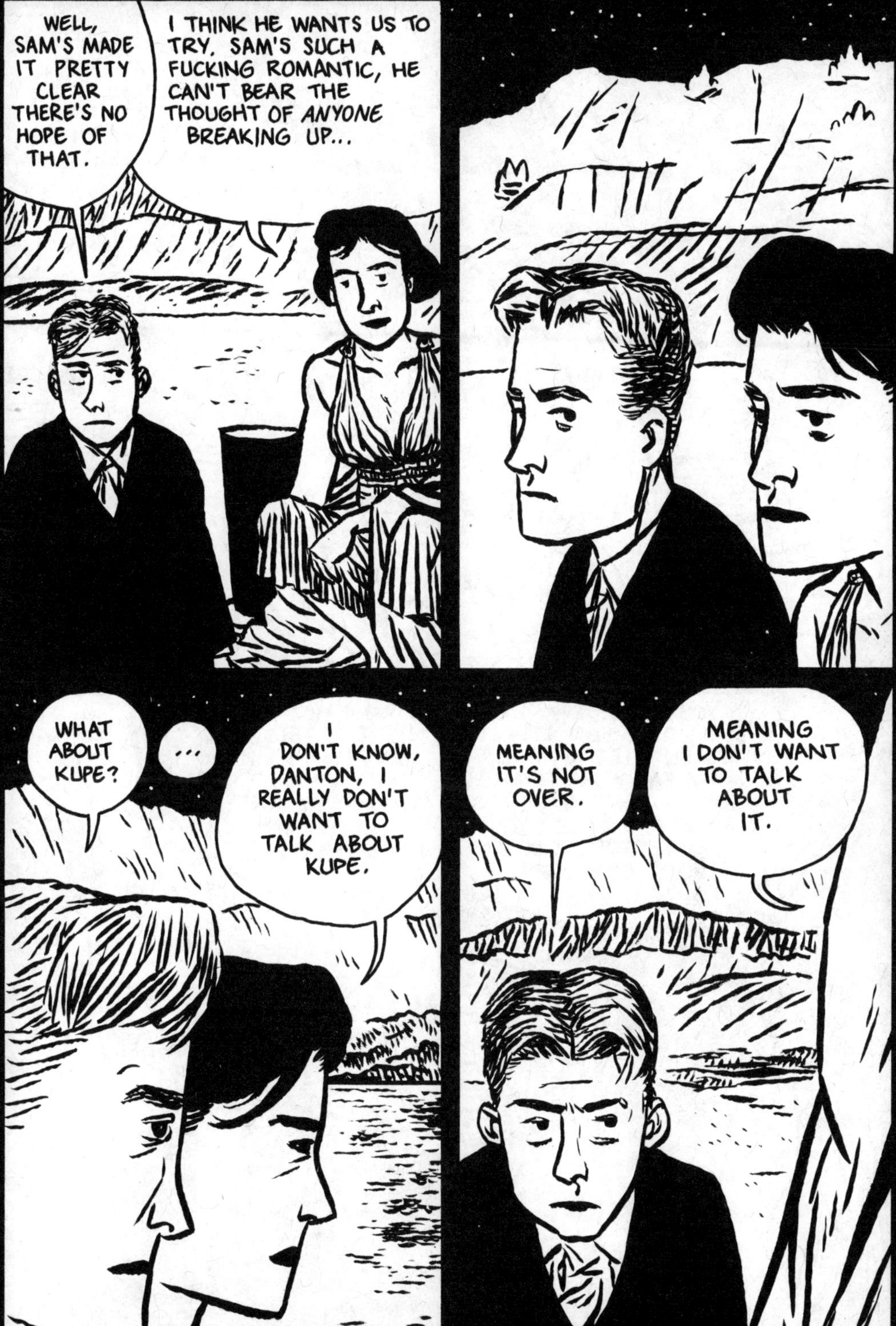
WELL, SAM'S MADE IT PRETTY CLEAR THERE'S NO HOPE OF THAT.
I THINK HE WANTS US TO TRY. SAM'S SUCH A FUCKING ROMANTIC, HE CAN'T BEAR THE THOUGHT OF *ANYONE* BREAKING UP...
WHAT ABOUT KUPE?
...
I DON'T KNOW, DANTON, I REALLY DON'T WANT TO TALK ABOUT KUPE.
MEANING IT'S NOT OVER.
MEANING I DON'T WANT TO TALK ABOUT IT.

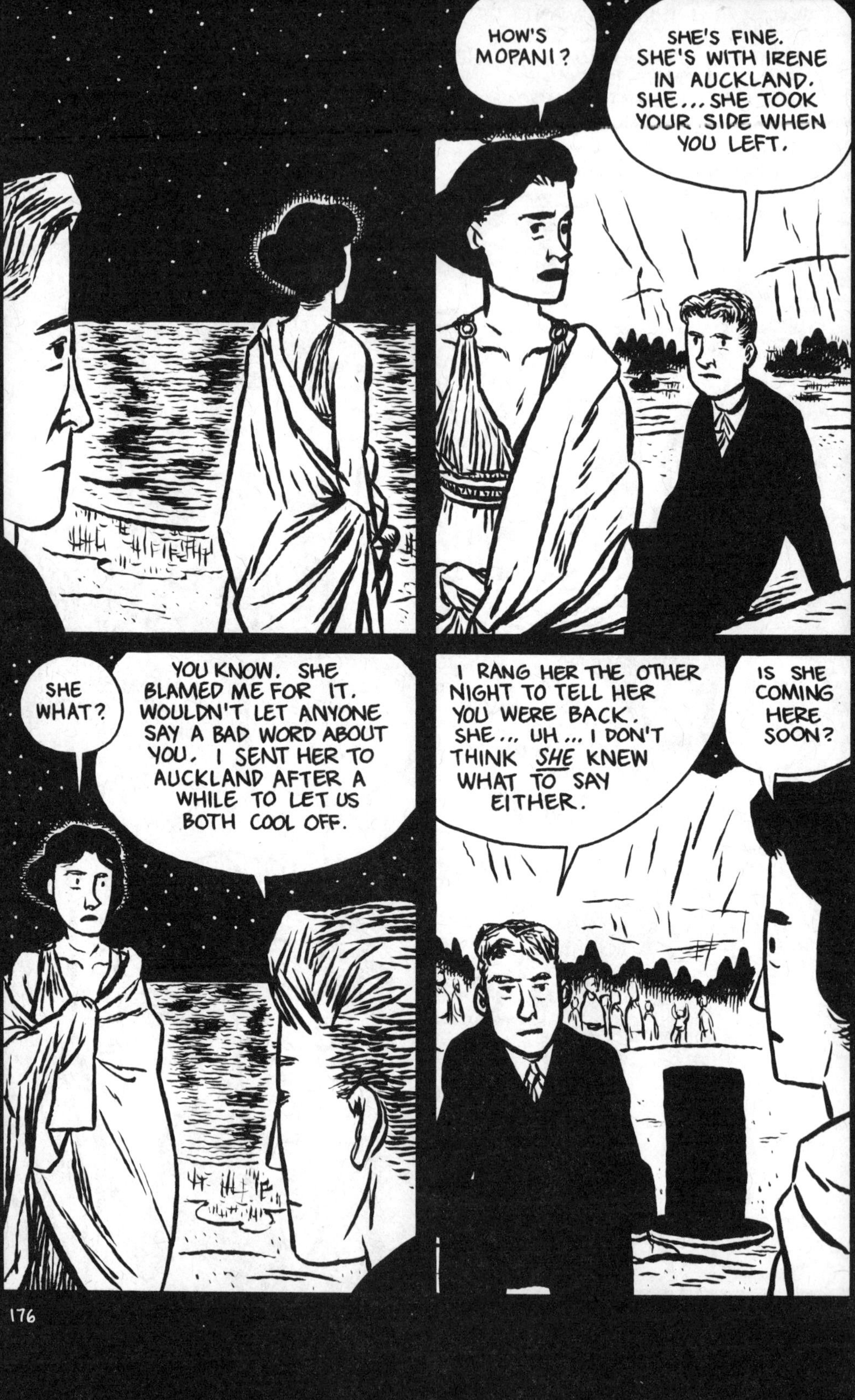
HOW'S MOPANI?
SHE'S FINE. SHE'S WITH IRENE IN AUCKLAND. SHE... SHE TOOK YOUR SIDE WHEN YOU LEFT.
SHE WHAT?
YOU KNOW. SHE BLAMED ME FOR IT. WOULDN'T LET ANYONE SAY A BAD WORD ABOUT YOU. I SENT HER TO AUCKLAND AFTER A WHILE TO LET US BOTH COOL OFF.
I RANG HER THE OTHER NIGHT TO TELL HER YOU WERE BACK. SHE... UH... I DON'T THINK SHE KNEW WHAT TO SAY EITHER.
IS SHE COMING HERE SOON?

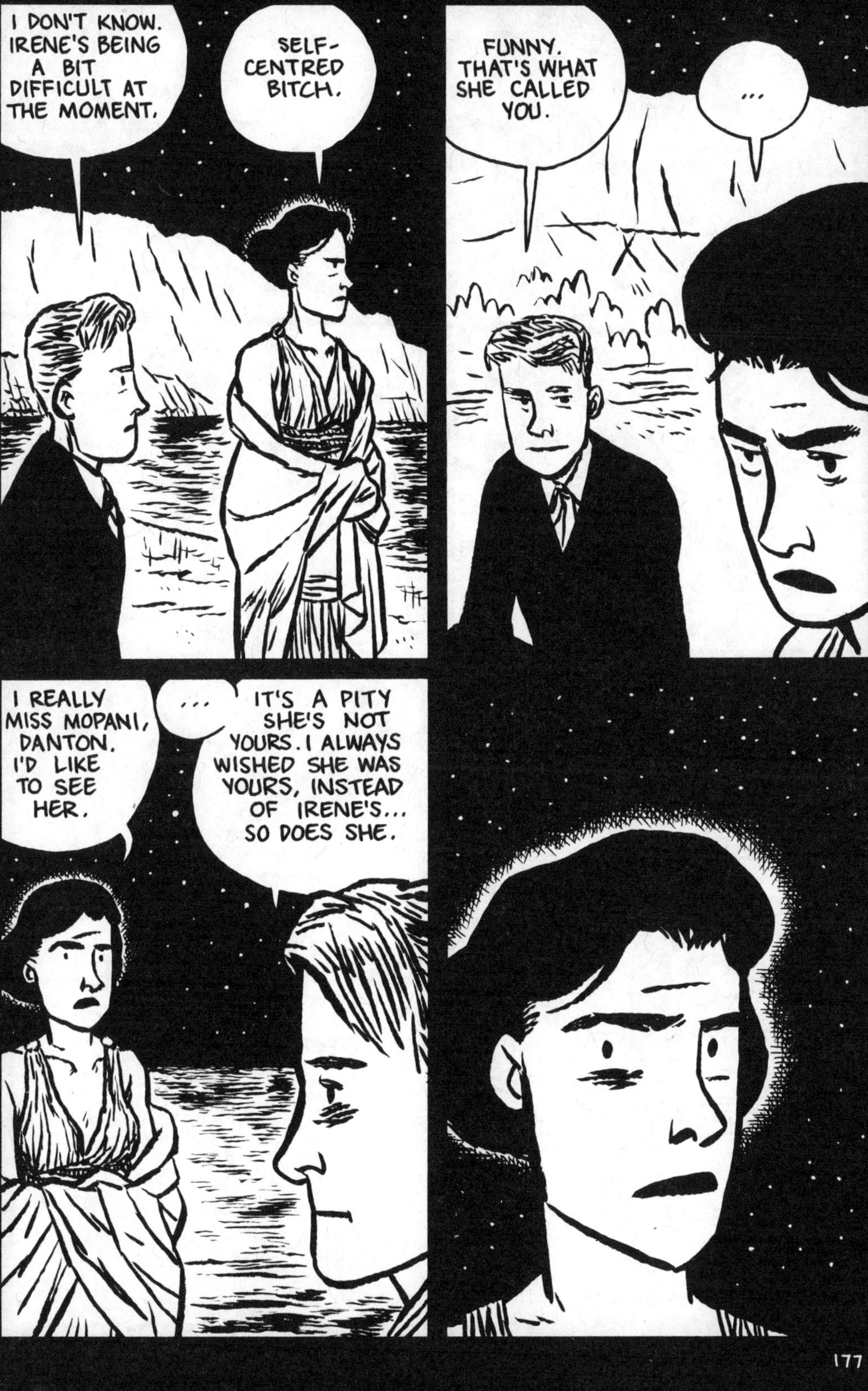
I DON'T KNOW. IRENE'S BEING A BIT DIFFICULT AT THE MOMENT.
SELF-CENTRED BITCH.
FUNNY. THAT'S WHAT SHE CALLED YOU.
...
I REALLY MISS MOPANI, DANTON. I'D LIKE TO SEE HER.
...
IT'S A PITY SHE'S NOT YOURS. I ALWAYS WISHED SHE WAS YOURS, INSTEAD OF IRENE'S... SO DOES SHE.

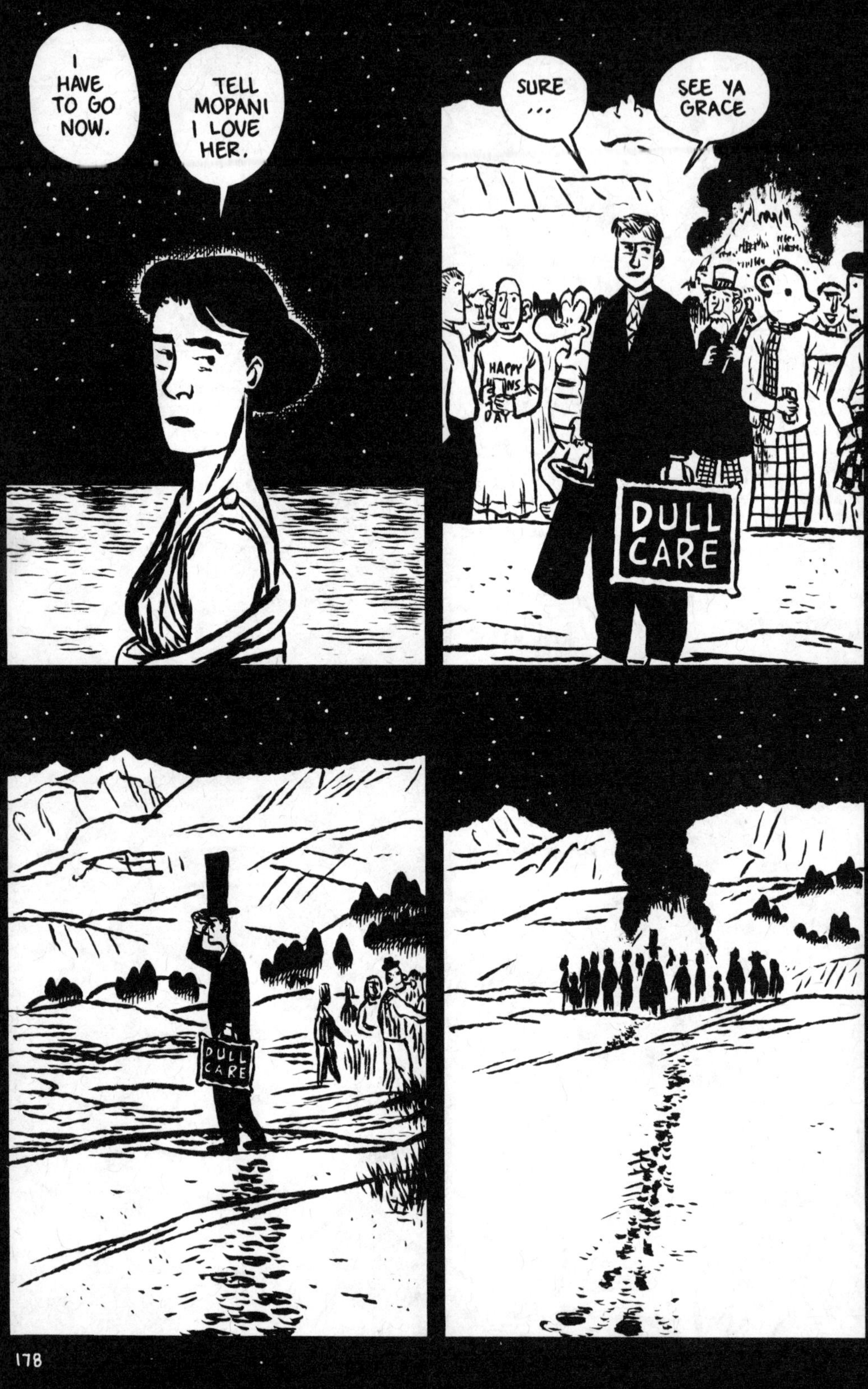
I HAVE TO GO NOW.
TELL MOPANI I LOVE HER.
SURE ...
SEE YA GRACE
DULL CARE
DULL CARE

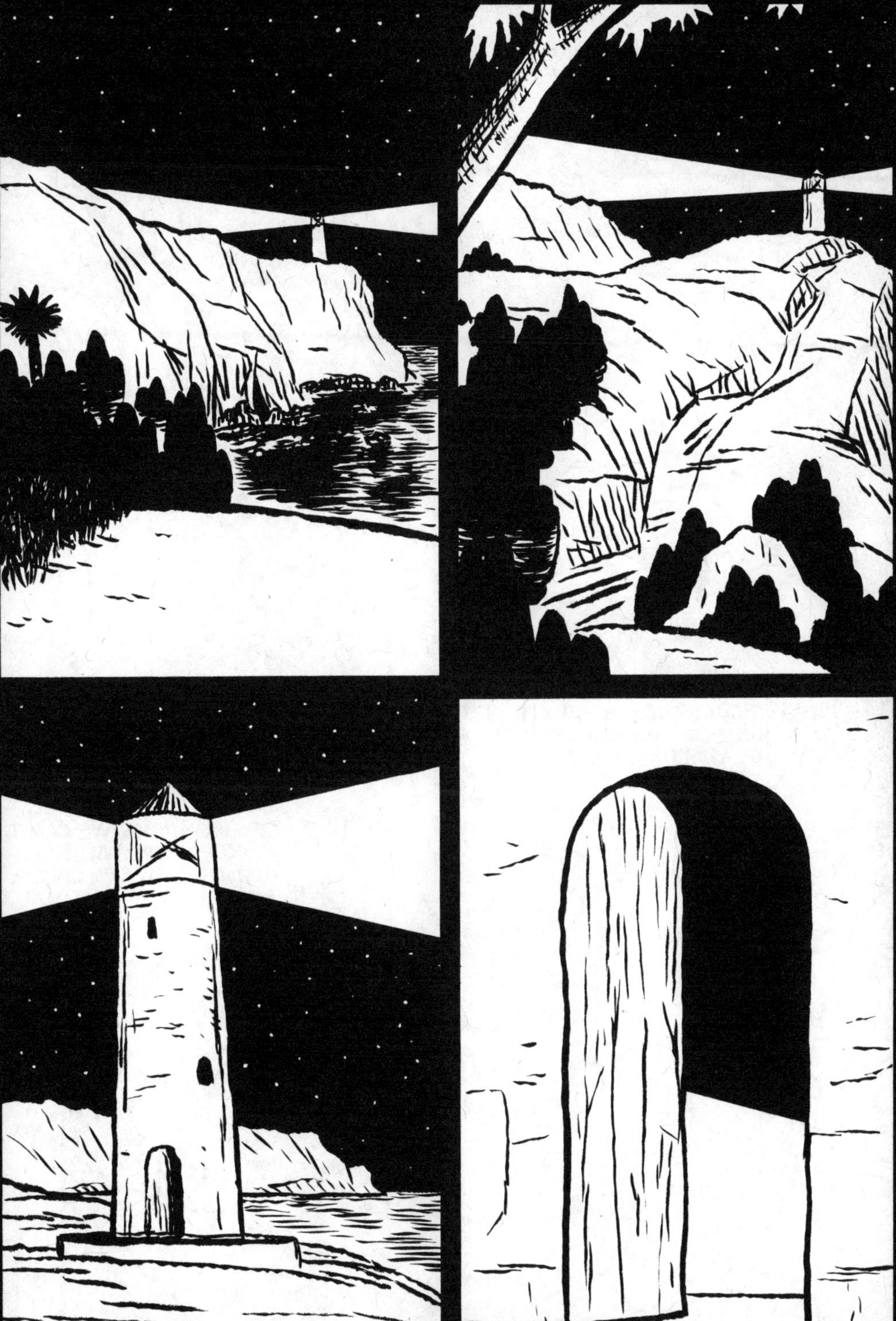

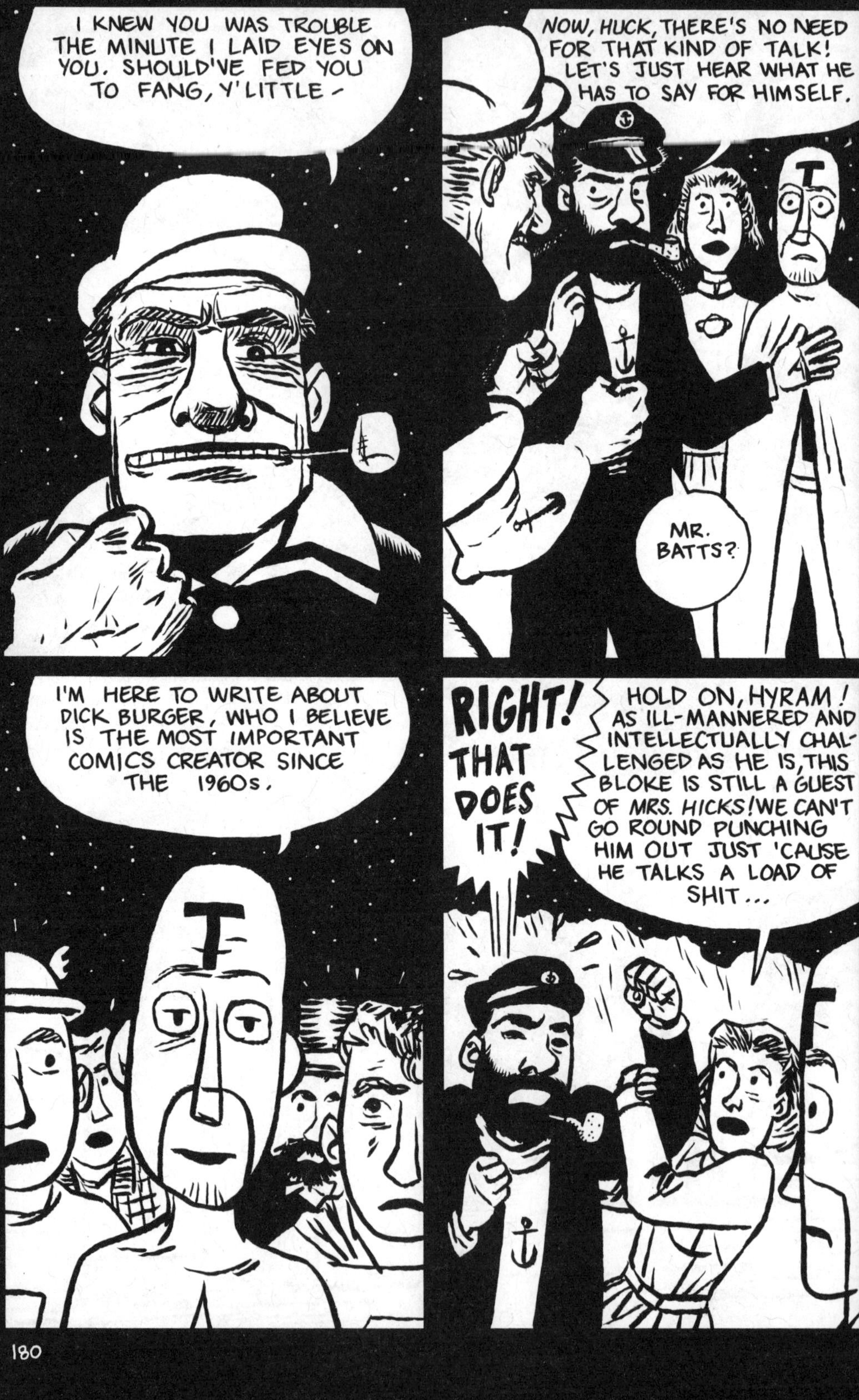
I KNEW YOU WAS TROUBLE THE MINUTE I LAID EYES ON YOU. SHOULD'VE FED YOU TO FANG, Y'LITTLE -
NOW, HUCK, THERE'S NO NEED FOR THAT KIND OF TALK! LET'S JUST HEAR WHAT HE HAS TO SAY FOR HIMSELF.
MR. BATTS?
I'M HERE TO WRITE ABOUT DICK BURGER, WHO I BELIEVE IS THE MOST IMPORTANT COMICS CREATOR SINCE THE 1960s.
RIGHT! THAT DOES IT!
HOLD ON, HYRAM! AS ILL-MANNERED AND INTELLECTUALLY CHAL-LENGED AS HE IS, THIS BLOKE IS STILL A GUEST OF MRS. HICKS! WE CAN'T GO ROUND PUNCHING HIM OUT JUST 'CAUSE HE TALKS A LOAD OF SHIT...

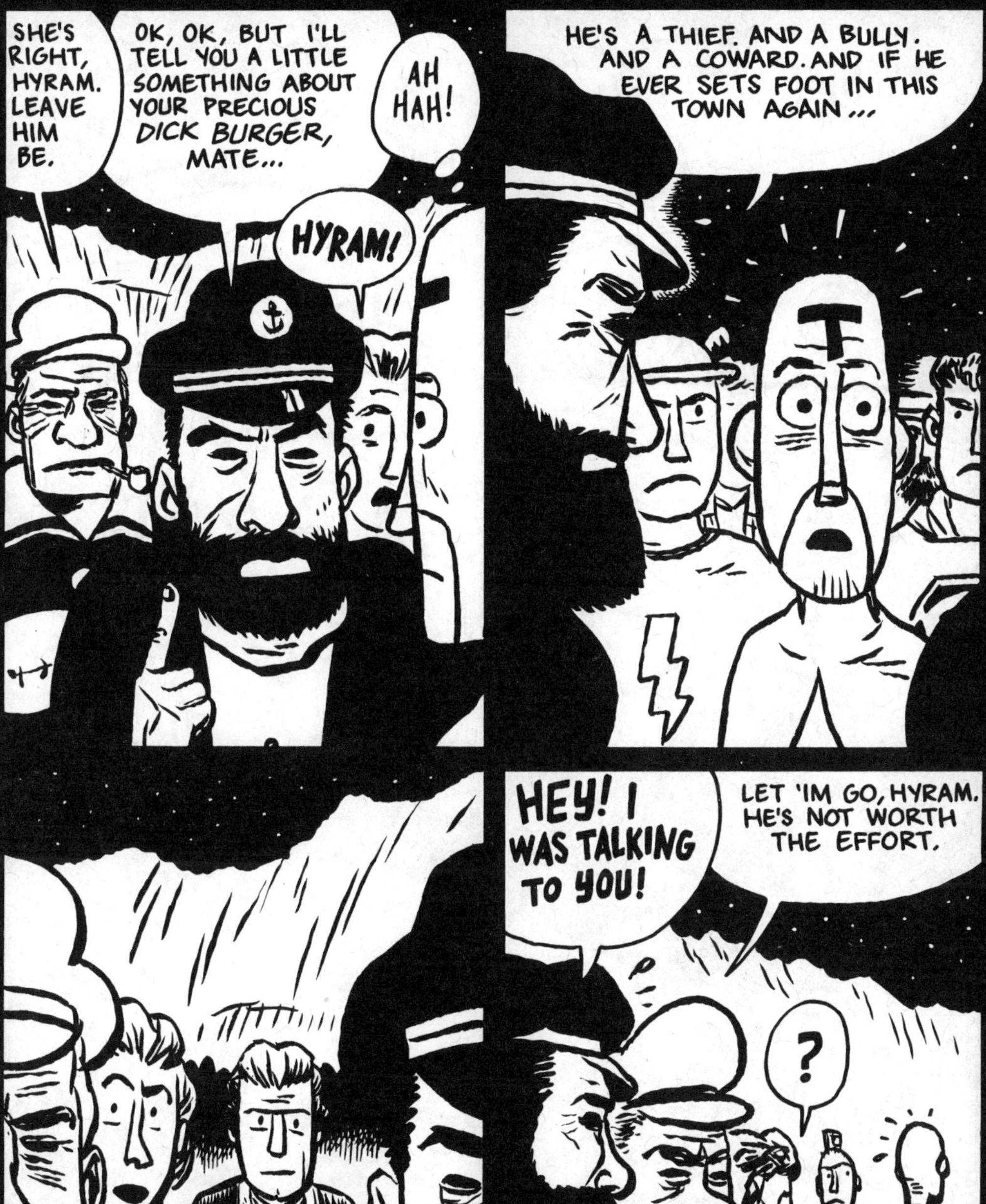
SHE'S RIGHT, HYRAM. LEAVE HIM BE.
OK, OK, BUT I'LL TELL YOU A LITTLE SOMETHING ABOUT YOUR PRECIOUS DICK BURGER, MATE...
AH HAH!
HYRAM!
HE'S A THIEF. AND A BULLY. AND A COWARD. AND IF HE EVER SETS FOOT IN THIS TOWN AGAIN...
HEY! I WAS TALKING TO YOU!
LET 'IM GO, HYRAM. HE'S NOT WORTH THE EFFORT.
?

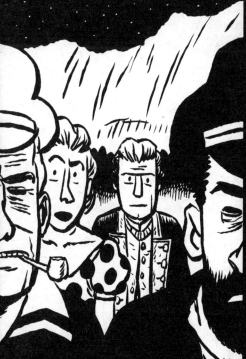

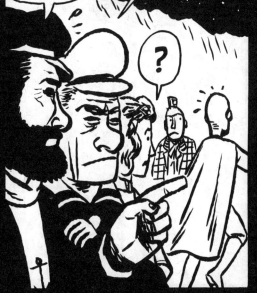

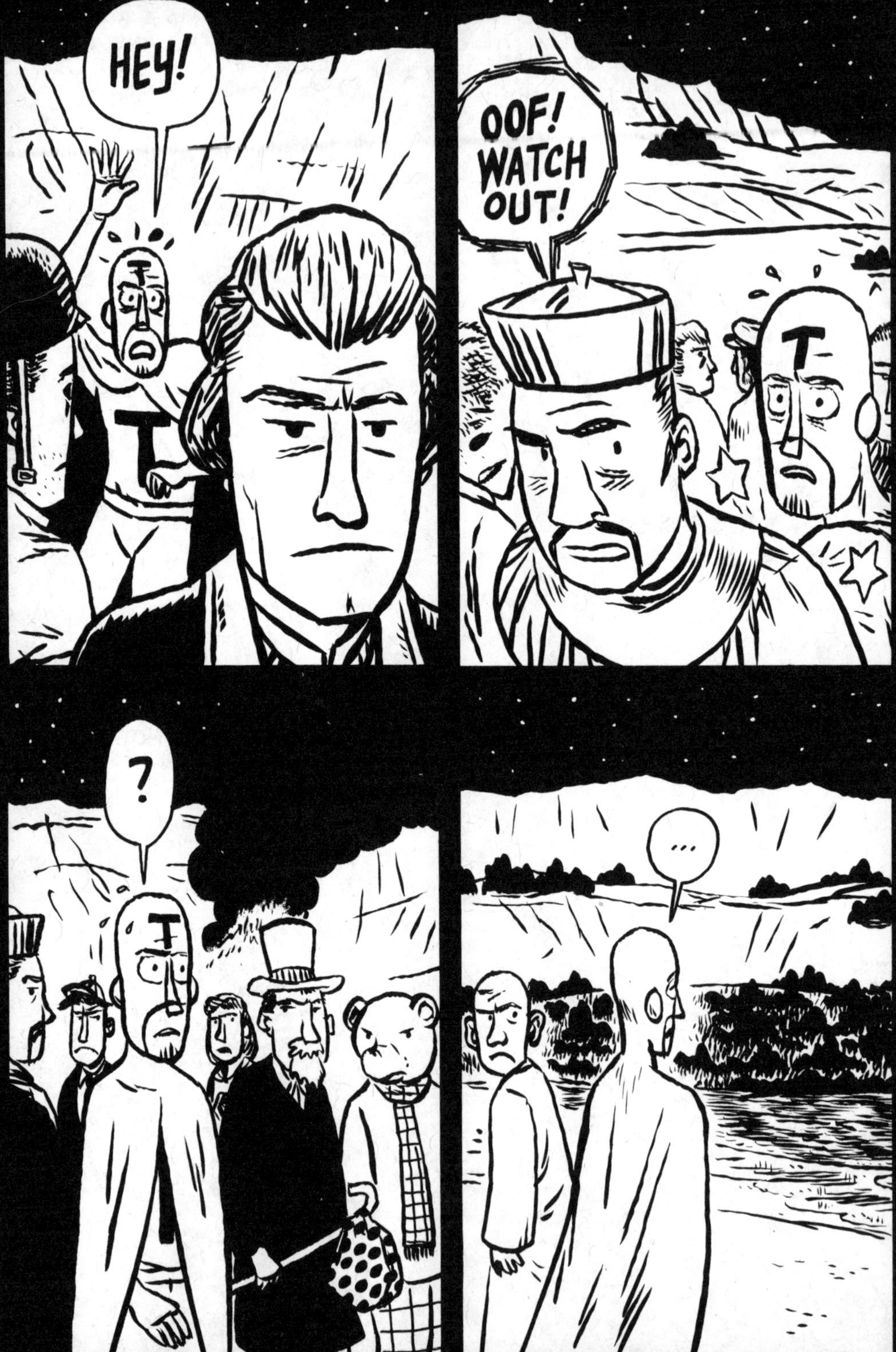
HEY!
OOF! WATCH OUT!
?
...

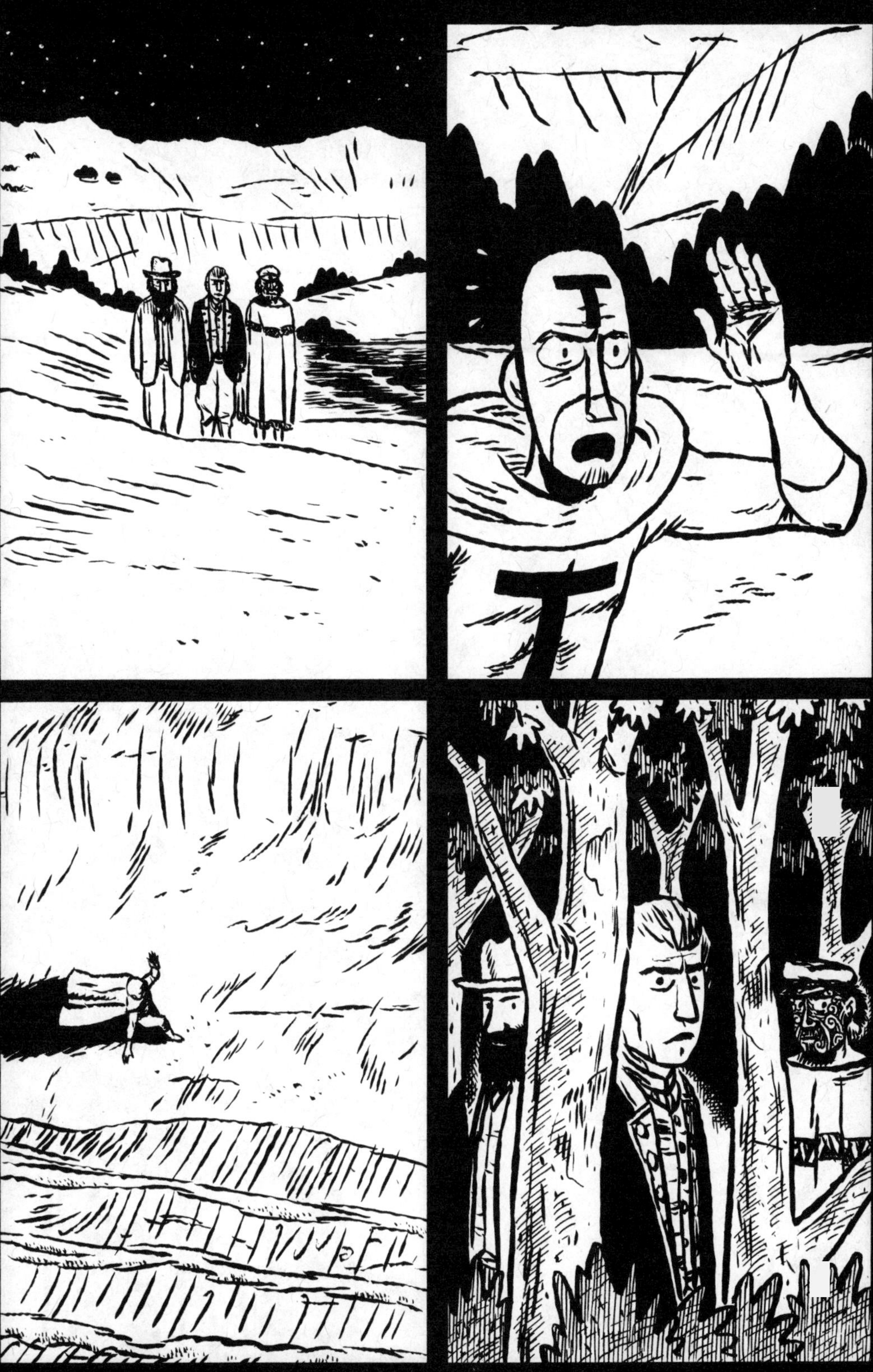

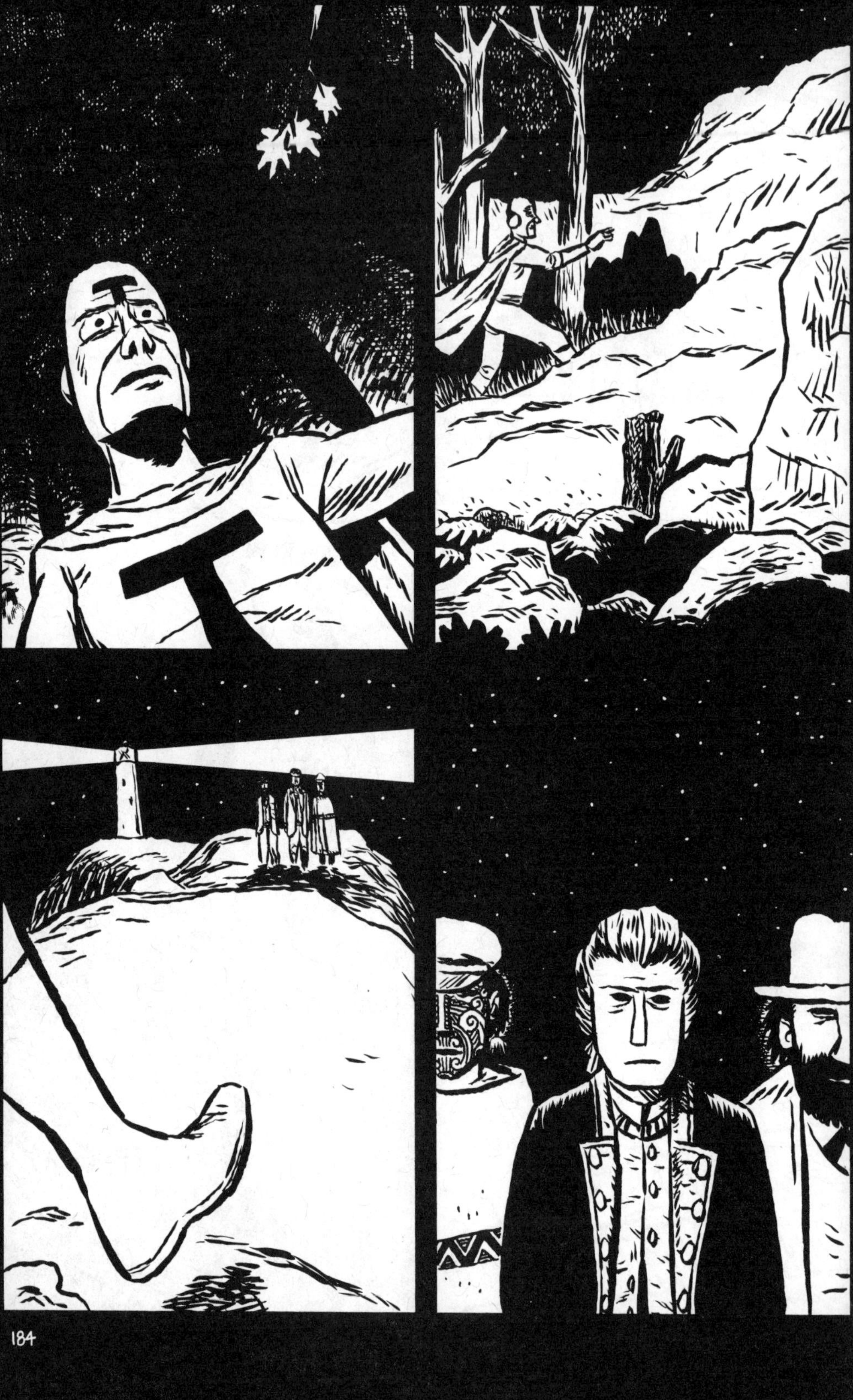

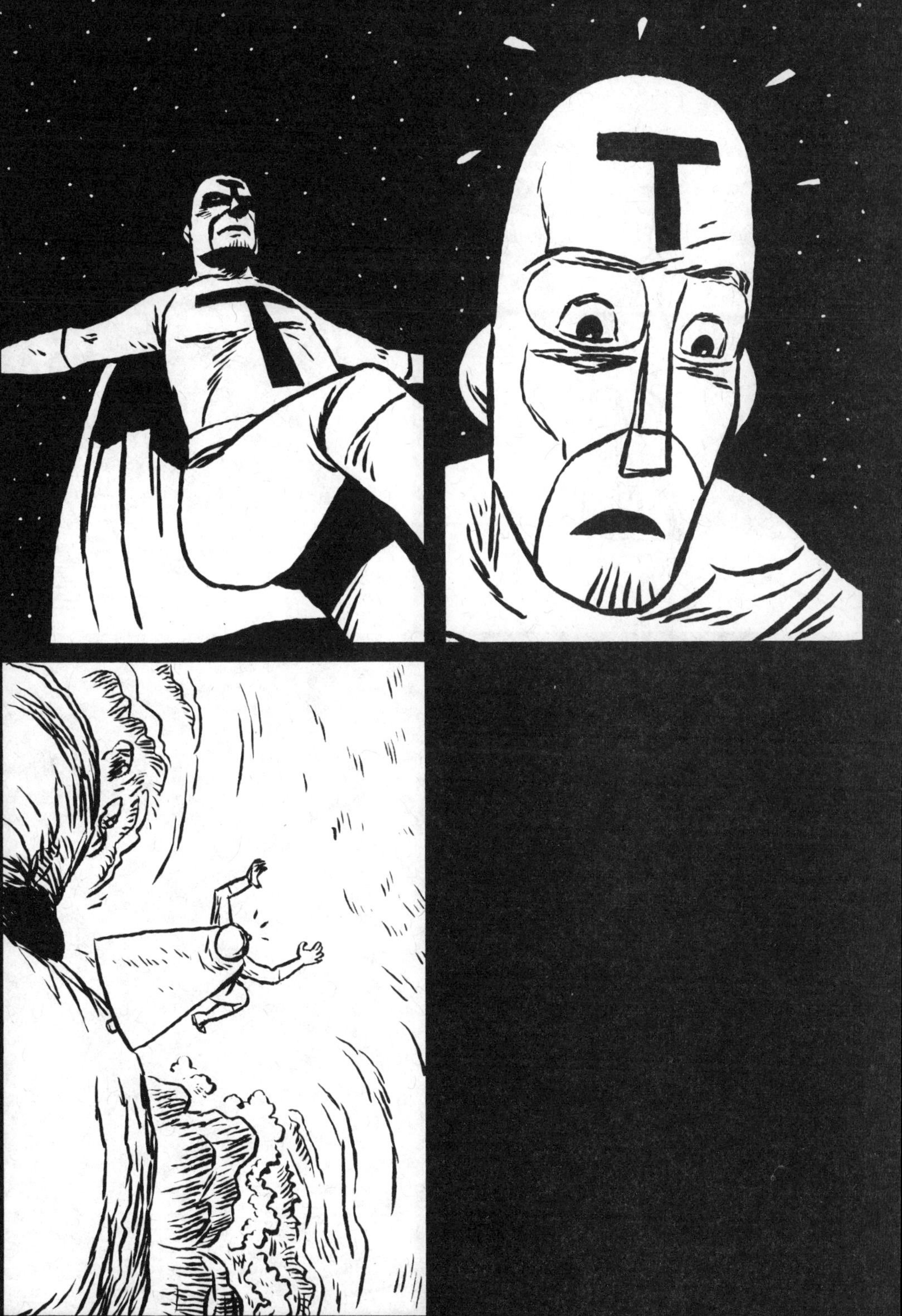

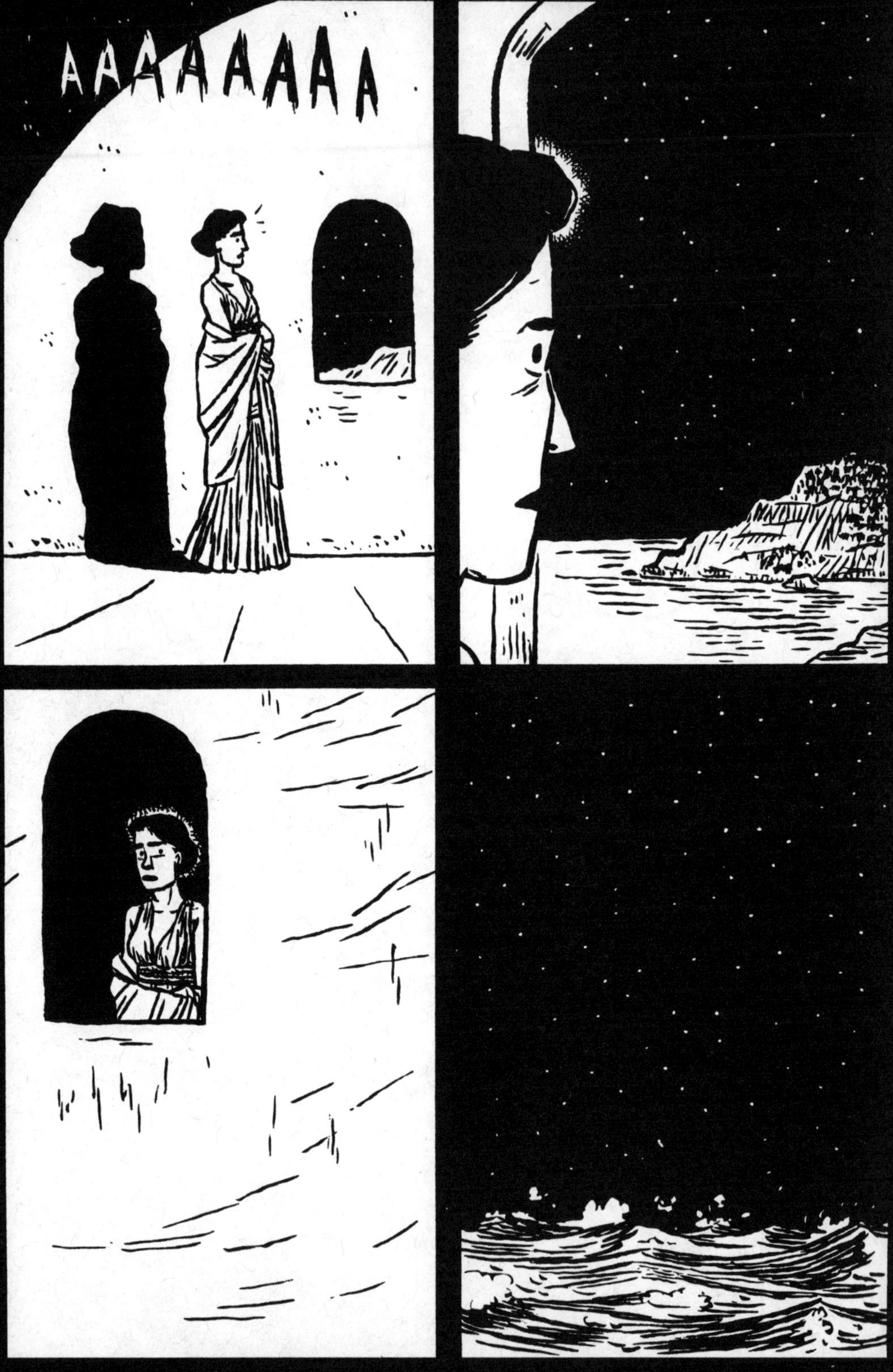
AAAAAAAA

Chapter Nine

"Inspiration! Who ever heard of
a comic artist being inspired?"
George Herriman, c.1902.

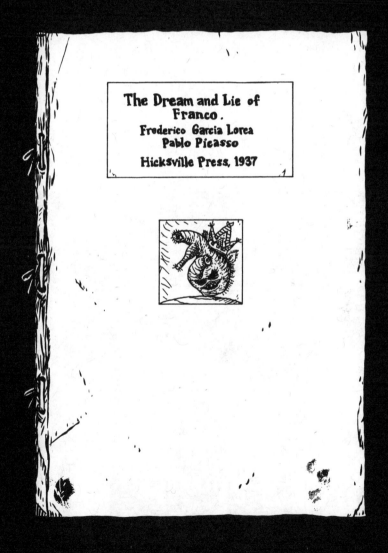

The Dream and Lie of
Franco.
Frederico Garcia Lorca
Pablo Picasso

Hicksville Press, 1937

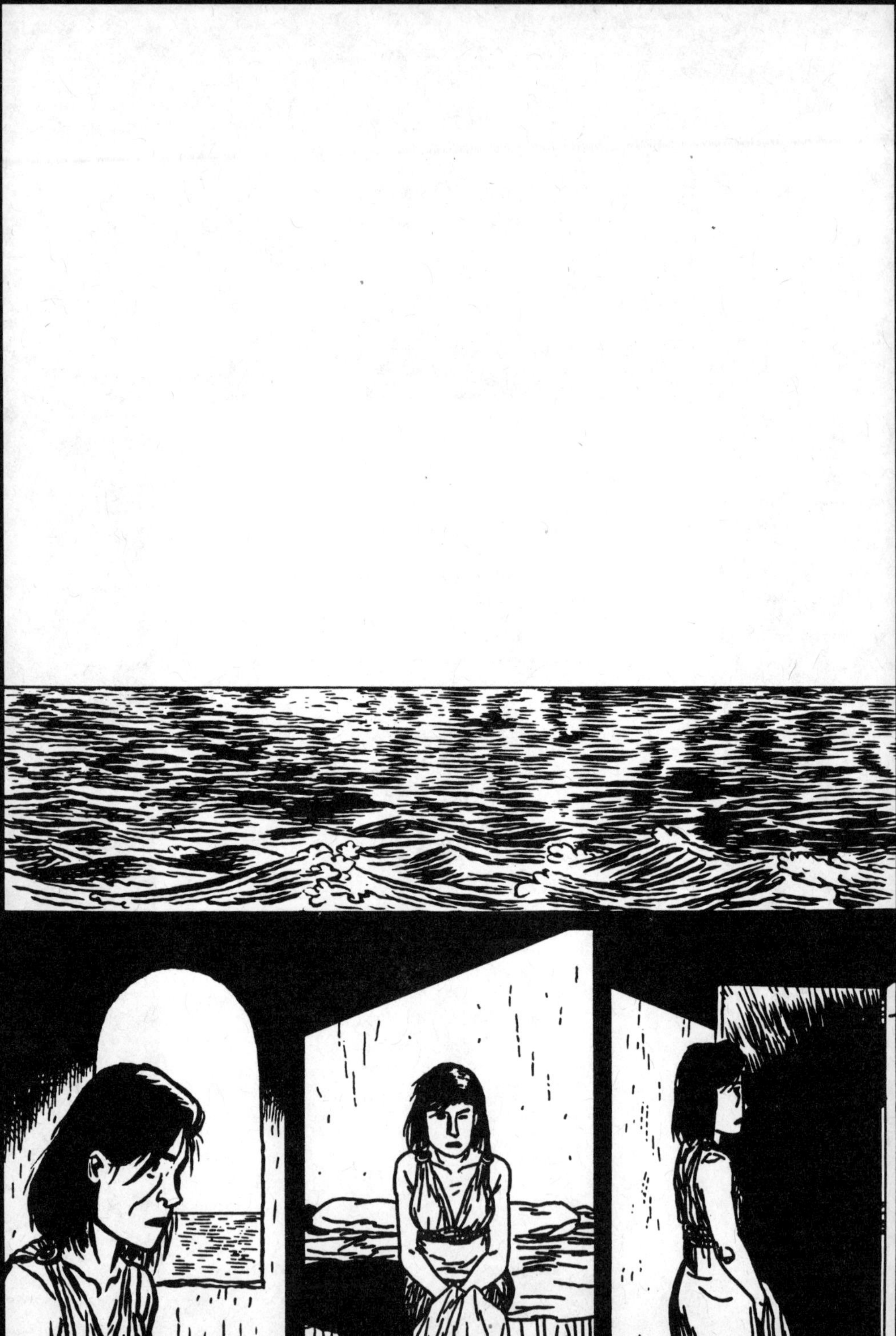

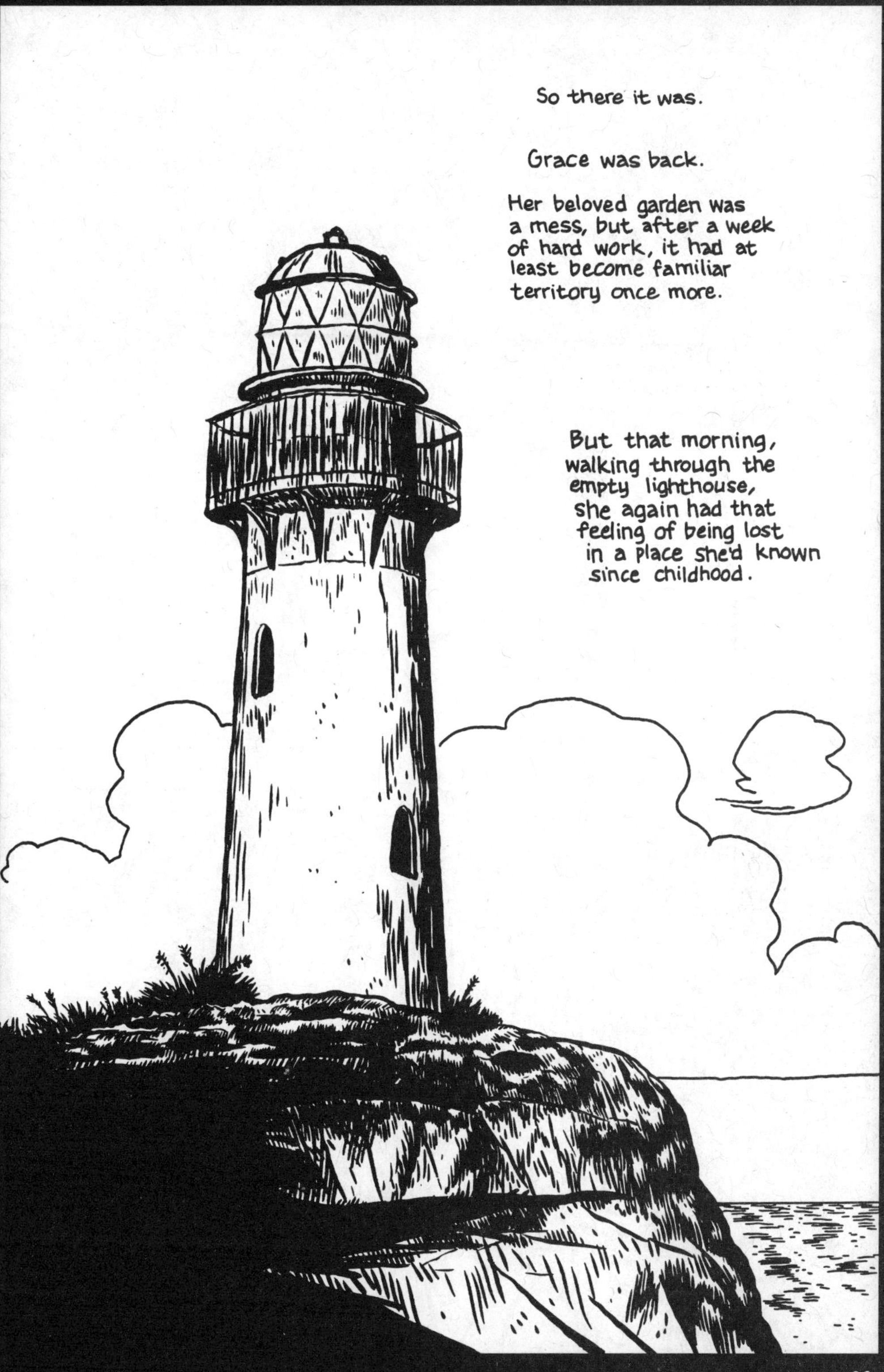
So there it was.
Grace was back.
Her beloved garden was a mess, but after a week of hard work, it had at least become familiar territory once more.
But that morning, walking through the empty lighthouse, she again had that feeling of being lost in a place she'd known since childhood.

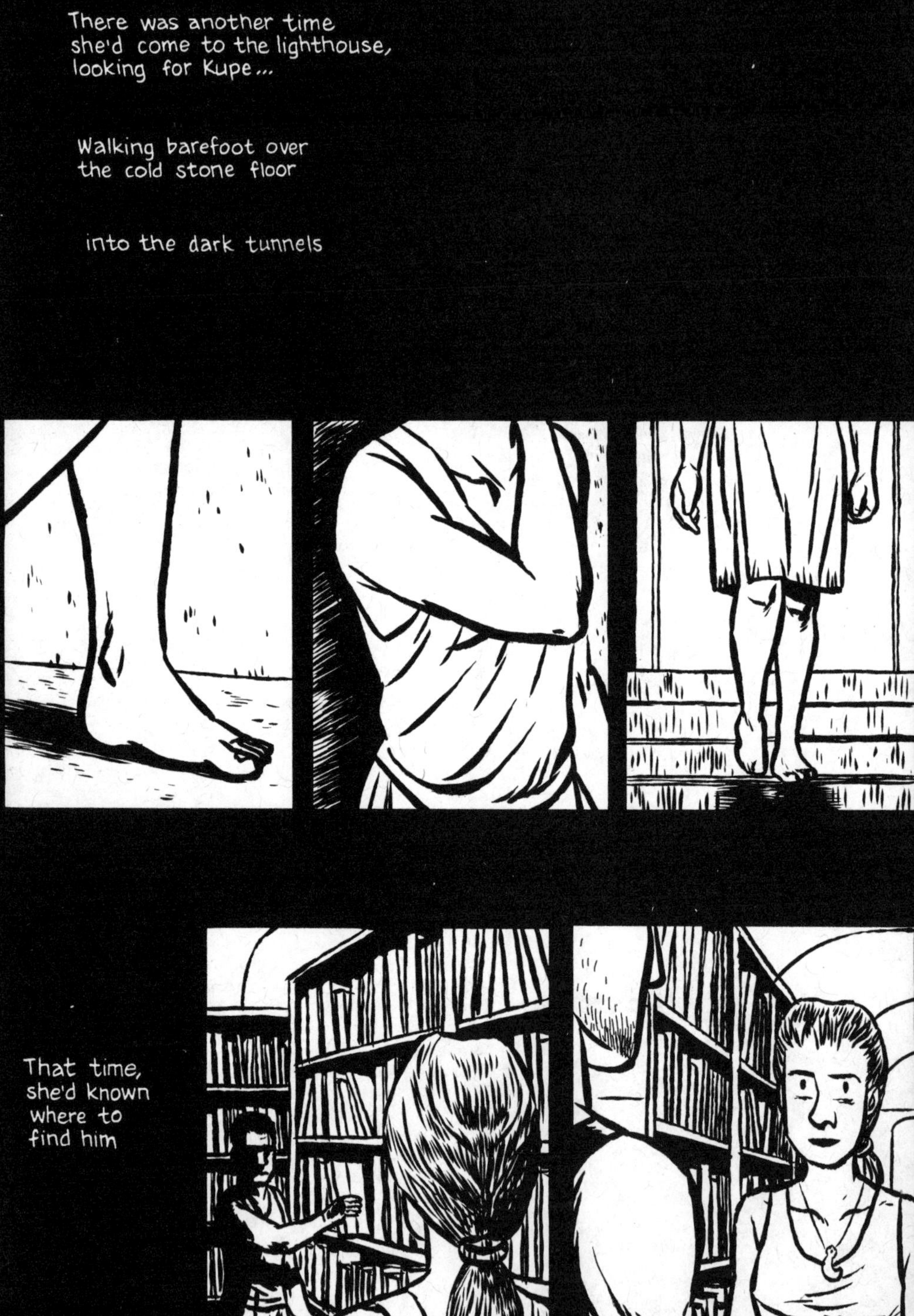
There was another time she'd come to the lighthouse, looking for Kupe...
Walking barefoot over the cold stone floor
into the dark tunnels
That time, she'd known where to find him

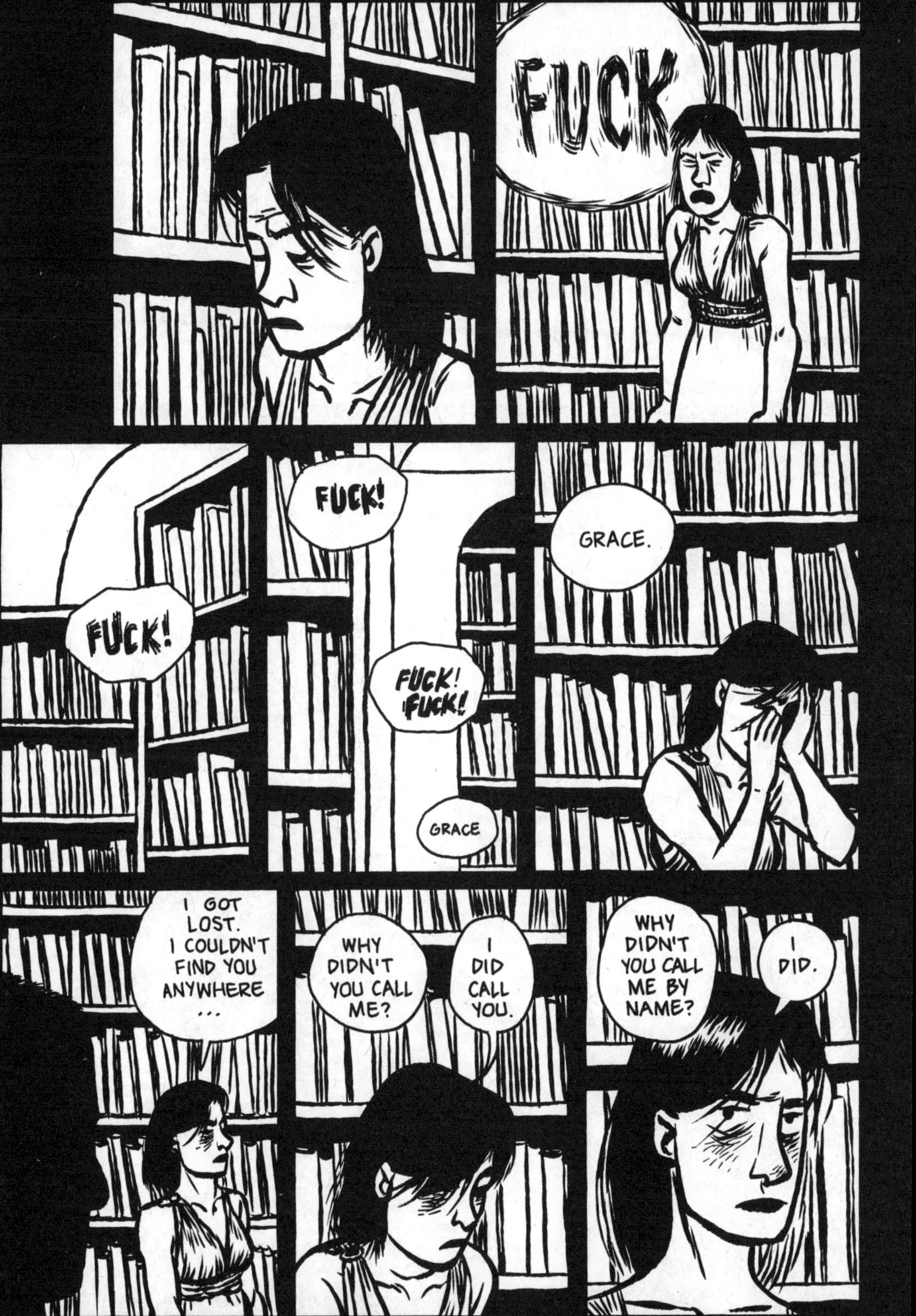
FUCK
FUCK!
FUCK!
FUCK! FUCK!
GRACE
GRACE.
I GOT LOST. I COULDN'T FIND YOU ANYWHERE ...
WHY DIDN'T YOU CALL ME?
I DID CALL YOU.
WHY DIDN'T YOU CALL ME BY NAME?
I DID.

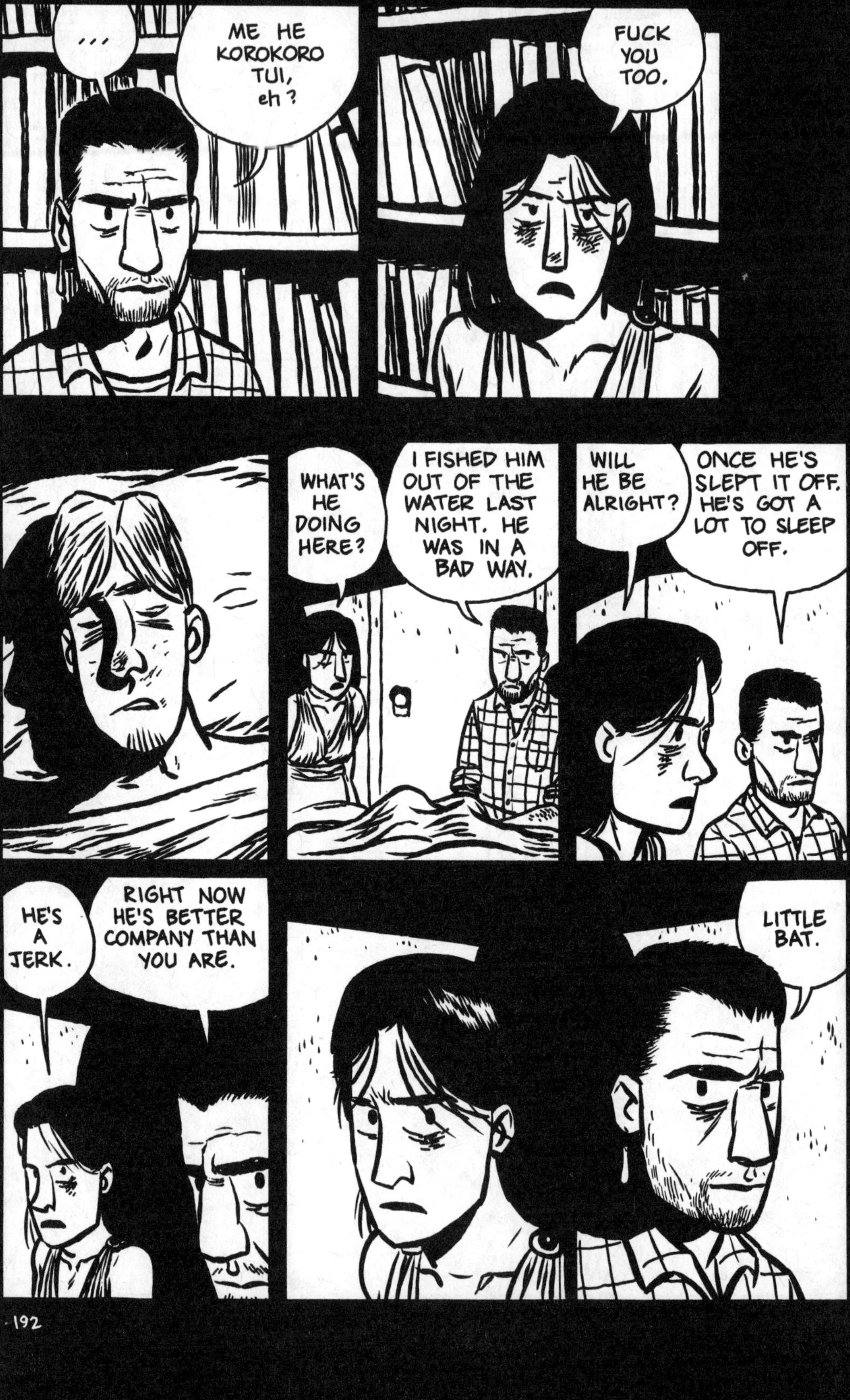
...
ME HE KOROKORO TUI, eh?
FUCK YOU TOO.
WHAT'S HE DOING HERE?
I FISHED HIM OUT OF THE WATER LAST NIGHT. HE WAS IN A BAD WAY.
WILL HE BE ALRIGHT?
ONCE HE'S SLEPT IT OFF. HE'S GOT A LOT TO SLEEP OFF.
HE'S A JERK.
RIGHT NOW HE'S BETTER COMPANY THAN YOU ARE.
LITTLE BAT.

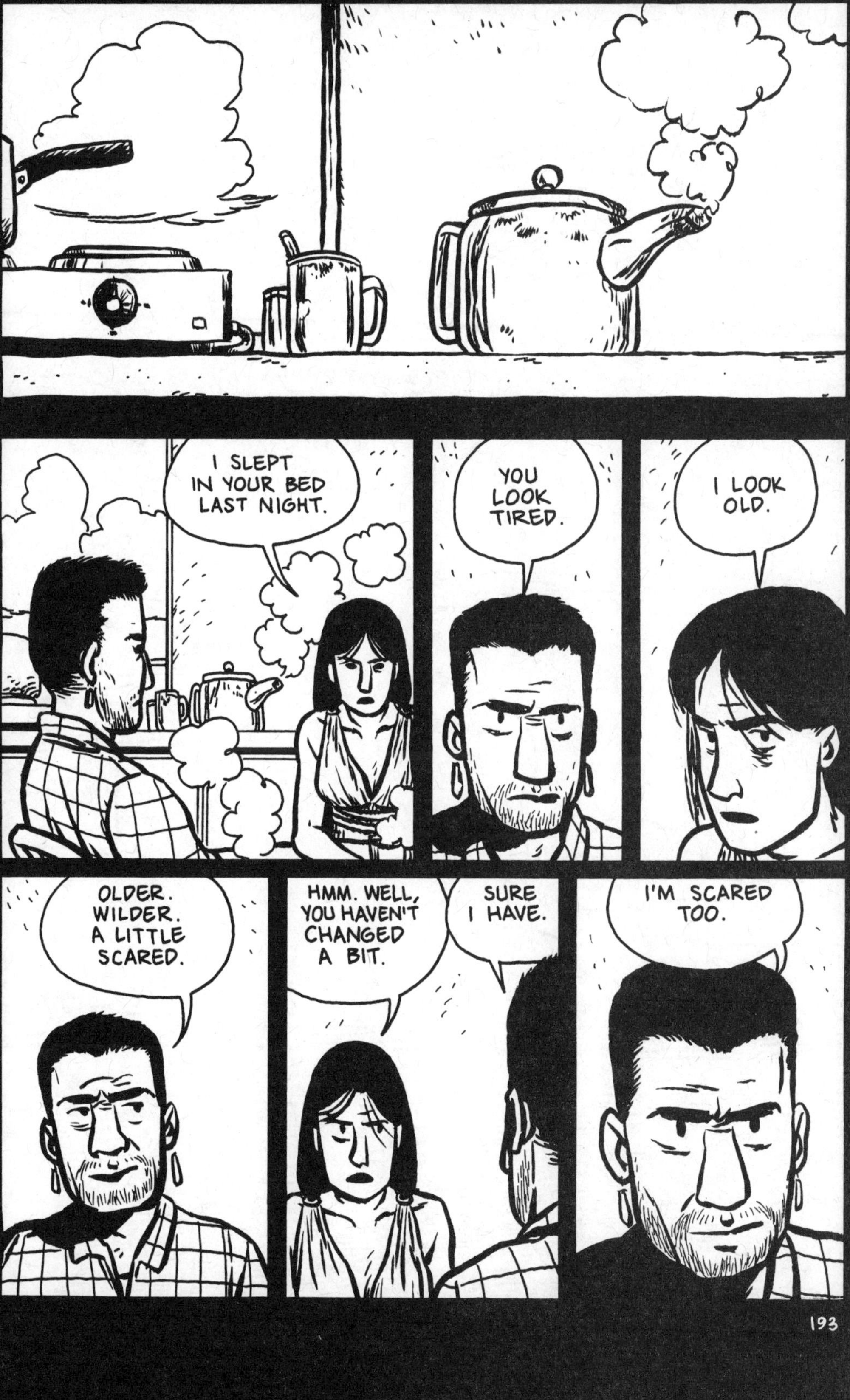
I SLEPT IN YOUR BED LAST NIGHT.
YOU LOOK TIRED.
I LOOK OLD.
OLDER. WILDER. A LITTLE SCARED.
HMM. WELL, YOU HAVEN'T CHANGED A BIT.
SURE I HAVE.
I'M SCARED TOO.

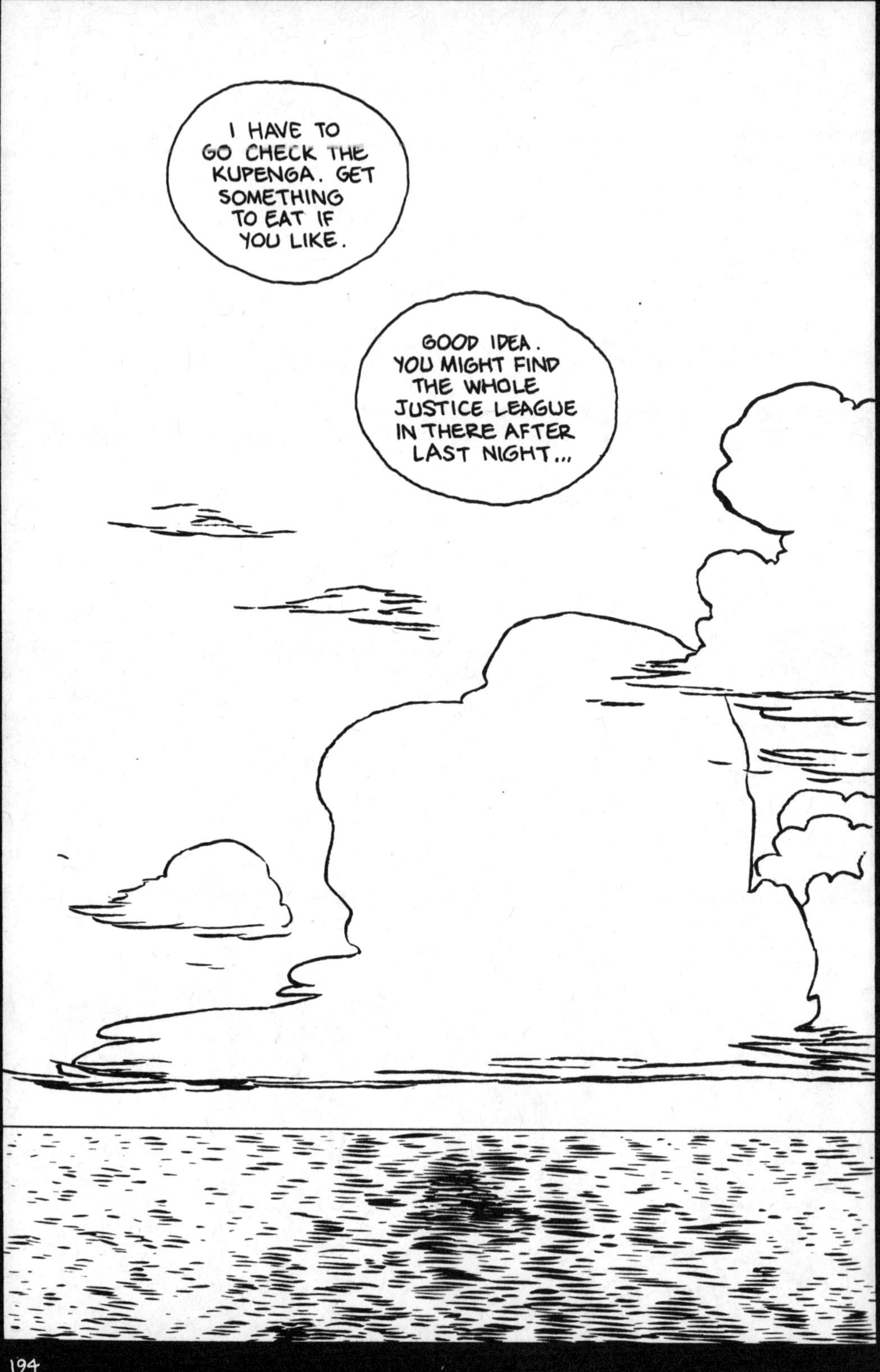
I HAVE TO GO CHECK THE KUPENGA. GET SOMETHING TO EAT IF YOU LIKE.
GOOD IDEA. YOU MIGHT FIND THE WHOLE JUSTICE LEAGUE IN THERE AFTER LAST NIGHT...

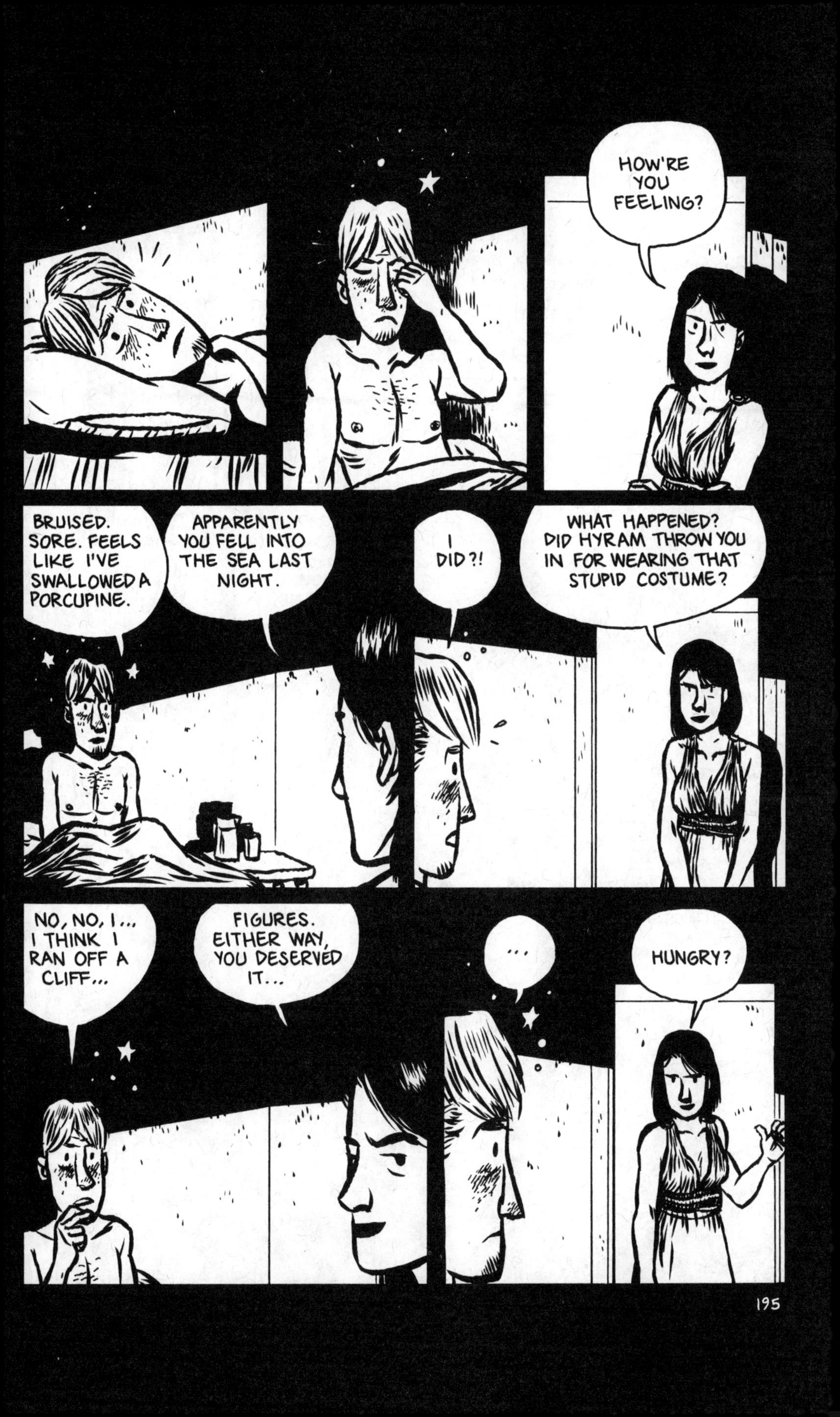
HOW'RE YOU FEELING?
BRUISED. SORE. FEELS LIKE I'VE SWALLOWED A PORCUPINE.
APPARENTLY YOU FELL INTO THE SEA LAST NIGHT.
I DID?!
WHAT HAPPENED? DID HYRAM THROW YOU IN FOR WEARING THAT STUPID COSTUME?
NO, NO, I... I THINK I RAN OFF A CLIFF...
FIGURES. EITHER WAY, YOU DESERVED IT...
...
HUNGRY?

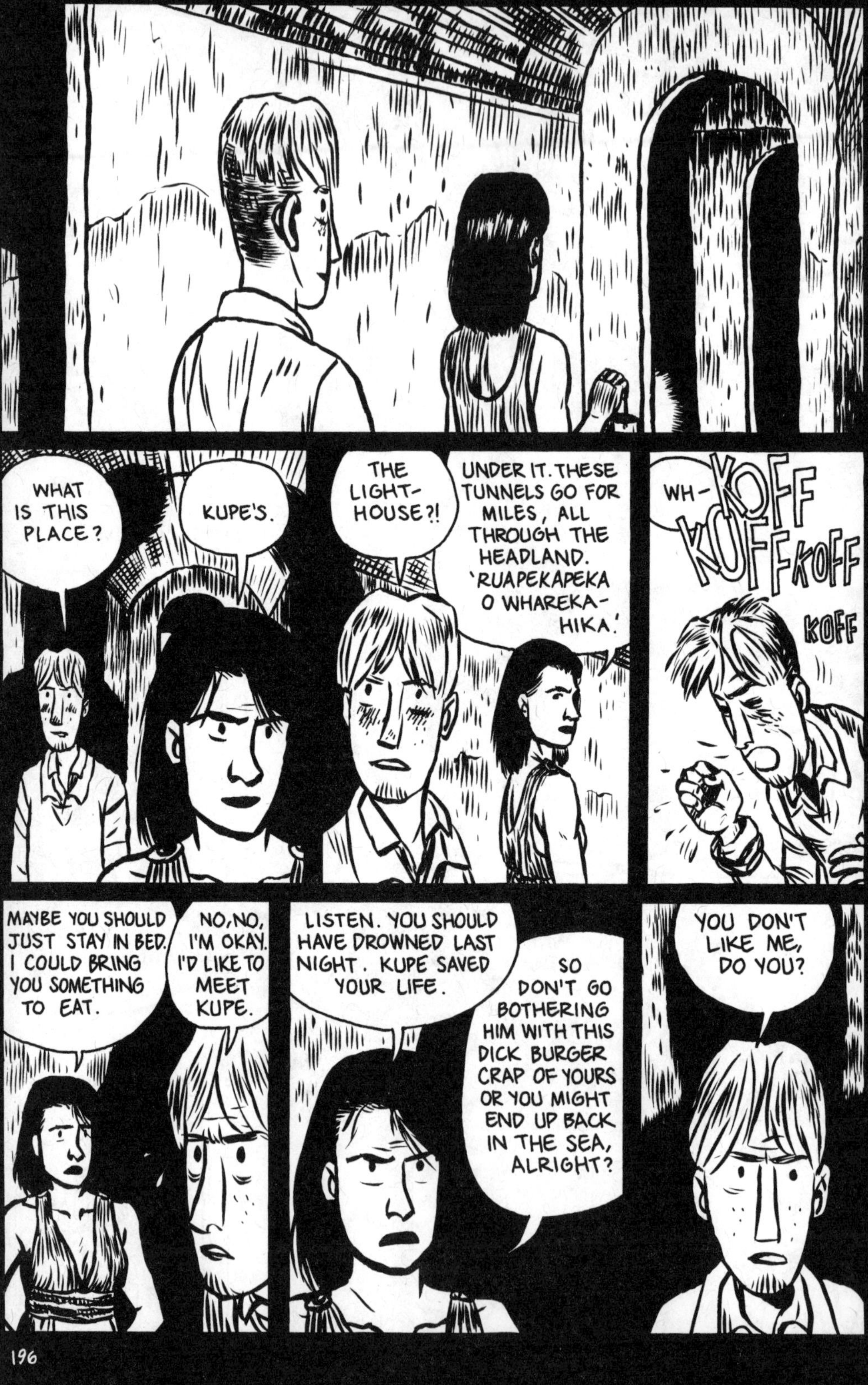
WHAT IS THIS PLACE?
KUPE'S.
THE LIGHT-HOUSE?!
UNDER IT. THESE TUNNELS GO FOR MILES, ALL THROUGH THE HEADLAND. 'RUAPEKAPEKA O WHAREKA-HIKA.'
WH-
KOFF KOFF KOFF KOFF
KOFF
MAYBE YOU SHOULD JUST STAY IN BED. I COULD BRING YOU SOMETHING TO EAT.
NO, NO, I'M OKAY. I'D LIKE TO MEET KUPE.
LISTEN. YOU SHOULD HAVE DROWNED LAST NIGHT. KUPE SAVED YOUR LIFE.
SO DON'T GO BOTHERING HIM WITH THIS DICK BURGER CRAP OF YOURS OR YOU MIGHT END UP BACK IN THE SEA, ALRIGHT?
YOU DON'T LIKE ME, DO YOU?

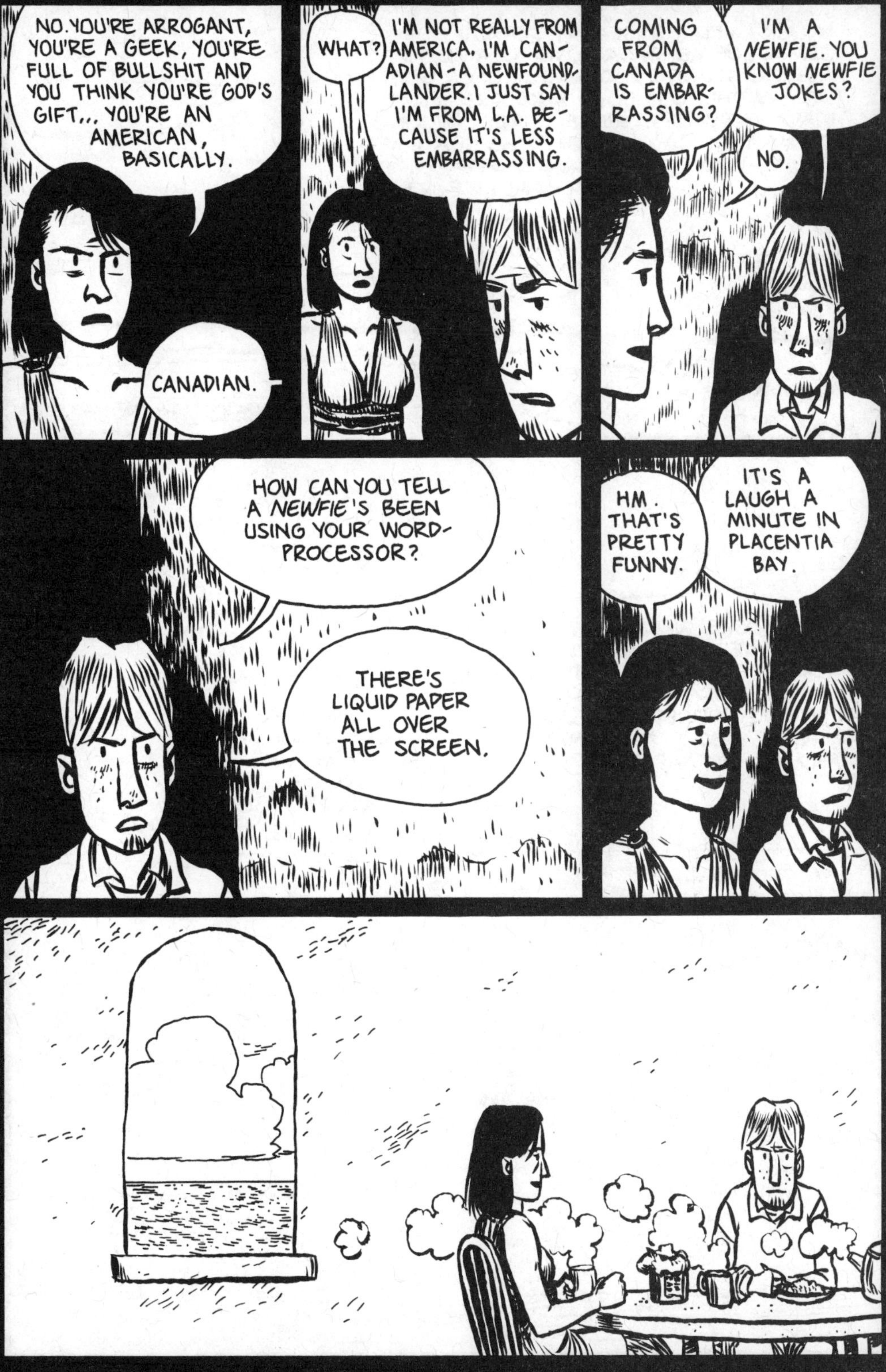
NO. YOU'RE ARROGANT, YOU'RE A GEEK, YOU'RE FULL OF BULLSHIT AND YOU THINK YOU'RE GOD'S GIFT... YOU'RE AN AMERICAN, BASICALLY.
CANADIAN.
WHAT?
I'M NOT REALLY FROM AMERICA. I'M CANADIAN - A NEWFOUNDLANDER. I JUST SAY I'M FROM L.A. BECAUSE IT'S LESS EMBARRASSING.
COMING FROM CANADA IS EMBARRASSING?
I'M A *NEWFIE*. YOU KNOW *NEWFIE* JOKES?
NO.
HOW CAN YOU TELL A *NEWFIE*'S BEEN USING YOUR WORD-PROCESSOR?
THERE'S LIQUID PAPER ALL OVER THE SCREEN.
HM. THAT'S PRETTY FUNNY.
IT'S A LAUGH A MINUTE IN PLACENTIA BAY.

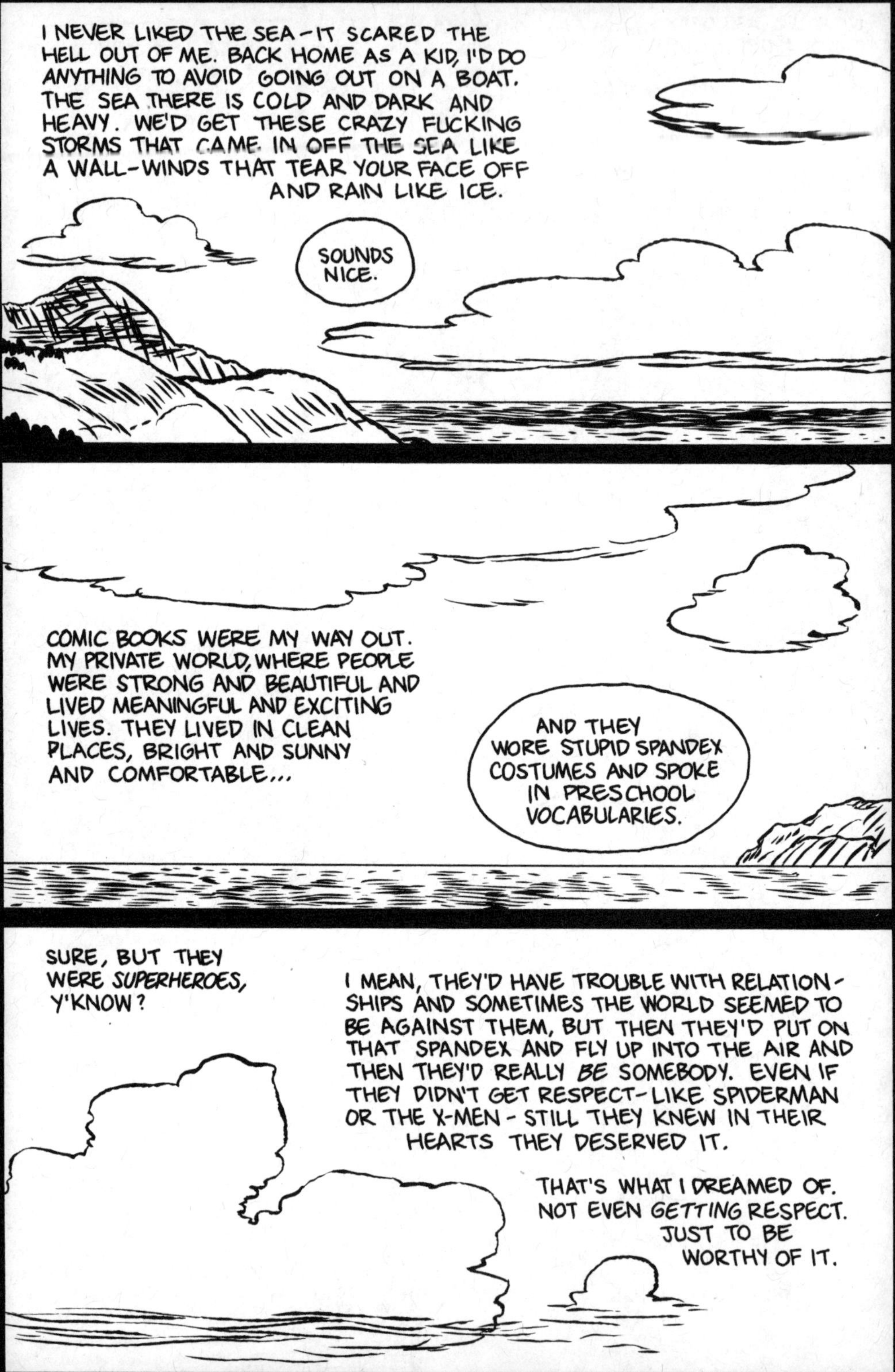
I NEVER LIKED THE SEA - IT SCARED THE HELL OUT OF ME. BACK HOME AS A KID, I'D DO ANYTHING TO AVOID GOING OUT ON A BOAT. THE SEA THERE IS COLD AND DARK AND HEAVY. WE'D GET THESE CRAZY FUCKING STORMS THAT CAME IN OFF THE SEA LIKE A WALL - WINDS THAT TEAR YOUR FACE OFF AND RAIN LIKE ICE.
SOUNDS NICE.
COMIC BOOKS WERE MY WAY OUT. MY PRIVATE WORLD, WHERE PEOPLE WERE STRONG AND BEAUTIFUL AND LIVED MEANINGFUL AND EXCITING LIVES. THEY LIVED IN CLEAN PLACES, BRIGHT AND SUNNY AND COMFORTABLE...
AND THEY WORE STUPID SPANDEX COSTUMES AND SPOKE IN PRESCHOOL VOCABULARIES.
SURE, BUT THEY WERE *SUPERHEROES*, Y'KNOW?
I MEAN, THEY'D HAVE TROUBLE WITH RELATIONSHIPS AND SOMETIMES THE WORLD SEEMED TO BE AGAINST THEM, BUT THEN THEY'D PUT ON THAT SPANDEX AND FLY UP INTO THE AIR AND THEN THEY'D REALLY *BE* SOMEBODY. EVEN IF THEY DIDN'T GET RESPECT - LIKE SPIDERMAN OR THE X-MEN - STILL THEY KNEW IN THEIR HEARTS THEY DESERVED IT.
THAT'S WHAT I DREAMED OF. NOT EVEN *GETTING* RESPECT. JUST TO BE WORTHY OF IT.

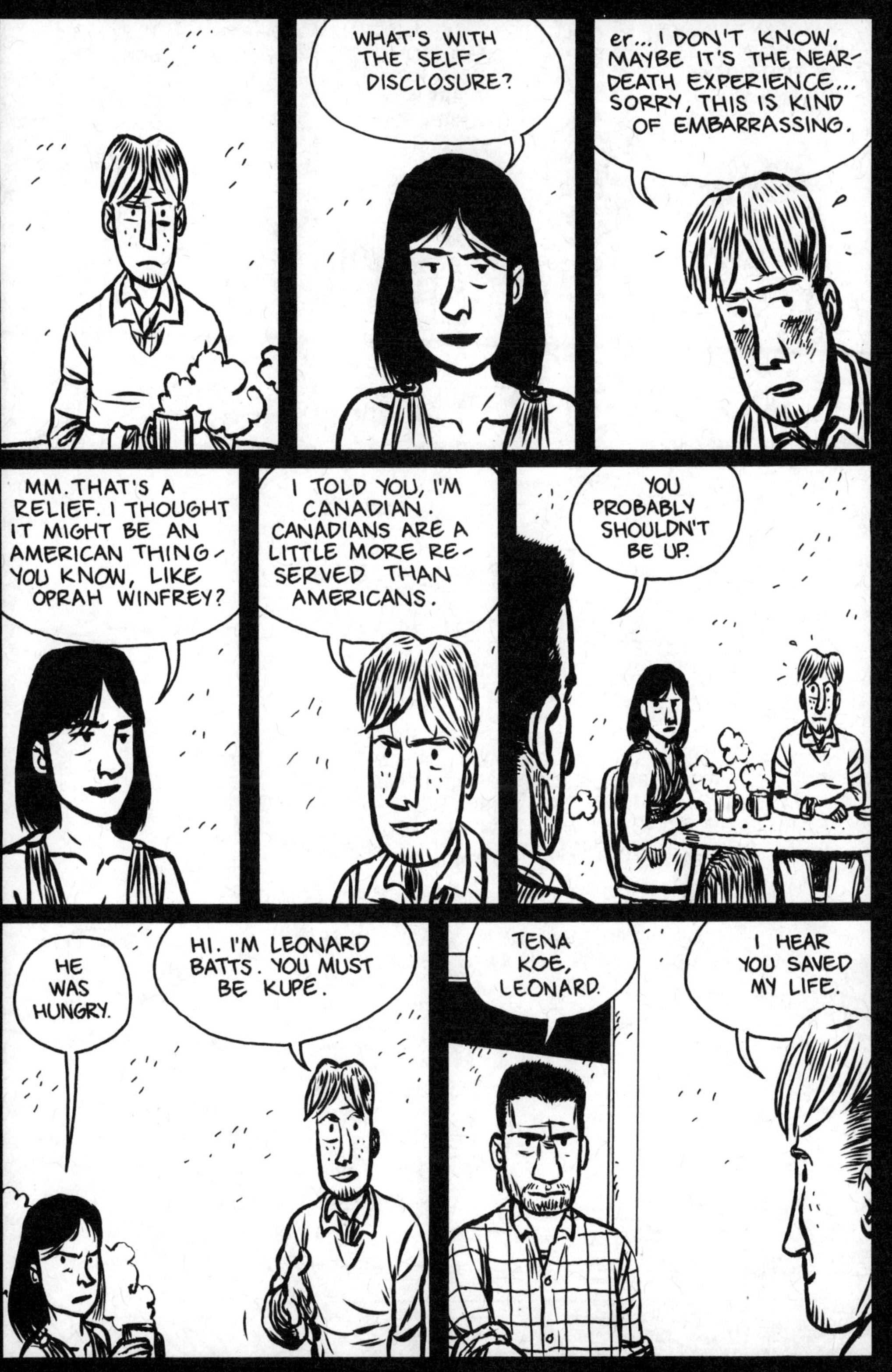

WHAT'S WITH THE SELF-DISCLOSURE?
er... I DON'T KNOW. MAYBE IT'S THE NEAR-DEATH EXPERIENCE... SORRY, THIS IS KIND OF EMBARRASSING.
MM. THAT'S A RELIEF. I THOUGHT IT MIGHT BE AN AMERICAN THING-YOU KNOW, LIKE OPRAH WINFREY?
I TOLD YOU, I'M CANADIAN. CANADIANS ARE A LITTLE MORE RE-SERVED THAN AMERICANS.
YOU PROBABLY SHOULDN'T BE UP.
HE WAS HUNGRY.
HI. I'M LEONARD BATTS. YOU MUST BE KUPE.
TENA KOE, LEONARD.
I HEAR YOU SAVED MY LIFE.

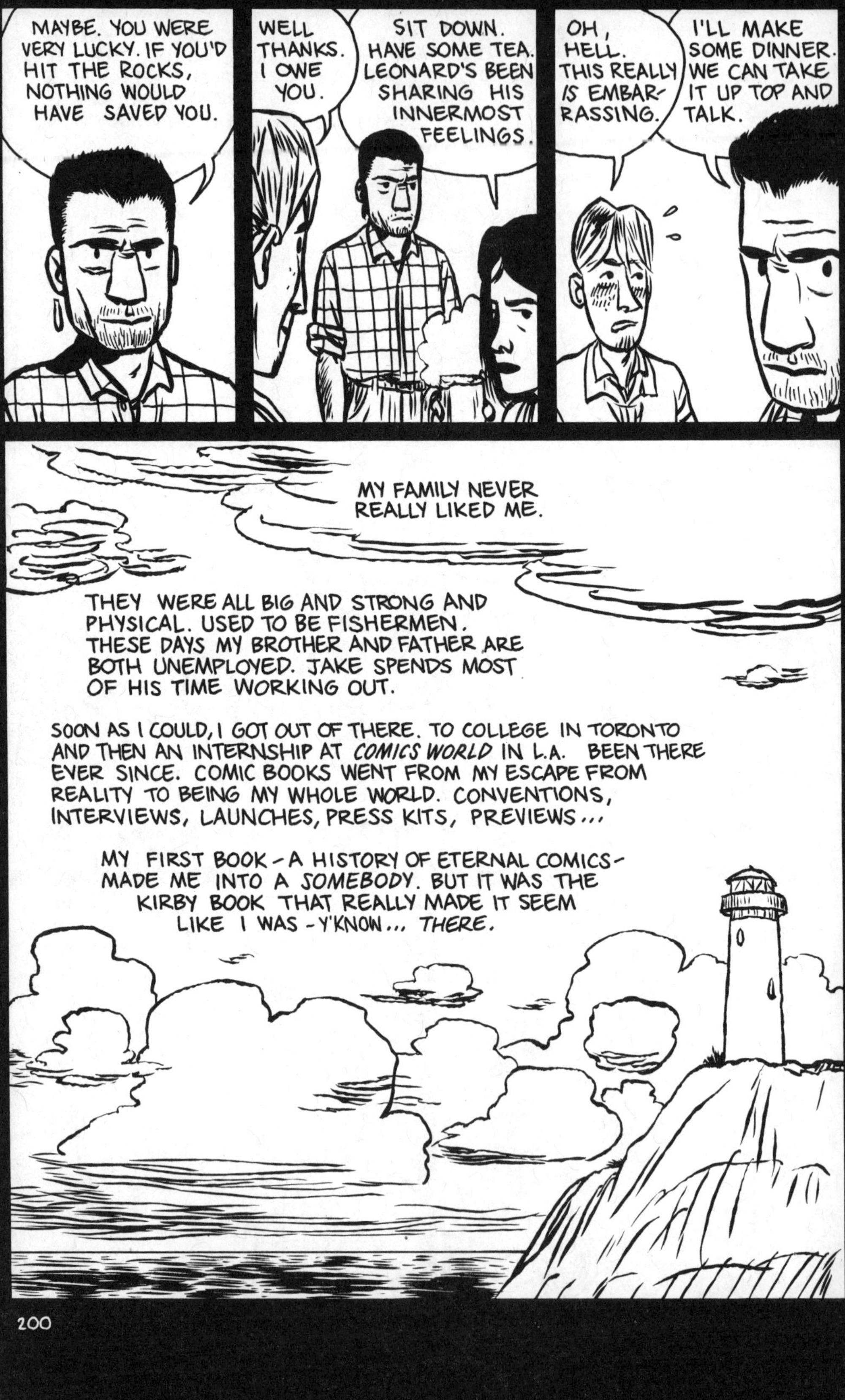
MAYBE. YOU WERE VERY LUCKY. IF YOU'D HIT THE ROCKS, NOTHING WOULD HAVE SAVED YOU.
WELL THANKS. I OWE YOU.
SIT DOWN. HAVE SOME TEA. LEONARD'S BEEN SHARING HIS INNERMOST FEELINGS.
OH, HELL. THIS REALLY *IS* EMBARRASSING.
I'LL MAKE SOME DINNER. WE CAN TAKE IT UP TOP AND TALK.
MY FAMILY NEVER REALLY LIKED ME.
THEY WERE ALL BIG AND STRONG AND PHYSICAL. USED TO BE FISHERMEN. THESE DAYS MY BROTHER AND FATHER ARE BOTH UNEMPLOYED. JAKE SPENDS MOST OF HIS TIME WORKING OUT.
SOON AS I COULD, I GOT OUT OF THERE. TO COLLEGE IN TORONTO AND THEN AN INTERNSHIP AT *COMICS WORLD* IN L.A. BEEN THERE EVER SINCE. COMIC BOOKS WENT FROM MY ESCAPE FROM REALITY TO BEING MY WHOLE WORLD. CONVENTIONS, INTERVIEWS, LAUNCHES, PRESS KITS, PREVIEWS...
MY FIRST BOOK - A HISTORY OF ETERNAL COMICS - MADE ME INTO A *SOMEBODY*. BUT IT WAS THE KIRBY BOOK THAT REALLY MADE IT SEEM LIKE I WAS - Y'KNOW... *THERE*.

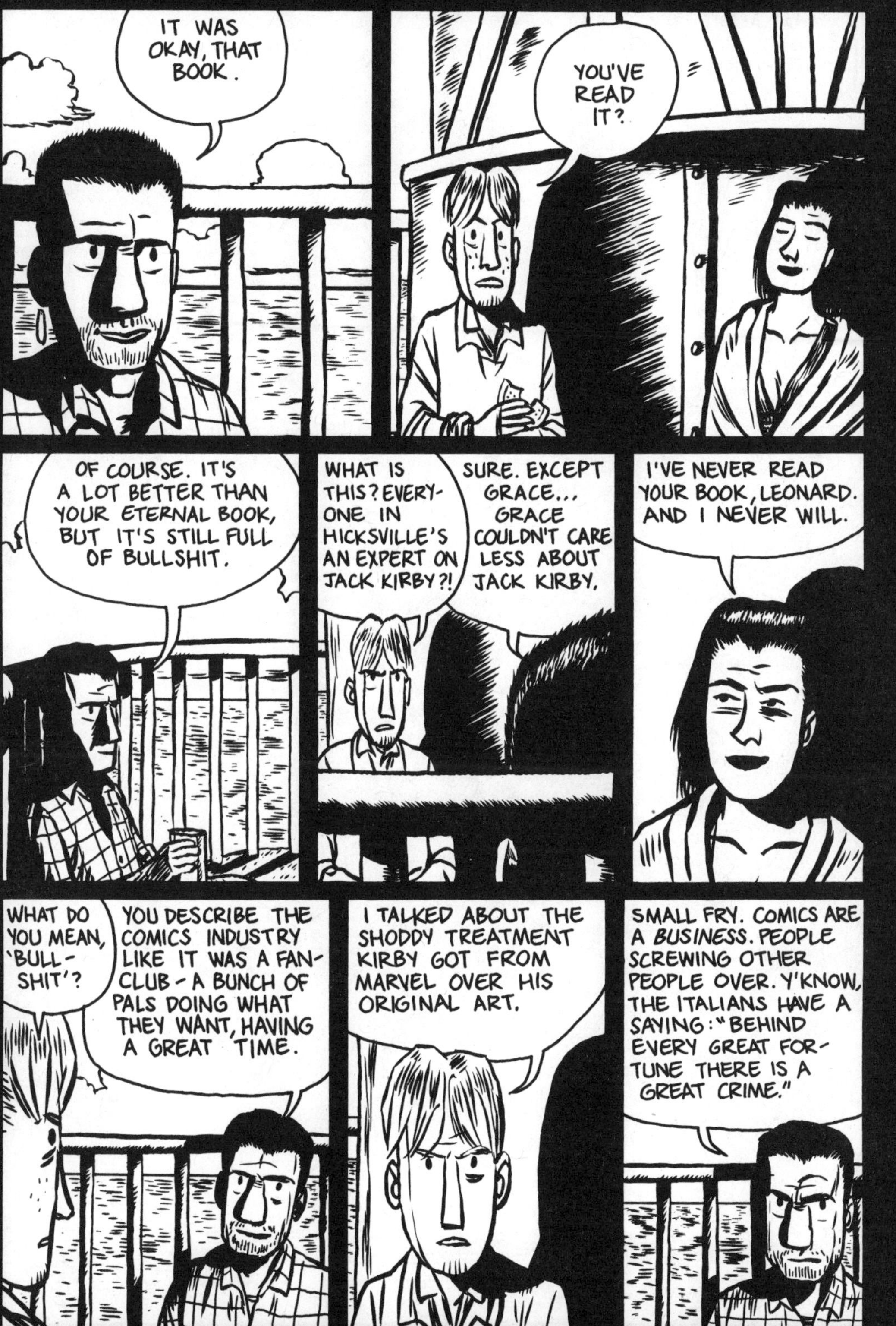
IT WAS OKAY, THAT BOOK.
YOU'VE READ IT?
OF COURSE. IT'S A LOT BETTER THAN YOUR ETERNAL BOOK, BUT IT'S STILL FULL OF BULLSHIT.
WHAT IS THIS? EVERY-ONE IN HICKSVILLE'S AN EXPERT ON JACK KIRBY?!
SURE. EXCEPT GRACE... GRACE COULDN'T CARE LESS ABOUT JACK KIRBY.
I'VE NEVER READ YOUR BOOK, LEONARD. AND I NEVER WILL.
WHAT DO YOU MEAN, 'BULL-SHIT'?
YOU DESCRIBE THE COMICS INDUSTRY LIKE IT WAS A FAN-CLUB - A BUNCH OF PALS DOING WHAT THEY WANT, HAVING A GREAT TIME.
I TALKED ABOUT THE SHODDY TREATMENT KIRBY GOT FROM MARVEL OVER HIS ORIGINAL ART.
SMALL FRY. COMICS ARE A *BUSINESS*. PEOPLE SCREWING OTHER PEOPLE OVER. Y'KNOW, THE ITALIANS HAVE A SAYING: "BEHIND EVERY GREAT FOR-TUNE THERE IS A GREAT CRIME."

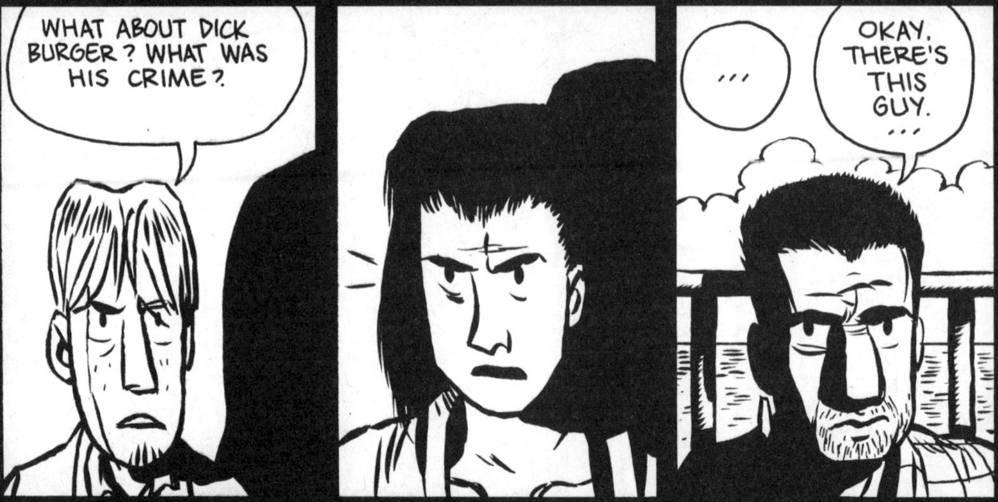
WHAT ABOUT DICK BURGER? WHAT WAS HIS CRIME?
...
OKAY. THERE'S THIS GUY. ...

HE'S NOTHING SPECIAL - JUST AN AVERAGE JOE TRYING TO KEEP HIS HEAD ABOVE WATER. THEN ONE DAY HE FINDS SOMETHING AND IT GIVES HIM AN INCREDIBLE POWER, ALMOST LIKE A GOD. NOW, IT'S SHEER CHANCE THAT THIS HAS HAPPENED TO *HIM* IN PARTICULAR. IT COULD HAVE BEEN *ANYONE*, BUT LUCKILY IT'S HIM, BECAUSE HE'S BASICALLY A GOOD BLOKE AND HE DECIDES TO USE THIS POWER TO BATTLE EVIL AND HELP PEOPLE OUT.

AND THAT GOES FINE AND HE BECOMES A HERO, RESPECTED AROUND THE WORLD. UNTIL ONE DAY WHEN HIS WORST ENEMY, WHOSE EVIL SCHEMES HE'S FOREVER FOILING, MANAGES TO STEAL HIS POWER. YOU SEE, THIS ENEMY HAS MADE A PACT WITH THESE MYSTICAL BEINGS WHO HELP HIM STEAL THE HERO'S POWER, ON ONE CONDITION: THAT HE USE IT TO DESTROY ALL LIFE ON EARTH. HE AGREES TO THIS BECAUSE HE THINKS HE'LL BE ABLE TO USE THE POWER TO DEFEAT THE MYSTICS AND THUS BE FREED FROM THEIR PACT. BUT HE'S WRONG. THE POWER FILLS HIM WITH A LUST FOR DESTRUCTION AND HE QUICKLY BECOMES THE MYSTICS' WILLING TOOL.

MEANWHILE OUR HERO IS BACK TO BEING AN ORDINARY GUY AGAIN. HE KNOWS WHAT HIS ENEMY MIGHT DO, BUT HE'S POWERLESS TO STOP HIM. STILL, HE'S A RESPONSIBLE SORT OF GUY, SO HE FIGURES HE HAS TO TRY.

HE GOES BACK TO THE TINY JUNK SHOP WHERE - TWENTY YEARS EARLIER - A DUSTY OLD ARTEFACT HAD GIVEN HIM THE POWER OF A GOD. AFTER FOLLOWING A LONG AND CONVOLUTED TRAIL, HE MANAGES TO FIND THE ARTEFACT - BUT TO NO AVAIL. THIS TIME IT SEEMS TO CARRY NO POWER.

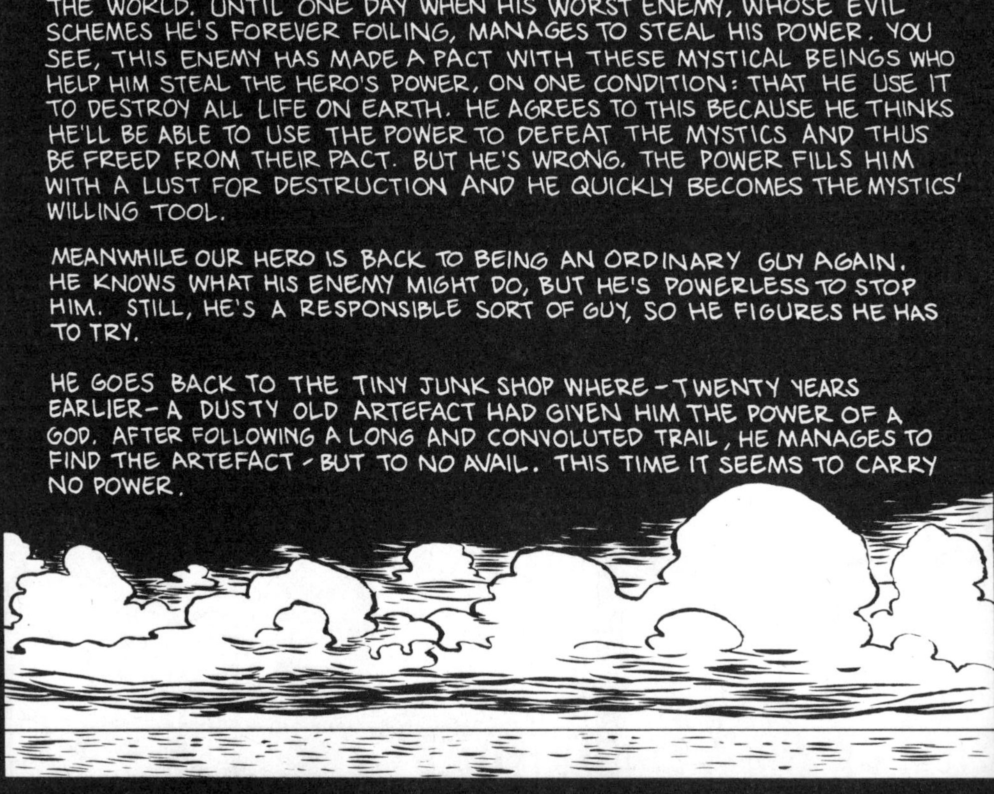

BUT OUR HERO CANNOT GIVE UP. HE RETRACES HIS OWN STEPS DURING
THE YEARS FOLLOWING THAT FIRST VISIT TO THE OLD JUNK SHOP, AND
AS THE STORY OF HIS CAREER AS A SUPERHERO UNFOLDS, HE BEGINS
TO DISCERN PATTERNS AND NOTICE DETAILS THAT HE HAD PREVIOUSLY
TAKEN FOR GRANTED. AND GRADUALLY THE SECRETS OF HIS LOST
POWER.

ALL THIS TIME HE'S BEING PURSUED BY HIS ENEMIES, BUT HE MANAGES
TO STAY ONE STEP AHEAD OF THEM, JUST BY THINKING AHEAD AND
ACCEPTING THE HELP OF GOOD PEOPLE. BUT FINALLY, HIS LUCK RUNS
OUT. HIS ENEMY FINDS HIM AND HE'S TRAPPED. AS HIS ENEMY
PREPARES TO DESTROY HIM, OUR HERO HOLDS THE OLD ARTEFACT
BEFORE HIM, AS A FUTILE SHIELD...

THE ENEMY UNLEASHES THE POWER — AND AS IT STRIKES THE ARTEFACT,
THERE IS A HUGE, CATACLYSMIC EXPLOSION.

THEN EVERYTHING FALLS QUIET.

AFTER WHAT SEEMS LIKE AN ETERNITY, OUR HERO AWAKES, AMAZED
THAT HE'S STILL ALIVE. HIS ENEMY HAS BEEN KILLED, AND THE POWER
SNUFFED OUT FOREVER AFTER DESTROYING ITS OWN SOURCE. THE
WORLD HAS BEEN SAVED.

AND SO OUR HERO RETURNS TO HIS ORDINARY LIFE, MORE CONTENTED
THAN HE HAS EVER BEEN. HE MARRIES, RAISES CHILDREN, RETIRES,
GROWS OLD.

NOW AND THEN, HE MISSES THE DAYS WHEN HE HAD THE POWER OF
A GOD. BUT FOR THE MOST PART, HE'S HAPPY WITH HIS LIFE.

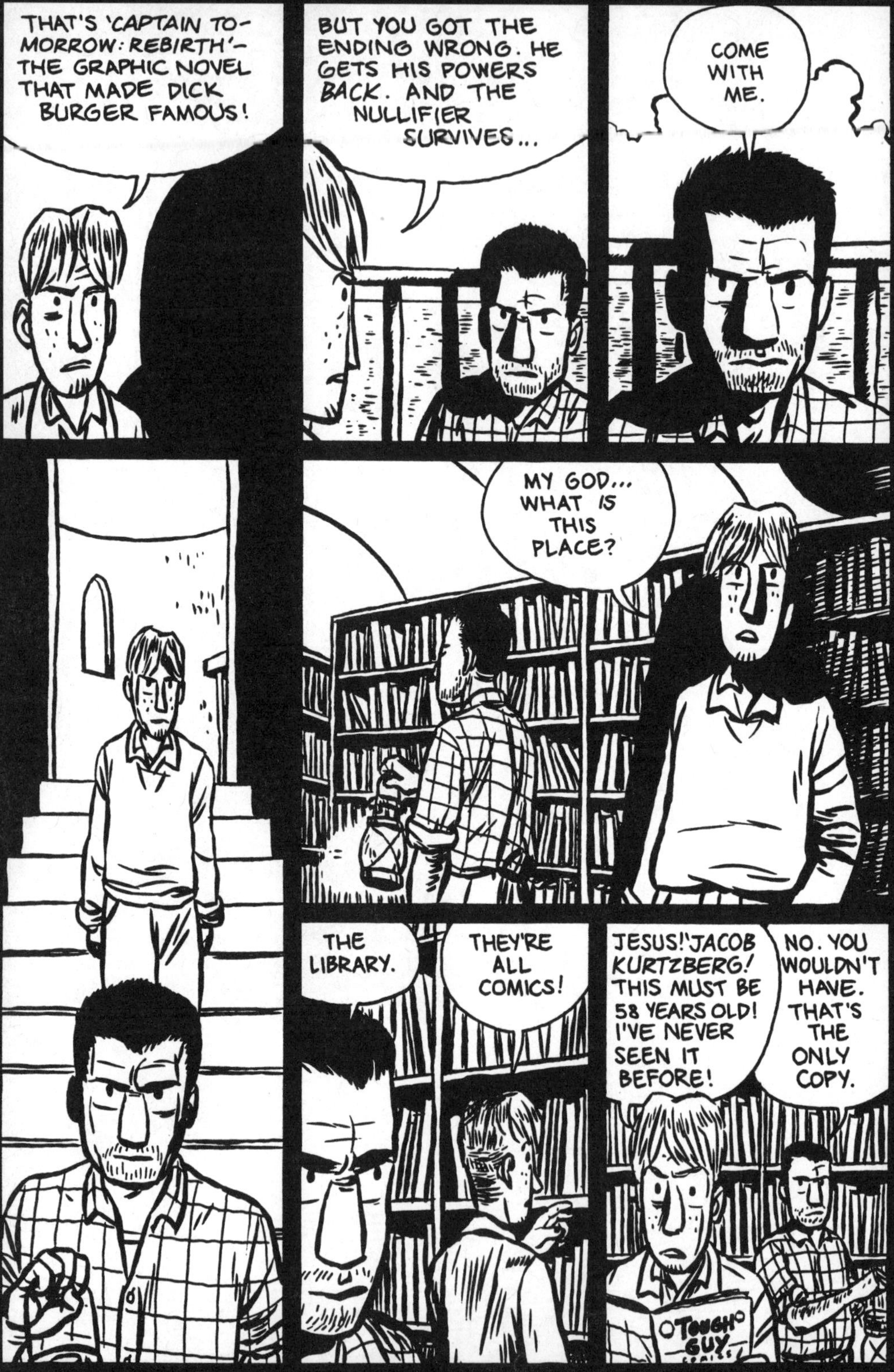
THAT'S 'CAPTAIN TOMORROW: REBIRTH'— THE GRAPHIC NOVEL THAT MADE DICK BURGER FAMOUS!
BUT YOU GOT THE ENDING WRONG. HE GETS HIS POWERS BACK. AND THE NULLIFIER SURVIVES...
COME WITH ME.
MY GOD... WHAT IS THIS PLACE?
THE LIBRARY.
THEY'RE ALL COMICS!
JESUS! JACOB KURTZBERG! THIS MUST BE 58 YEARS OLD! I'VE NEVER SEEN IT BEFORE!
NO. YOU WOULDN'T HAVE. THAT'S THE ONLY COPY.
TOUGH GUY

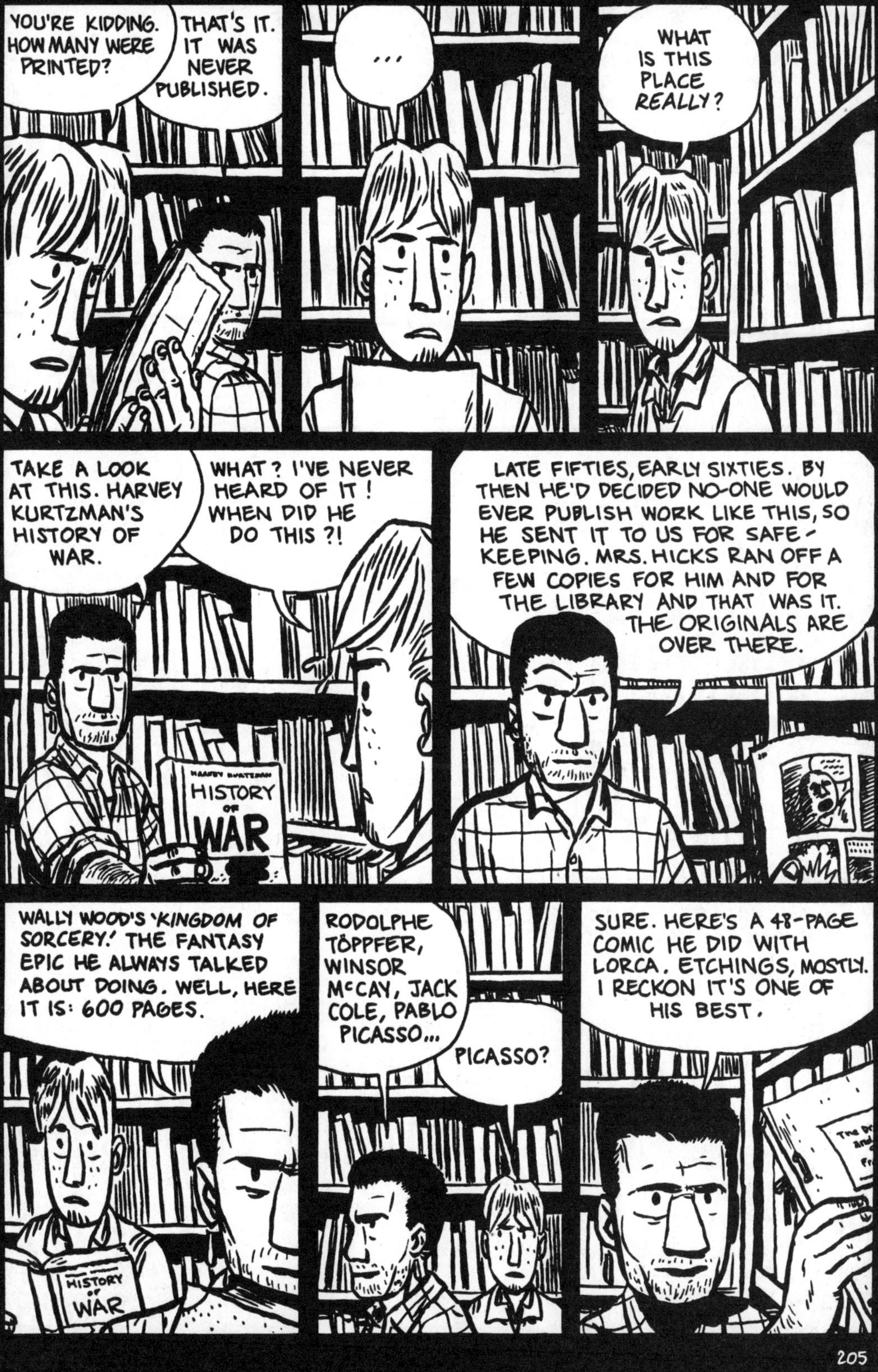

YOU'RE KIDDING. HOW MANY WERE PRINTED?
THAT'S IT. IT WAS NEVER PUBLISHED.
...
WHAT IS THIS PLACE REALLY?
TAKE A LOOK AT THIS. HARVEY KURTZMAN'S HISTORY OF WAR.
WHAT? I'VE NEVER HEARD OF IT! WHEN DID HE DO THIS?!
HISTORY OF WAR
LATE FIFTIES, EARLY SIXTIES. BY THEN HE'D DECIDED NO-ONE WOULD EVER PUBLISH WORK LIKE THIS, SO HE SENT IT TO US FOR SAFE-KEEPING. MRS. HICKS RAN OFF A FEW COPIES FOR HIM AND FOR THE LIBRARY AND THAT WAS IT. THE ORIGINALS ARE OVER THERE.
WALLY WOOD'S 'KINGDOM OF SORCERY.' THE FANTASY EPIC HE ALWAYS TALKED ABOUT DOING. WELL, HERE IT IS: 600 PAGES.
HISTORY OF WAR
RODOLPHE TÖPPFER, WINSOR McCAY, JACK COLE, PABLO PICASSO...
PICASSO?
SURE. HERE'S A 48-PAGE COMIC HE DID WITH LORCA. ETCHINGS, MOSTLY. I RECKON IT'S ONE OF HIS BEST.

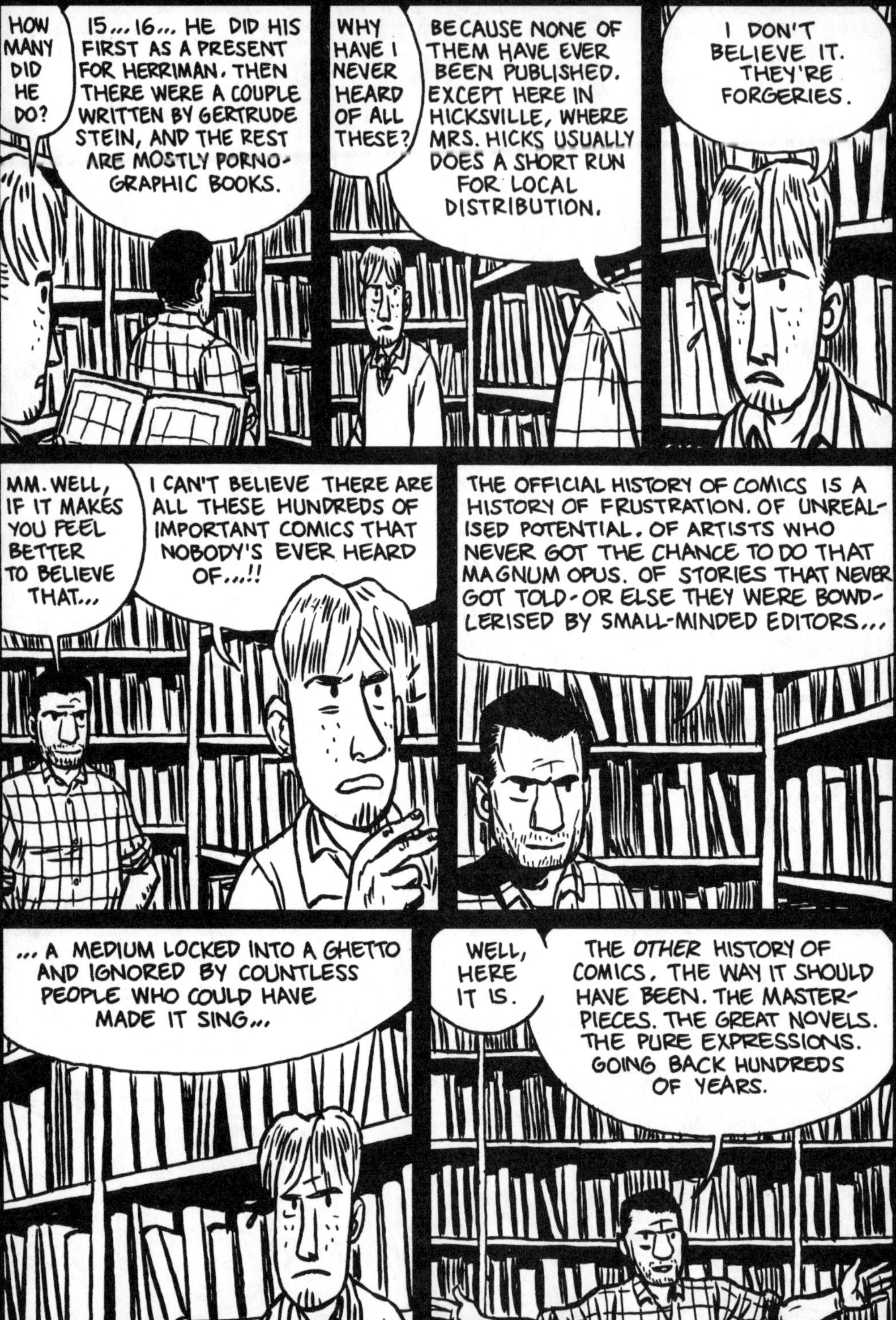
HOW MANY DID HE DO?
15... 16... HE DID HIS FIRST AS A PRESENT FOR HERRIMAN. THEN THERE WERE A COUPLE WRITTEN BY GERTRUDE STEIN, AND THE REST ARE MOSTLY PORNOGRAPHIC BOOKS.
WHY HAVE I NEVER HEARD OF ALL THESE?
BECAUSE NONE OF THEM HAVE EVER BEEN PUBLISHED. EXCEPT HERE IN HICKSVILLE, WHERE MRS. HICKS USUALLY DOES A SHORT RUN FOR LOCAL DISTRIBUTION.
I DON'T BELIEVE IT. THEY'RE FORGERIES.
MM. WELL, IF IT MAKES YOU FEEL BETTER TO BELIEVE THAT...
I CAN'T BELIEVE THERE ARE ALL THESE HUNDREDS OF IMPORTANT COMICS THAT NOBODY'S EVER HEARD OF...!!
THE OFFICIAL HISTORY OF COMICS IS A HISTORY OF FRUSTRATION. OF UNREALISED POTENTIAL. OF ARTISTS WHO NEVER GOT THE CHANCE TO DO THAT MAGNUM OPUS. OF STORIES THAT NEVER GOT TOLD - OR ELSE THEY WERE BOWDLERISED BY SMALL-MINDED EDITORS...
... A MEDIUM LOCKED INTO A GHETTO AND IGNORED BY COUNTLESS PEOPLE WHO COULD HAVE MADE IT SING...
WELL, HERE IT IS.
THE OTHER HISTORY OF COMICS, THE WAY IT SHOULD HAVE BEEN. THE MASTERPIECES. THE GREAT NOVELS. THE PURE EXPRESSIONS. GOING BACK HUNDREDS OF YEARS.

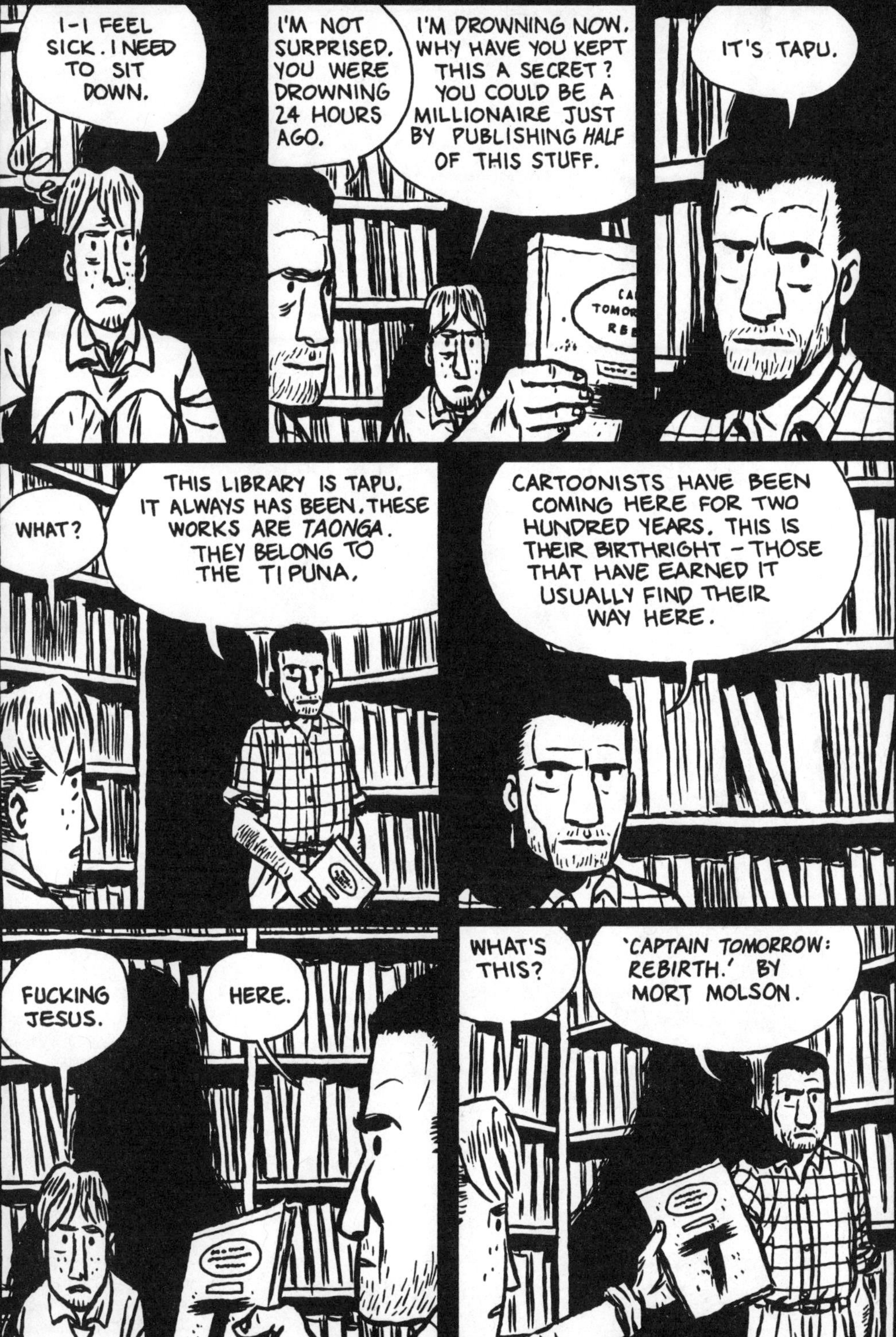

I-I FEEL SICK. I NEED TO SIT DOWN.
I'M NOT SURPRISED. YOU WERE DROWNING 24 HOURS AGO.
I'M DROWNING NOW. WHY HAVE YOU KEPT THIS A SECRET? YOU COULD BE A MILLIONAIRE JUST BY PUBLISHING *HALF* OF THIS STUFF.
IT'S TAPU.
WHAT?
THIS LIBRARY IS TAPU. IT ALWAYS HAS BEEN. THESE WORKS ARE *TAONGA*. THEY BELONG TO THE TIPUNA.
CARTOONISTS HAVE BEEN COMING HERE FOR TWO HUNDRED YEARS. THIS IS THEIR BIRTHRIGHT – THOSE THAT HAVE EARNED IT USUALLY FIND THEIR WAY HERE.
FUCKING JESUS.
HERE.
WHAT'S THIS?
'CAPTAIN *TOMORROW*: *REBIRTH*.' BY MORT MOLSON.

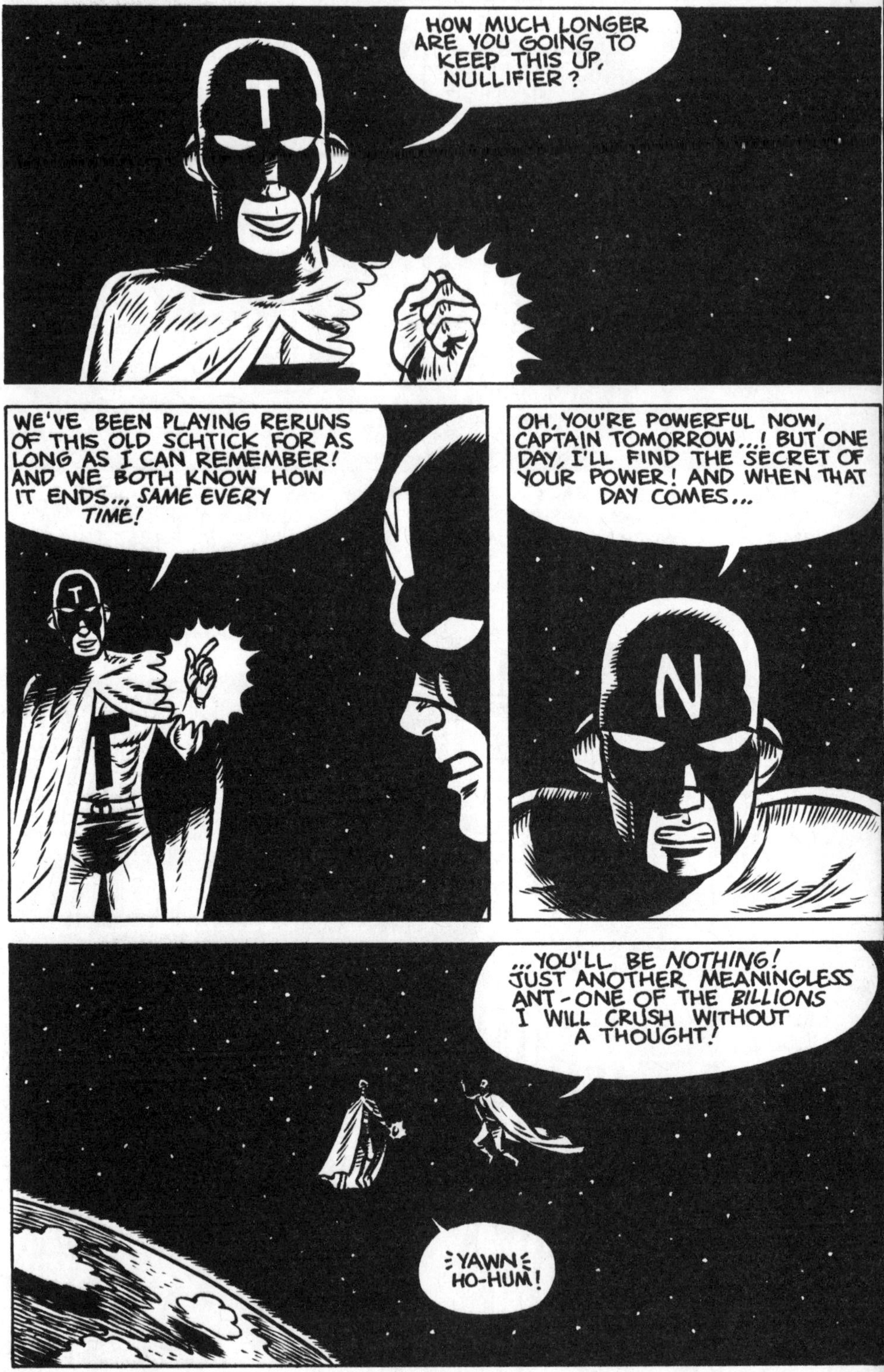
HOW MUCH LONGER ARE YOU GOING TO KEEP THIS UP, NULLIFIER?
WE'VE BEEN PLAYING RERUNS OF THIS OLD SCHTICK FOR AS LONG AS I CAN REMEMBER! AND WE BOTH KNOW HOW IT ENDS... SAME EVERY TIME!
OH, YOU'RE POWERFUL NOW, CAPTAIN TOMORROW...! BUT ONE DAY, I'LL FIND THE SECRET OF YOUR POWER! AND WHEN THAT DAY COMES...
...YOU'LL BE NOTHING! JUST ANOTHER MEANINGLESS ANT - ONE OF THE BILLIONS I WILL CRUSH WITHOUT A THOUGHT!
YAWN HO-HUM!

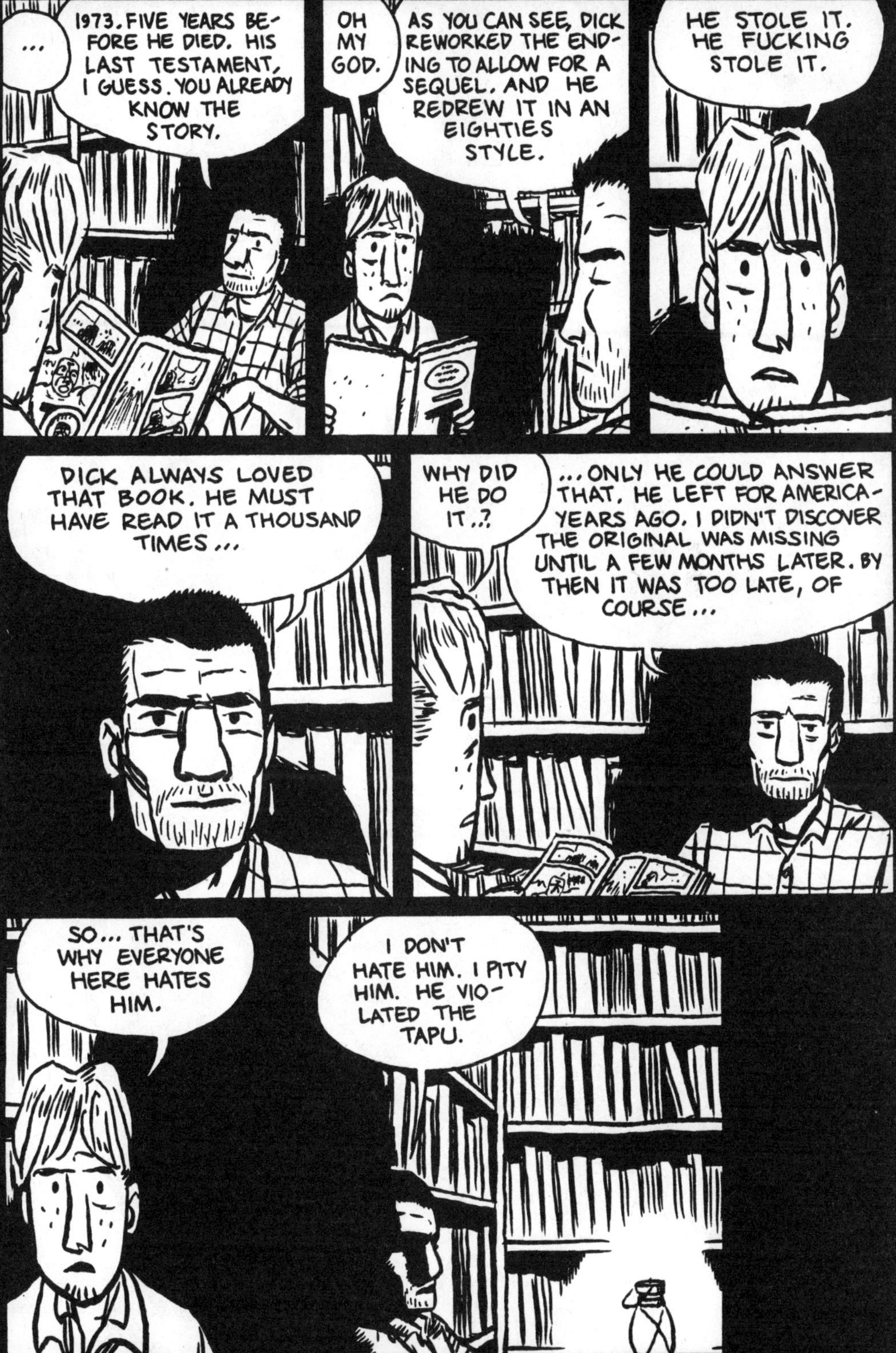
...
1973. FIVE YEARS BEFORE HE DIED. HIS LAST TESTAMENT, I GUESS. YOU ALREADY KNOW THE STORY.
OH MY GOD.
AS YOU CAN SEE, DICK REWORKED THE ENDING TO ALLOW FOR A SEQUEL. AND HE REDREW IT IN AN EIGHTIES STYLE.
HE STOLE IT. HE FUCKING STOLE IT.
DICK ALWAYS LOVED THAT BOOK. HE MUST HAVE READ IT A THOUSAND TIMES...
WHY DID HE DO IT..?
...ONLY HE COULD ANSWER THAT. HE LEFT FOR AMERICA YEARS AGO. I DIDN'T DISCOVER THE ORIGINAL WAS MISSING UNTIL A FEW MONTHS LATER. BY THEN IT WAS TOO LATE, OF COURSE...
SO... THAT'S WHY EVERYONE HERE HATES HIM.
I DON'T HATE HIM. I PITY HIM. HE VIOLATED THE TAPU.

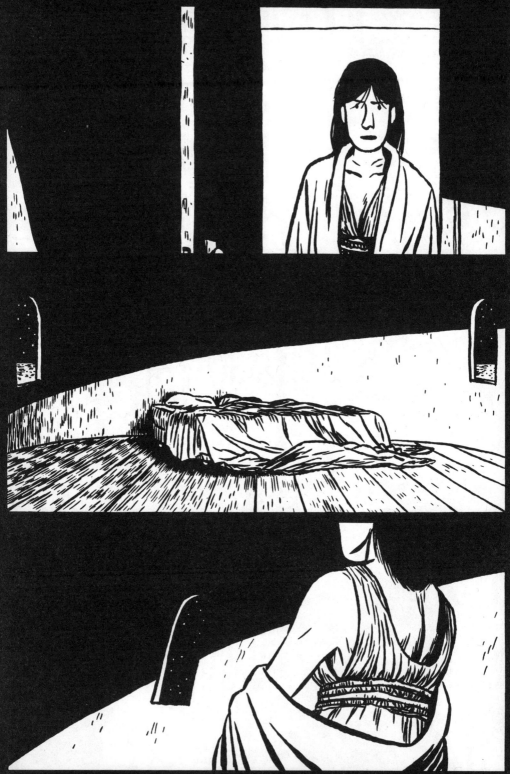

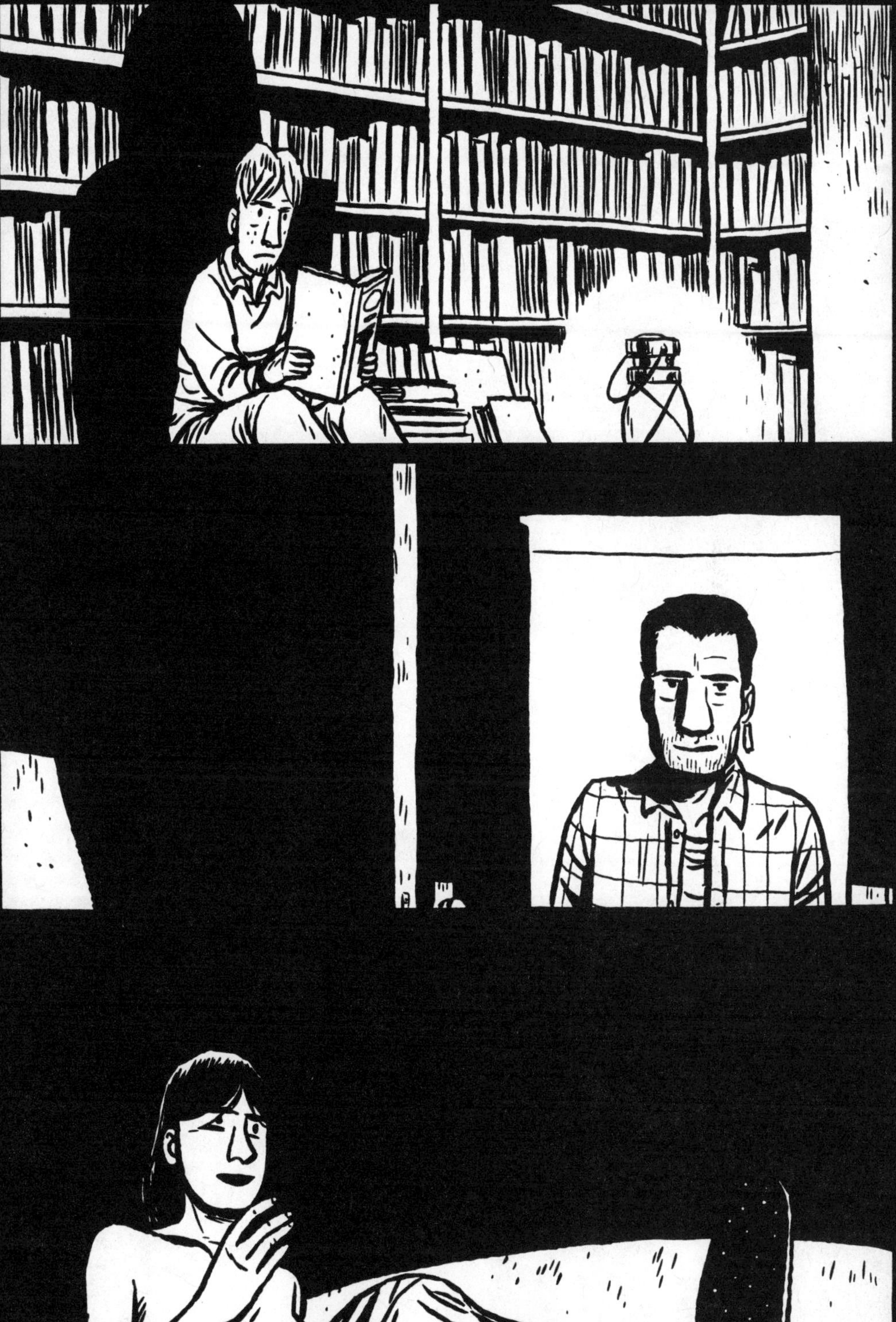

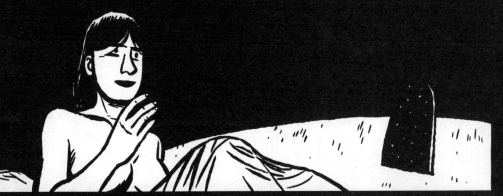

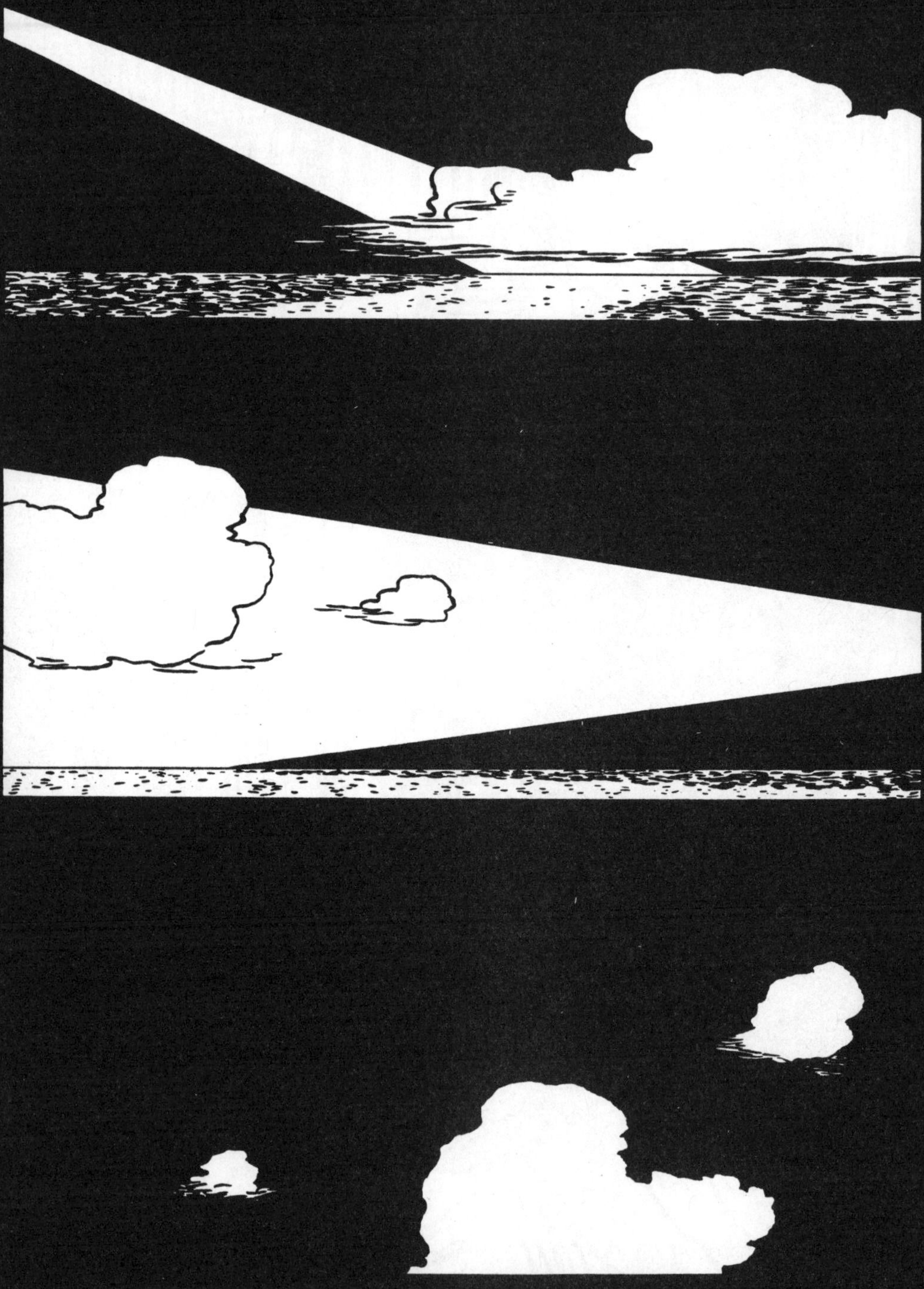

Chapter Ten

"Good is better than evil
because it's nicer."

Milton Caniff.

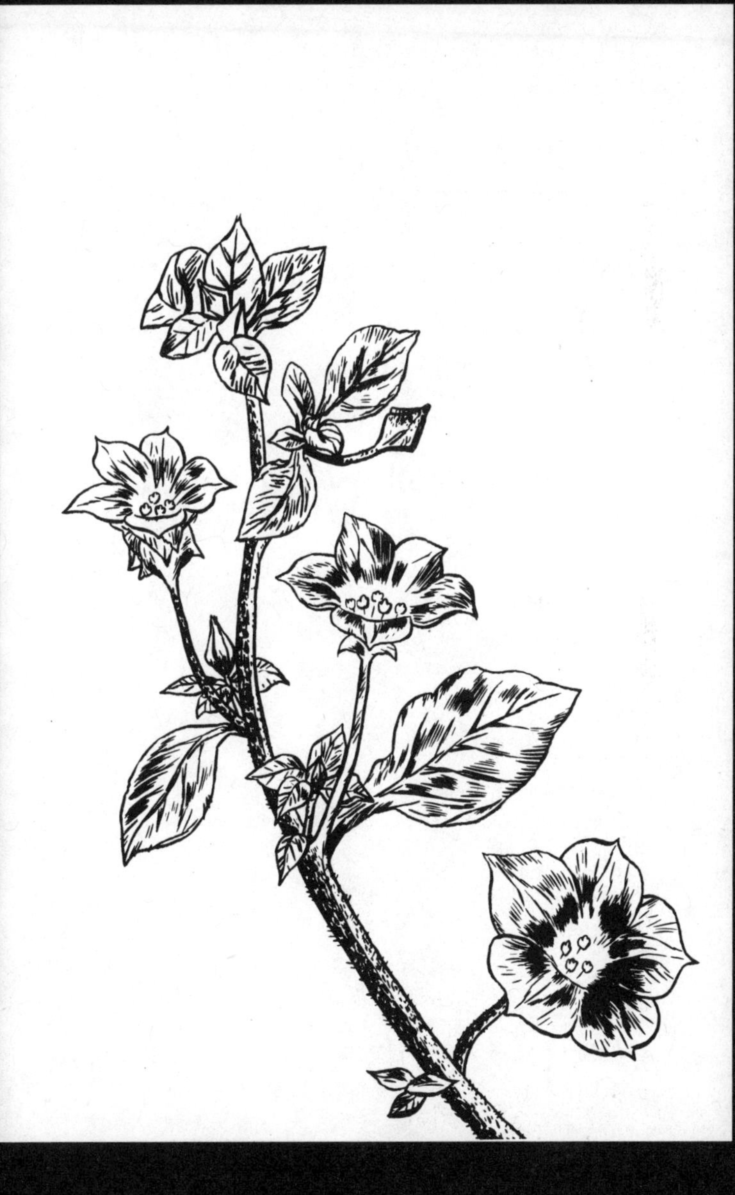

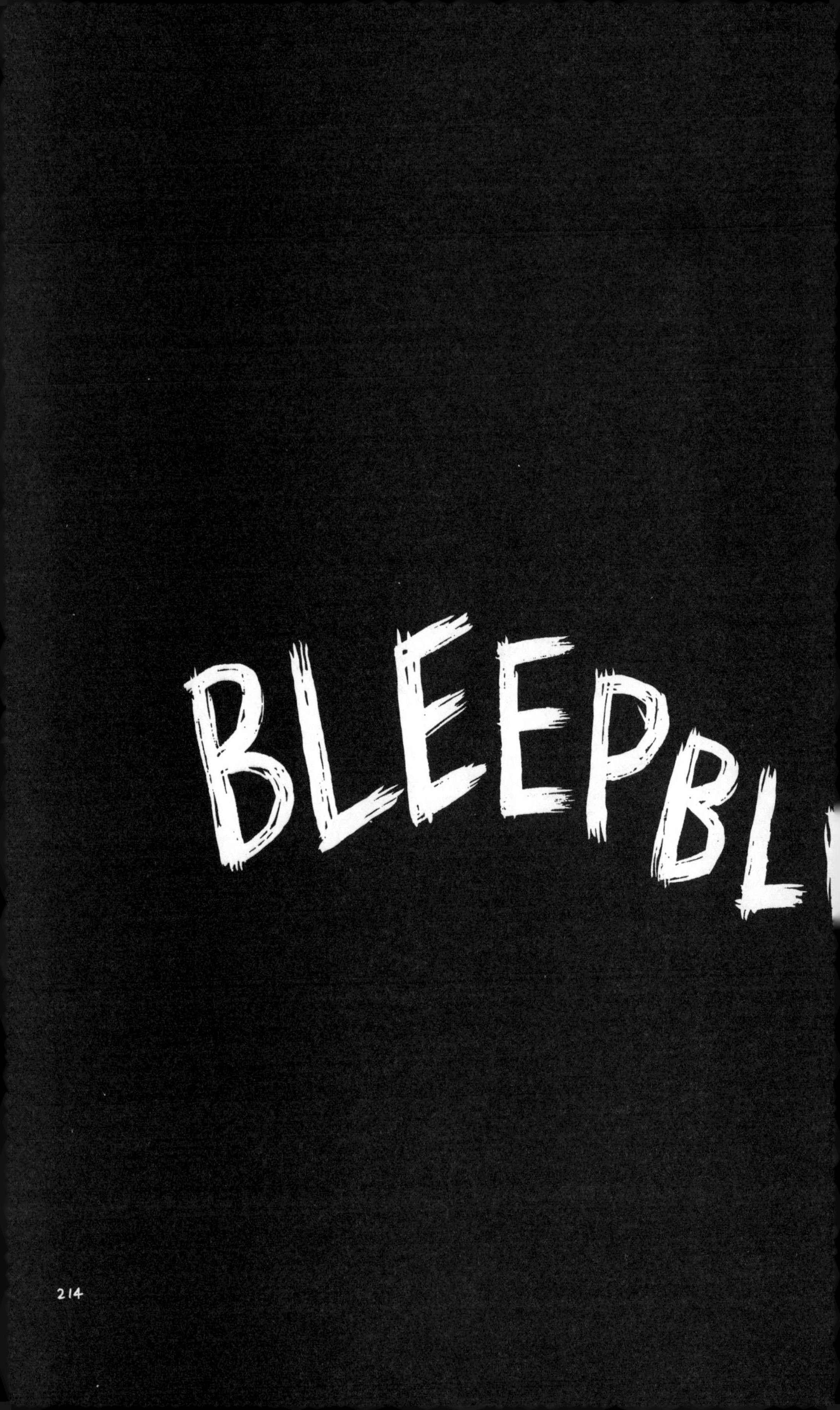
BLEEPBL

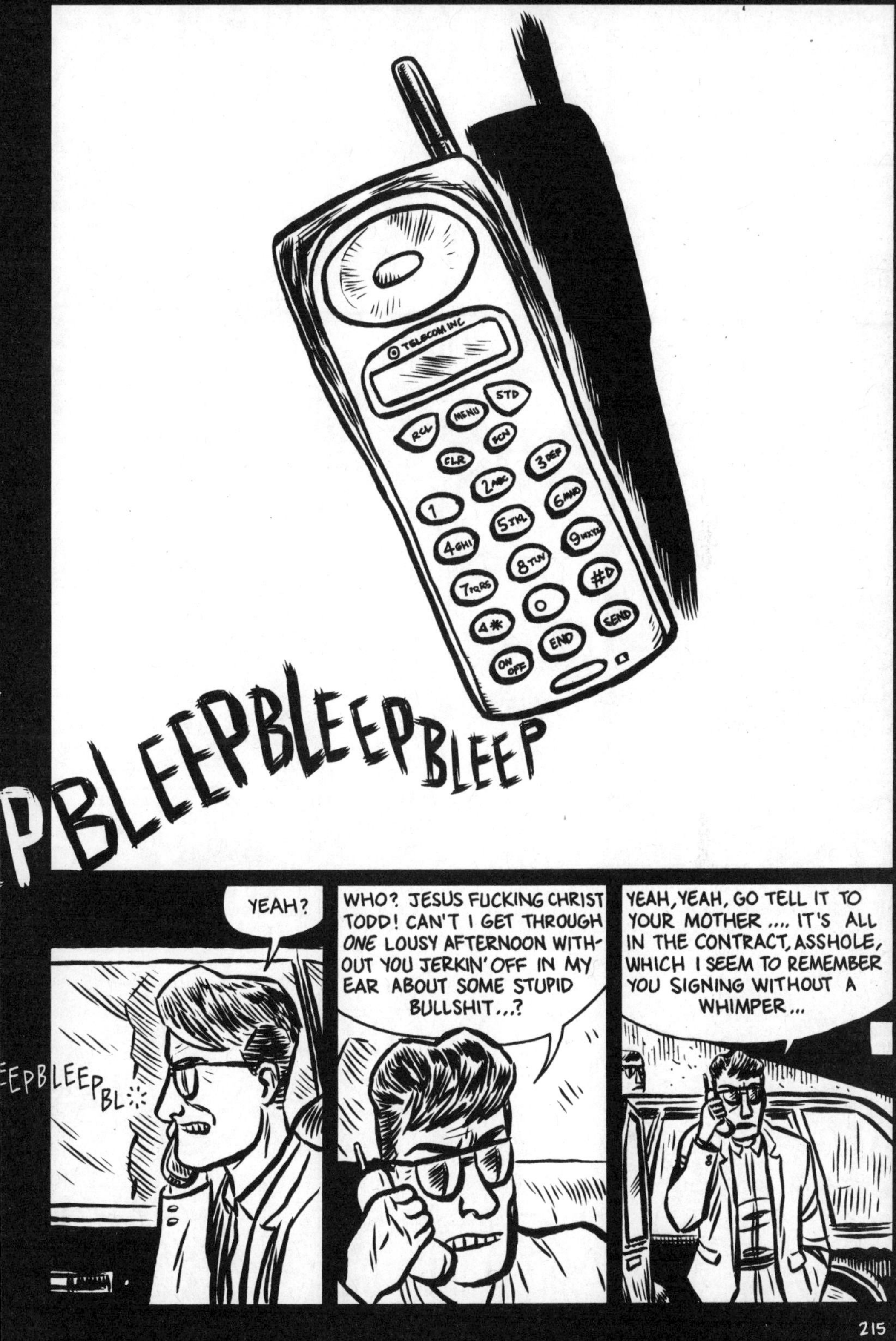
TELECOM INC
BLEEPBLEEPBLEEPBLEEP
YEAH?
EEPBLEEPBL
WHO? JESUS FUCKING CHRIST TODD! CAN'T I GET THROUGH *ONE* LOUSY AFTERNOON WITHOUT YOU JERKIN' OFF IN MY EAR ABOUT SOME STUPID BULLSHIT...?
YEAH, YEAH, GO TELL IT TO YOUR MOTHER .... IT'S ALL IN THE CONTRACT, ASSHOLE, WHICH I SEEM TO REMEMBER YOU SIGNING WITHOUT A WHIMPER...

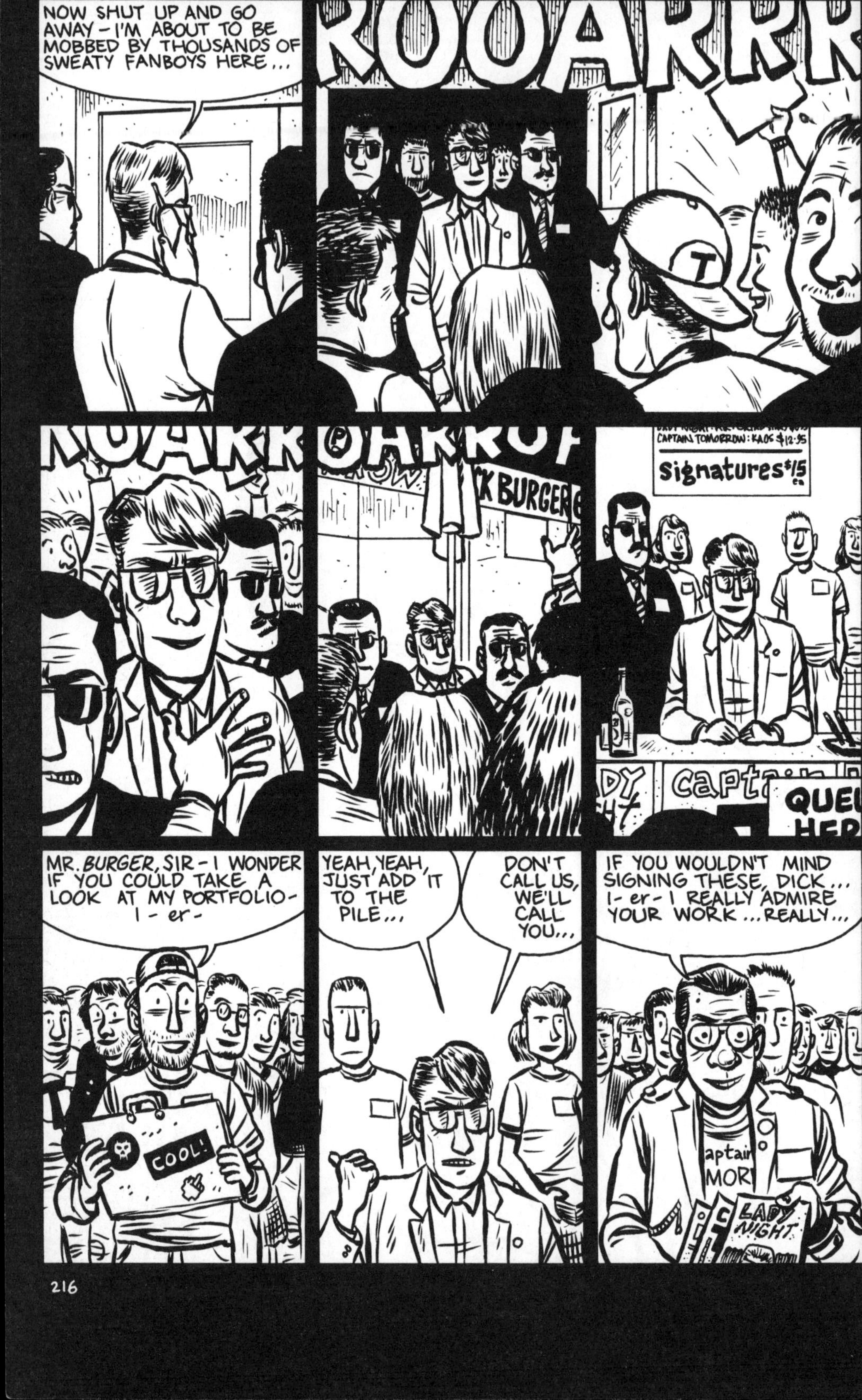
NOW SHUT UP AND GO AWAY - I'M ABOUT TO BE MOBBED BY THOUSANDS OF SWEATY FANBOYS HERE...
ROOARRR
CAPTAIN TOMORROW: KAOS $12.95
Signatures $15 ea
MR. BURGER, SIR - I WONDER IF YOU COULD TAKE A LOOK AT MY PORTFOLIO - I - er -
COOL!
YEAH, YEAH, JUST ADD IT TO THE PILE...
DON'T CALL US, WE'LL CALL YOU...
IF YOU WOULDN'T MIND SIGNING THESE, DICK... I - er - I REALLY ADMIRE YOUR WORK ...REALLY...
LADY NIGHT

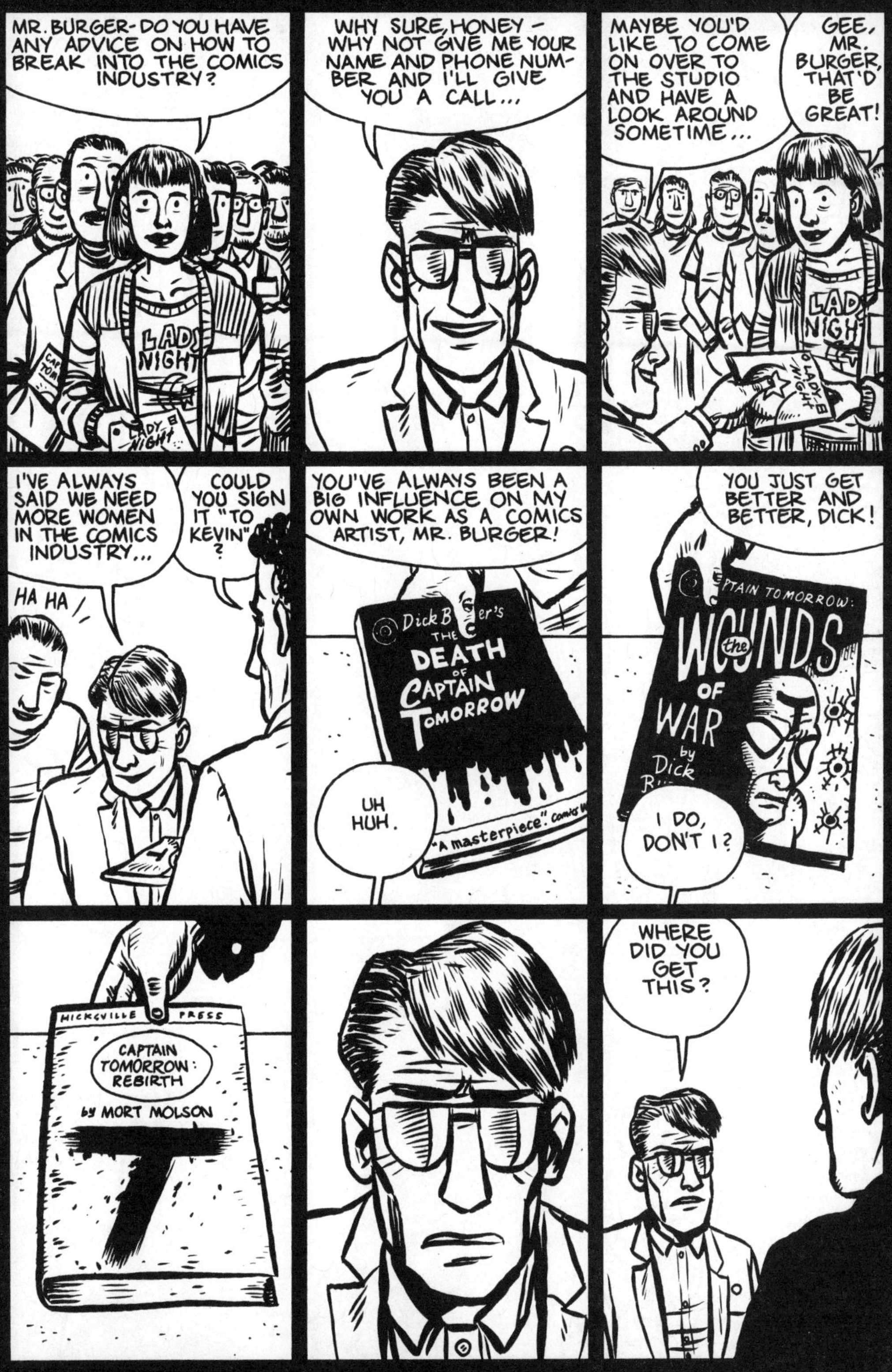
MR. BURGER- DO YOU HAVE ANY ADVICE ON HOW TO BREAK INTO THE COMICS INDUSTRY?
LADY NIGHT
WHY SURE, HONEY - WHY NOT GIVE ME YOUR NAME AND PHONE NUMBER AND I'LL GIVE YOU A CALL...
MAYBE YOU'D LIKE TO COME ON OVER TO THE STUDIO AND HAVE A LOOK AROUND SOMETIME...
GEE, MR. BURGER, THAT'D BE GREAT!
I'VE ALWAYS SAID WE NEED MORE WOMEN IN THE COMICS INDUSTRY...
COULD YOU SIGN IT "TO KEVIN"?
HA HA
YOU'VE ALWAYS BEEN A BIG INFLUENCE ON MY OWN WORK AS A COMICS ARTIST, MR. BURGER!
THE DEATH OF CAPTAIN TOMORROW
"A masterpiece."
UH HUH.
YOU JUST GET BETTER AND BETTER, DICK!
THE WOUNDS OF WAR
I DO, DON'T I?
HICKSVILLE PRESS
CAPTAIN TOMORROW: REBIRTH
by MORT MOLSON
WHERE DID YOU GET THIS?

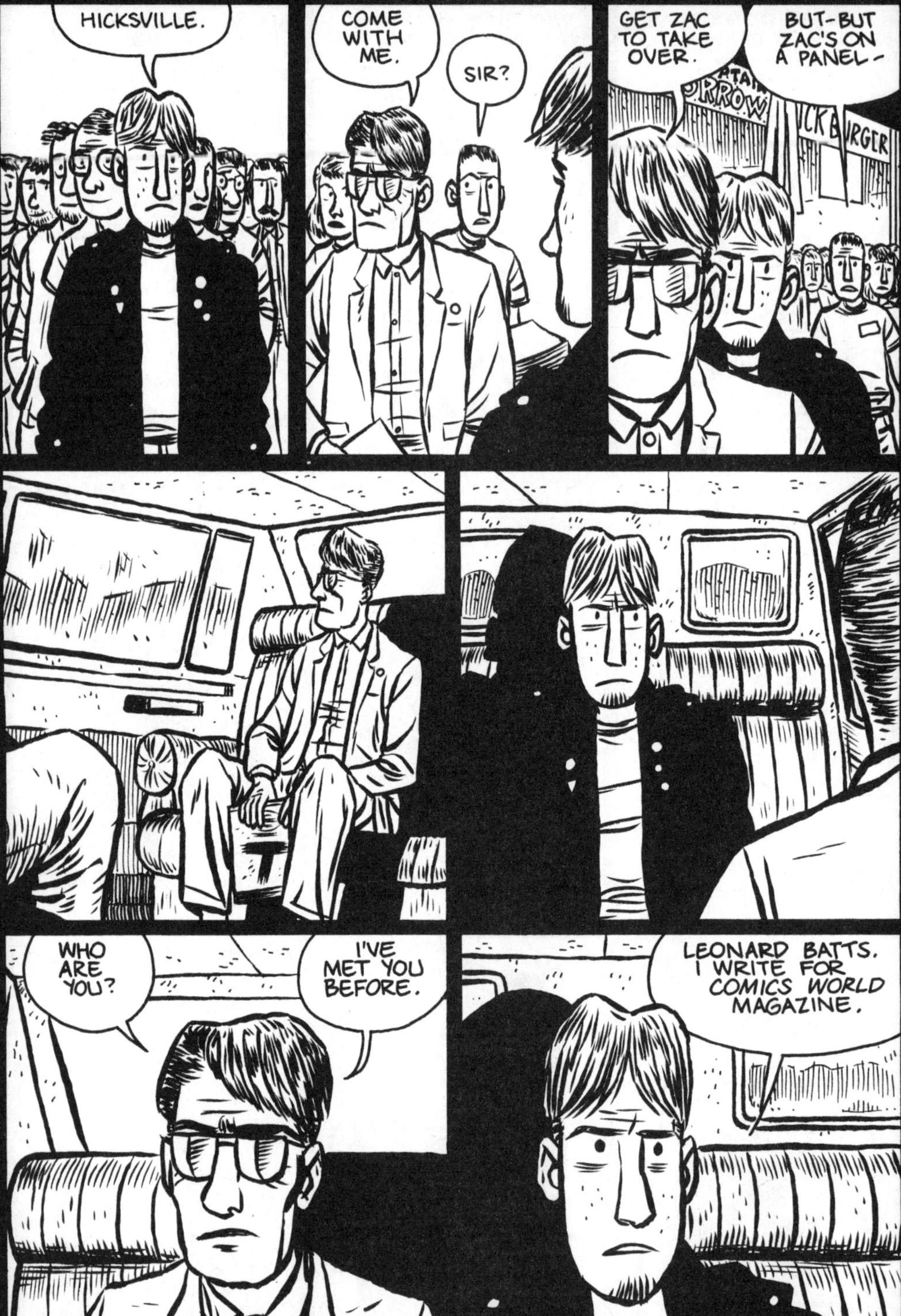
HICKSVILLE.
COME WITH ME.
SIR?
GET ZAC TO TAKE OVER.
BUT-BUT ZAC'S ON A PANEL-
WHO ARE YOU?
I'VE MET YOU BEFORE.
LEONARD BATTS. I WRITE FOR COMICS WORLD MAGAZINE.

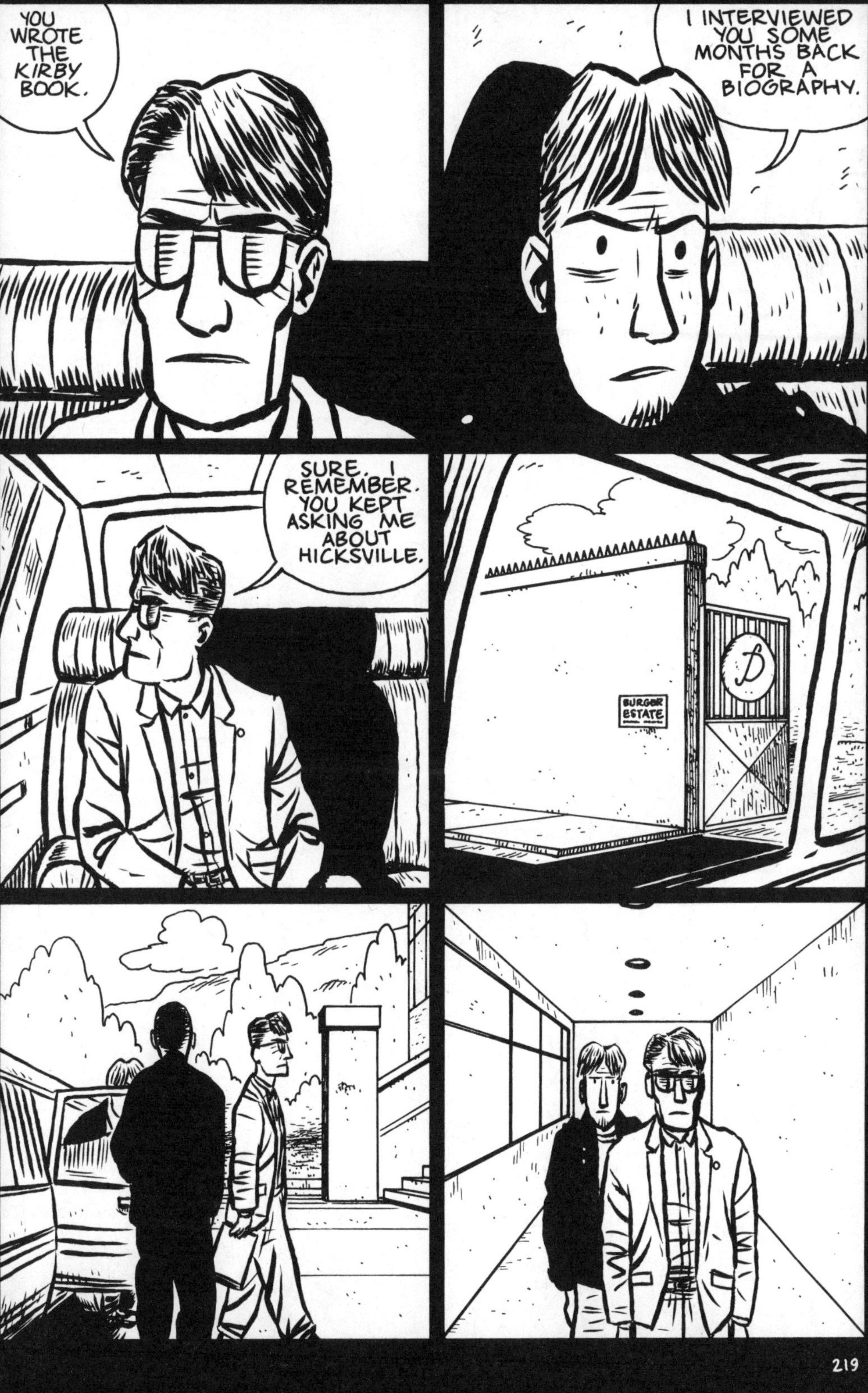
YOU WROTE THE KIRBY BOOK.
I INTERVIEWED YOU SOME MONTHS BACK FOR A BIOGRAPHY.
SURE. I REMEMBER. YOU KEPT ASKING ME ABOUT HICKSVILLE.
BURGER ESTATE

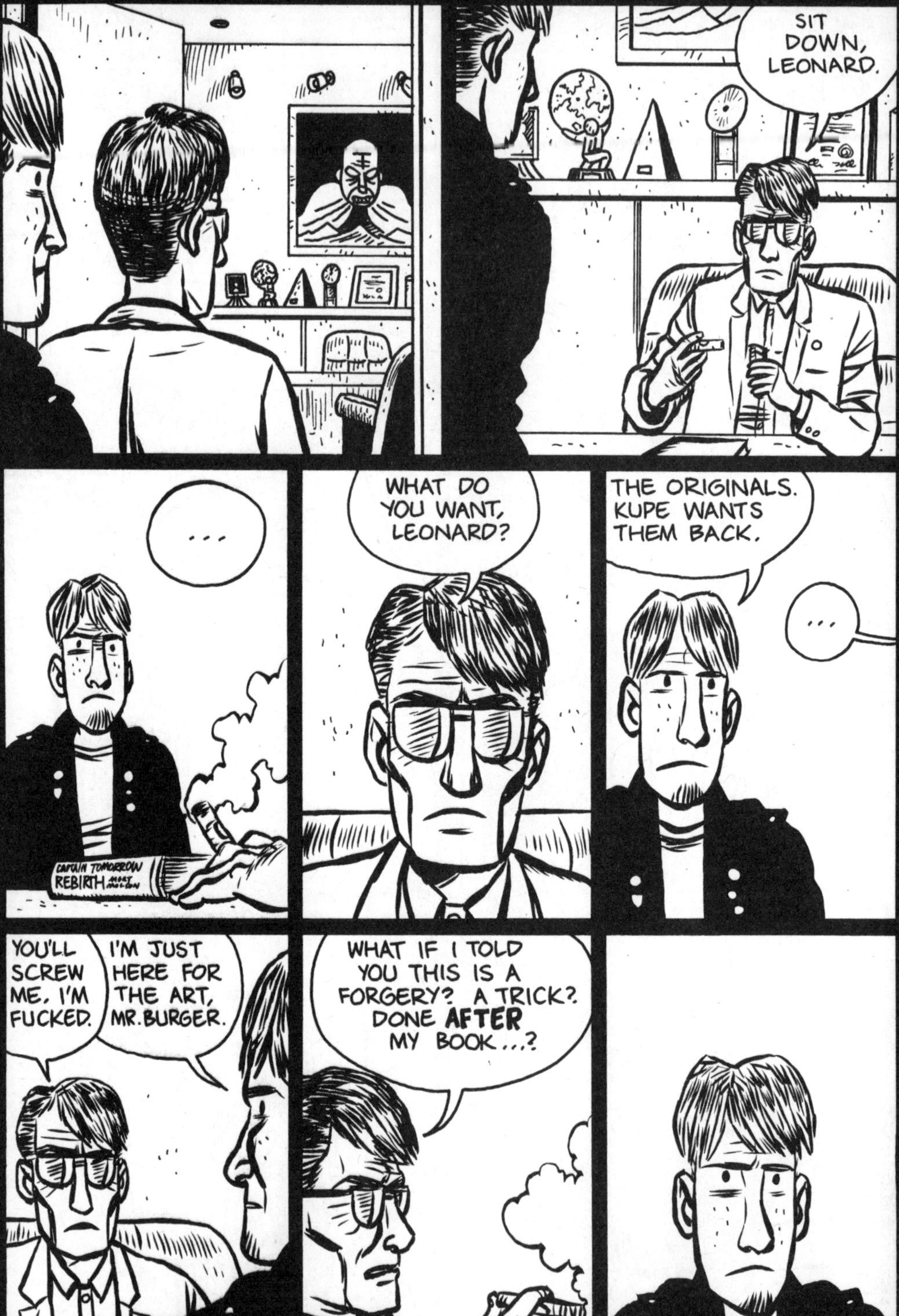
SIT DOWN, LEONARD.
...
CAPTAIN TOMORROW REBIRTH
WHAT DO YOU WANT, LEONARD?
THE ORIGINALS. KUPE WANTS THEM BACK.
...
YOU'LL SCREW ME, I'M FUCKED.
I'M JUST HERE FOR THE ART, MR. BURGER.
WHAT IF I TOLD YOU THIS IS A FORGERY? A TRICK? DONE **AFTER** MY BOOK...?

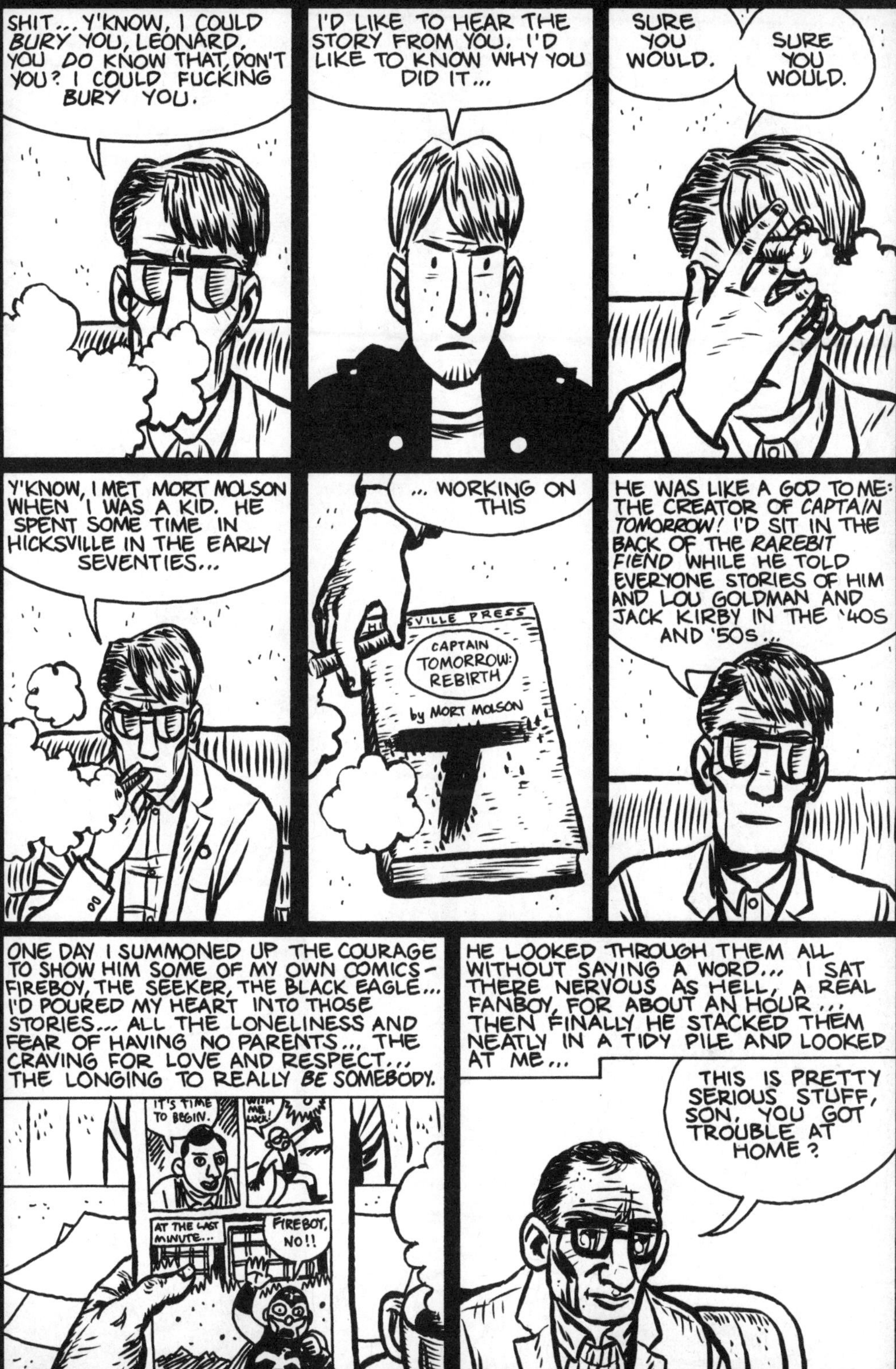

SHIT... Y'KNOW, I COULD BURY YOU, LEONARD. YOU DO KNOW THAT, DON'T YOU? I COULD FUCKING BURY YOU.
I'D LIKE TO HEAR THE STORY FROM YOU. I'D LIKE TO KNOW WHY YOU DID IT...
SURE YOU WOULD.
SURE YOU WOULD.
Y'KNOW, I MET MORT MOLSON WHEN I WAS A KID. HE SPENT SOME TIME IN HICKSVILLE IN THE EARLY SEVENTIES...
... WORKING ON THIS
SVILLE PRESS
CAPTAIN TOMORROW: REBIRTH
by MORT MOLSON
HE WAS LIKE A GOD TO ME: THE CREATOR OF CAPTAIN TOMORROW! I'D SIT IN THE BACK OF THE RAREBIT FIEND WHILE HE TOLD EVERYONE STORIES OF HIM AND LOU GOLDMAN AND JACK KIRBY IN THE '40S AND '50S...
ONE DAY I SUMMONED UP THE COURAGE TO SHOW HIM SOME OF MY OWN COMICS- FIREBOY, THE SEEKER, THE BLACK EAGLE... I'D POURED MY HEART INTO THOSE STORIES... ALL THE LONELINESS AND FEAR OF HAVING NO PARENTS... THE CRAVING FOR LOVE AND RESPECT... THE LONGING TO REALLY BE SOMEBODY.
IT'S TIME TO BEGIN.
AT THE LAST MINUTE...
FIREBOY, NO!!
HE LOOKED THROUGH THEM ALL WITHOUT SAYING A WORD... I SAT THERE NERVOUS AS HELL, A REAL FANBOY, FOR ABOUT AN HOUR... THEN FINALLY HE STACKED THEM NEATLY IN A TIDY PILE AND LOOKED AT ME...
THIS IS PRETTY SERIOUS STUFF, SON. YOU GOT TROUBLE AT HOME?

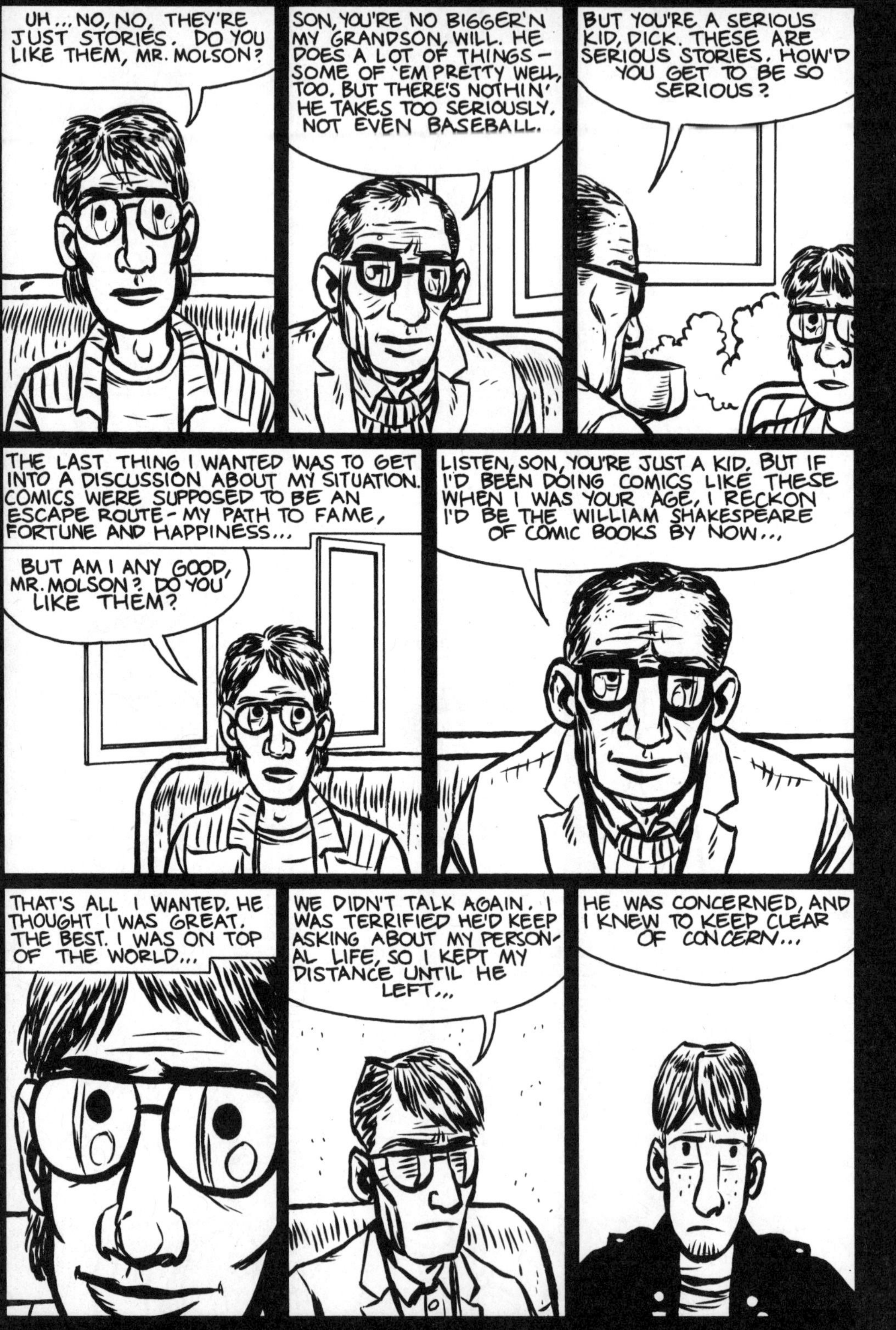
UH... NO, NO, THEY'RE JUST STORIES. DO YOU LIKE THEM, MR. MOLSON?
SON, YOU'RE NO BIGGER'N MY GRANDSON, WILL. HE DOES A LOT OF THINGS - SOME OF 'EM PRETTY WELL, TOO, BUT THERE'S NOTHIN' HE TAKES TOO SERIOUSLY. NOT EVEN BASEBALL.
BUT YOU'RE A SERIOUS KID, DICK. THESE ARE SERIOUS STORIES. HOW'D YOU GET TO BE SO SERIOUS?
THE LAST THING I WANTED WAS TO GET INTO A DISCUSSION ABOUT MY SITUATION. COMICS WERE SUPPOSED TO BE AN ESCAPE ROUTE - MY PATH TO FAME, FORTUNE AND HAPPINESS...
BUT AM I ANY GOOD, MR. MOLSON? DO YOU LIKE THEM?
LISTEN, SON, YOU'RE JUST A KID. BUT IF I'D BEEN DOING COMICS LIKE THESE WHEN I WAS YOUR AGE, I RECKON I'D BE THE WILLIAM SHAKESPEARE OF COMIC BOOKS BY NOW...
THAT'S ALL I WANTED. HE THOUGHT I WAS GREAT. THE BEST. I WAS ON TOP OF THE WORLD...
WE DIDN'T TALK AGAIN. I WAS TERRIFIED HE'D KEEP ASKING ABOUT MY PERSONAL LIFE, SO I KEPT MY DISTANCE UNTIL HE LEFT...
HE WAS CONCERNED, AND I KNEW TO KEEP CLEAR OF CONCERN...

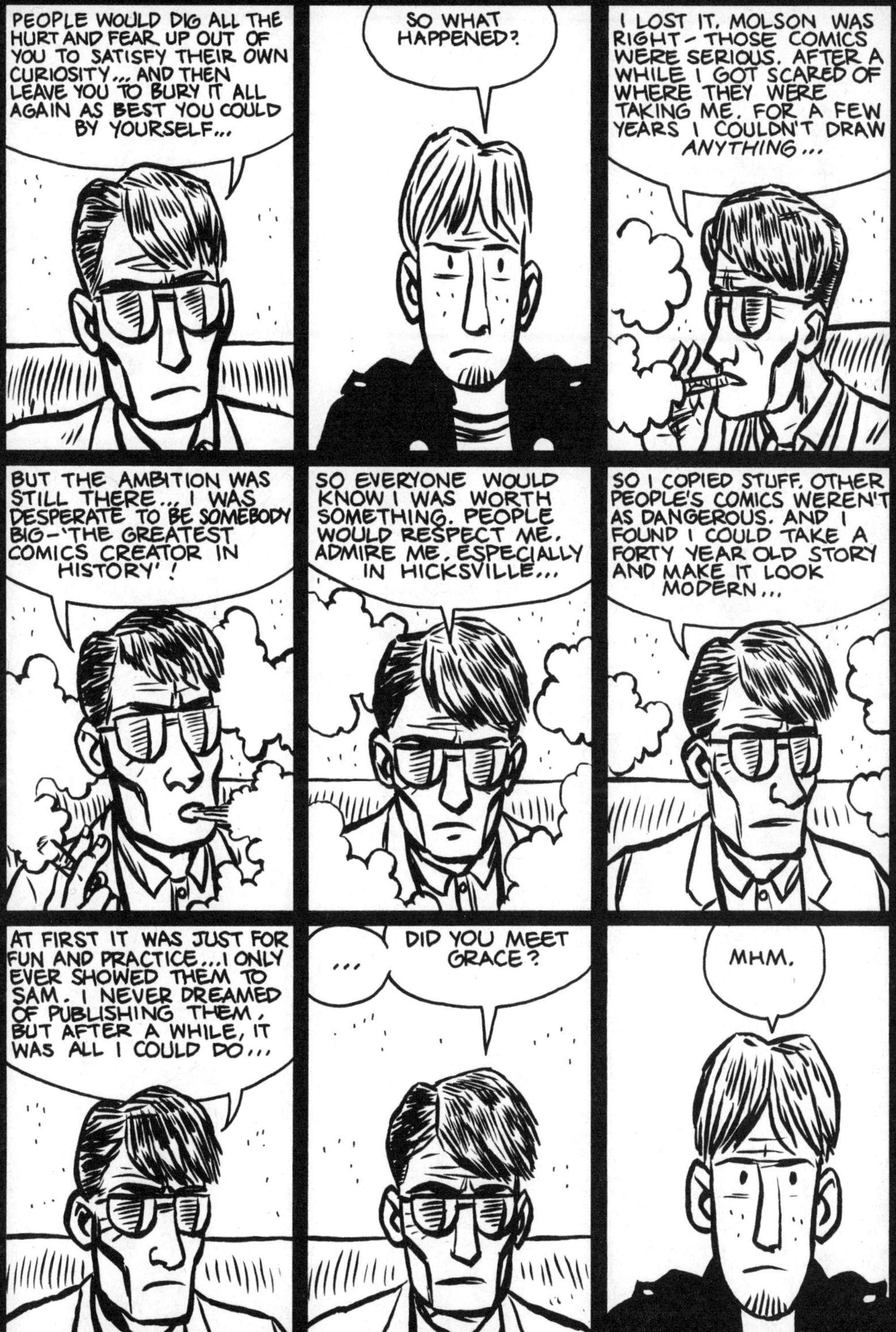
PEOPLE WOULD DIG ALL THE HURT AND FEAR UP OUT OF YOU TO SATISFY THEIR OWN CURIOSITY... AND THEN LEAVE YOU TO BURY IT ALL AGAIN AS BEST YOU COULD BY YOURSELF...
SO WHAT HAPPENED?
I LOST IT. MOLSON WAS RIGHT- THOSE COMICS WERE SERIOUS. AFTER A WHILE I GOT SCARED OF WHERE THEY WERE TAKING ME. FOR A FEW YEARS I COULDN'T DRAW ANYTHING...
BUT THE AMBITION WAS STILL THERE... I WAS DESPERATE TO BE SOMEBODY BIG-'THE GREATEST COMICS CREATOR IN HISTORY'!
SO EVERYONE WOULD KNOW I WAS WORTH SOMETHING. PEOPLE WOULD RESPECT ME, ADMIRE ME, ESPECIALLY IN HICKSVILLE...
SO I COPIED STUFF. OTHER PEOPLE'S COMICS WEREN'T AS DANGEROUS. AND I FOUND I COULD TAKE A FORTY YEAR OLD STORY AND MAKE IT LOOK MODERN...
AT FIRST IT WAS JUST FOR FUN AND PRACTICE... I ONLY EVER SHOWED THEM TO SAM. I NEVER DREAMED OF PUBLISHING THEM, BUT AFTER A WHILE, IT WAS ALL I COULD DO...
...
DID YOU MEET GRACE?
MHM.

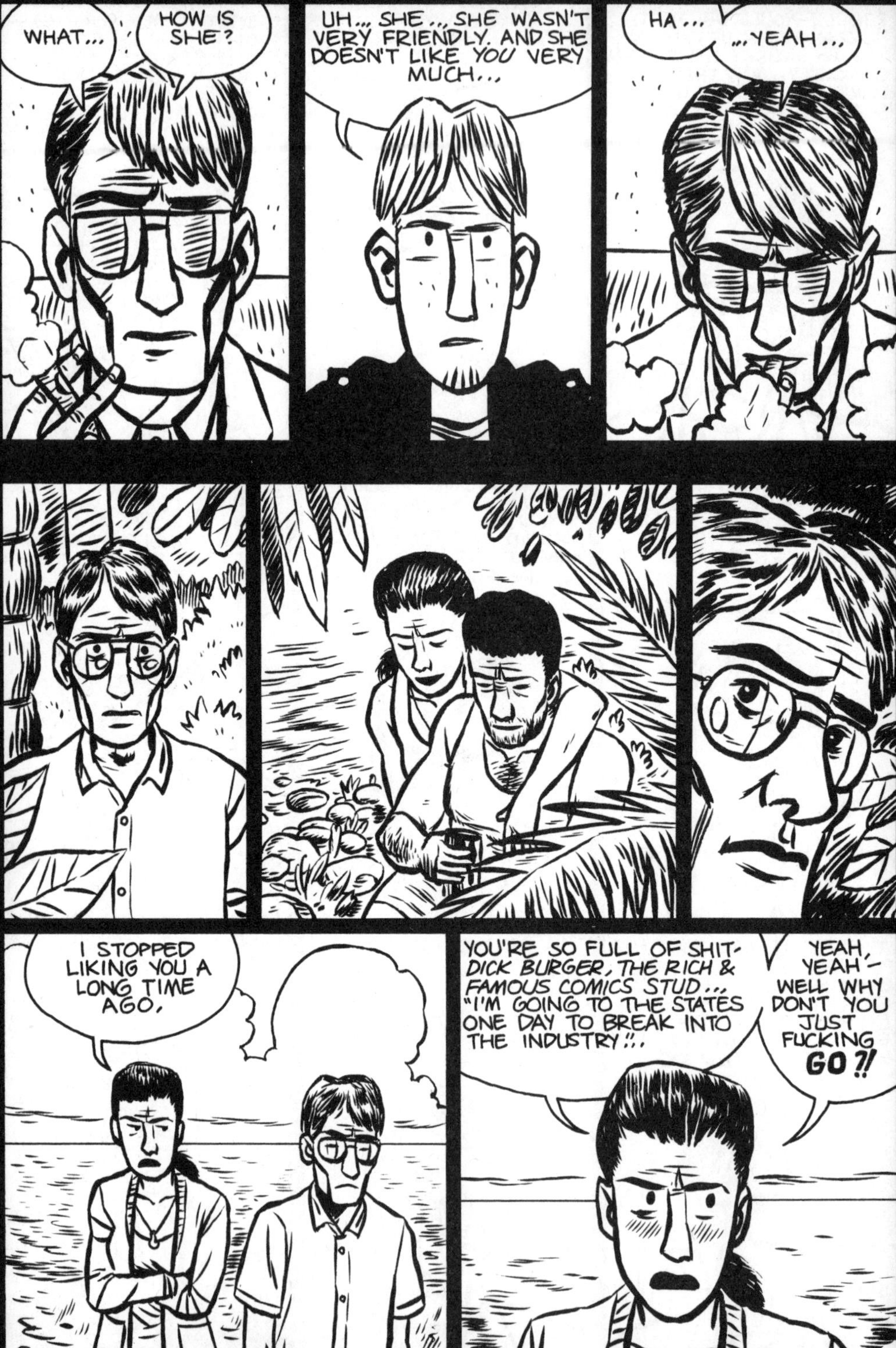

WHAT...
HOW IS SHE?
UH... SHE... SHE WASN'T VERY FRIENDLY. AND SHE DOESN'T LIKE YOU VERY MUCH...
HA...
...YEAH...
I STOPPED LIKING YOU A LONG TIME AGO,
YOU'RE SO FULL OF SHIT- DICK BURGER, THE RICH & FAMOUS COMICS STUD... "I'M GOING TO THE STATES ONE DAY TO BREAK INTO THE INDUSTRY!"...
YEAH, YEAH - WELL WHY DON'T YOU JUST FUCKING GO?!

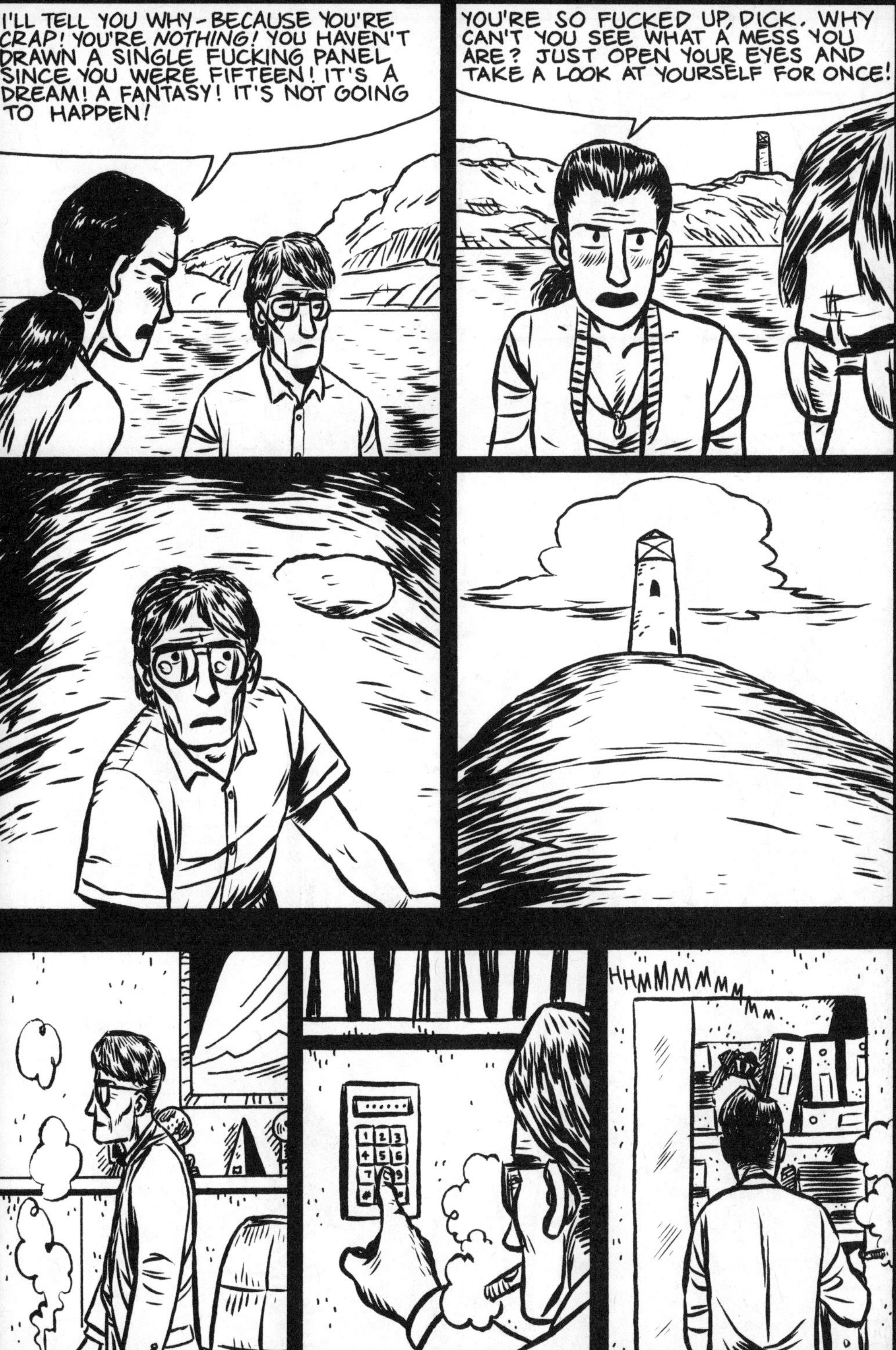

I'LL TELL YOU WHY- BECAUSE YOU'RE CRAP! YOU'RE NOTHING! YOU HAVEN'T DRAWN A SINGLE FUCKING PANEL SINCE YOU WERE FIFTEEN! IT'S A DREAM! A FANTASY! IT'S NOT GOING TO HAPPEN!
YOU'RE SO FUCKED UP, DICK. WHY CAN'T YOU SEE WHAT A MESS YOU ARE? JUST OPEN YOUR EYES AND TAKE A LOOK AT YOURSELF FOR ONCE!
HHMMMMMMMMM

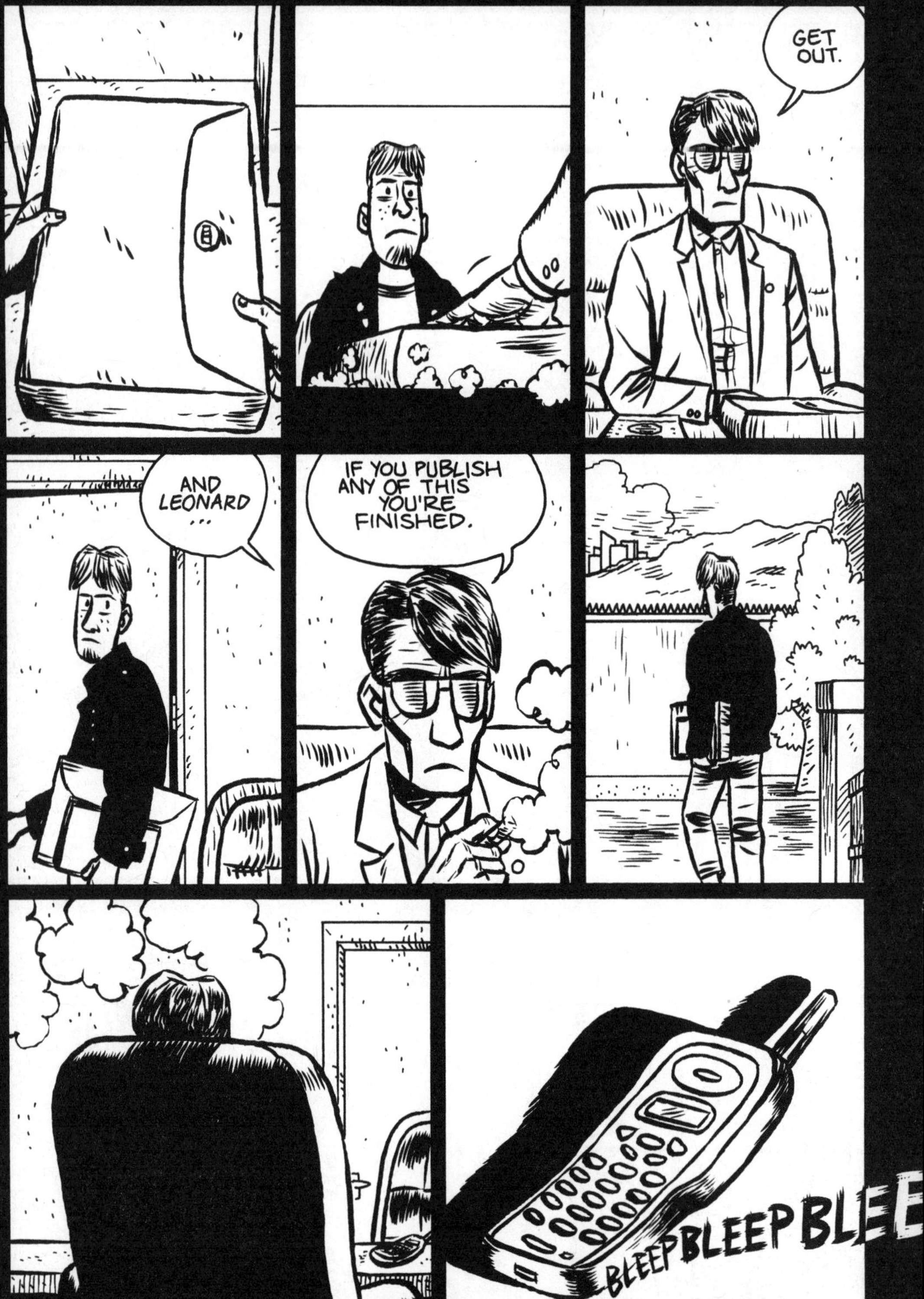
GET OUT.
AND LEONARD ...
IF YOU PUBLISH ANY OF THIS YOU'RE FINISHED.
BLEEP BLEEP BLEE

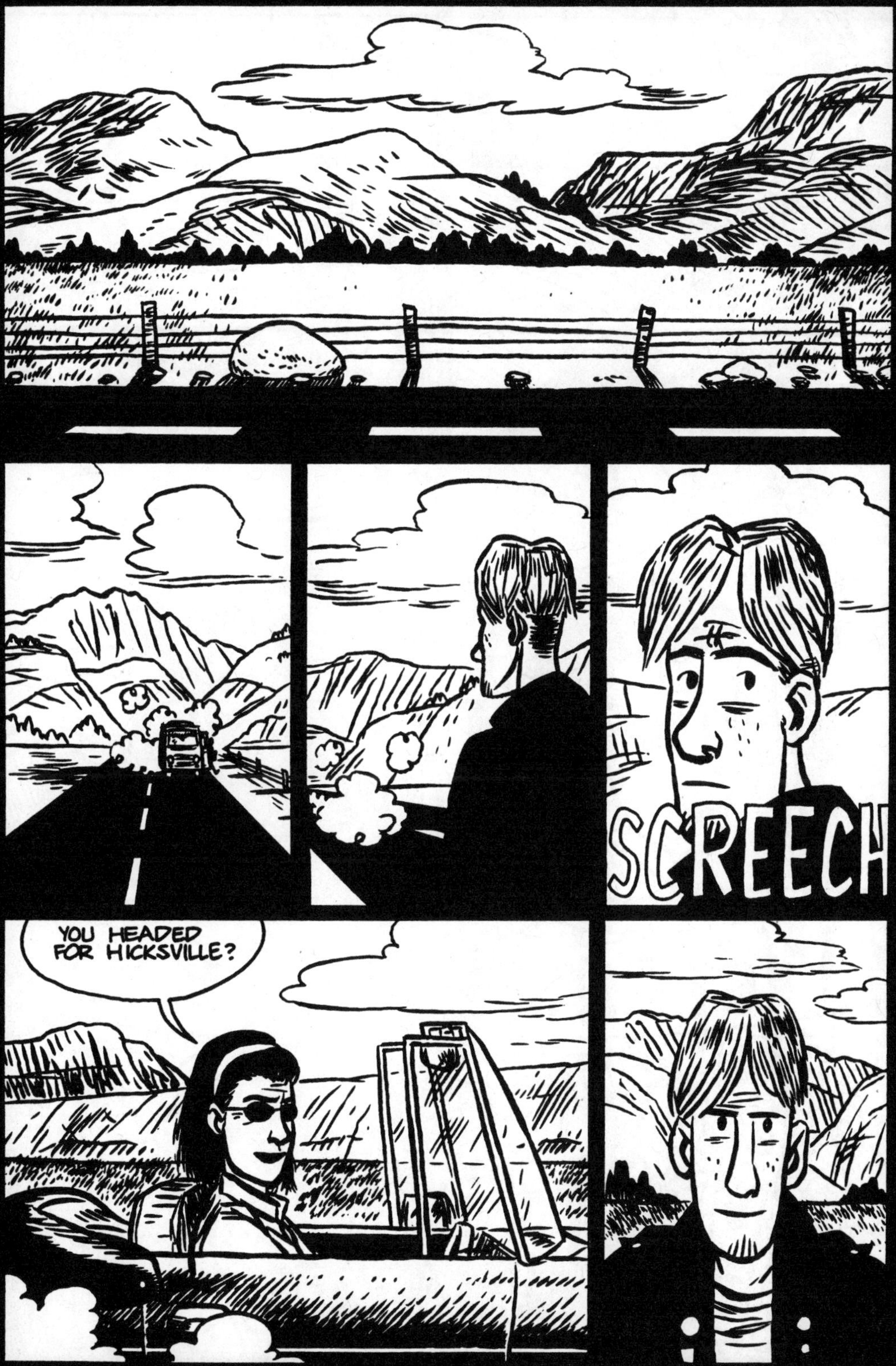
SCREECH
YOU HEADED FOR HICKSVILLE?

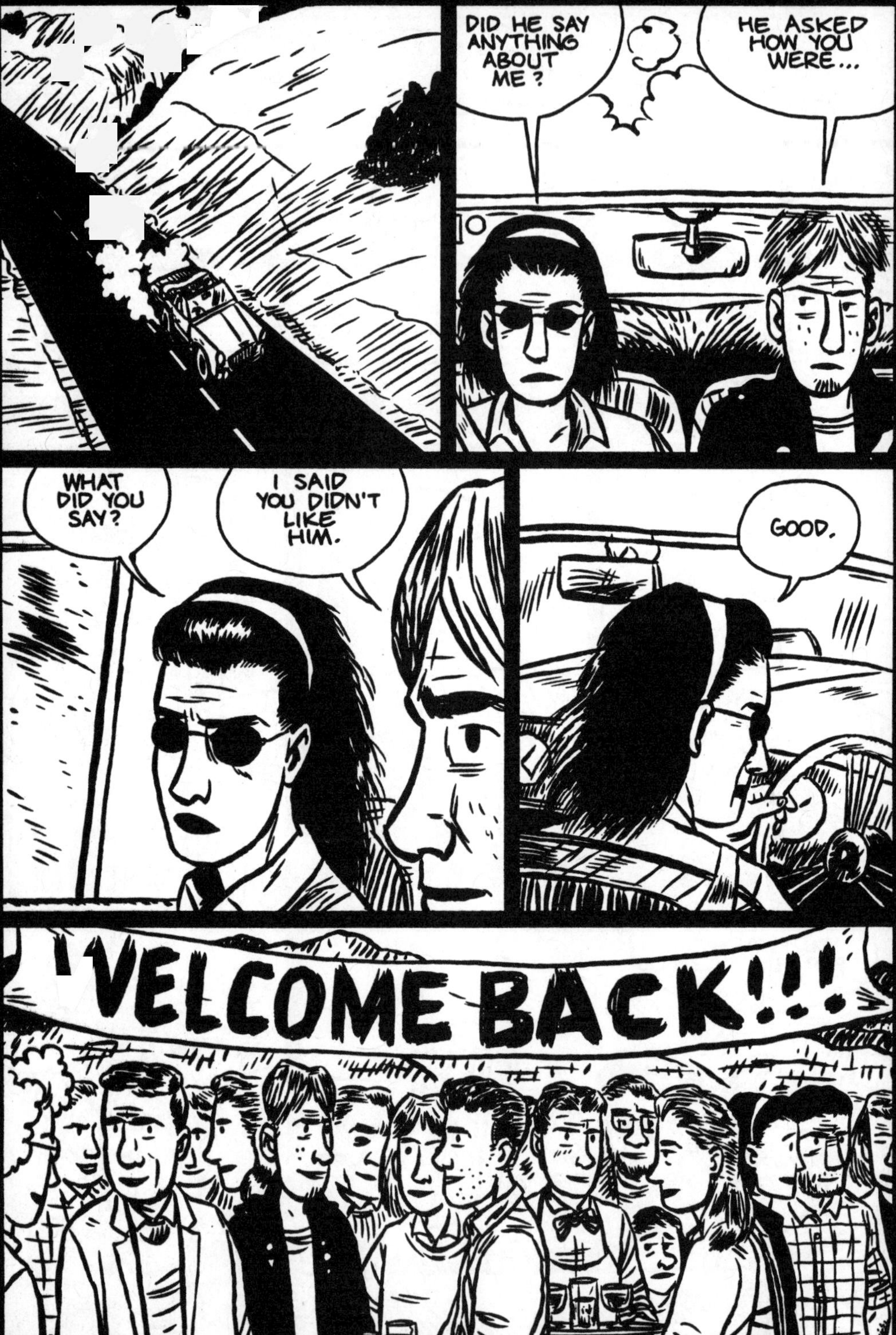

DID HE SAY ANYTHING ABOUT ME?
HE ASKED HOW YOU WERE...
WHAT DID YOU SAY?
I SAID YOU DIDN'T LIKE HIM.
GOOD.
VELCOME BACK!!!

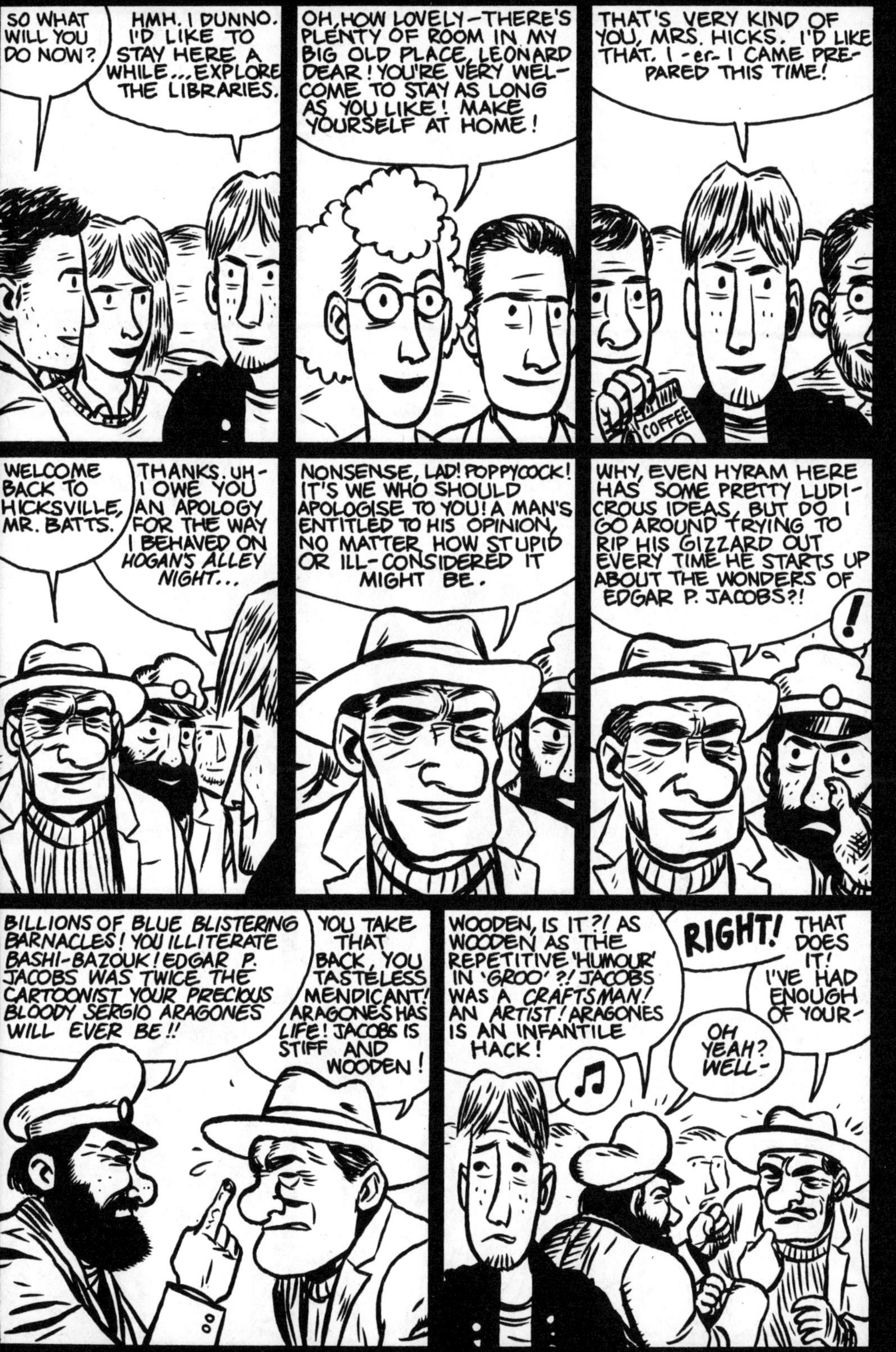
SO WHAT WILL YOU DO NOW?
HMH. I DUNNO. I'D LIKE TO STAY HERE A WHILE... EXPLORE THE LIBRARIES.
OH, HOW LOVELY—THERE'S PLENTY OF ROOM IN MY BIG OLD PLACE, LEONARD DEAR! YOU'RE VERY WELCOME TO STAY AS LONG AS YOU LIKE! MAKE YOURSELF AT HOME!
THAT'S VERY KIND OF YOU, MRS. HICKS. I'D LIKE THAT. I -er- I CAME PREPARED THIS TIME!
COFFEE
WELCOME BACK TO HICKSVILLE, MR. BATTS.
THANKS. UH- I OWE YOU AN APOLOGY FOR THE WAY I BEHAVED ON HOGAN'S ALLEY NIGHT...
NONSENSE, LAD! POPPYCOCK! IT'S WE WHO SHOULD APOLOGISE TO YOU! A MAN'S ENTITLED TO HIS OPINION, NO MATTER HOW STUPID OR ILL-CONSIDERED IT MIGHT BE.
WHY, EVEN HYRAM HERE HAS SOME PRETTY LUDICROUS IDEAS, BUT DO I GO AROUND TRYING TO RIP HIS GIZZARD OUT EVERY TIME HE STARTS UP ABOUT THE WONDERS OF EDGAR P. JACOBS?!
!
BILLIONS OF BLUE BLISTERING BARNACLES! YOU ILLITERATE BASHI-BAZOUK! EDGAR P. JACOBS WAS TWICE THE CARTOONIST YOUR PRECIOUS BLOODY SERGIO ARAGONES WILL EVER BE!!
YOU TAKE THAT BACK, YOU TASTELESS MENDICANT! ARAGONES HAS LIFE! JACOBS IS STIFF AND WOODEN!
WOODEN, IS IT?! AS WOODEN AS THE REPETITIVE 'HUMOUR' IN 'GROO'?! JACOBS WAS A CRAFTSMAN! AN ARTIST! ARAGONES IS AN INFANTILE HACK!
RIGHT!
THAT DOES IT! I'VE HAD ENOUGH OF YOUR-
OH YEAH? WELL-

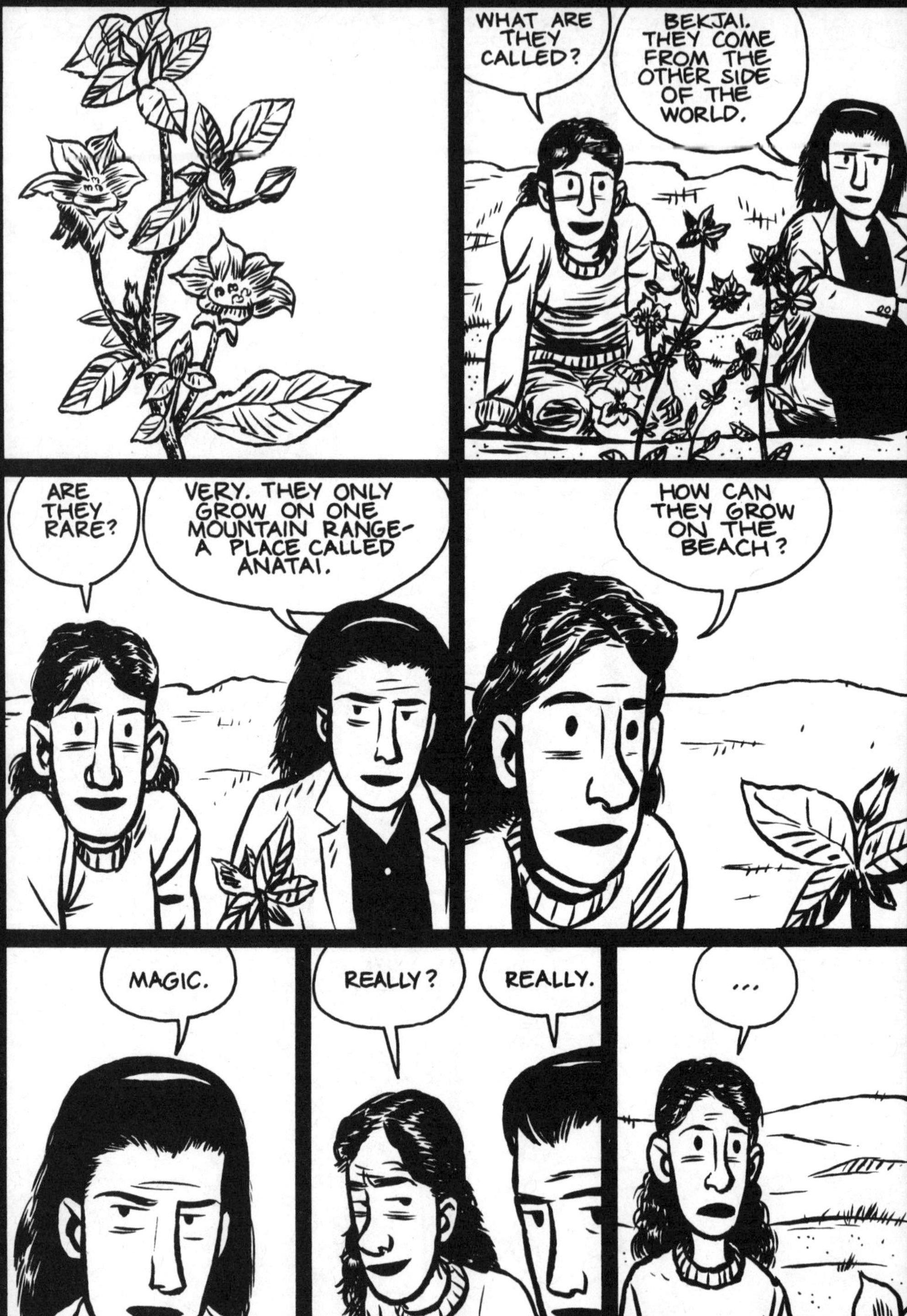
WHAT ARE THEY CALLED?
BEKJAI. THEY COME FROM THE OTHER SIDE OF THE WORLD.
ARE THEY RARE?
VERY. THEY ONLY GROW ON ONE MOUNTAIN RANGE- A PLACE CALLED ANATAI.
HOW CAN THEY GROW ON THE BEACH?
MAGIC.
REALLY?
REALLY.
...

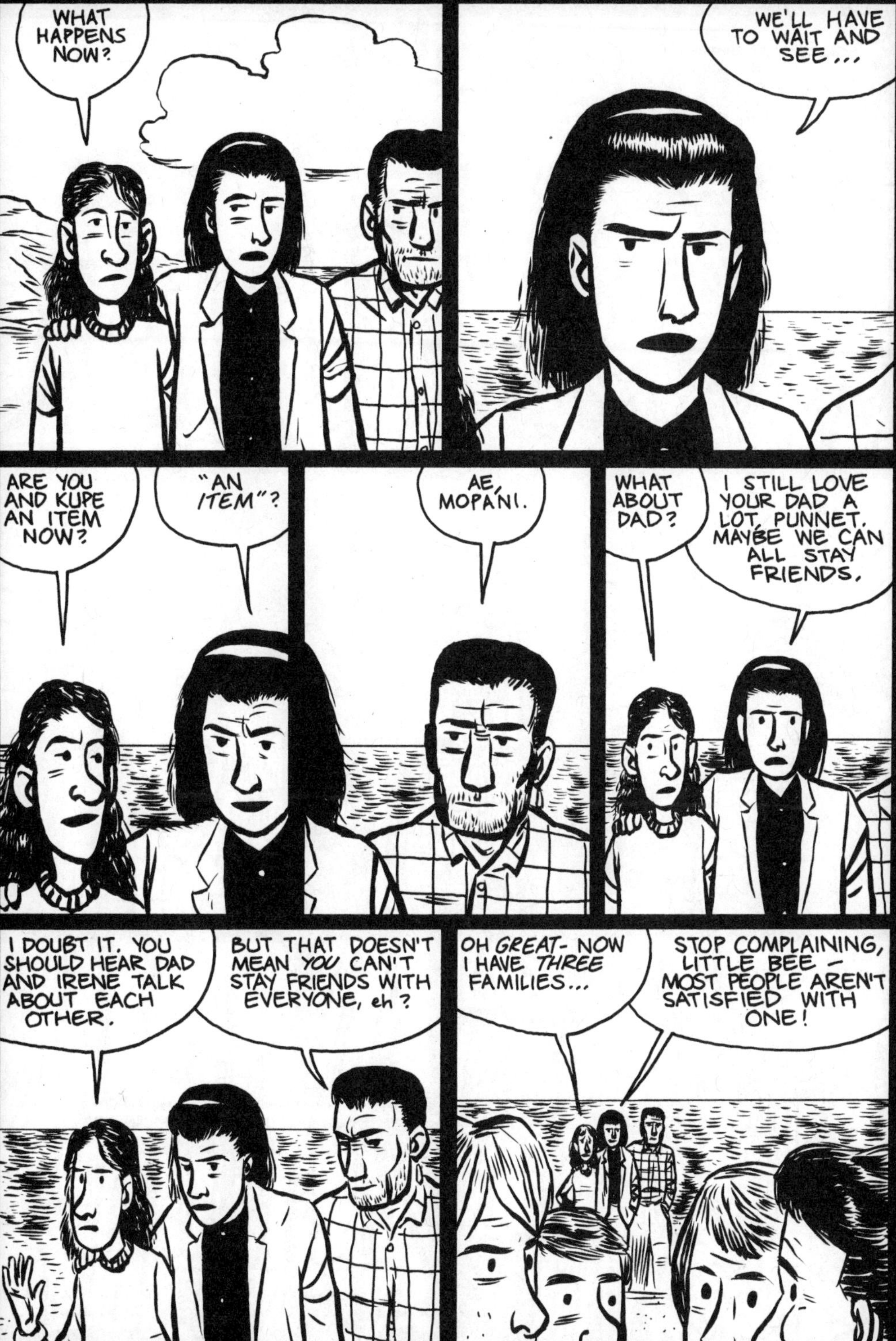
WHAT HAPPENS NOW?
WE'LL HAVE TO WAIT AND SEE...
ARE YOU AND KUPE AN ITEM NOW?
"AN *ITEM*"?
AE, MOPANI.
WHAT ABOUT DAD?
I STILL LOVE YOUR DAD A LOT, PUNNET. MAYBE WE CAN ALL STAY FRIENDS.
I DOUBT IT. YOU SHOULD HEAR DAD AND IRENE TALK ABOUT EACH OTHER.
BUT THAT DOESN'T MEAN *YOU* CAN'T STAY FRIENDS WITH EVERYONE, eh?
OH *GREAT*- NOW I HAVE *THREE* FAMILIES...
STOP COMPLAINING, LITTLE BEE - MOST PEOPLE AREN'T SATISFIED WITH ONE!

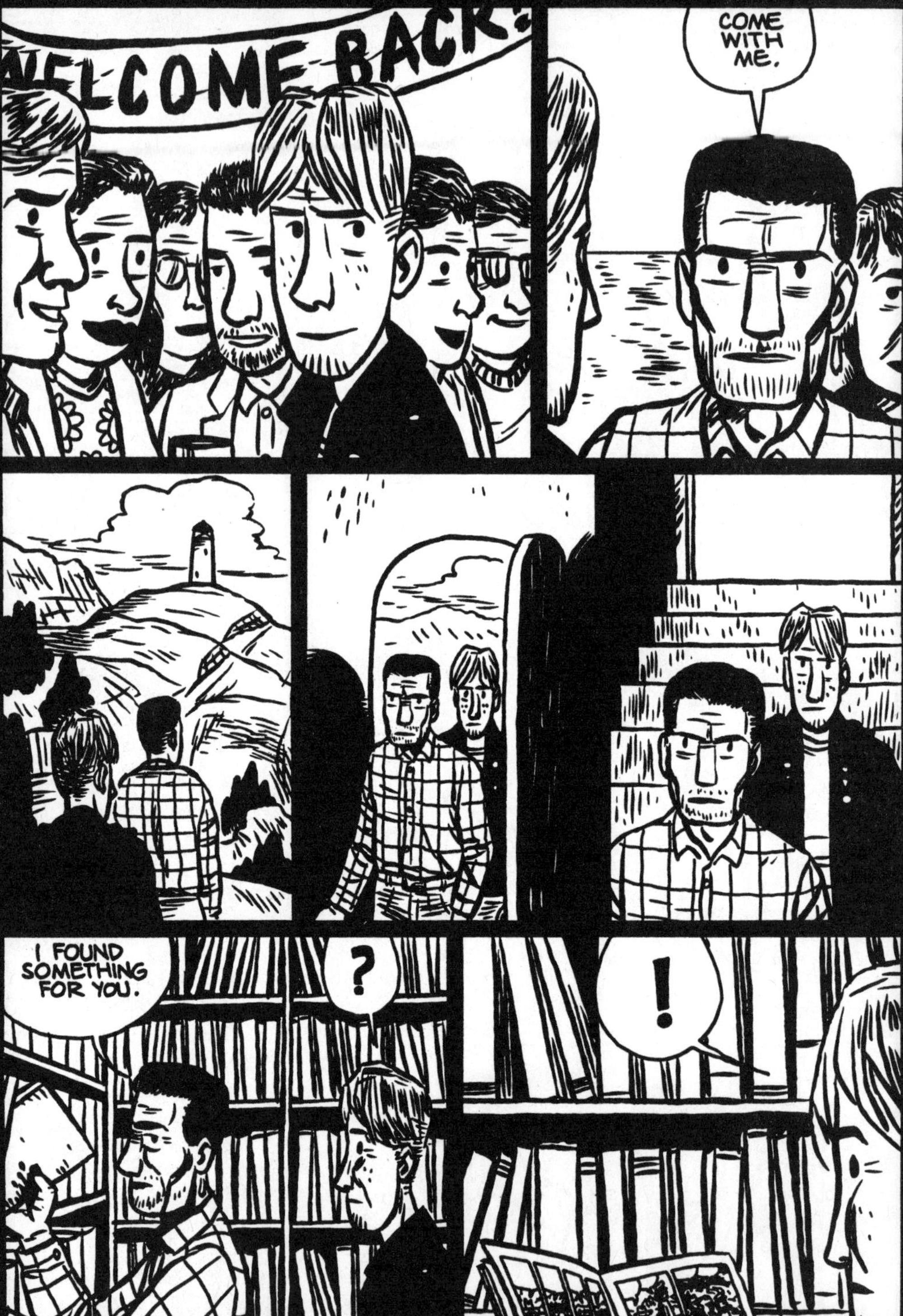
WELCOME BACK!
COME WITH ME.
I FOUND SOMETHING FOR YOU.
?
!

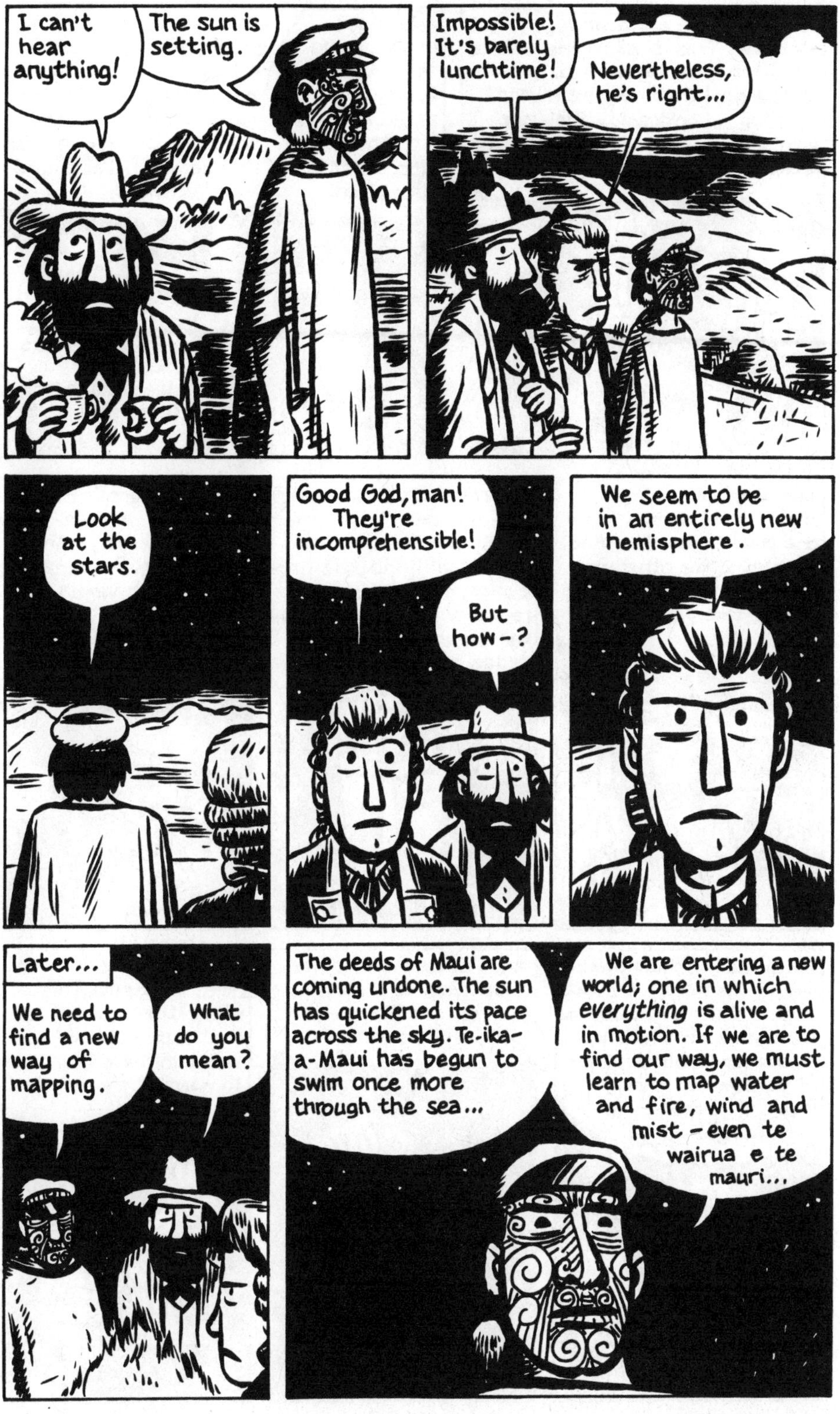

I can't hear anything!
The sun is setting.
Impossible! It's barely lunchtime!
Nevertheless, he's right...
Look at the stars.
Good God, man! They're incomprehensible!
But how-?
We seem to be in an entirely new hemisphere.
Later...
We need to find a new way of mapping.
What do you mean?
The deeds of Maui are coming undone. The sun has quickened its pace across the sky. Te-ika-a-Maui has begun to swim once more through the sea...
We are entering a new world; one in which *everything* is alive and in motion. If we are to find our way, we must learn to map water and fire, wind and mist - even te wairua e te mauri...

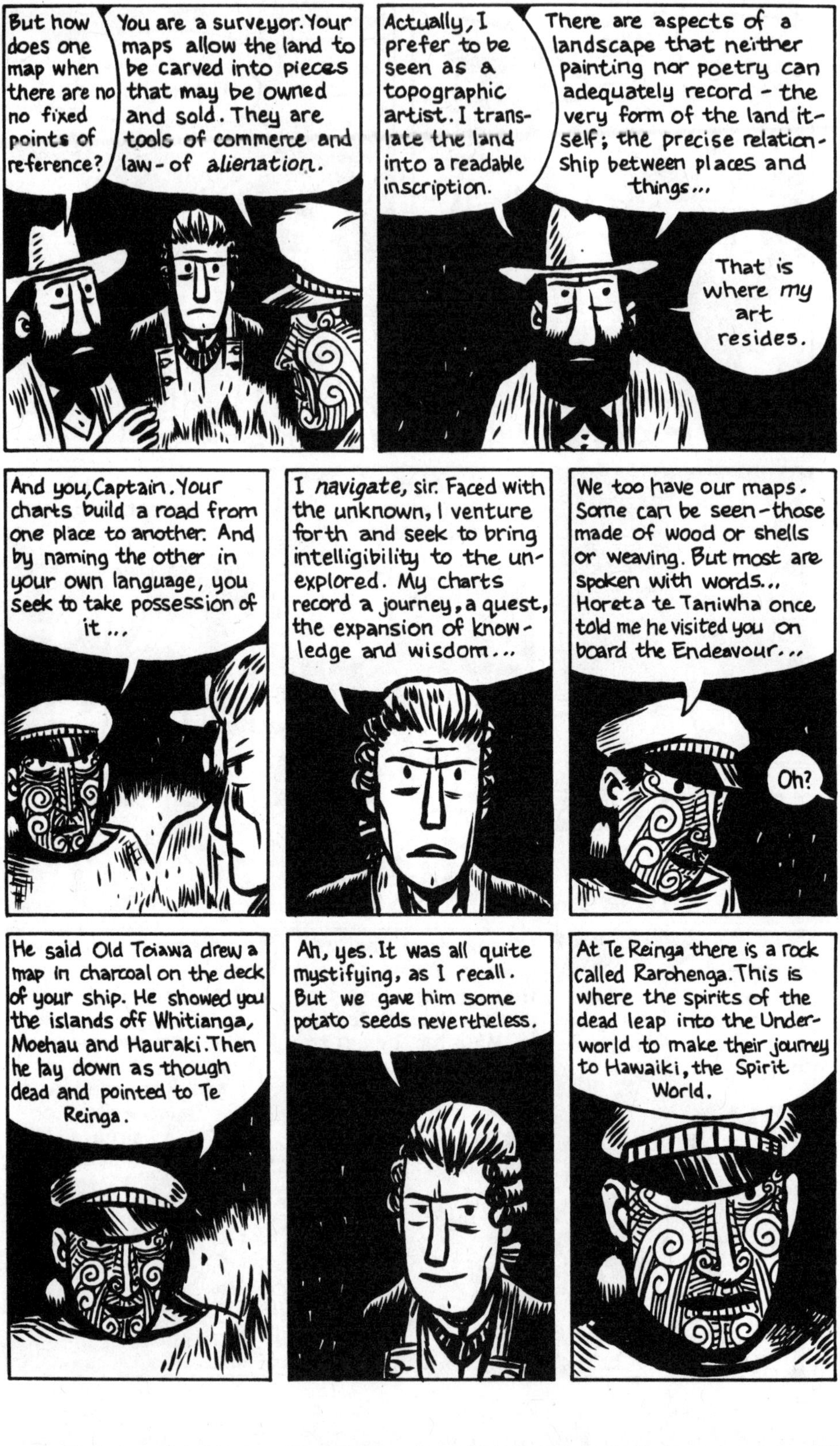
But how does one map when there are no no fixed points of reference?
You are a surveyor. Your maps allow the land to be carved into pieces that may be owned and sold. They are tools of commerce and law - of *alienation*.
Actually, I prefer to be seen as a topographic artist. I translate the land into a readable inscription.
There are aspects of a landscape that neither painting nor poetry can adequately record - the very form of the land itself; the precise relationship between places and things...
That is where *my* art resides.
And you, Captain. Your charts build a road from one place to another. And by naming the other in your own language, you seek to take possession of it...
I *navigate*, sir. Faced with the unknown, I venture forth and seek to bring intelligibility to the unexplored. My charts record a journey, a quest, the expansion of knowledge and wisdom...
We too have our maps. Some can be seen - those made of wood or shells or weaving. But most are spoken with words... Horeta te Taniwha once told me he visited you on board the Endeavour...
Oh?
He said Old Toiawa drew a map in charcoal on the deck of your ship. He showed you the islands off Whitianga, Moehau and Hauraki. Then he lay down as though dead and pointed to Te Reinga.
Ah, yes. It was all quite mystifying, as I recall. But we gave him some potato seeds nevertheless.
At Te Reinga there is a rock called Rarohenga. This is where the spirits of the dead leap into the Underworld to make their journey to Hawaiki, the Spirit World.

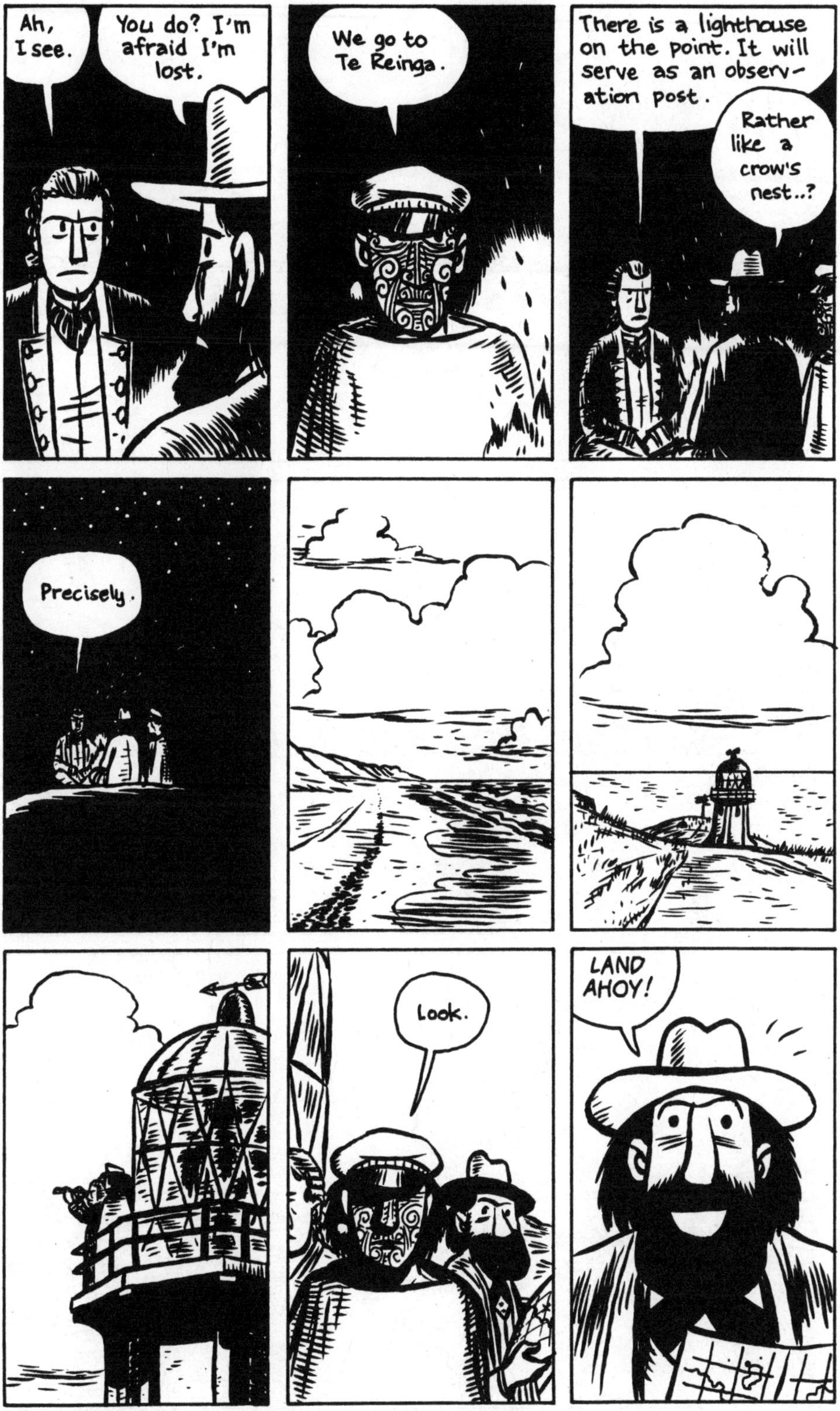
Ah, I see.
You do? I'm afraid I'm lost.
We go to Te Reinga.
There is a lighthouse on the point. It will serve as an observ-ation post.
Rather like a crow's nest..?
Precisely.
Look.
LAND AHOY!

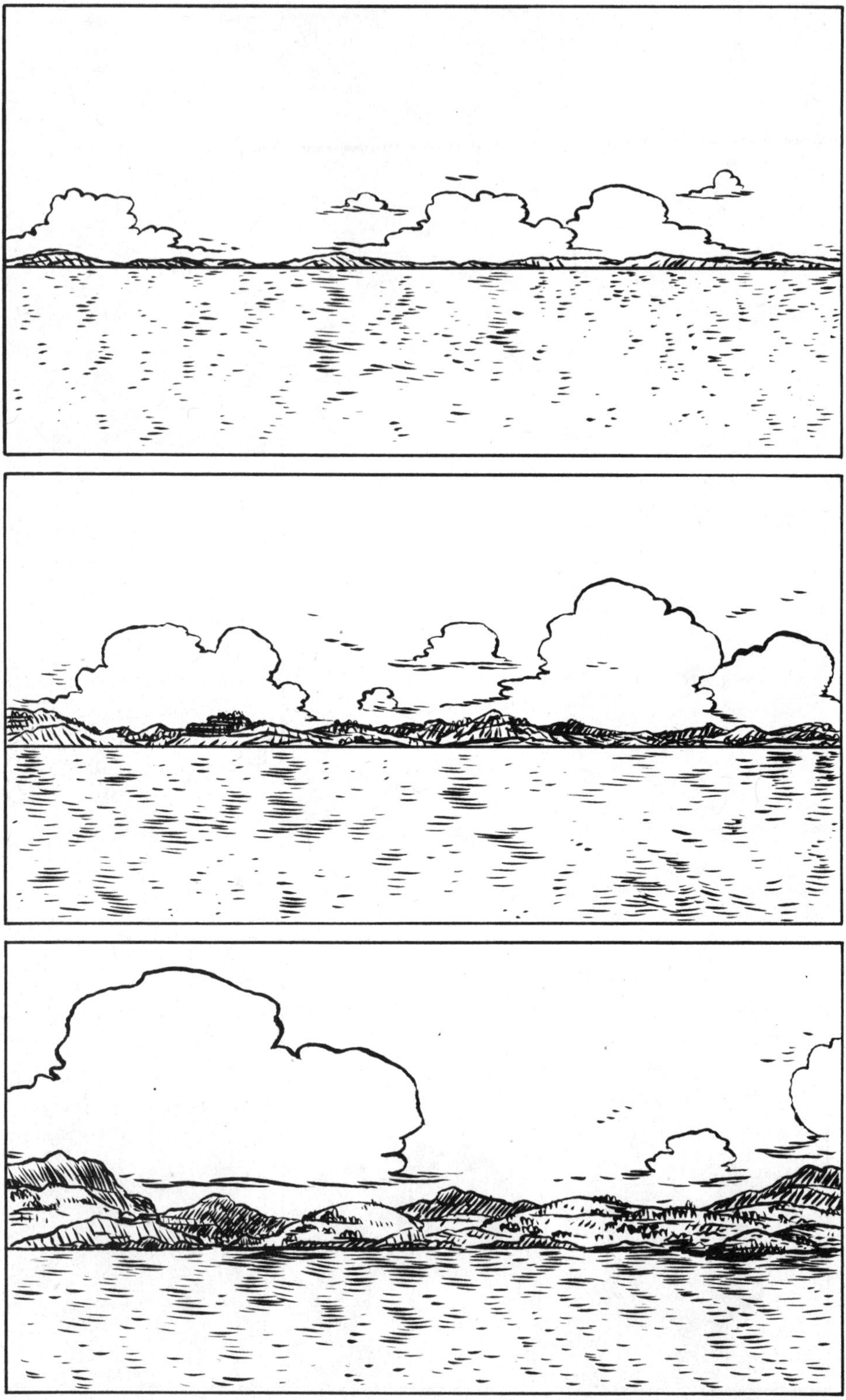

"Real or not - fact or unfact -
it was a beautiful vision."

George Herriman,
Krazy Kat.

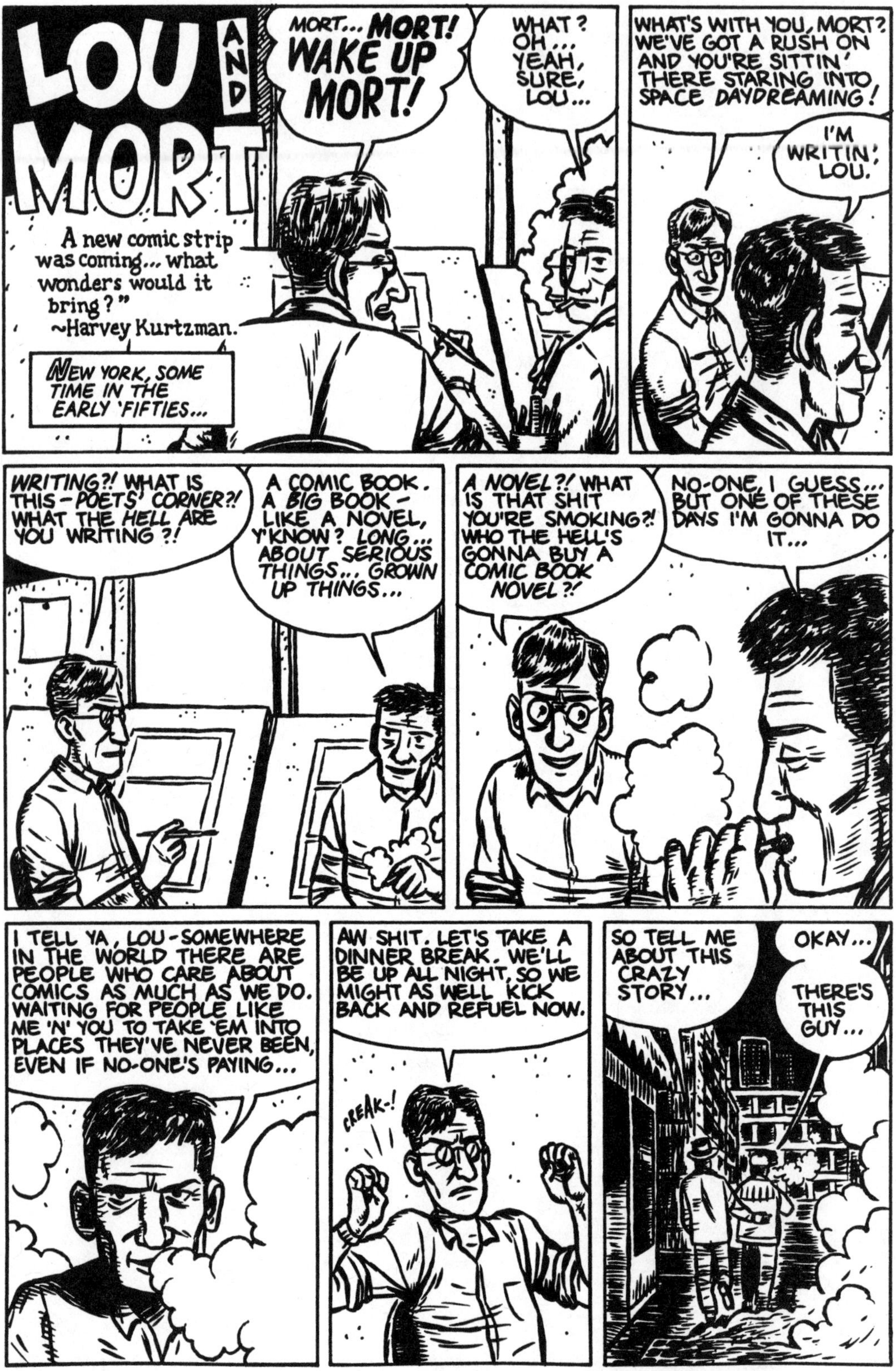
LOU AND MORT
"A new comic strip was coming... what wonders would it bring?" ~Harvey Kurtzman.
NEW YORK, SOME TIME IN THE EARLY 'FIFTIES...
MORT... MORT! WAKE UP MORT!
WHAT? OH... YEAH, SURE, LOU...
WHAT'S WITH YOU, MORT? WE'VE GOT A RUSH ON AND YOU'RE SITTIN' THERE STARING INTO SPACE DAYDREAMING!
I'M WRITIN', LOU.
WRITING?! WHAT IS THIS—POETS' CORNER?! WHAT THE HELL ARE YOU WRITING?!
A COMIC BOOK. A BIG BOOK—LIKE A NOVEL, Y'KNOW? LONG... ABOUT SERIOUS THINGS... GROWN UP THINGS...
A NOVEL?! WHAT IS THAT SHIT YOU'RE SMOKING?! WHO THE HELL'S GONNA BUY A COMIC BOOK NOVEL?!
NO-ONE, I GUESS... BUT ONE OF THESE DAYS I'M GONNA DO IT...
I TELL YA, LOU-SOMEWHERE IN THE WORLD THERE ARE PEOPLE WHO CARE ABOUT COMICS AS MUCH AS WE DO. WAITING FOR PEOPLE LIKE ME 'N' YOU TO TAKE 'EM INTO PLACES THEY'VE NEVER BEEN, EVEN IF NO-ONE'S PAYING...
AW SHIT. LET'S TAKE A DINNER BREAK. WE'LL BE UP ALL NIGHT, SO WE MIGHT AS WELL KICK BACK AND REFUEL NOW.
CREAK-!
SO TELL ME ABOUT THIS CRAZY STORY...
OKAY...
THERE'S THIS GUY...

—Dylan Horrocks. vii·97

GLOSSARY

and notes...

Action Comics: Issue #1 (June 1938) contains Superman's first appearance (by Jerry Siegel and Joe Schuster) and in 1996 was worth US$ 145,000.

Ae: "Yes" (Māori).

Kirk Alyn: (1910-1999) American actor, best known for playing Superman in his first live-action film appearances.

Anatai: a range of mountains in Cornucopia.

Aotearoa: Māori name for New Zealand; literally "Land of the long white cloud."

Sergio Aragones: (1937-) Spanish-born cartoonist, famous for his work in *Mad* magazine and his creation *Groo the Wanderer*. Once described as "the world's fastest cartoonist."

Arohanui: literally "big love" (Māori).

Auckland: largest city in New Zealand (population c. 1.4 million), situated on an isthmus and dominated by its harbours and a series of extinct volcanic cones. Also called Tāmaki-makau-rau – "Tāmaki of a thousand lovers."

Aunt May: Spiderman's kind elderly aunt.

Bach: (pronounced "Batch") New Zealand term for a sea-side holiday shack (derived from "bachelor").

H.M. Bateman: (1887-1970) cartoonist and social satirist, famous for a series of cartoons in the magazine *Tatler* depicting social gaffes, entitled 'The Man Who...'

Bekjai: a rare alpine flower from the Anatai Mountains, Cornucopia.

Lorena Bobbitt: (1970-) American woman who gained notoriety in 1994 after cutting off her abusive husband's penis.

Milton Caniff: (1907-1988) American cartoonist, creator of 'Terry and the Pirates' and 'Steve Canyon.'

Al Capp: (1909-1979) American cartoonist (born Alfred Caplin), creator of 'Li'l Abner.'

Jack Cole: (1918-1958) cartoonist, known for his manic inventiveness and practical jokes, who reportedly wept when other artists were assigned to draw his creation *Plastic Man*. He took his own life at the pinnacle of his career.

Captain James Cook, R.N.: (1728-1779) earliest English discoverer of New Zealand, who first circumnavigated the country in 1769-1770 in the *Endeavour*. Earned a reputation as one of the greatest explorers and cartographers of all time before being slain in Hawaii.

Cornucopia: a country once famous for cartography and magic. During the Middle Ages, travellers were reluctant to enter its borders for fear of sorcery and witchcraft, but Cornucopian cartographers were highly sought after for their skill. The landscape has remained largely unchanged since the Enlightenment. Its towns, roads and fields often seem designed to suit occult geomantic purposes rather than practical ones.

Crieste: capital city of Cornucopia.

Dairy: in New Zealand, a dairy is a small convenience store, selling mostly groceries and snacks.

D.B.: ('Dominion Breweries') a New Zealand beer.

Dire Straits: British soft-rock band.

Eisner Award: American award for comics. Named in honour of Will Eisner.

Will Eisner: (1917-2005) American cartoonist, best known as the creator of The Spirit and the ground-breaking graphic novel *A Contract With God* (1978).

Bekjai

Steve Englehart: (1947-) American writer who has worked in the comic book industry since 1971.

Eternal Comics: publisher of *Captain Tomorrow*, *Lady Night*, and many other popular comics. Now owned by Dick Burger.

Bud Fisher: (1885-1954) American cartoonist, creator of 'Mutt and Jeff.'

Whoopi Goldberg: (1955-) American actress and comedian.

Lou Goldman: (1920-) American cartoonist, famous for creating *Lady Night*.

Martin Goodman: (1908-1992) founder, publisher and managing editor of Marvel Comics until 1971.

Harvey Award: American award for comics, named in honour of Harvey Kurtzman.

Hauraki: "Northern Wind"- the North Island's Hauraki Gulf, beside which sits New Zealand's largest city, Auckland.

Hawaiki: the Spirit World and also the ancestral home of the Māori.

Charles Heaphy: (1820-1881) painter, draughtsman and surveyor employed by the New Zealand Company in 1839. Heaphy's paintings were used to promote New Zealand to potential settlers and he was involved in the surveying of the first British colonies at Port Nicholson and Nelson. During the Waikato War (1863-64), Heaphy became the only member of the colonial militia to receive the Victoria Cross. He later held various positions of public influence – including the Surveyor General of Auckland – and briefly entered politics.

George Herriman: (1880-1944) American cartoonist; creator of the newspaper strip *Krazy Kat*, which ran from 1913 until his death and was admired by e.e. cummings, Pablo Picasso, Robert Graves and Jack Kerouac, who called it an immediate progenitor of the Beat Generation.

Hicks Bay: also called 'Wharekahika' – sparsely settled bay near the tip of East Cape, New Zealand. Named after Lt. Zachary Hicks, one of Captain Cook's crew.

Hogan's Alley: American newspaper cartoon by R.F. Outcault which was instrumental in beginning the 'funny pages' boom at the end of the nineteenth century.

Hone Heke: (1810-1850) a leading chief of the Nga Puhi tribe; the first to sign the Treaty of Waitangi in 1840. Five years later he fought a remarkably successful war of independence against the British, which began when he cut down the British flagpole at Kororareka. His ally Kawiti has been credited with inventing modern trench warfare.

Lamington

Edgar P. Jacobs: (1904-1987) Belgian cartoonist and opera singer. In 1944 Jacobs entered a partnership with Hergé (Georges Remi) as colourist (and co-author) on *Tintin*. In 1947, however, Hergé ended their partnership after Jacobs demanded equal billing. Jacobs went on to achieve fame in his own right with his own series *Blake and Mortimer*.

Justice League: *The Justice League of America*, a popular superhero-team comic published by DC Comics.

Jack "the King" Kirby: (1917-1994, born Jacob Kurtzberg) cartoonist credited by many for the success of Marvel Comics in the 1960s and the creation of many famous characters, such as *Captain America* (co-created with Joe Simon), *the Hulk*, *the Fantastic Four*, etc. In the 1980s a controversy erupted over Marvel withholding his original artwork.

Kiwi: a small, flightless, shy, nocturnal bird; also New Zealand's national symbol.

Emil Kópen: (1914-) Cornucopia's most popular cartoonist, whose work has appeared in Cornucopian newspapers, magazines and books since he was a teenager. It is a mark of the esteem in which he is held in Cornucopia that his obscure and erotic comic strip *Irjan vir Pidz* is still printed in the otherwise highly conservative newspaper *Criesti Njad*. Outside his native country, however, he is almost completely unknown.

Kupe: according to some oral traditions, the original Kupe was the first polynesian navigator to discover Aotearoa. After exploring the coasts and naming many landmarks, he returned to Hawaiki to tell of his discovery. There followed a series of larger migrations – the Māori settlement of Aotearoa.

Kupenga: "nets" (Māori).

Harvey Kurtzman: (1924-1993) American cartoonist; creator of *Mad*, *Frontline Combat* and *Two-Fisted Tales*, among others. His war comics are famous for their meticulous research and commitment to historical accuracy.

Lady Night: superhero comic created by Lou Goldman in the 1950s and repopularised in the 1990s by Dick Burger.

Lamington: a cube of sponge cake coated in chocolate and dried coconut.

Tui

Lassie: canine hero of numerous films and books since 1940.

Stan Lee: (1922 – , born Stanley Lieber) editor, writer and publisher of Marvel Comics, who headed their rise to dominance of the market during the 1960s and 1970s. Is credited with the creation of such classic Marvel icons as *the Hulk*, *the Fantastic Four* and *Spider-Man*. Debate still rages, however, over the extent of Lee's contribution to these and other characters, compared with that of collaborators like Jack Kirby and Steve Ditko.

Frederico Garcia Lorca: (1899-1936) Spanish poet and dramatist, executed by fascists during the Spanish Civil War.

Winsor McCay: (1867?-1934) pioneer American newspaper cartoonist and animator; creator of *Little Nemo in Slumberland*, *Dreams of a Rarebit Fiend*, and *Pilgrim's Progress* among others.

Māori: the indigenous people (or 'tangata whenua'-"people of the land") of Aotearoa/ New Zealand.

Marae: Māori meeting house complex.

Maui: a significant figure in Māori legend; a trickster-hero and demi-god whose exploits include forcing the sun to slow its journey across the skies and fishing up the North Island from the sea.

"Me he korokoro tui": "The throat of a tui" – Māori proverb used to describe one who speaks beautifully. The tui is a native bird whose throat bears a white crest.

New Zealand Company: private company formed in 1839 to found British colonies in New Zealand.

Pakeha: Māori term for European settlers in New Zealand (origin obscure).

Pakiwaituhi: "comics" (Māori), from "pakiwaitara" (story) + "tuhi" (writing, drawing).

Pekapeka: native bat of New Zealand.

Pablo Picasso: (1881-1973) Spanish painter and fan of George Herriman's *Krazy Kat*.

Ed Pinsent: (1960 –) British cartoonist, who has been described as "the Philip Larkin of comics." His work has appeared in *Escape*, *Fox Comics*, *Fast Fiction* and countless self-published mini-comics, as well as in collections from Kingly Books and Slab-o-concrete.

Placentia Bay: a bay in Newfoundland, Canada.

Puriri: New Zealand native tree.

Puschkinia: flowering plant.

Puschkinia

The Rarebit Fiend: 'Dream of the Rarebit Fiend' was a comic strip created by Winsor McCay in 1904. 'Rarebit' is a dish made with melted cheese and other ingredients on bread or toast.

Rarebit

Chris Reynolds: (1960-) British cartoonist whose work has appeared in *Escape* magazine, *Mauretania Comics*, *Fast Fiction*, and various mini-comics. His graphic novel *Mauretania* was published in 1990 by Penguin Books.

Robin, the Boy Wonder: Batman's young sidekick.

Ruapekapeka o Wharekahika: "The Bat's Nest at Wharekahika." Affectionately known to locals as 'The Bat Cave.'

Julius Schwartz: (1915 - 2004) influential editor and writer at DC Comics.

William Shakespeare: (1564-1616) the 'George Herriman' of the stage.

Jim Shooter: (1951 -) managing-editor at Marvel Comics during the controversy-filled years of the 1980s, when cartoonists were agitating for royalties, creative control and greater recognition. Shooter gained a reputation as a loyal 'company man' and consequently became unpopular with creators' rights advocates. He was Marvel's most prominent spokesperson during the dispute over the return of Jack Kirby's artwork.

Joe Simon: (1913-) American cartoonist who collaborated for many years with Jack Kirby, including on the creation of Captain America.

Spiderman: popular Marvel Comics superhero created in 1962 by Stan Lee and Steve Ditko.

Gertrude Stein: (1874-1946) American-born poet, who, with partner Alice B. Toklas, hosted legendary parties for the bohemian set in Paris.

Taonga: "treasure, heirloom" (Māori).

Tapu: "holy, sacred; under ritual restriction or prohibition" (Māori).

Te Araroa: "The long path." A town on the East cape of New Zealand (near Hicks Bay), nestled between Whetumatarau Mountain and the long sweeping beach of Kawakawa Bay.

Te-Ika-a-Maui: "The fish of Maui." Māori name for the North Island of New Zealand.

Te Reinga: also called Te Rerenga Wairua, "the leaping place of the spirits." The northernmost point of New Zealand, from which the spirits of the dead leap on their journey to Hawaiki.

Horetā te Taniwha: (?-1853) leader of the Ngāti Whanaunga tribe who was a boy when Captain Cook first visited New Zealand. He later became a famous chief.

"Te wairua e te mauri": "the spirit and the life-force" (Māori), 'Mauri' is the force that binds together the body and the spirit.

Te-Waka-o-Maui: "The canoe of Maui." Māori name for the South Island of New Zealand.

"Tena koe": Māori welcome.

Osamu Tezuka: (1928-1989) Japanese cartoonist and animator, known as "The God of Manga."

Time Warner: giant global media conglomerate, owners of DC Comics.

Tipuna: "ancestors" (Māori).

Toiawa: eighteenth century rangatira (chief), probably of the Te Uri-o-Pou (or Ngāti Hei) tribe.

Rodolphe Töpffer: (1799-1846) Swiss writer, artist and educator who wrote and drew a series of extremely inventive 'picture stories' admired by Goethe. Sometimes called 'the father of the modern comic strip.'

Valja Domena: comic by Cornucopian cartoonist Emil Köpen, telling the story of a *Bethgemani* (or member of the order of witches).

Venom: fanged enemy of Spiderman.

Waka: Māori canoe.

Cincinatti Walker: (1975-) American movie actress.

Whitianga: "the crossing or ford." Beautiful bay on the Coromandel Peninsula.

Oprah Winfrey: (1954 –) American TV talk-show host and self-help celebrity.

Wally Wood: (1927-1981) American cartoonist. Three years before he took his own life, Wood said that "working in comics is like sentencing yourself to a life at hard labour in solitary confinement. If I had to do it all over again, I wouldn't do it..., And yet, I'm not sorry for where I am."

X-Men: Marvel Comics superhero team created in 1963 by Stan Lee and Jack Kirby.

Ziegfeld Follies: a series of American stage shows (1907-1931) famous for their pretty chorus girls.

Manuka

Notes to the Introduction:

2000 AD: British weekly science-fiction comic launched in 1977. Writers and artists included Pat Mills, Mike McMahon, Dave Gibbons, Brian Bolland, Alan Moore and Colin Wilson.

2001: A Space Odyssey: a comic book inspired by Stanley Kubrick's film of the same name, *2001* was written and drawn for Marvel Comics by Jack Kirby in 1976-1977.

Amphigorey: a collection of stories by American writer and artist Edward Gorey (1925-2000), published in 1972 and including such classics as 'The Curious Sofa,' 'The Doubtful Guest' and 'The Gashlycrumb Tinies.'

Batman: a superhero created in 1939 by Bob Kane and Bill Finger, who has since become one of DC Comics' most profitable brands.

Battle Picture Weekly: British war comic (1975-1988), initially created by Pat Mills and John Wagner. Many of the artists and writers from *Battle* later went on to create *2000AD*.

Captain Haddock: Tintin's close friend and companion, known for his irascible personality and colourful exclamations (e.g. "billions of blue blistering barnacles!").

Captain Marvel: comic book superhero created in 1939 by C.C. Beck and Bill Parker for Fawcett Comics. The character quickly became the most popular superhero in America, but a series of aggressive copyright infringement lawsuits by DC/National (the publishers of Superman) led to his demise in 1954. He was later revived by DC Comics in the 1970s.

Commando: British war comics published since 1961 in an unusual format (7 x 5½ inches, 68 pages).

Donald Duck: best remembered for the comic books written and drawn (anonymously) by Carl Barks (1901-2000).

Explorers on the Moon: the 17th Tintin adventure, published in French (as *On a Marché sur la Lune*) in 1954 and translated into English in 1959.

The Groke: in the Moomin stories, the Groke is a mysterious creature who craves warmth and friendship, but who is so cold that everything she touches freezes – including the grass she passes over.

Krazy: a British weekly humour comic published in the 1970s.

Mad: the earliest *Mad* comics of the 1950s were edited by Harvey Kurtzman and had a powerful cultural impact (Patti Smith once said "after *Mad*, drugs were nothing.").

Manuka: a prolific native New Zealand tree (Leptospermum scoparium). Also known as 'Tea Tree' (ever since Captain Cook boiled some of its leaves to make a hot drink).

Metal Men: a strange robotic superhero team created by Robert Kanigher, Ross Andru and Mike Esposito for DC Comics Showcase in 1962.

The Moomins: a series of children's novels written and illustrated by Tove Jansson (Finland, 1914-2001). The book shown here is *Moominpappa at Sea* (1965).

Notes

Our Army at War, featuring Sgt. Rock: American war comic published by DC Comics between 1952 and 1977. The comic's main hero, Sgt. Rock, was created in 1959 by Robert Kanigher and Joe Kubert. In the 1970s each story ended with the slogan "Make War No More."

Peanuts: American newspaper strip created in 1950 by Charles Schulz (1922-2000).

Pilote: a French comics magazine (1959-1989) which featured such popular series as Asterix the Gaul, Lt. Blueberry and Lucky Luke. The issue illustrated includes Jean Giraud's 'La Deviation.'

The Spirit: a comics series created by Will Eisner in 1940. In the 1970s Warren Publishing reprinted a number of classic *Spirit* stories in black and white magazine format.

Strips: an influential New Zealand comics magazine (1977-1987) which published work by Colin Wilson, Barry Linton, Joe Wylie, Laurence Clark, Kevin Jenkinson, Grant Major and others.

Terry and the Gunrunners: a New Zealand graphic novel by Bob Kerr and Stephen Ballantyne, published in 1982 and later turned into a children's TV series.

Tintin: The Adventures of Tintin is a series of comic books written and drawn by Belgian cartoonist Hergé (Georges Remi, 1907-1983).

Weird War: American supernatural war comic published by DC Comics between 1971 and 1983.

A *note about maps*:

The map on page 19 was drawn by Lt. (later Captain) James Cook, R.N., based on his first circumnavigation of New Zealand in 1769-1770.

A CHART OF NEWZELAND
OR THE ISLANDS OF
AEHEINOMOUWE AND TOVYPOENAMMU
Lying in the SOUTH SEA

The map of Aotearoa/New Zealand on page 22 was drawn in 1793 by Tuki Tahua and Ngahuruhuru, two Northland Māori abducted and taken to Norfolk Island at the request of its governor, who hoped they could train the island's convict labourers to dress flax. Being men, however, the two Māori knew little about the women's task of flax-processing. Tuki and Ngahuruhuru stayed on Norfolk Island for six months, as guests of the governor.

Their map was first drawn in chalk on the floor of the governor's mansion and then copied onto paper. The governor's secretary then annotated the map based on the two men's descriptions. Running the length of Te Ika-a-Maui (the North Island) is the path taken by the spirits of the dead on their journey to Te Reinga and thence to Hawaiki.

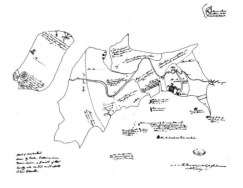

Tuki and Ngahuruhu's map is now held at the Public Record Office, London, England.

References:
J. Kelly, 'Tuki's Map of New Zealand,' *NZ Map Society Journal*, 1995
M. McKinnon (ed.), *New Zealand Historical Atlas*, Bateman (Auckland, 1997)
P. Barton, 'Maori Cartography and the European Encounter,' in D. Woodward and G. M. Lewis (eds), *Traditional Cartography in African, American, Arctic, Australian and Pacific Societies*, University of Chicago Press (Chicago, 1998).

Thank you

Terry Fleming
Louis Fleming
Abe Horrocks

Fergus Barrowman
Brian Biggs
David Billinghurst
Richard Bird
Jeremy Bishop
Tim Bollinger
David Brasting
Brad Brooks
Jonathan Brough
Chester Brown
Ed Brubaker
Mike Buckley
Peggy Burns
Bernard Caleo
Eddie Campbell
Richard Case
Lars Cawley
Nerilee Ceatha
Geoff Chapple
Matthew Chappory
Stu Colson
Comix@
Nick Craine
Malcolm Dale
Tom Devlin
Rob Edkins
Clemency Fleming
David Fleming
John Fleming
Richard Flynn
Nigel Gearing
Tony Gibson

Alex Gracewood
Ben Gracewood
Paul Gravett
Dominic Hannah
Tom Hart
Steve Heim
Tony Heim
Nigel Horrocks
Roger Horrocks
Shirley Horrocks
Simone Horrocks
Fran James
Adam Jamieson
Stephen Jewell
Sylvie Joly
Megan Kelso
Robyn Kenealy
Timothy Kidd
Jonathan King
Elizabeth Knox
James Kochalka
Arthur van Kruining
Roger Langridge
Chris Lander
Les Cartoonistes
 Dangereuses
Jon Lewis
Barry Linton
Edward Lynden-Bell
Paul MacQuibban
Sara-Jane MacQuibban
Scott McCloud

Heidi McDonald
Matt Madden
Jean-Christophe Menu
John Mitchinson
Toby Morris
Gregory O'Brien
Chris Oliveros
Jeffrey Paparoa Holman
Mark Paul
Tanya Paul
Tim Pilcher
David Raw
Peter Rees
Eric Reynolds
Eleanor Rimoldi
Alex Rimoldi
Diana Schutz
Eric Searleman
Seth
Kelly Sheehan
Keziah Singleton
Antony Spalding
Tom Spurgeon
Jay Stephens
Cornelius Stone
James Sturm
Andrew Thurtell (for giving
 life to Danton and Mopani)
Shelley Turner
Michel Vrána (without whom...)
Mark Williams

...and to everyone else
who's helped and supported
Hicksville and *Pickle*
over the years...

Dylan Horrocks
was born in 1966
and lives in New Zealand
with his wife and two sons.

He is the author of
the comic book series
Pickle and *Atlas*
and has written for
DC Comics, including
Hunter: The Age of Magic
and *Batgirl*.

His recent work
can be found at
hicksvillecomics.com

(drawing by Terry Fleming)

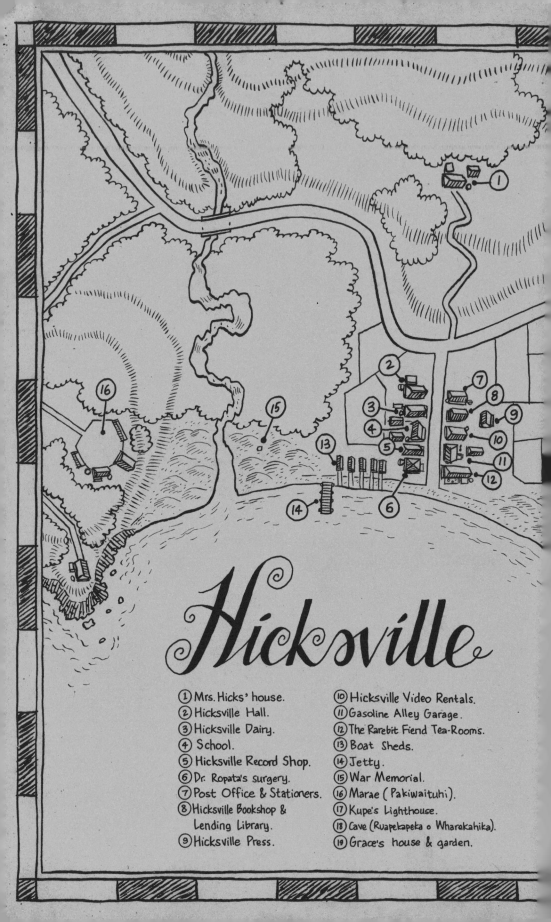

Hicksville

1. Mrs. Hicks' house.
2. Hicksville Hall.
3. Hicksville Dairy.
4. School.
5. Hicksville Record Shop.
6. Dr. Ropata's surgery.
7. Post Office & Stationers.
8. Hicksville Bookshop & Lending Library.
9. Hicksville Press.
10. Hicksville Video Rentals.
11. Gasoline Alley Garage.
12. The Rarebit Fiend Tea-Rooms.
13. Boat Sheds.
14. Jetty.
15. War Memorial.
16. Marae (Pakiwaituhi).
17. Kupe's Lighthouse.
18. Cave (Ruapekapeka o Wharekahika).
19. Grace's house & garden.